New Approaches to

Music

in the Elementary School

Fourth Edition

New Approaches to

Music

in the Elementary School

Lois Raebeck
Roosa School of Music
Brooklyn Heights, New York

Lawrence Wheeler
Manhattan School of Music, New York
North Merrick Union Free School District,
North Merrick, New York

wcb
Wm. C. Brown Company Publishers
Dubuque, Iowa

Dedicated to Liz and Al

Contents

Preface

Let us, for a moment, place ourselves in the role of the teacher who is confronted for the first time with the prospect of giving children a musical experience. If this be a classroom teacher, the apprehension felt in approaching this area of creativity may cause repression of the interesting ideas learned in music education courses. If the teacher is a music specialist, there may be more ease with the subject, but almost as much uncertainty, about how to make music an exciting experience for children. When the teacher's orientation to music has been primarily through pop-rock, there is an additional problem: how to deal with an attraction to a type of music that most educators consider only one facet of music literature.

Whatever the background of the teacher, the challenges are formidable: a multi-billion-dollar recording industry, which encourages children to insist that the highest priority be given to pop-rock; changing moral values and the resulting challenge to family life, which helps produce children with little responsibility or respect for authority; emphasis on instant gratification, whether it be through fast food establishments or television. The demands on the teacher of today are enormous.

How does one confront the changing attitudes of today without discarding the philosophy, methods, and materials of music education that have proven themselves valid throughout the years? Perhaps the first step is to accept the fact that we live in a pluralistic society. There is room for more than one approach, whether it be in the kind of music we teach or the structure of our family. Even the teacher committed to helping children understand and appreciate the great musical classics can explore rock music to expand conceptual understanding; and the recently graduated teacher, who believes traditional methods and materials are outmoded, can gain from trying to understand their contributions to present practices. The teacher who prefers an organized classroom can benefit from exploring more flexible classroom structures, just as the proponent of "open" classrooms can learn from the teacher who advocates organized, but creative, structured activity.

Whatever the background and orientation of the teacher, the questions are similar: What songs will these children enjoy? How can I present them so that growth will occur? What recordings of musical value will these children respond to? How should I present these for optimal musical growth? How do I initiate experiences in rhythms, playing instruments, creating songs, and giving these children—with their individual backgrounds and needs—creative musical experiences that will affect their overall musical and personal growth? What kind of classroom environment will help? What materials will I need? What attitudes and teaching techniques will encourage both personal and musical growth? Because of the pressures of the school day, many months or years can pass before these questions begin to be answered.

This book is an attempt to help the future classroom teacher or music specialist explore elementary school music and participate in activities that will help find some of the answers to these questions. It is an effort to answer the need for (1) concrete exposure to the wide range of musical activities appropriate for the elementary classroom, their relationship to each other and to the achievement of conceptual understandings and behavioral objectives; (2) knowledge of the techniques, materials, attitudes, and learning environments that can help implement these activities; (3) understanding of the relationship of achievement of conceptual understandings and behavioral objectives to enjoyment of music (aesthetic understanding and growth); (4) a guide for critical evaluation of the activities and approaches initiated; and (5) an opportunity for the teacher to discover how to enjoy participating in musical activities and thus attain a positive attitude toward music in the elementary school. In this text are both an overall view of the music program and many very specific ideas for activities, methods, approaches, and materials—all of which have been tested and proven successful in classroom situations.

It is hoped that through such an exposure the prospective teacher will begin to understand the need for careful planning, develop a personal philosophy and style in teaching, and gradually learn how to adapt plans to specific teaching situations. In short, this future teacher will be better prepared for the role of teaching music in the classroom—a role that demands extensive knowledge of activities, materials, techniques, skills, and concepts meaningful in the music program; the ability to plan for their best use; and the wisdom to evaluate the results.

To acquaint the prospective teacher with a viable way to plan musical experiences, the activities suggested in each chapter have been organized into a series of related activities. Each series contains experiences from several of the major areas of musical activity (rhythms, singing, listening, instrumental experiences, music reading), as well as an experience involving related arts. Each experience within the series is related to the same musical concepts and behavioral objectives.

Because this book often deals with the concrete rather than the abstract, a word of warning must be given. It is neither the intent nor the desire of the authors that any of these explicit suggestions be used as rigid formulas. On the contrary, such action would result in sterile teaching. These suggestions are offered to acquaint the teacher with some approaches and experiences that accomplish the aims of the music program. They are meant to stimulate the student's thinking and to serve as a point of departure. They should be modified at will to meet specific situations. When used in the college classroom they must be adapted for adults, who learn more quickly than children and who, because of thier maturity, bring more experience to each situation.

The authors are, of course, aware that there are many other valid approaches and procedures. They are also aware that no book can be comprehensive in the area of elementary music. Thus, this text presents only one possible approach to music for children.

This book attempts to survey the general elementary music program: (1) its philosophy; (2) its implementation; and (3) the resultant growth. It presents a concrete picture of the elementary music program, suggesting specific experiences for primary grades (grades one and two or level I), intermediate grades (grades three and four or level II), and upper grades (grades five and six or level III). Most experiences for level III may be adapted for the middle school. The book is organized in the following chapters:

1 Music in the Elementary School
2 Rhythmic Experiences
3 Singing Experiences: The Unison and Part-Song
4 Experiences with Instruments
5 Listening Experiences
6 Notational Experiences: Music Reading
7 Music in Special Activities: Special Clubs and Assembly Programs

The best possible use of this book does not require following the sequence of chapters. The college teacher may find it desirable to explore different sections of the book simultaneously, or to skip sections not deemed appropriate for the class. Care should be taken to avoid rigidly following the format of the book; rather, adapt its contents to specific situations. It may also be valuable to use ideas and experiences from this book in conjunction with activities from *Orff and Kodaly Adapted for the Elementary School* by the same authors and publisher.

Finally, the authors would like to explain their use of the masculine and feminine pronouns throughout the book. We have tried, through the device of alternating these pronouns as much as possible, to present men and women, girls and boys, equally—to suggest that the teacher of music may be either a woman or man; the student, a boy or girl. We sincerely hope that our book reflects our feeling that music may be experienced with equal enjoyment and skill by either sex, as a student or teacher.

Acknowledgments

The authors feel deeply indebted to friends, colleagues, teachers, and students who have contributed to the formation of the ideas in this book. To make an all-inclusive list would be difficult indeed, but to those who have given most directly of their time, effort, and understanding, we offer our sincere gratitude and thanks: Seymour Goldstein, Lillian Gordon, Sidney Hecker, Margaret Kelsey, Dr. John Manos, David Rosenthal, Alfred M. Smallens, Joseph and Clara Sugar, and Dr. Allan Toffler.

Our special thanks go to Joan Fyfe for various suggestions on individualization; to Mrs. Elizabeth Wheeler, for her expert secretarial work and illustrations for Cues to Music cards; and to the children whose pictures appear throughout the book: Melissa Hasler, Adrienne Hecker, Bruce Hecker, Roger Hecker, Neil Hicks, Jonathan Rosenthal, and Tina Weiss.

The authors would like to express their gratitude to the publishers whose cooperation made this volume possible. Special thanks are due those publishers who granted permission to reproduce songs, recording companies who made available their materials for research, companies who supplied photographs of their products, and the following children who appear in group pictures: Michael Bergantino, David Colasante, David Cooper, David Craig, Ian Craig, David Dick, Erika Ewing, Jane Goldstein, Matthew Goldstein, Kathryn Hawkins, Stacey Lowenthal, Jennifer Mahland, Stephanie Mitchell, Jennifer Okun, Elizabeth Perez, Varuth Suwankosai, Christopher Unger, and Nicole Zamora.

How to Use the Experiences in This Book

Do

1. Use suggestions in this book as guides only.
2. Be aware of the personal value inherent in each musical experience.
3. Be aware of musical growth inherent in each musical experience.
4. Let experiences evolve out of the human situation whenever possible.
5. Be flexible—change the approach when children's responses indicate a more fruitful course of action.
6. Guide children through well-planned experiences, appropriate questions, and suggestions.
7. Let children make suggestions, choices, and decisions whenever possible (i.e., how to dramatize a song, which rhythm instrument is best for accompanying a song, and so forth).
8. Be aware of many possible approaches, materials, and experiences.
9. Use your own as well as children's ideas for experiences.
10. Become thoroughly familiar with the experience before presenting any activity to children.
11. Be sure any experiences used are within children's capabilities.

Do Not

1. Use suggestions in this book as rigid formulas.
2. Let musical growth be the only goal of an experience.
3. Let enjoyment be the only goal of an experience.
4. Dictate experiences to children.
5. Stick rigidly to a course of action that is not working.
6. Tell children how they should respond to a specific activity.
7. Be disturbed when children's responses are not the same as yours.
8. Try to use all you know in the first week.
9. Be afraid to experiment.
10. Try any suggestion in this book without adequate preparation.
11. Use any suggestions that are beyond children's ability to respond with success.

Music in the Elementary School 1

The Role of Music in the Elementary School

Walk through an elementary school at almost any time of the day and listen. Is it nine o'clock? Then children are probably singing. "America" may be heard in one room, "The Star-Spangled Banner" in another. Music begins the school day.

Walk down a corridor. Why are children playing rhythm instruments in the hallway? Probably working out an orchestration for a song—part of the individualized instruction program for level II, grade 3.

Walk on, but watch out for the youngster hurrying toward you with a swinging trombone case; it's time for the group trombone lesson and she's in a hurry.

Don't miss that bulletin board display straight ahead. It's a related arts project—children from level I, grade 2, did those abstract drawings. Get their point? Music moves up. Music moves down. Music moves by step, by skip, by repeated tones just as lines and shapes in other art forms do.

Hear the part singing? That's the glee club rehearsing for next month's concert. They begin early—at 8:30 in the morning—in order to have a rehearsal of at least forty-five minutes. Yes, it is amazing how well fourth-, fifth-, and sixth-grade children can sing!

Let's walk down another corridor. We hear the music of *Aida*. Not surprising since the sixth-grade classrooms are located here, and *Aida* correlates so nicely with the sixth-grade social studies curriculum.

And so it goes, throughout the busy day that comprises life in an elementary school. We find that music can be experienced as an expression of patriotic feeling; as a means for individual growth; as a group effort; as a means of obtaining aesthetic satisfaction and encouraging creativity; as an aid in understanding an area of social studies. In these, as in many other ways, music plays a many-faceted role. In a world that has become increasingly materialistic and automated, it remains an art that can dynamically serve the human being. We discover in music unlimited sources of usefulness, as we initiate programs to cultivate the growth of the child.

Personal and Social Value to the Child

We find, first of all, that musical experiences planned with wisdom can give the child a most valuable gift—growth that is personal as well as musical. We learn how to initiate situations that hasten this type of growth in the child—situations that encourage the child to discover her own unique responses to music, and situations that encourage the child to express her own responses to music ever more fully and creatively.

It becomes apparent, too, that through the expanding self-knowledge, self-discipline, and self-expression, which comes from her own individual exploration and discovery, the child acquires a greater sense of her own worth. She also learns to work with others, since she experiences music in interaction with other children. Thus, the child perceives music as an art form through which the most basic human qualities can be expressed and re-created. We discover further that by hearing and exploring the music of other cultures and other times, the child begins to reach beyond her immediate social group to spin a thread of understanding of other people and other eras.

We see finally that when the child can identify music as an expressive force, she has acquired a source of recreation and joy that she can reach quickly and easily throughout life.

In all of these ways, we can hasten the child's personal growth and social adjustment through experiences with music.

Musical Value to the Child

What is the musical value of these experiences for the child? Though simply expressed, the implications of this question are far reaching, for it is through these experiences that the child decides first of all, whether music has any value for her—whether she should accept it as a worthwhile activity or reject it. Through these experiences she decides whether it is dull or interesting and whether, if interesting, she can successfully understand and participate in it.

For these reasons, we soon conclude that our first obligation to the child is to help her develop an attitude toward music that will ultimately tell her the value music can have for her personally.

1

As we proceed, it becomes apparent that we can obtain success in this most important of all objectives only if we remember above all else that all the experiences we initiate are meant to serve this goal. This knowledge helps us plan more wisely.

It tells us, first of all, that we must find ways to encourage the child to explore all the different activities through which she can experience music: rhythmic movement, singing, playing and learning about instruments, listening to music, reading music, creating music. During these activities we can help each child find the areas of music that will bring the deeply felt responses and successful achievement that result in the joy and wonder of music.

It tells us further that if we are to help the child learn to value music on the highest possible level—aesthetically—for the beauty it can give her, we must help her experience it through active participation, using both mind and emotions. For this reason we learn to encourage the conceptual understandings and achieve the behavioral objectives that can help the child enjoy music.

Thus, the value of music in the elementary school is fourfold. The child can:

1. Learn what music is
2. Discover what in music is most enjoyable to her
3. Discover her own musical aptitudes and skills
4. Learn to value music as an aesthetic experience involving mind and feelings

The teacher who gives the child these understandings has given her the best of the elementary school music program.

Music in the Curriculum

The child singing "America" in the exercises that open the school day is experiencing music as a means of expressing universal feelings. The child helping create an abstract mural relating direction in music to direction in space is experiencing music in relation to another art form. The child taking a trombone lesson, singing in a glee club, or studying the instruments of the orchestra is experiencing music as an activity important in its own right—valid because of its own unique qualities. The sixth-grade child listening to *Aida* is enjoying music valid because of its own beauty—the aesthetic satisfaction it can bring—as he enriches another area of study, Egypt.

These are some of the ways music fits into the curriculum. One activity encourages the child to use music as a means of expressing a feeling that is difficult to adequately verbalize. Another encourages the child to become involved with music simply because of the many values and satisfactions it has to offer. Still another

encourages the child to see music as a meaningful extension of another area of life and study. All these experiences are worthwhile. All contribute to the child's growth. They tell the child that music is, on one hand, an art that is unique and important in its own right; they tell him that it is, at the same time, an art that is related to and expressive of many areas of life. Ideally, musical experiences should be planned so that they relate to the curriculum in both ways. Thus, there should be time set aside during the week for musical experiences that are initiated simply because of the inherent value to the child—singing, listening, moving rhythmically—for no other reason than deepening the child's responsiveness to music. Simultaneously, however, there should be periods set aside to experience music that relates well to other areas of life and study. Such experiences give the child the connection between music and other areas of life, and have validity for this reason. A combination of both types of experiences gives the child a well-rounded and firmly grounded perspective of how music fits into the total life experience.

Environments for Musical Learning

As in all other areas of life, the environment helps shape the learning situation. We may well ask, therefore, what is an optimum environment for musical learning?

Until recently, most experiences with music in the elementary school took place in some kind of large group activity: music class, chorus, musical assembly programs, band, orchestra. And few would question the positive aspects of these large group experiences—the tremendous satisfaction and pride that comes from being part of a large, cohesive group and from sharing the feelings expressed in music with so many other human beings.

But what of the negative aspects? Does optimum musical learning and personal growth take place in a situation that by its very nature (and number of children) demands the dominance of the teacher and the conformity of the children? Because of the evolution of small group and individualized instruction in other subject areas, music educators have begun to question the confinement of all musical learning to large-group situations.

Is the "self" of each child being adequately elicited in these large groups? Does each child have sufficient opportunity to explore, experiment, inquire, hypothesize, conceptualize, and especially enjoy in her own way, at her own pace, in her own style? Or is the lip service paid to the development of individual capabilities too often just that—an ideal that often falls short of fulfillment because of groups so large that the teacher has no choice but to strive to reach the average child, leaving the "fast" child bored and the "slow" child frustrated and lost?

Many music educators have begun to suggest that it might be possible to alter the environment for musical learning to provide more flexibility so that children may not only benefit from experiences with large groups, but, in addition, have opportunities to obtain other types of self-fulfilling experiences through small-group and individualized experiences. And so, new methods, materials, and spatial arrangements have been and are being developed. The classroom is more and more a laboratory where children sometimes can work in ways more suited to their individual needs and styles: alone or in small groups, with the teacher, another adult, or even a peer as a guide or co-worker.

How, you may ask, does this work in practice?

Individualization (which includes small group activities) may begin on a very simple level. After a classroom experience exploring the concepts of loud and soft while learning a song, a small group might be given the opportunity to create a composition, using rhythm instruments, in which one section of the group plays softly and the other loudly. After some rehearsal, the class hears and analyzes the composition.

Or Larry, who knows a little about the guitar, might learn an accompaniment for the song. Or Elizabeth, who shows aptitude on the Autoharp, might help another child work out an Autoharp accompaniment. These small groups of children might be sent to the hallway, another section of the room, or other space provided for learning activities.

As children acquire the self-discipline needed to work alone and with others, more complex media can be used. Some teachers prepare a comprehensive series of games and projects related to musical concepts, in which children participate individually and in small groups, progressing sequentially at their own rate. Others use learning contracts—written contracts that the child signs, obligating her to work on a specific project in a sequential scale of projects. In addition, learning packets offer programmed instruction using taped lessons, filmstrips, charts, slides, and even special equipment, such as electronic keyboards. (There are specific examples in later chapters.)

Because of the need for adequate adult guidance and for a testing program to check on effectiveness, paraprofessionals or student teachers often work with small groups of children. Teaching machines function as teachers' aids to work with individual children. Computer centers are being developed to help test and assist in the instruction of children.

What, specifically, are all these innovations trying to accomplish? Basically, all individualized music programs are attempting to help each child attain a greater sense of her own worth, and a more complete realization of her own self through musical growth. In practice this means:

1. Beginning music instruction for each child at her own level instead of the level of the average child her age
2. Setting up a sequence of individual or small-group experiences through which each child can progress sequentially—working in her own style, at her own rate of progress toward goals that have been determined for her individually through testing; encouraging her to move on to the next level after mastering the concepts and skills on her present level
3. Offering a wide variety of area choices, concurrently, to meet the individual needs of children: reading music, writing music, creating verses or accompaniments to songs, listening and responding to music, creating recordings, practicing a second part to a song, playing musical games that test and reinforce musical knowledge, or, perhaps, simply verbalizing the interrelationship of concepts
4. Providing guidance and specific plans for continuous progress for each child who is working alone or with one or two others without constant supervision
5. Providing for continuous evaluation through testing and restructuring of instruction

What does the individualized instruction program imply for the music educator?

1. The teacher must know as much as possible about each child. What are her abilities, interests and hobbies, background, weaknesses and strengths, needs—musical and other? In addition to observation, a simple questionnaire can supply answers to these questions.
2. The teacher must become thoroughly acquainted with (a) the physical and psychological characteristics of each age level, (b) the musical activities appropriate for each level, (c) the conceptual understandings that can be encouraged on each level, and (d) the behavioral objectives relevant to each level. (See the chart at the end of this chapter.)
3. The teacher must decide what part individualized and small group activities and activities for the entire class play in musical growth. Should each concept, for example, be introduced in a group experience, then reinforced in an individualized experience? And, if so, what specific projects will be made available to reinforce each concept? On what projects can children be expected to work successfully alone or in small groups?
4. The teacher must give each child a diagnostic test to determine where he will begin on the sequential scale of activities planned and developed for individualized instruction. Such a test would indicate her conceptual understandings and behavioral skills.
5. The teacher must acquaint herself with and begin to provide for the materials needed for individualization, which might include:
    a. Teacher prepared games and projects
    b. Learning contracts
    c. Teaching machines
    d. Songbooks

e. Recordings
f. Cassette and tape recorders
g. Filmstrips and filmstrip projectors
h. Transparencies and overhead projectors
i. Instruments: piano, Autoharp, guitar, melody instruments, percussion instruments, and so on
j. Laminated charts illustrating musical concepts

6. The teacher and school administration must decide where to provide the individualized instruction: in the classroom, a music center, the hallway, a large closet, an empty classroom, or other facility?

7. The teacher must decide when to provide the individualized instruction. Will it be part of the regular music period—with time allotted to group instruction and to individualized instruction? Or will a schedule be set up for various activities: music listening for interested level I children at 10:00 A.M. in the music room; guitar for level II at 11:00 A.M., and so on.

8. Finally, the teacher must find a way of keeping a record of the progress of each child for himself, as well as for the child. Perhaps a paraprofessional or teacher trainee can help in this monumental task of testing and recording the progress of children and planning future programs for their development.

Although individualized music instruction in the public school setting is still in its infancy and is viewed by many with hesitancy and downright skepticism, others believe it is the answer to a need within the music curriculum. These advocates believe that individual instruction will not only encourage greater musical learning for all children, but also it will train people to work alone as well as with others and to develop initiative, resourcefulness, self-discipline, and self-realization.

Throughout this book there are specific experiences suggested for individualized instruction.[1]

Materials for Musical Learning

Whatever the environment for musical learning, the materials should be as accessible as possible. Ideally, the room in which musical experiences take place will be set up so that children take advantage of every possible opportunity to learn. Visual aids to reinforce musical learning (charts of note values related to rhythmic counting, pictures of instruments, and charts of hand signals with their corresponding syllables) should be hung on walls. Melody and accompanying instruments and record players should be easily available to children and teacher. Thus, the room itself will encourage musical learning through its visual aspects, as well as the availability of materials.

1. Joan Z. Fyfe, *Personalizing Music Education* (Sherman Oaks, Calif.: Alfred Publishing Co., Inc.) This is an excellent source of activities and specific information about individualized instruction.

What materials does a teacher need to teach effectively?

The teacher exploring ways of initiating musical activities with children will soon discover that some of the most profound musical experiences occur in the simplest of circumstances with a minimum of materials. A good song, perhaps, explored to the fullest can create a lasting memory of musical enjoyment for both teacher and children.

However, as we try to reach each child through the most available means, it soon becomes apparent that children respond in many different ways. We, therefore, must make use of all possible materials in order to succeed in meeting the many challenges before us.

In addition to the list of materials below, many teachers will want to build their own supplies of visual aids, including, for example:

1. Transparencies (made with a permanent marker) to be shown on an overhead projector:
   a. Rhythmic accompaniments to songs
   b. Original songs created by the class
   c. Descants to be used in a part-singing experiences
2. Flash cards to reinforce rhythmic, melodic, and other concepts:
   a. Rhythm patterns
   b. Melodic patterns
   c. Symbols for changes in meter, tempo, dynamics
3. Cues to Music cards to aid in listening experiences
4. Pictures to reinforce musical concepts (related arts)
5. Any materials for individualized instruction (musical games, work sheets, mimeographed sheets for learning contracts, etc.)

Note: Any materials using oak tag or heavy poster board should be laminated to extend durability.

Materials for Teaching Music

Instruments

Autoharp: twelve or fifteen bars, in tune

Chromatic resonator bells: with at least twenty removable bars, with a mallet for each bar

Diatonic step bells and a pair of mallets

Guitar or ukulele or both

Orff-designed instruments: xylophones, timpani, glockenspiels, metallophones, all with appropriate mallets

Piano: kept in good condition and in tune

Recorders: soprano, alto

Rhythm instruments: small drums, rhythm sticks, tambourines, maracas, claves, triangles, finger cymbals, cymbals, tone blocks, jingle bells, sand blocks, gong, temple blocks, etc.

Record Players

If possible, one for each classroom: in good condition and able to play 78, 45, and 33 rpm

Recordings

As many as possible for each level: to guide experiences in singing, rhythmic movement, listening, instruments, and to focus on the related conceptual understandings and behavioral objectives

Songbooks

One set of the basic song series you find most desirable. This should include teachers' guides, books for each child in each grade, recordings of songs, and so on.

Additional songbooks that contain material for individualization and other material you may want to use, not available in song series.

Cassette and Tape Recorders

To record material for singing, listening, instrumental experiences, or original compositions by children (The teacher should be aware of copyright laws.)

Films, Filmstrips, Transparencies, Audiotapes, Videotapes

Projectors and Screens

Opaque, overhead, filmstrip and film projectors with screens

The opaque and overhead projectors are often overlooked as aids in developing musical experiences in all areas of musical activity—rhythms, singing, instrumental, listening, or music-reading experiences. An imaginative teacher will think of many ways to use these machines. A few uses include the following:

1. Projecting musical notation on the screen for a more focused examination of the musical score in experiences with singing, instruments, listening
2. Projecting themes for examination of notation related to an abstract listening experience
3. Projecting words to songs that are in the public domain
4. Projecting pictures of instruments of an orchestra

5. Projecting illustrations in experiences with related arts, in order to focus on concepts pertinent to music as well as art
6. Projecting illustrations of a story (related to a listening experience involving story music) in order to stimulate a discussion about the ways music can tell a story; the teacher might:
   a. Tell a story, showing illustrations, then play the music
   b. Project illustrations as children hear the music
   c. Project an original filmstrip of illustrations that children create after they hear music
   d. Project illustrations of an actual story from a published text, after obtaining permission

Radio and Television

For special programs of benefit to musical growth

Miscellaneous

Beat board: A *beat board* is a board used for rhythmic dictation. It is approximately 1½ feet square. Four knobs are placed across the top. On each knob is a strip of red tape representing quarter notes, or the basic beat. Beneath the knobs are strips of white contact paper. The teacher beats a pattern on the knobs. Students clap it, count it, and write it below the appropriate knobs on the white contact paper, using a nonpermanent transparency marking pen so that it can be erased. Beat boards may be made for use with 4/4, 3/4, or 6/8 meters.

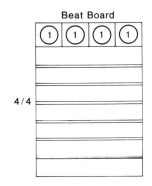

Beat Board

Pitchpipe (chromatic)

Tuning fork

Staff line and chalk

Music composition paper

Paper with large music staff printed on it

Any commercially produced flash cards and charts desired for developing melodic and rhythmic understandings

Textbooks to aid in teaching

Cues to Music Cards

Cues to Music cards, which are used in listening experiences, are large, laminated cards constructed on heavy poster board. On these cards are the main cues (themes) that tell the story of a musical composition. In addition to the theme, which may be either a melodic or rhythmic pattern, each card has on it one or more of the following:

1. A picture of the instrument or instruments that play the musical cue
2. A simple abstract or pictorial illustration of the situation taking place at the time of the cue in the music
3. A short word explanation of the situation

How are Cues to Music cards used? After a discussion with the children in which they are reminded of the wonderfully expressive powers of music—its ability to suggest a wide range of emotions and experiences—the teacher might explain that he will play a recording that suggests a story, and that he will use Cues to Music cards to help tell the story. He can then proceed, as follows:

1. Tell the title and composer of the composition and any information that is important to children's enjoyment of the musical story.
2. Tell the story, holding up each Cues to Music card as it appears in the story.
3. Teach class members to play any of the simple themes from the composition (using Cues to Music cards) on a melody instrument.
4. Play any themes that are too difficult for children to learn on a melody instrument.
5. Play a recording, holding up each card in sequence with the music.
6. Give each card to a child and have children holding Cues to Music cards arrange themselves in front of the room in the order in which their cue appears in the music. (Children may stand or sit, depending upon the length of the composition.)
7. Instruct children to hold their cues down except when their cue is played, at which time they hold it high for the class to see. (After repeated hearings, children can arrange themselves out of numerical order for a more challenging experience.)
8. Instruct the remainder of the class to listen and watch carefully and to raise their hands if they see someone miss a cue (fail to raise his card), so that the first one seeing the error can take the card of the person who missed his cue. (Remind the class that they are not to call out but to raise their hands if a cue is missed since the music must be heard at every moment.)
9. Play a recording as children hold up Cues to Music cards. (Children rarely miss their cues.)

Aside from the obvious satisfaction children get from this experience, other values are apparent:

1. Children gain an awareness of and an intimate acquaintance with the use of themes in a musical composition.
2. Children become concretely aware of the use of instruments, melodies, and rhythms suggesting changes of mood and pictorial images in music.
3. Children become intimately and enjoyably acquainted with a relatively long musical composition.
4. Children's attention is focused on musical notation.

Cues to Music cards can be made by the teacher or students with the help of music and art specialists. A procedure for making these cards follows:

1. Select a musical composition that suggests a story.
2. Become thoroughly acquainted with the story.
3. Listen to the music and become familiar with the specific themes that tell the story.
4. List the story actions that are suggested by the specific themes.
5. Prepare a large card (approximately eighteen by twenty-four inches) for each theme, placing on it one or more of the following items:
   a. The musical cue (theme)
   b. A picture of the instrument(s) playing the cue
   c. A picture or abstract drawing that suggests the situation represented by the theme
   d. A short word description of the action represented by the theme
   e. The number (on the back) of each card in the order it appears in the composition

The Teacher in the Elementary School

The Classroom Teacher

The classroom teacher is invaluable as an initiator and guide of musical experiences in the elementary school. In many schools he is the only person who teaches music to his students. He also has knowledge about the children in his class that other adults in the school environment do not possess.

He knows, first of all, who and what each child is. He knows the child's personality: her needs, abilities, problems, strengths and weaknesses, joys and sorrows, likes and dislikes. He knows why John reacts violently to one idea but accepts another easily. He knows why Susan always looks tired and the reason for Mary's general lack of enthusiasm. All of these understandings make it possible for the classroom teacher to make wise choices in materials and methods and to exercise proper timing in their use.

The classroom teacher has another type of knowledge other adults do not have. This is the knowledge of all the activities in the school day. He knows what has gone before and what will come later. He knows how each activity must dovetail into the other, why and when. This knowledge of the school day and the child makes the classroom teacher the most important person in the child's school life. This understanding of the child and her day gives him a vital role in shaping the child's musical growth and understanding.

How can the classroom teacher make the most of the opportunity he has to cultivate the child's musical growth? First and foremost, the classroom teacher must recognize the value of music for himself as well as for the child. He must see in music a means for personal growth and enjoyment, for there is little value in exploring method or materials in teaching music unless he feels convinced of these factors.

The teacher whose background has been so handicapped that he cannot place these values on music must be willing to grow musically with his class despite his personal limitations. Unless he has this willingness to explore music cooperatively, there obviously is little hope for a positive and dynamic music program developing in his classroom. With a willingness to explore and grow musically, however, even the "musically handicapped" teacher can discover new depths of creative expression within himself as he learns how to cultivate this in his classroom.

The classroom teacher must further accept the concept of music for all children. He must be able to accept the proposition that there are few "nonsingers." Except for the rare child who has a real physical disability, there are essentially only "weak" singers—children who have not yet discovered their singing voices. He must be willing to exert the special effort needed to help musically handicapped children to discover and develop their musical abilities.

Finally, to help the child respond with enthusiasm and grow musically, the teacher must be willing to discover and use music, methods, and materials that are suitable for his particular class.

How can the classroom teacher best prepare for initiating musical experiences in the classroom? In addition to giving careful thought to the attitudes necessary for stimulating musical growth, acquisition of some basic musical skills and experience in various musical activities are of utmost value. While these are probably best experienced before beginning teaching, they can be cultivated through individual efforts later, as well as through using the advice and help of the available music specialist or consultant.

First and foremost, the classroom teacher is most effective when he has some skill in singing or playing an instrument (recorder, Autoharp, guitar, ukulele, melody bells, or piano) so that he can have some means of expressing himself musically in the classroom. Further, the classroom teacher should have had the following experiences and understandings:

1. Firsthand experience in singing songs and playing instruments suitable for the elementary school.
2. Direct experience with creative activities: creating original words and melodies; understanding the most creative approaches to rhythms, listening, dramatizing, singing, and instrumental experiences.
3. A knowledge of the various types of musical activities to which the child responds and through which she achieves growth, as well as a knowledge of materials that can be useful in each area. (See the chart at the end of this chapter.)
4. An awareness of the desired musical growth (conceptual understandings and behavioral objectives) and the various means for promoting this growth. (See the chart at the end of this chapter.)
5. An awareness of the ways in which elementary school children respond to music, and the various ways that age, background, and special interests affect responses.

When we realize that musical experiences are only one aspect of a complex curriculum that includes many study areas, it becomes increasingly clear that the duties of the classroom teacher are indeed enormous. Because of these responsibilities, the classroom teacher needs more than a constructive attitude and adequate experiences and skills. There are aids he can rely on, which can make the task of teaching music easier and more effective.

The music consultant or specialist, when available, is probably the most effective of such aids and can help in many ways:

1. To create a sequence of experiences that will foster musical growth
2. To demonstrate ways to teach a song or initiate experiences in rhythms, listening, or playing instruments
3. To guide experiences that may be difficult for the classroom teacher
4. To suggest materials, activities, or approaches that encourage musical growth and enjoyment
5. To give individual assistance in cultivating musical skills, such as how to play the Autoharp, recorder, or other instrument
6. To make tape recordings that may be helpful in teaching a song,[2] initiating a rhythmic experience, or recording original songs composed by the class
7. To assist in creating and guiding individualized musical experiences
8. To suggest experiences combining music and related arts

---

2. Before making a tape recording of any song, it is important to be certain the song is in public domain or to secure permission to record it from the owner of the copyright.

There are other aids for the teacher seeking them. They are found in most schools and include:

1. The musically gifted children who can accompany the class, singing with guitar or piano; start a song and lead class singing; give reports; help other children play the Autoharp, and so on
2. Other teachers who can help guide more difficult experiences as well as give suggestions about materials or methods
3. Books on every aspect of the elementary school music program (see Appendixes)
4. Recordings of songs in the elementary song series used for teaching songs; recordings for listening experiences; and recordings that accompany filmstrips to aid in learning about instruments or telling a musical story (Suggested recordings are listed in appropriate chapters.)
5. Visual aids created by the classroom teacher or music specialist, collected from magazines, or purchased from commercial sources (films, filmstrips, audiotapes, videotapes, charts, flashcards)
6. In-service workshops given in the system or nearby school systems or colleges, which are available for the alert teacher who wants help
7. Tape and cassette recorders that may be used to record musical experiences initiated by the classroom teacher and later played for self-evaluation
8. Suggestions contained in the teacher's editions of the elementary song series used in the individual school
9. Musically gifted adults from the community who are willing to volunteer their services to enrich classroom activities
10. Radio and television programs conducive to musical growth

With effective use of these aids, a conscientious effort to prepare himself, and the willingness to explore music with his class, the classroom teacher can himself experience much of the satisfaction that music offers as he guides the child toward this most rewarding goal.

The Music Specialist

The music specialist is most commonly defined as the person who is employed to "teach" all the music in the school. All music experienced by the child is initiated by the specialist, leaving the classroom teacher with little or no responsibility for the music program.

There are, of course, advantages to this arrangement. The music specialist is highly skilled in music. He is aware of many approaches, techniques, and materials that aid the child's musical growth as well as the nature of the musical growth that should take place. In addition, the child is usually assured of a specific number of musical experiences, infrequent and brief though they may be.

The disadvantages of the arrangement are many. Since the music specialist is usually required to "cover" a great number of classes, he has, most often, far more to do than can possibly be done adequately. Normally, each class sees the specialist not more than once a week for twenty or twenty-five minutes. This means that experiences in music must be such that they can be initiated, experienced, and culminated within these twenty or twenty-five minutes. It means that the specialist has little or no opportunity to develop a meaningful experience or a continuity of experiences. It means that the specialist cannot possibly get to know the children, the overall curriculum, or the classroom teacher. The specialist cannot possibly acquaint children with all the areas of music, let alone give them the opportunity to explore these areas at frequent intervals in their own way. It means that music must remain an unrelated subject—an activity that comes for a few specific minutes each week and must be all too short and restrictively simple. It means, finally, that musical experiences for the child in such an arrangement must, of necessity, be incomplete, fragmentary, and generally unsatisfactory.

The Music Consultant

The music consultant is, by definition and fact, in a different position than the music specialist. He is most effective when assigned to no more than one or two schools as a person whose position is specifically designed to help the classroom teacher guide experiences in music. He is not a music supervisor for a number of schools. When he has a schedule of classes, these do not usually occupy the full week. He has time for work for and with individual teachers and children. Often, except for music clubs, there is no set schedule for the consultant's work, and he teaches by appointment with individual teachers who request or require help.

Under this arrangement, the classroom teacher is responsible for the musical experiences of the child just as he is responsible for other study areas. The responsibility of the music consultant is twofold: (1) to outline and clarify the philosophy of the music program and the activities, methods, and materials that best implement this philosophy; and (2) to give help in any form so that the classroom teacher can understand and guide the program.

The help the consultant gives the classroom teacher may take many forms:

1. Conferences to help clarify the various areas of the music program and to discuss specific ideas for musical experiences, approaches, techniques, and materials that best implement the program
2. Inspiration and stimulation through new ideas for approaches and materials that fit special situations

3. Individual and group workshops to help develop individual skills that help in the classroom (how to play the Autoharp, guitar, recorder, or song bells; how to sing specific songs; how to initiate specific music listening experiences)
4. Ideas for musical experiences that correlate meaningfully with other areas of the curriculum
5. Demonstrations in the classroom to help classroom teachers develop skills, understandings, and techniques
6. Preparation of transparencies for the overhead projector
7. Preparation of tapes for cassette or tape recorder for use by the classroom teacher
8. Guiding specific musical experiences that may be too difficult for classroom teachers (notating children's original songs, teaching difficult songs, rhythms, difficult listening experiences)
9. Helping to develop and guide individualized musical experiences

To explain the effectiveness of this arrangement one factor is perhaps more important than any other—time. Because of the flexibility of his schedule, the music consultant can give the classroom teacher help when and for as long as it is needed. His schedule can be arranged to meet special situations. He can schedule classes (to demonstrate or guide experiences needing his special skill) for the amount of time the class needs to have a successful experience—whether it be fifteen minutes or forty-five minutes.

The success of such a cooperative venture depends upon both music consultant and classroom teacher. Both must be eager to cooperate in developing an effective program. In addition, the consultant must have certain attributes to be most effective:

1. A positive attitude toward all teachers regardless of their musical abilities or personalities
2. The imagination and perseverance to discover and capitalize on the classroom teacher's individual strengths, minimizing his weaknesses and encouraging his musical efforts
3. Flexibility, organizational ability, self-discipline, and an optimistic philosophy

When the consultant has these qualities, it is possible to develop a team that can work together in a cooperative effort to give the child musical experiences that are most beneficial to him personally and musically. This team, made up of the classroom teacher who knows both the child and the curriculum well enough to guide musical experiences, and the music consultant who has the specialized knowledge and time to give the help necessary to insure success, is perhaps the most effective way currently available to insure that the child receives the most from his musical experiences in the elementary school.

The Music Supervisor or Coordinator

The music supervisor, or coordinator, differs from both music specialist and music consultant in the type of service he performs. Although his duties may sometimes be similar, most often his main responsibility is to plan, coordinate, and supervise the overall music program as taught by either classroom teachers or music specialists.

Thus, he is often responsible for the music programs of many schools—making periodic visits during the year to observe music classes and make suggestions for improvement.

Besides planning and supervising the general outlines of curricula in all the fundamental areas of music, he often serves as a resource person—helping teachers find appropriate songs and recordings and effective ways of presenting them, discussing problems (musical or otherwise) that arise in teaching, and, at times, giving demonstration lessons.

In general the supervisor plays somewhat the same role as the consultant, but, because he serves so many schools, is often unable to be as effective as is desirable.

Plans, Attitudes, and Problems in Teaching Music

Plans

Whether the teacher of music is a specialist, the classroom teacher, or a partnership of both, carefully considered plans are necessary to give children experiences that have meaning. Ideally, these plans will come from probing the reasons for initiating musical experiences. Why do we want children to have singing experiences? What kind of responses and attitudes do we hope to encourage from these experiences? From listening experiences? Rhythmic experiences? Experiences with instruments and music reading? What conceptual understandings and behavioral objectives do we hope to cultivate? And most important, how do we make the musical experiences we initiate relevant to children?

These are the questions every teacher must ask himself before he can plan significant musical experiences for children. These are the questions that will help develop an overview of the elementary music program, which he must have to be truly effective.

Some teachers will want to give what is perhaps the most that music has to offer—an aesthetic experience that can be used throughout life as a source of beauty and recreation. Some will want to give the child a form for expressing her own feelings and gaining a greater sense of her unique value. Some will want to give a means for sharing satisfying experiences with others, and feeling related, through music, to people everywhere.

Whatever the goal, the answers to these questions help in developing an overview of the elementary music program, but they do more. They suggest, first of all, a series of experiences, part of a spiral development plan related conceptually to the experiences that precede and follow. They suggest the methods and materials that help most in developing these experiences. Finally, they help us to plan effectively for each experience we initiate with children.

But knowing the goals and the precise experiences we believe will lead us closer to these goals is not enough. Each experience must be planned and developed in a way that will increase the possibility of its effectiveness. We cannot expect to walk into the classroom, even with a carefully considered philosophy, and initiate and guide a significant musical experience through instinct alone. Even the experienced teacher can rarely do this. Experience helps us to be more flexible, but it does not eliminate the need for careful planning. The wise teacher will plan each experience carefully in terms of his goals and then alter these plans whenever a better approach suggests itself. One type of plan follows:

Materials Needed
  1.
  2.

Activities Related to Major Musical Activity:
Rhythms, Singing, Instrumental, Listening,
or Music Reading
  1.
  2.

Related Musical Activities
  1.
  2.

Conceptual Understandings
  1.
  2.

Behavioral Objectives
  1.
  2.

Related Arts
  1.
  2.

Procedure
  1.
  2.

Evaluation
  1.
  2.

Ideas for Individualization, Follow-up, and Enrichment

If experiences are consistently recorded and evaluated, a fund of information can be built that will make teaching more effortless and more effective. (Suggestions for compiling these records are made at the end of each of these chapters: "Rhythmic Experiences," "Singing Experiences," "Experiences with Instruments," "Listening Experiences," and "Notational Experiences.")

Such a procedure, which includes setting goals, discovering and planning experiences that help attain these goals, and evaluating each experience in terms of these goals, is a good beginning to the fine art of teaching.

Attitudes

The plans are made. The teacher is well prepared to initiate an experience that will promote personal and musical growth. Are the materials ready? The record player? The music books? The visual aids? The rhythm instruments? All must be ready before initiating the experience. The best laid plan will go astray if the sequence must be broken to wait for a record player to warm up or rhythm instruments to be brought from the music room.

With adequate preparation of plans and materials we need only one other ingredient and that is a good attitude that will promote the best possible atmosphere. We need an attitude that says to the class, "I like and respect you, and I know you like and respect me. We enjoy being together. We are going to be responsive and respectful of one another to get the most from this interesting musical experience, just as we do from all our classroom experiences." Ideally, the teacher's attitude will gradually unfold as the relationship develops, telling each child that:

  1. She is musical to some degree and is becoming more so each day.
  2. She has something special to contribute to the class.
  3. She is participating well (when she is doing so).
  4. He likes the fact that she is trying even when she is not too successful.
  5. He will never call attention to her lack of success in any area in such a way that will embarrass her.
  6. He will be honest in evaluating her achievement.
  7. He wants, more than anything else, for her to express herself as fully as possible. However, he will not allow her to misuse her privilege, making it difficult for others to express themselves.
  8. He thoroughly enjoys the experience he is inviting her to participate in.
  9. He will not judge her if she does not respond; he will only be sorry that she cannot enjoy this experience.
  10. He wants her to contribute herself to the experience through questions, ideas, suggestions, and positive and negative reactions.

11. He has real concern for her and wants to know her better and help in any way he can.

Note: For children handicapped by physical, mental, or emotional disabilities, the teacher will want to observe these suggestions, and he will also want to adapt all activities and expectations to give these children successful musical experiences. Often this will mean simplifying the sequence and pace of activities.

The teacher will need time to convey all of these attitudes. He will think of others that have value. Most important will be his willingness to reexamine experiences he finds unsatisfactory, to see if his own attitude is at fault and, if so, to find the way to build an attitude that will have more positive effects on the group. Without an attitude that invites the child to respond, no plans, materials, or experiences can help.

Problems

Even the best laid plans sometimes go astray. The plans are carefully made according to the best goals. They include stimulating and challenging activities tailored to the interests and abilities of the age group. The materials are readily available. The attitude is just right. But the experience "falls apart." Why? What caused the failure? At what point did the experience go astray? What did I do or what did I not do? Every teacher must ask himself these questions. The answers are not easy and they differ for each teacher.

First of all, it is important to examine the class. There are classes that contain a number of incorrigible children—children who do not respond in any normal fashion. The teacher who has such a class cannot blame himself for every breakdown. He can only try to obtain the help of the administration and school psychologist in finding every possible way of helping these children learn to adjust to the group. (Some ways of dealing with this type of situation will be suggested later.)

Perhaps the breakdown was due to what started as a virtue—careful planning, but careful planning carried to a rigid routine. Unfortunately the first thing a teacher must learn is that a well-developed plan, though always necessary, must be constantly altered. Indeed, it must at times be discarded. Flexibility is perhaps the most important attribute a teacher can have—the ability to change midstream or toss the plan aside when it is not working. Remember the goal? It is to help the child explore music in all its areas and to help her discover which areas she most enjoys. When the child is working diligently toward that goal in a way that is contrary to "the plan," a tension leading to a breakdown of discipline can develop. Quite naturally then, the child, resenting curtailment of her free exploration, will show her resentment and often her classmates will join her. Unless the teacher is flexible enough to adjust his plans, a breakdown will result. The wise teacher will be sensitive to this situation and will adjust his thinking to allow the child to explore in her own way and at her own pace. He will, in this way, eliminate many of the breakdowns.

Other attitudes encourage breakdowns in experiences. One such attitude says, I am not sure just what I expect of you, or myself. The child senses this attitude immediately and responds negatively to it. It makes her uneasy and insecure. If she is at the age when testing authority and peer acceptance is important, this attitude gives her a chance to test authority; and off she goes, taking her classmates with her and causing a breakdown in the class activity. If, on the other hand, the teacher shows that he expects and will accept only the kind of behavior conducive to learning (though he can accept less than perfect achievement and is flexible in altering his plans) the child will be more inclined to cooperate. In the main, she wants to respect the teacher and she wants to be a good member of the group.

Still another attitude the teacher may have says I'm bored, or I don't like you or these activities. Though he may try, he cannot fool the child. She knows when he is honestly interested and involved she will not accept a reasonable facsimile. She can only be convinced by the real thing. She will normally respond to a teacher who enjoys what he is doing, puts himself into it, and uses his imagination fully.

What about the teacher who has examined his attitudes and believes that he truly has a flexible approach to classroom procedure, definite expectations regarding classroom behavior, and a sincere involvement in all musical activities? It is well, in this case, to reexamine the plan for the experience, to see if it provides interesting activities that the class can successfully achieve. In one of these areas, if he is honest with himself, the teacher will usually find the reason for the breakdown.

What if the class contains a child or children who have severe behavior problems? How can the teacher handle this situation in a way that guarantees constructive experiences for the entire class and helps the problem child cooperate with him and with the group? The answer is not a simple one.

The first step in resolving the problem is to remember that the teacher is responsible for the entire class, and, in all fairness, must provide an atmosphere conducive to constructive activity. When he is so convinced, he will probably follow the best course of action.

Secondly, even the most outwardly rebellious child wants firm limits on her behavior. Indeed, she is sometimes demanding such limits through behavior that she knows will be noticed and dealt with by the teacher. What this type of child needs, in addition to definite behavioral limits, is a more constructive way to get attention and respect. The teacher who can help her achieve this will be doing the child a great service and simultaneously improving the classroom atmosphere for all.

How can he accomplish this? Although there is no one clear-cut answer, these suggestions may help. The teacher may:

1. Try to know and understand the child: her problems, abilities, and interests.
2. Plan activities in which the problem child will be interested, challenged, and successful.
3. Call attention to each success the child experiences.
4. Find ways of giving the child responsibilities in the classroom, such as collecting and distributing books or helping with other similar responsibilities.
5. Talk to the child individually to clarify both the teacher's and the child's feelings about her behavior in the classroom and to focus attention on ways of improving her behavior. The teacher may:
   a. Try to discover and help the child discover why she behaves as she does.
   b. Try to discover ways of helping her behave differently.
   c. Make it quite clear to the child that the teacher wants her to enjoy the experiences initiated in the classroom, but that it is imperative that she behave so that others enjoy the experiences.
   d. Convey the idea to the child that the teacher will be most sorry if her behavior continues because (1) it means that she is still not enjoying or benefiting from musical experiences, and (2) it means that she will have to be punished.
6. Talk to her parents, the school psychologist, and the principal to find ways to help the child.
7. Remove her from the classroom, as a last resort, during the times that she is unable to behave, explaining to her that as much as you regret this action, she cannot remain in the classroom when she is preventing other children from enjoying musical experiences.

It is most effective, in any relationship with a truly disruptive child, if the teacher retains a detached attitude, which tells the child that he cares for her and believes that she suffers most from her disruptive behavior. This attitude on the part of the teacher sometimes convinces the child that antisocial behavior is not effective and encourages her to pursue behavior that may better satisfy the craving for attention. After the first steps toward more constructive behavior, it becomes possible to involve her in activities that, in themselves, have the potential for encouraging more responsible behavior—the activities that make up the interesting world of music.

Basic Musical Experiences

What are these experiences? What musical activities are basic to the elementary music program?

Were we to step into a classroom at this moment to observe a musical experience, it might be difficult to clas-

sify the activity. Singing? Yes, but look! Children are accompanying the song with instruments. Is this a singing or instrumental experience? Listening to a recording? Yes, but look again! One child is moving in rhythm to the recording as it plays. Is this a listening or rhythmic experience? Rhythms? Yes, but a child is notating the rhythm pattern on the board. Is this rhythms or music reading?

Experiences in music, to be meaningful, must overlap. Learning to sing a song is more significant and enjoyable when the child also learns to play an instrument in an appropriate rhythm. Learning to listen to music is easier when the child creates a rhythmic interpretation that clarifies the basic musical elements. Thus, the various types of musical experiences overlap and interweave to construct an interesting program. This list of basic musical activities indicates, in the broadest sense only, the musical experiences of the elementary school program:

1. Rhythmic experiences (bodily movement)
2. Singing experiences (unison and part singing)
3. Experiences with instruments (learning to play rhythm instruments, simple melodic and accompanying instruments and to identify and understand the instruments of the orchestra)
4. Listening experiences (learning to listen to music)
5. Experiences with music reading

These are the basic activities. They are the fundamentals for all experiences. They are the groundwork, the foundation of the music program. Though they cannot be separated from each other (for they are most often experienced in relation to one another), they are the individual components that make the framework of the program. They are the means to help the child achieve the basic goals of the elementary music program—to discover what music is and what in music is most enjoyable to her.

Creative Musical Experiences

How can learning a song become a creative musical experience? How can a listening experience or an experience in bodily movement elicit the creativity of a child? How can a note reading experience ever be called creative?

Webster's definition of *create* says: "To bring into being, to cause to exist. Hence, to invest with a new form."[3] Thus, the teacher who, in the process of encouraging a class to create a rhythmic accompaniment while learning a song, elicits ideas from Johnny for a drum pattern (| ⊓ | |), Judy for a pattern for the triangle (o), and Maryann for a pattern for the maracas (⊓⊓ | |), has, simultaneously, given them an experience in creativity. On the other hand, the teacher who tells

3. Webster's *New Collegiate Dictionary*, 2d ed, s.v. "create."

Judy, Maryann, and Johnny exactly what patterns to play has given them an experience that is sometimes valid in its own right, but is not creative.

The teacher who, in the process of encouraging a class to experience vocal exploration, asks her class to imagine that they are waking up early in the morning and then to make sounds—using their voices—typical of that early hour, is giving children a creative experience. The teacher who suggests possible sounds is giving an experience that may have validity in a certain context, but cannot be called creative.

Creative activity may come from different situations:

1. Situations requiring students to find their own imaginative solutions, using available resources: with a drum, triangle, and tone block create a composition using a steady beat, starting softly, growing louder, then diminishing.
2. Situations requiring children to make changes: How can we make the rhythmic dramatization of this song more effective? Would another instrument be more effective as an accompaniment to the song?

Why is it important to encourage creativity in musical experiences? Above all, it gives children a marvelous opportunity to discover their individuality. Their ideas are being used. Their judgment is being respected. Their personalities have been recognized as having value. In addition, creative experiences do the following:

1. Help children develop powers of discovery and imagination.
2. Help children learn to explore, experiment, make decisions, and evaluate results.
3. Help children trust their own decisions and their ability to contribute to the group.

For the teacher, creative experiences with children have their own rewards. Instead of being the leader and disciplinarian who must direct all activities to a group of conformists, the teacher, though still a guide, benefits from increased exposure to the ideas, feelings, and personalities of children. In addition, children normally respond with warmth and enthusiasm to the teacher interested in their ideas. Observing Johnny's reaction to a specific concept helps guide him through the sequence of musical growth.

The teacher will want some guidelines for creative activities.

1. The experience should insure success for the child:
   a. The problem presented for creative action should be clearly stated.
   b. The problem should be difficult enough to be challenging, but easy enough to be successfully completed.
   c. The atmosphere for the experience should be relaxed and without pressure.
   d. The problem should have many possible solutions.
   e. The problem should encourage children to explore, experiment, make decisions, and evaluate.
2. Each creative contribution must receive full respect. Encourage children to express their musical ideas. Initially, give no value judgment. The process—not the end result—is important.

The way a teacher guides an activity determines whether or not a creative experience occurs. When the teacher encourages children to use their minds and imaginations to develop a new form, they are being creative.

While it would be possible to devote an entire chapter of this book to exploring the creative approach, it is the authors' contention that creativity is so closely interwoven with teaching procedures, that it should be treated in conjunction with each area of activity. A partial listing of experiences that involve creativity, and are found throughout this book follows:

1. Creating rhythmic accompaniments to music, both songs and orchestral music
2. Creating rhythmic interpretations and dramatizations of music
3. Creating additional stanzas to songs
4. Creating original songs and operettas
5. Creating introductions, interludes, codas or contrasting sections (AB, ABA, rondo) for a song, for a rhythm or melody instrument
6. Creating orchestrations for songs, using Orff-type instruments
7. Creating descants and second parts to songs
8. Creating differences in musical form, rhythm, and expression while using the related arts

Evaluating Achievement of Conceptual Understandings and Behavioral Objectives

Perhaps the most difficult part of teaching music in the elementary school is evaluating musical growth. A child's reactions will often tell the perceptive teacher what the student is gaining personally from her experiences with music. It is more difficult to determine whether she is growing in conceptual understanding and achieving the appropriate behavioral objectives. Our first task is to understand the terms conceptual understandings and behavioral objectives.

Music is conceptually structured from many basic elements: rhythm, melody, texture, form, expression. In order to understand and enjoy music, it is necessary to comprehend the concepts relating to each of these elements—to feel them, to react to them, to internalize them, to reason about them. A real understanding of rhythm, for example, involves being able to hear, feel, respond to, and talk about the concept of a basic beat, simple and complex rhythm patterns, meters, and so on. An under-

...nding of melody and the other basic elements of music involves comprehension of the concepts that form these elements.

And so, in order to give children the fullest enjoyment of music—that kind of deep appreciation that comes from understanding as well as feeling—we encourage conceptual understandings. These enhance their enjoyment of rhythmic movement, singing, listening, and experiences with instruments, and reading music.

Behavioral objectives (skills) also contribute to this goal. Learning to hear a short melody and sing it back, learning to keep the beat, to play simple passages on a melody instrument are behavioral objectives that are major achievements for a five- or six-year-old. In addition, they are closely related to growth in conceptual understanding and contribute to musical enjoyment through the finest kind of experience—active participation. For the teacher they are a means of evaluating the child's cognitive, psychomotor skills.

A close perusal of the "Growth and Sequence Chart" following will help us see the relationship between musical activities and musical growth. As we explore each area of musical activity more thoroughly in the chapters following, we will begin to see how musical activities can lead to understandings of musical concepts; the interrelationship between concepts; and, finally, to an awareness of and insight into the largest units (elements) of music: rhythm, melody, texture, form, and expression. This musical growth will occur when children experience musical activities in a climate that encourages joyful experimentation, participation, inquiry, and discovery.

The wisdom and sensitivity of the teacher balances and interweaves musical activities. A skillful teacher fosters joy while he encourages growth in conceptual understandings and achievement of behavioral objectives. These goals of the skilled teacher are possible and eminently desirable if we are to give children the full enjoyment that comes from musical growth.

Growth and Sequence Chart

Primary Grades: Level I

Physical and Psychological Characteristics of the Child

Ages five and six

Muscular development incomplete and uneven, large muscles more developed than small muscles

Whole body usually involved in any rhythmic activity

Eyes still immature, tendency toward farsightedness, just learning to read

Enjoys constant activity, active participation, but fatigues easily

Imaginative, unselfconscious, trusting but aggressive, wants to be first

Competitive and boastful

Needs guidance, but in a discreet way

Most interested in immediate environment and the world of fantasy

Enjoys dramatizations, tends to become character he dramatizes

Needs to be encouraged, praised, recognized

Tends to be noisy and has a short attention span

Egocentric, apt to be stubborn and domineering

Responsive emotionally to environmental factors, sensitive and vulnerable

Ages six and seven

Muscular development slow but steady, small muscles better developed

More able to use parts of the body in rhythmic activity and less easily fatigued

Has longer attention span and is more interested in explanations

More logical in thinking, but still thinks primarily in concrete terms

At the beginning stages of self-consciousness, more introverted and thoughtful

Makes rapid strides in reading, can begin using song books, calmer

Tendency toward exaggeration, more talkative

Needs much encouragement and approval, increasingly sensitive to and aware of attitudes toward others

Musical Activities

Rhythms

Basic bodily movements: walk, run, skip, gallop, bend, push, clap, and so forth

Rhythmic interpretations: free movement (rhythmic exploration), rhythmic dramatizations of music and the spoken word, improvisations (created individually and as a group)

Echo clapping, stamping, snapping, patschen to internalize rhythm patterns, using these durations in all combinations in 4/4 and 3/4 meters:

Relating rhythmic movements to note values

Clapping with number notation, clapping and chanting to develop the inner ear and explore the voice

Action songs, finger plays, and singing games

Experiences with rhythm instruments, creating original accompaniments using rhythm instruments

Rhythmic activities to develop conceptual understanding and to achieve behavioral objectives

Singing by rote

Songs about home, school, community, special days and seasons; nonsense and fun songs; finger plays, action songs, singing games; original songs composed by the class; new verses to familiar songs, created by the class

Songs that develop rhythmic and dramatic interpretations and accompaniments

Syllables with hand signals, using pentatonic scale

Songs that help develop conceptual understandings and achieve behavioral objectives

Vocal exploration and improvisation

Instruments

Playing song bells: beginning with short, simple phrases and scale passages played by ear; later, playing extended phrases and using numbers, syllables, letter names in connection with song bells.

Playing Autoharp: during beginning experiences the teacher presses the button on one-chord songs as a child strums; later, one child presses the button as another strums.

Creating musical scale by making tuned water glasses.

Exploring rhythm instruments; creating original accompaniments, sound effects, and orchestrations using rhythm instruments.

Exploring piano, guitar, and orchestral instruments through listening activities.

Playing Orff-type instruments (xylophones, timpani, glockenspiels, metallophones) as accompaniments to songs and chants.

Instrumental experiences to develop conceptual understandings and to achieve behavioral objectives.

Listening

Listening and actively responding to story music, mood and picture music, marches, waltzes, lullabies, contemporary music, and music of other eras; the teacher or other adults or children singing or playing instruments

Listening, during all musical activities, to develop conceptual understandings and achieve behavioral objectives

Reading

Notating patterns experienced in echo clapping and in chants; do this on the board using stick notation, for example:

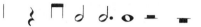

Hump-ty Dump-ty   sat on a wall.

Notating patterns tapped by teacher in circles on a board or beat board; these are tapped by the teacher, using the following notes and rests:

For example:

Recognizing rhythm patterns (formerly echo clapped) in notation of songs.

Singing syllables while using hand signals that follow a contour on the board; then using a staff, recognizing steps, skips, notes that stay in the same place.

Recognizing simple melody patterns (scale passages, skips, steps) from notation.

Responding rhythmically and associating symbols of note values to rhythmic counting and music that "walks" (|), "runs" (♪), suggests "giant steps" (♩), "skates" (♩.), and so on.

Exploring song books and musical scores (generally introduced in latter half of level I, second grade).

Conceptual Understandings

Rhythm

The rhythm of music generally has a basic beat, which contains both sound and silence and can vary in tempo from one musical composition to another.

Word or melodic rhythms may move with the basic beat or be longer or shorter in duration.

Rhythm has strong and weak beats (accented and unaccented notes) and swings in twos and threes (meter).

Rhythm consists of contrasting elements (durations): even and uneven, long and short.

The rhythm of music is related to bodily movements: some music "walks," some "runs," some suggests "giant steps."

These durations (note values) are related in the following ways:

| | = 🎵 | | = 𝄾
|| = ♩ | ♩ ♩ = 𝅝
||| = ♩. | 𝅝 = 𝄻
|||| = 𝅝 | ♩ = 𝄼

Melody

Melodies consist of phrases, which may be similar or different.

A melody may move from high to low or low to high, by step or by skip, or it may stay on the same level. Melodies may have repeated tonal patterns.

Some melodies, instruments, and voices (violins and sopranos, for example) are "high"; some are "low" (cellos and basses, for example).

When we sing, we sing a melody.

The melodic direction of a melody can be written in the musical score.

Texture—harmony

Music consists not only of melody and rhythm, but also of tones sounded simultaneously and heard as an accompaniment to melody (played on Autoharp, piano, guitar, ukulele, or in ensemble music to produce their own musical effects).

Two melodies sung simultaneously (as in a round or canon) produce a unique sound, which is different from the sound of a melody with an accompaniment.

Form

Repeated rhythmic or melodic patterns or phrases make music more meaningful, create form.

Music consists of phrases, each one a musical idea ending with a cadence.

In any one musical composition, there may be some phrases that are alike and some that are different.

Expression

Music may have many different moods. The mood of any musical composition is related to dynamics (loud or soft), tempo (fast or slow), and other expressive elements (accents and so on).

Use of different instruments or voices changes the tone, color, and the expressive qualities of the music.

Reading

The direction of a melody when heard is related to the contour created when drawn on the board or on the musical staff.

The movement of melodies by step, skip, or repeated tones, up or down, is seen in the musical score.

There is a rhythmic relationship between different durations of sound, which may be notated. For example:

Rhythm patterns in songs, and durational relationships in rhythmic counting and clapping may be notated.

The relationship between the numbers, syllables, or letter names used in singing experiences may be notated on the lines and spaces of the musical staff.

Behavioral Objectives: Skills

Rhythms

To keep time to music by using bodily movement, playing instruments, singing

To demonstrate ability to hear the basic beat and distinguish between the basic beat and word rhythms

To demonstrate ability to hear the difference between strong and weak beats (meter)

To discriminate and respond to music that suggests different bodily movements

To demonstrate ability to hear and respond to the difference between contrasting elements (even and uneven, long and short, staccato and legato)

To respond rhythmically to and associate symbols of note values to rhythmic counting and to music that "walks" (| | |), "runs" (🎵 🎵), suggests "giant steps" (♩), "skates" (♩.), and suggests "large giant steps" (𝅝)

To demonstrate rhythmic independence in echo clapping, stamping, snapping, patschen

To demonstrate the relationship between these durations:

$$| = \sqcap \qquad\qquad | = \xi$$

$$|\, | = \downarrow \qquad \downarrow \downarrow = \circ$$

$$|\, |\, | = \downarrow. \qquad \circ = \rule{8mm}{1mm}$$

$$|\, |\, |\, | = \circ \qquad \downarrow = \rule{8mm}{1mm}$$

To help create rhythmic interpretations and dramatizations of songs and instrumental music as well as original accompaniments using percussion instruments

Singing

To hear a short melody and repeat it accurately

To use voice with some freedom in experiences with vocal exploration and improvisation

To exercise some control in quality of singing as well as pitch and rhythm

To sing many songs, differing in rhythm, melody, texture, form, and expressive qualities

To begin to differentiate melodic directions and phrases

To help create original songs, rhythmic interpretations, and dramatizations of songs

To accurately sing intervals using sol, mi, la, do, and re (pentatonic scale) and use hand signals

Instruments

To play simple passages on melody instruments (song bells, xylophone, piano)

To strum Autoharp in rhythm as the teacher or another child presses buttons

To help create and play simple accompaniments on rhythm instruments for singing and listening experiences

To help create improvisations or soundscapes using rhythm or Orff-type instruments

To play simple ostinati as accompaniment to chants and songs, using Orff-type instruments

Listening

To listen to music and thus develop conceptual understandings and acquire skills in musical activities (singing, rhythms, instruments, reading)

To listen responsively to story music, mood or picture music, and abstract music

To hear and respond to similar and contrasting phrases and form

To hear and respond to differences in register, timbre, tempo, and dynamics

Reading

To identify differences in melodic direction (up, down, same) from notation

To identify difference between tonal patterns and phrases that are alike and different from staff notation

To identify and notate rhythm patterns experienced in echo clapping, chants, and songs, using:

To identify, sing, and play from notation simple melody patterns (scale passages, patterns that step, skip, or stay the same)

To sing songs from staff, in the pentatonic, using hand signals and syllables

---

Intermediate Grades: Level II

Physical and Psychological Characteristics of the Child

Ages seven and eight

Small muscles better developed, able to participate in activities involving finger coordination

Eyes more able to do close work

Verbalizes more easily but often noisy, argumentative, and bossy

Beginning to become aware of individual differences and more able to evaluate accomplishments

Feelings easily hurt, self-critical

Beginning of gang age; more and more influenced by his contemporaries of the same sex but still quite dependent on teacher for guidance and encouragement

Eager to experiment with new things but often lacks judgment

Dramatic and explosive, emotionally impatient

Enjoys organized group activities, games, folk dances

Cannot be depended upon to assume too much responsibility

Begins to enjoy making collections of objects

Still learns best through activity

Ages eight and nine

Overall growth slow and steady, small muscles well developed, eyes now able to do close work without strain, generally well coordinated

Interested in doing things well

Concerned about self; self-appraisal

Capable of independent thinking but

uncertain and has difficulty in making choices and decisions

Has strong sense of right and wrong and will challenge lack of fairness

Critical of others

Deepening of gang spirit with intense loyalties, often outspokenly critical of adults

Shows expanding interest in community and country but continued interest in the world of fantasy

Needs to have rules and regulations clearly defined but wants to participate in establishing them

Needs to be treated more as an adult

Enjoys being given definite responsibilities but becomes discouraged when too much pressure is exerted

Individual abilities become pronounced

Musical Activities

Musical activities developed in level I should be reinforced and expanded on all levels.

Rhythms

Basic bodily movements used individually and in combination to keep time and to step out note values and rhythm patterns

Clapping, stamping, finger snapping, patschen to internalize rhythm patterns, develop inner ear

Improvisation using clapping, snapping, patschen, stamping, entire body

Rhythmic rondo, through clapping, stamping, patschen, finger snapping

Conducting in various meters

Creative bodily movements (interpretations, dramatizations of music)

Singing games and simple folk dances

Use of rhythm instruments (original accompaniments created by individuals or class)

Making percussive sounds with body (clapping, snapping, patting, stamping) as rhythmic accompaniment to singing

Bodily movement to focus attention on a theme or form in listening experiences

Singing by rote and by note

Syllables with hand signals, in pentatonic, major, and minor modes

Vocal exploration and improvisation

Use of musical notation and music books as aids in learning a song

Folk songs of USA and other countries, patriotic songs

Songs for special days and holidays

Nonsense and fun songs

Action songs and singing games

Songs that correlate with other areas of study

New verses created by the class for familiar songs

Songs and operettas created by the class

Dialogue and echo songs, songs with chants or ostinati

Songs with descants

Harmonizing cadential endings of songs

Rounds

Melodic rondo

Two-part singing, using hand signals

Singing in canon, using hand signals

Instruments

Learning to play recorder or similar melody instrument

Playing song bells or similar instrument (phrases, scale passages, counter melodies, ostinato patterns, chord roots)

Creating rhythmic accompaniments using percussion instruments, for songs, to experience form (ABA), and to focus on themes and meter in music

Learning to accompany two-chord songs on Autoharp (first teacher and one child, then two children)

Making Autoharp chord charts for songs by ear

Playing ostinati on Orff-type instruments to accompany songs

Learning to recognize more band and orchestral instruments

Learning syllables, numbers or letter names in conjunction with playing melody instruments

Melodic improvisation on recorder

Rhythmic rondo using percussion instruments

Beginning instruction on band and orchestral instruments

Participating in club activities

Listening

To story music, mood or picture music, and abstract music

To the teacher, other adults, or other children sing or play instruments

For understanding of simple musical forms (ABA)

To focus on themes and expand understanding of notation (using theme cards, Cues to Music cards, and musical score)

For further understanding of texture in music (harmonic, polyphonic, electronic music)

For further understanding of the expressive elements of music

Reading

Recognizing, reproducing, and notating more complex relationships in duration in 2/4, 3/4, and 5/4 meters:

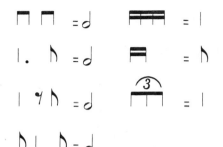

Recognizing chord tones in a melody from notation

Playing and sightsinging more complex phrases and simple melodies in 2/4, 3/4, and 4/4

Beginning to identify chordal progressions

Recognizing AB and ABA form through use of the score

Beginning to notate original songs and accompaniments

Beginning to use expressive markings as a way of indicating dynamics and tempo

---

Conceptual Understandings

Conceptual understandings developed on level I should be reinforced and expanded on all levels.

Rhythm

Music consists of rhythm patterns.

A rhythm pattern is a group of related durations.

Within each pattern, notes (durations) may be the same, longer, or shorter.

A strong pulse is sometimes felt after the initial sounding of a note, or as follows:

♩ | ♩ syncopation

♩. ♪ a dotted quarter note followed by an eighth note

These durations are related to each other in the following ways:

♫ ♫ = ♩

♩. ♪ = ♩

♩ ♪ = ♩

♬ = ♪

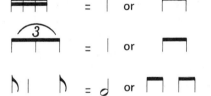

Six-eight (6/8) meter (compound) may be felt either as two groups of threes (1-2-3-4-5-6) or three groups of twos (1-2).

Five-four (5/4) meter may be felt as a group of threes and a group of twos (1-2-3, 1-2).

Melody

The range of a melody may be narrow or wide and is determined by its lowest and highest pitches.

All melodies are organized in some kind of scale.

Melodies written in the major, minor, or pentatonic scale have their own unique sound.

The end of a melody or the end of a section of a melody is marked by a cadence.

Texture

A group of related sounds produced simultaneously (chords) often accompanies songs.

These change to correspond to the melody.

Two or more melodies, the second (and any additional melodies) imitating the first exactly, create the texture of rounds and canons.

Counter melodies are melodies usually played or sung lower than the primary melody.

Descants are melodies usually played or sung higher than the primary melody.

Certain harmonic progressions indicate a point of rest (cadence).

Music that is constructed harmonically sounds different from music constructed contrapuntally or monophonically.

Some songs can be accompanied by one chord; others require two or three chords.

Some chords consist of a root and notes a third above and a fifth above that root.

The chordal progression I and V$_7$ appears in most songs.

Form

Some music is written in two sections, A and B, each one different from the other.

Some music is written in ABA form, which consists of three sections; the first and third are similar, the second, contrasting.

Rondo is a form with two or more sections contrasting and alternating with Section A (ABACA or ABACADA).

Expression

Our voices and musical instruments can produce differences in tone quality and mood.

Major or minor modes affect the mood of music.

Each instrument of the band and orchestra has its unique timbre and register that can change the mood and feelings expressed by music.

Reading

Chords played on the Autoharp (or other accompanying instruments) can be found outlined in the notation of a melody.

A sequence of tones suggesting a scale or part of a scale can often be found in the notation of a melody.

The rhythm of music is usually divided into measures, which are separated by bar lines.

Tempo, dynamics, and other expressive elements of a performance may be notated.

ABA form can be recognized from notation.

Behavioral Objectives: Skills

The behavioral objectives developed on level I should be reinforced and expanded on all levels.

Rhythms

To reproduce more complex rhythm patterns in echo clapping, stamping, snapping, and patschen, using the following new durational relationships in 2/4, 3/4, and 5/4 meters:

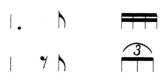

To conduct simple songs in meters that swing in twos or threes

To create rhythmic canons and rondos through clapping, snapping, patschen, stamping, in 2/4, 3/4, and 4/4 meters

To demonstrate greater rhythmic control in bodily movement used to step basic beat, note values, and rhythm patterns

To develop more complex rhythmic interpretations and dramatizations, singing games and folk dances

Singing

To sing more difficult songs with better tone quality, pitch accuracy, and expressiveness

To sing more difficult interval relationships with syllables, numbers, letter names, and hand signals

To sing more complex phrases from the musical score

To sing more independently dialogue and echo songs, ostinati with songs, simple counter melodies and descants, rounds and canons, and melodic rondos

To sing in two parts from hand signals

To demonstrate more originality in vocal exploration and improvisation

To help create more complex verses and songs

To sing in canon, using hand signals.

Instruments

To play simple songs on recorder or other melody instrument

To play more complex passages on melody instruments, aiding in singing and experiencing form

To create more complex rhythmic accompaniments using percussion instruments to experience meters, to focus on themes, form, and changes in mood

To play Autoharp independently: first one-chord, then two-chord songs (two children)

To create and read chord charts for Autoharp

To play more complicated ostinati or Orff-type instruments

To recognize the tone quality of more band and orchestral instruments

To use percussion instruments, recorder, and other melody instruments for improvising ABA and rondo form

Listening

To demonstrate the ability to listen more discriminately to focus on conceptual understandings

To hear chord changes in Autoharp accompaniments

To hear differences between harmonic and contrapuntal music through singing rounds and simple part-songs

To identify the difference between major and minor scale construction

To hear and identify the difference between AB, ABA, and rondo form

To differentiate between minuet, march, lullaby, waltz, rounds, and other types of composition

To hear and follow themes in abstract listening experiences

To differentiate aurally between music with and without a tonal center

To hear and identify cadences

Reading

To identify and reproduce from dictation more complex durations:

To identify from notation the range of a song

To identify and reproduce from dictation simple melodic patterns from songs

To identify the outline of a chord in the notation of songs

To identify scale passages in the notation of songs

To demonstrate ability to see the relationship between bar lines and meter

To begin to play and sightsing more complex phrases and simple melodies, using numbers, syllables, or letter names

To begin to identify the chordal progression I, V₇, I

To identify AB and ABA form from the musical score

To begin to notate original songs and accompaniments

To begin using expressive markings for tempo and dynamics in singing and playing

To begin reading notation for ostinati song accompaniments

Upper Grades: Level III

Physical and Psychological Characteristics of the Child

Ages nine and ten

Beginning of preadolescent period

Somewhat introverted, but beginning to be more loquacious

Rapid but uneven growth accompanied by awkwardness and restlessness

Wide range in maturity levels as well as abilities

Continuation of gang spirit, but generally accepts adult directives

Tendency toward fluctuation of interest in school work

Apt to be conflict between the sexes

Interest in larger world develops; own country, other countries, social concepts

Growth in ability to reason and think through own problems

Needs to share in making decisions, wants to be treated as an equal

Ages ten and eleven

Wide variation in level of physical maturity

Rapid growth often accompanied by inner conflicts

Is often overcritical, rebellious, uncooperative

Peers are all-important, influencing conduct as well as dress

Respects good sportsmanship and is more able to cooperate for the good of the group

Enjoys competition, is willing to work to acquire skills

Can understand and relate to broader social concepts

Interests are far-reaching

Girls often more mature than boys

Musical Activities

Musical activities developed on levels I and II should be reinforced and expanded on level III.

Rhythms

Making percussive sounds with the body as a rhythmic accompaniment to songs

Creating rhythmic rondo and canons through improvisations using clapping, snapping, patschen, and stamping

Performing rhythmic interpretations and dramatizations of music and the spoken word

Creating a rhythmic canon and accompaniments, using rhythm instruments

Conducting songs and orchestrations in varied meters

Dancing folk and square dances

Creating original dance steps

Singing by rote and by note

Art songs, patriotic songs, songs for special days and holidays, nonsense and fun songs, folk songs of the world

Songs that correlate with other areas of study and life, ethnic songs

Using music books to help learn a song

Using syllables and hand signals in unison and two-part singing

Dialogue and echo songs

Songs with chants, descants, counter melodies

Rounds and canons

Songs harmonized in thirds and sixths

Songs harmonized using chord roots or by vocal chording

Harmonizing by ear

Original songs and operettas

School chorus

Instruments

Continuing to play soprano recorders

Enriching singing and listening experiences through playing recorders

Continuing to play Autoharp (three-chord songs by ear and by reading chord charts)

Continuing to play rhythm instruments to explore form, to enrich listening experiences, and to accompany singing (emphasis on Latin American rhythms)

Learning to classify instruments of the band and orchestra into families, according to sight and sound

Continuing to play Orff-type instruments as song accompaniments

Beginning guitar and ukulele

Individual children begin to accompany classroom singing using guitar, ukulele, and piano

Continuing to create original introductions, interludes, and codas using melody and rhythm instruments

Listening

To story music, mood and picture music, abstract music

To selections from operas, operettas, and the musical theater

To the teacher, other adults, and children singing or playing instruments

To children's concerts

To create dramatizations of story music

To focus on themes, by ear and through use of theme and Cues to Music cards

To focus on expressive elements in music

To create instrumental accompaniments to music

To focus on form (ABA, fugue, theme and variations, rondo and other)

For greater understanding of texture (twelve-tone scale, electronic music, polytonality)

Reading

Recognizing, reproducing, and notating more complex relationships in duration:

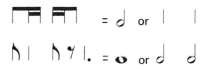

Singing and playing from notation in 6/8 and 7/4 meters (as well as 2/4, 3/4, and 4/4)

Learning to understand, recognize, and play major, minor, and pentatonic scales

Using key signature to help identify scales

Learning to use time signatures to interpret notation and accent

Notating original songs and accompaniments

Learning to recognize rondo form from notation

Singing and playing themes for listening experiences

Conceptual Understandings

Conceptual understandings developed on levels I and II should be reinforced and expanded on level III.

Rhythm

Rhythm controls any melody.

These durations are related to each other in the following ways:

$$ \flat \,|. \quad = \; d \; \text{or} \; | \quad | $$

$$ \sqcap \;\sqcap. \quad = \; d \; \text{or} \; | \quad | $$

$$ \sqcap \; \sqcap \quad = \; d \; \text{or} \; | \quad | $$

$$ \flat \,| \quad \flat \, \gamma |. \;\; = \; o \; \text{or} \; d \quad d $$

Melody

In addition to major, minor, and pentatonic, some melodies are organized in the whole tone scale, tone row, or mode.

A melody based on a major, minor, or modal scale has a tonal or key center to which all tones relate.

Songs constructed in the major, minor, modal, or pentatonic scale have unique

sound qualities, as do compositions constructed in the whole tone scale or tone row.

Texture

Music may be monophonic, homophonic, or polyphonic.

When many tones sound simultaneously, the texture is thick; when only a few tones sound and they are spaced far apart, the texture is thin.

In major and minor scales, certain fundamental chordal progressions are used; one common progression is the I, IV, V_7, and I chords.

Chords to accompany songs are constructed in a specific way, usually with a root, a note a third above, and a note a fifth above that root.

When there is a key center, music has tonality.

When two different key centers are used simultaneously, bitonality or polytonality results.

When no key center is used, atonality results.

Form

Theme and variations is a form in which a theme is stated then repeated in altered arrangements.

A fugue is a form in which a theme is announced, followed by an "answer" in another voice, then imitated by one or more voices.

An opera is a drama set to music.

An opera contains many small musical forms: overture, recitative, aria, chorus, duets, trios, quartets, and ballets.

Expression

We can blend and balance our parts in singing and playing to create an expressive tone quality.

The way we "phrase" in singing and playing affects the expressive qualities of the music.

The nature of the rhythm, tonal organization, texture, instrumentation, tempo, and dynamics of any musical composition affects the expressive qualities of the composition.

Different cultures produce unique expressive qualities in music.

Contemporary music has new timbres, rhythms, pitch organizations, and textures, which create expressive qualities quite different from earlier music.

Reading

Major, minor, modal, pentatonic, and whole tone scales have their own unique notational relationship.

Songs reflect the notational relationship of the scale involved.

Key signatures relate to the scale (tonality) upon which the song is constructed.

Time signatures (2/4, 3/4, 4/4, and so on) indicate the number of beats to a measure (top number) and the kind of note that gets one beat (bottom).

Behavioral Objectives: Skills

Behavioral objectives developed on levels I and II should be reinforced and expanded on level III.

Rhythms

To remember and reproduce longer rhythm patterns, through clapping, snapping, patschen, and stamping, using these new durational relationships:

To participate in creating a rhythmic rondo, canon, and improvisations in 5/4 and 7/4 meters

To participate and help create more complex folk dances, rhythmic interpretations, and dramatizations

To help create original dance steps

To conduct a short musical composition

To help create more sophisticated, original compositions for rhythm instruments

Singing

To sing a wide variety of songs, including dialogue and echo songs, songs with descants and counter melodies, chants, songs harmonized in thirds and sixths, using chord roots or vocal chording

To blend and balance parts to produce a pleasing tone quality, to phrase musically, and to sing more expressively

To hear and reproduce from memory more complicated melodic patterns both in singing songs and in echo-singing solfeggio with hand signals, including canon

To help create sophisticated original songs and operettas

To use conceptual understandings to facilitate learning songs

Instruments

To play more complex songs (including two-part songs) and improvisations on the recorder

To use the recorder to enrich listening and singing experiences

To play three-chord songs on Autoharp, both by ear and by reading chord charts

To play more difficult passages on melody instruments, including original introductions, interludes, codas, and themes for listening

To use rhythm instruments to play more sophisticated accompaniments and improvisations

To play simple accompaniments for singing using guitar or ukulele

To play more sophisticated accompaniments using Orff-type instruments and orchestrations

To distinguish, by ear, instruments of the band and orchestra, understanding the family to which each belongs

Listening

To hear and explain how differences in texture, rhythm, melody, form, tempo, dynamics, instrumentation, and interpretation affect the expressive qualities of music

To demonstrate understanding of the difference between program and abstract music

To demonstrate the ability to enjoy some of the world's great musical literature

To demonstrate familiarity with many types of musical expression: folk songs, art songs, ballet, opera, symphony, concerto, suite

To identify new forms in music: rondo, theme and variations, fugue

To follow themes in music with increasing ease, utilizing Cues to Music and theme cards

To demonstrate familiarity with opera as a musical form

To participate in some of the forms used in opera

Reading

To recognize, reproduce, and notate rhythmically more complex durational relationships:

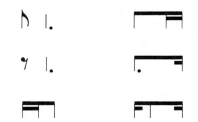

To read notation in 6/8 and 7/4 meters

To explain major, minor, and pentatonic scale construction

To use key signatures to interpret tonality

To notate original songs, with teacher assistance if necessary

To identify from notation rondo form

To play themes for listening experiences

To identify familiar chordal progressions (I, IV, V_7, I)

To identify from notation melodic sequences in songs

To use meter signature to interpret notation and accent

To identify from notation homophonic and polyphonic music

Rhythmic Experiences 2

Rhythm is, for most children, the element through which they first experience and explore the world of music. Long before he can sing a tune, for example, the child responds rhythmically to the movement it suggests. Long before he can articulate what an orchestral composition suggests to him, he shows us, with his body. The rhythm of music is, for him, a natural extension of the rhythmic movement he has experienced from birth. From the first regular breathing felt as an infant, through the creeping, crawling, and walking stages, he has known the feeling of rhythm. His enjoyment and need for rhythmic motion is observed endlessly as he walks, runs, skips, and hops. The satisfaction he obtains from the exploration of rhythmic movement, the release of energy that is so satisfying to him, and the pride he feels in the discovery of increased muscular coordination and new-found ability to express himself through bodily movement are evident to the most casual observer.

For all these reasons, experiences with rhythm are not only the most natural element through which children can first be helped to explore music, but also are vitally important in giving children a physical release that invariably improves their learning behavior.

Aims of Rhythmic Experiences

1. To expand the child's innate enjoyment of rhythmic movement
2. To help the child develop an increasing ability to hear, feel, and respond to rhythm in music
3. To help the child develop the conceptual understandings and achieve behavioral objectives related to rhythmic experiences (For a list of conceptual understandings and behavioral objectives related to each age level, see the chart at the end of chapter 1.)
4. To develop an increasing freedom and spontaneity in the child's rhythmic response

Relationship of Rhythmic Experiences to Other Musical Activities

All musical experiences involve rhythm. The teacher may ask, however, whether there are times when rhythm should be emphasized during experiences in which the primary emphasis is singing, listening, exploration of instruments, or music reading. The answer is, of course, yes. Whenever focusing upon the rhythm can encourage increased enjoyment or musical growth the child should be encouraged to hear, feel, and respond to the rhythm of the music. Indeed, the imaginative teacher will make a conscious effort to weave rhythmic experiences into other musical activities (singing, listening, playing, reading). It is through this kind of interweaving that the various elements of music form a related whole.

How does the teacher encourage children to hear, feel, and respond to rhythm in experiences that primarily concern another musical activity? Throughout the chapters in this book, there are suggestions for such emphasis on rhythm. They include:

1. Encouraging children to respond to the rhythm of music through bodily movement.
   a. Basic bodily movements
   b. Rhythmic interpretations
   c. Free movement (rhythmic exploration)
   d. Rhythmic dramatizations
2. Encouraging children to create rhythmic accompaniments using rhythm instruments. (See chapter 4.)

For detailed suggestions about emphasizing rhythm in singing, listening, and other activities, refer to these specific chapters in this book.

Rhythmic Activities

Rhythmic activities are specifically structured to give children experiences in responding to music through bodily movement. They are experiences that help children hear, feel, and respond to all the elements of music through appropriate rhythmic movement. There are lists of music for rhythmic activities at the end of this chapter.

Whatever the "conceptual focus" in any rhythmic activity—be it rhythm, melody, texture, form, expression, or music reading—when the "activity focus" is rhythmic, children are helped toward musical growth and enjoyment through some kind of rhythmic movement.

Rhythmic movement activities carry the opportunity for a vital, fulfilling experience or the possibility of a

e. They give the child the opportunity to cultivate his creative imaginative powers.
f. They help the child achieve a greater enjoyment of music.

3. Guidelines for the teacher
   a. Accept any serious effort made by children to interpret music rhythmically. Always use a positive approach. Withhold value judgments.
   b. Help children hear the important elements in music, without demanding a specific response.
   c. If possible, focus attention on successful interpretations without making other children feel inadequate.
   d. Use experiences from the world of make-believe as well as from real life to help children get the feeling for interpretive movement.
   e. If children are especially self-conscious about moving rhythmically, the teacher may want to structure initial experiences so that children sit on the floor with their eyes closed and move only the upper parts of their bodies.

Free Movement

1. A sequence for developing an experience in free movement[1]
   a. Children listen to the music.
   b. Children decide what it makes them want to do rhythmically without suggestions from any other source.
   c. Children move in their own way to the music.

2. Value to the child of experiences with free movement
   a. They give the child the opportunity to use his own resources, without outside influence—to hear, feel, and respond to the basic elements of music: rhythm, melody, form, texture, expression.
   b. They give him the opportunity to explore and nurture his own responses to music.
   c. They help him become aware of his ability to hear differences in music and to respond to these differences, thus increasing his enjoyment of music.

3. Guidelines for the teacher
   a. In initial experiences with free movement—before the child has had the opportunity to test his own responses and gain confidence—the teacher may help by using devices that establish the basic beat or the general feeling of the music or both.
   b. As children show ability to respond, however minimally, encourage them to follow their rhythmic impulses in interpreting music.

1. Free movement is rhythmic exploration of music done without suggestions or restrictions from the teacher.

Rhythmic Dramatizations

1. Types of rhythmic dramatizations
   a. Children can create rhythmic dramatizations of the spoken word (stories adapted by the teacher; poetry, such as the Japanese Haiku; fairy tales; American Indian and African folk tales).
   b. Children can create dramatizations of music written to tell a story.
   c. Children can create dramatizations of music that suggests a story, because of the composer's expressive use of the elements of music.

2. A sequence for developing a rhythmic dramatization of the spoken word
   a. Adapt and simplify a story or poem so that the rhythmic movement suggested is obvious to children, occurs frequently enough to hold their interest, and is within their ability to understand and perform.
   b. Children should become familiar with the story or poem before dramatizing. (An exception to this occurs with improvisational stories in which the teacher adapts the story line, on the spot, to the actions of children.)
   c. Children should discuss the story or poem: how it can best be dramatized rhythmically; where in the room the characters move; what rhythmic accompaniment will be played for each character; and who will play each character.
   d. Children should experiment with different movements in the dramatization, associate these movements to the rhythmic accompaniment, change and experiment until the dramatization is effective.

3. A sequence for developing a rhythmic dramatization of music
   a. Children listen to the music to hear how it suggests a story. (When the music has been written to tell a story, the teacher may or may not decide to tell children the story before they hear the music.)
   b. Children create a general story outline, based on the expressive elements of the music.
   c. The teacher helps children become aware of the specific musical cues (rhythm, melodies, tempo changes, dynamics, instrumentation) that suggest each part of the story.
   d. Children create, through experimentation, rhythmic movements that illustrate each part of the story.

4. Value to the child of experiences with rhythmic dramatizations
   a. They give him the satisfaction of enjoying a familiar and well-loved activity (story telling) with an added dimension: the rhythmic pulse, felt inwardly and expressed through rhythmic movement.

b. They give him greater enjoyment of music as he hears, feels, and responds to differences in rhythm, melody, texture, form, and expression.

c. They give him the opportunity to experiment with his ideas, relating rhythmic movement to musical elements.

d. They allow him to be creative and feel the self-esteem and group rapport that accompany this kind of activity.

5. Selecting appropriate music for rhythmic dramatizations

a. Music should have strong rhythmic impulses that immediately suggest a specific response.

b. The length of the music must fit the attention span of the group. Kindergarten or first-grade children will listen thoughtfully for only a few minutes; as they grow older, they will gradually extend this period.

c. It must be of a melodic and rhythmic construction that the group can understand and remember. Kindergarten and first-grade children will respond successfully to two or three melodies or rhythm patterns if they are easily heard and repeated. Gradually they can understand a more complicated structure.

6. Guidelines for developing a rhythmic dramatization of music

a. The teacher should know the music and the musical elements that suggest a story.

b. An outline of the musical cues (melodic and rhythmic) that suggest the dramatization can be very valuable. The following are outlines of two compositions:

Composition One
Melody A slow, sustained
Melody B fast
Melody A slow, sustained

Composition Two
Melody A skipping rhythms, violins
Melody B walking rhythms, trumpets
Melody A skipping rhythms, violins
Melody C slow, percussion
Melody A skipping rhythms, violins

c. The teacher who plans rhythmic movements to dramatize each section will be better able to guide children in a rhythmic dramatization. Though she will not want to tell them her ideas, she will be more apt to act instinctively to help them find their own.

d. The teacher should allow children to experiment with ideas for rhythmic movement that dramatizes the story and to demonstrate and select the ideas that seem to work best.

e. The teacher should provide a climate that allows children to express their ideas, experiment with them, and evaluate them without being judgmental.

In addition to knowing the types of activities to introduce, the teacher should learn the conceptual understandings and behavioral objectives connected with these activities at each age level. (See "Growth and Sequence Chart," chapter 1.) She should ask herself, for example, when planning an experience using basic bodily movements, What concepts related to rhythm or melody can be the focus of this experience? Should the conceptual understandings be related to form, texture, expression? What behavioral objectives can be achieved? She should decide what medium to use for the experience: piano, drums, recordings, or clapping? The teacher should also know that any music or accompaniment for rhythmic experiences should have these characteristics:

1. The rhythm (or rhythmic accompaniment) must be easily understood and felt by the child. That is:

a. Music for basic bodily movements must obviously suggest its intended movement: marching, skipping, running, galloping, skating, or other.

b. Music for initial experiences with interpretive rhythms must suggest only one strong mood or picture, which has potential for varied interpretations. (Later experiences can use music with varying moods.)

c. Music used for rhythmic dramatization must always give strong, definite cues that can suggest a story. (Many different stories might evolve from these cues.)

2. The tempo must be comfortable for the child so that he is not pushed to increase his muscular coordination. Thus he will use his body rhythmically according to his own rate of development. (For the very young, this often means that the teacher must follow the beat of the child.)

3. The accompaniment used must be long enough to be satisfying and enjoyable, but short enough to hold the child's interest.

So that experiences can be planned to help the child with difficulties, the teacher should know as much as possible about the child:

1. What muscular coordinations are difficult for him?

a. Skipping, galloping, swaying, or other of the basic bodily movements?

b. Movements involving the large muscles (the whole body, legs, or arms)?

c. Movements involving the smaller muscles (hands and fingers)?

2. In what tempo (slow, moderate, or fast) can he comfortably respond using these basic movements?
3. Is he able to hear and respond rhythmically to music that creates a mood or picture (interpretive rhythms)?
4. What units are difficult for him to hear: the basic meter, the strong and weak beats, the phrase, or the musical construction (form)?
5. Does he have difficulty expressing his response or participating in a group interpretation or dramatization?

While we can give general answers to some of these questions (the average child can gallop before he can skip; large muscles are used before small; young children can generally move at a fast tempo more easily than at a slow tempo), still, individual differences do exist among children of the same age, and must be considered if maximum growth is to occur.

The teacher will want to provide physical conditions for satisfactory rhythmic movement. Whenever possible, use a large room. When the classroom must be used, arrange it for the maximum amount of space and allow only as many children on the floor as can comfortably move in the space available.

It is important, too, that the atmosphere encourages successful experiences. Since children enjoy rhythmic experience so much that they sometimes bubble over with disruptive enthusiasm, the teacher must be especially firm in asking them not to talk or touch each other as they participate. She must help children understand that quiet and cooperation are essential so that they can hear and respond to the music, and have the freedom to express themselves through rhythmic movement.

Finally, the teacher should find ways to interlace rhythmic activities with other types of activity, so that the child receives all possible opportunities to achieve conceptual understandings and behavioral objectives so important to the enjoyment of music. Experiences involving the related arts, singing, listening, instruments, and music reading should reinforce concepts.

When rhythmic experiences are based on these things:

1. Knowledge of the types of activities
2. Awareness of the related conceptual understandings and behavioral objectives
3. Appropriate medium and music for each experience
4. Individual characteristics of the child
5. Physical facilities and atmosphere most conducive to successful experiences
6. Successful interweaving of related arts and other musical activities

the teacher can feel satisfied that she has provided the groundwork for a continuing, rhythms program that will help children enjoy hearing, feeling, and responding to rhythm in music.

Figure 2.1
Keeping the beat, photograph by Elizabeth Wheeler

In the sections that follow there are suggestions for experiences focusing on concepts related to each of the basic elements of music structure: rhythm, melody, form, texture, expression, and notation.

Rhythmic Concepts

Level I

Materials Needed
1. A rhythm instrument for each child
2. Pictures illustrating strong beat and weak beat
3. Record player
4. Recordings[2]
   a. Composition by Ussachevsky, Folkways Records, album no. FX 6160
   b. March (*Nutcracker* Suite) by Tchaikovsky, RCA Victor *Basic Record Library for Elementary Grades* recording WE 72, or Bowmar *Orchestral Library* recording BOL 071, or Holt, Rinehart and Winston *Exploring Music* recording 28
   c. "Soldier's March" by Schumann, RCA Victor *Basic Record Library for Elementary Grades* recording WE 72
   d. March by Hollaender, RCA Victor *Basic Record Library for Elementary Grades* recording WE 72
   e. "Kangaroos" (*Carnival of the Animals*) by Saint-Saëns, Bowmar *Orchestral Library* recording BOL 064
   f. "Fog and Storm" (*Harbor Vignettes*) by Donaldson, Bowmar *Orchestral Library* recording BOL 066
5. Music Cue charts

2. Recordings listed are one possible choice of music that children may enjoy as they focus on conceptual understandings or behavioral objectives. The teacher should freely substitute other recordings whenever she can better meet her objectives by so doing.

Rhythmic Activity
Basic bodily movements

Related Musical Activities
1. Listening
2. Playing rhythm instruments
3. Creating accompaniment for rhythm instruments

Conceptual Understandings
1. The rhythm of music generally has a strong basic beat that contains sound and silence.
2. Some music has a weak beat.
3. The rhythm of music is related to bodily movements: some music moves at a moderate tempo ("walks"); some music moves quickly ("runs"), and so on.

Behavioral Objectives
1. To keep time to music through bodily movement
2. To respond to music with appropriate bodily movements
3. To demonstrate the ability to hear the difference between music with a strong beat and music with a weak beat

Related Arts
Comparing strong and weak beat in music with strong and weak beat in art
1. Figure 2.2. View of Bonnefont Cloister, looking northeast, showing herb garden (strong beat)
2. Figure 2.3. View of the Cloisters, the West Terrace (weak beat)

Procedure
1. Basic beat in a game, "Feel the Beat in Your Feet"
   a. If space is available, have the children form a circle. (If not, children may stand near their chairs.)
   b. Tell children to try to feel their hearts beat. (Children may put their hands on their hearts or wrists to feel a pulse.)
   c. Tell them they are going to try to put that heartbeat in as many parts of the body as possible. Discuss all the places it might be put (in the feet, toes, hands, fingers, hips, nose, eyelids, and so on).
   d. Explain that you will begin by putting the beat in one part of your body, and that they are to listen and watch, then echo you exactly. They are then to keep the beat going wherever you put it, until the person to your right tells them to feel it in some other part of the body, at which time they are to echo that person, keeping the beat in the new part by moving that part until the next person in line speaks. The game will continue until everyone has had the opportunity to put the beat in a

Figure 2.2
Museum view, the Cloisters-Gardens, view of Bonnefont Cloister, looking northeast, showing herb garden. Photograph from the Metropolitan Museum of Art. The Cloisters Collection.

Figure 2.3
Museum view, the Cloisters-Exteriors, view of the Cloisters, the West Terrace. Photograph from the Metropolitan Museum of Art. The Cloisters Collection.

new part of the body. Remind children to try to keep the beat going at its initial speed and to keep it going without pause throughout the game.

e. Begin by saying:

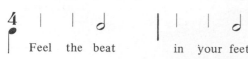

Feel the beat in your feet.

as you step the basic beat in place. Signal the class to echo, then turn to the person to your right, signaling him to say "Feel the beat, in your . . . ." and the class to echo him, putting the beat in a new place. If the class does not understand the procedure, stop, clarify, and begin again. (Not all children on level I will be able to keep the beat perfectly throughout the game and should not be expected to do so.)

2. Putting the beat into rhythm instruments
   a. Display the rhythm instruments. Ask for volunteers to put the beat into one of the instruments:

Feel the beat with your sticks.

When several have done so, distribute all the instruments. Have rhythm sticks feel the beat, followed by other instruments.

   b. Add an accompaniment, using drum, piano, or recording as the entire class "feels the beat."

3. Observing strong and weak beats in illustrations
   a. Display illustrations demonstrating strong beat and weak beat.
   b. Ask children which picture makes them think of music with a strong beat. (figure 2.2) Why? (Help them to see that the repeated arches give us the same feeling as repeated pulsations.)
   c. Ask them why figure 2.3 seems to suggest a weak beat. (In this photograph there are only suggestions of arches, in two small groups. There is no strong repetition of lines or shapes as in figure 2.2.)
   d. Ask the children if they can think of other things they see around their houses, neighborhoods, or on the way to school that suggest a strong beat. They may think of a fence, with repeated vertical slats, a row of trees, or their seats, if arranged in rows.

4. Playing rhythm instruments, using a weak beat
   a. Ask the children to think for a moment how it would sound if they played their rhythm instruments with a very weak beat.
   b. Tell them to wait for your signal, then play with a weak beat. Give the signal.

   c. Discuss the difference in the sound they produced with a weak beat from the sound they produced with a strong beat. Could they feel the beat inside? Were they playing the beat together? Was it a fuzzy kind of feeling? (Ask any other appropriate questions.)

5. Strong and weak beats in music, composition by Ussachevsky and March from *Nutcracker* Suite by Tchaikovsky
   a. Tell the children you are going to play a composition. Ask them to listen carefully to determine if the music has a strong beat that can be clapped or a weak beat that cannot be clapped. Play the recording of Composition.
   b. Encourage the children to tell you what they heard. Could they clap the beat? Did they hear something in the rhythm that made them want to make strong, definite movements? Or was it a weak beat? (If necessary, play the recording again, to clarify. The composition is made on a tape recorder. There is little or no repetition of a rhythmic or melodic pattern—nothing that would suggest a repetition of movement or a basic pulse.)
   c. Tell the children to listen to another piece of music to determine if it has a strong beat they can clap. Play March.
   d. Encourage the children to tell you what they heard. Could they clap the beat? Did the music make them want to move? If necessary, play the recording again.

6. Basic bodily movements to music with a strong beat
   a. Ask for volunteers to demonstrate what bodily movement the march suggests. If necessary, ask questions similar to the following: "Does the music make you want to run?" "Is it fast?" "Is the music moving at a moderate tempo—making you want to walk?" (Children will probably want to march to the music.)
   b. Let a group of children do the movement deemed most appropriate, as you play the recording. Repeat, letting other children move, until all have had the opportunity to participate.

7. Creating an orchestration of March, using rhythm instruments (For guidelines and detailed suggestions for one possible orchestration see chapter 5, "Listening Experiences.")

8. Evaluating children's ability to hear the difference between music with a strong beat and music with a weak beat
   a. Distribute papers to the children on which the following has been printed:

Music Cue Chart	
1. Strong beat	Weak beat
2. Strong beat	Weak beat
3. Strong beat	Weak beat
4. Strong beat	Weak beat

b. Tell the children that you will play four musical compositions and that you would like them to circle the words that best describe the beat of each (strong beat or weak beat). Play the following:
   (1) "Soldier's March" by Schumann (strong beat)
   (2) "Kangaroos" (*Carnival of the Animals*) by Saint-Saëns (weak beat)
   (3) "Fog and Storm" (*Harbor Vignettes*) by Donaldson (weak beat)
   (4) March by Hollaender (strong beat)
   (The teacher may want to substitute other recordings, perhaps including a "pop" recording. Further, she may want to play only a part of each selection—just enough to give the feeling of a strong or weak beat.)
c. Have the children check their answers against the correct answer. Discuss the answers, focusing on the musical elements that give the feeling of a strong or weak beat. Strive to minimize any feelings of inadequacy, which may arise. Poor test results would suggest the need for further experiences with this concept.

Rhythmic Experiences That Focus on Rhythmic Concepts

Level I

Discovering the Basic Bodily Movements
1. Ask the children to name all the parts of their bodies that can move.
2. Encourage volunteers (first individuals, then groups) to demonstrate what each part of the body can do as the class claps rhythm. (Legs can walk, run, hop, and so on; hands can clap, tap, wave, and so on.)
3. Through class discussion and positive comments, thoroughly explore each suggestion, emphasizing the variations possible (walking slowly, as though tired; walking quickly, as though eager to get home; walking like father, mother, a policeman, an elephant, and so on).

Level I

Discovering the Basic Bodily Movements Suggested by the Music
"The Ball" from *Children's Games* by Bizet, RCA *Adventures in Music* grade 1, vol. 1, LES-1000

1. Initiate a discussion about the instruments of the band and orchestra in which children focus on the instruments most likely to "run" (violins, flutes) and those most likely to "walk" (bass tubas, trombones).
2. Play enough of "The Ball" for children to determine the type of movement suggested and the instruments used. Discuss: Does it walk or run? Is it fast or slow? (It runs and is fast.)
3. Select volunteers to demonstrate the movement suggested until one child runs. (If the class has difficulty in hearing the rhythm, play the recording and have them clap the rhythm.)
4. Select several children to run, letting them run long enough to feel the rhythm and mood, then letting each select a child to take his place.

Level I

Creating Rhythmic Interpretations Based on a Person, Animal, or Machine
Machine Rhythms, Classroom Materials recording CM 1077

1. Through discussion, help the children focus on people, animals, and machines that move slowly and those that move quickly. When do people move slowly? When they are tired, or carrying bundles? What kind of animals move slowly? What kind of machines move slowly?
2. Tell children to listen and try to feel the rhythm inside while you play an accompaniment (or recording) for a person, animal, or machine moving slowly. They should raise their hands when they have an idea for becoming such a person, animal, or machine.
3. Play an accompaniment, using piano, drums, or a recording such as "Machine Rhythms." Select volunteers to interpret the music. Make positive comments about interpretations that most successfully incorporate the rhythm of the accompaniment. Let the class guess what kind of animal, person, or machine children depict.

Level I

Feeling Meter, through Basic Bodily Movements
"Little Miss Muffet"

1. Say "Little Miss Muffet" for the children, emphasizing the rhythmic flow of the words and the strongly accented syllables.

$\begin{smallmatrix}6\\8\end{smallmatrix}$ Rhythm of Words
Basic Beat

Lit - tle Miss Muf - fet
Sat on a tuf - fet,
Eat - ing her curds and whey.
There came a spi - der
And sat down be - side her,
And fright - ened Miss Muf - fet a - way.

2. Select three or four children to say the rhyme with you as the class taps their fingers lightly in any rhythm desired.
3. Have individuals demonstrate their rhythm as the rhyme is repeated. Have the class select a preferred pattern. (Some children may tap word rhythms, others may tap the basic beat.)
4. Have half the class say the rhyme as the other half clap the selected pattern. Switch groups.
5. Have the class select rhythm instruments that would best accompany the rhyme, using the pattern selected. (If the pattern reflects the rhythm of the words, tone blocks or rhythm sticks might be best; if it reflects the primary accents, triangle or finger cymbals may be preferable.)

Level I

Focusing on Rhythm That Moves in Twos and Threes, through Echo Clapping

1. Clap the notation at the right. Have students echo on repeats.
2. To add variety, tell the children you will play the patterns on a drum and that they should echo using whatever you call: snap, clap, pat knees, stamp.

Cape Cod Chantey

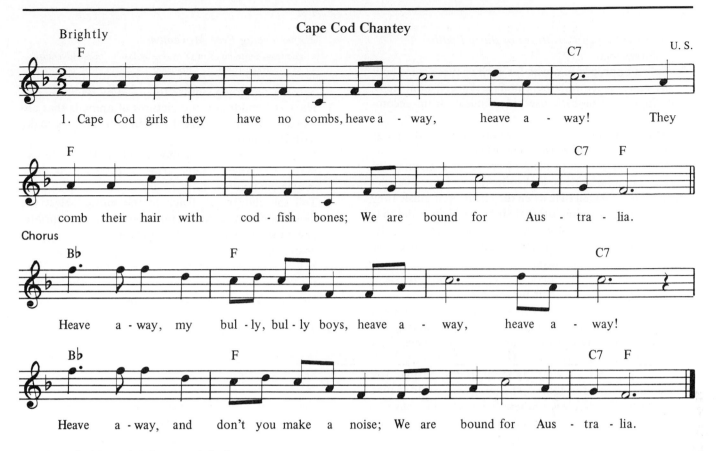

Brightly

F

C7

U. S.

1. Cape Cod girls they have no combs, heave a - way, heave a - way! They comb their hair with cod - fish bones; We are bound for Aus - tra - lia.

Chorus

Bb   F   C7

Heave a - way, my bul - ly, bul - ly boys, heave a - way, heave a - way!

Bb   F   C7   F

Heave a - way, and don't you make a noise; We are bound for Aus - tra - lia.

2. Cape Cod boys they have no sleds, heave away,
heave away!
They slide down hill on codfish heads;
We are bound for Australia.

3. Cape Cod cats they have no tails, heave away,
heave away!
They blew away in heavy gales;
We are bound for Australia.

Arranged from *Heritage Songster* by Dallin and Dallin, © 1966 by Wm. C. Brown Company Publishers, Dubuque, Iowa. (in public domain)

Level I or II

Focusing on Music That Moves in Twos and Threes, through Bodily Movements

1. Have children choose partners and do the following:

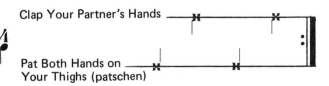

Clap Your Partner's Hands

Pat Both Hands on Your Thighs (patschen)

2. Ask what kind of a song this would best accompany, a song that moves in twos or a song that moves in threes (twos). Have the class sing a song similar to "Cape Cod Chantey," as they use the pattern to accompany it.

3. Ask children how their accompaniment might be changed to fit a song that swings in threes (by adding another clap on the partner's hands).

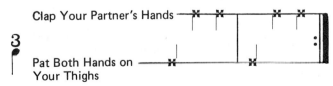

Clap Your Partner's Hands

Pat Both Hands on Your Thighs

4. Have the children think of a song they know that moves in threes, and you accompany it as they sing. Some possible songs are: "On Top of Old Smokey," "Santa Lucia," "My Bonnie," and "Sweet Betsy from Pike."

Responding to Variations in Basic Bodily Movements

1. Select appropriate music for each of these basic bodily movements: walking, running, skating, giant steps, skipping. (You may use piano music, drum accompaniment, or recordings.)
2. Make certain everything is ready for a rapid change from one kind of music to another.
3. Divide the class into as many groups as needed: walkers, runners, skaters, and so forth.
4. Tell the children that when they hear their music they are to start moving, using their entire bodies, and that when their music stops they are to stop immediately. Remind them not to touch anyone, and to move only when their music plays.
5. Play just enough music so that each group has a chance to perform their movement.
6. Tell the children you will play the music for each movement in rapid succession, in no particular order. They must listen carefully and move only when their music plays.
7. Play portions of each type of music, using any sequence or order desired, changing frequently so that children will not know when to expect their music.
8. Children will enjoy focusing on the notation for each of these bodily movements. See "Notational Concepts: Music Reading" in this chapter.

Level I or II

Strong and Weak Beats in Music That Moves in Twos

1. Select one of these recordings: "Marche Militaire" by Schubert, Bowmar *Orchestral Library* recording BOL 067 or "Stars and Stripes Forever" by Sousa, RCA *Adventures in Music* grade 4, vol. 2, LES-1005.
2. Play the recording, clapping on strong beats and encouraging the class to join you.
3. Ask how this music would best be counted: one, two or one, two, three. (one, two)
4. Have the class listen to the recording as they count one, two and clap on one only.
5. Through experimentation, have the class select a different motion for the second (weak) beat (patting head, knees, desks or snapping fingers).
6. Play the recording as the class claps on beat one and does another motion on two.
7. Repeat until all suggestions have been used.

Level II

Experiencing Free Movement
Gigue from Suite no. 3 in D Major by Bach, RCA *Adventures in Music* grade 1, vol. 1, LES-1000

1. Select a recording similar to Gigue by Bach.
2. Have the children bring pictures of animals that are moving. Discuss different movements animals make with their legs.
3. Have the class discuss movements that people can make with their hands, arms, and legs. List these movements on board.
4. Tell the children to listen to the music, select the movement or movements that seem most appropriate, and raise their hands when they are ready to demonstrate.
5. Select a few volunteers to move to the music. Stop the music before the children tire. Give other groups an opportunity to demonstrate movement.

Level II

Experiencing 4/4 Meter, through Ball Bouncing

1. Select a recording similar to one of the following: "Cortege of the Sadar" by Ippolitov-Ivanov, Bowmar *Orchestral Library* recording BOL 067 or March (*Summer Day*) by Prokofieff, RCA *Adventures in Music* grade 1, vol. 1, LES-1000.
2. Play the recording as you count one, two, three, four, clapping on one and encouraging the class to participate.
3. Ask for a volunteer to join you. Explain that instead of clapping on one, you will bounce a ball.
4. Play the recording, counting one, two, three, four in rhythm. On the first beat of measure 3, bounce the ball to a child. Have him bounce it back on the first beat of the next measure. Repeat until he and the class understand what to do.
5. Have the class form a circle. Let them practice counting and bouncing the ball on one, first without the recording, then with the recording.

Level II

Creating a Rhythmic Dramatization
"The Little White Donkey" from *Histoires* no. 2 by Ibert, RCA *Adventures in Music* grade 2, vol. 1, LES-1001

1. Tell the class to listen carefully to the recording to hear what story it may suggest. Play the recording.
2. Discuss the story ideas suggested by the children, encouraging them to focus on the exact musical elements that suggest various parts of the story (changes in tempo, dynamics, rhythm, instrumentation).

3. Have the class vote for the story idea they think best fits the music.
4. Have the class listen again to decide exactly what happens during each section of music. Write their ideas on the board. One class suggested:

Section 1
  (A) Jogging rhythm and lovely melody: A man and his family are rolling West in a covered wagon. A dog runs along beside, nipping at the horses' hooves and barking now and then.

Section 2
  (B) Loud chord: The dog runs off to chase a rabbit. The father is angry about the delay and scolds the dog when he returns. The dog hangs his head in shame.

Section 3
  (A) Jogging rhythm and lovely melody: The family continues its journey in the covered wagon.

5. Elicit ideas for dramatizing each section. Let volunteers demonstrate. Have the class decide which they like best and where in the room the dramatization will take place.
6. Select characters to dramatize. Through discussion and experimentation, improve the dramatization until it reflects the predominant musical elements.

Level II

Focusing on Fast and Slow Tempi, through a Game

1. Make two large cards (from oak tag) on which the words *fast* and *slow* have been printed:

Fast	Slow

2. Select a song that children can easily sing or play on the recorder.
3. Select a child to be "it." Tell him he must play or sing the song in the tempo indicated on the card shown. Select a child to hold cards. If the child who is "it" succeeds in playing or singing the song in the tempo indicated by the card, he then gets to hold the cards and selects someone else to be "it." If he is unable to complete the song or changes tempo, he is out and the teacher selects another person to be "it." (The teacher may want to form two teams, girls competing with boys.)

Level II

Creating a Rhythmic Dramatization

"March and Comedian's Gallop" from *The Comedians* by Kabalevsky, RCA *Adventures in Music* grade 3, vol. 1, LES-1002 or Holt, Rinehart and Winston *Exploring Music* recording 110

1. Tell the children you will play a recording that may suggest a story to them. Play "March and Comedian's Gallop."
2. Through discussion focusing on musical elements, have the class decide whether the music describes people or animals and what these people or animals are doing in the various parts of the music. (One class decided the first section describes several people creeping along a dark cave, trying to find the way out, frightened by imaginary animals coming from dark corners.)
3. Ask for volunteers to dramatize the first section, letting many children experiment, until the class decides which idea best fits the music and why.
4. Help the class work out a dramatization of the second section in a similar manner.

Level I, II, or III

Focusing on the Basic Beat, through Creating a Machine, Using Basic Bodily Movements

This experience may be adapted to any level by making it more or less complex and using more or fewer children. Level I may find it more manageable if only a few children participate and if extensive discussion and help from the teacher precede the experience. Levels II and III may be able to involve more of the class and create quite complicated machines. In addition, the experience may be adapted to create "Movement Soundscapes," each child doing an appropriate movement and sound, in place, depicting a holiday, a seasonal sport, the country, the city, a baseball game, and so on.

1. Tell the children that they will build a machine. Ask for a volunteer to be the first part of the machine, explaining that he simply comes to the center and moves a part of his body in a steady rhythm, simulating part of a machine.
2. When the child is doing so, invite other children, one at a time, to become another moving part of the machine. Explain that each new part should relate to the parts already in motion. For example:
   a. A child moving his right arm back and forth like a piston creates a space under his arm where another part may go in and out in rhythm.
   b. At the precise moment that a child's right hand reaches its farthest point in space, a hammer might hit it or a fastener rotate it to tighten a cap.
   c. The legs of the child starting the machine building might be parted, inviting two arms, perhaps, to move rhythmically back and forth between them.
3. Stress that each child's movement should:
   a. Relate in some way to another movement.
   b. Reinforce the basic pulsation established.

Creating a Rhythmic Dramatization Based on the Spoken Word

1. Tell this American Indian myth, developed by the Musquakie (Fox) Indians, which tells one version of how the constellation known as the Great Bear came to exist:

Section A

It is said that once, a long time ago, in early winter, three men went out to hunt for a bear. A little dog named Hold Tight, followed along behind them. Along the river they went, and into the woods, climbing higher and higher and higher, until they came to the place where the shrubs and low bushes grew.

After a long time, they came to a trail that led to a cave on a hillside. There they stopped. Which one of them would go into the cave to look for the bear? Finally the oldest said he would go, and into the cave he crawled, poking with his bow to drive out the bear.

Section B

He had been poking only a few minutes, when out came the bear! Out of the cave he ran. Past the hunters he ran and off to the North, to the place from whence comes the cold.

After him went the youngest hunter, to drive him back. Back came the bear—but this time, in order to avoid the hunters, he ran to the East, to the place from whence comes the daylight.

After him went the hunter who was next oldest. And back came the bear. But this time he ran to the West, to the place where the sun goes down. And after him went all the hunters, followed by Hold Tight.

Off they went—mile after mile—but suddenly, as the hunters looked down, they saw Grandmother Earth below them. The bear was taking them into the sky! But there was nothing they could do—it was too late. Higher and higher they went.

Section C

Finally they caught the bear, and killed him. They put on a great pile of sumac and maple branches, where they butchered him, which is the reason these trees turn red—the color of blood—every fall.

Then the hunters lifted the bear's head and threw it to the East. That is why the group of stars in the shape of a bear's head appears before sunrise each winter morning.

Then the hunters picked up the bear's backbone. They threw it to the North. That is why the group of stars that outlines the bear's backbone appears in the northern, winter sky.

And if you want to know what happened to the hunters and their dog Hold Tight, just look into the sky until you find them, for there they are—all year round—four bright stars in a square (the bear) and, behind them, three big, bright stars (the hunters) and one tiny, dim star (Hold Tight). For the hunters and their little dog are doomed to move around the sky forever.

And that is the end of the story.[3]

2. With the help of the class, make a list on the board of the actions that outline the story. For example:
   a. The hunters go off to hunt.
   b. The little dog Hold Tight follows them.
   c. They climb higher and higher up the mountains.
3. Through discussion and experimentation, help the class decide how each character would move throughout Section A of the story (walk or run, fast or slow, large movements or small), having individual children demonstrate their ideas.
4. Have the class decide where in the room each part of Section A will take place.
5. Select volunteers to dramatize Section A, accompanying them on a drum as you tell the story. Discuss for improvements.
6. Continue similarly until all three sections have been dramatized.
7. Children may enjoy:
   a. Adding percussion instruments for sound effects
   b. Having classmates be the narrator
   c. Dramatizing other Indian myths

Level II or III

Strengthening Rhythmic Independence, through a Rhyme

1. Teach the following by having children pat their knees and clap their hands as they listen to you, joining in when they are able. (Repeat many times.)

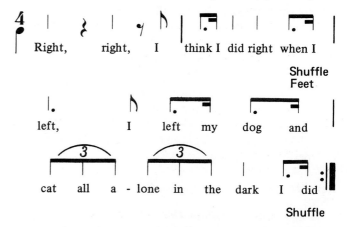

3. Adapted from Franz Boas, *Handbook of American Indian Languages*, pt. 1, Bureau of American Ethnology, Bulletin no. 40 (Washington, D.C., 1911). Linguistic text recorded by William Jones, translated and revised by Truman Michelson.

2. When children know the rhyme, have them form a circle and chant as they walk, shuffling their feet as indicated so that the foot mentioned in the rhyme steps at the appropriate moment.

Melodic Concepts

Level I or II

Materials Needed
1. Copy of "Eena, Deena, Dina, Duss"
2. Illustration depicting upward and downward motion, highs and lows
3. Record player
4. Recording of "The Swan" (*Carnival of the Animals*) by Saint-Saëns, Bowmar *Orchestral Library* recording BOL 064, RCA *Adventures in Music* grade 3, vol. 2, LES-1003, or Holt, Rinehart and Winston *Exploring Music* recording 28
5. Music Cue charts
6. Music and melody instrument for evaluation procedure

Rhythmic Activities
1. Basic bodily movements
2. Interpretive movements

Related Musical Activity
Listening

Conceptual Understandings
1. Melodies consist of phrases, which may be similar or different.
2. A melody may move from low to high or high to low, by step or skip, or it may move to a note on the same pitch level.

Behavioral Objectives
1. To differentiate between contrasting melodic directions
2. To differentiate between phrases that are similar and phrases that are different

Related Arts
1. Experiencing phrase in a rhyme ("Eena, Deena, Dina, Duss")
2. Observing upward and downward direction in a picture (figure 2.4, view of Verrazano Bridge)

Procedure
1. Experiencing the feeling of a phrase and direction through the rhyme, "Eena, Deena, Dina, Duss"

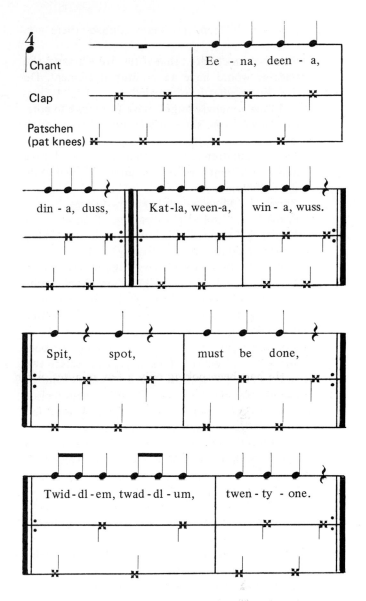

a. Have the children begin a patschen-clap pattern with you, as notated in the rhyme, then echo each phrase when you say it. Repeat, varying the rhythmic accompaniment, until children know the rhyme. (Stamp, finger snap, or patschen snap may be substituted for patschen clap.)
b. Put the chant on the board:
Eena, deena, dina, duss,
Katla, weena, wina, wuss,
Spit, spot, must be done,
Twiddlem, twaddlum, twenty-one.

c. Ask the children how many phrases there are. (four)

d. Remind the children that if this were a song, the phrases would have an additional element. Do they know what it is? (melody)

e. Ask how a melody might move from note to note. (up, down, step, skip, or stay on the same pitch level)

f. Ask the children for ways to make these phrases move with their voices. One group decided to do the following:

Phrase 1 Move voices from low to high.
Phrase 2 Move voices from high to low.
Phrase 3 Stay on the same pitch level (at a moderate pitch—neither too high nor too low).
Phrase 4 Move voices from high to low.

g. Ask the class how they might show the direction of their voices with their hands, and let them experiment as they chant, using the direction decided upon for each phrase.

h. Ask for volunteers who will move their entire bodies in the direction of each phrase. Select two students for each phrase. Have the class chant the rhyme, moving their hands to show the direction of the voices, as the volunteers move. Repeat, letting other children move as the class chants.
(The teacher may expand the experience by having children decide whether they want voices and bodily movements to move by step or skip as does a melody.)

2. Observing direction in an illustration
a. Have the children look at figure 2.4 or a similar picture.
b. Discuss the picture: Is anything moving up in this picture? Down? Are there highs and lows? Focus on the lines and shapes that create the contour (ups, downs, highs, and lows). In music, differences in pitch create the contour.

3. Experiencing phrase and direction through rhythmic response to "The Swan" by Saint-Saëns
a. Remind the children of their experiences hearing phrases in poetry and song. Remind them we know when a phrase ends because we seem to hear a "period" (in music, called a cadence). Tell the children that you will play a recording and when they think they hear a new phrase they are to raise their hands.

Figure 2.4
View of Verrazano Bridge, New York, photograph by David Rosenthal

b. Play the recording of "The Swan." If necessary, help the children hear phrases by raising your hand at the beginning of a new phrase.

c. Divide the class into two groups. Tell the children that this time as they hear the music, group 1 is to clap the strong beats of the first phrase and every alternate phrase thereafter, and group 2 is to pat their knees on the strong beats of the second phrase and every alternate phrase thereafter. Play the recording as the class claps and pats.

d. Discuss the kinds of phrases heard. What was the general mood created? Flowing or erratic? Did anyone hear phrases that moved primarily upward? Primarily downward? Both upward and downward? (All types were represented.)

e. Tell the children you would like group 1 to move their arms in the direction suggested by the first phrase and every alternate phrase and group 2 to move their arms in the direction suggested by the second phrase and every alternate phrase. Remind the children to move their arms in the spirit and mood of the music.

f. Play the recording. Help the children, if necessary, by moving your arms with each group.

g. Ask the class if they can think of ways to move their entire bodies to suggest the direction in which each phrase moves. After each suggestion, let one child from each group demonstrate, moving on his phrases only as the recording plays. Write the suggestions on the board and let the class vote for those they like. One group suggested the following:

For phrases moving primarily downward: walk slowly, stepping with each strong beat and moving your arms slowly downward.

For phrases moving primarily upward: from a crouched position move upward in a circling motion, until standing with hands raised above head.

For phrases moving both downward and upward: walk slowly moving your arms slowly down or up, as the music suggests.

h. Have group 1 form a circle leaving space between each child. Tell this group to move on the first phrase and every alternate phrase, using the suggestions voted upon, but feeling free to make any changes they think more effectively interpret the phrase direction.

i. Play the recording as group 1 moves. Make positive comments about the children whose movements effectively interpret the phrase direction or mood or both.

j. Have group 2 form a circle inside the circle made by group 1. Ask them to move on the second phrase and every alternate phrase in the opposite direction of group 1.

k. Play the recording as group 2 moves, group 1 watching.

l. Tell the children that this time both groups may move on their phrases. Remind them to listen carefully so they hear when to move, and to make movements that express both direction and mood.

m. Correct any misunderstandings, playing the music again, if necessary, to help the children understand what to do and to develop facility.

4. Evaluating the children's ability to hear differences in melodic direction

a. Distribute papers upon which the following has been written:

Music Cue Chart

1. Phrase moves mostly up.	Phrase moves mostly down.
2. Phrase moves mostly up.	Phrase moves mostly down.
3. Phrase moves mostly up.	Phrase moves mostly down.
4. Phrase moves mostly up.	Phrase moves mostly down.

---

b. Tell the class that you arc going to play four musical phrases, and that they are to circle the phrase on the Music Cue chart that best describes each. Play the following on the piano, recorder, or other melody instrument:

(1) Mostly down

(2) Mostly up

(3) Mostly up

(4) Mostly down

Rain, Leaves, Snow, and Sun

Lois Raebeck

	Em			Am			Em			B7	
1. The	rain's	fall	- ing	light	- ly	a	- round	us	to	- day,	Oh
2. The	leaves ___	are	fall	- ing	a	- round	us	to	- day,		Oh
3. The	snow - flakes	are	fall	- ing	so	si	- lent	- ly	down,		With
4. The	sun ___	is	shin	- ing	so	big	and	so	round,		It

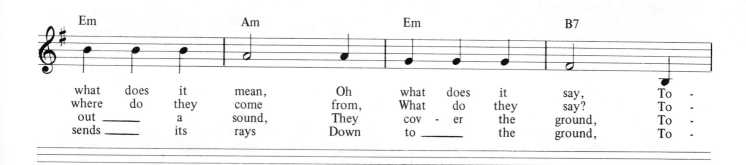

	Em			Am			Em			B7	
what	does	it	mean,	Oh	what	does	it	say,	To	-
where	do	they	come	from,	What	do	they	say?	To	-
out ___	a	sound,	They	cov	- er	the	ground,	To	-
sends ___	its	rays	Down	to ___	the	ground,	To	-

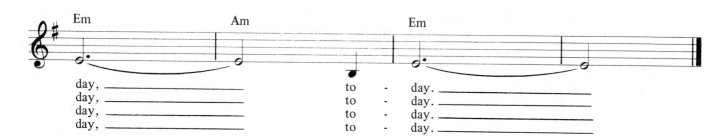

	Em		Am			Em		
day, ___		to	- day. ___
day, ___		to	- day. ___
day, ___		to	- day. ___
day, ___		to	- day. ___

Rhythmic Experiences That Focus on Melodic Concepts

Level I

Experiencing Melodic Direction, through Rhythmic Dramatization

1. Tell the children to find a place on the floor and turn into tiny little snowflakes. Tell them to listen and, as the music you play moves upward, to imagine a snow storm is piling more and more snow on them, until they grow slowly into a huge snowman. After the music reaches the highest point, it will slowly move downward, telling them that the sun has come out and is slowly melting them to the ground.
2. Improvise or play a slowly ascending melody on the piano as children move very slowly into a huge snowman. Then play a slowly descending melody as they melt away.

Level I

Experiencing Melodic Direction, through Rhythmic Dramatization
"Rain, Leaves, Snow, and Sun"

1. Ask the children to listen to a song that describes rain, leaves, snow, and sun. Sing "Rain, Leaves, Snow, and Sun."
2. Ask the children what direction the words and melody suggest. (downward)
3. Encourage the children to dramatize each verse, focusing on melodic direction.

Level I

Experiencing Melodic Direction, through a Game Using Basic Bodily Movements
"Find the Button"

1. Tell the children to listen to your piano accompaniment and tell you what kind of movement it suggests to them: walking, running, skipping, or other.

Happy Are They

Sturdily

Israeli Round
Fine

Hap - py are they who in friend - ship Will - ing - ly work to - geth - er.
Hin - ay mah tov u - mah na - im She - vet a - chim gam ya - chad.

Hap - py are _____ they who ____ in peace u - nit - ed,
Hin - ay mah ____ tov u - mah na - im, _____

D. C. al Fine

Work to - geth - er, Will - ing - ly work to - geth - er.
She - vet a - chim, She - vet a - chim gam ya - chad.

From Book 5, of *Discovering Music Together*. Used by permission of the Follett Publishing Company.

2. Play or improvise music with a slow tempo, for walking.
3. Tell the children they are going to play "Find the Button." The object is to find a button, which will be hidden. The person who is "it" will have to look for the button, while he moves in the walking rhythm just played. When the melody goes up that indicates the person who is "it" is getting warm. When the melody goes down he is cold and should change direction.
4. Show the class the button. Select a child to be "it," and have him close his eyes. Select a volunteer to hide the button so that all will see where it is hidden.
5. Remind the child to walk in rhythm to the music and to change the direction of the search according to what the music tells him by its melodic direction.
6. When the child finds the button have him select someone else to be "it," then hide the button as all watch except "it."

Level I

Experiencing Melodic Direction, through Free Movement

Andantino from *Raymond Overture* by Thomas, RCA Victor *Basic Record Library for Elementary Grades* recording WE 78

1. Select a recording similar to Andantino.
2. Make strips of paper, approximately two feet long and two inches wide, from colored tissue paper.
3. Give each child two strips of paper.

4. Remind the children of all their experiences with melodic direction (melodies that move up and melodies that move down).
5. Tell the children you are going to play a recording and that when they feel the mood and melodic direction, they may move their strips of paper in the direction the music suggests. (If space is limited, have a few children move at one time.)

Level II or III

Experiencing Phrase Differences, through Basic Bodily Movements
"Happy Are They"

1. Review with the children the various percussive sounds they themselves can make. For example:
   a. Clapping with flat hands
   b. Clapping with cupped hands
   c. Clapping with three fingers, two fingers, one finger
   d. Patting knees, shoulders, heads
   e. Snapping fingers
   f. Clicking tongue
2. Teach "Happy Are They" by having the children:
   a. Identify the number of phrases by ear
   b. Select, through experimentation, a different percussive sound for each phrase
   c. Accompany the song as they sing it in unison, then as a round

Textural Concepts

Level II or III

Materials Needed
1. Pictures illustrating texture and no texture
2. Copy of "This Old Hammer"[4]
3. Autoharp or guitar, if used
4. Copy of "Row, Row, Row Your Boat"

Rhythmic Activities
1. Basic bodily movements
2. Rhythmic dramatization

Related Musical Activities
1. Singing a round and song with chant
2. Playing the guitar or Autoharp

Conceptual Understandings
1. Music can consist not only of a single melody, but also of tones sounded simultaneously (as an accompaniment or in ensemble to create its own musical effect).
2. Songs are generally accompanied by a group of related sounds produced simultaneously (chords), which must be changed to correspond to the melody being accompanied.

Behavioral Objectives
1. To sing a round and a chant with pitch accuracy and rhythmic independence
2. To demonstrate greater rhythmic independence and control
3. To demonstrate the ability to hear differences in texture

Related Arts
Examining pictures to explore texture in the visual arts
1. Figure 2.5 *Homage to the Square – Precinct* by Joseph Albers (no texture)
2. Figure 2.6 *Bird's-Eye View of the Great New York and Brooklyn Bridge, and Grand Display of Fire Works on Opening Night* (texture)

Procedure
1. Experiencing texture through the visual arts
   a. Display *Homage to the Square* and *Bird's-Eye View.* Ask children to examine both and describe the differences between them.

4. Songs suggested are one possible choice of material children may enjoy as they focus on conceptual understandings or behavioral objectives. The teacher should freely substitute other songs whenever she can better meet her objective by so doing.

Figure 2.5
Homage to the Square – Precinct by Joseph Albers. Oil on composition board. 31-¾ × 31-¾". 1951. The Metropolitan Museum of Art, George A. Hearn Fund, 1953.

   b. Discuss the differences. Which has the feeling of many different things happening at once? Name things that are happening simultaneously. Does *Homage to the Square* suggest activity? Are many things happening simultaneously? Focus on the idea that *Homage to the Square* has little or no texture. It seems flat. *Bird's-Eye View,* on the other hand, seems to be active on many different levels at the same time. It has texture.
   c. Ask what in music gives the feeling that many things are happening at once? (Two or more tones or sounds, heard simultaneously.) Discuss the ways in which the class has experienced this kind of music—music with texture. Perhaps they will name some of the following:
      (1) Singing a song with a chant or counter melody
      (2) Singing a round
      (3) Singing with accompaniment (piano, Autoharp, guitar, Orff instruments)
      (4) Chanting with a rhythmic accompaniment (clapping, stamping, etc.)
      (5) Chanting with accompaniment of Orff instruments
      (6) Playing percussion instruments as an accompaniment to singing
      (7) Listening to orchestral music
      (8) Interpreting or dramatizing songs or orchestral music
      (9) Creating a percussive accompaniment to orchestral music

Figure 2.6
Bird's-Eye View of the Great New York and Brooklyn Bridge, and Grand Display of Fire Works on Opening Night.
The Metropolitan Museum of Art, The Edward W. C. Arnold Collection of New York Prints, Maps, and Pictures. Bequest of Edward W. C. Arnold, 1954.

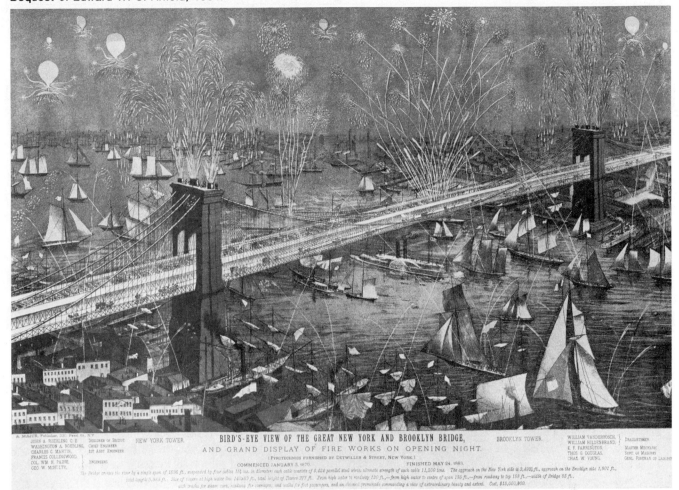

2. Experiencing texture through dramatizing a song with a chant, "This Old Hammer"
Prior to this experience, ask a child who plays the Autoharp or guitar to learn the accompaniment for "This Old Hammer."

   a. Sing "This Old Hammer" for the class.
   b. Ask the class if the song had texture. (No. It was a single melody, sung without accompaniment.)
   c. Tell the class that they are going to add texture. Teach them the following chant by having them pat their knees or stamp-clap as they sing with you:

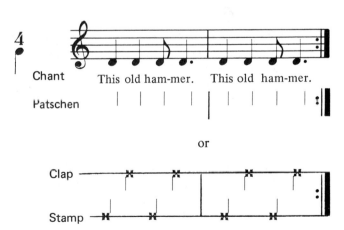

This Old Hammer

This old ham-mer _____ killed John Hen-ry, _____

This old ham-mer _____ killed John Hen-ry, _____

This old ham-mer _____ killed John Hen-ry, _____ But it

won't _ kill me, _____ won't kill me. _____

From *One Tune More (Songs of America)* © 1961 by World Around Songs. Used by permission.

d. When they are singing the chant easily, continue patting your knees or stamping and clapping as you sing the melody. Begin melody on the third beat of the chant, the word "hammer."

e. Ask who can sing the melody with you. Select a few children to sing with you and repeat the song as the class chants.

f. Continue adding children to sing the melody until the two parts are nicely balanced and children can sing without help. (If desired, select one child to lead the chant and one to lead the melody.)

g. Ask the class how they can add more texture. (They may suggest using an accompaniment.)

h. Ask the child who has prepared an accompaniment on guitar or Autoharp to accompany the class as they sing the melody and chant. Discuss ways that the accompaniment adds to the texture (through related chords).

5. This book can be obtained from World Around Songs, Rt. 5, Burnsville, NC 28714 at an extremely low fee. World Around Songs is an excellent source of song material for every aspect of elementary-school music. Books include songs from the United States as well as other countries.

i. Ask the children if they know the story of John Henry. If not, tell them this story.
In the 1870s, when the C & O railroad was being built, and men had to drive steel into the rock to make holes for blasting charges, John Henry was known as the champion steel-driver in the country. Legend has it that he died trying to prove that he could do more work than a steam drill.

j. Ask for ideas for dramatizing the song. Encourage children to experiment, discuss experimentations, and select the dramatization they think best suits the story. (Children may choose to have a few children work at hammering the steel into the rock, swinging their hammers and bodies with the rhythm of the chant.)

k. Repeat the song with chant, as a few children dramatize.

l. Discuss the performance. How many activities contributed to the texture? (four) Was there a balance between chant, melody, and accompaniment? Did the dramatization rhythmically fit the song? Repeat, improving the dramatization in ways suggested by the class, and letting other children dramatize. When the children are ready,

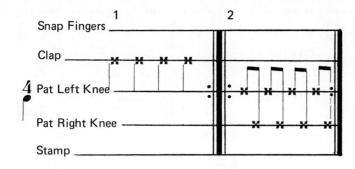

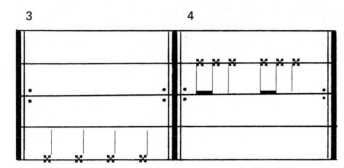

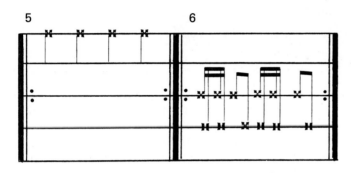

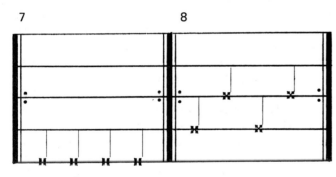

switch parts, children singing the melody now sing the chant and vice versa.

3. Experiencing texture through a rhythmic game, "Change Game"
   a. Tell the children you would like them to experience texture using rhythm.
   b. Ask them to do as you do and to continue until you say "change." Start clapping in a steady beat as in measure 1, above. Encourage the children to join you. When they are clapping with you, change to measure 2. (Children should not join

you until you say "change.") After repeating measure 2 a few times, say "change." When children are performing measure 2 with you, add measure 3. Continue the game.
4. Experiencing texture through round clapping ("Row, Row, Row Your Boat")
   a. Tell the children to sing "Row, Row, Row Your Boat" with you, in unison. Ask them if it had texture. (no)
   b. Divide the class into two groups. Have them sing "Row, Row, Row Your Boat" as a round. Ask them if it has texture now? (yes)
   c. Ask the class to step the basic beat as they sing and clap to the song in unison.
   d. Ask the class to clap "Row, Row, Row Your Boat" as they sing the song inside (internalize).
   e. Divide the class into two sections. Select two children who understand rhythm to be leaders. Let each section practice clapping the round with its leader, singing the round inside. Then clap as a two-part round.
   f. Ask the class if this performance had texture. (yes)
   g. Repeat, switching parts.
5. Evaluating children's perception of texture
   a. Tell the class you would like them to create texture.
   b. Divide the class into four groups and select a leader for each. (Assign children to a group in which they will be successful.)
   Group 1 Present a musical experience with no texture.
   Group 2 Present an experience with texture, using rhythm only.
   Group 3 Present an experience with texture using rhythmic movement and rhythm instruments.
   Group 4 Present an experience with texture using rhythmic movement and singing.
   c. Give groups adequate opportunity to experiment with their presentations before presenting them to the class.

Rhythmic Experiences That Focus on Textural Concepts

Level I

Exploring Texture, through Basic Bodily Movements
"Eggs, Butter, Cheese, Bread"

1. Teach the rhyme "Eggs, Butter, Cheese, Bread" by having the class echo each phrase as they maintain a steady clap-patschen (pat knees) accompaniment with you.

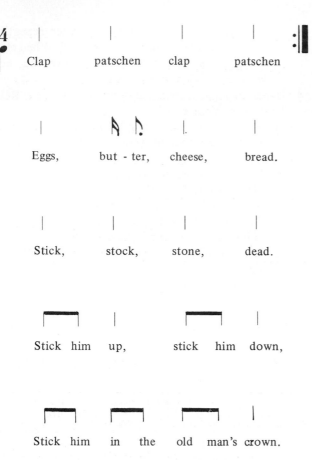

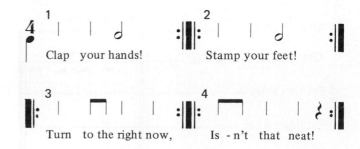

2. Have the children perform the chant as a round, using the following sequence:
   a. Class begins the chant, with bodily movement.
   b. You begin the chant when the children begin measure 2.
   c. Repeat, adding a few children to your part.
   d. Keep adding more children to your part until the two parts are balanced.
   e. If the class has a rich rhythmic background, divide the children into four groups. Select a leader for each and perform as a four-part round.

Level II or III

Experiencing Texture by Creating a Rhythmic Canon
"Stamp, Clap"

1. Teach this pattern in the following manner:
   a. Have the class imitate the measures in this sequence: first two measures, third measure, fourth measure, third and fourth measures.

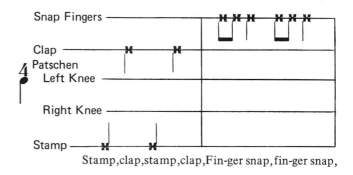

2. Expand and change the experience in any of these ways:
   a. Change the rhythmic accompaniment, using stamping, finger snapping.
   b. Encourage the children to sing the chant, using sol, la, and mi.
   c. Add the following accompaniments:

Alto Xylophone   Alto Glockenspiel

   d. Encourage the children to internalize the chant, thinking all the words inside except the first and last, which are spoken aloud.

Level I

Experiencing Texture, through Basic Bodily Movements That Accompany a Chant
"Clap Your Hands"

1. Have the children form a circle, then echo and imitate you as you say and do the following:

b. Have the class perform the entire pattern with you.

c. When the class knows the pattern well, divide into four groups. Have them do the pattern as a four-part round, each new group beginning a measure apart.

d. If necessary, use the words to simplify movement patterns for the class.

Level II

Experiencing Texture by Creating a Canon, Using Bodily Movement

1. Have the children form a circle and clap a basic beat as they say the following:

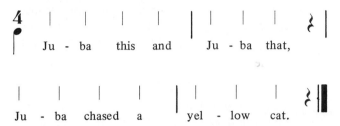

2. Teach the children a game using this chant. As all chant, the first child in the circle will watch you and on your signal will make the motions he just saw you do. The child to his right will watch the first child and do the motions he saw the first child do. The third child will watch the second child, and so on, around the circle.

3. Begin chanting the rhyme, using some movement such as clapping. Repeat the verse, changing to a second movement such as stamping and signaling the first child to begin chanting as he does the first motion (clapping). Repeat the rhyme, changing motion for each repetition.

Level II or III

Experiencing Texture by Creating an Echo Canon, Using Bodily Movement

Tell the class that you would like them to perform a rhythmic canon. Remind them that a rhythmic canon is like a round—one part begins, the other part follows, imitating exactly the first part, generally one measure apart. Tell the children to listen, and upon your signal, to begin, imitating exactly what they see and hear you do, as they listen to the new pattern.

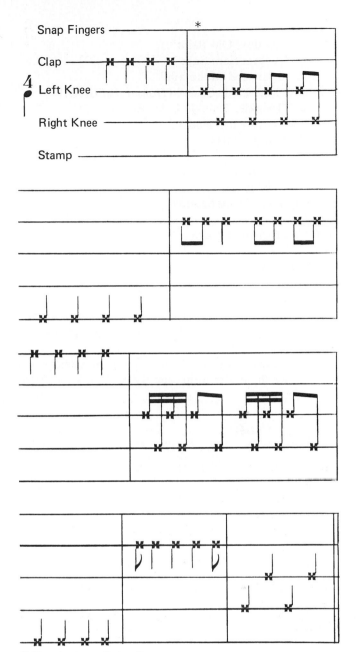

* Class begins on first pattern.

Concepts Related to Form

Level II

Materials Needed

1. Twelve equilateral triangles each with six-inch sides, and seven rectangles each six inches by four inches, all made from oak tag

2. A drum for accompanying bodily movement

3. Record player and recording: "March Past of the Kitchen Utensils" (*The Wasps*) by Vaughan Williams, RCA *Adventures in Music* grade 3, vol. 1, LES-1002

4. Copies of:
   a. "Goodby, Old Paint"
   b. "A Ram Sam Sam"
   c. "Sourwood Mountain"
   d. "Susie Little Susie" (*Hansel and Gretel*)
   e. "Twinkle, Twinkle Little Star"
5. A melody instrument
6. Music Cue charts

Rhythmic Activities
1. Basic bodily movements
2. Rhythmic dramatization

Related Musical Activities
1. Singing
2. Listening

Conceptual Understandings
1. Repeated musical phrases are used to create form.
2. Some music consists of two contrasting sections, A and B.
3. Some music consists of two contrasting sections and creates composite forms, as: ABA, AABA, AABBA, ABABA.

Behavioral Objectives
1. To demonstrate the ability to respond through bodily movement to differences in rhythm and melody
2. To demonstrate the ability to hear and respond to differences in form (AB, ABA, AABA, AABBA, ABABA)
3. To help create a rhythmic accompaniment using basic bodily movements

Related Arts
Observing form through arrangements of familiar shapes
1. Triangles
2. Rectangles

Procedure
1. Experiencing form through the visual arts
   a. Display one triangle and one rectangle, from those made.
   b. Tell the children that one of these will be A and the other B. Ask which they would like to be A. (Let us assume the rectangle is A.)
   c. Display the rectangle followed by the triangle. Ask the class to identify the form created by this arrangement. (AB)

   d. Ask who can create an ABA form from rectangles (A) and triangles (B).

   e. Continue in this way, encouraging individual children to create the following forms from rectangles and triangles: AABA, AABB, AABBA, ABABA.
2. Experiencing form through bodily movement in response to visual aids
   a. Remind the children that music can create the same forms they have created using shapes. Ask how music creates differences in form. (Instead of similar and contrasting shapes, music has similar and contrasting phrases created by melody and rhythm.)
   b. Tell the children that you will take one of the elements of music—rhythm—and create a form. Tell them to listen so that they can tell you what form you have created. Beat the following on the drum:

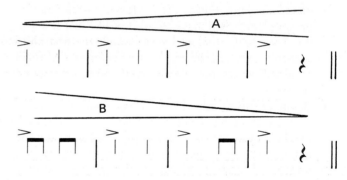

   c. Ask the class how many phrases you beat on the drum. (two) Were they similar or different? (different) Have the class clap the two phrases as you play them on the drum.
   d. Ask a child to arrange the triangles and rectangles to show you the form created.

   e. Ask for volunteers to experiment with movement using the entire body, to represent phrase A. Beat the drum pattern for them, many times, until the class has selected the movement they like best. (Children may decide to march, accenting the first beat of each measure or throwing their arms upward on the first beat.)

f. Ask for volunteers to experiment with movement for phrase B. Beat the drum pattern for them until class has selected an appropriate movement. (Children may decide to move their feet exactly in the rhythm of the beat—running and walking. They may decide to make circles in the air with their arms, one circle for each two measures. They may decide to leap during each measure.)

g. Select several volunteers to do the bodily movements for A and for B. Play the A and B patterns, using a steady beat, as the children do their movements. Repeat, allowing other children to participate.

h. Ask how an ABA form could be created with these bodily movements. (By repeating movement for A after the movement for B.) Encourage the children to create an ABA form, as you accompany them on the drum.

i. Continue in this way, helping children create the following forms: AABA, AABBA, ABABA.

3. Experiencing AABBA form by adding bodily movements as an accompaniment to a song

a. Ask the children how to identify a form in a song. (Through similar and contrasting melodies.)

b. Ask the class to patschen clap clap in a steady rhythm with you.

c. When the class can do this, ask them how they can alter the pattern as they maintain a steady beat. They may suggest one of the following:

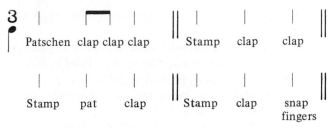

Encourage the children to experiment with each suggestion until they feel and maintain a steady rhythm.

d. Tell them that you will sing or play a song as they perform the first rhythmic accompaniment (patschen clap clap) to the first melody (A). When they hear a different melody (B), they are to change to a second pattern, (select one of those practiced). If A melody reoccurs, they should return to the first accompaniment.

e. Have the class begin the accompaniment for A. When they are ready, begin singing (or playing) "Goodby, Old Paint." Emphasize the second melody slightly to underline the change.

f. Discuss the song, focusing on the form (AABBA) and clarifying any problems encountered in the rhythmic accompaniment. Repeat the song, if necessary.

g. Select someone to arrange the rectangles and triangles to illustrate the form.

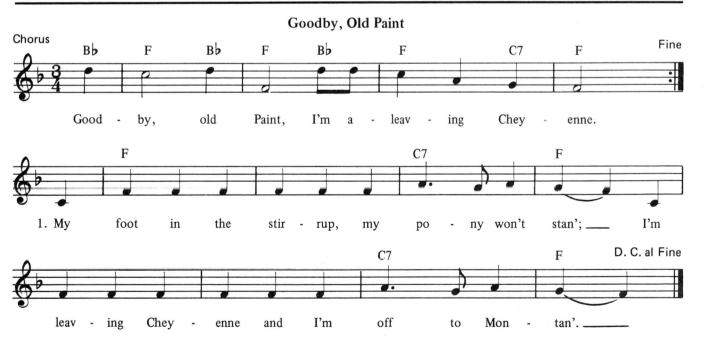

Goodby, Old Paint

Good - by, old Paint, I'm a - leav - ing Chey - enne.

1. My foot in the stir - rup, my po - ny won't stan'; ___ I'm

leav - ing Chey - enne and I'm off to Mon - tan'. ___

2. I'm riding old Paint and I'm leading old Fan;
   Goodby little Annie, I'm off for Montan'.

3. Oh, keep yourself by me as long as you can;
   Goodby little Annie, I'm off for Montan'.

Adapted from *Heritage Songster* by Dallin and Dallin, © 1966 by Wm. C. Brown Company Publishers, Dubuque, Iowa. (in public domain)

h. Ask for volunteers to accompany sections A and B.

i. Divide the class into three groups: one group to sing, another to accompany A, a third to accompany B. Repeat, switching parts.

j. Children might enjoy using rhythm instruments for an accompaniment.

4. Experiencing form through rhythmic dramatization, "March Past of the Kitchen Utensils" from *The Wasps* by Vaughan Williams

   a. Tell the children to listen and tap their knees on the first section, A. When they hear a totally different melody and rhythm, B, they should tap their heads. If A reoccurs, they should resume tapping their knees. Play the recording of "March Past of the Kitchen Utensils." (The basic form is ABA. Although both A and B sections have two different phrases, the overall ABA form is easily heard.)

   b. Have a child arrange the rectangles and triangles to define form:

c. Discuss the difference in mood created by each section. (Children may decide that A is steady, marchlike, dignified while B is dancelike and rollicking.)

d. Ask for several volunteers to experiment with bodily movements for A. Play the recording, repeating until some good ideas emerge.

e. Ask for volunteers to experiment with bodily movements for B.

f. Select children to perform movement for sections A and B. (If room is available, and children work well in a large group, the entire class may interpret the piece.)

g. Children may enjoy creating a dramatization of the story, which is described in the Teacher's Guide, grade 3, volume 1, "Adventures in Music."

5. Evaluating children's perception of form

   a. Distribute papers on which the following Music Cue chart has been printed.

   b. Tell the children to listen to the following four selections and circle the form each suggests. Play the songs on a melody instrument. (Songs may be prerecorded.)

   c. Discuss, answering any questions regarding form.

Music Cue Chart

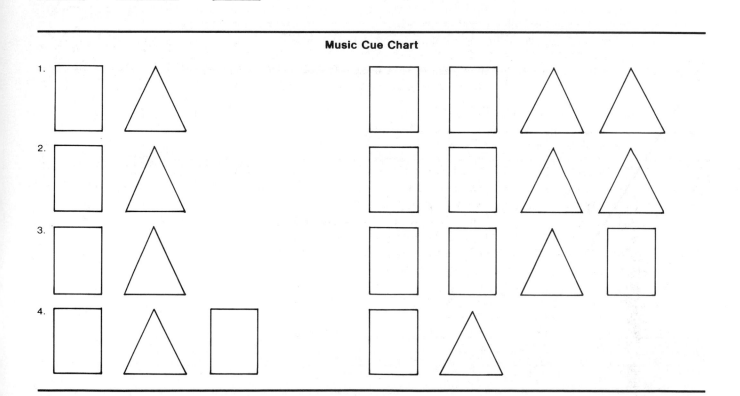

A Ram Sam Sam

Morocco

AB

A ram sam sam, a ram sam sam, Gu - li

gu - li gu - li gu - li gu - li ram sam sam. A ra - fi, a

ra - fi, Gu - li gu - li gu - li gu - li gu - li ram sam sam.

Adapted from *A Pocket Full of Songs,* Collected by Piet Kriethof. © World Around Songs. Used by permission.

2.

Sourwood Mountain

American Folk Song

AABB

1. Chick - en crow - in' on Sour - wood moun - tain, Hey de ing dang did - dle al - ly day.
2. So many pret - ty girls I can't count 'em, Hey de ing dang did - dle al - ly day.

My true love, she lives in Letch - er, Hey de ing dang did - dle al - ly day.
She won't come and I won't fetch 'er, Hey de ing dang did - dle al - ly day.

2. My true love's a blue-eyed daisy, Hey . . .
   If I don't get her I'll go crazy, Hey . . .
   Big dog bark, and little one bite you, Hey . . .
   Big girl court, and little one slight you, Hey . .

3. My true love lives up the river . . .
   A few more jumps and I'll be with 'er
   My true love lives up the holler . . .
   She won't come and I won't foller . . .

Adapted from *A Pocket Full of Songs,* © World Around Songs. Used by permission.

3.   Susie, Little Susie

AABA   Engelbert Humperdinck

Su - sie, lit - tle Su - sie, pray what is the news?

The geese are go - ing bare - foot be - cause they've no shoes!

The cob - bler has leath - er and plen - ty to spare,

Why___ can't he make the poor goose a new pair?_____

Adapted from *Heritage Songster* by Dallin and Dallin, © 1966 by Wm. C. Brown Company Publishers, Dubuque, Iowa. (in public domain)

---

4.   Twinkle, Twinkle Little Star

ABA   Old Folk Tune
                                                                                                          Fine

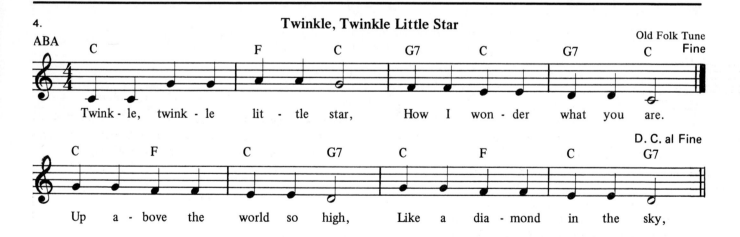

Twink - le, twink - le lit - tle star, How I won - der what you are.

                                                                                          D. C. al Fine

Up a - bove the world so high, Like a dia - mond in the sky,

Rhythmic Experiences That Focus on Concepts Related to Form

Level I

Experiencing Form by Creating a Rhythmic Dramatization

"Golliwog's Cakewalk" (*Children's Corner* Suite) by Debussy, RCA Victor *Basic Record Library for Elementary Grades* recording WE 78 or Bowmar *Orchestral Library* recording BOL 076

1. Read or tell the story of a golliwog as described in the manual accompanying RCA Victor WE 78. Discuss the story with children, focusing on how elements of music might tell this story.
2. Play the recording. Discuss the musical elements that tell the story, and put an outline on the board:

Section A Tunes 1 and 2 (each played twice) The golliwogs strut in a circle around the cake.

Section B Golliwogs go to the center one at a time, to do their rhythmic gyrations.
Section A Golliwogs strut in a circle as before.

3. Play the recording, having children raise their hands when they hear Section B.
4. Ask for volunteers to show movements for golliwogs in B section. Play the recording.
5. Select children to be golliwogs and dramatize Sections A and B. Play the recording. Discuss. Allow further experimentation. Encourage other children to dramatize.

Level I

Creating a Rhythmic Dramatization in ABA Form
"Here Comes a Giant"

1. Chant the following, which represents section A, playing the drum rhythm notated above each line:

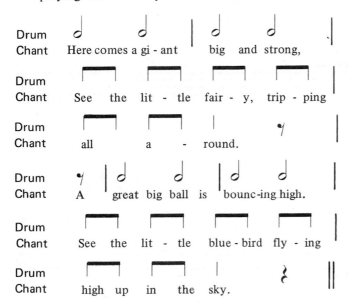

2. Encourage the children to experiment until they find ways of dramatizing each line.
3. Ask the children where these characters may be going. Through discussion and experimentation, help the children create an ABA form by having the characters come and go to the place decided, using the chant above, A. B section may consist of bodily movement expanding the story as one class suggested:

Section A The four characters come to a party in the forest.
Section B At the party a few other friends join them, and all do a dance. (Each child may improvise his own rhythmic movement in place, as the drum beats eight measures of quarter notes, or the class may create a group dance.)

Section A The four characters return home, using the same procedure as in the initial A.

Note: See p. 62 for another exercise using "Here Comes a Giant."

Level II or III

Experiencing AABA Form in a Rhythmic Dramatization
"Drill, Ye Tarriers"

1. Teach "Drill, Ye Tarriers" (next page) and encourage the class to create a rhythmic dramatization based on the text.
2. When children know the song, ask them to listen, then echo the patterns you clap:

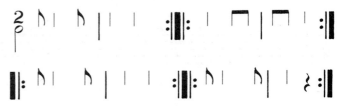

Repeat until children can clap the entire pattern. Notate, if desired.
3. Select children to play the following instruments as the class claps the pattern. Add one instrument at a time.

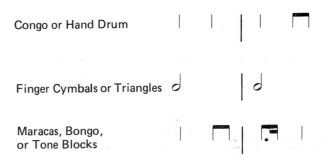

4. When the class and selected children can perform rhythm patterns (for B section) tell them verses one and two of the song will be A. Immediately following the chorus of the second verse, on the first beat of the next measure, they will begin B. A will be repeated in the form of verse three.

Level II or III

Experiencing Form by Creating a Rhythmic Dramatization
"Alla Siciliana" (*Royal Fireworks Music*) by Handel

1. Without telling the children the title, play the first few bars of the recording. Encourage the children to share their reactions to the melody. (Is it slow or fast? Solemn or bright?) Have them listen and raise their hands each time the melody occurs, as they decide what kind of person it describes and what he or she is doing.

Drill, Ye Tarriers

With Zeal

Thomas Casey

1. Ev'-ry morn-ing at sev-en o'-clock There's twen-ty tar-ri-ers a-work-ing at the rock, And the boss comes a-long and he says, "Keep still, and come down heav-y on the cast-iron drill."

Chorus

So drill, ye tar-ri-ers drill, And drill, ye tar-ri-ers drill! Oh, it's work all day for sug-ar in your "tay," Down be-yond the rail-way, And drill, ye tar-ri-ers drill!

(After the last chorus, repeat ad. lib. getting softer.)   (loud)

And drill, and blast, and fire!

2. Our new foreman is Dan McCann,
   I'll tell you true, he's a real mean man;
   Last week a premature blast went off,
   And a mile in the air went Big Jim Goff.

3. Next time pay day came around
   Jim Goff was short one buck, he found,
   "What for?" says he, then this reply,
   "You're docked for the time you were up in the sky."

2. Help the children hear the music and develop ideas for dramatizing Melody B in the same way.
3. One class developed this plan for the music:

Melody A

Melody B

Melody A Sixteen slow beats ♩. (♩ ♩ ♩), four measures. The queen walks sixteen steps.

Melody B Eight slow beats ♩ ♩ ♩ ♩ , two measures. The child runs up to the queen.

Interlude Eight slow beats ♩ ♩ ♩ ♩ , two measures. The child pleads with the queen.

Melody A Sixteen slow beats ♩. (♩ ♩ ♩), four measures. The queen walks sixteen steps.

Melody B Eight slow beats ♩. (♩ ♩ ♩), two measures. The child runs up to the queen.

Interlude Eight slow beats ♩. (♩ ♩ ♩), two measures. The child pleads with the queen.

Melody A Sixteen slow beats ♩. (♩ ♩ ♩), four measures. The queen walks sixteen steps.

Interlude Eight slow beats, two measures. The child pleads.

Conclusion Eight slow beats, two measures. The child pleads anew (two beats, arm gestures). The queen says, "Yes" (two beats, nods her head). All bow and curtsy to each other (four beats).

Expressive Concepts

Level I, II, or III

Materials Needed
1. Hand drum
2. Illustrations depicting smooth, flowing lines and sharp, pointed lines
3. Recordings:
   a. "Fantasia" on *Greensleeves* by Vaughan Williams, RCA *Adventures in Music* grade 6, vol. 2, LES-1008
   b. "Pizzicato Polka" (Ballet Suite no. 1) by Shostakovich, RCA *Adventures in Music* grade 1, vol. 1, LES-1000
   c. "Bydlo" (*Pictures at an Exhibition*) by Moussorgsky, RCA *Adventures in Music* grade 2, vol. 1, LES-1001 or Bowmar *Orchestral Library* recording BOL 097
   d. "Children's Dance" (*Merry Mount* Suite) by Hanson, RCA *Adventures in Music* grade 3, vol. 1, LES-1002
   e. "The Swan" (*Carnival of the Animals*) by Saint-Saëns, RCA *Adventures in Music* grade 3, vol. 2, LES-1003
   f. "March and Comedians' Gallop" by Kabalevsky, RCA *Adventures in Music* grade 3, vol. 1, LES-1002
   g. "Aquarium" (*Carnival of the Animals*) by Saint-Saëns, Bowmar *Orchestral Library* recording BOL 064.
4. Music Cue charts

Rhythmic Activities
1. Basic bodily movements
2. Rhythmic interpretation

Related Musical Activity
Listening

Conceptual Understandings
1. Music may have many different moods including happy, sad, smooth, flowing, detached, and jolting.
2. The mood of any composition is related to dynamics, tempi, and other expressive elements.

Behavioral Objectives
1. To demonstrate the ability to hear and respond to the difference between contrasting expressive elements
2. To help create a rhythmic interpretation of orchestral music

Figure 2.7
Legato by Joseph Sekac, North Merrick Union Free School District, North Merrick, New York.

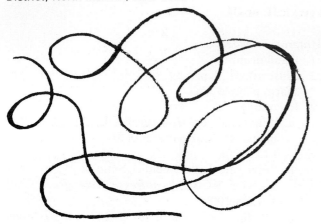

Figure 2.8
Staccato by Susan Haack, North Merrick Union Free School District, North Merrick, New York.

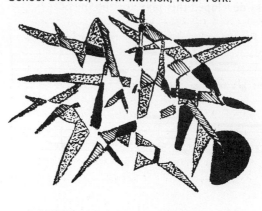

Related Arts
Observing expressive elements through the visual arts
  1. *Legato*
  2. *Staccato*

Procedure
1. Experiencing expressive elements through the visual arts
   a. Display figures 2.7 and 2.8.
   b. Through discussion, help the children focus on the different mood created by each picture, asking questions similar to the following, but adapted to the appropriate grade level:
      (1) What comes to mind when you look at *Legato:* movement that is fast or slow, smooth or disjointed? Things that flow or leap, are calm or excited?
      (2) What comes to mind when you look at *Staccato:* a soft, round ball of fur or electronic flashes? A calm summer day or a thunder storm?
   c. Ask the children what contributes to the different moods of these drawings. (Flowing lines, suggesting curves, in *Legato* create an entirely different mood from the sharp, disjointed lines and shapes in *Staccato.*)
   d. Ask how music would create these moods. (Smooth, flowing music would suggest *Legato.* Detached, disjointed music would suggest *Staccato.*)
2. Experiencing expressive elements through a game, "Happy Face"
   a. Tell children we will play a game while creating some of the expressive elements in art and music.
   b. Ask them to listen to the drum and do the following:

   (1) On the first beat of the drum make a happy face.
   (2) On the second beat of the drum make a happy body.
   (3) On the third beat of the drum make a happy motion.
   (4) On the fourth beat of the drum "freeze" (become statues).
   c. Remind them to make only one movement for the first two drum beats, to make no sounds, and to touch no one.
   d. Play the four drum beats.
   e. Follow the same procedure for these and other moods that the children suggest:
      (1) Angry (2) Funny (3) Sad (4) Happy
3. Experiencing the expressive elements through bodily movement ("Fantasia" on *Greensleeves* by Vaughan Williams and "Pizzicato Polka" by Shostakovich)
   a. Discuss all the moods that people can express using their arms, encouraging children to demonstrate each suggestion by moving their own arms.
   b. Tell the children to listen and decide what arm motions would be appropriate for the music. Play just enough of "Fantasia" to suggest the mood and motions.
   c. Ask the children to find space in the room and move their arms according to the mood. (Play the recording until the second section, introduced with a strongly accented note by violins.)
   d. Discuss the mood and the musical elements that create this mood. (A beautiful, flowing, legato, sad melody written in the minor mode and played by violins and harps creates the mood.)
   e. Make positive comments about interpretations.
   f. If desired, give children the opportunity to interpret music with their entire bodies.

Note: Children on level I may enjoy using short strips of colored tissue paper as an additional expressive element.

g. Ask the children to listen to music that expresses a different mood and to decide what arm motions would be appropriate. Play "Pizzicato Polka."

h. Follow the procedure outlined in 3c through 3e of this section to encourage further exploration of expressive elements.

i. Ask the children to find pictures in magazines or art books that express similar moods.

j. The teacher may collaborate with the art specialist and let children use an art period for creating drawings of these selections. If so, use this procedure:

    (1) Have the children imagine their arms are long pencils, drawing lines in the air to music.

    (2) Play the music as children draw in the air.

    (3) Ask a responsive child to draw his lines on the board as the music plays.

    (4) Distribute paper and crayons. Ask children to draw as the music plays. Caution against too many lines and trying to draw realistic shapes.

    (5) Allow time for the children to color their designs.

4. Experiencing expressive elements through a rhythmic dramatization ("Bydlo" from *Pictures at an Exhibition* by Moussorgsky)

a. Without explanation, play the recording. Clap, using large arm movements to suggest the slow, heavy, ponderous feeling of the music. Adapt clapping and arm movements to changes in the music. Encourage the class to participate.

b. Ask what mood the music suggests. What elements help portray this mood: tempo, dynamics, instrumentation?

c. Ask what kind of picture the music describes. If they have difficulty, ask these or similar questions:

    (1) Is the music describing something that moves slowly or quickly?

    (2) Is this an animal, machine, or person?

    (3) What is it doing? Where is it going?

    (4) Where are we in relation to this object?

One class thought of a parade of tired soldiers approaching. As they come closer, the music grows louder. After they pass, the music grows softer, until they disappear.

d. As children dramatize their ideas, encourage other children to demonstrate their suggestions for improvement. Explore and dramatize all ideas.

e. The class may enjoy comparing their story with the composer's, described in the teacher's guide accompanying the record.

5. Evaluating children's perception of the expressive elements in music:

a. Distribute papers on which the following has been printed:

Level I or II

Music Cue Chart

1. Smooth and flowing	Detached and disjointed
2. Smooth and flowing	Detached and disjointed
3. Smooth and flowing	Detached and disjointed
4. Smooth and flowing	Detached and disjointed

Level III

Music Cue Chart

1. Tempo	Dynamics	Instrumentation	Texture
2. Tempo	Dynamics	Instrumentation	Texture
3. Tempo	Dynamics	Instrumentation	Texture
4. Tempo	Dynamics	Instrumentation	Texture

For level I or II, ask children to circle the words that best describe each piece. For level I play a short fragment of these pieces; for level II play more of each. For level III, tell the children to circle the words that describe the musical element most important in creating the mood. Play the following:

    (1) "Children's Dance" (*Merry Mount* Suite) by Hanson (detached)

    (2) "The Swan" (*Carnival of the Animals*) by Saint-Saëns (smooth)

    (3) "March and Comedians' Gallop" by Kabalevsky (detached)

    (4) "Aquarium" (*Carnival of the Animals*) by Saint-Saëns (smooth)

b. Discuss answers with the children, focusing on the musical elements of each selection.

Rhythmic Experiences That Focus on Expressive Concepts

Level I

Exploring Expressive Concepts by Creating a Rhythmic Interpretation

1. Select one of the following:

a. "Bydlo" (*Pictures at an Exhibition*) by Moussorgsky, RCA *Adventures in Music* grade 2, vol. 1, LES-1001

b. "Dwarfs" by Reinhold, RCA Victor *Basic Record Library for Elementary Grades* recording WE 71

c. "Elephants" (*Under the Big Top*) by Donaldson, Bowmar *Orchestral Library* recording BOL 064

2. Without telling the title, play the recording and clap strong beats. Encourage the class to join you.

3. Repeat, moving your arms in rhythm above your head, to your sides, and to the front.
4. Ask children:
   a. Does the music tell about something fast or slow? (slow)
   b. Does the music tell about something big or little? (big)
   c. What musical elements help portray these large, slow-moving things? (Focus on tempo, dynamics, instrumentation.)
   d. What people, animals, plants, and machines move slowly or take big steps?
5. Ask the class to think of a person, animal, plant, or machine that is slow and big, as they listen to the recording.
6. Select several children to interpret the music. Have the class guess what each child did, letting children who guess correctly take the place of the child on the floor. Continue until all volunteers have the opportunity to interpret.

Level I

Exploring Expressive Concepts by Creating a Rhythmic Interpretation
1. Select one of the following records:
   a. "Ballet of the Sylphs" by Berlioz, RCA *Adventures in Music* grade 1, vol. 1, LES-1000
   b. "Waltzing Doll" by Poldini, RCA Victor *Basic Record Library for Elementary Grades* recording WE 78
   c. "Gavotte" (*Mlle. Angot* Suite) by Lecocq, Bowmar *Orchestral Library* recording BOL 066
2. Without telling the title, play the recording, then ask the children these questions, focusing on tempo, dynamics, and instrumentation:
   a. Does this music make you think of giants or elves? (elves)
   b. Does it remind you of raindrops or a snow storm? (raindrops)
   c. Does it sound more like dancing or stamping? (dancing)
   d. Does it sound more like a butterfly or an elephant? (butterfly)
   e. Does it sound more like a music box or a big brass band? (music box)
3. Ask the children what the music suggests, and how to use their arms, legs, and bodies to interpret it.
4. Select volunteers to interpret. Play the recording. Make positive comments about interpretations that fit the mood. Let children guess what each volunteer was doing, then select other children to interpret.

Level I

Exploring Expressive Concepts, through Free Movement
Adagio by Corelli, RCA Victor *Basic Record Library for Elementary Grades* recording WE 71

1. Play the recording of Adagio. Begin rhythmically tapping your forefingers on the desk, encouraging the class to imitate you.
2. Ask the children what their feet would do if they followed the rhythm of their forefingers. (run or tiptoe, except during the middle and end sections, when they would walk slowly)
3. Ask the class to raise their hands when they hear slow music. Play the recording.
4. Select volunteers to move to the music. Remind them to (1) listen and do what the music suggests, (2) change movement when music suggests, (3) refrain from touching other children, (4) move freely in any available space.
5. Discuss, making positive comments about movement, and focusing on musical elements (tempo, dynamics, instrumentation). Let others who desire move.

Level I

Experiencing Expressive Concepts, through Bodily Movement
1. Tell the children you are going to play a game in which their bodies will express many different feelings, just as music does.
2. Tell them to move freely but not to touch anyone or make sounds.
3. Tell them to:
   a. Shout with your bodies.
   b. Whisper with your bodies.
   c. Lie on the floor and feel how hard it is.
   d. Get up and keep your bodies just as hard.
   e. Make a movement as soft as cotton, as a puppy.
   f. Make yourself as floopy as a Raggedy Ann doll.
   g. Make yourself as stretched as a taut rubber band.
   h. Carry an elephant, a feather.[6]

Level II

Experiencing Expressive Concepts by Creating a Rhythmic Interpretation
"Clowns" by Mendelssohn, RCA Victor *Basic Record Library for Elementary Grades* recording WE 71

1. Discuss the game "charades" with the children. Tell them that in "musical charades" the teacher plays a record and they must decide whether the music is telling about something big or little, fast or slow,

6. Sue Richheimer, "Motivational Techniques for Creative Movement," *Keeping Up With Orff-Schulwerk in the Classroom* vol. 1, no. 4, (© March 1974): p. 72.

heavy or light. They must know which musical elements tell them these things.

2. Play the recording and discuss what the music tells.
3. Ask the children to think of a specific person, animal, machine, or other object that is little, fast, and light. What movements could they make to suggest such a person, animal, or object? Play the recording.
4. Select a volunteer to demonstrate his idea as the recording plays. Let the class guess what he is depicting. The child who guesses correctly replaces the first child. Repeat until many have participated.

Level I, II, or III

Experiencing Expressive Concepts, through Free Movement
"Sham B'Eretz Yisrael"

Modify the terminology of this experience when using it for level II or III.

1. Discuss the country of Israel. Tell the class you will play an Israeli dance tune and they should think of a fitting movement.
2. Play "Sham B'Eretz Yisrael." Discuss, encouraging exploration: Does the tune suggest walking or running? Is it fast or slow? Happy or sad? Heavy or light?
3. Select volunteers to move. Repeat the melody. Ask for positive comments. Let other volunteers demonstrate their movements as you repeat the melody.

Level I, II, or III

Focusing on Expressive Concepts by Becoming "Musical Sculptors"

1. Select a recording that suggests legato movement.
2. Have the children choose partners—one to be the sculptor, the other the clay. Have the "clay" sit on floor, near the sculptor.

3. Tell the sculptor to listen to the music and, in rhythm, sculpt the "clay" into the arms, legs, head, and body of any statue desired. Remind them to create something reflecting the mood of the music, and to be gentle with the "clay."

Notational Concepts: Music Reading

Level II

Materials Needed

1. Cards showing rhythm patterns and expressive markings: cards should be approximately eight inches by four inches so all children can easily see them. Place rhythmic counting on the back of each card.

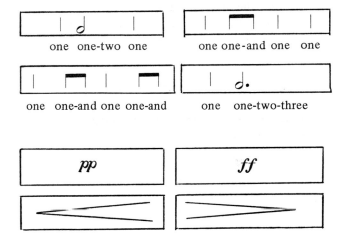

2. A copy of "Every Night When the Sun Goes Down."
3. "Country Gardens," arranged by Percy Grainger, RCA Victor *Basic Record Library for Elementary Grades* recording WE 76.
4. Blank paper and a pencil for each child.

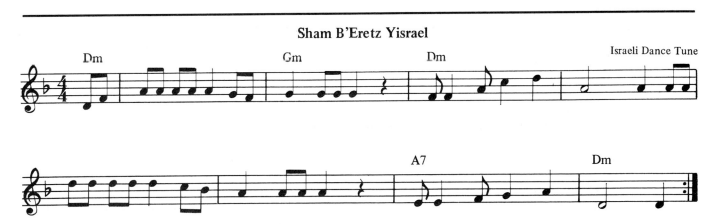

Sham B'Eretz Yisrael

Israeli Dance Tune

From *The Songs We Sing*, by Harry Coopersmith. Published by The United States Synagogue Commission on Jewish Education. Used by permission.

Figure 2.9
Merced River, Yosemite Valley, by Albert Bierstadt. The Metropolitan Museum of Art, Gift of the sons of William Paton, 1909.

e. Have the children draw their contours on paper. Encourage volunteers to show the class their drawings.

f. Ask what in the picture creates the contour? (lines and shapes)

g. Ask what in music can create a contour? (A melody creates a contour in sound. When notated, it creates a contour we can observe.)

4. Using free movement to focus on melodic contours created by different melodies (*Country Gardens* arranged by Percy Grainger)

Tune 1

Tune 2

Tune 3

Themes from Percy Grainger's *Country Gardens* Copyright, 1919, 1946, by G. Schirmer, Inc. Used by permission.

a. Remind the children that music has many moods and, as you play the recording, they should decide how it makes them feel. (Do not tell them the title.)

b. Play the recording of the first tune only.

c. Place the melodic direction of the first tune on the board.

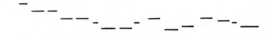

d. Have the children hum or sing the tune on a neutral syllable (la) as they follow the direction (contour) with their hands.

e. Have them select an appropriate title. (They may call it: "Happy Tune," "Dancing Tune," "Jumping Tune," "Hop, Skip, and Jump Tune.")

f. Ask the class to clap their hands lightly with this tune, as you point to the blank notation. Play the recording.

g. Tell the children to watch as you connect the notes to create a contour.

h. Ask the class to think about what the contour suggests.

i. Place the blank notation of the second tune on the board.

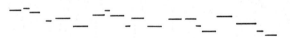

j. Tell the children that this is another tune within the composition. Ask how it looks different from the first tune. (The second tune skips about; the first tune descends stepwise.)

k. Play the recording as the children (1) clap lightly in rhythm each time they hear the second tune, (2) hum or sing the tune on a neutral syllable as they follow the direction with their hands, and (3) watch as you draw the melody's contour. Then have them select a title for the tune.

l. Place the blank notation of the third tune on the board.

m. Have the children compare the melodic direction of this tune with the other two tunes. (The third tune skips in an upward and downward direction.)

n. Repeat step k for the third tune.

o. Ask the children to help you make a plan of the music. As they hear the tunes, they are to raise one, two, or three fingers to indicate which tune is being played. Play the recording and place the following on the board:

Tune numbers in the order they appear on the recording

1			2
{	2	{	1
	1		3
	3	{	2
{	2	{	1
	1		1
	1	{	2
			1

Note: Tune 1 always plays with the last half of tune 2.

p. Ask the class to plan rhythmic movements that would fit the first tune. Tell them to feel free to perform any appropriate movement.

q. Select volunteers to demonstrate their ideas as you play the recording. Ask for positive comments about the movements of the volunteers.

r. Repeat steps p and q for the second and third tunes.

s. Play the recording, having three groups of children (one group for each tune) move to their tunes as they occur.

t. Repeat, letting other children participate.

5. Evaluating children's perception of notational symbols related to rhythm, melody, and expression

a. Distribute Music Cue charts similar to the following:

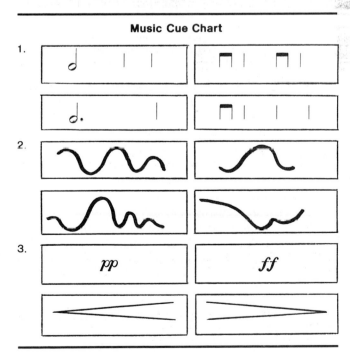

Music Cue Chart

b. Ask the children to circle the pattern you clap, after number one. (Clap pattern two.)

c. After number two, have children circle the picture that fits the melody you play. Play the following:

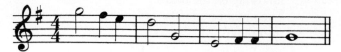

d. After number three, tell the children to circle the card showing the dynamics you use in playing a melody. Repeat the melody for number two using a crescendo. (third card)

e. Check the answers with children, clarifying any misconceptions.

Rhythmic Experiences That Focus on Notational Concepts

Level I

Focusing on Notation, through Basic Bodily Movements

1. Prepare and laminate five note charts, each approximately twelve by eighteen inches, using the following notes:

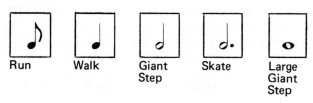

2. Collect recordings (or other music) for walking, running, giant steps, skating, and large giant steps. A drum may be substituted for music.

3. Hold each note card for children to see, and do the following:

   a. Tell them what bodily movement is associated with each note.

   b. Let them discuss the differences between notes.

   c. Have volunteers illustrate the bodily movements associated with each note value.

4. Play music for walking. Ask which bodily movement and which note fit the music. Have a child walk to the music, while he holds the quarter note. Select others to accompany him.

5. Repeat step 4 for the other notes, until there is a group of children representing each note value.

6. Explain that you would like to play a game. The directions are:

a. Each group (walk, run, small giant step, and so on) stands behind its leader.

b. When they hear their music, they move in the way practiced.

c. When their music stops, they stop immediately.

7. To give the groups a feeling for their movement, play the music for each one. Then repeat, changing music frequently.

(To maintain groups, without children moving in lines, give each child a different color ribbon to identify his group: red ribbons for quarter or walking notes, yellow for eighth or running notes, and so on.)

Level I

Focusing on Notation, through a Rhythmic Dramatization
"Here Comes a Giant"

1. After the experience on p. 51 using "Here Comes a Giant," place notation for the drum accompaniment above the words of the chant on the board.

2. Have the children count and clap notation.

3. Have some children accompany the chant with appropriate rhythm instruments as others dramatize it.

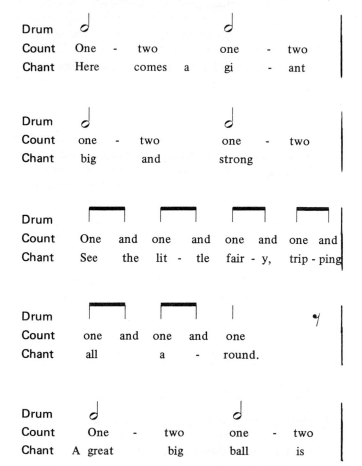

Drum			
Count	one - two	one - two	
Chant	bounc - ing	high.	

Drum				
Count	One and	one and	one and	one and
Chant	See the	lit - tle	blue - bird	fly - ing

Drum				
Count	one and	one and	one	
Chant	high up	in the	sky.	

Level I

Focusing on Notation, through a Clapping Game and Chant

1. Select a chant, such as the following:

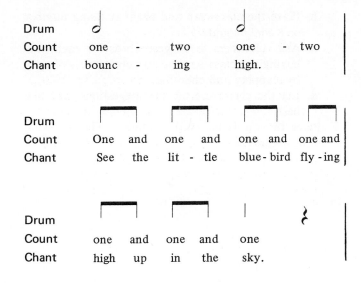

2. Make and laminate cards approximately four by six inches representing the notation for each phrase:

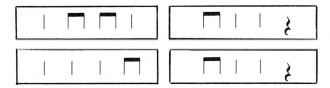

3. Display the cards but not in the correct order.
4. Review the chant by clapping and chanting it with the children, first using words, then number notation.

5. Clap the first card. Which phrase does it represent, and where does it belong? Continue until all cards are in the proper order.

Level II

Learning Notation, through Round Clapping
"Are You Sleeping"

Note: Previous to this experience children should have had extensive experience in echo canon.

1. Have the children sing "Are You Sleeping."
2. Use each measure of the song as an echo clap-back, clapping and counting:

One one one one   one one one - two

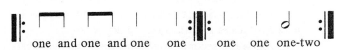

one and one and one   one   one one one-two

3. Clap and count the first measure, having the class echo. Have a volunteer notate the rhythm on the board. Continue with subsequent measures until the pattern is notated:

4. Have the children clap and count the pattern.
5. Tell the children you would like them to make a canon using "Are You Sleeping" as the first part and the notated clapping pattern as the second part. Explain that they begin clapping two measures after beginning the song.
6. Signal for the class to sing and, two measures later, to begin clapping the canon. Help by singing and clapping with them. Repeat the canon several times. Erase the notation from the board and have the children sing and clap the canon as a memory-training exercise.

Level II

Focusing on Notation for Two Kinds of Bodily Movements

"Entrance of the Little Fauns" by Pierné, Bowmar *Orchestral Library* recording BOL 067

1. Write the following on the board:

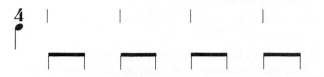

2. Explain that some music suggests two rhythms occurring at the same time.
3. Play the recording. Clap the basic beat (a walking rhythm) and encourage children to join you.
4. Ask which note value is associated with this beat. (quarter note) Have a child point to it on the board.
5. Play the recording again, as a volunteer walks and the class claps. Select several children to walk as the recording plays and the class claps.
6. Running is the second movement the music suggests. Treat this rhythm as you did the first (in steps 2–5).
7. When the children feel both rhythms, ask one group to walk and another to run in rhythm with the music.

Level II or III

Focusing on Rhythmic Notation by Creating and Notating Chants

1. Invite the class to select a favorite topic (sports, cars, holidays, and so forth). Help them create a four-line poem in the following manner:
   a. Place this notation on the board, omitting the counting.

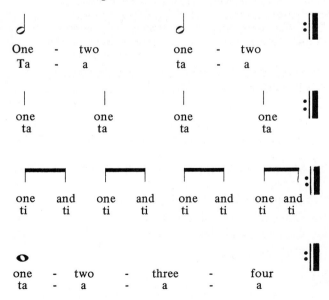

   b. Have the class clap and chant it, using number or Kodaly counting.
   c. Ask volunteers to suggest words for each line, having the class test the appropriateness of each by clapping and chanting.
   d. Let the class vote for the suggestions they like best.
2. Place the words below the notation. The following were suggested:

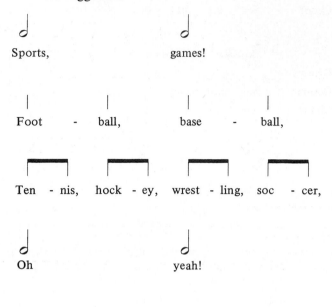

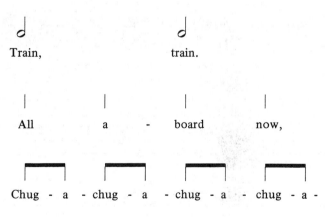

o
Whoooooooooooo!

3. Children may enjoy:
   a. Selecting a rhythm instrument to play each note value (i.e.: half note, triangle; quarter note, tone block; eighth note, maracas; whole note, large cymbals).
   b. Chanting rhyme as an echo canon, group two beginning as group one begins second line.

Individualizing Rhythmic Experiences

The teacher interested in giving children individualized experiences in rhythm will want to introduce each musical concept in a group experience. When children have begun to grasp the concept, the teacher may divide them into small groups for individualized activities. Following are suggestions for such activities.

Level I

"Roll-a-Rhythm," Game 1
For two or three children

Reproduce Rhythm Patterns 1 and the answer sheet on heavy cardboard, then laminate.

Rhythm Patterns 1

Instructions: (1) Player one rolls two dice. (2) He claps and counts the pattern written beside the number shown on the dice. If correct, he gets one point. (Other children check the answers.) (3) The other players take turns. (4) The first player to win fifteen points wins the game.

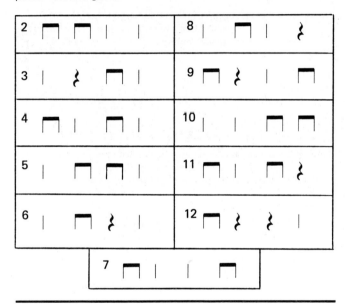

Answer Sheet

2. One and one and one one
3. One rest one and one
4. One and one one and one
5. One one and one and one
6. One one and rest one
7. One and one one one and
8. One one and one rest
9. One and rest one one and
10. One one one and one and
11. One and one one and rest
12. One and rest rest one

Level I or II

"Roll-a-Rhythm" Game 2
For two or three children

Reproduce Rhythm Patterns 2 and the answer sheet.

Rhythm Patterns 2

Instructions: (1) Player one rolls two dice. (2) He claps and counts the pattern written beside the number shown on the dice. If correct, he gets one point. (Other children check the answers.) (3) The other players take turns. (4) The first player to win fifteen points wins the game.

Answer Sheet

2. One-two one and one
3. One one and one-two
4. One and rest one-two
5. One-two rest one and
6. One-two-three one and
7. One and one-two one
8. One-two rest rest
9. One-two-three one
10. One one and one-two
11. One and one-two-three
12. One rest rest one

Level I or II

"Beat the Rhythm" Game
For seven or more children

1. Divide the children into two teams and choose a class leader.
2. Write this on the board:

Leader

◯ ◯ ◯ ◯

Team 1   Team 2

◯ ◯ ◯ ◯   ◯ ◯ ◯

3. Explain the game:
    a. The leader taps a rhythm pattern in the top row. (Remember, he does not write in the circles, he only taps the pattern.) For example, he may tap this rhythm:

    b. The first person from either team to mark the correct notation in his team's circles scores one team point.
    c. The leader continues to tap rhythms in the top row of circles. Competing team members continue trying to be first to write correct notation for each pattern tapped. The team that scores fifteen points first is the winner.

Level II

"Halloween Rhythm" Game
For one child

1. Reproduce copies of the following:

Halloween Rhythm

The first column consists of Halloween words and phrases. Clap and chant each word or phrase. Listen for each syllable and for short and long sounds. Write the rhythmic notation in the empty space. For example: Halloween—

Halloween Words and Phrases	Rhythmic Notation
Owls and witches	
Ghosts scaring	
Pumpkin lanterns	
Trick or treat	
Goblins and bats	
Pumpkins bouncing	
Witches flying	
Boo!	
Cats creeping	
Owls screeching	
Candles burning	
Whooooooooooo!	
I'll get you!	

---

2. Make a copy of the answer sheet on a heavy cardboard and laminate it. Have the children check their own work against the answer sheet.

Answer Sheet

Owls and witches	♫ ♫	Witches flying	♫ ♫
Ghosts scaring	♩ ♫	Boo!	♩
Pumpkin lanterns	♫ ♫	Cats creeping	♩ ♫
Trick or treat	♫ ♩	Owls screeching	♫ ♫
Goblins and bats	♫ ♩ ♩	Candles burning	♫ ♫
Pumpkins bouncing	♫ ♫	Whooooooooooo!	𝅝
		I'll get you!	♫ ♩

Note: Since there is room for individual interpretation, the teacher will want to check children's work and acknowledge answers that are correct, though different from the answer sheet.

Level I or II

Recordings for Individualizing Rhythmic Experiences
For one child or a small group

Note: All recordings are structured so that children can follow them without help. All are available from Educational Record Sales, 157 Chambers St., New York, New York 10007.

Level I
Finger Play, vols. 1 and 2
Classroom Rhythms
Animal Rhythms
Rhythms from the Land of Make Believe
Interpretive Rhythms

Level II
Rhythms of Cowboys and Indians
Machine Rhythms

Level III
"Match the Pattern" Game
For one person
1. Reproduce copies of the following:

Match the Pattern

Instructions
(1) Quietly clap and chant the name of each state.
(2) Examine the notations and clap each state to determine which pattern it creates.
(3) Write the state beneath the pattern it fits.
(4) Check your answers with the answer sheet.

Write the names of these states under the appropriate rhythm patterns.

1. Maine	9. Pennsylvania
2. Utah	10. Idaho
3. Mississippi	11. Kansas
4. Texas	12. Alabama
5. Michigan	13. Iowa
6. California	14. New York
7. Georgia	15. Tennessee
8. Colorado	16. Massachusetts
	17. Washington

18. Oklahoma
19. West Virginia
20. Arkansas
21. Delaware
22. Minnesota
23. Illinois
24. Florida
25. North Dakota
26. Oregon

2. Prepare this answer sheet on a heavy cardboard and laminate it.

Answer Sheet

Maine	U-tah	Mich-i-gan	Cal-i-for-nia
	Tex-as	Id-a-ho	Col-o-ra-do
	Geor-gia	I-o-wa	Penn-syl-va-nia
	Kan-sas	Ten-nes-see	Al-a-bam-a
	New York	Wash-ing-ton	Mas-sa-chu-setts
		Ar-kan-sas	O-kla-ho-ma
		Del-a-ware	West Vir-gin-ia
		Il-li-nois	Min-ne-so-ta
		Flor-i-da	North Da-ko-ta
		Or-e-gon	Mis-sis-sip-pi

Discussions and Reports

1. Discuss the idea that all musical experiences involve experiences with rhythm, giving specific examples and illustrations.

2. Through discussion, clarify the differences between basic bodily movements, free movement, rhythmic interpretation, and rhythmic dramatization, showing the interrelationship, yet distinctive characteristics of each.

3. Plan to initiate an experience in one of the following for level I: (1) free movement (rhythmic exploration), (2) rhythmic interpretation, or (3) rhythmic dramatization. Write a paper describing the physical conditions you want, for optimum results; the emotional atmosphere you want and the way you might create it; the types of movement you hope to see; and the personal growth and conceptual development you might expect.

4. Select a conceptual understanding related to rhythm, melody, texture, form, expression, or reading, and appropriate to level I, II, or III. (See the chart in chapter 1.) Following the suggestions listed on pages 21 through 27, plan a strategy for a rhythmic experience revolving around the conceptual understanding chosen.

5. Prepare a report explaining ways that other arts, life experiences, and the environment can help children understand musical concepts related to rhythm.

6. Prepare a report explaining ways to introduce basic bodily movements to a level II class that has no previous experience. Give specific ideas for making the experience sophisticated enough to maintain interest.

7. Prepare a report explaining how to use "rock" to achieve conceptual understandings and behavioral objectives. State the level intended.

8. Write a paper describing your experiences in learning about movement. Describe both positive and negative influences. Discuss how the latter might have been eliminated.

9. Discuss ways rhythmic experiences can focus on melody, texture, form, expression, and note reading.

10. Compile a list of music appropriate for rhythmic experiences that focus on (1) rhythm, (2) melody, (3) texture, (4) form, (5) expression, and (6) note reading.

11. Discuss ways of encouraging uninhibited self-expression in the rhythmic activities suggested in this chapter.

12. Experiment with a set of rhythm instruments. Play each, and free associate to the sound. Write a paper giving your characterization of the sound of each instrument.

13. Find a poem suitable for a specific elementary grade, which also suggests dramatization. Write a paper explaining how you would help children create a rhythmic dramatization.
14. Find a folk tale that suggests dramatization and is interesting to a specific grade because of its relevance to other studies. Write a paper showing how you would help children create a dramatization of the story.
15. Observe a rhythmic experience in an elementary classroom. Write a report describing approaches, techniques, materials, activities, and general classroom atmosphere.
16. Discuss the general suggestions throughout this chapter in relation to creativity versus rigidity. How might these be used creatively in an actual teaching situation set?
17. Using the "Rhythmic Activities Evaluation" chart, keep a log of all successful rhythmic activities. This chart may be a basis for an expanding source of possible rhythmic activities for the elementary school.
18. Prepare an individualized activity, involving concepts related to rhythm, for a small group.

Activities to Develop Skills and Practice in Initiating Musical Experiences

1. Prepare a strategy that focuses upon specific conceptual understandings and behavioral objectives related to rhythm, melody, texture, form, expression, or music reading involving (1) rhythmic interpretation or dramatization, (2) a related musical activity, (3) a related arts activity, and (4) an activity for evaluating children's perception of the conceptual focus. Specify the level intended (level I, II, or III). Present your strategy to the class. Evaluate: How does the use of related arts or other musical activities make the experience more successful?
2. Plan an experience for level I children using basic bodily movements and focusing on the concept that music generally has a strong beat. Initiate and guide the experience. Through class discussion, evaluate the results in terms of (1) successful participation and (2) increased understanding of the concept.
3. Select one of the experiences listed under "Rhythmic Experiences That Focus on Rhythmic Concepts." Analyze, making any additions or changes you think necessary for a successful experience. Interweave other musical activities or related arts. Decide on conceptual understandings and behavioral objectives. Develop an activity for evaluating the children's perception (Music Cue chart). Initiate and guide the experience with the class. Through discussion, ana-

lyze the results in terms of (1) enjoyment and (2) increased perception added through related arts and other musical activities.
4. Prepare a plan for basic bodily movements for level I. Using a drum for accompaniment help the children feel and express the differences among walking, running, skipping, and hopping. Initiate and guide the experience with the class. Evaluate the results.
5. Select music for interpretive rhythms from available recordings, feeling free to use only parts of selections. Prepare, initiate, and guide an experience for level II—one that gives children the opportunity to hear and express two different moods in music. Evaluate the results.
6. Examine the experiences listed under "Rhythmic Experiences That Focus on Melodic Concepts." Using any ideas suggested by these plans as a departure point, create an experience in rhythm for either (level I, II, or III) in which the concept focus is related to melody. Initiate and guide the experience with the class. Evaluate the results.
7. Examine the strategy for level II or III, "Textural Concepts." Make any alterations desirable for a more successful experience. Initiate and guide the experience with the class. Evaluate.
8. Examine the strategy for level II, "Concepts Related to Form." Make any alterations desirable for a more successful experience. Initiate and guide the experience with the class. Evaluate.
9. Select, from the Growth and Sequence chart in chapter 1, conceptual understandings and behavioral objectives related to expression for levels II or III. Using the ideas suggested as a departure point, plan a strategy using rhythmic dramatization, a related musical activity, a related arts activity, and an activity for evaluating the children's perception of the conceptual focus. Initiate and guide the experience. Evaluate for (1) enjoyment, (2) increased conceptual understanding, and (3) achieved behavioral objectives.
10. Following the basic plan of the strategy for level II, "Notational Concepts: Music Reading" create your own strategy stating the level intended. Including a rhythmic activity, related musical activity, specific conceptual understandings and behavioral objectives, as well as related arts and an activity for evaluating students' perception. Initiate and guide the experience. Through discussion, evaluate results.
11. Examine the Music Cue charts and analyze them in terms of their effectiveness for evaluating growth in conceptual understandings. Design your own plan for evaluating such growth in a specific conceptual area: rhythm, melody, texture, form, expression, or music reading. Relate your plan to specific musical growth experiences.

Rhythmic Activities Evaluation Chart

Level	Type of Rhythmic Activity				Type of Accompaniment (Recording, Song, Other)	Conceptual Understandings	Behavioral Objectives	Related Musical Activities	Related Arts	Evaluation
	Basic Bodily Movement	Rhythmic Interpretation	Free Movement	Rhythmic Dramatization						

Recordings, Piano Music, and Materials for Rhythmic Experiences

Recordings for Basic Bodily Movements

Walking or Marching	Composer	Recording
Air Gai (*Iphigénie in Aulis*)	Gluck	RCA LES-1000
"Changing of the Guard, The" (*Carmen* Suite no. 2)	Bizet	RCA LES-1003
"Children's March"	Goldman	HRW 18
Classroom Rhythms	Raebeck	CM 1037
"Colonel Bogey March"	Alford	BOL 54/067
"Farandole" (*L'Arlesienne* Suite no. 2)	Bizet	RCA LES-1009 and HRW 68
March (*Love for Three Oranges*)	Prokofieff	RCA WE 76 and BOL 54/067
March (*Nutcracker* Suite)	Tchaikovsky	RCA WE 72, BOL 58/071 and HRW 28
March (*Summer Day* Suite)	Prokofieff	RCA LES-1000
"Marche Militaire"	Schubert	RCA WE 73 and BOL 54/067
March in F	Anderson	RCA WE 71

"March of the Little Lead Soldiers"	Pierné	RCA WE 77 and BOL 54/067
"March of the Siamese Children"	Rodgers	BOL 54/067
"March of the Toys" (*Babes in Toyland*)	Herbert	RCA LES-1001
"March Past of the Kitchen Utensils" (*The Wasps*)	Williams	RCA LES-1002
"March—Trumpet and Drum"	Bizet	BOL 53/066
"Military March"	Anderson	RCA WE 71
Parade (*Divertissement*)	Ibert	RCA LES-1000
"Petite Ballerina" (Ballet Suite no. 1)	Shostakovich	RCA LES-1001
"Pomp and Circumstance"	Elgar	BOL 54/067
"Semper Fidelis"	Sousa	RCA LES-1003, and HRW 27
"Soldiers' March"	Schumann	RCA WE 72
"Stars and Stripes Forever"	Sousa	BOL 54/067 HRW 59 and RCA LES-1005
"Tiptoe March"	Anderson	RCA WE 71
"Toreador Song" (*Carmen*)	Bizet	RCA WE 74
"Walking Song" (*Acadian Songs and Dances*)	Thomson	RCA LES-1000
"Washington Post March"	Sousa	HRW 37

Running

Adagio	Corelli	RCA WE 71

Sources of recordings are given only when compositions have been recorded by companies whose materials are most commonly used in the elementary schools. Compositions that are easily available from commercial recording companies are listed without reference to company or record number because of the frequency with which these change.

"Ball, The" (*Children's Games*)	Bizet	RCA LES-1000
Ballet	Gluck	RCA WE 71
"Entrance of the Little Fauns"	Pierné	BOL 54/067
"Etude Joyeuse"	Kopylov	RCA WE 71
"Farandole" (*L'Arlesienne* Suite)	Bizet	RCA LES-1009 and HRW 68
"Flying Birds"	Anderson	RCA WE 71
"Pizzicato Polka" (Ballet Suite no. 1)	Shostakovich	RCA LES-1000
"Running Game"	Gurlitt	RCA WE 72
"Running Horses"	Anderson	RCA WE 71
"Run, Run" (*Memories of Childhood*)	Pinto	RCA WE 77
"Run, Run, Run"	Concone	RCA WE 72

Skating

"Argonaise" (*Le Cid*)	Massenet	RCA LES-1000 and HRW 610
"German Waltz—Paganini"	Schumann-Glazunov	BOL 53/066
"Petite Ballerina" (Ballet Suite no. 1)	Shostakovich	RCA LES-1001
Rosenkavalier Suite	Strauss	RCA LES-1009
"Skaters Waltz, The"	Waldteufel	RCA WE 74, BOL 55/068
"Tinikling"	Folk Dance	HRW 513
"Valsette"	Borowski	RCA WE 71
Waltz (*Les Patineurs*)	Meyerbeer	RCA LES-1001
Waltz (*Masquerade* Suite)	Khachaturian	RCA LES-1005
Waltz (*The Sleeping Beauty*)	Tchaikovsky	RCA LES-1004
Waltzes nos. 1, 2 and 9	Brahms	RCA WE 72
Waltz no. 1 (*Faust Ballet Music*)	Gounod	RCA LES-1002
"Waltz on the Ice" (*Winter Holiday*)	Prokofieff	RCA LES-1003

Giant Step

Air Gai (*Iphigénie in Aulis*)	Gluck	RCA LES-1000
"Cortege of the Sardar"	Ippolitov-Ivanov	BOL 54/067
"Gnomes"	Reinhold	RCA WE 71
"Jumping"	Gurlitt	RCA WE 72
March (*Alceste*)	Gluck	RCA WE 72
"Pantomime" (*The Comedians*)	Kabalevsky	RCA LES-1000
"Procession of the Sardar" (*Caucasian Sketches*)	Ippolitoff-Ivanoff	RCA WE 76
"War Song" (*Miniatures*)	Reinhold	RCA WE 75
"Wheelbarrow Motive"	Anderson	RCA WE 71

Large Giant Step

"Dagger Dance" (*Natoma*)	Herbert	RCA LES-1002
"Dwarfs"	Reinhold	RCA WE 71
March	Hollaender	RCA WE 72
March (*Iphigénie in Aulis*)	Gluck	RCA WE 75

Skipping

"Badinerie" (Suite no. 2 in B Minor)	Bach	RCA LES-1002
Gigue (*Cephale et Procris*)	Grétry	RCA LES-1000
Gigue (Suite no. 3 in D Major)	Bach	RCA LES-1000
"Kalvelis"	Folk Dance	HRW 68
"Plain Skip"	Anderson	RCA WE 71
"Play Party Time"	Folk Dance	HRW 511
"Roberts, The"	Folk Dance	HRW 410
"Skipping Theme"	Anderson	RCA WE 71
"Texas Star"	Folk Dance	HRW 512
"Theme for Skipping"	Anderson	RCA WE 71
"Virginia Reel"	Folk Dance	HRW 410

Galloping

Air Gai (*Iphigénie in Aulis*)	Gluck	RCA LES-1000
"Badinerie" (Suite no. 2 in B Minor)	Bach	RCA LES-1002
Finale (*William Tell* Overture)	Rossini	HRW 68 and RCA LES-1002
"Galloping Horses"	Anderson	RCA WE 71
Gigue (*Cephale et Procris*)	Grétry	RCA LES-1000
Gigue (Suite no. 3 in D Major)	Bach	RCA LES-1000
"Haymaker's Jig"	Folk Dance	HRW 510
March	Prokofieff	BOL 54/067
"Pony Trot" (*Under the Big Top*)	Donaldson	BOL 51/064
"Scherzo" (Septet in E-flat, op. 20)	Beethoven	HRW 110

Recordings for All Categories of Basic Bodily Movements

Activities for Individualization in Movement and Music	Hallam and Glass	AR 49
Animals and Circus		BOL 51/064
Classroom Rhythms		CM 1037
Classroom Rhythms "Animal Rhythms"		CM 1044
Classroom Rhythms "Rhythms from the Land of Make-Believe"		CM 1055
Classroom Rhythms "Rhythms of Cowboys and Indians"		CM 1067
Creative Movement and Rhythmic Expression		AR 533
Creative Rhythms	Ruth Evans (5 albums)	Bowmar/Noble
Feel of Music	Hap Palmer	AR 556
Holiday Rhythms two pianos	Wood and Turner	Bowmar/Noble
Ideas, Thoughts and Feelings	Hap Palmer	AR 549
Marches		BOL 54/067
Mod Marches	Hap Palmer	AR 527
Movin'	Hap Palmer	AR 546
Nature and Make Believe		BOL 52/065
Perceptual Motor Rhythm Games	Capan and Hallam	AR 50
Rhythmic Activity two pianos	Bassett and Chestnut	Bowmar/Noble
Rhythm is Fun piano and drum	Inez Schubert	Bowmar/Noble
Rhythm Time two pianos	Wood and Turner	Bowmar/Noble

Note Values: Recordings with Filmstrips

Exploring Music Reading	Raebeck	CM 1047
Introduction to Music Reading	Raebeck	CM 1013

2/4 Meter

Air Gai (*Iphigénie in Aulis*)	Gluck	RCA LES-1000
Gigue (*Cephale et Procris*)	Grétry	RCA LES-1000
Gigue (Suite no. 3 in D Major)	Bach	RCA LES-1000

"Hoedown" (*Rodeo*)	Copland	HRW 512 and RCA LES-1007
"Knightsbridge March" (*London* Suite)	Coates	RCA LES-1007
March (*Soirees Musicales*)	Rossini-Britten	RCA LES-1000
"Marche Militaire"	Schubert	BOL 54/067
"March Past of the Kitchen Utensils" (*The Wasps*)	Williams	RCA LES-1002
"Stars and Stripes Forever"	Sousa	HRW 59 and RCA LES-1005
"Tambourin" (Ballet Music, *Cephale et Procris*)	Grétry	RCA LES-1001

3/4 Meter

"Carillon" (*L'Arlesienne* Suite no. 1)	Bizet	HRW 49
"German Waltz—Paganini"	Schumann-Glazunov	BOL 53/066
Minuet	Mozart	BOL 53/066
Minuet (*Don Giovanni*)	Mozart	HRW 511
Minuetto (*L'Arlesienne* Suite no. 1)	Bizet	RCA LES-1005
"Petite Ballerina" (Ballet Suite no. 1)	Shostakovich	RCA LES-1001
Rosenkavalier Suite	Strauss	RCA LES-1009
"Skater's Waltz, The"	Waldteufel	BOL 55/068 and RCA WE 74
"Tinikling"	Folk Dance	HRW 513
Waltz (*Les Patineurs*)	Meyerbeer	RCA LES-1001
Waltz (*Masquerade* Suite)	Khachaturian	RCA LES-1005
Waltz (*The Sleeping Beauty*)	Tchaikovsky	RCA LES-1004
Waltz in C-sharp Minor	Chopin	HRW 37
"Waltz of the Doll" (*Coppelia*)	Delibes	RCA LES-1000
"Waltz on the Ice" (*Winter Holiday*)	Prokofieff	RCA LES-1003
Waltz no. 1 (*Faust Ballet Music*)	Gounod	RCA LES-1002

4/4 Meter

"Cortege of the Sardar"	Ippolitov-Ivanov	BOL 54/067
"Dagger Dance" (*Natoma*)	Herbert	RCA LES-1002
March (*Summer Day* Suite)	Prokofieff	RCA LES-1000
"March of the Toys" (*Babes in Toyland*)	Herbert	RCA LES-1001
"March—Trumpet and Drum"	Bizet	BOL 53/066
"Pantomime" (*The Comedians*)	Kabalevsky	RCA LES-1000
"Semper Fidelis"	Sousa	HRW 27

Legato Rhythms

Andantino	Thomas	RCA WE 78
"Ballet of the Sylphs" (*Damnation of Faust*)	Berlioz	RCA LES-1000
"Barcarolle" (*Tales of Hoffman*)	Offenbach	RCA LES-1002
"Berceuse" (*Dolly,* op. 56, no. 1)	Fauré	RCA LES-1001
"Berceuse" (*Firebird* Suite)	Stravinsky	RCA LES-1000
"Chopin" (*Carnaval*)	Schumann-Glazunoff	BOL 53/066
"Cradle Song"	Hauser	RCA WE 73
"Cradle Song" (*Children's Games*)	Bizet	RCA LES-1000

"En Bateau"	Debussy	BOL 53/066 and HRW 110
"Flying Birds"	Anderson	RCA WE 71
"Fountain Dance" (*Wand of Youth* Suite no. 2)	Elgar	RCA LES-1001
"German Waltz—Paganini"	Schumann-Glazunoff	BOL 53/066
"Londonderry Air"	Grainger	BOL 60/073
"Love's Dream after the Ball"	Czibulka	RCA WE 71
Rosenkavalier Suite	Strauss	RCA LES-1009
"Serenata"	Moszkowski	RCA WE 78
"Skater's Waltz, The"	Waldteufel	BOL 55/068 and RCA WE 74
"Swan, The" (*Carnival of the Animals*)	Saint-Saëns	BOL 51/064, HRW 28 and RCA LES-1003
"Valse Gracieuse"	Dvorak	RCA WE 73
"Valse Serenade"	Poldini	RCA WE 71
Waltz	Schubert	RCA WE 72
"Walzer"	Gurlitt	RCA WE 72
Waltz no. 1 (*Faust Ballet Music*)	Gounod	RCA LES-1002
Waltz, op. 9b, no. 1	Schubert	RCA WE 74

Staccato Rhythms

Air de Ballet	Jadassohn	RCA WE 72
"Ballet of the Unhatched Chicks" (*Pictures at an Exhibition*)	Moussorgsky	RCA LES-1000
"Come Lasses and Lads"	English Folk	RCA WE 73
"Dance of the Little Swans" (*Swan Lake*)	Tchaikovsky	RCA LES-1000
"Dance of the Sugar Plum Fairy" (*Nutcracker* Suite)	Tchaikovsky	BOL 58/071 and HRW 28
"Etude Joyeuse"	Kopyloff	RCA WE 71
"Intermezzo" (*The Comedians*)	Kabalevsky	BOL 53/066
"Jumping"	Gurlitt	RCA WE 72
March (*Summer Day* Suite)	Prokofieff	RCA LES-1000
"Marche Militaire"	Schubert	BOL 54/067 and RCA WE 73
"March of the Toys" (*Babes in Toyland*)	Herbert	RCA LES-1001
"March Past of the Kitchen Utensils" (*The Wasps*)	Williams	RCA LES-1002
"Petite Ballerina" (Ballet Suite no. 1)	Shostakovich	RCA LES-1001
"Pizzicato" (*Fantastic Toyshop*)	Rossini-Respighi	BOL 53/066
"Pizzicato Polka" (Ballet Suite no. 1)	Shostakovich	RCA LES-1000
"Running Game"	Gurlitt	RCA WE 72
"Run, Run, Run"	Concone	RCA WE 72
"Skipping Theme"	Anderson	RCA WE 71
"Sparks"	Moszkowski	RCA WE 71
"Street Boy's Parade" (*Carmen*)	Bizet	RCA WE 74
"Toreador Song" (*Carmen*)	Bizet	RCA WE 74
"Village Dance"	Liadoff	BOL 53/066
"Wild Horseman, The"	Schumann	RCA WE 78

Phrase

Barcarolle (*Tales of Hoffman*)	Offenbach	RCA LES-1002
"Berceuse" (*Dolly,* op. 56, no. 1)	Fauré	RCA LES-1001

"Crested Hen, The"	Folk Dance	HRW 48
"Hungarian Dance" no. 5	Brahms	BOL 55/068
"Knightsbridge March" (*London* Suite)	Coates	RCA LES-1007
"Petite Ballerina" (Ballet Suite no. 1)	Shostakovich	RCA LES-1001
"Swan, The" (*Carnival of the Animals*)	Saint-Saëns	HRW 28, BOL 51/064 and RCA LES-1003
Waltz (*Les Patineurs*)	Meyerbeer	RCA LES-1001

Recordings and Piano Music for Rhythmic Interpretations

Adagio	Corelli	RCA WE 71
Air Gai (*Iphigénie in Aulis*)	Gluck	RCA LES-1000
"Argonaise" (*Le Cid*)	Massenet	RCA LES-1000 and HRW 610
"Ball, The" (*Children's Games*)	Bizet	RCA LES-1000
"Ballet of the Sylphs" (*Damnation of Faust*)	Berlioz	RCA LES-1000
"Ballet of the Unhatched Chicks" (*Pictures at an Exhibition*)	Moussorgsky	RCA LES-1000
"Barcarolle" (*Tales of Hoffman*)	Offenbach	RCA LES-1002
"Berceuse" (*Dolly*, op. 56, no. 1)	Fauré	RCA LES-1001
"Bydlo" (*Pictures at an Exhibition*)	Moussorgsky	RCA LES-1001
"Can-Can" (*The Fantastic Toyshop*)	Rossini-Respighi	RCA LES-1001
Childhood Rhythms (Five Albums—Ruth Evans)		Bowmar/Noble
"Children's Dance" (*Merry Mount* Suite)	Hanson	RCA LES-1002
Children's Symphony, Third Movement	McDonald	RCA LES-1001
"Circus Music" (*The Red Pony*)	Copland	RCA LES-1002
Classroom Rhythms "Animal Rhythms" (side one prepares children; side two is music only)		CM 1044
Classroom Rhythms "Interpretive Rhythms" (same as above)		CM 1050
Classroom Rhythms "Machine Rhythms" (see "Animal Rhythms")		CM 1077
Classroom Rhythms "Rhythms from the Land of Make-Believe" (see "Animal Rhythms")		CM 1055
Classroom Rhythms "Rhythms of Cowboys and Indians" (see "Animal Rhythms")		CM 1067
"Clowns" (*Under the Big Top*)	Donaldson	BOL 51/064
"Colonel Bogey March"	Alford	BOL 54/067
"Cradle Song" (*Children's Games*)	Bizet	RCA LES-1000
Creative Rhythms	P. James (22 records)	AED series Bowmar/Noble
"Dagger Dance" (*Natoma*)	Herbert	RCA LES-1002

"Dance-a-Story about Balloons"		RCA LE-104
"Dance-a-Story about Flappy and Floppy"		RCA LE-106
"Dance-a-Story about Little Duck"		RCA LE-101
"Dance-a-Story about Noah's Ark"		RCA LE-102
"Dance-a-Story about the Brave Hunter"		RCA LE-105
"Dance-a-Story about the Magic Mountain"		RCA LE-103
"Dance-a-Story about the Toy Tree"		RCA LE-107
"Dance-a-Story at the Beach"		RCA LE-108
"Dance of the Little Swans" (*Swan Lake*)	Tchaikovsky	RCA LES-1000
"Entrance of the Little Fauns"	Pierné	BOL 54/067
"Etude Joyeuse"	Kopylov	RCA WE 71
"Fairies and Giants" (*Wand of Youth* Suite no. 1)	Elgar	RCA LES-1002
"Farandole" (*L'Arlesienne* Suite no. 2)	Bizet	RCA LES-1009 or HRW 68
Finale (*William Tell* Overture)	Rossini	RCA LES-1002 or HRW 68
"Fountain Dance" (*Wand of Youth* Suite no. 2)	Elgar	RCA LES-1001
Fun with Rhythm (3 records)		Bowmar/Noble
"German Waltz—Paganini"	Schumann-Glazonov	BOL 53/066
Gigue (*Cephale et Procris*)	Grétry	RCA LES-1000
Gigue (*Suite no. 3 in D Major*)	Bach	RCA LES-1000
"Hoedown"	Copland	HRW 512 and RCA LES-1007
Holiday Rhythms (Album—4 records)		Bowmar/Noble
"Hornpipe" (*Water Music*)	Handel	RCA LES-1001 and HRW 59
"Jack-in-the-Box" (*Mikrokosmos* Suite no. 2)	Bartok	RCA LES-1001
"Jumping"	Gurlitt	RCA WE 72
"Laranjeiras" (*Saudades do Brazil*)	Milhaud	RCA LES-1001
"Leap Frog" (*Children's Games*)	Bizet	RCA LES-1000
"Little Bird"	Grieg	BOL 52/065
"Little White Donkey" (*Histoires* no. 2)	Ibert	RCA LES-1001
"Londonderry Air" (Irish Tune from County Derry)	Grainger	RCA LES-1005
March (*Iphigénie in Aulis*)	Gluck	RCA WE 75
March (*Love for Three Oranges*)	Prokofieff	RCA WE 76, BOL 54/067
March (*Nutcracker* Suite)	Tchaikovsky	RCA LES-1000, BOL 58/071, HRW 28
March (*Soirees Musicales*)	Rossini-Britten	RCA LES-1000
March (*Summer Day* Suite)	Prokofieff	RCA LES-1000
"March and Comedians Gallop" (*The Comedians*)	Kabalevsky	RCA LE/LES-1002 and HRW 110
"Marche Militaire"	Schubert	RCA WE 73 and BOL 54/067
March in F	Anderson	RCA WE 71
"March Little Soldier"	Pinto	RCA WE 77

Title	Composer	Recording
"March of the Dwarfs"	Grieg	BOL 52/065 and RCA WE 79
"March of the Toys" (*Babes in Toyland*)	Herbert	RCA LES-1001
"March Past of the Kitchen Utensils" (*The Wasps*)	Williams	RCA LES-1002
Once Upon a Time Suite	Donaldson	BOL 52/065
"Pantomime" (*The Comedians*)	Kabalevsky	RCA LES-1000
"Parade" (*Divertissement*)	Ibert	RCA LES-1000
"Petite Ballerina" (*Ballet* Suite no. 1)	Shostakovich	RCA LES-1001
"Pizzicato Polka" (*Ballet* Suite no. 1)	Shostakovich	RCA LES-1000
"Puss-in-Boots and the White Cat" (*Sleeping Beauty*)	Tchaikovsky	RCA LES-1002
Rhythmic Activity		Bowmar/Noble
Rhythm is Fun		Bowmar/Noble
Rhythm Time		Bowmar/Noble
Rosenkavalier Suite	Strauss	RCA LES-1009
"Royal March of the Lion"	Saint-Saëns	BOL 51/064 and HRW 28
"Running Game"	Gurlitt	RCA WE 72
"Run, Run, Run"	Concone	RCA WE 72
"Season Fantasies"	Donaldson	BOL 52/065
"Shepherds' Dance" (*Amahl and the Night Visitors*)	Menotti	RCA LES-1005
"Skaters Waltz"	Waldteufel	BOL 55/068 and RCA WE 74
"Slavonic Dance" no. 7	Dvorak	RCA LES-1005
"Spanish Dance" no. 1 (*La Vida Breve*)	Falla	RCA LES-1009
"Swan, The" (*Carnival of the Animals*)	Saint-Saëns	BOL 51/064, HRW 28 and RCA LES-1000
"Tambourin" (*Cephale et Procris* Ballet Music)	Grétry	RCA LES-1001
"Tarantella" (*The Fantastic Toyshop*)	Rossini-Respighi	RCA LES-1003
"Theme for Skipping"	Anderson	RCA WE 71
"Under the Big Top"	Donaldson	BOL 51/064
"Valsette"	Borowski	RCA WE 71
"Viennese Musical Clock" (*Hary Janos* Suite)	Kodaly	RCA LES-1001
"Walking Song" (*Acadian Songs and Dances*)	Thomson	RCA LES-1000
Waltz (*Les Patineurs*)	Meyerbeer	RCA LES-1001
Waltz no. 1 (*Faust* Ballet Music)	Gounod	RCA LES-1002
"Waltz of the Doll" (*Coppelia*)	Delibes	RCA LES-1000
"War Song" (*Miniatures*)	Reinhold	RCA WE 75
"Wheelbarrow Motive"	Anderson	RCA WE 71
"White Peacock, The," op. 7, no. 1	Griffes	RCA LES-1009

Piano Music	Composer	Publisher
Albums of Selected Pieces	Bartok	E.C. Schirmer
Carnival of the Animals	Saint-Saëns	Durand and Co.
Enfantines	Block	C. Fischer
Fifteen Children's Pieces	Kabalevsky	Leeds Music
Fifty Selected Studies	Heller	G. Schirmer, Inc.
First Book of Creative Rhythms	R.B. Salfran	Holt, Rinehart and Winston
Master Series for the Young	Grieg (and other composers)	G. Schirmer, Inc.
Meet Modern Music (collection)	E.B. Barnett	Mercury Music
Montessori and Music	Butolph	Schocken Books
Music in Motion	Moussorgsky	Willis
Pictures at an Exhibition	Burgmüller	G. Schirmer, Inc.
Twenty-Five Easy and Progressive Studies		G. Schirmer, Inc.

Recordings for Free Movement: Rhythmic Exploration

Title	Composer	Recording
Adagio	Corelli	RCA WE 71
Air Gai (*Iphigénie in Aulis*)	Gluck	RCA LES-1000
"Animals and Circus"		BOL 51/064
"Argonaise" (*Le Cid*)	Massenet	RCA LES-1000 and HRW 610
"Badinerie" (Suite no. 2 in B Minor)	Bach	RCA LES-1002
"Ball, The" (*Children's Games*)	Bizet	RCA LES-1000
"Ballet of the Sylphs" (*Damnation of Faust*)	Berlioz	RCA LES-1000
"Ballet of the Unhatched Chicks" (*Pictures at an Exhibition*)	Moussorgsky	RCA LES-1000
"Barcarolle" (*Tales of Hoffman*)	Offenbach	RCA LES-1002
"Berceuse"	Ilyinsky	RCA WE 73
"Can-Can" (*The Fantastic Toyshop*)	Rossini-Respighi	RCA LES-1001
Childhood Rhythms (Ruth Evans)		Bowmar/Noble (Album)
"Children's Dance" (*Merry Mount Suite*)	Hanson	RCA LES-1002
"Cradle Song"	Hauser	RCA WE 73
"Dagger Dance" (*Natoma*)	Herbert	RCA LES-1002
"Dance of the Comedians" (*Bartered Bridge*)	Smetana	BOL 56/069
"Dance of the Little Swans" (*Swan Lake*)	Tchaikovsky	RCA LES-1000
"Dance of the Moorish Slaves" (*Aida*)	Verdi	RCA WE 73
Dances, Part I		BOL 55/068
Dances, Part II		BOL 56/069
"Dwarfs"	Reinhold	RCA WE 71
"Entrance of the Little Fauns"	Pierné	BOL 54/067
"Etude Joyeuse"	Kopylov	RCA WE 71
"Farandole" (*L'Arlesienne* Suite no. 2)	Bizet	RCA LES-1009 and HRW 68
Fun with Music		Bowmar/Noble (Album)
"Gavotte" (*Mlle. Angot* Suite)	Lecocq	BOL 53/67
"German Waltz—Paganini"	Schumann-Glazunov	BOL 53/67
Gigue (*Cephale et Procris*)	Grétry	RCA LES-1000
Gigue (Suite no. 3 in D Major)	Bach	RCA LES-1000
"Happy and Light of Heart" (*Bohemian Girl*)	Balfe	RCA WE 72
Holiday Rhythms		Bowmar/Noble (Album)
"Hornpipe" (*Water Music*)	Handel	RCA LES-1001 and HRW 59
"Jumping"	Gurlitt	RCA WE 72
March (*Iphigénie in Aulis*)	Gluck	RCA WE 75
March (*Nutcracker* Suite)	Tchaikovsky	BOL 58/071 and RCA WE 72

Title	Composer	Recording
March (*The Love for Three Oranges*)	Prokofieff	BOL 54/067 and RCA WE 76
March in F	Anderson	RCA WE 71
"March of the Little Lead Soldiers"	Pierné	BOL 54/067
"March of the Toys" (*Babes in Toyland*)	Herbert	RCA LES-1001
"March Past of the Kitchen Utensils" (*The Wasps*)	Williams	RCA LES-1002
"Pantomime" (*The Comedians*)	Kabalevsky	RCA LES-1000
"Petite Ballerina" (Ballet Suite no. 1)	Shostakovich	RCA LES-1001
"Pictures and Patterns"		BOL 53/068
"Pizzicato Polka" (Ballet Suite no. 1)	Shostakovich	RCA LES-1000
Polka	Lecocq	BOL 53/068
"Red Pony, The" (*Circus Music*)	Copland	RCA LES-1002
Rhythmic Activity		Bowmar/Noble (Album)
Rhythmic Play		Bowmar/Noble (Album)
Rhythm is Fun		Bowmar/Noble (Album)
Rhythm Time		Bowmar/Noble (Album)
Rosenkavalier Suite	Strauss	RCA LES-1009
"Run, Run" (*Memories of Childhood*)	Pinto	RCA WE 77
"Run, Run, Run"	Concone	RCA WE 72
"Season Fantasies"	Donaldson	BOL 52/065
"Skaters Waltz, The"	Waldteufel	RCA WE 74, BOL 55/068
"Spanish Dance" no. 1 (*La Vida Breve*)	Falla	RCA LES-1009
"Tambourin" (*Cephale et Procris* Ballet Music)	Grétry	RCA LES-1001
"Tarantella" (*The Fantastic Toyshop*)	Rossini-Respighi	RCA LES-1003
"Tarantelle"	Saint-Saëns	RCA WE 72
"Valsette"	Borowski	RCA WE 71
"Walking Song" (*Acadian Songs and Dances*)	Thomson	RCA LES-1000
Waltz (*Les Patineurs*)	Meyerbeer	RCA LES-1001
Waltz no. 1 (*Faust* Ballet Music)	Gounod	RCA LES-1002
"Waltz of the Doll" (*Coppelia*)	Delibes	RCA LES-1000
"Waltz of the Flowers" (*Nutcracker* Suite)	Tchaikovsky	BOL 58/071 and HRW 28
"War Song" (*Miniatures*)	Reinhold	RCA WE 75
"Wheelbarrow Motive"	Anderson	RCA WE 71

Recordings for Rhythmic Dramatizations

Title	Composer	Recording
Air Gai (*Iphigénie in Aulis*)	Gluck	RCA LES-1000
"Amaryllis"	Ghys	RCA WE 90
"An American in Paris"	Gershwin	
"Ballet of the Sylphs" (*Damnation of Faust*)	Berlioz	RCA LES-1000
"Ballet of the Unhatched Chicks" (*Pictures at an Exhibition*)	Moussorgsky	RCA LES-1000
"Ballet Petit"	Donaldson	BOL 53/066
"Barcarolle" (*Tales of Hoffman*)	Offenbach	RCA LES-1002
"Bee, The"	Schubert	RCA WE 79
"Berceuse" (*Firebird* Suite)	Stravinsky	RCA LES-1000
Billy the Kid	Copland	RCA LM-2195
"Bydlo" (*Pictures at an Exhibition*)	Moussorgsky	RCA LES-1001
"Can-Can" (*The Fantastic Toyshop*)	Rossini-Respighi	RCA LES-1001
"Carillon" (*L'Arlesienne* Suite no. 1)	Bizet	HRW 49
Carnival of the Animals	Saint-Saëns	BOL 51/064 and HRW 28
"Circus Music" (*The Red Pony*)	Copland	RCA LES-1002
"Dagger Dance" (*Natoma*)	Herbert	RCA LES-1002
"Dance of the Chinese Dolls"	Rebikoff	RCA WE 80
"Dance of the Gnomes"	Liszt	RCA WE 82
"Danse Macabre"	Saint-Saëns	RCA LM 2056 and BOL 59/072
"Departure" (*Winter Holiday*)	Prokofieff	RCA LES-1001
"Fairies and Giants" (*Wand of Youth*)	Elgar	RCA LES-1002
Finale (*William Tell* Overture)	Rossini	RCA LES-1002 or HRW 68
Firebird Suite	Stravinsky	
"Flight of the Bumblebee"	Rimsky-Korsakoff	BOL 52/065
Gigue (*Cephale et Procris*)	Grétry	RCA LES-1000
"Gnomes"	Reinhold	RCA WE 71
"Golliwog's Cakewalk"	Debussy	
"In the Hall of the Mountain King" (*Peer Gynt*)	Grieg	RCA LES-1003
"Leap Frog" (*Children's Games*)	Bizet	RCA LES-1000
Listen and Do Series (Vol. 1, 2, 3, and 4)		Audio Education, Inc.
"Little White Donkey, The" (*Histoires* no. 2)	Ibert	RCA LES-1001
March (*Soirees Musicales*)	Rossini-Britten	RCA LES-1000
"March and Comedians Gallop" (*The Comedians*)	Kabalevsky	RCA LES-1002 and HRW 110
"March of the Dwarfs"	Grieg	RCA WE 79 and BOL 52
"March of the Gnomes"	Rebikoff	RCA WE 79
"March of the Little Lead Soldiers"	Pierné	BOL 54/067 and RCA WE 77
"March of the Tin Soldiers"	Tchaikovsky	RCA WE 73
"March of the Toys" (*Babes in Toyland*)	Herbert	RCA LES-1001
"March Past of the Kitchen Utensils" (*The Wasps*)	Williams	RCA LES-1002
"March—Trumpet and Drum"	Bizet	BOL 53/066
Mother Goose Suite	Ravel	BOL 57/070
Nutcracker Suite	Tchaikovsky	BOL 58/071 and HRW 28
"Of a Tailor and a Bear"	MacDowell	RCA WE 78
"Pantomime" (*The Comedians*)	Kabalevsky	RCA LES-1000
"Parade" (*Divertissement*)	Ibert	RCA LES-1000
"Petite Ballerina" (Ballet Suite no. 1)	Shostakovich	RCA LES-1001
"Pizzicato Polka" (Ballet Suite no. 1)	Shostakovich	RCA LES-1000
"Puss-in-Boots and the White Cat" (*Sleeping Beauty*)	Tchaikovsky	RCA LES-1002
"Rodeo"	Copland	RCA LM-2195

Rosenkavalier Suite	Strauss	RCA LES-1009
"Season Fantasies"	Donaldson	BOL 52/065
"Shepherds' Dance" (*Amahl and the Night Visitors*)	Menotti	RCA LES-1005
"Sorcerer's Apprentice"	Dukas	RCA LM-1803 and BOL 59/072
"Street in a Frontier Town" (*Billy the Kid*)	Copland	RCA LES-1009
"Swan, The" (*Carnival of the Animals*)	Saint-Saëns	HRW 28 and RCA LES-1003
"To a Water Lily"	MacDowell	RCA WE 79
"Under the Big Top"	Donaldson	BOL 51/064
"Witch, The"	Tchaikovsky	RCA WE 73
"Witches Dance"	MacDowell	RCA WE 81

Recordings and Materials for Experiences with Rhythm Instruments

Recordings
Audio Education Inc. (American Book Co.)
    Rhythm Band Patterns (2 vols.)
Bowmar/Noble Records
    Childhood Rhythms
    Creative Rhythms
    Fun with Music
    Rhythm Is Fun
    Rhythm Time
    Rhythmic Activity
Classroom Materials Company
    Exploring the Rhythm Instruments CM 1032
    Introducing the Rhythm Instruments CM 1020
    Our First Rhythm Band, Vol. 1 CM 1066
    Our First Rhythm Band, Vol. 2 CM 1075
Educational Activities
    Modern Tunes for Rhythms & Instruments Hap Palmer
Folkways
    Play Your Instruments and Make a Pretty Sound Ella Jenkins
Holt, Rinehart and Winston, Inc.
    Exploring Music Series
Musical Sound Books
    Fun with Rhythm
RCA Victor
    Adventures in Music elementary series
    Basic Record Library for Elementary Grades

AR: Educational Activities
BOL: Bowmar/Noble Orchestral Library
Bowmar/Noble Albums (piano and two pianos)
CM: Classroom Materials Co.
HRW: Holt, Rinehart and Winston *Exploring Music* (First number refers to grade; remaining numbers refer to album. Thus "510" means grade 5, album 10.)
RCA LES: RCA Victor *Adventures in Music* series
RCA WE: RCA Victor *Basic Record Library for Elementary Grades*

Singing Experiences
The Unison and Part-Song

3

Singing can be important to the child's personal as well as musical development. Thus, its usefulness is often discovered at a very early age. Listen to the rise and fall of the voice of the infant in his crib as he makes little sounds to himself. Listen to children playing together, barely able to talk but already chanting. Listen to the chant grow into a simple melody as the child grows. Listen to an adult humming or whistling. Because of a very basic need, all are using, quite unconsciously, a language that is universal—that of singing.

Singing is, indeed, a universal language. In addition, it is the most natural and direct way of making music. It gives intimate contact with the expressive elements of music—rhythm, melody, tone color, texture, and form.

Singing is not just a musical experience: it goes beyond. It gives the child a way of expressing and releasing her many emotions, strengthening her sense of identity, and better relating to her environment. Further, as she sings the songs that tell of other people and cultures, she learns to identify with the feelings of others, and the feelings generated in the classroom take on a depth and cohesiveness not always developed in other activities.

Thus, singing may be one of the most important musical experiences for the child in the elementary school.

Aims of Singing Experiences

1. To expand the child's innate enjoyment of singing.
2. To help the child sing, both in unison and part singing: more easily and naturally; with an ever widening vocal range; in tune; and with a pleasing and expressive tone quality.
3. To help the child achieve the conceptual understandings and behavioral objectives related to singing experiences. (For a list of conceptual understandings and behavioral objectives related to each age level, see the chart at the end of chapter 1.)

Selecting the Song

A song may be beautiful or funny. Its text may be based on fantasy or realism. It may be a unison song or a part-song. It may have a catchy rhythm or a lovely flowing melody. It may tell a good story or be interesting to a particular group because of other classroom or world happenings. It may be a spiritual, work song, folk ballad, sea chantey, patriotic song, or art song; a song that promotes ethnic understandings or a song that illuminates another culture; a song that has mellowed with age or a new song from the popular idiom. If the song seems to have lasting value (the children learning it will want to sing it at later times in their lives), obviously is attractive to the age group, and is within the scope of the children's ability to learn, it is worth teaching. The alert teacher will have a wealth of these songs ready and waiting for the right time to present them to the class.

He will, of course, also know other criteria for selecting a song. For example, is the range of the song appropriate for the age? It is well to remember that while a first grader normally has a range of from middle C to A above (a sixth) which gradually expands, the current trend to imitate favorite "rock" singers has contributed to a more restricted vocal range for children in the upper elementary grades. Further, some boys in the late fifth- and sixth grades have changing voices, with a drastically reduced range. (Suggestions for helping boys with this problem are in the section of this chapter entitled "Vocal Exploration and Aids for the Weak Singer."

At what point, it may also be asked, should the part-song be introduced? When the child can sing many songs in tune, with a pleasing tone quality (often in the latter part of level I), she is ready for initial part-singing experiences:

Chants to songs
Echo (dialogue) songs
Simple ostinati to pentatonic songs

When she reaches level II, she will be ready to sing:
Descants
Counter melodies
Harmonized cadences
Easy rounds and canons

On level III part-singing experiences will include:
Singing chord roots
Harmonizing in thirds and sixths
Vocal chording (chordal progressions)
Harmonizing by ear

Teaching the part-song has its own special challenges. For suggestions see the section in this chapter entitled "Textural Concepts."

Motivating Interest in the Song

The teacher's way of motivating interest will depend primarily on why he selected the song and how he intends to teach it. If he selected it because of the beauty of its melody, he must convey this quality of the song quickly. Sometimes singing it simply, but meaningfully, will be enough. Sometimes focusing on various aspects of the melody as it is heard will bring about the desire to learn it. Perhaps the teacher will write part of the melody on the board, letting the class see its contours, and follow it visually as it is played or sung. Perhaps the teacher will teach a child to play part of the song on melody bells or will himself play the melody.

If the song is illustrated in the songbook, the teacher may use this to stimulate the child's interest. He may also provide reproductions of paintings that show a related emotion or mood.

If the song's unique quality is its rhythm, the teacher may clap it or play it on a rhythm instrument, letting the class join him, first clapping, then using a few rhythm instruments. There can be, through this approach, a complete involvement with the song's rhythm, even before the class hears the song.

If the song's focus is the text or the story it tells, very often discussion of this element will create student interest.

Somehow the teacher must relate the song to the lives of children—to their feelings; their appreciation for melody, rhythm, mood, or drama; their studies, out-of-school activities, or people they know or may want to know. Whether they are fifth- and sixth-grade boys, increasingly reluctant to sing because of negative influences and peer pressure, or first-graders, hesitant because they lack control of their singing voices, the teacher must make the song relevant and encourage participation. Somehow he must do this so that motivating the song and teaching the song unite. If the teacher cannot achieve this, he probably has chosen the wrong song or motivating procedure.

Teaching the Song

When the teacher has chosen a song, has studied its unique qualities, has planned an enjoyable singing experience, and has motivated the children, learning the song will occur quickly, easily, and naturally. The teacher will be more able to give this satisfying experience to children if he has answered the questions in the following paragraphs.

Should the song be taught by rote or by note? Throughout the elementary grades, children will learn a majority of songs by rote. However, in late first grade or early second grade, the teacher can begin to focus children's attention on various simple aspects of musical notation. As children develop some knowledge of notation, such as recognition of scale passages in a melody or repeated rhythmic and melodic patterns, the teacher can use these specific understandings in teaching songs.

Should the teacher sing the song or use a recording? The teacher who feels adequate in singing should sing often with the class, using a recording only when it can contribute something beyond his ability, such as a recording of a two-part song, or an interesting accompaniment or interpretation of a song. Children generally will prefer their teacher's voice to a recording. When the teacher knows the song well, enjoys it, and is able to convey this to the children, imperfections in vocal technique are of minor concern. Use of a pitch pipe or any available melody instrument can insure starting on a suitable pitch. However, the teacher should guard against excess concern with beginning each song on exactly the pitch indicated. It is often necessary to start on a lower pitch to avoid strain and to stay within the vocal range of children. In addition, it is wiser to keep spontaneity in singing experiences than to be unduly concerned with pitch accuracy.

Upon what musical concepts can the song focus to encourage growth in conceptual understandings and fulfillment of behavioral objectives?

1. Rhythmic concepts
   Does the song have a rhythmic pull that will entice children? Does it encourage bodily response or rhythmic accompaniment? Do its rhythmic characteristics easily focus on conceptual understandings and behavioral objectives related to rhythm? If so, stress rhythmic concepts.
2. Melodic concepts
   Does the melody have a quality to which children will respond? Does its contour, or the way in which it progresses (by step, skip, up or down) suggest a focus on conceptual understandings or behavioral objectives related to melody? If so, stress melodic concepts.
3. Textural concepts
   Is the song a part-song? Will the class be able to perform it? Does it lend itself to accompaniment by children, using guitar, Autoharp, or Orff instruments? If so, stress concepts related to texture.
4. Concepts related to form
   When the song is heard, will it suggest a form created through similar and contrasting phrases? If so, stress concepts related to form.
5. Expressive concepts
   When heard, does the song strongly suggest expressive qualities to which children will respond? Can the children understand and re-create these qualities? If so, stress concepts related to expression.
6. Notational concepts
   Are there melodic or rhythmic patterns or phrases that can be the focus for exploring notation? Does the score suggest a focus on the conceptual understandings or behavioral objectives related to notation? If so, stress concepts related to music reading.

What kind of responses does the song suggest, and how can these responses stress important musical concepts and involve children while they learn the song? The teacher should know many different ways to repeat a song, so that children can enjoy learning a song by rote. Listening to a song over and over, and mimicking the teacher as he sings it is not a very stimulating or satisfying procedure.

Anything that gets children involved with the song is stimulating. Anything that involves physical, emotional, and intellectual resources and needs, and gives the feeling of success, achievement, and growth is satisfying.

Therefore, it is imperative for the teacher to ask (1) what responses best fit the song; (2) which of these responses would be most stimulating and satisfying for children; and (3) which would encourage conceptual understanding and fulfillment of behavioral objectives. According to the answers to these questions, the following may be used:

1. Bodily movement
   When the rhythm or the text of the song suggest rhythmic dramatization or basic bodily movements, such as walking, running, skipping
2. Creating an accompaniment
   When the rhythm or melody of the song suggest an accompaniment with rhythm or melody instruments
3. Immediate participation in singing
   When the song has a "chime-in" phrase, a refrain, or a chant that can be quickly learned

How can other musical experiences (rhythms, listening, instrumental, or music reading) enrich the singing experience? It is important to remember that interaction exists among the various types of musical activities. Rarely will an isolated singing experience occur, because, for enjoyment or musical growth, other activities will become part of the experience. The teacher will find, for example, that to develop a rhythmic concept, she will encourage children to dramatize a song; to develop understandings of notation, she will teach children to play a short phrase on the melody bells; to help them hear the second part in a two-part song, she will initiate a listening experience.

The imaginative teacher will freely and eagerly use any musical activity to further enjoyment and musical growth—even when the primary activity is singing.

Are there other art forms to interweave with singing to further musical growth and enjoyment? Concepts found in music often appear in other arts. A child learning to hear and recognize the notation of repeated rhythmic patterns may be helped by observing patterns in a painting. Learning that a melody, when notated, creates a contour is reinforced by discovering the contour that a city skyline creates. Texture, defined in a painting or photograph, becomes aural in music. The phrase, experienced in poetry, becomes more easily identifiable in music. Helping children relate the concepts of music to those in other arts not only hastens musical growth, it enriches immeasurably the whole learning process.

What is the best possible sequence for teaching children the song? When the teacher has answered the foregoing questions, she is ready to make a detailed plan for teaching. The value of such a plan is twofold: (1) the choice of approach and techniques is more apt to encourage the maximum musical growth and enjoyment; and (2) the teacher who becomes well prepared and secure is thereby more flexible in his teaching. This flexibility will allow him to adapt his plans to incorporate children's suggestions. A plan for a singing experience should include:

1. Materials needed
2. Specific songs
3. Related musical activities
4. Conceptual understandings and behavioral objectives
5. Related arts
6. Correlation with other subjects, when appropriate
7. A specific strategy including:
   a. Interweaving other musical activities and related arts to reinforce conceptual understandings
   b. Focusing on musical concepts and behavioral objectives
   c. Encouraging enjoyment, response, and suggestions from the children
   d. Introducing the song (specific words or activities to be used) to motivate participation and foster musical discovery
   e. Allowing children to hear the song, and respond musically or intellectually before singing the entire song
   f. Helping children understand, respond to, and express the mood and text of the song
8. Ideas for individualization, follow-up, and enrichment
9. Evaluation

The following sections provide suggestions for experiences focusing on concepts related to each of the basic musical elements: rhythm, melody, form, texture, expression, and notation.

Rhythmic Concepts

Level I

Materials Needed
1. Drum and other percussion instruments
2. Illustrations of fast and slow
3. Copy of "Train Is A-Coming"

4. Recordings:
   a. "Flight of the Bumblebee" by Rimsky-Korsakov, Bowmar *Orchestral Library* recording BOL 52/#5073
   b. "Wheelbarrow Motive" by Anderson, RCA Victor *Basic Record Library for Elementary Grades* recording WE 71
   c. "Traumerei" by Schumann, Bowmar *Orchestral Library* recording BOL 076
   d. "Run, Run, Run" by Concone, RCA Victor *Basic Record Library for Elementary Grades* recording WE 72
5. Music Cue charts

Singing Activities
Learning "Train Is A-Coming"

Related Musical Activities
1. Playing percussion instruments
2. Rhythmic dramatization
3. Listening

Conceptual Understandings
1. The rhythm of music generally has a basic beat, which can vary in tempo.
2. These durations (notes) are related to one another in the following way:

Behavioral Objectives
1. To demonstrate ability to hear basic beat in different tempi
2. To demonstrate through a rhythmic activity the relationship between a quarter note and an eighth note and other long-short durational patterns
3. To hear a short melody and repeat it accurately
4. To begin to differentiate between contrasting melodic directions

Related Arts
Observing fast and slow movement in illustrations
1. Boy running
2. Girl running
3. Boy creeping
4. Elephant walking slowly

Procedure
1. Experiencing the concepts of fast and slow through the visual arts
   a. Display illustrations similar to figure 3.1a-d.

Figure 3.1
a, Boy running, photograph by David Rosenthal; b, girl running, photograph by Elizabeth Wheeler; c, boy creeping, photograph by David Rosenthal; d, elephant walking slowly, photograph by Lois Raebeck.

a

b

b. Tell the children to examine the pictures carefully to see what they have in common. (If children have difficulty deciding that they all show movement, ask them to listen as you play a drumbeat, and to tell you which picture or pictures match the beat you are playing. Play a fast drumbeat. Children will no doubt select the pictures of the boy and girl running.)
c. Select a volunteer to play a moderately fast drumbeat. When the beat is steady, select volunteers to move to the rhythm of the drum. Make positive comments about children moving with the beat.
d. Ask for a volunteer to play the drum in a rhythm suggested by the elephant moving and the boy creeping. When the beat is steady, select children to move to the rhythm of the drum.

maracas, sand blocks, and voices, let children experiment making different kinds of sounds (gaining speed, slowing down, and fading into the distance).

b. Tell the children you will play the basic beat of a slow freight train (| | | |), and they should clap their hands with you. Play quarter notes on the drum as the children clap their hands.

c. Tell the children you will change to the basic beat of an express train. Invite them to alternate patting their right and left thighs as you play the drum. (♫♫)

d. Tell the children to maintain the basic beat of a freight train as you play the basic beat of an express train. Play the rhythm of the express train on the drum as children pat their thighs in the rhythm of the freight train.

Freight train | | | |

Express train   ♫ ♫ ♫ ♫

e. When class can do the above, have them try *stepping* the beat of the freight train as they *clap* the rhythm of the express train.

3. Experiencing differences in duration, tempo, and melodic direction, by learning and dramatizing a song ("Train Is A-Coming") while adding percussive accompaniment

a. Tell the class you will sing a song about a train and you need a few children to move as a freight train does. Select a few responsive volunteers to move with your drumbeat. When they are moving together in a slow, steady rhythm, begin singing "Train Is A-Coming" in the same tempo.

b. Ask the class if they heard any repeated tonal patterns in the song. ("Oh, yes") Ask if it moved up or down. Have the children sing this pattern and show direction with their hands.

c. Select some children to move as an express train does. Help them establish the rhythm of eighth notes. Begin singing, encouraging the class to pat express-train rhythm on their thighs and sing "Oh, yes" patterns.

d. Put the notation of the two trains on the board:

Freight train | | | |

Express train   ♫ ♫ ♫ ♫

e. Ask the children how many claps or steps the express train takes to one step or clap of the freight. (two) If children are familiar with the

e. If two drums are available, have groups and drummers perform on your signal: group one moving in a fast tempo when you call "fast," group two moving when you call "slow." Try to "catch" them by calling "fast" and "slow," encouraging quick responses.

f. Invite the children to bring other pictures showing differences in tempo.

2. Experiencing differences in duration and tempo by simulating the rhythms of a slow freight train and a fast express train

a. Discuss with the children their experiences with trains: recent trips by train; different kinds of trains they have seen; nearby towns that may be reached by train; and different kinds of train sounds, such as "choo-choo," "toot-toot." Using

Train Is A-Coming

Spiritual

1. Train is a-com-ing, Oh, yes,
Train is a-com-ing,___ Oh, yes, Train is a-com-ing,
Train is a-com-ing, Train is a-com-ing, Oh, yes.

2. Better get your ticket, Oh, yes, *(2 times)*
   Better get your ticket, *(2 times)*
   Better get your ticket, Oh, yes.

3. Train is a-leaving Oh yes, *(2 times)*
   Train is a-leaving, *(2 times)*
   Train is a-leaving, Oh, yes.

names of these notes, remind them that the notation for the freight train is quarter notes; for the express, eighth notes.

f. Ask which rhythm instrument would best make the sound for each train. (One class selected sand blocks for the freight train, maracas for the express train.) Let individual children practice playing, each in the proper rhythm, as the class sings the song.

g. Ask the class which train's rhythm would best suit each verse of this song. (One class decided the rhythm of the express train would best fit verses one and three, the rhythm of the freight train for verse two.)

h. Select children to be the train, moving in the rhythm decided upon for each verse. Select children to accompany each rhythm, using percussion instruments. Have the "train" for the first verse begin moving, with accompaniment. When they are moving steadily, begin singing, encouraging the children to join you.

i. Ask the children for ideas for further dramatizing the song. They may decide to:
   (1) Let some children be passengers, buying tickets from the ticket seller, then boarding the train.
   (2) Select a child to play the triangle for a train bell ringing at the station, and a conductor to call, "All aboard!" as an interlude between verses two and three.
   (3) Have some people be trees waving in the breeze.

j. Make certain the class plans the following:
   (1) The location (in the room) of the station
   (2) The direction of the train, both approaching and leaving the station
   (3) The location of the ticket seller and waiting passengers
   (4) The location of other "characters" (trees, and so on)
   (5) The actors to portray the train, passengers, ticket seller, and trees

Bass Xylophone

Alto Xylophone

Timpani

Alto Metallophone

Alto Glockenspiel

Triangle

Maracas and
Sand Blocks

k. Help the children dramatize the song.
l. Teacher may add the orchestration shown on this page.
4. Evaluating the children's ability to hear the difference between music that has a fast basic beat and music that has a slow beat
a. Reproduce and distribute this Music Cue chart.

Music Cue Chart	
1. Slow	Fast
2. Slow	Fast
3. Slow	Fast
4. Slow	Fast

b. Tell children you will play four compositions, and they should listen then circle the word that best describes each. Play the following or similar compositions:
   (1) "Flight of the Bumblebee" by Rimsky-Korsakov (fast)
   (2) "Wheelbarrow Motive," by Anderson (slow)
   (3) "Traumerei" by Schumann (slow)
   (4) "Run, Run, Run" by Concone (fast)

Note: The teacher may want to substitute other recordings, including, perhaps, a "pop" recording favorite of the class. Further, he may want to play only a part of each selection, just enough to give the feeling of "fast" or "slow."

Singing Experiences That Focus on Rhythmic Concepts

Level I or II

Experiencing Rhythm, through Finger Plays and Action Songs

Teach the following or similar action songs, by singing them and using actions suggested by the words. Encourage the children to join you.

Eency Weency Spider

Action Song

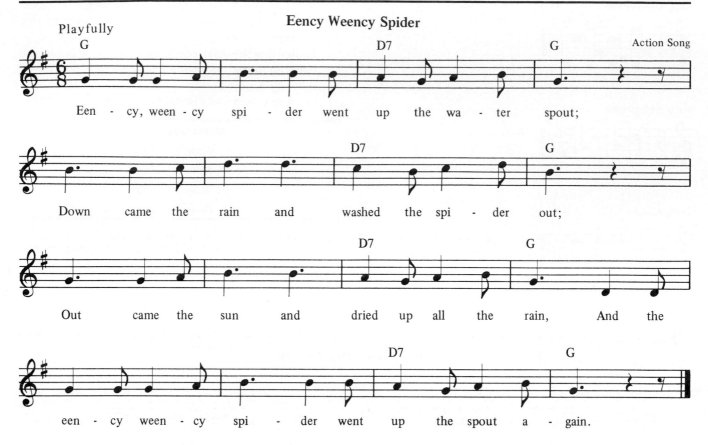

Een - cy, ween - cy spi - der went up the wa - ter spout;

Down came the rain and washed the spi - der out;

Out came the sun and dried up all the rain, And the

een - cy ween - cy spi - der went up the spout a - gain.

The words of this song suggest actions. Represent the motion of the spider by touching the tip of the index finger on one hand to the tip of the thumb on the other and alternating them as the hands move up and down.

Arranged from *Heritage Songster* by Dallin and Dallin, © 1966 by Wm. C. Brown Company Publishers, Dubuque, Iowa. (in public domain)

This Old Man

Steadily

England

1. This old man, he played one, He played nick - nack on my thumb. With a

nick - nack pad - dy whack give the dog a bone! This old man came roll - ing home.

2. This old man, he played two,
   He played nick-nack on my shoe.

3. This old man, he played three,
   He played nick-nack on my knee.

4. This old man, he played four,
   He played nick-nack on my door.

5. This old man, he played five,
   He played nick-nack on my hive.

6. This old man, he played six,
   He played nick-nack on my sticks.

7. This old man, he played sev'n,
   He played nick-nack till elev'n.

8. This old man, he played eight,
   He played nick-nack on my gate.

9. This old man, he played nine,
   He played nick-nack on my spine.

10. This old man, he played ten,
    He played nick-nack over again.

This popular children's song from England serves for a variety of activities. It is a familiar marching rhythm, a favorite counting song, and is excellent for pantomime.

Arranged from *Heritage Songster* by Dallin and Dallin, © 1966 by Wm. C. Brown Company Publishers, Dubuque, Iowa. (in public domain)

One Finger, One Thumb

1. One fin-ger, one thumb, keep grow-ing; One fin-ger, one thumb, keep grow-ing; One

fin-ger, one thumb keep grow-ing; We'll all be hap-py and gay!

2. One finger, one thumb, one hand, keep growing, etc.
3. Add: . . . two hands, etc.
4. Add: . . . one arm, etc.
5. Add: . . . two arms, etc.
6. Add: . . . one leg, etc.
7. Add: . . . two legs, etc.
8. Add: . . . sit down, get up, etc.

From *For Happy Singing* © 1958 by World Around Songs. Used by permission.

Under the Spreading Chestnut Tree

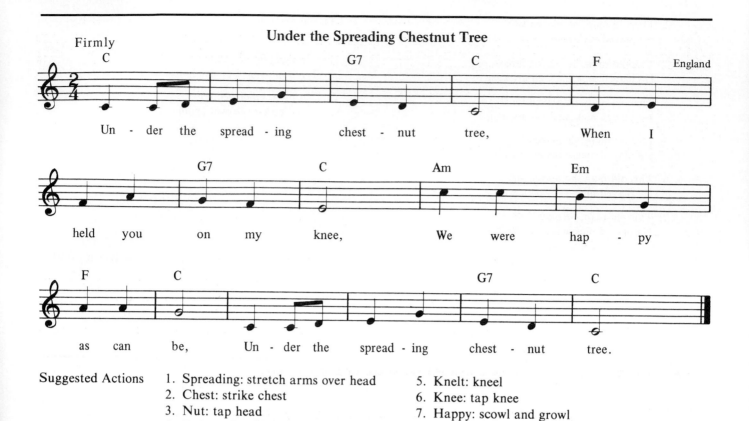

Firmly

Under the spread - ing chest - nut tree, When I held you on my knee, We were hap - py as can be, Un - der the spread - ing chest - nut tree.

Suggested Actions
1. Spreading: stretch arms over head
2. Chest: strike chest
3. Nut: tap head
4. Tree: same as spreading
5. Knelt: kneel
6. Knee: tap knee
7. Happy: scowl and growl

Arranged from *Heritage Songster* by Dallin and Dallin, © 1966 by Wm. C. Brown Company Publishers, Dubuque, Iowa. (in public domain)

Level I or II

Experiencing Rhythm, through Singing Games
Teach the following games by singing as you do the actions, first with a small group of children, then with the entire class. Encourage children to join in the singing.

Kagome

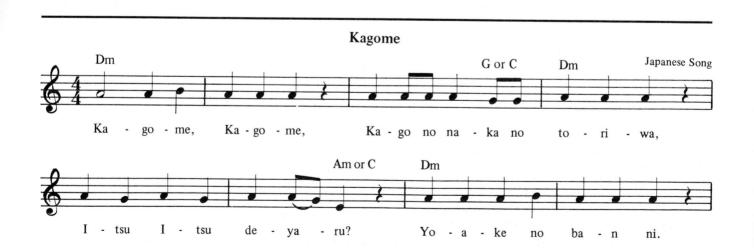

Ka - go - me, Ka - go - me, Ka - go no na - ka no to - ri - wa, I - tsu I - tsu de - ya - ru? Yo - a - ke no ba - n ni.

Tsu - ru to ka - me to   su - bet - ta,   U - shi - ro no sho - nen   da - a - re?

English Translation

(In Japan the crane and the turtle are symbols of
long life.)

The bird in the cage, the bird in the cage,
When will the bird get out of the cage?
On a dark night, toward the dawn,
The crane and the turtle misstepped.
Who is right behind you?

Players stand in circle holding hands. One person is "it" and stands in center, blindfolded.
Players walk or skip around the circle while they sing the song. When the song ends they must
stop. "It" then tries to guess the name of the person standing directly in back of him. If he
guesses right the person whom he has named becomes "it." If he guesses wrong, he must be
"it" again.

From *Hi Neighbor*, Book 2, publ. by U.S. Committee for UNICEF, United Nations, N.Y. Used by permission.

The Old Brass Wagon

Square Dance Rhythm

Midwestern U. S.

1. Cir - cle to the left, the old brass wag - on,
Cir - cle to the left, the old brass wag - on, Cir - cle to the left, the
old brass wag - on, You're the one my dar - ling.

2. Circle to the right, the old brass wagon, etc.
3. Swing, oh swing, the old brass wagon, etc.
4. Promenade around, the old brass wagon, etc.
5. Swing your partner, the old brass wagon, etc.
6. Break and swing, the old brass wagon, etc.
7. Promenade in, the old brass wagon, etc.

Arranged from *Heritage Songster* by Dallin and Dallin, © 1966 by Wm. C. Brown Company Publishers, Dubuque, Iowa. (in public domain)

Sandy Land

1. Make my liv - ing in san - dy land,
2. Hie, come a - long my pret - ty lit - tle miss,

Make my liv - ing in san - dy land, Make my liv - ing in
Hie, come a - long my hon - ey, Hie, come a - long my

san - dy land, La - dies fare thee well! _____
pret - ty lit - tle miss, I won't be home till Sun - day.

3. Raise big taters in sandy land, (3 times)
    If you can't dig 'em I guess I can.

4. How old are you, my pretty little miss?
    How old are you, my honey?
    She answered me with a ha, ha, ha,
    "I'll be sixteen next Sunday."

5. One more river I'm bound to cross. (3 times)
      'Fore I see my honey.

6. Will you marry me, my pretty little miss?
    Will you marry me, my honey?
    She answered me with a ha, ha, ha,
    "I'll run and ask my mama."

7. Hump back mule I'm bound to ride, (3 times)
    'Fore I see my honey.

8. Hop come along, my pretty little miss,
    Hop come along, my honey,
    Hop come along, my pretty little miss,
      Marry you next Sunday.

Formation: Single circle, by partners, facing in.

Action: (1) In and out: With hands joined all take four steps in toward the center, lifting hands; and four steps back, dropping hands. Repeat in and out again. (2) Right and left: Partners face each other so that men will move counterclockwise, girls clockwise. Starting with right hands joined, partners pass right shoulders. Loose right hands, and each advances and takes the next one by left hand, which makes the man go outside, girl in. Continue this around the circle until partners meet. (Use as many verses as are required, depending on size of group). (3) Double L swing: Continue in the same direction, as in right and left, but now hook elbows and turn each one completely around, first with right arms joined, then left arms with the next, until partners meet again. (4) Promenade in a circle by partners: For the promenade partners join crossed hands, girl on the right, walk or skip once around the circle counterclockwise.

From *Handy Party Book* © 1940 by Lynn Rohrbough. Published by World Around Songs. Used by permission.

Kye Kye Kole
(Che Che Kole)

Ghana

Che - che - koo - lay, che - che - koo - lay, Che - che Ko - fi sa

che - che Ko - fi - sa Ko - fi - sa - lan - ga, Ko - fi - sa - lan - ga,

Ca - ca - shi lan - ga, ca - ca - shi lan - ga Koom - ma - dye - day.

Players stand in circle. One person is "it" and stands in the center with hands on head and sings "Che che koolay." (Words are only nonsense.) The other players repeat, with hands on heads. "It" sings next phrase with hands on shoulders, others follow; the next phrase with hands on hips, and finally the last with hands grasping ankles. Others repeat each phrase.

As "it" finishes, he falls to ground; others follow. Then, without warning, "it" gets up. He tries to tag one of the other players, who scramble to their feet and run away as fast as they can. However, they must not start getting up until "it" does. Anyone who is tagged becomes "it" for the next round.

From *Hi Neighbor*, Book 2, publ. by U.S. Committee for UNICEF, United Nations, N.Y. Used by permission.

Looby Loo

U.S.

Swinging Rhythm

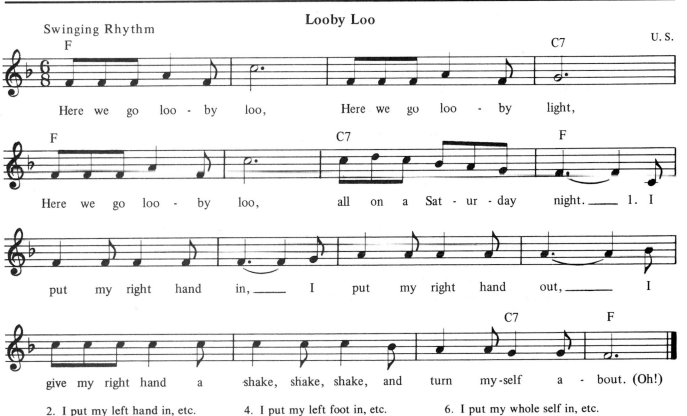

Here we go loo - by loo, Here we go loo - by light,

Here we go loo - by loo, all on a Sat - ur - day night. 1. I

put my right hand in, I put my right hand out, I

give my right hand a shake, shake, shake, and turn my-self a - bout. (Oh!)

2. I put my left hand in, etc.
3. I put my right foot in, etc.

4. I put my left foot in, etc.
5. I put my head right in, etc.

6. I put my whole self in, etc.

This old singing game originally was played with children at bath time. Now children skip to the music and pantomime the words.

Arranged from *Heritage Songster* by Dallin and Dallin, © 1966 by Wm. C. Brown Company Publishers, Dubuque, Iowa. (in public domain)

Bow Belinda

1. Bow, bow, O Be - lin - da, Bow, bow, O Be - lin - da,

Bow, bow, O Be - lin - da, Won't you be my part - ner?

2. Right hand around, oh, Belinda, etc.
3. Left hand around, etc.
4. Both hands around, etc.
5. Back to back, etc.
6. Promenade around, etc.

Formation: Longways for five, six, or seven couples.

```
              O  O  O  O  O  O   (girls)
Top                                         Bottom
              X  X  X  X  X  X   (boys)
```

Figures: Easy-going, but brisk, walking step, verses 1–5.

1. Top boy and bottom girl meet, fall back to places—eight counts; top girl and bottom boy the same—eight counts.
2. Same couples swing with right hands, once around.
3. Same with left hands, once around.
4. Corners swing with both hands. Join hands straight across, left in right and right in left, and swing once around, clockwise.
5. Top boy and bottom girl forward, go around each other clockwise, passing right shoulder to right shoulder, and fall back to places without turning around—eight counts; top girl and bottom boy the same.
6. All take crossed hands (right in right and left in left) and, facing the top, follow first couple who swing out to their left and skip straight to the bottom—eight counts—where the first boy swings his partner over to the girls' side and they raise an arch quickly at the bottom place; all the others go under the arch and return to places with a new couple at the top—eight counts. This figure should be completed in the sixteen counts of the tune.

Repeat all these figures as many times as there are couples.

Collected by Richard Chase, Glade Spring, Virginia

Adapted from *Second Fun and Folk Song Proof Book*, published by World Around Songs. Used by permission.

Ach Ja

German

When my fa-ther and my moth-er Go a-journey-ing to the fair; Ach
What ___ if they have no mon-ey They're as rich as an-y there; Ach

ja! Ach ja! Tra la la, tra la la, tra la

la la la la la, Tra la la, tra la la, Tra la

la la la la la, Ach ja! Ach ja!

The Game: Partners join adjacent hands, the man with his left hand toward the center of the circle and with the girl on his right. They walk four slow steps counterclockwise around the circle; partners then face each other, release hands, and bow very simply by bending at the hips, on "ja," then turn back to back and bow again, on "ja."

Repeat from the beginning.

Chorus: Partners face each other, join hands, and sidestep to man's left for four steps. Finish with bows as before.

Repeat, moving in the opposite direction. Then each man moves forward and takes the next girl as partner, and the whole dance is repeated.

Adapted from *Second Fun and Folk Song Proof Book*, published by World Around Songs. Used by permission.

Sambalele

Brazilian Folk Song

Sam - ba - le - le is a sick one, He missed the danc - ing and
But if our feet be - gin tap - ping, Sam - ba - le - le will stop

good fun. nap - ping! Sam - ba, sam - ba, sam - ba - le - le - le

Pick up your feet and you'll dance oh so spright - ly. soon smile so bright - ly!
Stamp out the beat and you'll

Adapted from *Amigos Cantando*, © 1948 World Around Songs. Used by permission.

Level I, II, or III

Identifying and Responding to Rhythm Patterns

1. Select a song with a repeated rhythm pattern. (In "Old Brass Wagon" ▬▬▬▬ | is repeated. In "Sambalele" ▬▬ is repeated.)
2. Play or sing the song.
3. Ask for volunteers to clap the rhythm pattern. (Repeat the song, if necessary.)
4. Play or sing the song again, as the class claps pattern whenever it occurs.
5. Have the class think of other ways of accompanying the pattern (stamping it, patting head, and so on).

Level I, II, or III

Identifying a Song through Its Rhythm

1. Have children list on the board several songs they know.
2. Tell the class to think word rhythms of each song as they join you in clapping these rhythms.
3. Ask for volunteers to clap one song, while the rest of the class guesses which one it is. The person who guesses the song may clap the next song.

Level II or III

Developing Rhythmic Independence by Singing a Song, Walking a Basic Beat, or Clapping a Changing Accent Pattern

1. Select an appropriate song in 4/4 meter.

2. Have the children walk in a circle, stepping the basic beat (| | | | | | | |) and clapping the accents, changing the position of the accent on each measure:

3. When the children can do this, play or sing the song as they walk and clap, changing the accent as notated. Encourage the class to sing along.

Level II or III

Playing "Pass the Beat" to Aid in Learning a Song

1. Select a song in 4/4 meter appropriate for the age.
2. Clap this ostinato:

3. Select five children to clap the ostinato in this manner: the first child claps the first note only; the second child claps the second note; the third child claps the third note; the fourth child claps the fourth note; the fifth child claps the fifth note. Let them practice until they can do it smoothly. If children have difficulty with the set of eighth notes, simplify by using only four children, one child clapping set of eighth notes.
4. When they can do it easily, sing the song.
5. Repeat many times, asking different children to clap the ostinato and more children to sing, until the class knows the song.

English by C. S. Demos

Greek Folk Song

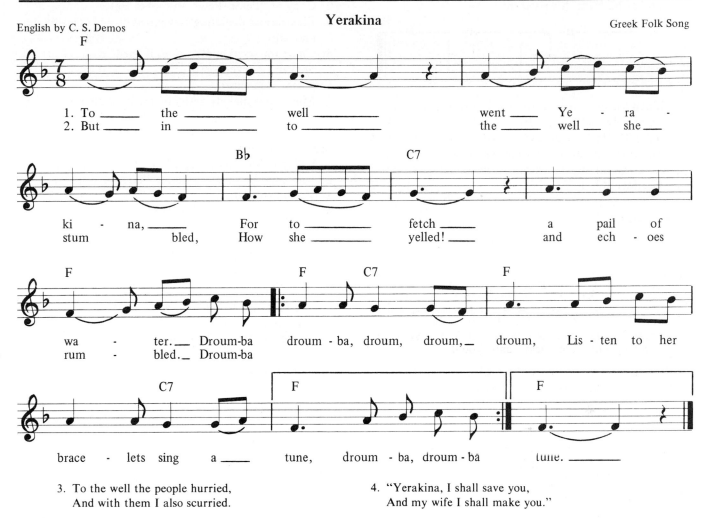

1. To _____ the _____ well _____ went _____ Ye - ra -
2. But _____ in _____ to _____ the _____ well ___ she ___

ki - na, _____ For to _____ fetch _____ a pail of
stum bled, How she _____ yelled! ___ and ech - oes

wa - ter.___ Droum-ba droum - ba, droum, droum,__ droum, Lis - ten to her
rum - bled.___ Droum-ba

brace - lets sing a _____ tune, droum - ba, droum - ba tune. _____

3. To the well the people hurried,
   And with them I also scurried.

4. "Yerakina, I shall save you,
   And my wife I shall make you."

Adapted from *Friendly Folk Songs,* published by World Around Songs. Used by permission.

6. If desired, use a wood block, tambourine, maracas, guiro, and hand drum for the ostinato pattern.

Level III

Experiencing Rhythm by Creating a Rhythmic Accompaniment
"Sambalele"

This approach may be used with any song having a strong rhythmic pulse.

1. Sing or play a recording of "Sambalele," asking children to clap any rhythm they think suitable, experimenting as much as they desire.
2. Ask for volunteers to clap their rhythms as you sing or play the song. Let the class choose the pattern they like best and notate it on the board.
3. Have the class choose an appropriate rhythm instrument for playing the selected pattern.
4. Let a few children play the pattern on instruments as an accompaniment to the song.

5. Using the same procedure, have the class select a second pattern to be played on contrasting instruments.
6. Divide the class into three groups; one group plays the first pattern, one group plays the second pattern, and the third group sings. Repeat, interchanging groups.
7. Add other instruments. Keep transparent texture of ensemble. Instruments should serve as a rhythmic accompaniment to singing.

Level III

Experiencing Meter by Creating a Rhythmic Accompaniment
"Yerakina"

By adapting the accompaniment, this approach may be used with songs in 2/4, 3/4, and 4/4 meter.

1. Teach the class this pattern:

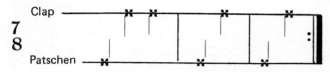

2. When the class can do the pattern easily, begin playing or singing "Yerakina."
3. Have the class select rhythm instruments to play with the patschen (drum, perhaps) and the claps (sticks, perhaps). Invite the class to begin singing whenever they feel able to do so.

Level I, II, or III

Experiencing the Difference Between Strong and Weak Beats by Accompanying a Song

Select an appropriate song in 2/4, 3/4, or 4/4 meter and have the class sing as they do rhythmic movements:

	Beat One Strong beat	Beat Two Weak beat	Beat Three Weak beat	Beat Four Weak beat
Level I				
4/4	Clap	Pat thighs	Pat thighs	Pat thighs
3/4	Clap	Pat thighs	Pat thighs	_____
2/4	Clap	Pat thighs	_____	_____
Levels II and III				
2/4	Bounce ball	Catch ball	_____	_____
3/4	Step and bounce ball	Catch ball	Change to other hand	_____
4/4	Step and bounce ball	Catch ball	Change to other hand	Change back to original hand

Level II or III

Experiencing Meter by Conducting Songs in 2/4, 3/4, and 4/4

1. Select a familiar song in 2/4, 3/4, or 4/4 meter.
2. Teach the conducting pattern. Let the children who master the pattern conduct as the class sings.

 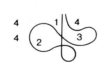

Melodic Concepts

Level I

Materials Needed
1. Copy of "Hickety, Pickety"

2. Copy of "Peter, Peter, Pumpkin Eater"
3. Illustrations depicting movement up and down by step and skip
4. Chart for vocal exploration, if used
5. Soprano glockenspiel
6. Music Cue charts
7. Music and melody instrument for evaluation procedure

Singing Activities
1. Syllables with hand signals
2. Learning the song and game "Hickety Pickety"
3. Vocal exploration
4. Learning the song "Peter, Peter, Pumpkin Eater"

Related Musical Activities
1. Rhythmic dramatization
2. Listening

Conceptual Understanding
A melody may move from high to low or low to high, by step or skip, or it may stay on the same level.

Behavioral Objectives
1. To identify contrasting melodic directions (up, down; by step, skip, or same pitch)
2. To accurately sing back intervals using sol and mi
3. To use the voice with more freedom in vocal exploration

Related Arts
Observing movement up and down, by step and skip in the visual arts

1. Girl climbing ladder by step
2. Boy moving downward by skip

Procedure
1. Experiencing melodic direction through singing syllables with hand signals

Hand Signals

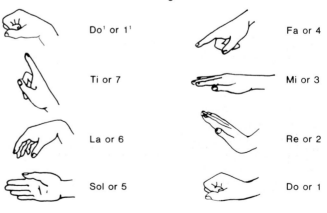

Note: In any scale the first seven tones are noted with syllables only. Tones from high do and up are indicated with a "1" above each syllable; tones below low do are indicated with a "1" below the syllable.

a. Tell children that you will sing their names, using hand motions, and that they should imitate you (both voice and hand). Using the hand signals for sol and mi, go around the room, singing the names of the children, encouraging them to echo you each time. For example:

(S   M)
San - dy,   Ju - lie,   Jon - a - than,

Dav - id,   Dar - ren,   Lo - is,   Al - fred,

E - liz - a - beth,   Law - rence,   Ja - nie

b. Ask children to imitate you and do the following, with hand signals.

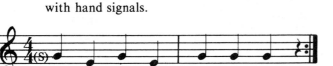
Rob - in,   Al - ice,   Burt,   and   Jon.

Jen - nie and Ken - nie,   Jean and Bob.

Ralph and Rich - ard,   Joan and Jim,

May   and Ger - al - dine, Jean - nette and Chazz!

c. Ask the children which note is higher, sol or mi. (sol)

d. Select two children, one taller than the other. Tell the class to sing sol when you pat the head of the taller child; to sing mi when you pat the head of the shorter child. Proceed slowly, patting each head without establishing any pattern, until children in the class can respond easily by singing the appropriate syllable.

2. Experiencing high and low (sol and mi) by learning a song and game, "Hickety Pickety"
   a. Tell the children to think of something high (a mountain, a tree, a tall building) and, on your signal, to freeze into that shape.
   b. Tell the children to think of something low (an ant, grass, a snake) and, on your signal, to freeze into that shape.
   c. Tell the children you will sing a song. When they hear the last word, they are to freeze into a high or low shape. Sing the following:

Hick - e - ty, pick - e - ty,   me oh my.

Take   your   choice   now,   low   or   high.

d. When children have frozen into their high or low positions, go about the room tapping the heads of children who have high positions when you sing sol and the heads of children who have low positions when you sing mi.

e. Later, have children sing the song again, letting a child sing sol and mi, as you tap the heads of children in high and low positions. (As an alternative, each child tapped can sing the appropriate syllable.)

3. Experiencing high and low through vocal exploration
   a. Put the following two sets of notation on the board or display it on previously prepared oak tags:

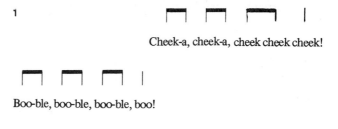
Cheek-a, cheek-a, cheek cheek cheek!

Boo-ble, boo-ble, boo-ble, boo!

2

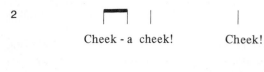

Cheek - a cheek!   Cheek!

Boo - ble boo!   Boo!   Boo!

b. Ask the children to say the words with you. Encourage them to follow the rhythm notated.

c. Ask why some words are printed low and some high. (The words printed low are to be spoken in a low voice, the words printed high in a high voice.)

d. Encourage them to say the words again in low and high voices indicated by the position of the words. Repeat, encouraging the class to say the words softly, loudly, quickly, slowly, but always using high or low voice indicated.

e. When they can do this easily, help them create their own words (or low and high sounds). They may also enjoy making a soundscape for seasons and holidays.

4. Experiencing movement up, down, by step or skip, through the visual arts

a. Display pictures similar to figures 3.2a and b.

b. Ask the children to examine the pictures to see how they are similar and how different.
   Similar They both show a child moving on steps.
   Different (1) One shows a girl, one a boy. (2) One shows upward motion, one downward. (3) One shows movement by step, one by skip.

5. Experiencing melodic direction by step and skip while learning "Peter, Peter, Pumpkin Eater"

a. Tell the children you will sing a song and accompany yourself on the soprano glockenspiel. Tell them to listen and show melodic direction with their hands.

b. Sing and play "Peter, Peter, Pumpkin Eater," holding the glockenspiel vertically (lowest note on bottom) so the class can easily see. (Instead of playing every note, the teacher may want to play only the first note of each measure, except in the next to the last measure, to help children follow melodic direction.)

c. Remind the children of steps and skips they observed in figures 3.2a and b. Ask if they heard any steps in this song. If children have difficulty, repeat the song as they move their hands indicating melodic direction, and you draw the melodic contour on the board as follows:

---- ---- ---- ---- ---- ----
---- ---- ---- ----

Figure 3.2
a, Girl climbing a ladder by step, photograph by Margaret Kelsey; **b**, boy moving downward by skip, photograph by David Rosenthal.

a

b

d. Ask if the contour of steps reminds them of figure 3.2a or 3.2b. (girl climbing a ladder by step, 3.2a)

e. Ask the children if they heard any skips in this song. If they are uncertain, repeat the song as

Peter, Peter, Pumpkin Eater

Lois Raebeck

Pe - ter, Pe - ter, Pump - kin Eat - er, Had a wife and could - n't keep her.

Put her in a pump - kin shell, And there he kept her ver - y well.

Mis - sus Pe - ter Pump - kin Eat - er Swore that he would nev - er keep her.

Climbed out - side the pump - kin shell, But where she is I'll nev - er tell!

children move their hands indicating steps and skips, and you draw the melodic contour of lines that skip:

```
----
      ----  ----
            ----     ----    ----  --
                                       --      ---
```

f. Ask if the contour of skips reminds them of figure 3.2a or 3.2b. (boy moving downward by skip, 3.2b)

g. Ask the children who can sing the song with you to do so as you point to the steps and skips the melody creates.

h. The teacher may proceed according to the interest and ability of the class:

(1) She may have the class continue singing the song, using words or syllables and hand signals, and having individuals point to blank notation on the board.

(2) She may let individual children learn to play the song on melody bells or glockenspiel.

(3) She may help children create a dramatization of the song. One class, through discussion and experimentation, created the following: During the first half, Peter (mov-

ing in the rhythm of the song) pursues his wife, catches her, and puts her in a big, imaginary, pumpkin shell, then goes away. During the second half, Missus Peter Pumpkin Eater climbs until she escapes the pumpkin shell, then creeps away.

6. Evaluating children's ability to hear the differences in melodic movement

a. Reproduce and distribute the following Music Cue chart:

Music Cue Chart				
1.	Up	Down	Step	Skip
2.	Up	Down	Step	Skip
3.	Up	Down	Step	Skip
4.	Up	Down	Step	Skip

b. Tell the children you will play four tunes and they should circle the two words that describe each. If the tune goes up in steps they should circle the words "up" and "step." Make certain they understand.

c. Using any available melody instrument, play the following:

1.   Up Skip

2.   Down Step

3.   Down Skip

4.   Up Step

Singing Experiences That Focus on Melodic Concepts

Level I

Focusing on Repeated Melodic Patterns and the Intervals Sol, Mi, and Do
"I'm a Person"

1. Have the children identify objects in the classroom (chairs, tables, etc.); animals; and different groups of people (mothers, fathers, boys, girls, aunts, and uncles).
2. Tell the children you will sing a song that tells about being a person, and they should listen for the repeated phrase. Sing the first verse. (They will hear "sol, mi, do" of "No I'm not!" repeated.)
3. If children have had previous experiences singing sol, mi, do, ask if this phrase sounds familiar and identify the syllables.
4. Put the phrase on the board so they can see how it looks in notation, and have them sing it with words, syllables, and hand signals.

Sol   mi   do
No   I'm   not!

I'm a Person
Lois Raebeck

2. Are you a coat? No I'm not! Are you a hat?
   No I'm not! Are you a dog, or are you a cat?

3. Are you the wind? No I'm not! Are you the air?
   No I'm not! Are you a horse, or are you a bear?

4. Are you a train? No I'm not! Or an airplane? No I'm not! Are you the snow, or are you the rain?

5. Are you a tree? No I'm not! Or a bumblebee? No I'm not! Are you the lock, or are you the key?

6. Are you a clock? No I'm not! Or a warm sock? No I'm not! Are you a stone, or are you a rock?

When the group knows the song, let half sing the part of the "leader," half that marked "children," then switch.

"I'm a Person" from *Who Am I?* © 1970 by Lois Raebeck.

5. Ask the children to sing the phrase when it occurs, as you sing the entire song.
6. Children will enjoy learning to play the phrase on the xylophone, while learning the song.

Level I or II

Focusing on Melodic Direction and Interval Relationships by Echo-Singing Syllables with Hand Signals

1. Give the children experiences singing syllables with hand signals similar to that described in the section, "Melodic Concepts." Add syllables gradually, in this sequence:

Level I	*Level II*
Sol mi	Sol mi la do re fa
Sol mi la	Sol mi la do re fa ti
Sol mi la do	
Sol mi la do re	

When children can successfully echo sing "sol mi" phrases, teach them to echo sing "sol, mi, la" phrases, "sol, mi, la, do" phrases, and so on.

2. Give them many experiences singing rhymes, echo singing with hand signals, and incorporating each new syllable. For example:

Here's sulk - y Sue,

What shall we do?

Turn her face to the wall

Till she comes to.

Level I or II

Focusing on Skips and Steps
"Row Your Boat"

1. When children can identify melodies that skip or step downward, have them sing "Row Your Boat." Ask half the class to sing it again, omitting the last phrase, "Life is but a dream."
2. Ask the other half of class if the omitted phrase: (1) went up or down, (2) by step or skip. (down, stepwise)
3. Have the other half sing "Row Your Boat," omitting the phrase "Merrily, merrily, merrily, merrily."
4. Ask the first group if the omitted phrase: (1) went up or down, (2) by step or skip. (down, by skip)
   The teacher may use this procedure on all levels, with many songs, asking children to identify other concepts. For example, he may sing a familiar song using hand signals and syllables, then ask children to identify an omitted syllable, note, or phrase.

Level I or II

Singing Syllables, with Hand Signals While Learning a Popular Song
"Do-Re-Mi" from *The Sound of Music* by Rodgers and Hammerstein

Teach the children "Do-Re-Mi" using hand signals.

Row Your Boat

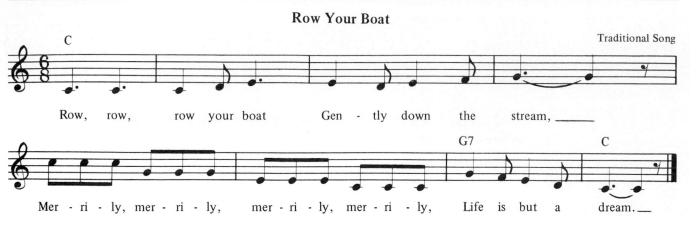

Traditional Song

Row, row, row your boat Gen - tly down the stream, _____

Mer - ri - ly, mer - ri - ly, mer - ri - ly, mer - ri - ly, Life is but a dream. __

Tongo

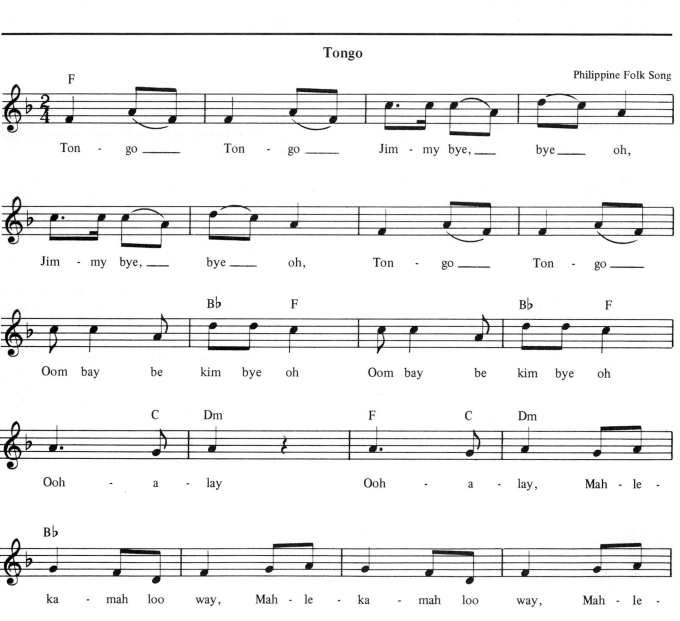

Philippine Folk Song

Ton - go _____ Ton - go _____ Jim - my bye, ___ bye ___ oh,

Jim - my bye, ___ bye ___ oh, Ton - go _____ Ton - go _____

Oom bay be kim bye oh Oom bay be kim bye oh

Ooh - a - lay Ooh - a - lay, Mah - le -

ka - mah loo way, Mah - le - ka - mah loo way, Mah - le -

ka - mah loo way, Mah - le - ka - mah loo way.

"Tongo" may also be sung, as in the country of its origin, with a leader singing each phrase, and the group echoing.

Adapted from *Tayo'y Umawit*, © 1962 by World Around Songs. Used by permission.

Level II

Focusing on Repeated Melodic Patterns
"Tongo"

1. Write these patterns on board:

a.

D M D

b.

S S S M L S M

c.

S S M L L S

d.

M R M

e.

R M R D L₁ D

2. Tell the class you will play a melodic pattern and someone should tell you which one you played. Play pattern number five. Have a child identify it. Discuss contour it creates. Do the same for each of the other patterns.

3. Have the class sing each pattern with letter names or syllables.

4. Have the class write numbers one through five on a sheet of paper. Tell them you will sing a song, and, beside number one, they should write the number of times they hear the first phrase on the board. Sing "Tongo." Repeat, for second, third, fourth, and fifth phrases. Check answers: (1) 4, (2) 2, (3) 2, (4) 2, (5) 4.

5. Tell the class you will sing the song and they should sing phrase one whenever it occurs. Sing "Tongo." Repeat, each time having the class sing another phrase and finally the entire song.

Level II

Focusing on Chord Tones and Scale Passages
"On Top of Old Smoky"

1. Have the class sing the first verse of "Old Smoky" (page 102), indicating the direction of the melody with their hands.

2. Distribute resonator bells and have the children form the C scale by experimenting with the bells. When they have determined the correct arrangement have them stand in sequence, facing the class.

3. Have the children play the C scale, ascending and descending, as the class sings, first using letter names, then numbers and syllables.

4. Have the children play a C chord. Remind the class a chord is several notes sounding together:

C chord

5. Ask class to sing first pattern of song: "On Top of Old Smok-." ("Y" on "Smok-y" is not part of the pattern.)

6. Ask them what this pattern reminds them of. (C chord) Have the children play this pattern.

7. Have the class sing the song, listening for the number of times they hear the C E G C pattern. (once in complete form, a second time with high C omitted) Have the class sing verse one as children with C E G C bells play when the pattern occurs.

8. Ask the children with F E D C bells to play a descending pattern. Ask children if that reminds them of anything. Have the class sing the first verse again, this time with the F E D C bells playing at the end.

9. Have the class sing the song as children play the two patterns when they occur (C E G C and F E D C).

10. Help the children discover the bell parts for the remainder of the song.

On Top of Old Smoky

On top of old Smok-y _____ All cov-ered with snow, _____ I

lost my true lov-er _____ By_ court-ing too slow. _____

2. Oh, courting is pleasure, and parting is grief,
   But a false-hearted lover is worse than a thief.

3. A thief will just rob you of all that you save,
   But a false-hearted lover will lead to the grave.

4. The grave will decay you and turn you to dust,
   Not one in a million a poor girl (boy) can trust.

5. They'll kiss you and squeeze you and tell you more lies,
   Than the rain drops from heaven, or stars from the skies.

6. They'll swear that they love you, your heart for to please,

But as soon as your back's turned, they'll love who they please.

7. It's raining and hailing this cold, stormy night,
   Your horses can't travel, for the moon gives no light.

8. So put up your horses and give them some hay,
   And come sit beside me as long as you stay.

9. My horses aren't hungry; they don't want your hay.
   I'm anxious to leave, so I'll be on my way.

10. (Repeat the first verse.)

Arranged from *Heritage Songster* by Dallin and Dallin, © 1966 by Wm. C. Brown Company Publishers, Dubuque, Iowa. (in public domain)

Level I, II, or III

Focusing on Melody Patterns by Creating a Song
These suggestions are tailored to level II. The teacher should adapt them when working with level I or III.

1. Help the children select a topic for a short, four-line song. (Assume they select Halloween.) Tell them each line will end with:

Ooooooooooooo

2. Ask for ideas for the first line (words only), and use the first, good idea (or combination of several ideas). Write it on the board. Let us assume "Hal-low-een is com-ing; you bet-ter beware!" is suggested.

3. Have the entire class say that line with your phrase at the end. Ask the class to raise their hands if they

have an idea for the second line. Select the best (or a combination of several) suggested. Write it on the board, under the first line. Continue until four lines have been selected. Let us assume this is the poem:

Halloween is coming; you better beware! Oooooooooooooo
Witches and spooks are out to scare! Oooooooooooooo
Pumpkins boo! Bats fly too! Oooooooooooooo
All are out to scare poor you! Oooooooooooooo

4. Help the class create a melody by: (1) having the entire class sing the first line together; (2) asking for volunteers to sing their melody ideas for line one; (3) selecting the best first line and notating it on board; (4) having the class sing the first line and experiment singing a second line immediately afterwards; (5) having volunteers sing their second line ideas alone; and (6) proceeding similarly through the third and fourth lines. One class created the following:

Halloween Is Coming

Hal - low - een is com - ing; you bet - ter be - ware! Oooooooo

Witch - es and spooks are out to scare! Oooooooo

Pump - kins boo! Bats fly too! Oooooooo

All are out to scare poor you! Oooooooo

Textural Concepts

One of the better ways for children to experience the feeling of texture is by singing the part-song. This experience, at least in initial stages, is a challenge for both child and teacher, but it can be rewarding as well. Problems arise when the teacher expects too much too soon. Presenting the type of part-singing experience most suitable for children's stage of musical development is of prime importance.

Thus, when children have had experience singing difficult unison songs, chants, echo songs, and simple ostinati to a pentatonic song, they are ready for the challenge of singing descants, counter melodies, harmonized cadences, and simple rounds and canons. The teacher should be aware of several teaching guidelines for these:

1. Learning descants (written above the melody) is easier than learning counter melodies (normally written below the melody).
2. Harmonizing-cadences—breathing-points or points of rest in a song—are an excellent introduction to singing in harmony, giving children a feeling for the cadence, and preparing them for later experiences harmonizing songs in thirds and sixths.
3. Learning rounds and canons is easier after learning descants, counter melodies, and harmonized cadences.

In addition to a proper sequence for experiencing part singing, it is also important to give children simple preliminary experiences that prepare them for the challenge of singing one part while hearing another. One such activity, available when students can sing with hand signals, consists of initiating part singing through having half the class sing simple melodic sequences from hand signals given by the teacher's right hand, as the other half sings from hand signals given by the left hand. (This activity will be treated later in the chapter.) Any ensemble activity that demands the concurrent singing of two or more parts develops the independence needed for part singing.

A simple guide for teaching the two-part song can include:

1. Teaching melody as though it were a unison song.
2. Singing the new part as the class sings the melody.
3. Playing the new part on a melody instrument (song bells, recorder, piano) as the class sings the melody.
4. Teaching a few children to play the new part on a melody instrument; letting these children introduce the new part by playing it as the class sings the familiar melody. (Children can also learn to play both parts, using different melody instruments for each part. Thus they hear the relationship between parts before learning to sing them.)

5. Using a recording (or making a recording, when songs are in the public domain) designed to assist in teaching part-singing.

A general outline for teaching a round or canon can include:

1. Teaching a round as a unison song
2. Having several children who know the melody sing it alone
3. Explaining voice entrances
4. Having a small group and the teacher sing it as a round (group begins, teacher joins)
5. Selecting a few children to sing the second part with you
6. Having two small groups sing the round alone
7. Dividing the class into two parts and having them sing the round
8. Following the same procedure to teach a three-part round

Singing the roots of chords as a lower part is another simple and effective way of creating a second part. This method encourages boys with changing voices to sing, for these chord tones are generally within their range. Since most elementary-school song series provide chording plans for many songs, it is comparatively simple to encourage children to discover and sing chord roots. In earlier experiences it is advisable to use songs built on two chords; later, songs built on three chords may be used. For example, in Book 6 of *Music*, published by Silver Burdett, the chords suggested for the song "The John B. Sails" are G, C, and D$_7$. By singing G, C, and D chord roots a second part is created.

Harmonizing in thirds and sixths becomes a welcome challenge for children with previous experiences in part singing. The teacher should remember that in initial experiences, songs harmonized should have parallel thirds or sixths below the melody. Most part-songs in the elementary series are harmonized below the melody. These offer children a good opportunity to use the musical score as an aid in part singing. The two-part-song plan suggested earlier can be used to introduce songs harmonized in thirds and sixths.

Vocal chording (singing chordal progressions) is a natural outgrowth of previous part-singing, Autoharp, and song bells experiences. Since the success of vocal chording depends on training the ear to listen discriminately, this must always be the major emphasis in vocal chording experiences.

Progressing from the simple to the complex, the natural sequence in vocal chording is as follows:

1. Two-part chording to songs constructed on two chords
2. Two-part chording to songs constructed on three chords

3. Three-part chording to songs constructed on two chords
4. Three-part chording to songs constructed on three chords

A simple procedure to involve children in experiences with vocal chording follows:

1. Prepare a chart of the chord plan, for use on the overhead projector. An example of a plan for the three-chord song, "Mama Don't 'Low," (found later in this chapter) follows:

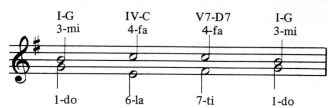

2. When children have learned how to sing the chordal progressions, help them to associate and sing the following:

Figure 3.3
a, I chord: The teacher holds up her hand with index finger extended. **b,** IV chord: The teacher holds up her hand with four fingers extended. **c,** V$_7$ chord: The teacher holds up her hand with all five fingers raised.

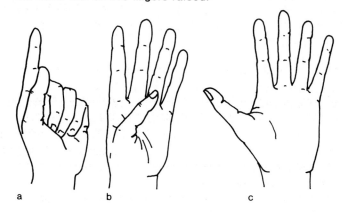

Harmonizing by ear—hearing and singing spontaneously a part that harmonizes with the melody of a song—can occur after children learn to hear harmonic relationships. The teacher can hasten this process by building new activities on past experiences and introducing new activities. A simple guide to these experiences includes:

1. Teaching children to sing chord tones heard from Autoharp accompaniments
2. Teaching children to harmonize songs in parallel thirds, without using the score
3. Teaching children to hear and sing the third and fourth degrees of the scale, the fifth and sixth degrees of the scale, or the first and seventh degrees of the scale when harmonizing the I, IV, and V$_7$ chords

There are advanced part-singing activities in the chapter "Notational Experiences: Music Reading."

Level II or III

Materials Needed
1. Illustrations showing texture
2. A plan for the singing soundscape, on oak tag or board
3. Copy of "I'm on My Way"
4. Copy of "Dona nobis pacem"
5. Autoharp
6. Music and melody instrument for evaluation procedure
7. Music Cue charts

Singing Activities
1. Singing in two parts, through following hand signals
2. Creating a singing soundscape
3. Singing an echo song, "I'm on My Way"
4. Singing the song "Dona nobis pacem" in various ways to experience music that is monophonic, homophonic, and polyphonic

Related Musical Activities
1. Accompanying song with Autoharp, ukulele, or guitar
2. Listening
3. Rhythmic accompaniment to a song

Conceptual Understandings
Music that is monophonic (melody only) sounds different from music that is homophonic (melody with harmony) or polyphonic (two or more melodies sounding simultaneously).

Behavioral Objectives
1. To begin hearing the difference between music that is monophonic, homophonic, and polyphonic
2. To be able to reproduce, with others, music that is homophonic and polyphonic
3. To sing in two parts from hand signals
4. To demonstrate more freedom in vocal exploration

Related Arts
Observing texture in the visual arts: *Manchester Valley* by Joseph Pickett

Procedure
Children should have had previous experience singing with hand signals.
1. Focusing on texture by singing in two parts and using hand signals
   a. Tell the class to listen, then echo you. Sing the following using hand signals:

S L S M   S M D

D D D S   S L D'

D' T D'   D' L S   M R D

b. When the class can echo easily, using hand signals, tell them to try to sing a melody while watching your hand signals. Use the following, signaling very slowly and helping, by singing any note necessary:

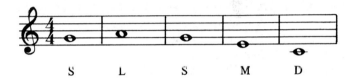

S L S M D

M S L S D'

c. When class can easily sing this, divide them into two groups; one group will sing the notes indicated by your right hand; the other will sing the notes indicated by your left hand. Using right and left hands as indicated, give signals for the following:

Group One (right hand)

Group Two (left hand)

S L S M   D
S L S M

continued on next page

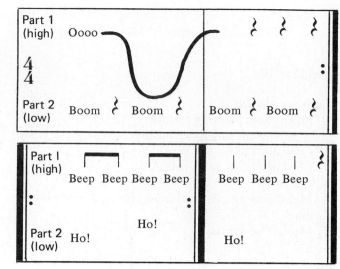

d. Give the class many experiences of this kind, gradually increasing the melodic and rhythmic complexity.

2. Observing texture in the visual arts
   a. Display picture similar to figure 3.4.
   b. Ask children how many different activities are described. (A train chugging down tracks, trees blowing, flag waving, lighted windows suggesting people working inside houses, water wending its way downward, etc.)
   c. Ask what this picture most nearly resembles: a unison song or a three-part song with accompaniment. (the latter, because of the varied texture)
   d. Compare ways texture is created in art and music.

3. Experiencing texture by creating a singing soundscape
   a. Ask the class to close their eyes and listen. After a few seconds, ask them what sounds they heard, and write their responses on the board. They may hear people walking, clock ticking, car or other machine sounds from outside. Remind them that throughout the day they are hearing a whole texture of sound (soundscape), not organized as it is in music.
   b. Display on the board or previously prepared oak tag something similar to the following:

c. Explain the chart. Part 1 uses a higher voice than part 2. It starts high on "Oooo" and descends for the first measure, then ascends, ending on first beat of second measure. Then it repeats. (The second half is self-evident. Part 2 is performed in a low voice, except for the second "Ho," which is slightly higher.)

d. Have the children practice each part until they know exactly what to do. Then divide the class into two groups, one for part 1, one for part 2. Give the signal to begin and conduct unobtrusively. If they have difficulty, select individual leaders for each part.

e. Encourage children to experiment with their own ideas for sounds; substitute them in chart above.

4. Experiencing texture by singing an echo song ("I'm on My Way")
   a. Ask the children to echo as you do the following:

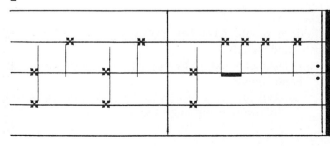

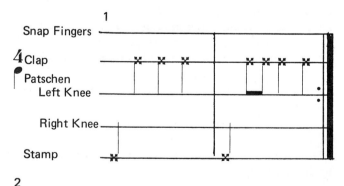

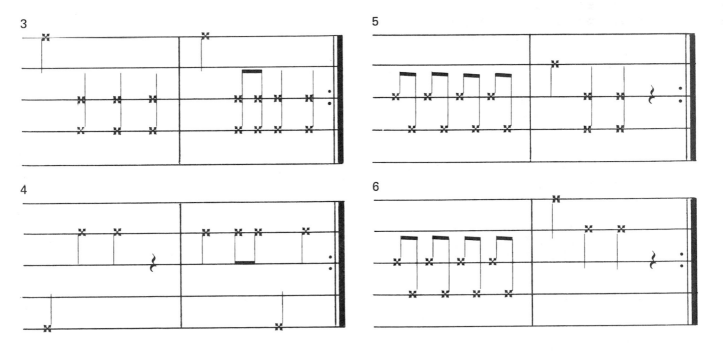

I'm on My Way

Adapted from *Great Days*, © World Around Songs. Used by permission.

b. Ask the children to echo a song as they accompany themselves with a patsch-clap pattern. When a steady beat is established, begin singing, encouraging them to echo each phrase.

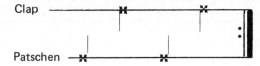

c. Discuss the performance and resolve any difficulties. Ask the class what mood the song creates. Is it a happy or a sad song? Ask for suggestions for improving the expressive qualities of their singing (faster, slower, softer, louder, with a brighter tone, different accompaniment, and so on). Repeat the song, incorporating their suggestions.

d. When the class can easily echo the song, add a few children to the group for part 1 and repeat the song.

e. Add other children to part 1, until parts are balanced.

Note: Children will enjoy creating their own verses. One class created the following:

2. We've found a song,
It's the song for us.
                    (Repeat)
We're on our way,
And we won't turn back.
We're on our way,
Oh yes, we're on our way.

3. We've found a road,
It's the road for us.
                    (Repeat)
We're on our way,
And we won't turn back.
We're on our way,
Oh yes, we're on our way.

5. Exploring different types of texture (monophonic, homophonic, and polyphonic) while learning a song, ("Dona nobis pacem"). Children should know the song before this experience. Use round familiar to class.

a. Through discussion, remind children of the different kinds of texture they have experienced (singing alone, singing with Autoharp or piano accompaniment, singing two-part songs or a round, accompanying songs and chants with Orff-type instruments).

b. Have the class explore the different kinds of texture that can be experienced through a round. Have them sing "Dona nobis pacem" (page 110) in unison. Write "monophonic" on the board. Explain that the texture created by singing in unison was monophonic. Ask them to describe the sound. Emphasize that it was a single melody with no accompaniment.

c. Write the word "homophonic" on the board. Ask what must be added to create a texture that is homophonic.

d. Select a volunteer to accompany on Autoharp as the class sings.

e. Discuss the difference between monophonic and homophonic texture. (Children may say homophonic sounds thicker, or fuller.)

f. Place the word "polyphonic" on the board. Ask the class what kind of texture this describes. (More than one melody sounded at one time.)

g. Tell class they have heard this texture many times, each time they sang a round. Divide the class into three groups and sing "Dona nobis pacem." (If there is difficulty, have the class sing in two parts.)

h. Discuss the sound created, comparing it with the unison sound and song sung with Autoharp accompaniment. Encourage children to describe the difference in sounds. If they have difficulty verbalizing, they may draw illustrations to show differences in monophonic, homophonic, and polyphonic texture:

Figure 3.5
a, Monophonic sound; b, homophonic sound; c, polyphonic sound.

a   Monophonic

b   Homophonic

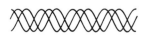

c   Polyphonic

Dona Nobis Pacem

From *We Sing of Life*. Permission was granted by the American Ethical Union, copyright 1955: The American Ethical Union Library Catalog number 54:11625.

6. Evaluating the ability of children to identify texture that is monophonic, homophonic, and polyphonic
   a. Distribute Music Cue charts.
   b. Tell the children you will play four different musical selections, and they should circle the correct answers on their papers. Play the first selection; have the children circle the correct answer. Play remaining selections.

Music Cue Chart

	Monophonic	Homophonic	Polyphonic
1.	Melody alone	Melody with harmony	Two or more melodies
2.	Melody alone	Melody with harmony	Two or more melodies
3.	Melody alone	Melody with harmony	Two or more melodies
4.	Melody alone	Melody with harmony	Two or more melodies

1. Melody Alone

2. Melody with Harmony

3. Two or More Melodies

4. Melody Alone

Singing Experiences That Focus on Textural Concepts

Level I

Learning a Song with a Chant
"Ten Little Indians"

1. Discuss chants and their use in culture (to accompany Indian dancing, ask gods for rain, and so on.) Introduce the chant by singing it, using a melody instrument for accompaniment as the class sings "Ten Little Indians" (page 112).

Chant

2. Teach the class the chant. Teach a child to play it on a melody instrument. Practice together until the child knows the rhythm.
3. Divide the class: one group to sing the chant, as a child accompanies on the melody instrument; one to sing the melody.

Level II

Learning a Song with a Chant
"Lone Star Trail"

Chant

1. Teach this chant, melody (page 113), and accompaniment as described in the previous exercise, "Ten Little Indians."
2. As an enriching experience the children can play the following, or similar ostinati on Orff-type instruments, song bells, or recorder, to accompany class singing:

Ostinato 1   Ostinato 2

Ten Little Indians

Arranged from *Heritage Songster* by Dallin and Dallin, © 1966 by Wm. C. Brown Company Publishers, Dubuque, Iowa. (in public domain)

Level II or III

Learning a Song with a Chant
"Zum Gali Gali"

1. Write on the board:

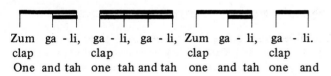

2. Teach the chant by having children pronounce words, say words in rhythm, clap strong beats, chant rhythmic counting, and finally sing.
3. When they know the chant, select child to lead as you sing the melody (page 114). Add a few children to the melody part until class is equally divided, half singing chant, half singing melody. Switch parts.

Level II

Learning an Echo Song
"Old Texas"

1. Have the class begin:

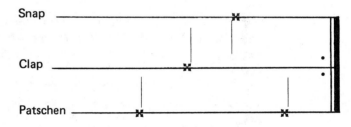

2. Ask them to echo each phrase of "Old Texas" (page 115). Begin singing, helping them if necessary by doing the accompaniment with them, and signaling them to echo.

Level II or III

Learning an Echo Song by Using Hand Signals
"Every Night When the Sun Goes Down"

For a copy of the song, see the "Music Reading" section of chapter 2.

Give children a warm-up experience singing syllables with hand signals. Show hand signals for the first phrase of "Every Night." Have the class sing. Use the same procedure for other phrases in the song. Help sing, if necessary.

Lone Star Trail

Steadily

U. S. Cowboy

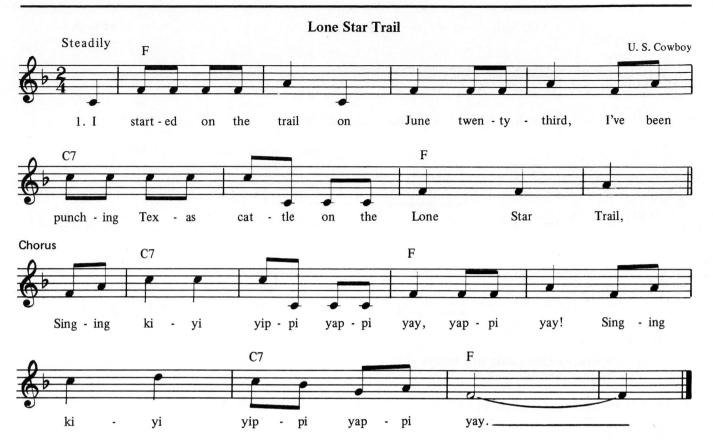

1. I start - ed on the trail on June twen - ty - third, I've been punch - ing Tex - as cat - tle on the Lone Star Trail,

Chorus

Sing - ing ki - yi yip - pi yap - pi yay, yap - pi yay! Sing - ing ki - yi yip - pi yap - pi yay. _____

2. I'm up in the morning long before daylight,
And before I'm sleeping, the moon is shining
bright, etc.

3. My feet are in the stirrups, and my rope is at
my side,
And I never yet have seen the horse that I can't
ride, etc.

4. Oh, it's bacon and beans about every day,
And I'd just about as soon be eating prairie hay,
etc.

5. Now my seat is in the saddle, and my hand is on
my rope,
And my eye is on the dogies, I'm a good cow
poke, etc.

6. With my knees in the saddle and my seat in the
sky,
I'll continue punching cattle in the sweet by and
by, etc.

Arranged from *Heritage Songster* by Dallin and Dallin © 1966 by Wm. C. Brown Company Publishers, Dubuque, Iowa. (in public domain)

Zum Gali Gali

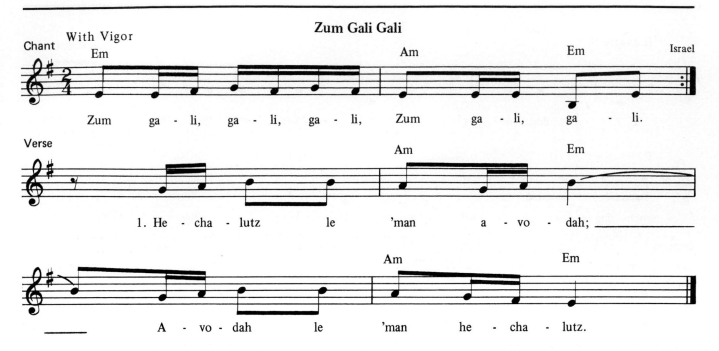

Chant — With Vigor — Em — Am — Em — Israel

Zum ga - li, ga - li, ga - li, Zum ga - li, ga - li.

Verse — Am — Em

1. He - cha - lutz le 'man a - vo - dah; _____

Am — Em

A - vo - dah le 'man he - cha - lutz.

2. Avodah le 'man hechalutz;
   Hechalutz le 'man avodah.

3. Hechalutz le 'man hab'tulah;
   Hab'tulah le 'man hechalutz.

4. Hashalom le 'man ha'amim;
   Ha'amim le 'man hashalom.

Use the chant as an introduction, an interlude between verses, or sing it continuously as a second part. Pronounce Hebrew words phonetically. The following verses in English may substitute the Hebrew:

1. As we toil we'll sing along.
   We will sing the whole day long.

2. And when night begins to fall,
   We will dance and sing 'til we fall.

Level II

Learning a Round
"Kookaburra"

1. Explain to children what a kookaburra is. (The kookaburra is a large kingfisher bird, native to Australia and New Guinia. It makes a weird, raucous, laughlike sound.)
2. Write on the board:

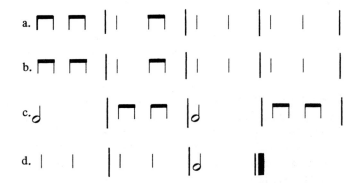

Old Texas

Deliberately

F

Cowboy

1. I'm going to leave _____ old __ Tex - as now, _____
They've plowed and fenced _____ my __ cat - tle range, _____

C7

F

_____ They've got no use _____ for the long - horned cow. _____
_____ And the peo - ple there are __ all so strange. _____

2. I'll take my horse, and I'll take my rope,
I'll hit the trail upon a lope;
Say *adiós* to the Alamo,
And turn my face towards Mexico.

Arranged from *Heritage Songster* by Dallin and Dallin, © 1966 by Wm. C. Brown Company Publishers, Dubuque, Iowa. (in public domain)

Kookaburra

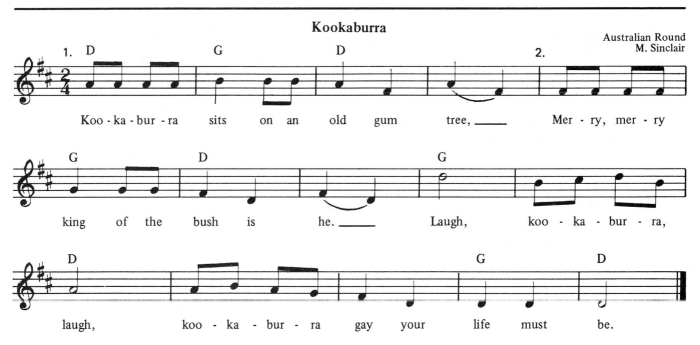

Australian Round
M. Sinclair

1. D   G   D   2.

Koo - ka - bur - ra sits on an old gum tree, ____ Mer - ry, mer - ry

G   D   G

king of the bush is he. ____ Laugh, koo - ka - bur - ra,

D   G   D

laugh, koo - ka - bur - ra gay your life must be.

Adapted from *101 Rounds for Singing*, published by World Around Songs. Used by permission.

3. Explain that this is "stick notation" for the round. Sing the round, pointing to the notation.

4. Tell the class you will sing the melody, using "la," and you will stop at any point. They are to tell you the note on which you stopped. Do this several times, until the class can follow you easily.

5. Ask the class to sing only on phrase *b,* as you sing the entire round. Repeat, class singing phrase *a* only, then phrases *c* and *d* only.

6. Assign each of four phrases to sections of the class. Have the class sing the song, each group singing its assigned phrase at the proper time.

7. Select volunteers to sing the round as you sing the second part. (Children begin first, you begin when they reach the second phrase.) Divide the class into two groups and sing the two-part round. When they can do this successfully, have them try to sing it as a three-, then a four-part round.

All Night, All Day

Level II or III

Learning a Song with a Descant
"All Night, All Day"

1. Teach the melody. When the class can sing it independently, play or sing this descant as they sing the melody. Repeat. Write it on the board:

2. Show the class the score for the song. Ask the children which melody line is descant. (upper) Ask how many phrases are in the song. (eight) Have individual children identify each phrase. Ask the children how many times the phrase on the board appears in descant. (twice, in phrases one and three) Focusing on melodic direction, skips, and steps, teach a child to play this phrase on song bells.
3. Have the class sing the melody as you sing the descant, and the child plays song bells during phrases one and three.
4. Use the same procedure to teach children to recognize and play on song bells phrases two and six (which are alike), four and eight (which are alike), and five and seven (which are alike).
5. When children can play the entire descant, have the class hum as children play their phrases. Divide the class into three groups and perform the song as follows:
   (1) Children playing song bells
   (2) Group singing melody
   (3) Group singing descant
6. Have the three groups practice the song until they play it well. Switch groups: group singing the melody sings the descant, group singing the descant sings the melody.

Level II

Learning to Sing a Song with a Counter Melody
"Swing Low, Sweet Chariot" and "All Night, All Day"

1. Teach each of these songs: "Swing Low, Sweet Chariot" (page 118) and "All Night, All Day."
2. When children can sing them easily, with a steady rhythm, divide the class into two groups, one to sing "Swing Low, Sweet Chariot" and the other "All Night, All Day." Have the group singing "Swing Low" begin first, on the up beat, the other group entering on the next beat. Conduct unobtrusively, to keep them together.
3. Have them listen to the texture created by the two melodies sung together.

Level II

Learning a Song with a Harmonized Cadence
"My Lord, What a Morning"

1. Teach as a unison song.
2. Discuss harmonized cadences with the class: what they are, how they are created and how they add interest to a song. Write on the board:

3. Have the class sing the melody (page 118) as you play the harmony.
4. Explain that the notes with the stems going down are the harmonizing part of the song. Play harmonizing notes as the class listens and a child points to notes.
5. Teach a child to play harmony part on a melody instrument.
6. Have class sing the harmony part as a child accompanies on an instrument.
7. Select a small group to sing the harmony as a child accompanies on an instrument. Have the class sing the melody and the small group sing harmony on cadence. Repeat, having other children sing harmony on cadence, until all who desire have had the opportunity to sing harmony.

Level III

Learning to Sing Chord Roots
"Oh, Mary Don't You Weep"

Children should know the song before this experience.

1. Make certain children understand that a chord root is the bottom note upon which chords are built.
2. Distribute resonator bells for roots to the chords you will play on the Autoharp (C, D, and G bells). Play each chord, having individuals decide which bell (chord root) goes with each.
3. Have the children sing chord roots to chords you play on the Autoharp.
4. Display the song (page 119). Ask what the letters above music mean. (They indicate chord roots and chords to accompany song.) Write on the board:
   G   D   D   G   C   G   D   G
5. Teach a child to play them on resonator bells, as the class sing and follow pitch directions with their hands.
6. Divide the class into two groups: one to sing chord roots, as a child accompanies; the other to sing the melody.

Swing Low, Sweet Chariot

Spiritual

Swing low, sweet char-i-ot,___ Com-ing for to car-ry me home.

Swing_ low, sweet char-i-ot,___ Com-ing for to car-ry me home.

Verse

I looked o-ver Jor-dan and what did I see,___

Com-ing for to car-ry me home, A band___ of an-gels

com-ing af-ter me,___ Com-ing for to car-ry me home.

2. If you get there before I do,
   Coming for to carry me home,
   Tell all my friends I'll be there, too,
   Coming for to carry me home.

3. The brightest day I ever saw,
   Coming for to carry me home,
   When Jesus washed my sins away,
   Coming for to carry me home.

4. I'm sometimes up and sometimes down,
   Coming for to carry me home,
   But still my soul feels heavenward bound,
   Coming for to carry me home.

Adapted from *Heritage Songster* by Dallin and Dallin, © 1966 by Wm. C. Brown Company Publishers, Dubuque, Iowa. (in public domain)

My Lord, What a Morning

My Lord, what a morn-ing, My Lord, what a morn-ing, O___

my Lord, what a morn - ing, When the stars be - gin to fall.

1. You'll hear the trum - pet sound,
2. You'll hear the an - gels sing, To wake the na - tions un - der - ground,
3. You'll hear the Chris - tians shout,

Look-ing to my God's right hand, When the stars be - gin to fall.

Adapted from arrangement from *Folk Songster* by Dallin and Dallin, © 1967 by Wm. C. Brown Company Publishers, Dubuque, Iowa. (in public domain)

Oh, Mary Don't You Weep

1. Oh, Ma - ry don't you weep, don't you mourn.

Oh, Ma - ry don't you weep, don't you mourn. Phar - aoh's ar - my got

drown - ded; Oh, Ma - ry don't you weep.

2. When I get to heaven, gonna sing and pray;
   Nobody there gonna send me away.
   Pharaoh's army got downded;
   Oh, Mary don't you weep.

   (Repeat verse 1 after each verse.)

3. One of these nights about twelve o'clock,
   This world's gonna reel and rock. etc.

4. Sister, how I wish I could
   Stand where the Children of Israel stood. etc.

5. I'm goin' to heaven, gonna put on my wings,
   And watch them crown Him King of Kings. etc.

6. I'm gonna wear a starry crown.
   Golden slippers and a snow-white gown. etc.

7. I'm goin' to heaven with the angel band.
   Gonna stay forever in that Promised Land. etc.

Arranged from *Folk Songster* by Dallin and Dallin, © 1967 by Wm. C. Brown Company Publishers, Dubuque, Iowa. (in public domain)

Level II or III

Learning to Sing a Melodic Canon in the Pentatonic Scale

1. Have the children echo you as you do the following, with hand signals:

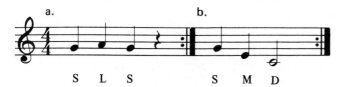

a.

S L S

b.

S M D

c.

S S D¹

d.

M R D

e.

D S L S D D

f.

S S L S D D

g.

S S S L D¹ D M

h.

S L S M R D D

2. Ask the children to follow you as they would in a round. Tell them to listen, then sing the phrase they just heard, as they continue listening to the next part. (They will always be behind you, as in a round.) Begin singing the following. Children should begin when you reach the first note of the second measure.

Loo
D S L S D D

S S L S D D S S S L D¹

D M S L S M R D D

Level II

Harmonizing Thirds Below the Melody
"Kum Ba Yah"

1. Make certain the class knows the melody. Tell them you will play a lower part on a melody instrument as they sing the melody. Remind them to listen to both parts.
2. Put the notation on the board. Discuss the direction each part moves throughout the song, noting that both parts move in parallel directions (except in the next to the last measure, on the word "Kum").
3. Play the low part, having the class hum as they follow it on the board.
4. Divide the class in half: half singing the melody, half the low part. Repeat, switching parts.

Level II or III

Learning to Sing Chordal Progressions (Vocal Chording) Using Two Chords, in Two Parts
"He's Got the Whole World in His Hands"

1. Place chord plan where the students can see it, on chalkboard or previously prepared oak tag:

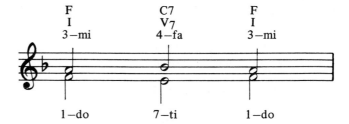

F	C7	F
I	V7	I
3—mi	4—fa	3—mi

1—do   7—ti   1—do

Kum Ba Yah

Slowly
Spiritual

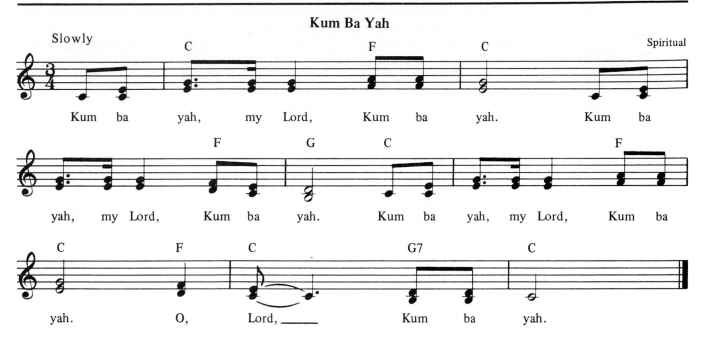

Kum ba yah, my Lord, Kum ba yah. Kum ba

yah, my Lord, Kum ba yah. Kum ba yah, my Lord, Kum ba

yah. O, Lord, _____ Kum ba yah.

2. Someone's crying, Lord, Kum ba yah.
3. Someone's singing, Lord, Kum ba yah.
4. Someone's praying, Lord, Kum ba yah.

Adapted from *A Pocket Full of Songs,* published by World Around Songs. Used by permission.

He's Got the Whole World in His Hands

1. He's got the whole world _____ in His hands. _____ He's got the

whole world _____ in His hands. He's got the whole world _____

in His hands. _____ He's got the whole world in His hands.

Adapted from arrangement from *Folk Songster* by Dallin and Dallin, © 1967 by Wm. C. Brown Company Publishers, Dubuque, Iowa. (in public domain)

2. Play the progression of the low part (F, E, F) on a melody instrument, noting melodic direction. Repeat, having the children sing and show melodic direction with their hands or hand signals.

3. Teach a child to play the progression on a melody instrument. Have a few children sing the low part using numbers, syllables, letter names, or a neutral sound, as an accompanying instrument plays. Add other children to this group until approximately half the class is involved.

4. Repeat the same procedure for the high part, using a contrasting melody instrument.

5. Have those singing the same part stand together. Have them sing, following your directions, as follows:

Right hand   ―――   ―――
Left hand   ―――   ―――

6. Adopt a plan for indicating chordal progressions. (For example, the second finger of the teacher's right hand could be raised to indicate the singing of the I chord, the second and third fingers of the left hand to indicate the V_7 chord.)

7. Tell the class that as you count one-two-three-four, they should sing the proper notes of the chord you indicate on count one, hold note until the next count one, at which time they will sing another chord. Follow this procedure until the class can easily sing from one progression to the other.

8. Follow a similar procedure, this time singing the song and signaling the class to sing appropriate chordal progressions. When the class can easily sing chordal progressions, divide it into three groups: melody, high harmony part; low harmony part; and accompanying melody instruments.

Level II

Harmonizing by Ear, Using Song Bells
"Hot Cross Buns"

1. Teach the song. As the class sings the song, play song bells a third above the melody, as follows:

2. Have the class softly hum the melody as they listen to the song bells.

3. Select a few children to sing the added part, accompanied by song bells.

4. Have the class sing the melody as the small group sings the new part, with song bells accompanying. Repeat, eliminating the song bells.

5. Repeat, adding children to the group singing the upper part, until the class is evenly divided. Switch parts and sing the song again.

Level II

Harmonizing by Ear, Using the Autoharp
"Down in the Valley"

After vocal chording experiences, children can expand their skills in harmonizing two-chord songs by ear. When they can do this spontaneously, introduce three-chord songs in a similar manner.

1. Play G chord on the Autoharp. Ask the children to listen as you play the chord again, and, on your signal, to sing a neutral sound (oo, ah, oh) for any note they hear, holding this note until signaled to stop. Play the chord. Signal children to sing, hold the chord, and stop. (Two- or three-part harmony should result. If not, explain the procedure again and practice until the class succeeds.)

2. Play D_7 chord on the Autoharp and repeat the procedure in step 1.

3. Tell the children you will play G and D_7 chords several times. Each time you play a chord they are to sing a note (on signal) and hold it until signaled to stop. Play chords G, D_7, G, D_7, G. Practice until the children can respond successfully.

4. Place the following chart on board:

G	D_7	G	D_7	G
down	low	blow	blow	blow

5. Tell the class they have been singing this chordal plan using notes from the G and D_7 chords. Tell them to follow the same procedure, but sing the words indicated instead of a neutral sound. Practice until successful.

6. To the chart on board add the additional words of the song:

G D_7
Down in the valley, the valley so *low,*
                                G
Hang your head over, hear the wind *blow.*
                                D_7
Hear the wind blow, dear, hear the wind *blow,*
                            G
Hang your head over, hear the wind *blow.*

Hot Cross Buns

Hot cross buns! Hot cross buns! One a pen-ny, two a pen-ny, Hot cross buns!

Down in the Valley

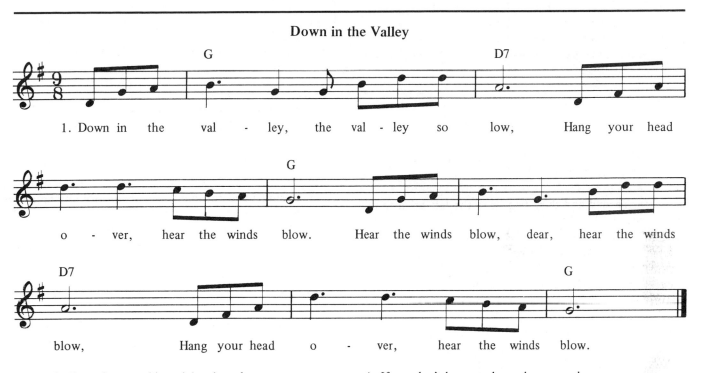

1. Down in the val - ley, the val - ley so low, Hang your head
o - ver, hear the winds blow. Hear the winds blow, dear, hear the winds
blow, Hang your head o - ver, hear the winds blow.

2. Roses love sunshine, violets love dew;
Angels in heaven know I love you.
Know I love you, dear, know I love you,
Angels in heaven know I love you.

3. Write me a letter containing three lines;
Answer my question, "Will you be mine?"
"Will you be mine, love, will you be mine?"
Answer my question, "Will you be mine?"

4. If you don't love me, love whom you please;
But hold me close, love, give my heart ease.
Give my heart ease, love, give my heart ease,
While there is time, love, give my heart ease.

5. Build me a castle forty feet high,
So I can see him as he goes by.
As he goes by, love, as he goes by,
So I can see him as he goes by.

Arranged from *Folk Songster* by Dallin and Dallin, © 1967 by Wm. C. Brown Company Publishers, Dubuque, Iowa. (in public domain)

7. Explain they are to sing all the words in the rhythm of the song, changing tones only where indicated on the chart. Practice several times, making certain that children understand they are not to sing the melody.

8. Select a small group to sing the harmony. Select another small group to sing the melody. Have the two groups sing together, helping the harmony part, if necessary. Add other children to the two parts until all are participating.

Concepts Related to Form

Level II

Materials Needed
1. Pictures illustrating form
2. A plan for the experience in vocal exploration
3. Rhythm instruments

Figure 3.6
a, Photogram, illustrating form; **b**, photograms, illustrating ABA form; **c**, photograms, illustrating AB form; **d**, photograms, illustrating ABACA form.

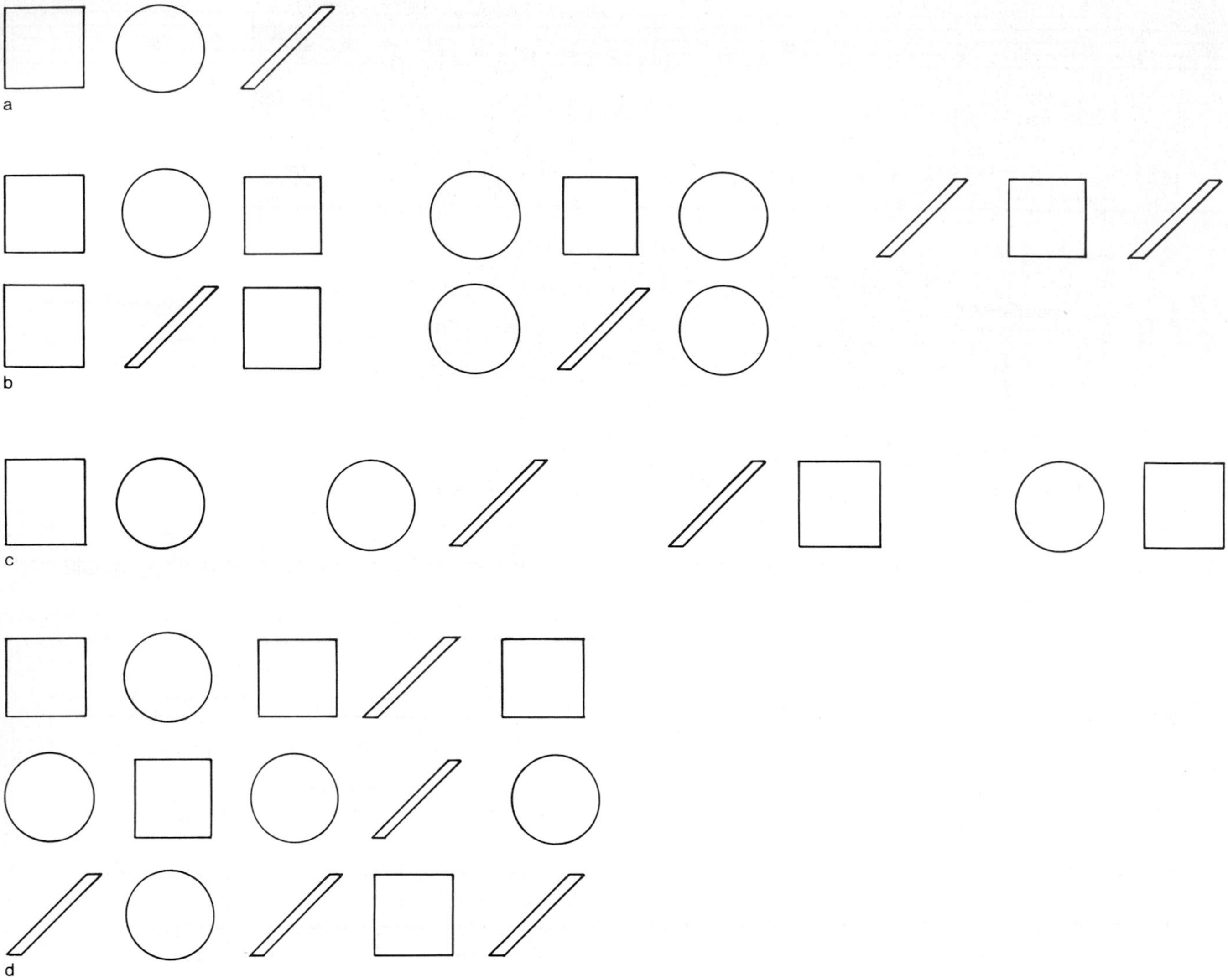

4. Recording of "Barcarolle" *(Tales of Hoffman)* by Offenbach, RCA *Adventures in Music* grade 3, vol. 1, LES–1002
5. Theme from "Barcarolle"
6. Melody instrument
7. A copy of "All Through the Night"
8. A copy of the melody for the evaluation procedure

Singing Activities
1. Vocal exploration
2. Learning the song "All Through the Night"

Related Musical Activities
1. Playing rhythm instruments
2. Listening

Conceptual Understandings
1. Repeated musical phrases often make music more meaningful.
2. Some music is written in two sections, A and B, each different from the other.
3. Some music is written so that it uses a combination of two contrasting sections, all A's alike and all B's alike. For example: ABA, AABA, AABBA, ABABA.
4. Rondo form is a musical form consisting of two or more sections alternating with section A (ABACA or ABACADA).

Behavioral Objectives
1. To demonstrate ability to recognize, by ear, the difference between AB, ABA, and rondo form
2. To demonstrate more imagination and freedom in vocal exploration and improvisation

Figure 3.7
Photograms by Elizabeth Wheeler

3. To demonstrate ability to create more complex rhythmic accompaniments in experiences with form

Related Arts
Experiencing form through the visual arts: Photograms illustrating form (fig. 3.6a–d)

Procedure
1. Focusing on form through the visual arts
   a. Draw figure 3.6a on the chalkboard.
   b. Ask the children how they would make an **ABA** form, using two of these shapes. Children may suggest any of the photograms in figure 3.6b.
   c. Ask how they would create an AB form (fig. 3.6c).
   d. Ask how they would create an ABACA form (fig. 3.6d).
   e. Ask the class to draw an abstract design illustrating ABA form, using these shapes in any combination. Encourage them to use their imaginations and try to create something unique. One class made illustrations similar to those in figure 3.7.
   f. Children may enjoy creating sounds that relate to the shapes, thus having an experience in vocal exploration. For example:

Circles (round sounds)	Lines
ooooo	pick
loooo	stick
moooo	pfft
coool	sttt
zoool	kuckt

2. Focusing on form through vocal exploration and clapping
   a. Display the following:

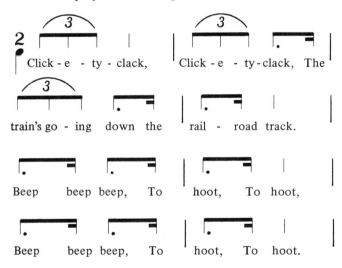

Click - e - ty - clack, Click - e - ty - clack, The train's go - ing down the rail - road track. Beep beep beep, To hoot, To hoot, Beep beep beep, To hoot, To hoot.

   b. Have the class observe the notation as you chant and clap the rhyme and decide the form, AB or ABA. Chant and clap the rhyme, using different pitch levels for each phrase. In the second line, produce the "hoot to hoot" passages higher than the "Beep beep beep, To" passages.
   c. Ask what form is represented. (AB)
   d. Ask for volunteers to chant and clap the rhyme with you, and encourage them to experiment with their voices, expressing the feeling of the rhyme. Discuss the vocal explorations, letting other children experiment until the class decides on a style most appropriate for the rhyme.

e. Ask how they rhyme can be made into an ABA form. (by repeating the first line after the second line) Perform the rhyme in ABA form.

f. Display rhythm instruments and ask for suggestions as to which would best accompany A. Let the children experiment and vote for the instrument(s) they prefer. (One class decided on tone blocks.) Repeat the chant as the children accompany, using the selected instrument.

g. Let children experiment with instruments of a different tone quality for B line, and vote for the instrument(s) they prefer. (One class chose the tambourine.) Have the class repeat the chant, as some children accompany the B line and others the A line, with the selected instruments. Discuss and make any appropriate changes to improve the performance.

h. Ask the class how they might create an ABACA form from this chant. (Children might improvise four measures—the same length as each of the other sections—using percussion instruments or contrasting vocal sounds.) Let them experiment, having the class perform A and B as a few children improvise C.

i. Add the notation for the C and two additional A sections so that children can observe the rondo form, ABACA, clearly. Repeat the chant in rondo form.

3. Focusing on form by creating a rhythmic accompaniment to "Barcarolle" (*Tales of Hoffman*) by Offenbach

a. Write the following on the board (or use a previously prepared laminated chart):

M F F M M R F F M

M R F F M M

b. Play this tune on a melody instrument. Play again, inviting the children to hum or sing syllables with you.

c. Tell the children this is the main theme, A, in a recording they will hear. Ask them to raise their hands each time they hear A.

d. Play the recording. Each time the children raise their hands write A on the board.

e. Ask the children if they heard any different melodies. (They might have noticed a section at the

beginning, in the middle, and at the end.) Explain that there is a long introduction before A and a section at the end called a *coda*, which completes the composition. Write on the board:

Introduction
A
A
Coda

f. Ask the children if they heard a different middle section—a section in which one melody imitates another at a lower pitch. Tell them to raise their hands when they hear this section. Help, if necessary, when B occurs and write B on the board between the two A sections:

Introduction
A
B
A
Coda

g. Play the recording again and have the children lightly clap their hands on A and pat their knees on B. Help the children, if necessary.

h. Ask the children which percussion instrument might best fit A. Invite them to experiment and vote for the one they prefer. (One class chose the triangle because its tone was soft, like the melody.) Select several children to play the triangle for A sections, using the repeated quarter- and eighth-note pattern. Ask the class to decide which instrument would best accompany B. Play the recording. Help the children begin A and B sections.

i. Help the children select and practice with an instrument for B, in the same manner. One class used the orchestration below:

A first eight measures, triangles alone
second eight measures, triangles and maracas
B tambourine throughout
A same as above
Coda triangles alone, fading away softly

j. To enrich the experience the teacher may use the background information in the Teacher's Guide, which accompanies the recording.

4. Focusing on form while learning "All through the Night"

a. Sing "All through the Night."

b. Ask the children how many melodies they heard in the song. If they have difficulty, sing it again.

c. Have the children clap their hands on the first melody, A, and tap their shoulders on the second melody, B.

All through the Night

Welsh
Ceiriog Hughes

Sleep my child and peace at-tend thee, All through the
Guard-ian an-gels God will send thee, All through the

night. Soft the drow-sy hours are creep-ing;
night.

Hill and vale in slum-ber steep-ing. I my lov-ing

vig-il keep-ing, All through the night.

Adapted from *Joyful Singing,* © 1962 by World Around Songs. Used by permission.

d. Discuss the song. Is it in **AB, ABA,** or **AABA** form? (AABA) Is it loud or soft? (soft) Is it quiet or robust? (quiet) Should the pattern for an accompaniment be smooth or detached. (probably smooth)

e. Ask the class to select an appropriate rhythm instrument for the A sections. Select individual children to sing the song with you, as one child plays the accompaniment. Repeat, letting others experiment with instruments until the class selects the preferred instrument and pattern.

f. Repeat step e for the B section. One class adopted the following:

Section A ♩   ♩   Finger Cymbals

Section B | | | | Tone Block

g. Select children who will accompany as the class sings. Divide the class into two groups: one group to sing A sections, the other B sections. Sing the song. Repeat, switching groups and allowing other children to accompany.

h. Children will enjoy enriching the experience by:
   (1) Having one child sing a solo, the class joining on the phrase, "All through the night"
   (2) Learning to play the song, or A sections, on a melody instrument

5. Evaluating children's ability to create these forms: **AB, ABA, ABACA** and **AABB**

   a. Have the children do the following patschen-clap accompaniment, as they listen to you sing the proverb. Repeat until the children can sing with you.

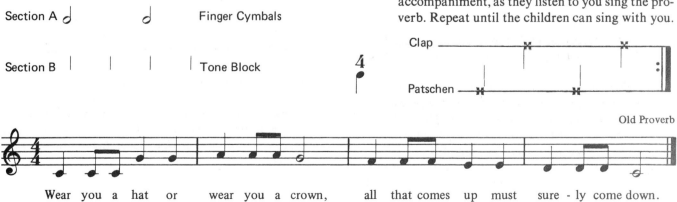

Old Proverb

Wear you a hat or wear you a crown, all that comes up must sure-ly come down.

Hey, Betty Martin

Briskly

U. S.

1. Hey, Bet-ty Mar - tin, tip - toe, tip - toe, Hey, Bet - ty Mar - tin, tip - toe fine. Hey, Bet - ty Mar - tin, tip - toe, tip - toe, Hey, Bet - ty Mar - tin, tip - toe fine.

2. Can't find a boy, a boy to please her,
   Can't find a boy to please her mind;
   She hopes to find a boy to please her,
   She hopes to find a certain kind.

3. I found a boy, a boy to please me,
   I found a boy to please my mind.
   I found a boy, a boy to please me,
   I found a boy, a certain kind.

Arranged from *Heritage Songster* by Dallin and Dallin, © 1966 by Wm. C. Brown Company Publishers, Dubuque, Iowa. (in public domain)

b. When the children know the melody and words, divide them into five groups. Each group will create a different form from this melody. (If necessary, discuss ways these forms are created.)

Group	Form
one	AB
two	ABA
three	AABB
four	ABACA

c. Tell the children that B and C must be approximately the same length as A and that they may be created by:
   (1) Using a different melody
   (2) Creating a rhythmic section, using rhythm instruments
   (3) Creating a rhythmic section, using bodily movement (clapping, snapping, stamping, patschen)

d. Give the children ample time to experiment, helping if necessary. Then let them perform their newly created forms. (It is possible to evaluate what children have learned without insisting that they accomplish their task unaided.)

Singing Experiences That Focus on Concepts Related to Form

Level I

Learning a Song in Uniary Form
"Hey, Betty Martin"

1. Sing the song, clapping softly on each beat.
2. Ask the class why soft clapping is appropriate. (Because the word "tiptoe" suggests a soft clap.)
3. Ask for volunteers to tiptoe as you sing.
4. Tell the children that as you sing you will draw a picture of the song on the board. Draw the contour similar to that in figure 3.8.
5. Ask children to examine the pictures made by each phrase. Are they similar? (Yes. The first and third are alike; the second and fourth are alike. All phrases begin the same.)
6. Have the children sing the song as you point to the contour of each phrase.
7. Help children explore other possible movements and lyrics to match. For example: "Hey, Betty Martin, skip a little, skip a little. Hey, Betty Martin, skip down the line."

Lullaby

Gently   C   G7   Johannes Brahms

1. Lul - la - by and good - night, with__ ro - ses be - dight,__ with__

down o - ver__ spread is__ ba - by's wee bed;   C   Lay thee

F   C   G7   C

down now and rest, May thy slum - bers be blest; Lay thee

F   C   G7   C

down now and rest, May thy slum - bers be blest.

Adapted from arrangement from *Heritage Songster* by Dallin and Dallin, © 1966 by Wm. C. Brown Company Publishers, Dubuque, Iowa. (in public domain)

Figure 3.8
Contour of "Hey, Betty Martin"

Phrase 1   Phrase 3

Phrase 2   Phrase 4

Level II

Learning a Two-Part Song in AB Form
"Lullaby" by Brahms

1. Have children do the following two patterns with you:

Pattern 1

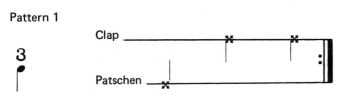

Pattern 2

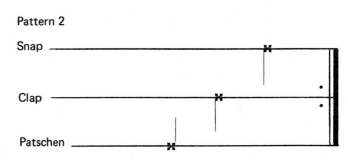

2. Tell the class you will sing a song that may be familiar. Tell them to start with pattern 1 and continue until they hear a change of melody, at which time they are to switch to pattern 2. Have the class start pattern 1 in a steady rhythm, then you begin singing. Children should change on "down" of the third phrase. If they have difficulty, repeat.

3. Ask the class the form of the song. (AB)

4. To teach the song, display the music and words, using an overhead projector or the chalkboard. Have the children use the two patterns as they sing. Introduce a second part by playing it on a melody instrument, as the class sings the melody. Have the class sing the new part, accompanied by the melody instrument.

Old Dan Tucker

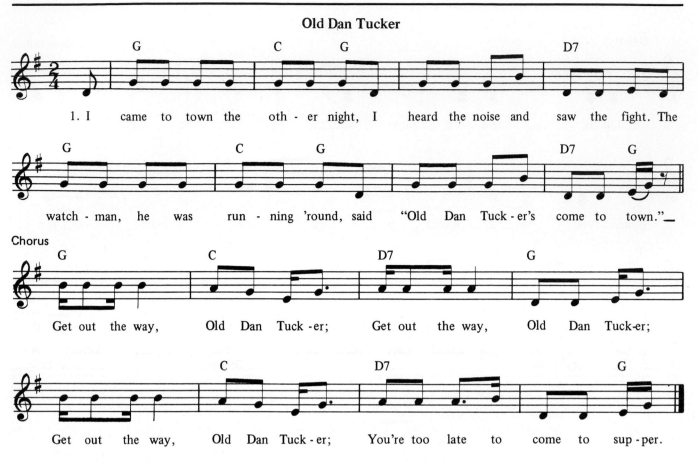

1. I came to town the oth-er night, I heard the noise and saw the fight. The watch-man, he was run-ning 'round, said "Old Dan Tuck-er's come to town."

Chorus

Get out the way, Old Dan Tuck-er; Get out the way, Old Dan Tuck-er; Get out the way, Old Dan Tuck-er; You're too late to come to sup-per.

2. Old Dan Tucker was a fine old man; he washed his face in the frying pan;
He combed his hair with a wagon wheel, and died with a toothache in his heel.

3. Now, Old Dan Tucker and I fell out, and what do you think it was all about?
He borrowed my old setting hen and didn't bring her back again.

4. Old Dan began in early life to play the banjo and win a wife,
But every time a date he'd keep he'd play himself right fast asleep.

5. Now, Old Dan Tucker he came to town to swing the ladies all around;
Swing them right and swing them left then to the one he liked the best.

6. And when Old Dan had passed away they missed the music he used to play;
They took him on his final ride and buried his banjo by his side.

Arranged from *Folk Songster* by Dallin and Dallin, © 1967 by Wm. C. Brown Company Publishers, Dubuque, Iowa. (in public domain)

Then have a few children sing the second part (with accompaniment), as the class sings the melody. Repeat, adding voices to the lower part until the class is equally divided.

Level II

Learning a Song in AABA Form
"Goodbye Old Paint"

For suggestions for teaching this song, see chapter 2, "Rhythmic Experiences."

Level II

Learning a Song in AABB Form
"Old Dan Tucker"

1. Help the children explore the different percussive sounds they can make without moving from their seats, using fingers, hands, legs, and feet. Let individuals demonstrate and the class select sounds they like best. For this exercise, assume the four are:
   a. Stamping foot
   b. Clapping hands

Roll, Jordan, Roll

Roll, Jor-dan, roll, Roll, Jor-dan, roll, I

Group

want to go to heav-en when I die to hear old Jor-dan roll.

Verse

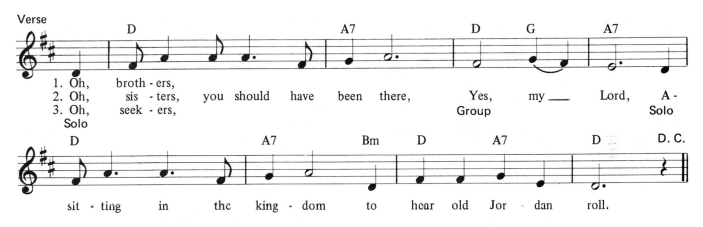

1. Oh, broth-ers,
2. Oh, sis-ters, you should have been there, Yes, my ___ Lord, A-
3. Oh, seek-ers,

Group   Solo

Solo

sit-ting in the king-dom to hear old Jor-dan roll.

Arranged from *Folk Songster* by Dallin and Dallin, © 1967 by Wm. C. Brown Company Publishers, Dubuque, Iowa. (in public domain)

c. Snapping fingers

d. Patting knees

2. Have the class make each percussive sound on the count of "one" as they count "one-two" four times:

Count	1	2	1	2	1	2	1	2
	stamp		stamp		stamp		stamp	
	clap		clap		clap		clap	
	snap		snap		snap		snap	
	pat		pat		pat		pat	

3. Have the class perform four measures for each sound.

4. Select volunteers to do percussive sounds as you sing "Old Dan Tucker."

5. Ask the class how many phrases they heard in the song. (four) Are any alike? (The first two are alike. The third and fourth are similar.) To clarify, repeat the song, with accompaniment. Place the following on the board and ask the form of the song:

AB   AABB   AABA   ABA

(It is in AABB form.)

6. Repeat the song, adding children to the percussive accompaniment group until half are performing accompaniment and half are singing. Then switch parts.

Level III

Learning a Song in ABA Form

"Roll, Jordan, Roll"

1. Tell the children to experiment with a rhythmic accompaniment as you sing the first two lines (chorus) of "Roll, Jordan, Roll." Ask for volunteers to demonstrate their rhythmic accompaniment and to sing the chorus as they demonstrate. Have the class select its favorite accompaniment. The child whose pattern is chosen should select an appropriate percussion instrument and play the accompaniment as the class sings.

2. Tell the class to listen to the verse and find a different accompaniment. Sing the verse as the class experiments. Let individuals demonstrate their accompaniment as you sing the verse again. Follow the same

procedure for selecting an accompaniment for the verse. Write accompaniments on the board:

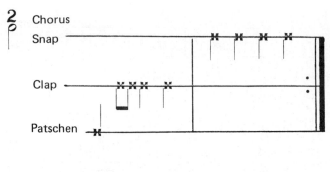

3. Explain that the song begins with the chorus, followed by the verse and the chorus once again. Ask what kind of form this creates: AB, ABA, or other. (ABA)
4. Have the class sing the song, doing rhythmic accompaniment at their seats, as two children play rhythm instruments.
5. Children may enjoy having individuals sing the verses as solos, to emphasize the ABA form.

Expressive Concepts

Level III

Materials Needed
1. Illustrations of expressive concepts in visual arts
2. A paragraph from a newspaper, one copy for each child
3. Percussion (rhythm) instruments
4. Recording of "Fog and Storm" (*Harbor Vignettes*) by Donaldson, Bowmar *Orchestral Library* recording BOL #53/066.
5. Pictures of instruments of the orchestra, if possible
6. Copy of "Mama Don't 'Low"

Singing Activities
1. Vocal exploration
2. Learning the song "Mama Don't 'Low"
3. Applying expressive concepts to a familiar song.

Related Musical Activities
1. Using rhythm instruments to accompany vocal exploration
2. Listening
3. Rhythmic interpretation of music
4. Rhythmic accompaniment to a song

Conceptual Understandings
1. The mood of any musical composition is related to tempo, dynamics, rhythm, tonality, and instrumentation used.
2. Our voices can produce differences in tone quality and mood.

Behavioral Objectives
1. To demonstrate ability to control voice and sing more expressively
2. To demonstrate awareness of ways that rhythm, tonality, tempo, dynamics, and instrumentation affect the expressive qualities of music

Related Arts
Examining a picture that illustrates expressive qualities: *Endeavor* by Felix Delmarle

Procedure
1. Focusing on expressive concepts in the visual arts
   a. Display *Endeavor* by Felix Delmarle (fig. 3.9), or a similar picture.
   b. Ask the children the following:
      (1) Does this picture suggest tranquility or urgency? Intense energy or passivity? (urgency, energy)
      (2) How does the artist achieve this effect? (Through use of sharp, jagged lines that are being pulled forcibly in one direction)
      (3) What do you think the artist is trying to say? (Perhaps the artist is saying the man and horse are pulling a tremendous weight, trying to "move mountains.")
   c. Tell the title of the picture and relate the title to their previous observations.
   d. Ask the children this question: In a musical composition, how would a musician achieve the effect created by this picture?
      (1) Would the rhythm be flowing and legato, or detached and staccato?
      (2) Would the melody be singable or have many wide intervals and abrasive leaps?
      (3) Would the texture have a clearly stated tonal center, in major or minor perhaps, or be dissonant, with no tonal center?
      (4) What instruments might be used?
      (5) Would the tempo be fast or slow?
      (6) Would the dynamics be loud or soft?
2. Focusing on expressive concepts through vocal exploration, using a paragraph from a newspaper article
   a. Place on the board:

   Dynamics   loud and soft
   Tempo   fast and slow
   Rhythms   even and uneven
   Tonality   major, minor, and pentatonic

b. Discuss each. Make certain children understand how to reproduce each vocally.

c. Tell the children you will show how a simple newspaper article can be changed by altering the expressive elements. Distribute copies of the following:

"The Glenwood Academy of Music, received a large grant, from the National Endowment for the Arts, it was announced yesterday. The Academy was selected as one of eighty-two cultural organizations, to receive a grant. The grant was awarded on the basis of artistic quality, need, and the ability to match grant dollars at least three to one."

d. Have the children read article aloud, together, pausing at each comma and period.

e. Tell class you would like everyone to sing the article together, starting on your signal. Remind them to pause whenever there is a period or comma. Give the class the signal to sing. If they have difficulty, discuss various ways their improvisation might proceed. Then repeat.

f. When the children can sing the article, have them select one of the expressive elements (dynamics, for example), decide what dynamics they want to use, and sing the article again.

g. Select individual children to sing the article, using the dynamics they selected. Have the class vote on the dynamics they prefer, using these dynamics in their singing.

h. Follow a similar procedure with tempo, tonality, and rhythm until the class has chosen the dynamics, tempo, tonality, and rhythm they prefer for their article. If class does not agree, let them select several alternative ways of singing the article, writing each on board:

	1	2	3
Dynamics	loud	soft	soft
Tempo	slow	slow	fast
Rhythm	even	uneven	uneven
Tonality	major	minor	major

i. After each performance, discuss the way the article seemed to change with changes in expressive elements.

j. Have the class examine available rhythm instruments. Encourage experimentation with instruments to find an accompaniment to their singing. Discuss the mood that different instruments create; for example, compare a triangle to a tone block.

3. Focusing on expressive concepts through creating a rhythmic interpretation of "Fog and Storm" (*Harbor Vignettes*) by Donaldson

   a. Display available pictures of instruments of the orchestra or write the names of the instruments on the board:

English horn	harp	percussion
bassoon	flute	trumpet
bass fiddle	clarinet	trombone
violin	French horn	cello

   b. Write the following on the board:

Tempo	Dynamics	Rhythm
slow	very soft	steady beat
moderately fast	soft	uneven
fast	moderately loud	
very fast	loud	

   c. Tell the children you will play a recording, and they should listen carefully to discover which instruments play and which words, written on the board, best describe the music. Play "Fog and Storm."

   d. Discuss the music. Did one tempo predominate? Dynamics? Rhythm?

   e. Tell the children, as you play the recording, you will raise your hand from time to time. When you do this, you will select a volunteer to circle words on the board that describe the tempo, dynamics, or rhythm that predominates. Play the recording, raising your hand at times when these are easily identifiable.

   f. Repeat, having selected children circle the instrument they hear when you raise your hand.

   g. Discuss the mood created and encourage children to suggest what the music might be portraying. Then tell them the title.

   h. Ask who would like to interpret the music by being the fog and the storm. Select several children to do so. Ask them to listen and feel internally the tempo, dynamics, rhythm, and general mood. After their interpretation, discuss more successful interpretations. Repeat, having other children move.

4. Focusing on expressive concepts by learning "Mama Don't 'Low"

   a. Teach the children the following rhythmic accompaniment.

b. When children can do this easily, sing "Mama Don't 'Low" as they accompany you.

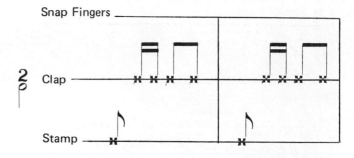

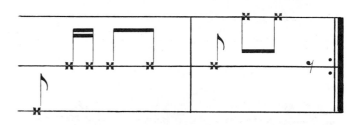

c. Ask the children to experiment, using different expressive devices, to see how this changes the song. Ask them to name expressive elements and list them on the board. For example:

moderately loud	crescendo	fast
loud	decrescendo	slow
loud	staccato	legato
soft		

d. Ask for volunteers to sing the song with you, using each of these expressive elements. The rest of the class should do the rhythmic accompaniment. Use the first-listed expressive element for the first verse, the second for the second verse, and so on.

e. Ask the class which expressive elements best fits with each verse. One class selected the following:

Verse	Expressive Element
1	moderately loud
2	soft, slow, and legato
3	loud and fast
4	crescendo
5	very staccato, moderately loud
6	soft and fast

f. Divide the class: one group to sing, the other to do the rhythmic accompaniment. Have them perform the song, using the expressive elements chosen. Repeat, switching groups.

5. Evaluating children's ability to use expressive elements in singing

Mama Don't 'Low

1. Ma-ma don't 'low no ban-jo play-in' 'round here;_____
   Ma-ma don't 'low no ban-jo play-in' 'round here._____
   I don't care what ma-ma don't 'low, gon-na play my ban-jo an-y-how.
   Ma-ma don't 'low no ban-jo play-in' 'round here._____

2. Mama don't 'low no slide trombones round here, etc.
3. Mama don't 'low no fancy singin' round here, etc.
4. Mama don't 'low no bass slappin' round here, etc.
5. Mama don't 'low no talk or chatter round here, etc.
6. Mama don't 'low no two-step dancin' round here, etc.

Arranged from *Folk Songster* by Dallin and Dallin, © 1967 by Wm. C. Brown Company Publishers, Dubuque, Iowa. (in public domain)

a. Review expressive devices, if necessary: discuss expressive ways to sing a song and write these on the board:

very slow	very soft	crescendo
slow	soft	decrescendo
moderately	moderately	staccato
fast	loud	legato
fast	loud	

b. Divide the class into groups. Tell each group to select a familiar song, decide which expressive devices they will use, practice, and perform it for the class. Before singing, they should give you a slip of paper indicating expressive devices they will use.

c. Discuss the performances, focusing on positive elements of each performance and expressive devices used.

Singing Experiences That Focus on Expressive Concepts

Level II

Focusing on Expressive Concepts by Learning a Song
"Erie Canal"

1. Tell the children to listen, as you sing a song, for the expressive elements which describe the song. For

Erie Canal

al - ways know your neigh - bor, You'll al - ways know your pal, If you've

ev - er nav - i - gat - ed on the E - rie Ca - nal.

Arranged from *Heritage Songster* by Dallin and Dallin, © 1966 by Wm. C. Brown Company Publishers, Dubuque, Iowa. (in public domain)

example, is the rhythm even or uneven, interesting or uninteresting? Is the tempo fast or slow? Are the dynamics loud or soft?

2. Sing the song. Children will probably say the rhythm is uneven and interesting; tempo is neither fast nor slow, but "in between"; dynamics are loud.

3. Ask the children to tap rhythmic accompaniment as you sing.

4. Let individuals demonstrate the rhythmic accompaniment they tapped and the class vote for the one they prefer. Then divide the class into two groups, one to do the rhythmic accompaniment and one to sing with you. One class chose this accompaniment: ♪ ♩. ♩ for the verse and this | | | | for the chorus.

5. Children may also enjoy adding percussion instruments as an accompaniment.

Level III

Focusing on Expressive Concepts by Learning a Song
"Sometimes I Feel Like a Motherless Child"

1. Write on the board:

C Major

A Minor

2. Have eight children select the resonator bells for the C major scale. As they play it, ascending and descending, have the class sing the letter names and then syllables. Repeat, changing children and bells where

necessary, this time playing and singing the A minor scale.

3. Encourage children to tell the mood created by each scale.

4. Tell the children to listen to a song and decide whether it is constructed around a major or minor scale. Sing or play "Sometimes I Feel Like a Motherless Child" (page 138). (It is constructed around the E minor scale.) Encourage children to tell the mood this song expresses. Ask if they think the scale used is the primary factor in creating this mood or are there other expressive elements that contribute (rhythm, melody, tempo, dynamics).

5. To focus on the repeated do-mi and mi-re-do-la patterns, teach the children syllables and hand signals for the song. To focus on the mood created by the minor chords, teach Autoharp accompaniment.

Level III

Focusing on Expressive Concepts by Learning a Song
"Sinner Man"

1. Write the words to "Sinner Man" (page 139) on the board. Have the class examine them and think about the different emotions expressed by the words and the incorporation of these emotions into their singing. Ask them to choose an element for each verse.

2. Write expressive elements selected on the board.

3. Tell the children you are going to sing the song, following their instructions for expression. When they can, they should begin to sing with you, using the expressive qualities.

4. Discuss the performance and make any changes children decide would improve the quality of the singing and more appropriately interpret each verse.

Sometimes I Feel Like a Motherless Child

1. Some - times I feel like a moth - er - less child; _____
Some - times I feel like a moth - er - less child; _____
Some - times I feel like a moth - er - less child, _____
long way _____ from home; _____
long way _____ from home. _____

2. Sometimes I feel like I'm almost gone; (three
   times)
   A long way from home; a long way from home.

3. Sometimes I feel that the night is long; (three
   times)
   A long way from home; a long way from home.

4. Sometimes I feel that I haven't a friend; (three
   times)
   A long way from home, a long way from home.

Adapted from arrangement from *Folk Songster* by Dallin and Dallin, © 1967 by Wm. C. Brown Company Publishers, Dubuque, Iowa. (in public domain)

Sinner Man

2. Run to the rock, the rock was a-melting, (three times)
3. Run to the sea, the sea was a-raging, (three times)
4. Run to the moon, moon was a-bleeding, (three times)
5. Run to the Lord, "Lord, won't you hide me?" (three times)

6. Oh, sinner man, you should-a been a-praying, (three times)
7. Run to the Devil, Devil stood a-waiting, (three times)
8. Run to the trees, trees were a-swaying, (three times)
9. Fall to the earth, earth was a-rolling, (three times)

Repeat verse 1.

Arranged from *Folk Songster* by Dallin and Dallin, © 1967 by Wm. C. Brown Company Publishers, Dubuque, Iowa. (in public domain)

Notational Concepts: Music Reading

Level III

Materials Needed
1. Illustration showing contour in the visual arts
2. Copy of rhythmic notation, for a number game.
3. Copy of "All My Trials," on previously prepared oak tag or transparency
4. Materials used in notating an original song
5. Copies of Music Cue charts

Singing Activities
1. Learning "All My Trials"
2. Singing an original song

Related Musical Activities
1. Creating a song
2. Focusing on rhythmic notation through a rhythm game
3. Listening for differences in contour and rhythm

Conceptual Understandings
1. The direction of a melody when heard (up, down, same) is related to the contour created when it is drawn on the chalkboard or on the musical staff.
2. There is a rhythmic relationship between different durations of sounds that may be notated.
3. A sequence of tones suggesting a scale or part of a scale is often in the notation of a melody.

Behavioral Objectives
1. To identify differences in melodic direction (up, down, same) from notation
2. To recognize and reproduce rhythmic notation of:

3. To identify scale passages in notation of song
4. To notate original songs, with assistance

Related Arts
Focusing on contour through the visual arts: *Farm Fields*
by Rainey Bennett

Procedure
1. Focusing on contour through the visual arts
   a. Display the illustration in figure 3.10 or one sim-
      ilar to it.
   b. Ask the children to examine the picture to see
      how many things suggest direction—movement
      up and down. Help them perceive the following,
      letting volunteers point out the contour of each
      item suggested.
      (1) The road moving up and to the left
      (2) The hill above and to the right of that road,
          which slopes gently down to the center right
      (3) A second, gently sloping hill, which begins
          in the center of the picture and moves
          toward the farmhouse and barn
      (4) The hills at the bottom, one sloping up to
          the right, one to the left; the farmer standing
          at the foot of these hills
      (5) The shapes on the bottom left, which sug-
          gest rocks
   c. Ask children if they can see how the artist empha-
      sizes the contour. (Help them see the use of dark
      hills and trees against a light sky, the vertical
      lines of trees contrasting horizontal lines of sky
      and clouds.)
   d. Ask children what in music creates contour,
      movement up and down. (A melody creates con-
      tour in sound. When notated it creates contour on
      the musical staff or board.)
   e. Ask children what in music would make the con-
      tour of a specific melody different from that of
      another similar melody. (Any change in tempo,
      dynamics, texture, or expression emphasizes the
      distinctive quality of the melody and its contour.)

f. Have the children sing a familiar song, following the contour of the melody with their hands. Help them experiment, changing tempo, dynamics, expression, and texture (adding an accompaniment perhaps) to show how the contour, though remaining the same, has a change of emphasis through these other changes.

2. Focusing on rhythmic notation by playing the "Number Game" (Children should have previous experience clapping and counting these note values. For guidance in initiating this type experience see chapter 6 "Music Reading Experiences." The teacher may want to substitute familiar rhythm patterns for those in this game.)

a. Place these on the board:

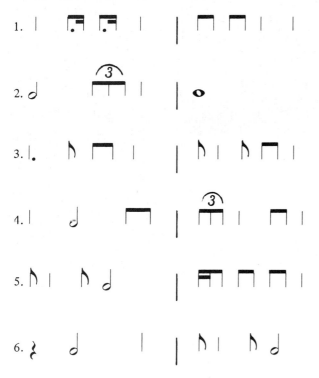

b. Review the rhythm patterns notated in numbers 1–6 by having the class clap and count each.

c. Tell the class you would like to play the "Number Game" with them. Explain that if you say number 5, someone volunteers to clap and count number 5. If you say number 51, someone volunteers to clap and count number 5, then number 1, without missing a beat in between. If you say number 642, someone claps number 6, number 4, then number 2.

d. When children understand, begin calling numbers.

3. Focusing on notation while learning "All My Trials"

a. Tell the class you will sing a song that may be familiar and they should try indicating melodic direction with their hands. Sing "All My Trials" (page 142), indicating melodic direction.

Figure 3.11
Melodic contour of "All My Trials"

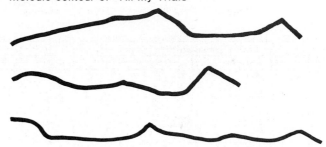

b. Ask the children if they heard any scale passages or skips in the song. (Both occur.) If they hesitate, sing the song again, having the children follow the melodic direction with their hands.

c. Tell the children as you sing you are going to draw the melodic contour on the board. Invite them to help you sing and watch the contour emerging. Something similar to figure 3.11 should result.

d. Ask the children to examine the contour to see where the melody moves by step and where it moves by skip. Invite individuals to point to these sections.

e. Display notation for "All My Trials." Ask for volunteers to point to scale passages and skips.

f. Place the following rhythm patterns on the board. Ask for volunteers to clap and count them, and then indicate where they occur in the song:

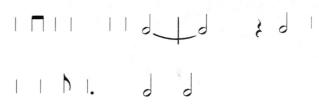

g. Ask for a volunteer to point to the notes as you and the class sing the song. Repeat, letting other children point.

h. Discuss the text with class, and ask how they might use their voices to best express the feeling of the song. Sing the song, using their suggestions.

i. Invite a child who is adept at the Autoharp or guitar, to learn the accompaniment and accompany.

4. Focusing on notation while creating an original song

a. Following a sequence similar to that suggested on page 102 of this chapter, help the class create an original song. When the song is completed and notated on board, continue to step b of this exercise.

All My Trials

Hush lit-tle ba - by, don't you cry; _____ You

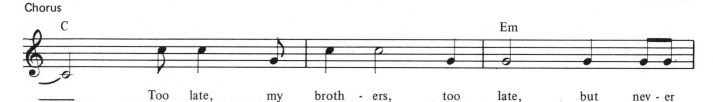

know your ma - ma _____ was born to die. _____

All my trials, _ Lord, soon be o - ver. _____

Chorus

_____ Too late, my broth - ers, too late, but nev - er

mind. _____ All my trials, _____ Lord,

soon be o - ver. _____

2. The Jordan River is mighty cold;
   It chills the body, but not the soul.
   All my trials, Lord, soon be over.

3. I have a little book, 'twas given to me,
   And every page spells liberty.
   All my trials, Lord, soon be over.

4. If religion were something money could buy,
   The rich would live and the poor would die.
   All my trials, Lord, soon be over.

5. A little tree grows in Paradise,
   And the faithful call it the tree of life.
   All my trials, Lord, soon be over.

6. And when I die, I'm bound to go
   To the Promised Land where there's no woe.
   All my trials, Lord, soon be over.

7. And there I'll wear a starry crown,
   Have angel wings, and a snow-white gown.
   All my trials, Lord, soon be over.

Adapted from arrangement from *Folk Songster* by Dallin and Dallin, © 1967 by Wm. C. Brown Company Publishers, Dubuque, Iowa. (in public domain)

b. Ask the class to examine the notation and to look for:

scale passages   rhythm patterns
steps   meter indication
skips   general contour
melody patterns and
    sequences

c. Have the volunteers point to any scale passages, sections that move by step or skip, melody or rhythm patterns. Have a volunteer follow the general contour as the class sings the melody.

d. Help the class discover and place on the staff the key signature and meter.

e. Have the class clap and count familiar rhythm patterns and sing the song using syllables or numbers, as volunteers point to notes.

f. Have the class copy the song on music paper. At a later date, volunteers might copy the song on a large piece of oak tag, so that all can examine it for further enjoyment and learning.

5. Evaluating the ability of children to perceive differences in melodic contour and rhythm by examining notation

a. Distribute Music Cue charts similar to the following:

b. Play number 1b of the Music Cue chart. Repeat and have the children circle the melody they think you are playing. Follow the same procedure for number 2.

c. Tell the children you will tap a rhythm pattern from number 3, and they should circle the pattern they hear. Follow the same procedure for number 4.

d. Tell the class the correct answers and discuss any difficulties they had.

Singing Experiences That Focus on Notational Concepts

Level I

Focusing on Notation while Learning a Song
"Little Red Caboose"

1. Place this on the board:

| | | | |
chug   chug   chug   chug

2. Explain that this represents a slow train. Have the class say and clap chugs slowly.

Music Cue Chart

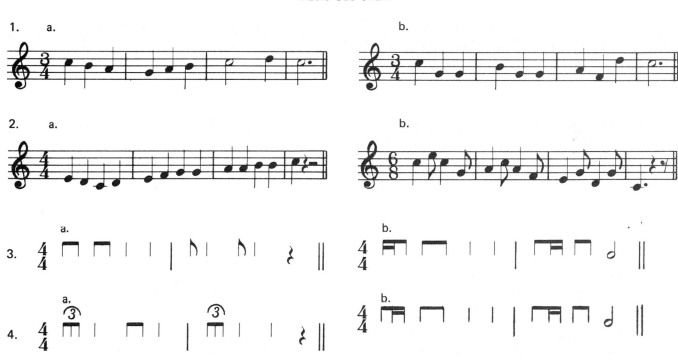

Little Red Caboose

Camp Song

Lit - tle red ca - boose, lit - tle red ca - boose,

Lit - tle red ca - boose be - hind the train, _____ the train. _____

Smoke - stack on his back, go - ing down the track,

Lit - tle red ca - boose be - hind the train. _____ train. (Too - too - too!)

3. Let one child walk, in rhythm, as the class claps and says the chugs. Repeat, adding other children to the walking group.
4. Place the following on the board. Explain that this represents a fast-moving train:

chug - a chug - a chug - a chug - a

5. Have the class examine the notation for both trains and tell you how the notes differ.
6. Have the class decide which rhythm best fits "Little Red Caboose" by having them clap and say the rhythm of the slow train, then fast train, as you sing the song.
7. When the class can say the chosen rhythm as they hear the song, select a child to be the train, moving in rhythm as the class claps and says the chugs. Add other children until a good-sized train develops. Have the train say the chugs and the class sing the song.

Level I

Focusing on Notation While Learning a Song
"Hot Cross Buns"

This experience may be adapted for any level, by using any song that children can easily sing, using syllables.
1. Write this on the board:

     M
       R
         D

2. Point to these syllables in various sequences. Have the children sing, using hand signals.
3. When children have had adequate experience singing different sequences, write the following on board:

M R D   M R D   D D D D R R R R M R D

4. Have the children clap and count the rhythm, then sing the syllables in rhythm, as they use hand signals. Ask them the name of the song.
5. Put the first note on the staff. Then ask individual children to notate the remainder of the song, with help from the class.

Hot Cross Buns

Michael, Row the Boat Ashore

1. Mich - ael, row the boat a - shore, al - le - lu - ia. Mich - ael,

row the boat a - shore, al - le - lu - ia.

2. Sister, help to trim the sail, alleluia,
   (twice)(Repeat verse 1 after each verse.)
3. River Jordan's deep and wide, alleluia, (twice)
4. River Jordan's chilly and cold, alleluia, (twice)

Arranged from *Folk Songster* by Dallin and Dallin, © 1967 by Wm. C. Brown Company Publishers, Dubuque, Iowa. (in public domain)

Level I or II

Focusing on Notation through Examining Phrases of a Familiar Song
"Michael, Row the Boat Ashore"

This experience may be adapted for any song on any level when children are familiar with the notation.

1. Put the four phrases of the song on four separate large oak tags, as in a-d, and laminate:

d

2. Have the class sing "Michael, Row the Boat Ashore," following the melodic direction with their hands, or, if possible, using syllables and hand signals.
3. Display the four cards, *not* in proper order. Tell the class these cards represent the notation for "Michael, Row the Boat Ashore." Ask who can find the card for the first phrase and put it at the beginning. Select volunteers to arrange the other cards in the proper order. Discuss the melodic and rhythmic characteristics of the song that helped children place the cards in the correct order.
4. Have the class sing the song by following notation and using syllables, then words.

Level II

Notation in a Song
"Doktor Eisenbart"

Doktor Eisenbart

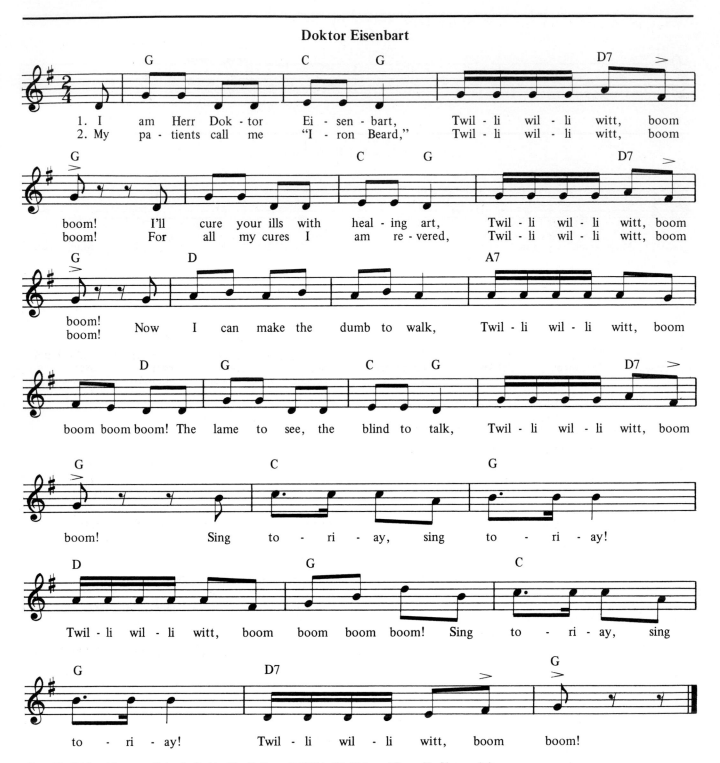

From *The Bridge of Song* compiled and edited by Max V. Exner. © 1957 by World Around Songs. Used by permission.

1. Place rhythmic notation and words on the board:

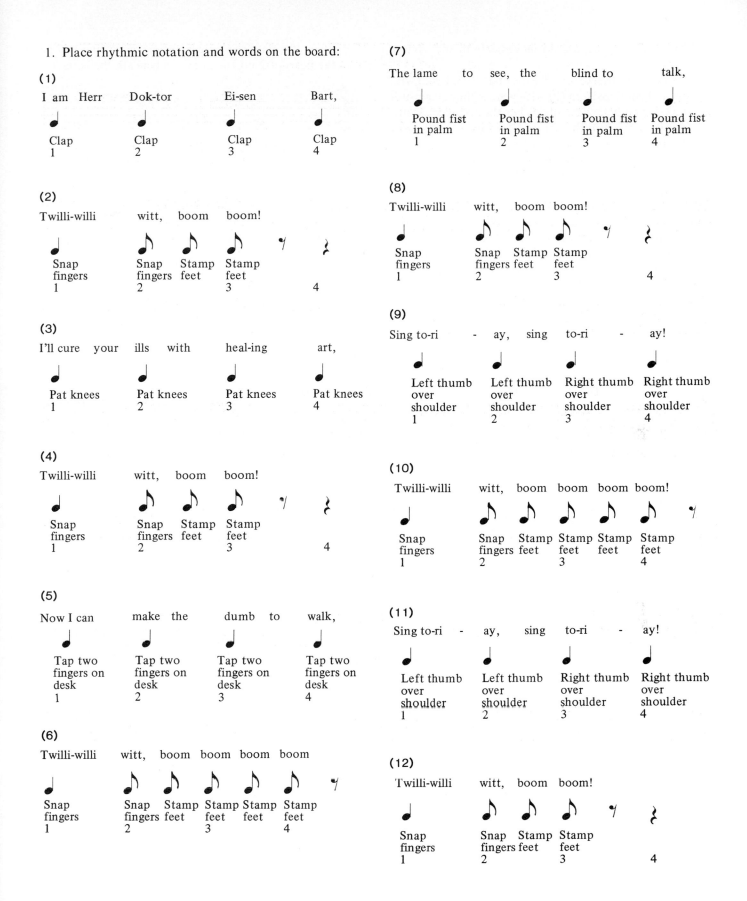

2. Sing the song as you do movements in the rhythm indicated.
3. Ask the children to practice the first "Twilli-willi witt, boom boom" pattern (2) with you, as they sing words and do bodily movements. When they can do it easily, do the same with the second "Twilli-willi witt, boom boom boom boom" pattern (6).
4. Sing the entire song, having children join on the "Twilli-willi-witt boom boom" patterns.
5. Ask the class to practice the "Sing to-ri-ay" pattern.
6. Sing and do movements for the entire song, asking children to join you on the "Twilli-willi witt boom boom" and "Sing to-ri-ay" patterns.
7. Ask children to practice line (7) with you. Sing the entire song, children joining you on all lines they have practiced.
8. Add lines (5), (3), and (1), one at a time, in the same manner.
9. Let the class sing and do movements for the entire song.

Level I

Focusing on Notation while Singing a Song
"Pit, Pat, Well-a-Day"

You may use this procedure on any level, if you select a rhyme or song appropriate for the age of the children.
1. Have the class echo as you do the following, using first syllables and hand signals, then words:

2. Show the class the song notation by writing this on the board. (Omit the numbers beneath the notes.)

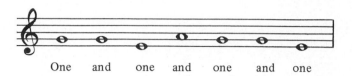

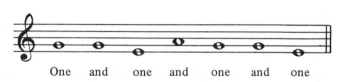

3. Remind the children that this is a picture showing the direction our voices move. Have the children sing the song using syllables, then words, as you point to the notes.
4. Ask the children to help fill in the notes so they show rhythm as well as direction. Help them clap and count each measure, then fill in the notes.
5. Orchestrate, using Orff-type instruments, if desired.

Level I, II, or III

Focusing on Notation in Titles of Familiar Songs
1. Have the class list familiar song titles on the board, clap and chant each, and write the notation beside each. Level I might list and notate the rhythm of:

Zebra Dun

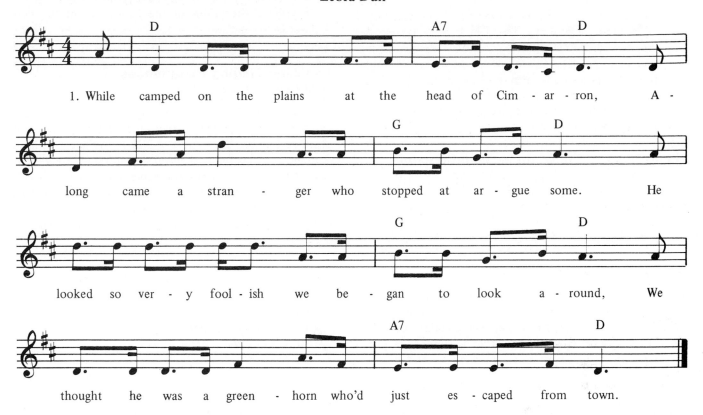

1. While camped on the plains at the head of Cim - ar - ron, A -
long came a stran - ger who stopped at ar - gue some. He
looked so ver - y fool - ish we be - gan to look a - round, We
thought he was a green - horn who'd just es - caped from town.

2. He said he'd lost a fine job on the Santa Fe
   And was headed o'er the plains to strike the
   Seven D.
   He didn't say what happened, just some trouble
   with the boss,
   And asked if he could borrow a good, fat saddle
   hoss.

3. This tickled the boys, and they laughed right up
   their sleeves,
   "We will lend you a fine hoss, as fat, sir, as you
   please,"
   Then Shorty grabbed a lariat and roped the
   Zebra Dun,
   And gave him to the stranger, and waited for
   the fun.

4. Old Dunny was an outlaw who had grown so
   awful wild,
   He could paw the moon down and jump more
   than a mile,
   But Dunny stood there quietly as if he didn't
   know,
   Until we got him saddled and ready for to go.

Arranged from *Folk Songster* by Dallin and Dallin, © 1967 by Wm. C. Brown Company Publishers, Dubuque, Iowa. (in public domain)

2. Have the class find rhythm patterns notated in other songs.

Level III

Focusing on Notation while Learning a Song
"Zebra Dun"

1. Ask the class if they can hear one rhythm pattern repeated many times, as you sing the song.

2. Sing "Zebra Dun," articulating the dotted eighth- and sixteenth-note figure.

3. Ask the class what pattern they heard. Write each suggestion on the board. If no one hears the dotted eighth- and sixteenth-note pattern, put it on the board and have the class clap and chant it.

4. Show the class the notation for the song and have them find ♪. | whenever it occurs. List on the board the various combinations in which it appears.

5. Have a volunteer play 𝄽 or 𝄽 on a hand drum or tone block as the class sings.

Using Rock to Focus on Musical Concepts

At a recent gathering of the Music Educators National Conference, the prevailing theme was "From Rock to Bach." This, simply stated, is a concept many teachers have adopted to take children from where they are (rock) to where we hope they may come to be (at home with even the ultimate of classical composers, Bach).

Many teachers have found that giving rock a place in the classroom helps break down the barrier against other types of music. As children focus on musical concepts in rock, the polarization between popular and classical music breaks down, and a wider acceptance results.

Following is a suggestion for using rock to focus on rhythmic concepts.

Level III

Using a Rock Composition to Focus on Rhythmic Concepts
"Scattin' "

1. Write ♪ ♪ on the board. Have the class
   syn-co-pah
   clap this rhythmic ostinato as you play "Scattin' " on a piano or melody instrument.
2. Ask the class to count the times they hear this rhythm pattern, as you play "Scattin' " again. (twelve)
3. Repeat, having the children clap and count each time this pattern occurs.
4. Using the overhead projector, show the melody. Select volunteers to point to the syncopation patterns.
5. Have the class clap and count the rhythm of the song.
6. Write 𝄽 𝄽 | 𝄽 | 𝄽 ♫ on the board. Have the children clap this ostinato as you play "Scattin'."
7. Select a child who knows the rhythm to play it on the tambourine as the class sings the song and you accompany on a melody instrument. (See page 152.)
8. Write | 𝄾 ♪ 𝄾 ♪ on the board. Have the class clap this ostinato to the song.
9. Select a child to play this ostinato on claves. Have the class sing the song, accompanied by tambourine and claves.

10. Divide the class into groups of four or five children to write new words to the melody. Students may make rhythmic alterations of the melody to fit the new words.

Enriching Singing Experiences with Creative Activities

When the child has learned a song in such a way that it has become truly a part of her, she will want to sing it again and again. Sometimes it will be sufficient to keep the song in this category—a well-loved friend brought out now and then for another enjoyable few minutes.

However, when the teacher sees joy emanating from his class because of a song he has taught well, he should know the possibilities for further experiences that can enrich the song.

Enriching the song can take place in a variety of ways:

1. Creating a rhythmic accompaniment (bodily movement or rhythm instruments) for the song
2. Dramatizing the song
3. Illustrating the song
4. Creating a large-scale dramatization that uses the song, appropriate rhythms, and other related songs
5. Creating other stanzas
6. Learning to accompany the song on Autoharp, ukulele, guitar, or piano
7. Learning the song (or sections of it) on melody instruments (melody bells or recorder)
8. Creating introductions, interludes, or codas for melody or rhythm instruments
9. Creating an orchestration, using Orff-type instruments
10. Creating an ABA form, with B section being an improvised rhythmic experience

Although the choice of the specific enriching activity should arise from a discussion between the teacher and the class, the teacher can best guide this choice by being aware that the enriching activity will be most successful when: (1) it seems to fit the song so naturally that it is a direct outgrowth of the learning process (i.e., *children* suggest adding verses, adding an instrument, dramatizing, and so forth); (2) it creates an immediate, positive response from the children; (3) it is within the ability of the children to accomplish successfully.

A song that tells a story, such as "A Frog Went A-Courtin" will naturally suggest illustration or dramatization. A song or portion of a song that is not too difficult to play, might be learned on the recorder, especially if its text suggests an instrumental accompaniment. A song such as "Hush, Little Baby" will suggest creating additional verses that use the same rhyming patterns as the song.

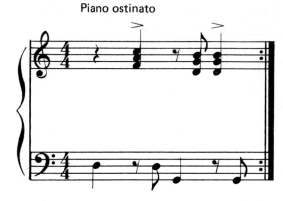

Piano ostinato

Last measure

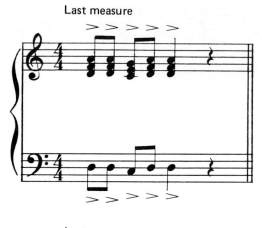

Piano ostinato (easy)

Last measure

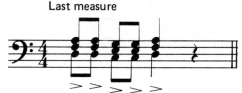

As the teacher grows more aware of these possibilities and shares them with the children, they, in turn, more readily contribute ideas that can be used.

Level I

Dramatizing a Song
"Frog Went A-Courting"

1. After the class has learned the song and decided to dramatize it, let them "set the stage" by establishing the following:
   a. Where Mister Frog lives. (He will come riding from there.)
   b. Where Miss Mousie lives. (Mister Frog will ride to her home.)
   c. Where Mister Frog will sit before taking Miss Mousie on his knee.
   d. The location of the hollow tree (site of the wedding).
   e. The homes of the other characters.
2. Select characters. As each is chosen, discuss that character's basic movements with the class. Have them sing the verse as the actor practices.

3. Have the class decide whether they will sing all parts, or if Mister Frog and Miss Mousie will sing their own parts (in verses three and four). Emphasize that all should sing when it is the class' turn.
4. After the class performs the dramatization, discuss ways to improve it. Have other children dramatize, incorporating suggestions.

Level I or II

Creating Additional Stanzas to a Song
"Hush, Little Baby"

1. When the class knows the song, sing it with them. After the final verse, you continue singing, "If you're the sweetest little baby in town, Mommie's goin' to buy you a . . . ." Stop singing. Ask the children what else they would like Mommie to buy that rhymes with "town." If they cannot think of a word, help them by suggesting, for instance, "pretty red gown."
2. Continue singing, indicating to the children to sing with you:
   "And if that pretty red gown turns blue,
   Mommie's goin' to buy you a . . . ."

Frog Went A-Courting

England

1. A frog went a-court-ing and he did ride, uh, huh! _____

_____ A frog went a-court-ing and he did ride, uh, huh! _____

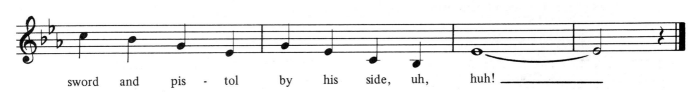

_____ A frog went a-court-ing and he did ride, a

sword and pis-tol by his side, uh, huh! _____

2. He rode right to Miss Mousie's door, uh, huh!
   He rode right to Miss Mousie's door, uh, huh!
   He rode right to Miss Mousie's door
   Where he had often gone before, uh, huh!

3. He took Miss Mousie on his knee, etc.
   Said, "Miss Mousie, will you marry me?" uh,
   huh!

4. "Without my Uncle Rat's consent, etc.
   I couldn't marry the president!" uh, huh!

5. Uncle Rat gave his consent, etc.
   So they got married and off they went, uh huh!

6. Now, where will the wedding supper be? etc.
   Away down yonder by the hollow tree, uh, huh!

7. Who's going to make the wedding gown? etc.
   Old Miss Toad from the lily pond, uh, huh!

8. Now, what will the wedding supper be, etc.
   Two big green peppers and a blackeyed pea, uh,
   huh!

9. Now, the first to come was a big white moth,
   etc.
   She spread down a white table cloth, uh, huh!

10. If you want this song again to ring, etc.
    Make it up yourself and start to sing, uh, huh!

Arranged from *Heritage Songster* by Dallin and Dallin, © 1966 by Wm. C. Brown Company Publishers, Dubuque, Iowa. (in public domain)

Hush, Little Baby

American Traditional

Hush, lit-tle ba-by, don't say a word,

Mom-mie's goin' to buy you a mock-in' bird. If that mock-in'

bird don't sing, Mom-mie's goin' to buy you a dia-mond ring.

If that diamond ring turn brass,
Mommie's goin' to buy you a lookin' glass.

If that lookin' glass gets broke,
Mommie's goin' to buy you a billy goat.

If that billy goat don't pull,
Mommie's goin' to buy you a cart 'n' bull.

If that cart 'n' bull turn over,
Mommie's goin' to buy you a dog named Rover.

If that dog named Rover don't bark,
Mommie's goin' to buy you a horse 'n' cart.

If that horse 'n' cart break down,
Still be the sweetest little baby in town.

As sung by Jean Ritchie

From "One Tune More" *(Songs of America)* © 1956 by World Around Songs. Used by permission.

Ask the children for a word that rhymes with "blue"—perhaps a "yellow shoe." If it rhymes, use the first word they suggest, even if it is a nonsense word.

3. Continue adding verses. Some classes will make up many verses, some classes a few.

Note: For level II, the teacher may want to create a different verse 1 and use "Poppa" instead of "Mommie." For example:

Hey boy, hey boy, where you been?
Up to Chicago and back again!
Hey boy, hey boy, have you heard?
Poppa's goin' to buy you a brand new pen!

Other verses can be changed to fit the temperament of the age.

Level I or II

Creating a Dramatization, Using Rhythms and Related Songs

1. Have the children list and review the Indian songs they know. They may know the following: "Ten Little Indians," "The Zulu Warrior," "Magic Tom-Tom."

2. Review the following rhythms:

Galloping Rhythm

Giant Steps

Paddling Rhythm

Ev'rybody Loves Saturday Night

Sierra Leone

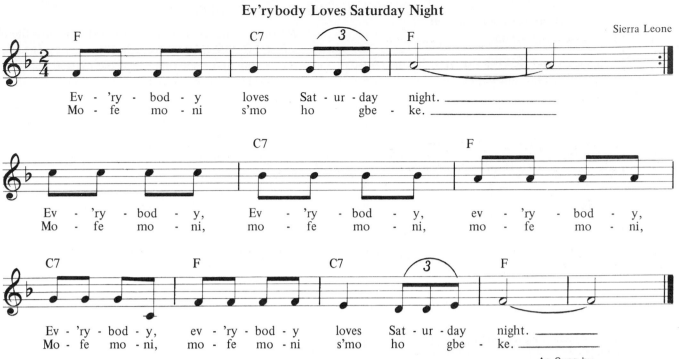

Ev - 'ry - bod - y loves Sat - ur - day night. _____
Mo - fe mo - ni s'mo ho gbe - ke. _____

Ev - 'ry - bod - y, Ev - 'ry - bod - y, ev - 'ry - bod - y,
Mo - fe mo - ni, mo - fe mo - ni, mo - fe mo - ni,

Ev - 'ry - bod - y, ev - 'ry - bod - y loves Sat - ur - day night. _____
Mo - fe mo - ni, mo - fe mo - ni s'mo ho gbe - ke. _____

As Sung by
Emmanuel Aryeequaye Hyde

Pronounciation: Maw-fay mo-nee s'maw haw be-kay.

Children also enjoy singing this song in these languages.
French: Tout le monde aime samedi soir.
Spanish: Nos gústa a tódos la nóche de sábado.
Italian: Place a tutti sabato sera.
Yiddish: Yeder ainer gleicht Shabes bei nacht.

3. Have the children experiment with Indian dance steps to drum accompaniment.
4. Divide the class into four groups.
    a. Zulu tribe, who is going to invite several other tribes to a festival
    b. Tribe one, who lives across the lake
    c. Tribe two, who lives on other side of forest
    d. Tribe three, who lives down the road and owns horses
5. Help the class decide how each tribe will come to the festival. (Tribe one might paddle canoes; tribe two might creep slowly across the forest, with their bows and arrows ready to shoot dangerous animals; tribe three might gallop down the road on horses.)
6. Have the class decide where in the room each tribe "lives." The Zulu tribe must live in the center of the room.
7. Tell the tribes, when they hear their particular drum rhythm, they should begin moving and continue until the drum stops. Play the appropriate drum rhythms, letting each tribe practice. Encourage a good bodily response.

8. Ask the children what entertainment they would like at the festival. List these on the board. (They may sing Indian songs, either as solos or together; some children may do original Indian dances, play drum solos, and so on.)
9. Have each tribe choose a chief. Let the Zulu chief announce the program of entertainment.
10. Have each tribe go to its "home," listen for its rhythm, then move to the festival, where members will sit cross-legged in a semicircle.
11. Play rhythms for the tribes to go to the festival. When the program is over, send the tribes home by playing their rhythms. Discuss the drama with the children, eliciting ways to improve it.
12. Help the class create an original story, incorporating familiar songs and rhythms that relate to Indians or another theme. Ideally this type of sequence would develop over a period of time, in conjunction with other classroom activities and studies.

Level I, II, or III

Creating a Rhythmic Accompaniment
"Ev'rybody Loves Saturday Night"

1. After the song (page 155) is familiar, begin a soft, spontaneous rhythmic accompaniment as the class sings.
2. As the class joins you, experiment with different rhythms and sound effects, indicating the class should imitate you. The following might be used:

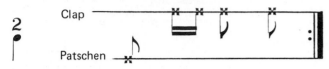

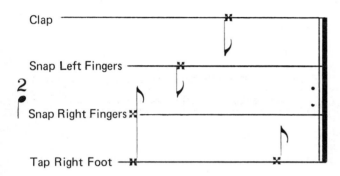

3. Sing many verses, while the class experiments with rhythmic accompaniments. Remind them to keep rhythms soft, so that it *accompanies* their singing.
4. Ask individuals to demonstrate their rhythmic accompaniment as the class sings.
5. Have the class vote for the accompaniment they like for each verse. Write the patterns on the board and sing the song, using these accompaniments.
6. Let the class choose rhythm instruments to accompany each verse.
7. Select children to play them, as the class sings and performs rhythmic accompaniments.

Level II or III

Creating a Rhythmic Interpretation
"Joshua Fit the Battle of Jericho"

When children know the song, encourage them to experiment with movements that would best express the feeling for each section of the song. Let several children experi-

ment with movements for each section, as the class sings. One class developed the following:

Refrain: Children assume a strong stance with their legs apart. On the two strong beats in each measure, they swing first their right, then their left arms, with a vigorous outward motion.

Verse one: Children throw their arms outward, as if addressing a throng, and turn slowly in a semicircle, then turn back.

Verse two: Children crouch low on the floor, with head, arms, and torso curled under. They slowly move upward, expanding their arms until they are tall, upright, and their arms are stretched up and out.

Verse three: Children take long strides, changing direction on every step. Their right hands are cupped to their mouths as though blowing a horn.

Individualizing Singing Experiences

Activities in this section will help children reinforce concepts already experienced in large groups.

Level I or II

Recordings for Individualizing Singing Experiences

These are recordings for one child or a small group. They are structured so that children can follow them with little or no help from the teacher, and are available from Educational Record Sales, 157 Chambers Street, New York, New York 10007.

Level I
Johnny Can Sing Too, Vols. 1, 2, and 3
Song Dramatizations for Children

Level II
Echo Songs and Rhythms
Classroom Sing Along

Level II

Song Rhythms
For one child

1. Reproduce copies of the "Song Rhythms" game on page 158. Be sure that children understand the directions.

Joshua Fit the Battle of Jericho

Negro Spiritual

Refrain Fast and Triumphant

Josh - ua fit the bat - tle of___ Jer - i - cho,___ Jer - i - cho,___

Jer - i - cho,___ Josh - ua fit the bat - tle of___ Jer - i - cho, And the

walls came tum - blin' down! Oh!___ down!

Verse

1. You may talk a - bout your King of Gid - e - on,___ You may

talk a - bout your King of Saul, There's none like good ol'

Josh - u - a___ At the bat - tle of Jer - i - cho.

2. Up to the walls of Jericho, He marched with
   spear in hand.
   "Go blow them ram-horns!" Joshua cried,
   "Cause the battle am in my hand!"

3. Then the lamb-ram sheep horns began to blow,
   The trumpets began to soun'
   Ol' Joshua commanded the chil'ren to shout,
   And the walls came tumblin' down! Oh!

Adapted from *A Proof Book of Spirituals and Folk Hymns*, published by World Around Songs. Used by permission.

Song Rhythms

Clap and chant each line of the song until you understand the rhythm. Then fill out the remaining rhythmic notation for each line, writing the notation for each syllable directly above it.

Rhythmic Notation

Line of Song   Are   you sleep-ing? Are you sleep-ing?

Rhythmic Notation

Line of Song   Broth - er   John?   Broth - er   John?

Rhythmic Notation

Line of Song   Morn-ing bells are   ring - ing,

                 Morn-ing bells are   ring - ing,

Rhythmic Notation

Line of Song   Ding   dong   ding!   Ding dong ding!

2. Prepare the answer sheet, laminate it, and have children check their own work.

Answer Sheet

Rhythmic Notation

Line of Song   Are   you sleep - ing?   Are you sleep - ing?

Rhythmic Notation

Line of Song   Broth-er   John?   Broth - er   John?

Rhythmic Notation

Line of Song   Morn-ing bells are   ring   -   ing,

                 Morn-ing bells are   ring   -   ing,

Rhythmic Notation

Line of Song   Ding   dong   ding!   Ding dong ding!

3. When children are familiar with the words and rhythm of a song, they can use it for "Song Rhythms." Some familiar pieces are "Caisson Song," "America," and "America the Beautiful."

Level II

Name the Syllable Game
For one person

1. Reproduce the following. Laminate the answer sheet.

Name the Syllable Game

Instructions: Assuming sol to be on the second line, mark the syllable names under each whole note. Use only the first letter of each syllable. Check your answers with the answer sheet.

Answer Sheet

1. S M S	6. D R M L
2. S L S M	7. T D¹ D¹ S
3. S D¹ D¹	8. L T D¹ D
4. D¹ L S	9. D¹ D M S
5. M S S D	10. M R D T

Level I or II

Draw the Note Game
For one child

Reproduce the following. Laminate the answer sheet.

Draw the Note Game

Instructions
1. Find the place where sol is indicated on each staff.
2. Draw a whole note in the line or space indicated by the syllable written below the staff.
3. Check your answers with the answer sheet.
4. Sing the intervals in each pattern (level II).

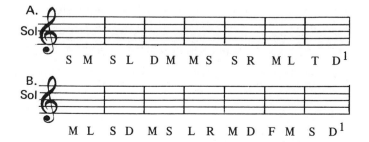

Answer Sheet

A.

S M S L D M M S S R M L T D¹

B.

M L S D M S L R M D F M S D¹

Level II or III

Arrange the Cards Game
For one child

1. Prepare and laminate these cards. The number below the notation should appear on *back* of each card.

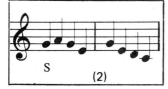

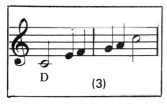

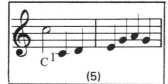

2. Prepare and laminate this answer sheet.

Answer Sheet

4.	6.
10.	3.
8.	7.
1.	9.
2.	5.

3. Using a cassette recorder, record the notation on each card in the order listed on the answer sheet. Record in each of these ways:
   a. Singing syllables, accompanied by a melody instrument
   b. Singing letter names, accompanied by a melody instrument
   c. Playing a melody instrument alone
4. Give these instructions to the child playing the game:
   a. Shuffle the cards.
   b. Using a cassette recorder that plays only (does not record), listen to the recording and sing when possible.
   c. Arrange the cards in the order heard on the cassette.
   d. Check your order with the answer sheet. (Numbers are on the backs of cards.)

Vocal Exploration and Aids for the Weak Singer

Children find their singing voices at different ages. Some children can sing many songs using a wide pitch range by the time they enter first grade; others of that age seem to have almost no singing voices at all. However, a majority of first graders can sing in a limited range, usually from middle C to the A above.

How does the teacher proceed so that weak singers have an optimum opportunity to become strong singers, those who have a limited pitch range develop a wider range, and all children learn to use their voices as fully as possible? First of all, the teacher can assume that, given an adequate number of rewarding singing experiences, most children can become strong singers. Any judgment of a child's singing ability should be withheld until she has had ample opportunity to explore her voice, perhaps at the age of ten or eleven. At this time the problem, if it still exists, can be discussed openly. Discussion or open labeling of a singing problem at an early age is only detrimental to the child's development and, indeed, can create a permanent inhibition and negative attitude toward singing.

Proceeding on this basis, then, the teacher will want to give all children the opportunity to explore their voices: to discover their range; how loud or soft, how fast or slow they can sing; to discover that they can make funny and serious sounds, happy and sad sounds, short and long sounds, hisses and growls. Often, through this type of free exploration children will discover their singing voices.

Among the most helpful things a teacher can do are these: create a free, relaxed atmosphere in which each child feels that she *wants* to sing, and provide songs that capture the imagination and elicit only enjoyable, positive feelings about singing.

What other aids are there for the weak singer in the first few grades? Action songs, dialogue songs, singing games, and songs that the child dramatizes all help her to "loosen up," relax, and enjoy singing. Songs with repeated chime-in phrases or choruses that turn the child's attention to particular intervals help too, for, in a dynamic and unconscious way, they focus both ear and voice on pitch relationships.

For the teacher who wants to work more directly on singing problems, there are other activities that help children. When used with care, in an enjoyable context, without any special emphasis on singing difficulties, these too can be helpful. They include imitative tone calls, in which the teacher sings a short phrase or interval, such as "Yoo hoo, how are you?" (sol mi, sol sol mi) or "Good morning" (do sol mi), and the child answers, using the same tones. Effective, too, for the child who can sing only in a low range, is a song or game imitating things that start low and go high, such as a fire siren or the wind. The reverse helps the child who sings only in a high range. It is also helpful to sing songs in the range most comfortable for the majority of the class, finding ways to expand the range gradually.

It is helpful to accompany singing activities with bodily movment and hand signals, which emphasize the vocal direction. It must be stressed, however, that all experiences be approached in a spirit of enjoyment and fun—not drill.

As children grow older—ten or eleven—the teacher will have problems with two groups of children: those who have never learned to control their singing voices, and boys whose voices are suddenly beginning to change or have changed. For boys with changing voices, the challenge is to keep them singing within their range. Thus, the teacher may encourage them to sing chord roots of songs, low harmony parts, chants, and the low phrases of a round.

What can the teacher do to help older children who have never learned to control their singing voices? At this age it is possible to state simply and frankly—without any value judgment—that some people do have difficulties singing, but these difficulties have solutions. For children who are willing to face their singing problems and try singing, it is sometimes extremely effective to form a

"sing club." When organized to give positive reinforcement, such a club can make dramatic changes in attitude and singing ability. It can work seriously, openly, and cooperatively on children's problems, using techniques as in earlier years, but on a more sophisticated level. By careful listening and use of physical movements (hands) and instruments (with singing) the child can discover his singing voice, often in six or seven meetings. This indicates that the problem was superficial and needed only understanding and practice to solve.

Level I

Exploring the Voice through Chanting, Bodily Movement, and Vocal Improvisation

This experience should be extended over as many days as necessary. A penny whistle, if available, will be helpful for this experience.

1. Ask children to close their eyes and listen to a sound you make, then tell you what it reminds them of. Blow your penny whistle or use your own voice to simulate the sound of a fire siren, starting as low and sliding as high as possible, then back down. Ask children what they thought of.

2. Ask children to make this sound with you. Using your voice and showing the pitch directions with your hands or entire body (stooping to floor, rising on tiptoes), help the children sing from low to very high, letting their voices slide up and down. (Do not insist on unison singing)

3. Let individual children, then the entire class, experiment. Repeat until the class is using the fullest possible range.

4. Tell the class to imagine that an animal is caught in a tree. Starting and stopping on your signal, they should make the sound of the animal. Signal them to start. Make positive comments about the freest and most effective sounds.

5. Tell the class to make sound effects for a story about a fire department rescue of an animal caught in a tree. When the story begins, they are to make the sounds of the fire engine coming, blowing its siren. Upon your signal, they are to make the sounds of the animal in the tree, and on the next signal the sounds of the fire engine leaving, after having saved the animal. Draw a picture on the board to show what will be happening. (See fig. 3.12.)

Note: The animal sounds should correspond to those made by the class.

6. Signal the class to begin. Conduct each section unobtrusively, giving signals for animal sounds and the fire engine. Make positive comments about successful attempts. Repeat, interspersing group attempts with individual attempts, until the class feels their performance is effective.

Figure 3.12
A picture of the sound effects for a vocal improvisation story.

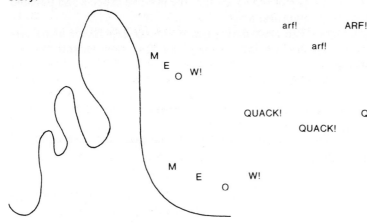

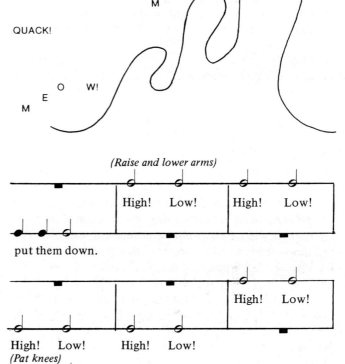

7. Tell the children there is more to the story of the animal caught in the tree. Tell them to listen and echo you. Do the following, making the movements and using a high or low voice, as suggested by the words.

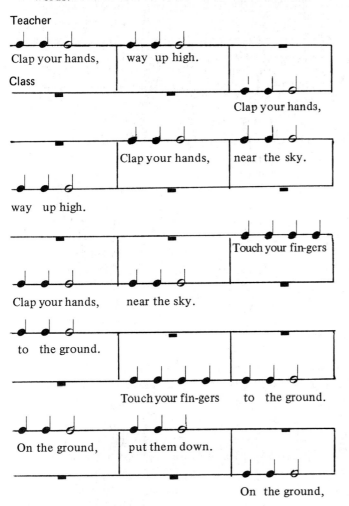

Teacher

Clap your hands, way up high.

Class

Clap your hands,

Clap your hands, near the sky.

way up high.

Touch your fin-gers

Clap your hands, near the sky.

to the ground.

Touch your fin-gers to the ground.

On the ground, put them down.

On the ground,

put them down.

(Raise and lower arms)

High! Low! High! Low!

High! Low!

High! Low! High! Low!
(Pat knees)

Ho, ho, ho!

High! Low! Ho, ho, ho!

8. When the class can do this easily, explain that before the fire engine came, some children were playing a clapping game near the tree. They stopped long enough to watch the firemen free the animal and depart again.
9. Have the children perform the entire story: the clapping game, the sound effects for the fire engine and animals, and the clapping game again.

Level II or III

Exploring the Voice through Vocal Improvisation, Illustrated

Use a tape or cassette recorder for this experience.

1. Write the following on the board:
   high   low   loud
2. Discuss the meaning of each, clarifying that high does not mean loud; it means high in pitch, as the ceiling

is high; similarly, low does not mean soft, it means low in pitch, as the floor is low; loud, however, may be high or low.

3. Have the class practice making sounds that are high, low, loud, and soft, using a neutral syllable, such as lah, lay, or loo.

4. Ask the class to think of words (real or make-believe) that sound high, low, and loud. Write these on the board. One class thought of the following:

High	Low	Loud
skyyy	down	shout!
highhhh	deeeep	yell!
sky-high	looooow	bowl!
mountain	dungeon	loud!
peak	bottom	ouch!
yi yi	boooom	yowl!
eeeeek		

5. Divide the class into three groups: one to make high sounds when you point to the word "high"; two to make low sounds; three to make loud sounds. Tell the children to select the word they will sound when their category is called. Remind groups one and two that their words should always be moderately loud. Only group three is to be loud. Point to the categories several times, but not in consecutive order.

6. Draw something similar to the following on the board:

```
H  HH                        H   HH  H   H
     H   H
         Loud              Loud       Loud

Loud

     Loud            Loud
               L

         LL   LL   L    L    L
```

7. Tell the class that "H" stands for high, and "L" stands for low, and ask them to say the words they practiced when you point to their category. Beginning at the upper left and moving from left to right, point to each letter, using a steady rhythm. (Two letters close to each other represent a quicker repetition of sounds.)

8. Discuss. Ask whether the position of H's and Louds means something. (It is a signal to raise voices higher or lower, according to their position on the board.)

9. Tell the class you will follow the indications on the board, moving quickly when two letters are close to one another. Conduct, indicating rhythm and pitch changes.

10. Select a talented child to be the conductor. Let other children have the opportunity to conduct. After each performance, discuss the positive aspects and possible improvements.

11. The class may enjoy a similar experience using different words—happy, sad, fast, slow, or soft.

Level II or III

Exploring the Voice through Creating an Environmental Soundscape

The teacher will need a tape recorder, and each child will need a paper and pencil.

1. Distribute paper and pencil.

2. Ask what the word "environment" means. Through discussion, elicit the idea that it includes all our surroundings, both man-made and natural.

3. Write this on the board and have the children copy it on their papers:
   Man-Made Sounds   *Nature's Sounds*

4. Ask the class to list sounds in each category.

5. Give children a few minutes to make their lists. Answer questions and help them, if necessary, by asking questions like these: "If you're camping in the forest, what do you hear?" (birds, mosquitoes, trees blowing in the wind, and so on) "At the beach?" (surf, sea gulls)

6. Have many children read their lists. Write their ideas on the board. Following is a partial list of sounds thought of by one class:

Man-Made Sounds	Nature's Sounds
jet planes	rain
man walking	wind
man talking	birds
fire siren	dogs
cars	cats
car horns	waves
lawnmower	sea gulls
vacuum cleaner	crickets
guitar—folk, electric	bumblebees
telephone	flies
doorbell	mosquitoes
clock	snow
	sleet

7. Ask which sounds they like best and erase all but the six most popular sounds. Have the class help you arrange these in order from the softest to loudest.

Man-Made Sounds	Nature's Sounds
man walking	crickets
church bell (in distance)	bumblebees
lawnmower	rain
folk guitar	birds
fire siren	dogs
jet plane	wind howling in a storm

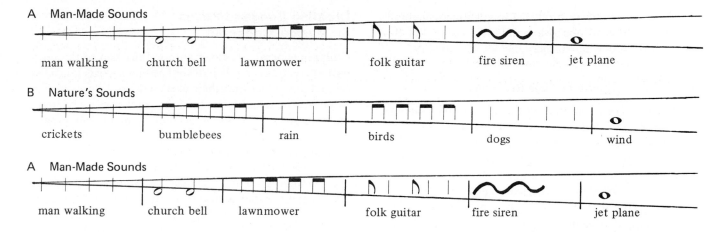

A Man-Made Sounds

man walking   church bell   lawnmower   folk guitar   fire siren   jet plane

B Nature's Sounds

crickets   bumblebees   rain   birds   dogs   wind

A Man-Made Sounds

man walking   church bell   lawnmower   folk guitar   fire siren   jet plane

8. Ask if they can make these sounds. Let them experiment.

9. Tell class you will point to each of these sounds, and they are to make their voices reproduce each. Remind them to use any vocal sound necessary to create the illusion they desire.

10. Point to the sounds until the class has had ample time to experiment with each.

11. Discuss the experiments. Ask which were easier, and which more difficult to produce.

12. Tell the class to make each sound for exactly one measure in 4/4 meter. Tell them to move from soft to loud in each category, starting and ending with man-made sounds. (ABA form) If you need to clarify, draw the plan on the board, as above.

13. Conduct the class through ABA form, helping them keep the beat and follow dynamics.

Level I

Aiding the Weak Singer through Use of Chime-in Phrases That Tell a Story

Johnny Can Sing Too, vol. 2, Classroom Materials Recording CM 1026

1. Ask the children to name, identify the pitch (high or low), and demonstrate familiar sounds, such as those heard about the house or made by toys and animals.

2. Tell them they will hear familiar sounds on a recording, and they should imitate these sounds.

3. Play the recording, encouraging participation. (Older children will listen to the entire record; younger to one side at a time.)

4. Discuss the story.

5. Have the children practice each sound, drawing pictures in the air to show the pitch changes. Give special attention to weak singers.

6. Help the children play sounds on melody bells. Give weak singers special opportunities.

7. Repeat the recording and practice the sounds until children can successfully make them.

8. Assign several children to sing each part (Grandfather's clock, water faucet, and so on), putting weak and strong singers together.

9. Help the children dramatize the story, as they sing with the record.

Recordings and Other Aids for Teaching the Song

Some teachers feel unable to sing well enough to teach a song. Although this is a problem, there are solutions. Often a change of attitude sufficiently solves the problem; the teacher summons the courage to use his voice.

What about the "nonsinging" teacher? First and foremost, he will be wise to consider himself a teacher who does not yet sing. Experience has taught us that a true nonsinger is a rarity. Given freedom from inhibitions, which many have experienced in singing, and the opportunity to develop awareness of pitch differences, most nonsingers can become singers. The nonsinging teacher should forget pride and learn, with the children, to enjoy singing and use his ear as a guide. There are aids to help him, both in teaching songs and in developing his own singing ability.

Song Leaders

Song leaders in his class will become apparent. The boy or girl who learns the song almost immediately can and should help teach it to the class. Guarding against the overuse of one such child, the teacher should share responsibility with all capable children in the class.

Melody Instruments

Melody instruments are easy to play. They can help the teacher learn as well as teach a song. Many songs can be learned on a recorder, xylophone or melody bells, thus enabling the teacher to teach the song without singing it. The wise teacher will be aware and ask assistance of children in the class who can play melody instruments.

Records and Cassette or Tape Recorders

Using records can become such an art that the non-singing teacher can develop a very fine singing class. Most songs from the basal song series are recorded, and the accompanying teacher's manuals often contain suggestions for optimal use of recordings. A recording can be substituted for most experiences throughout this book that suggest singing. For the teacher who needs concrete help in developing a singing class, recordings, such as *Johnny Can Sing Too* (Classroom Materials Recordings, vols. 1, 2, and 3), which are designed to help young children find their singing voices, can be of inestimable value.

The teacher can also use cassette and tape recorders, not only to play commercially prepared tapes but also to make special recordings for teaching aids. The advantage here is that the teacher may reach beyond his own abilities to use the talents of others (such as the music teacher) in preparing tapes. Cassette and tape recordings may be used in many ways, including the following:

1. Recording (or having someone else record) an entire song not otherwise available.
2. Recording the accompaniment for a song.
3. Recording the harmony of a part-song.
4. Recording all but one phrase of a familiar song, perhaps having children focus on the missing phrase: Does it move up or down, by step or skip?
5. Recording a rhythmic accompaniment to a song.
6. Recording songs and rhythm instrument and accompaniments created by children.

The teacher should remember that only songs in the public domain may be recorded without permission from the copyright holder. He should remember also that some cassette recorders are made for playback purposes only, to avoid erasure.

Overhead Projector

With the availability of the overhead projector, the teacher has an invaluable aid in teaching a song. It is now possible to put a song or a portion of a song on a transparency and project it on a large screen while facing the class. Since the room can remain light, the teacher can work with ease. Thus, a teacher can help the class examine the nature of the melody, rhythm, form, harmony, or text, and point to any aspect under consideration. He can also prepare overlays and first show the melody, then add an overlay to show the harmony, and so on. In addition, commercial transparencies for teaching music are now available.

Creating Songs to Focus on Musical Concepts

Children generally respond with enthusiasm to the prospect of creating song. Whatever hesitancy exists is usually related to the fear that their ideas will not be of sufficient value. As the song evolves, and the teacher uses children's ideas, positive feelings of accomplishment and growth begin to develop, and self-doubt gives way to joy in creating or helping to create a song.

But what does the child learn from such an experience? What growth in conceptual understanding and achievement of behavioral objectives occur? Musically, because she is enjoying the experience, the child makes rapid strides. In the most dynamic way possible, by creating music, she learns these things:

1. Melodies can move up and down, by step or skip, as well as stay on the same pitch. This does make a difference in the effect created.
2. Melodies can be written in different keys. This does make a difference in the effect created and in the pitch.
3. Melodies can move in twos or threes, and it does make a difference.
4. Melodies can be written in the major or minor mode, and it makes a difference.
5. It is important to understand notation so that one can read notated melodies.
6. Music reading is something one can understand.
7. Melodies can be orchestrated (using percussion instruments or Orff-type instruments) to create various effects.
8. Melodies can be accompanied by guitar. Different melodies require different accompanying chords.
9. Tempo and dynamics help determine the mood of a melody or song.
10. Phrase repetition can unify a song.
11. Cadences "end" a phrase or song.

Personally and socially the child grows too. She learns these things:

1. Her ideas have value that others may accept and use.
2. Others also have good ideas.
3. By working cooperatively with a group, fine projects can be developed and enjoyed.
4. Composers are people like herself who have developed their talents to a greater extent.

The child enjoys and learns from this experience. But how can a teacher develop and guide such a project? For the teacher with a musical background, or the music specialist, the matter becomes fairly simple. These teachers can more easily remember and notate the melodies children sing. Other teachers will probably need help from a music specialist or teaching aids, such as the tape or cassette recorder.

In any case, it is wise to give children preparatory experiences so that they have some background for writing songs. Earlier experiences might include adding original words or verses to songs, and writing melodies for poems.

With these experiences as part of their background, children can naturally and easily join in creating song. What, then, is a good plan for proceeding? This is one possible approach:

1. Through discussion, help the class select a song topic.
2. Help the class choose the lyrical message they wish to convey and the mood they wish to create.
3. Help them compose a simple, rhythmic poem. (It is far easier to create a four-line song with many verses than a longer song with a few verses.)
4. Suggest that the class rhythmically clap and chant poem. (Initiate clapping and chanting and participate with the class.) Repeat, until the class feels the rhythm of the poem. Put the poem on the board, and let the class help you find and underline the accented syllables. Put bar lines in appropriate places.
5. Ask the class to sing the first line only, when you say "sing," and to raise their hands if they like the tune they create.
6. Tell the class to sing. Sing softly with them, but stop before they imitate you. If they do not sing, ask them to try again, this time starting high and descending. If reticence persists, repeat, this time starting low and ascending. (Specific suggestions sometimes give children confidence.)
7. Ask volunteers to sing their melodies. Make positive comments. When you hear an acceptable tune, sing it for the class and suggest that it be used. If the class agrees, write it on the board. (Your objective is to give children feelings of success, so they will proceed with confidence. Do not expect the class to produce a perfect song.)
8. Ask the class to sing this first line with you several times.
9. Ask for a volunteer to sing the second line, explaining that the class will sing the first line with her, and she will continue, singing the second line alone. Have other children sing their lines until you hear an acceptable second line. Ask the class if they think this line goes well with the first line. If they agree, notate it on the board.
10. Continue in this manner until the song is completed.
11. Have the class write the song on a large cardboard.
12. Ask if they would like to add a rhythmic or guitar accompaniment. On another day, help children with these ideas, using suggestions from chapter 4, "Experiences with Instruments."

Additional Enrichment Activities

When the relationship between teacher and child fosters free expression of ideas and responsiveness to musical experiences, both will become aware of singing as a means for self-expression and of relating to the outside world. The wise teacher will encourage such experiences by taking cues from children and by making suggestions at appropriate times.

These are valuable enrichment experiences:

1. Compiling a list of favorite songs
2. Sharing songs with other classes
3. Allowing time in singing periods for requests
4. Encouraging children to sing, for the class, songs they learned elsewhere
5. Encouraging children who play guitar to accompany songs
6. Developing an assembly program from songs learned in class
7. Discovering and learning songs related to other areas of study
8. Inviting outside guests to sing for class
9. Encouraging solo and small group singing
10. Helping children build a scale using water glasses, and teaching them to play songs or parts of songs using this scale
11. Encouraging children to prepare a bulletin board showing pictures of people singing

Discussions and Reports

1. Through discussion, explore the idea that all children innately love to sing.
2. Prepare a report indicating the criteria necessary for selecting a song for levels I, II, and III.
3. Select a song appropriate for level I, II, or III. After answering questions listed under "Teaching the Song" earlier in this chapter, write a strategy, following the outline on page 79.
4. Select a conceptual understanding related to rhythm, melody, texture, form, expression, or reading, appropriate to level I, II, or III. (See the Growth and Sequence chart in chapter 1.) Following the suggestions on pages 78–79 of this chapter, plan a strategy for a singing experience revolving around the conceptual understanding chosen.
5. Prepare a report showing ways to use other arts, living experiences, and the environment to help children understand musical concepts.
6. Discuss the advantages of planning singing experiences so that they involve related musical activities (listening, rhythms, and so on) as well as related arts.
7. Select a behavioral objective related to singing and appropriate to level I. Plan a singing experience, fol-

lowing suggestions listed on page 79 of this chapter, that will help children achieve this objective.

8. Discuss the characteristics of songs for focusing on rhythmic concepts, melodic concepts, concepts related to texture, form, expression, and reading.

9. Find and list songs that would best be taught focusing on rhythmic concepts, melodic concepts, concepts related to texture, form, expression, and reading.

10. Prepare a report describing your elementary school singing experiences. Describe the positive and negative influences on your attitude toward and skill in singing.

11. Select one of the experiences for individualization. Evaluate its strengths and weaknesses. Make suggestions for improvement.

12. Discuss the merits and limitations of the section "Vocal Exploration and Aids for the Weak Singer." Add other ideas for vocal exploration.

13. Through discussion, define and clarify the various kinds of part singing: chants, echo songs, ostinati to a pentatonic song, descants, counter melodies, harmonized cadences, rounds, canons, chord roots, songs in thirds and sixths, vocal chording, harmonizing by ear.

14. Through discussion define *relationship between parts, balance between parts,* and *blend of parts.* Explore the idea that it is important for the child to hear the relationship, balance, and blend of parts.

15. Through discussion, define the word *texture* in music. List ways children can experience texture.

16. Prepare a plan for teaching one of the following: a song with a chant; an echo song; a round or canon; a song with descant, counter melody, or harmonized cadence.

17. Write a report discussing the types of part-singing experiences you have had, the factors that helped you to participate successfully, and your general reaction to part-singing activities.

18. Prepare a plan for teaching a chant, using a melody instrument to help teach the second part.

19. Discuss the importance of having part-singing experiences by rote before attempting part-singing experiences through note reading.

20. Discuss ways to use a recording for teaching a part-song. Prepare a plan for using a recording to teach one of the following: a song in thirds or sixths, a song with descant or counter melody.

21. Observe an elementary school chorus in rehearsal. Write a report discussing approaches, techniques, materials, and attitudes observed.

22. Discuss this chapter, focusing on creativity versus rigidity.

23. Discuss songs children enjoy as contrasted to adult tastes. Indicate the implications for teaching children.

24. Discuss using ethnic music and music from the current popular idiom to foster musical growth and understanding.

25. If possible, observe singing activities in an elementary classroom. Write a paper describing the approaches, techniques, materials, and attitudes observed.

26. Using the "Singing Activities Evaluation Chart," keep a log of class singing activities. (This chart can be a basis for an expanding source of possible singing activities for the elementary grades.)

Activities to Develop Skills and Practice in Initiating Musical Experiences

1. Prepare a strategy that focuses on specific conceptual understandings and behavioral objectives related to rhythm, melody, texture, form, expression, or music reading and involves (1) teaching a song, (2) a related musical activity, and (3) an experience with related arts. Specify the level intended (level I, II, or III).

2. Prepare a plan for teaching a song to level I. Use basic bodily movements to focus on rhythmic concepts and involve children in immediate participation. Teach the song. Discuss the ways that bodily movements encouraged enjoyment, rhythmic exploration, and growth in conceptual understanding.

3. Prepare a plan for teaching a song to level II. Use concepts related to form, melody, or expression as the focal point. Teach the song. Evaluate the results to determine whether this method encouraged conceptual understandings, behavioral objectives, and enjoyment.

4. Select a song for level III in which the conceptual focus is on music reading. Prepare a teaching plan and present it to the class. Through discussion, evaluate the plan to determine whether it helped achieve conceptual understanding, behavioral objectives, and enjoyment.

5. Select an experience on vocal exploration. Initiate and guide the experience. Through class discussion, evaluate the results.

6. Select a song that has a good, available recording. Prepare a plan for teaching the song, using the recording. Initiate and guide the experience. Evaluate it in terms of enjoyment and ease in learning.

7. Prepare, initiate, and guide a plan for using a melody instrument to help teach a song. Discuss growth and enjoyment created through use of the instrument.

8. Prepare and initiate an experience whereby the class creates additional stanzas to a familiar song. Discuss ways this activity encourages creativity.

9. Select several related songs for a specific grade. Teach, using a different approach for each.

10. Prepare a unit of singing experiences for a specific age, using an environmental theme of current ecological significance. Present it to the class. Through discussion, evaluate it in terms of (1) human values, (2) enjoyment and relevance, (3) conceptual understandings and behavioral objectives.
11. Prepare and present a strategy for level III, using ethnic materials (song, related musical activity, and related arts). Show how this plan can foster musical enjoyment, musical development, and awareness of other cultures.
12. Select a song from the current popular idiom. Prepare a teaching plan that encourages musical enjoyment and conceptual growth. Present it and evaluate results.
13. Prepare a plan for level II for using a melody instrument to teach a song with a chant, an echo song, a round or canon, or a song with a counter melody or descant. Initiate and guide the experience. Through class discussion, evaluate the results.
14. Prepare a plan for level III for using a recording to teach a song with a chant, descant, counter melody, harmonized cadence, echo song, round or canon. Initiate and guide the experience. Through discussion, evaluate it.
15. Create a chant for a familiar song. Prepare a teaching plan. Initiate and guide the experience. Evaluate results, through class discussion.
16. Create an individualized activity using rhythmic or melodic concepts. Initiate with an individual or group from the class. Have the class evaluate it.

Singing Activities Evaluation Chart

Level	Song	Book and Page	Ideas for Immediate Participation	Conceptual Understandings	Behavioral Objectives	Related Musical Activities	Related Arts	Evaluation

Supplementary Song Collections

Book Title	Author	Publisher
African Songs		WAS
American Ballads and Folk Songs	Lomax and Lomax	Macmillan
American Folk Songs for Children	Seeger	Doubleday
American Folk Tales and Songs	Chase	New American Library
American Negro Songs and Spirituals	Work	Bonanza
American Songbag, The	Sandburg	Harcourt, Brace & World
Amigos Cantando		WAS
An Elizabethan Songbag	Raebeck	E. B. Marks (Belwin)
Bells of Rhymney, The	Seeger	Oak
Best Loved American Folk Songs	Lomax	Gosset & Dunlap
Bicinia Americana, vol. 1	arr., Burkart	Keeping Up with Music Education
Bluegrass Songbook, The	Cyporyn	Macmillan
Book of Ballads, Songs, and Snatches	Shekerjian	Harper & Row
Burl Ives Sea Songs		Ballentine
Calypso Song Book	Attaway	McGraw-Hill
Cantos de Juventud	Spanish	WAS
Carl Sandburg's New American Song Bag		Associated Music
Celebration of Life	Ritchie	Gordie Music
Chansons de Notre Chalet		WAS
Children's Songs from Japan	White and Akiyama	E. B. Marks (Belwin)
Come Friends		WAS
Ditty Bag, The	Tobitt	Plymouth Music Co.
East-West Songs		WAS

Echoes of Africa in Folk Songs of the Americas	Landeck	Van Rees	New Song Fest	Best and Best	Crown
Energy and Motion Songs	Zaret and Singer	Argosy	New Treasury of Folk Songs, The	Glazer	Bantam Books
Experiment Songs	Zaret and Singer	Argosy	150 American Folk Songs to Sing, Read, and Play	Erdi	Boosey and Hawkes
Fireside Book of Children's Songs	Winn and Miller	Simon & Schuster	One Tune More		WAS
Fireside Book of Folksongs	Boni	Simon & Schuster	Pagoda, The (Chinese)		WAS
Fireside Songs Book of Birds and Beasts, The	Yolen, Green, and Parnall	Simon & Schuster	Pocket Full of Songs, A		WAS
			Richard Dyer-Bennet Folk Song Book		Simon & Schuster
Folk Song Jamboree	Marais and Miranda	Ballentine Books	Rique Ran (South American)		WAS
Folk Songs of North America	Lomax	Doubleday	Seasons in Song	Zimmerman	Witmark
Folk Songs of U.S.A.	Lomax and Lomax	Meredith Press	Sesame Street Song Book	Raposo and Moss	Simon & Schuster
Folk Songster	Dallin and Dallin	Brown	Seventy Simple Songs with Ostinati	Chatterley	Novello
Folksongs for Fun	Brand	Berkley Pub. Corp.	Sing and Celebrate	Whitaker	Silver Burdett
			Sing and Strum	Snyder	Mills
Folksongs and Footnotes	Bikel	Meridian Books	Sing a Song with Charity Bailey		Plymouth
For Happy Singing		WAS			
Forty-six Two-Part American Folk Songs for Elementary Grades	arr., Bacon	Kodaly Musical Training Institute	Sing a Tune		WAS
			Sing It Yourself: 220 Pentatonic American Folk Songs	Bradford	Alfred
French Folk Songs		E. B. Marks (Belwin)	Sing Together Children		WAS
			Songs Children Like		Asso. for Childhood Educ.
Fresh New Day Songbook		Up With People			
Git on Board	Landeck	E. B. Marks (Belwin)	Songs for All Seasons and Rhymes without Reasons	Marquis	Marks
Good Fellowship Songs		WAS	Songs for Our Small World	Garlid and Olson	Schmitt, Hall & McCreary
Grandma Sings	Danish Songs	WAS			
Great Songs of the Sixties	Okun	Quadrangle Books (Belwin)	Songs for Singin'	Lynn	Chandler Publ. Co.
			Songs from South Africa	Marais	G. Schirmer
Guiana Sings		WAS	Songs in Motion	Richards	Fearon
Handy Play Party Book, The		WAS	Songs of All Time		WAS
Hap Palmer Songbook (two vols.)		Educational Activities	Songs of the Hills and Plains	Wilson	Schmitt, Hall & McCreary
Happy Meeting (Czech)		WAS	Songs of the Wigwam		WAS
Heritage Songster	Dallin and Dallin	Brown	Songs to Grow On	Landeck	E. B. Marks (Belwin)
Holiday Songbag	Obenshain	Shawnee Press	Space Songs	Zaret and Singer	Argosy
Japanese Songs		WAS			
Jim Along Josie	Langstaff and Langstaff	Harcourt Brace Jovanovich	Survival Songbook	Morsel and Mathews	Sierra Club
Joyful Singing		WAS	Swiss Alpine Songs		WAS
Just Five (Collection of Pentatonic Songs)	Kersey	Belwin Mills	Takin' Off for the Day Songbook		Up With People
Just Five Plus Two	Kersey	Belwin Mills	Treasury of Folk Songs	Kolb	Bantam Books
Leadbelly Songbook, The		Oak	Twice Fifty-five Community Songs (two vols.)		Summy-Birchard
Little Book of Carols		WAS	Upbeat, Main Street Songbook		Up With People
Little Calypsos	Krugman and Ludwig	Carl Van Roy (Peripole)	Vermont Sings		WAS
Look Away (Negro Songs)		WAS	Voices in Song	Richardson	Willis
Merry Hours (Hungarian)		WAS	Wake Up and Sing	Landeck and Crook	E. B. Marks (Belwin)
More Nature Songs	Zaret and Singer	Argosy	Weather Songs	Zaret and Singer	Argosy
More Songs to Grow On	Landeck	E. B. Marks (Belwin)			
Music for Fun, Music for Learning	Birkenshaw	Holt, Rinehart and Winston			
Nature Songs	Zaret and Singer	Argosy			
Negro Sings a New Heaven	Grissom	Dover			

Note: World Around Songs (WAS) offers a unique service. From an extensive list of excellent songs can be chosen titles for custom-made song collections containing from 16 to 100 pages. The convenient size and reasonable cost of these publications make them valuable as supplementary classroom materials and for use in singing assemblies. For further information about these custom-made books as well as a list of their standard publication, write: World Around Songs, Rt. 5, Burnsville, North Carolina, 28714.

Weavers' Song Book, The	DeCormier	Harper & Row
Wide Horizons		WAS
Work and Sing		WAS
World in Tune, The		WAS
World of African Song	Makeba	Quadrangle

Collections of Descants	Composer	Publisher
Descants to Sing for Fun	Foltz	Mills Music Co.
Great Songs of Faith	The Krones	Niel A. Kjos
Intermediate Descants	The Krones	Niel A. Kjos
More Descants to Sing for Fun	Foltz, Shelley	Mills Music Co.
Our First Songs to Sing with Descants	Krone	Niel A. Kjos
Our Third Book of Descants	The Krones	Niel A. Kjos
Songs for Fun with Descants	The Krones	Niel A. Kjos
Songs to Sing with Descants	Krone	Niel A. Kjos

Collections of Rounds and Canons		
Catches for Three, Four, and Five Voices	Lawton	Music Press
Catch that Catch Can	Taylor, Windham, Simpson	E. C. Schirmer
Easy Canons	Reichenback	Music Press
Fifty Simple Rounds	Lawrence	Novello
Round and Round They Go	Daniel	Summy-Birchard
Rounds and Canons	Wilson	Hall & McCreary
Rounds and Rounds	Taylor	Wm. Sloane

Supplementary Recordings

Title	Composer	Recording
Activity Songs for Kids		Sch R7523
Adventures in Rhythm	Jenkins	Sch R7682
American Folk Songs for Children	Seeger	Folkways 7601
American Playparties	Seeger	Folkways 7674
Animal Folk Songs for Children	Peggy Seeger	Sch R7551
Birds, Beasts, Bugs, and Bigger Fishes	Seeger	Folkways 7611
Birds, Beasts, Bugs, and Little Fishes	Seeger	Folkways 7610
Burl Ives Sings Songs for All Ages		Columbia
Call and Response Rhythmic Group Singing		Sch R7638
Camp Songs	Seeger and Darling	Folkways 7628
Children's Activity Songs	Richardson	Sch R7678
Children's Jamaican Songs and Games	Bennett	Folkways 7250
Classroom Sing Along		CM 1054
Counting Games and Rhythms for the Little Ones	Jenkins	Sch R7679
Creative Music for Exceptional Children		CM 1025
Discovery!		Sch 11050
Early Childhood Songs	Jenkins	Sch R7630
Exploring Music Reading		CM 1047
Finger Play, vol. 1		CM 1043
Finger Play, vol. 2		CMF1046
Folk Songs	Clauson	RCA
Folk Songs for Young People	Seeger	Folkways 7532
Folk Songs of Africa		Bowmar 154
Folk Songs of Canada		Bowmar 139
Folk Songs of Japanese Children		Bowmar 157
Folk Songs of Latin America		Bowmar 145
Folk Songs of Our Pacific Neighbors		Bowmar 141
Folk songs of the U.S.A.		Bowmar 143
Gosh, What a Wonderful World!		Sch R7025
Introduction to Music Reading		CM 1013
Jambo and Other Call and Response Songs and Chants	Jenkins	Folkways FC 7661
Johnny Can Sing Too, vol. 1		Cm 1014
Johnny Can Sing Too, vol. 2		CM 1026
Johnny Can Sing Too, vol. 3		CM 1052
Join into the Game	Glazer	Columbia
Learning as We Play		Sch R7659
Let's Sing and Act Together		Cm 1057
Little Johnny Brown	Jenkins	Sch R7631
More Learning as We Play		Sch R7658
More Music Time and Stories	Bailey and Sahlein	Folkways 7528
More Songs to Grow On	Mills	Folkways 7676
Musical Experiences for Basic Learning Readiness: Who Am I		Cm 1068
Musical Experiences for Basic Learning Readiness: I Go to School		CM 1076
Musical Plays for Special Days		Sch R7560
Music Time	Bailey	Folkways 7307
Negro Folk Songs for Young People	Leadbelly	Folkways 7533
Nursery Rhymes for Dramatic Play		CM 1051
One, Two, Three, and a Zing Zing Zing		Folkways 7003
Play Your Instruments and Make a Pretty Sound		Folkways 7665
Rhythm and Game Songs for the Little Ones, vol. 2		Sch R7680
Rhythms and Songs for Exceptional Children		CM 1021
Rhythms of Childhood	Jenkins	Sch R7653
Seasons for Singing	Jenkins	Folkways 7656
Sing a Song of Holidays and Seasons		Bowmar/Noble
Sing a Song of Home and Community		Bowmar/Noble
Singing Games		RCA WE 87
Sing'n Do (five albums)		Sing'n Do
Skip Rope		Sch R7649
Song Dramatizations for Children		CM 1048
Songs to Grow On		Sch R7501
Twelve Joyous Carols from Around the World		WAS

Twelve Songs for All Year Long		Sch R7626
Whoever Shall Have Some Good Peanuts	Hinton	Sch R7530
You Can Sing It Yourself		Folkways 7624
You'll Sing a Song and I'll Sing a Song	Jenkins	Folkways 7664
You Too Can Sing		CM 1031

Note: Recordings of importance in teaching and easily available from commercial recording companies are listed without reference number because of the frequency with which these change.

CM—Classroom Materials Co.
RCA WE—Basic Record
   Library for Elementary
   Grades
Sch—Scholastic
WAS—World Around Songs

Experiences with Instruments 4

A musical instrument is a fascinating object to the child. Whether it be a simple melody instrument, a band or orchestral instrument, a rhythm instrument, or an accompanying instrument, it has an aura of magic for him. He likes to examine it, touch it, listen to it, compare its sounds with other instruments, and, above all, play it.

Playing it, even in the most elementary fashion, gives him a feeling of accomplishment. He takes pride in demonstrating each newly acquired skill: shaking and tapping the tambourine in rhythm; playing a new note on the recorder; or playing melodies that skip, step, or remain on the same level, on the song bells. The transition from playing song bells to playing a recorder gives a feeling of progress. Becoming a member of the school band or orchestra is a desirable achievement. All of these experiences give the child the satisfaction that comes from seeing his newly developed skills serve him in creating something beautiful.

Because of the satisfaction he feels, the child is willing to accept restrictions and controls for which he would normally have little tolerance. He will persevere in his efforts to master his instrument or to wait his turn while others receive assistance. Because he senses the importance of what he is doing, he is willing to cooperate with the group and learns that, through this kind of cooperation, gratifying experiences can result.

In addition to these personal benefits, experiences with instruments can benefit musical growth. Because the child experiences making music firsthand, he understands the musical concepts of duration, meter, phrase, form, tempo, dynamics, pitch, instrumentation, melodic patterns, and interval relationships more quickly and concrete. Verbalization of these elements begins to have meaning, for he understands them in the best possible way—through experiencing them.

Aims of Experiences with Instruments

1. To expand the child's interest in musical instruments.
2. To give the child the opportunity to know and experiment with many instruments: rhythm, melody, accompanying, and orchestral.
3. To give the child the opportunity to develop skill in playing one or more of these instruments.
4. To help the child develop the conceptual understandings and behavioral objectives related to experiences with instruments. (For a list of conceptual understandings and behavioral objectives related to each age level, see the "Growth and Sequence Chart" at the end of chapter 1.)

Classification of Instruments

Children enjoy exploring a wide variety of instruments, including:

1. Rhythm instruments
2. Simple melody instruments: song bells (melody bells), diatonic xylophone, chromatic xylophone, step bells, resonator bells, and Orff-type instruments
3. Recorder
4. Accompanying instruments: Autoharp, ukulele, guitar, and piano
5. Band and orchestral instruments

Experiences with Rhythm Instruments

Activities involving rhythm instruments attract the child. He enjoys these instruments so much that he does not mind the self-discipline and concentration they sometimes demand. Although he enjoys playing these instruments, his growth in conceptual understanding and achievement of behavioral objectives depends upon how they are introduced and used. When the child discovers that each instrument speaks in its own "voice" and has its own rhythmic style, the potential for musical growth is enhanced. With this approach, the child begins to think of them as authentic instruments—members of the percussion family through which he can either communicate his own ideas and feelings or emphasize the rhythm patterns of a familiar nursery rhyme, poem, or song. When his experiences with rhythm instruments are integrated with other musical experiences a natural growth sequence occurs whereby he can begin using percussion instruments to experience music abstractly. Thus, in intermediate and upper grades he can play instruments in canon, learn to improvise B and C sections of a rondo, and learn to play from notation.

What experiences are enjoyable as well as beneficial? While it is impossible to give a definitive list, some basic experiences include:

Figure 4.1
Rhythm instruments, photo courtesy of The World of
Peripole, Inc., Browns Mills, N.J. 08015

1. Introductory experiences with rhythm instruments
    a. Discovering the distinctive tone quality of each—
       how it is best played to produce different qualities
       of sound
    b. Learning to use each instrument as a means of
       communication
    c. Learning to accompany simple chants and
       rhythms
    d. Learning to use instruments in question and
       answer (phrase building) experiences
    e. Learning to hear and reproduce the rhythm of the
       melody, meter, strong and weak beats, and recur-
       ring rhythm patterns
2. Use of rhythm instruments to cultivate conceptual
   understandings and behavioral objectives related to
   rhythm, melody, texture, form, expression, in these
   experiences:
    a. Singing
    b. Listening
    c. Rhythms (including rhythmic improvisation)
    d. Music reading

The teacher should have a thorough knowledge of
rhythm instruments, how they are best played, and the
sound qualities of each. The chart on this page may be
helpful.

The rhythm band, in the traditional sense, will not
be discussed in this book. It is the authors' contention that
the use of the term *rhythm band* often creates a mechanical ensemble. When the response involves group playing,
it can be considered a rhythm band; however, the main
concern here will be to help children focus on the expressive and conceptual elements of music.

The teacher who initiates experiences using rhythm
instruments should be thoroughly prepared: she should
know her long term goals and those for individual experiences. In addition, she should plan experiences that

Instrument	Type Music Best Accompanied	How Played
Cymbals	Accents, climaxes	Strike together or strike single cymbal with soft or wire beater.
Finger cymbals	Soft, slow music, long notes, accents, ringing effects, filling rests	Hold one in left hand, other perpendicularly above in right hand; cymbal in right hand taps cymbal in left hand.
Gong	Special sound effects	Strike with soft mallet.
Hand drum	Accents, meter	Strike with a stick, mallet, fist, flat hand, closed hand, or tap lightly with fingers. Different sounds result when a drum is struck in the center, side or edge. Different sizes and shapes of drums produce different sound qualities.
Jingle bells	Fast, jingly music	Hold in left hand; hit left hand with right fist.
Maracas	Running, fast music, shaking effects	Same as for jingle bells or make circular motion.
Tambourine (with or without head)	Accents, shaking effects	Tap on edge or shake.
Timpani	Meter	Play with soft mallets.
Tone block (many shapes and sizes)	Walking music, accents, short notes, basic beats	Level I, hit "body" of tone block with stick. Level II or III, place tone block in cupped left hand; strike tone block with stick.
Triangle	Slow music, long notes, accents, ringing effects	Hold in left hand (be careful not to touch triangle); strike with mallet held in right hand.

encourage the child himself to discover these goals. Further, she will need to establish a rule for playing rhythm
instruments, which will promote an atmosphere conducive
to making music. Children should understand that they
play only at times specified, and that without this rule
time is wasted and little musical gratification is attained.

When the teacher is well prepared and plans for the
child's full participation in each activity, the experience
involving rhythm instruments can be one that is satisfying
to the child in the musical growth he attains and the
enjoyment he experiences.

Children enjoy making their own rhythm instruments. For the teacher who wishes to give her children
this experience, there are instructions for making rhythm
instruments later in this chapter.

Introducing the Rhythm Instruments: Level I

Materials Needed
1. A set of rhythm instruments, including these:
   rhythm sticks   sand blocks   cymbals
   tone blocks   triangles   finger cymbals
   maracas   drums   jingle bells
2. Pictures illustrating related but contrasting objects
3. Recording of "Shadows" by Schytte, RCA Victor *Basic Record Library for Elementary Grades* recording WE 90
4. Music Cue charts

Instrumental Activities
Exploring the rhythm instruments and creating an accompaniment for a recording

Related Musical Activity
Listening

Conceptual Understandings
1. Use of different instruments changes the timbre and feelings expressed.
2. The mood of any musical composition is related to tempo.
3. Repeated musical ideas (rhythmic or melodic patterns) or phrases make music meaningful.

Behavioral Objectives
1. To begin hearing differences in tone color produced by percussion instruments
2. To maintain steady musical pulse by playing rhythm instruments
3. To hear similar phrases and the form they produce and to respond by playing percussion instruments to accompany the music
4. To show how changes in tempo change mood

Related Arts
Examining pictures of related but different objects to discover how they produce different reactions (using fig. 4.2)

Procedure
1. Examining pictures of related but different objects to discover how they produce different reactions
   a. Display a picture similar to that in figure 4.2.
   b. Ask the children to name objects they see. (grapefruit, grapes, apples, bananas)
   c. Ask the children to describe each, focusing on the different image each gives. (A banana is long, slightly curved, with a yellow skin; a grape is small, and round, and, in this case, dark, and so on.)
   d. Ask children if they get different taste sensations when they look at different fruits.

Figure 4.2.
Fruits, photograph by David Rosenthal

    e. Ask what they have in common.
    f. Continue discussing the fruits, emphasizing that though they are members of the same family they create different reactions.
    g. Explain that they will also have different reactions to different rhythm instruments.
2. Experiencing differences in tone color and mood while being introduced to the rhythm instruments
   a. Hold up rhythm sticks. Tell the class what they are and demonstrate how to play them.
   b. Ask the children what rhythm sticks sound like (i.e., a clock ticking, woodpecker pecking, heels clicking, and so on).
   c. Distribute pairs of rhythm sticks to several children. Tell them to experiment until they hear your signal to stop. Give them a few seconds to experiment.
   d. Tell the children to listen for a section or sections that rhythm sticks might accompany. Play the recording of "Shadows."
   e. Discuss, focusing on contrasting moods created by the two sections of the piece. Was one faster than the other? Was one section repeated? Which section would sound best with rhythm sticks?
   f. Write *ABA* on the chalk board. Assuming the children elect to accompany A, write on the board:
   Section A   rhythm sticks
   Section B
   Section A   rhythm sticks
   If the children are not already familiar with ABA form, discuss, making certain they understand how it is created.
   g. Tell the class when they hear section A, they are to accompany, using their index fingers as rhythm sticks. Play the recording and help the children, if necessary.
   h. Have the children with rhythm sticks accompany as you play the recording; the rest of the class is "playing" index fingers.

i. Hold triangle for children to see. Repeat above steps a-c procedure to introduce the triangle.
j. Have the children decide which section would be most effective with the triangle. (assume B)
k. Ask if B is faster or slower than A. (slower) Compare the moods of the two sections and discuss the effect of tempo and instrumentation on these moods.
l. Tell the children that as the recording plays they should tap the rhythm stick sections (A) and clap the triangle (B) sections. Play the recording, helping them by tapping and clapping at appropriate times.
m. Tell those playing sticks and triangles to accompany the recording as others tap and clap.
n. On another day, introduce the remaining instruments, following this procedure:
   (1) Display the instrument. Tell the children what it is and show how it is played.
   (2) Play it for them.
   (3) Ask them to focus on its sound, noting the mood it expresses and the tone color it creates.
   (4) Distribute instruments to several children in the class.
   (5) Let them listen to "Shadows" to determine what section would best be accompanied by the instrument.
   (6) Let them play the instrument, accompanying the recording and other instruments selected.
o. An effective instrumentation for "Shadows" can be the following:

Section A

Rhythm Sticks

Tone Blocks

Maracas

Sand Blocks

Jingle Bells

Section B

Triangles

Drums

Cymbals

Finger Cymbals

3. Evaluating children's ability to hear differences in timbre of the various instruments
   a. Reproduce a Music Cue chart similar to the one on page 175 and distribute it.
   b. Tell the children you will play six different rhythm instruments. They are to shut their eyes. When you play the first, you will say "number one." They are to write 1 beside the picture of the instrument they heard; when you say "number two" they will write 2 beside a picture, and so on. (A cassette may be prepared in advance to facilitate this experience.)
   c. Play instruments and have children mark answers. Discuss their answers, focusing on differences in tone color.

How to Make Rhythm Instruments

Children on level III or middle school will enjoy a project in which they are challenged to make rhythm instruments. When money is not available for rhythm instruments, this is an especially fruitful project.

Drums

Round Cereal Box Drum: Make a finger painting on heavy paper, large enough to cover the top and bottom of a round cereal box. Cut two pieces to fit the top and bottom of the box and staple them on. Decorate the box by painting or covering it with colorful construction paper. Bind finger painting and construction paper together with mystic tape. Shellac to preserve.

Coffee Can Drum: Play on plastic top. Decorate sides, if desired.

Indian Water Drum: Fill a coffee can with water. Using heavily shellacked string, tightly bind a circular rubber head made from inner tube over the can. Decorate the drum with colorful yarns.

Steel Drums: Collect coffee cans with plastic tops of various sizes. Turn upside down and play on bottom of can.

Drumsticks

Make drumsticks from doweling, whittled sticks, broom handles, or pencils. To get a soft drumstick head, attach cotton or twine to one end.

Guiros

Cut two, twelve-inch sticks from broom handles or bamboo poles. Notch one stick every half inch.

Cymbals

Attach wooden knobs (cut from an old broom) to old kitchen saucepan covers.

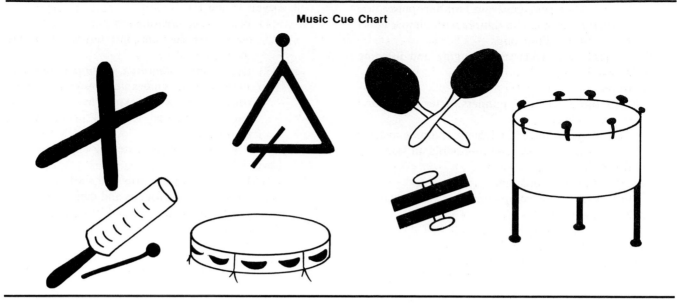

Tambourines

To the top of round, cardboard cereal box covers, attach buttons, bottle tops, or jingle bells. Aluminum pie plates may also be used.

Rhythm Sticks or Claves

Cut two, twelve-inch pieces of wood from a broom handle, doweling or bamboo poles. Sandpaper and paint these.

Sandblocks

Glue or staple sandpaper to two blocks of wood approximately 3 inches long and 1½ inch high.

Triangles

Suspend, then strike large nails or old door hinges.

Maracas

Insert sand, rice, peas, or seeds into any hollow container (juice can) that can be tightly shut and is small enough to be held easily in one hand.

Wind Chimes

Collect old, ice tray dividers. Strike gently in a vertical motion.

Experiences with Simple Melody Instruments

Experiences with simple melody instruments can begin in kindergarten or first grade. These instruments appeal to the small child. He can easily learn to play two- or three-note melodic figures taken from familiar songs, simple intervals, scale passages from songs, and even entire songs (when they are short and simple). This can be an enjoyable adjunct to both singing and listening experiences,

Figure 4.3

Photo of song bells courtesy of The World of Peripole, Inc., Browns Mills, N.J. 08015.

while it adds to conceptual understandings and achievement of behavioral objectives. Therefore, these experiences should continue and expand throughout the elementary grades.

In this section chromatic song bells will be used to represent the simple melody instruments. For the most effective use of these instruments, the following sequence of activities might be used:

1. First experiences (all in level I and related to singing activities)[1]
   a. Introduction to the instrument
   b. Playing short, repeated melodic figures, which move by step, from familiar songs

1. A helpful instruction book for song bells is *Make Music with the Bells* by McLaughlin and Dawley, published by the Carl Van Roy Company (distributed by Peripole, Inc.). Should a psaltery be available, the teacher may find *The Psaltery Book,* by Satis N. Coleman (distributed by Oscar Schmidt International Corporation) useful.

c. Playing scale passages from familiar songs

d. Playing short melodic figures with simple intervals, from familiar songs

2. Later experiences (related to singing and listening activities)

a. Level I

(1) Introduction of numbers, letter names, and syllables

(2) Playing longer and more complex melodic figures that include more difficult skips

b. Level II

(1) Playing chord roots

(2) Playing accompaniments to pentatonic songs

c. Levels II and III

(1) Playing and creating descants, counter melodies, introductions, interludes, and codas to songs

(2) Developing a chording accompaniment for songs using removable (resonator) bells (direct outgrowth of experiences with Autoharp and related to vocal chording and recorder)

(3) Playing themes for listening experiences

d. Level III

(1) Playing songs in thirds and sixths

(2) Accompanying rounds and canons

Figure 4.4
Pictures of Studio 49 Orff instruments, courtesy of Magnamusic-Baton, Inc., 10370 Page Industrial, St. Louis, Mo. 63132

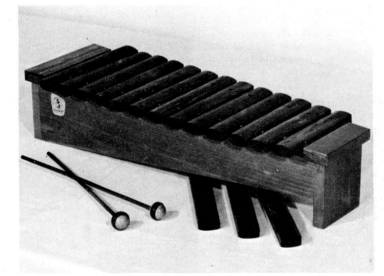

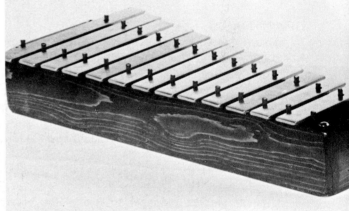

The teacher should explore the various approaches to find those most effective for these experiences. Approaches will vary with the age of the children and the nature of the experience. Generally, the child will respond most enthusiastically when:

1. He hears the instrument played in a musical way.
2. He explores the instrument, to discover its sound and how it makes this sound; to ascertain the various moods it creates and how they contrast with other instruments.
3. He, with help, produces a good tone quality and develops a technical facility, proceeding at his own pace.
4. He plays the instrument in various activities: as a solo; as an accompaniment to singing, rhythmic, and listening activities; in an ensemble with others.
5. He senses the teacher's respect for and enjoyment of the musical value of the instrument.

Introducing the Song Bells: Level I

Materials Needed
1. A set of chromatic song bells
2. A copy of "Chatter with the Angels"
3. Illustration depicting patterns

Instrumental Activity
Playing the song bells

Related Musical Activity
Singing

Conceptual Understandings
1. A melody may have a repeated tonal pattern.
2. Melodies may move up or down, by step or skip.

Behavioral Objectives
1. To hear a short melody and repeat it
2. To play simple passages on melody instruments

Related Arts
Observing patterns in the visual arts (using fig. 4.5)

Procedure
1. Exploring the song bells
   a. Show the class the song bells. (Hold song bells vertically with the high notes at the top so children can more easily visualize high and low concepts.)
   b. Ask these, or similar questions:
      (1) Does anyone know the name of this instrument?
      (2) How many white keys does it have?
      (3) How many black keys?
   c. Play a short melody on song bells. Ask class what the sound reminds them of.

(1) Is the tone loud or soft?
(2) Is it sweet or harsh?
(3) Is it like a clock or a bell?
(4) Is it like a butterfly or an elephant?
   d. Demonstrate how the mallet bounces off the keys, suggesting that children practice in the air as you play the song bells.
   e. Ask for a volunteer to play the white keys.
   f. Ask for a volunteer to play the black keys.
   g. Ask for a volunteer to play all the keys going up. (Ask the class to follow the rising pitch level by moving their hands in an upward direction as the child plays.)
   h. Ask the class what other direction can be played. (going down) Select a volunteer to play descending notes as the class follows the downward movement with their hands.
   i. Select a volunteer to play the keys going up and down as the class indicates the pitch levels with their hands.
2. Focusing on patterns through the visual arts
   a. Ask the children if they know what a pattern is. (something repeated)
   b. Ask them to name some things in print that have patterns. (material for dresses, curtains, linoleum, other floor coverings, sneakers) Encourage children to find patterns in the room.
   c. Ask them to name patterns in their living habits. (going to bed at a certain hour, getting up, eating, going to school, and so on)
   d. Ask them to name patterns in sound. (Songs have repeated melodies and rhythms. Chants have repeated phrases. When they play rhythm instruments, they often repeat rhythm patterns.)
   e. Ask if they can think of patterns in movement (for example, repeated steps made in interpretive movement or in folk dancing).
   f. Display the following, or a similar illustration:

Figure 4.5
Patterns photograph by Lois Raebeck

Chatter with the Angels

With Spirit

Negro Folk Song
Traditional Words

1. Chat-ter with the an - gels soon in the morn - ing, Chat-ter with the an - gels in that land! Chat-ter with the an - gels soon in the morn - ing, Chat-ter with the an - gels, Join that band! I hope to join that band and chat-ter with the an - gels all day long! I hope to join that band and chat-ter with the an - gels all day long!

2. March with the angels, etc.
3. Dance with the angels, etc.
4. Skip with the angels, etc.

Used by permission of American Book Company.

g. Tell them this is a picture of material for a dress. Ask what is repeated to make a pattern. (the daisy)

h. Ask children why we like patterns in so many areas of our lives—helping them to see that patterns, by repeating something we like, give meaning and focus.

3. Learning to play a three-note melodic pattern in a familiar song, "Chatter with the Angels" Children should know the song before this experience is introduced.

a. Review the song. As the last three notes are sung (AGF) emphasize the direction of the pattern by moving your hand downward. Ask the children to join you.

b. Ask the children how many times this pattern occurred in the song. If necessary, sing the song again, having them count the times the pattern is sung. (four)

c. Mark the first note on the board and ask a volunteer to draw the second and third.
   Teacher's mark _____
   Child's marks   _____
                                    _____

d. Ask the class:
   (1) Are the three notes in this melodic pattern close together or far apart? (close)
   (2) Do they move by step or skip? (step)
   (3) Do they move up or down? (down)

e. Tell children you will play the first note on the song bells and then ask someone to play the last

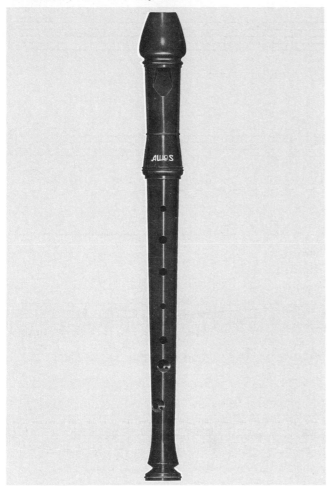

two notes. Play the first note. Select a volunteer to play the last two notes.

f. Have a volunteer play all three notes.

g. Sing the first verse with the class as a child plays the three-note melodic pattern at the end of each line.

h. Select other children to play the three notes for the second, third, and fourth verses.

Experiences with a Recorder

Experiences with the recorder are usually most valuable when initiated in the middle of the third grade. The child of this age is ready for the challenge and opportunity for musical growth he receives through music-making in this exciting new way.

Children invariably respond with enthusiasm when they discover they can play a familiar tune or tongue the fast passages of the *William Tell* Overture. At these times, too, they demonstrate new abilities: use of the ear in the selection or rejection of notes that create the mel-

ody; new awareness of contrasts in rhythm, melody, and tempo. All skills develop in the best possible way, from feeling, hearing, seeing, and playing.

For these reasons, all children in the elementary school should have the opportunity to play the recorder. Supplying children with an instrument and instruction book need not be a problem. When parents know the aims and objectives of the program, they are usually willing to purchase the instrument and book, both of which are inexpensive. In addition, school administrators will often provide funds for children who cannot afford these materials.

Making the most of this opportunity for musical growth requires careful planning, which allows for experiences that are integrated with singing and listening activities as well as those that focus on the instrument. Through this two-faceted approach, the child puts his newfound information and skill into functional usage— playing the same notes in new patterns and varied rhythms in familiar songs or in themes heard later in listening experiences. Such an application of information and skill helps the child focus on pitch relationships. By coupling his rhythm and pitch understandings, he develops skill in music reading.

What steps should be included in a procedure for teaching children the recorder? The following, which is only one of many possible approaches, should be developed over a period of months. Ample time should be allotted for children to consolidate each new concept by using it in many different songs.

1. Teaching the class to sing songs from available series, which can be used later to transfer technical information learned on recorder to singing activities.
2. Introducing the recorder to the child.
   a. How to hold it
   b. How to produce a good tune
   c. How to play notes B, A, and G and songs using these notes
3. Relating information to singing experiences by having children play sections of familiar songs containing notes B, A, and G.
4. Teaching the half note rhythmically and a song on the recorder incorporating the half note. (Similar experiences should be given to introduce eighth notes, dotted half notes, and whole notes as they appear in songs.)
5. Teaching high C, by using a song that combines it with B, A, and G, such as "Soaring Jets."
6. Relating the new knowledge to singing activities by having the class play sections of a familiar song containing high C.
7. Teaching high D by using songs (such as, "The Old Gray Goose") that combine this with other notes previously taught.

Soaring Jets

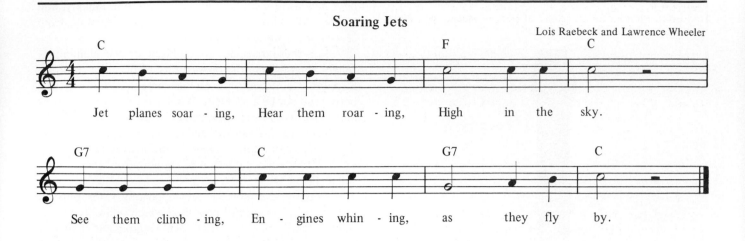

Lois Raebeck and Lawrence Wheeler

Jet planes soar - ing, Hear them roar - ing, High in the sky.

See them climb - ing, En - gines whin - ing, as they fly by.

The Old Gray Goose
(Go Tell Aunt Rhody)

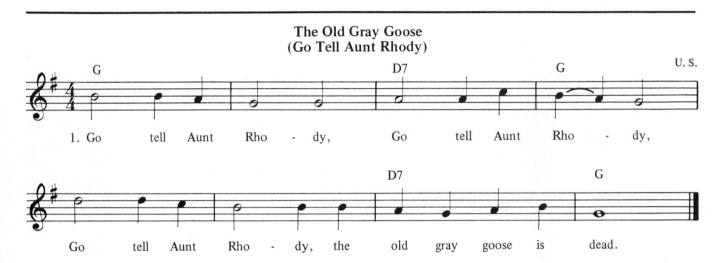

U. S.

1. Go tell Aunt Rho - dy, Go tell Aunt Rho - dy,

Go tell Aunt Rho - dy, the old gray goose is dead.

2. The one she was saving
   To make a feather bed.

3. She died in the mill pond,
   Standing on her head.

4. The goslings are crying,
   Because the goose is dead.

5. The gander is weeping,
   Because the goose is dead.

Adapted from arrangement from *Heritage Songster* by Dallin and Dallin, © 1966 by Wm. C. Brown Company Publishers, Dubuque, Iowa. (in public domain)

8. Consolidating all technical information by having the class play many songs or sections of songs using this information.
9. Teaching new notes, E, D, C, and F and songs using these notes.
10. Teaching the C scale and a song using the C scale.
11. Teaching B♭ and F♯ and songs using these notes.

Later experiences can continue into the fourth, fifth, and sixth grades and can include these:

1. Continuing to learn songs on recorder, which expand knowledge and skill
2. Using the recorder to learn new songs
3. Using the recorder to enrich singing, through playing or creating interludes, codas, and descants
4. Using the recorder to support part-singing
5. Playing themes to enrich listening activities
6. Creating songs

The following guidelines may be helpful to the teacher making use of the available elementary song series to find songs containing tonal groups for each stage of learning to play the recorder:

1. All elementary songbooks available should be used in order to obtain adequate material.
2. Except when the entire song is played, songs selected should have short, repeated melodic figures or phrases that can easily be played.
3. Complicated rhythmic or melodic patterns should be avoided unless children have the skill to play them. Songs can be shortened.
4. New notes and note values should be applied to many songs before proceeding to more advanced concepts.
5. Songs should relate to the ability, interest, and skill of the class.

Introducing the Recorder: Level II

Materials Needed
1. Recorder for each child
2. Instruction book for each child
3. Copies of "Mr. B, Mr. A, and Mr. G" and "Old MacDonald"

Instrumental Activity
Playing the recorder

Related Musical Activity
Singing

Conceptual Understandings
1. A melody may move up or down by step or skip or it may stay on the same level.
2. These durations are related to one another:

$$| \ = \ \gamma \qquad \quad \downarrow = \ | \ |$$

Behavioral Objectives
1. To begin to hear direction and durations in a melody
2. To play the notes B, A, and G on the recorder
3. To play a simple song on the recorder
4. To play phrases of a familiar song on the recorder

Related Arts
The teacher may want to plan an experience with related arts similar to others suggested throughout the book.

Procedure
1. Introducing the recorder
   a. Prior to discussion and initiation of the recorder program, invite children from the fourth, fifth, or sixth grade to play several selections on the recorder.
   b. At a later date, demonstrate the instrument in class to arouse children's interest. Discuss these questions:
      (1) How many holes does it have? (eight—seven on top, one on the bottom)
      (2) Did you notice which end I blew? (mouthpiece)
      (3) How did I change the notes? (by covering holes with fingers)
      (4) Did I use more fingers for high notes or for low notes? (low)
      (5) What song would you like me to play? (Suggest several you know.)
   c. Have recorders and instruction books ready for distribution. Before distributing, clarify the following through discussion:
      (1) The need to place names on books and recorders.
      (2) Rules for playing the recorder in the classroom. Establish the following:
         (a) Recorders are to be played only at times agreed upon by teacher and class.
         (b) Recorders are to be taken home only at times agreed upon by teacher and class.
   d. Ask children *not* to open boxes containing recorders until told to do so.
   e. Distribute recorders and books. Ask children to write their names on books immediately.
   f. Ask them to remove recorders from boxes and place them on their desks.

Figure 4.7
Fingering chart for the soprano recorder, two octaves.

fingering chart for soprano recorder

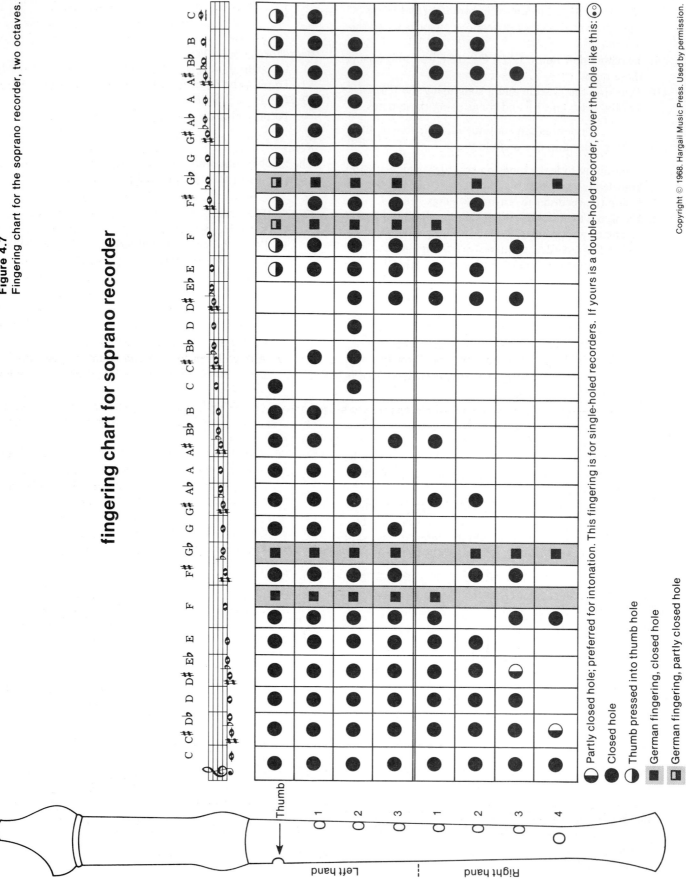

◖ Partly closed hole; preferred for intonation. This fingering is for single-holed recorders. If yours is a double-holed recorder, cover the hole like this: ⦿

◖ Partly closed hole

● Closed hole

◑ Thumb pressed into thumb hole

■ German fingering, closed hole

▣ German fingering, partly closed hole

g. Ask them to place their left hands behind their backs. Explain when they pick up their recorders they are to grasp the small end with the right hand. Check to be certain children are holding their recorders properly.

(Because of the importance of establishing proper habits for holding and playing the recorder in initial experiences, and because of children's individual differences in coordination, this step must be detailed so that children are not confused. If they establish good habits in the beginning experiences, they will learn each new skill more easily. Otherwise, successive skills may become too difficult and children may become discouraged and lose interest.)

h. Ask children to cover the single hole on the back of the recorder with their left-hand thumb. Check to make certain all children are doing this correctly.

i. Ask children to leave thumbs of left hand over single hole on back and place their left hand pointer fingers over the first hole on top.

j. Ask children to say the word "doo" softly.

k. Ask the class to put the recorders to their lips and say "doo" softly as they blow.

l. Place B on the board. Ask children around which line this note is written, what kind of a note it is, and the name of the note. (third line, quarter note, B)

m. Add two additional quarter-note B's, a quarter rest, and the time signature to the B on the board.

n. Ask how many B's there are on the board (three) and the name of the rest on the last beat. Explain, if necessary, that the rest indicates silence and that the quarter note and rest each get one beat in 4/4 meter.

o. Ask children to count "one, one, one, one." When they have established a steady rhythm, play the measure several times, then signal the class to stop counting.

p. Tell the class you would like them to play the notes as you did, while you point to notes on board and count.

q. Tell them not to start playing until you signal, "one, one, ready, play." Establish a steady rhythm, then signal the class to play. Count for them as you point to notes. When they can play the measure easily, signal them to stop.

r. Teach notes A and G in the same manner.

s. Add the notes A and G to the board until you have the composition "Mr. B, Mr. A, and Mr. G." (Chords have been added here for the teacher who wishes to accompany on Autoharp or guitar.)

t. Ask individual children the names of the last five notes and ask volunteers to play them.

u. Have the entire class play these last five notes several times. Establish the rhythm; signal them to start, count, and point to notes.

v. Ask children to clap and count as you play the song. Start them clapping and counting before you play.

w. Have the class play as you clap and count, establishing a steady rhythm, then signaling them to begin.

x. The class may enjoy dividing into groups, one playing, one singing, and later switching parts.

y. They may enjoy playing by ear the familiar song "Hot Cross Buns" using these notes.

2. Relating a tonal pattern, previously learned on the recorder, to the song, "Old MacDonald"

a. Have the class sing "Old MacDonald."

b. Write this on the board:

c. Have the class sing, using letter names, syllables, and rhythmic counting. Through discussion,

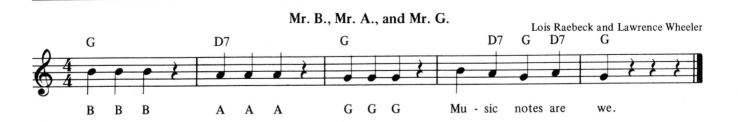

Mr. B., Mr. A., and Mr. G.

Lois Raebeck and Lawrence Wheeler

B B B A A A G G G Mu - sic notes are we.

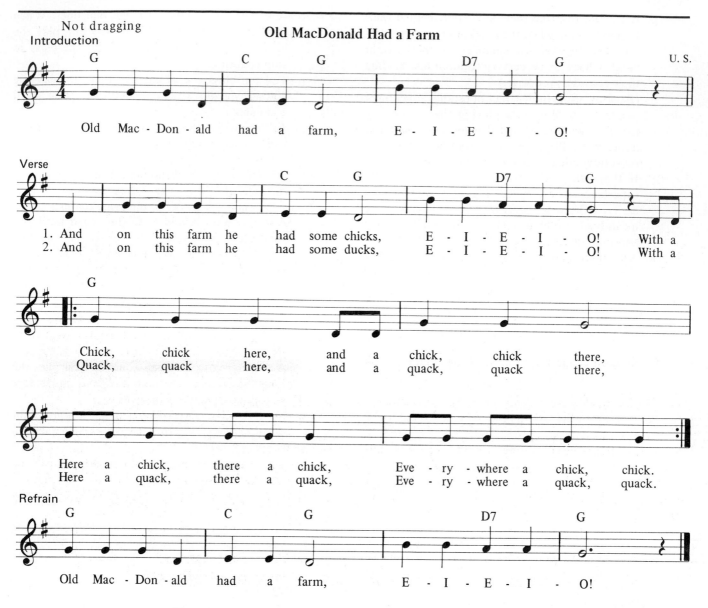

Old MacDonald Had a Farm

Sing the introduction only once. The first verse (without repeat) and refrain follow in order. After the second verse, repeat the section of the first verse between the repeat signs before the refrain. Additional verses may be added using the names and sounds of various farm animals, for example:

3. Turkey: gobble, gobble   4. Pig: oink, oink

After each new verse, sing the parts of all previous verses between the repeat signs in reverse order before singing the refrain. Following the last verse and all repeated sections, sing the refrain louder and slower for the final time.

Arranged from *Heritage Songster* by Dallin and Dallin, © 1966 by Wm. C. Brown Company Publishers, Dubuque, Iowa. (in public domain)

emphasize that two quarter notes equal one half note. Ask what the little figure after the half note is. (a half rest, two beats in 4/4 meter)

d. Ask to what words we sing these notes in "Old MacDonald." (E-I-E-I-O)
e. Ask children how many times they hear this pattern in the song. (three times)
f. Ask for volunteers to play the pattern on the recorder at appropriate times as the class sings.
g. Repeat, letting other children play the pattern.

Experiences with Accompanying Instruments

What are accompanying instruments? Although there is an impressive list of such instruments, the following are most often used in the elementary school:

Autoharp
Ukulele: classroom use is an outgrowth of club activity.
Guitar: classroom use is an outgrowth of club activity.
Piano: most suggestions for Autoharp, ukulele, guitar, and resonator bells can be adapted for piano.
Resonator bells or xylophones
Orff-type instruments

How does the teacher initiate the child's first experiences in playing these instruments? Accompanying instruments are probably best introduced in the most natural and obvious way—to accompany singing. With this as his initiation the child gradually becomes aware of the sight and sound of each instrument, and he feels at ease as he learns to play them. Experiences with any accompanying instrument will be most successful when the child is allowed to proceed at his own pace in these areas:

1. Exploring the instrument
2. Learning to play simple, one-chord accompaniments
3. Adding more chords and more complex rhythmic patterns gradually

The Autoharp

Autoharp chords are changed by pressing buttons. Because it is portable, inexpensive, and played easily, the Autoharp is an excellent accompanying instrument and will be used in this book, along with the guitar, to represent the accompanying instruments.

The teacher's greatest problem with the Autoharp will usually be that all children want to play the one available instrument. This problem, however, need not be too difficult if the teacher keeps each step simple, so that children can respond quickly and successfully, thus eliminating long, frustrating waiting periods as a child struggles to master a skill beyond his ability. In addition, such a method of proceeding allows for frequent successful participation for all children.

Figure 4.8
The term Autoharp (R) is a registered trademark, in the United States and Canada, of Oscar Schmidt International, Inc. Autoharps are made by O.S.I., Garden State Rd., Union, N.J. 07083.

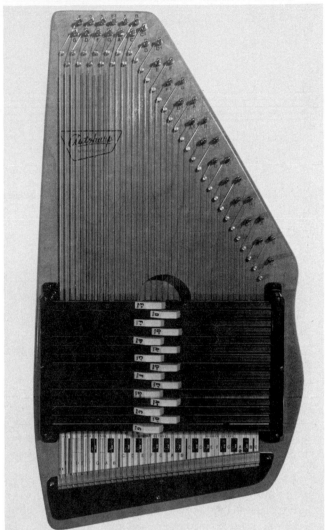

What is a possible sequence of experiences for children to explore the Autoharp? One plan might be:

1. Level I
   a. Introducing the Autoharp
   b. Learning to strum as the teacher presses chord buttons and the class sings
   c. Learning to press button for one-chord songs as another child strums
2. Level II
   a. Learning to press button and strum one-chord songs as the class sings
   b. Learning to press chord buttons for two-chord songs as another child strums
   c. Learning to press buttons and strum two chords as the class sings

See-Saw, Margery Daw

Old Rhyme

See - saw, Mar - ger - y Daw,

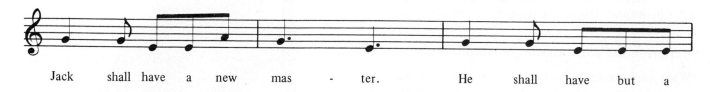

Jack shall have a new mas - ter. He shall have but a

pen - ny a day, be - cause he won't work an - y fas - ter.

3. Level III
   a. Learning to press chord buttons for three-chord songs as another child strums
   b. Learning to press buttons and strum three-chord songs as the class sings

After the child has had some experience in accompanying, the teacher should use this excellent opportunity to expand the child's understanding of chords and chord relationships in songs. To do this, she should give him two kinds of experiences in playing chordal accompaniments:

1. Experience in following chord markings found above the music of many songs in the elementary series
2. Experience in discovering for himself which chords can be used to accompany a song

With these experiences and the mastery of the skills previously suggested, conceptual understandings and achievement of behavioral objectives will expand and the child will participate successfully in another area of musical activity.

Introducing the Autoharp: Level I

Materials Needed
1. Autoharp
2. Copy of "See-Saw, Margery Daw"

Instrumental Activity
Playing the Autoharp

Related Musical Activity
Singing

Conceptual Understanding
Music consists not only of melody and rhythm, but of tones sounded simultaneously and heard as an accompaniment.

Behavioral Objective
To strum the Autoharp in rhythm, as the teacher or another child presses buttons

Related Arts
The teacher may want to use an experience with the visual arts, focusing on texture, found elsewhere in the book.

Procedure
1. Learning to strum Autoharp as teacher presses chord buttons
   a. Have the class sing "See-Saw, Margery Daw" as you accompany on the Autoharp.
   b. Ask volunteers to demonstrate the motion your hand makes as you play Autoharp.
   c. Ask the class if they would like to try strumming in the air. Suggest they all strum at the same time, with you, making long, steady strokes.
   d. When they can strum easily in rhythm, have them pretend they have Autoharps on their desks, which they strum as they sing and you accompany.

e. Ask the class if the Autoharp sounded the same as their singing. If not, what was different? Help the children focus on the concept that music consists not only of melody and rhythm, but of tones sounded simultaneously and heard as an accompaniment.

f. Select a volunteer to strum the Autoharp. Before beginning, remind him to strum steadily. Have him practice. If necessary, help him by strumming in the air or by gently guiding his arm.

g. Select other volunteers to strum the Autoharp.

h. After many children have tried it, select one to strum as you press chord buttons and sing with the class.

Introducing the Guitar

No music program in the elementary school can be complete today without some use of the guitar. Long an instrument used to convey the folk tales, feelings, and frustrations of an occasional troubadour, the guitar has now become the instrument accepted by today's youth as their musical medium of self-expression.

There are many kinds of guitars, all requiring a slightly different technique and adjustment. For beginning experiences the classic model (round hole, nylon strings, wide neck) is preferable, since its nylon strings are easier to press, and the wide neck leaves more space between the strings for fingers of the right hand to fit when playing finger-style. One or two guitars of this type should be available for classroom use.

What place does the guitar have in the music program? Students on level II will enjoy tuning the guitar to two tones (C and G or D and A) and using it to strum accompaniments to one-chord songs or provide a bordun accompaniment in an Orff orchestration. Use of the capo makes it possible to play in several other keys.

Children on level III will enjoy joining a guitar club in which they learn to play simple accompaniments using the regular tuning. This activity will be treated in the final chapter of this book.

Introducing the Guitar: Level II

Materials Needed
1. Guitar
2. Copy of "Poor Tom"

Instrumental Activity
Playing the guitar

Related Musical Activities
1. Singing
2. Reading

Conceptual Understandings
1. Music consists not only of melody and rhythm but of tones sounded simultaneously and heard as an accompaniment to a melody.
2. Some songs can be accompanied by one chord; others require two, three, or more chords.

Behavioral Objective
To play a simple accompaniment to singing, using a guitar

Related Arts
The teacher may want to use an experience with the visual arts focusing on texture, found elsewhere in this book.

Procedure
1. Becoming acquainted with the guitar
   a. Point out and discuss the parts of the guitar listed below, eliciting any information children may have and making certain they understand the purpose of each part.
      (1) Tuning pegs: each string is attached to a peg. When the peg is tightened, the pitch of the string is made higher; when loosened, the pitch is made lower.
      (2) Frets: Each fret marks a place where, if a finger is pressed against the string and the string is plucked, a specific pitch will sound. Frets are placed one half step apart.
      (3) Neck and its fingerboard: The neck holds the fingerboard and the frets.
      (4) Six strings: The strings are tuned to E, A, D, G, B and E. By pressing a string at any one point, the string is made shorter, the amount of vibrating material is changed and the pitch is raised.
      (5) The sound hole: The sound hole allows the tone produced by the vibrating strings to enter the body of the guitar, where it is magnified.
      (6) Sounding board: The sounding board picks up the vibrations made by strings and helps magnify the tone.
      (7) Bridge: Strings are fastened at one end to the bridge.
   b. Have children count the strings.
   c. Have children find and play the string with the lowest pitch.
   d. Have children find and play the string with the highest pitch.
   e. Have children find the tuning peg connected to
      (1) Lowest pitched string (E)
      (2) Highest pitched string (E)
      (3) Strings in between (A, D, G, and B)

Figure 4.9
Holding the guitar, photograph by David Rosenthal

2. Learning how to hold the guitar
   A straight-backed chair with no arms should be available.
   a. Ask a volunteer to help demonstrate holding the guitar. Have him sit in a chair, holding the guitar, as follows:
      (1) The right knee is crossed over the left knee.
      (2) The guitar rests on the right knee; the fingerboard points to the left; the curve of the guitar fits over the right thigh; the left hand

curves behind the fingerboard above the nut; the ball of the left thumb is at the back of the neck of the guitar, above the first fret; the right arm is crooked, with the elbow resting on the body of the guitar just above the sounding hole; the right hand is at right angles to the strings, above the sounding hole; the guitar is pressed close to the chest.
   b. Let other children practice holding the guitar. Stress the importance of correct position.
3. Learning to play a one-chord song, "Poor Tom", with a D and A tuning, using a capo.
   a. Tune the guitar strings as follows:

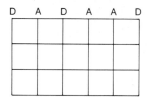

   b. Place the capo just below the second fret. (Below on a guitar refers to the direction toward the tuning pegs.)
   c. Ask children to strum with you as you sing the song. Strum your right thumb downward across all strings as follows:

   | | | | |

   strum   strum   strum   strum

   d. Ask for a volunteer to strum as the class sings with you. Repeat, letting different children accompany until the class knows the song.
   e. Give the class other experiences accompanying one-chord songs: "Hey, Ho! Nobody Home" (in chapter 6), "Zum Gali Gali" (in chapter 3), "Shalom Chaverim."

Poor Tom

Martha Grubb

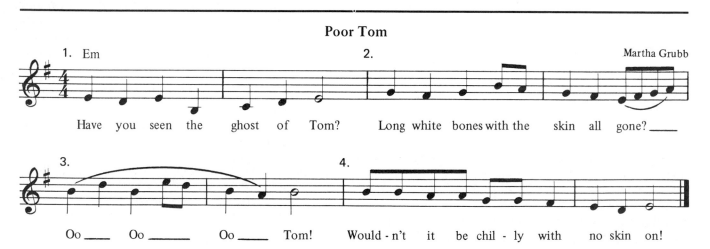

From *101 Rounds for Singing*, published by World Around Songs. Used by permission.

Figure 4.10
Piano learning lab, photo used by permission of Musitronic,
Inc., Owatonna, Minnesota 55060

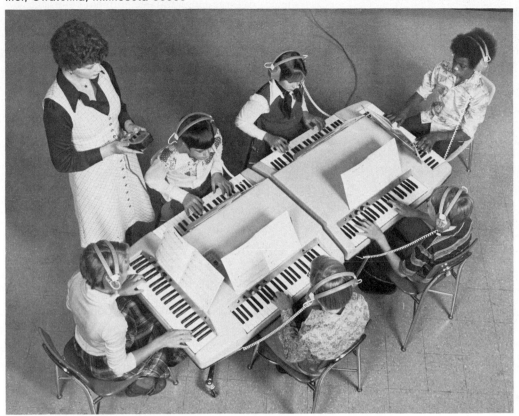

Piano in the Classroom

Classroom piano instruction presents many challenges to the teacher. In one classroom there may be children working on the first level as well as the fourth level, children with little or no knowledge of melodic and rhythmic notation, and children with considerable understanding from experience with the piano or other instruments. How does a teacher handle this diversity of abilities?

One answer is to use learning contracts or learning packets. For the teacher who wants to give a child the opportunity to work at his own pace and select his own objectives, methods, and materials for specific musical projects, the learning contract has value. A child may thus commit himself to a specific project, draw up (with help from the teacher) and sign a contract, and proceed on his own level.

For the teacher who wants to give children the opportunity to work on musical objectives individually, at their own pace, and on their own level, but in relation to a sequentially structured program, learning packets may be preferable. With these each musical concept is first presented in a group situation, then pursued individually by using a learning packet. The packet relates directly to the concept and contains all the necessary information

and materials: prerequisite learning, behavioral objectives, time limit, equipment needed, materials needed, optional bonus activities, and evaluation procedure.

Teachers may create their own learning packets by finding materials from many sources. (Songs may be cut from old music books, pasted on cards, and laminated, for example.) A system of marking packets according to their place in the sequential program may be devised. (The simplest level can be indicated on materials for each packet by small green dots, for example, with other levels being assigned other colors.)

Six levels of difficulty for learning packets for supplementing a program of classroom piano could be the following:

1. Notes with a range of a fifth, using simple rhythm patterns
2. Notes within an octave, with simple rhythm patterns
3. Songs with F♯
4. Songs using B♭
5. Songs in 6/8 meter with more complicated rhythms
6. Songs with chromatic alterations and complicated rhythmic patterns

Learning Packet for Piano Level II

With modification, this learning packet can also be used for melody bells, recorder, Autoharp, ukulele, or guitar.

Prerequisite Learning

1. Understanding of these durational relationships

2. Understanding of the melodic relationship of notes on the treble-clef staff
3. Knowing (from experiences with melody bells) where to find notes from the treble clef on the piano

Behavioral Objective

Learning to play songs, within a range of five notes, with rhythmic and melodic accuracy

Time Limit

Three or four class periods of thirty minutes each (less, if possible)

Equipment Needed

1. Piano lab with earphones
2. Plain paper
3. Manuscript paper
4. Pencil

Required Materials

1. Songs
   a. "Hot Cross Buns"
   b. "Merrily We Roll Along"
   c. "Fais Do Do"
   d. "The Old Gray Goose"
   e. "Good News"
2. Major scale formula sheet
3. Chord-construction sheet

Optional Bonus Activities

1. On the piano learn the melody of "Grandma Grunts," "When the Saints Go Marching In," and "Bought Me a Cat." (These songs are included in the packet.)
2. Write and play C, F, or G major scale. (See major scale formula sheet on scale construction.)
3. Write and play C, F, or G chord. (See chord-construction sheet.)
4. Create a song (words are optional).
5. Write words and music of a commercial heard on television.

Evaluation Procedure

1. Record on cassette a performance for the class of the melody of three songs and one optional bonus activity. Discuss the problems involved in these activities.
2. Give an oral or taped report on how scales are constructed by half and whole steps. Include in your report why F♯ is used in the G scale and B♭ in the F scale.
3. Explain how a chord is built from notes in a scale.
4. Prepare a written summary of what you have learned from the activities in this packet.
5. Indicate the grade you think you should receive for the project and have a conference with your teacher.

Proceed to learning packet for piano, level III.

Chord Construction

Chords are built upward, in thirds, on every degree of the scale. If a chord is built on a line, the two notes above will be on the next two lines; if a chord is built on a space, the two notes above will be on the next two spaces.

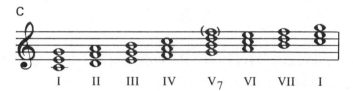

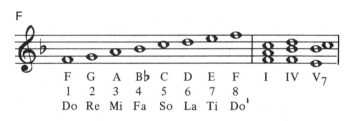

These three primary chords (I, IV, and V, in the keys of C, G, and F) are used to accompany many songs in the elementary series. These chords are indicated in most of the elementary songbooks to facilitate children's learning to play the Autoharp.

Evaluating the Ability to Recognize the Sound of Song Bells, Recorder, Autoharp, Guitar, and Piano

1. Reproduce and distribute the following chart. (The teacher may want to eliminate any instruments from the Music Cue chart that children have not studied.)

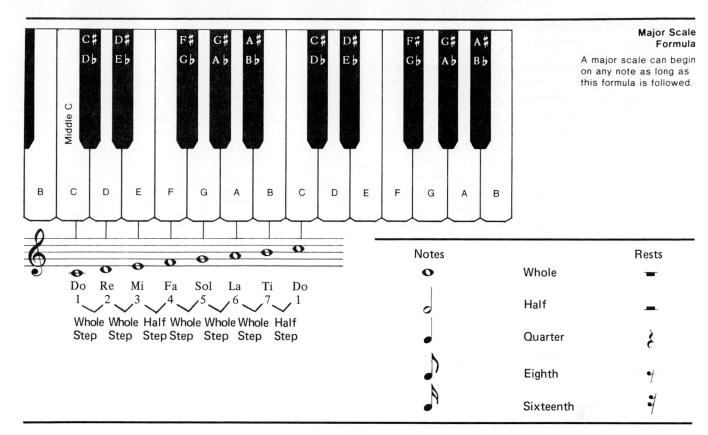

A major scale can begin on any note as long as this formula is followed.

Middle C

B C D E F G A B C D E F G A B

C# D# F# G# A# C# D# F# G# A#
Db Eb Gb Ab Bb Db Eb Gb Ab Bb

Do Re Mi Fa Sol La Ti Do
1   2   3   4   5   6   7   1
Whole Whole Half Whole Whole Whole Half
Step Step Step Step Step Step Step

Notes		Rests
𝅝	Whole	▬
𝅗𝅥	Half	▬
♩	Quarter	𝄽
♪	Eighth	𝄾
𝅘𝅥𝅯	Sixteenth	𝄿

Music Cue Chart

1.	Song bells	Recorder	Autoharp	Piano	Guitar
2.	Song bells	Recorder	Autoharp	Piano	Guitar
3.	Song bells	Recorder	Autoharp	Piano	Guitar
4.	Song bells	Recorder	Autoharp	Piano	Guitar
5.	Song bells	Recorder	Autoharp	Piano	Guitar
6.	Song bells	Recorder	Autoharp	Piano	Guitar
7.	Song bells	Recorder	Autoharp	Piano	Guitar
8.	Song bells	Recorder	Autoharp	Piano	Guitar

2. Discuss each instrument, focusing on its unique sound and how the sound differs from other instruments. Tell children to close their eyes and listen as you play one of these instruments. When you have finished, they are to open their eyes and circle the instrument heard, after number 1. On the recorder, play the melody listed for number 1. Have children circle their answer. Continue, following the same procedure, for numbers 2–8. (The teacher may want to use recordings or prepare a cassette for this experience.)

(1) Recorder (melody 1)
(2) Guitar (accompaniment 1)
(3) Song bells (melody 2)
(4) Autoharp (accompaniment 2)
(5) Piano (melody 1)
(6) Guitar (accompaniment 2)
(7) Song bells (melody 1)
(8) Autoharp (accompaniment 1)

Melody 1

Melody 2

Accompaniment 1
Play these chordal progressions:

D   D   G   G A_7 A_7 D

Accompaniment 2
Play these chordal progressions:

A   A   D   D E_7 E_7 A

Experiences with Band and Orchestral Instruments

What is a violin? What does it look like? To what section of the orchestra does it belong? How is its sound produced? How does one change the pitch? What moods can it evoke? Do you recognize its sound? The child will eagerly answer these questions as he gains familiarity with band and orchestral instruments in a relaxed and enjoyable way.

His familiarity with instruments begins in kindergarten and primary grades as he hears interesting recordings that introduce these instruments. By hearing many recordings the child will automatically begin to discriminate between the sounds made by each instrument. As he begins to recognize the violin, the trumpet, and the oboe, as well as other instruments, he will enjoy identifying these instruments as he hears them in music-listening experiences.

When the child can identify different instruments, he will respond enthusiastically the invitation to participate in firsthand experiences with an instrument that he can see, hear, and perhaps touch. This experience, if offered by a child from an upper grade who can talk about as well as play the instrument, has added meaning, since it then becomes evident that playing an instrument is something the child himself might someday achieve.

The child entering the fourth grade often has the opportunity to study an instrument with a music specialist and to play in a band or orchestra. It is at this age that he is ready and eager to make a thorough study of each instrument of the band and orchestra and to find the answers to questions of pitch changes, tone production, and tone qualities. It is at this age, too, that he enjoys exploring the use of instruments to express varied moods in more abstract music which he experiences in his listening activities. The teacher should prepare to meet this curiosity with experiences which allow the child to answer these questions as completely as possible.

Note: Instrumental instruction is generally assigned to a music specialist.

Introducing Band and Orchestra Instruments: Level II

Materials Needed
1. Four large cardboards on which pictures of each family of the orchestra have been placed. (Do not use the names of instruments, only pictures.)

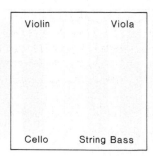

Violin	Viola
Cello	String Bass

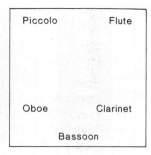

Piccolo	Flute
Oboe	Clarinet
Bassoon	

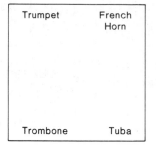

Trumpet	French Horn
Trombone	Tuba

Snare Drum	Tympani
Bass Drum	Other Percussion

2. *Instruments of the Orchestra,* RCA Victor LES–6000, or a similar recording.
3. Any instruments available for demonstration.
4. Music Cue charts.

Related Musical Activity
Listening

Conceptual Understanding
Each instrument of the band and orchestra has a unique sound, which affects the mood and feelings expressed.

Behavioral Objective
To recognize differences in tone quality between the instruments of the band and orchestra

Related Arts
The teacher may wish to create an experience with related arts similar to that used in the introduction to rhythm instruments, in this chapter.

Procedure
1. Exploring the four sections of the orchestra
   a. Place the four cards where they can be seen by all children.
   b. Remind the class that the orchestra is divided into four sections: brass, strings, woodwinds, and percussion. Ask if someone would like to point out the card showing pictures of brass instruments. Select a volunteer. Select other volunteers to identify the other three sections.

c. Select a volunteer to name all the instruments of the brass section. Have the class identify those he fails to name. Select other volunteers to name the instruments of the other three sections.

d. Explain that the instruments are grouped together in sections because they have common physical characteristics. Generally their pitch and tone is produced and changed in the same way.

2. Examining how the tone is produced and the pitch changed

a. Explain that something must vibrate to produce a tone. Pitch is changed by either shortening (to raise pitch) or lengthening (to lower pitch) the vibrating substance.

b. Ask what vibrates on stringed instruments. (strings) If one is available, demonstrate by plucking a string and having the class observe its vibration.

c. Ask how the pitch is changed. (by pressing the strings against the fingerboard, at various points, with the fingers)

d. Ask which stringed instrument produces the highest notes and why. (the violin, because it has the shortest strings) Select a child to point to the violin. Ask which instrument makes the next highest tones (viola) and ask a child to point to it. Proceed similarly for the cello and stringed bass.

e. Ask the class if they can identify the sounds made by instruments of the string section. Tell them you will play a recording and, when they know which instrument is being played, to raise their hands. Tell the class you will select a child to point to the instrument playing. This child may continue pointing out various instruments (as you play various recordings) until he misses. He will then select another volunteer to take his place.

f. Play the recording of the instruments in the string section, until children readily recognize each instrument.

g. Proceed similarly for the other three sections of the orchestra. Bring to children's attention these facts:

Section	How Tone Is Produced	How Pitch Is Changed
Brass	Lips vibrate, causing the air being blown into the instrument to vibrate.	Press valves and tighten or loosen lips; either will change the length of the air column being blown into the instrument and thus change the pitch. Exception: the trombone slide is pushed out or pulled in, to lengthen or shorten the column of air.
Woodwinds	On the clarinet one reed vibrates and creates a vibrating column of air. On the oboe and bassoon, two reeds vibrate. The flute is actually more like a brass instrument but is in the woodwind family because it was originally made of wood.	Close the holes and lengthen the column of vibrating air, or open the holes and shorten the vibrating column of air.
Percussion	The surface, which is struck, vibrates.	Of all the members of the percussion section, the pitch of only the drums can be changed. By tightening or loosening the drumhead, the pitch is raised or lowered, except in the case of the tympani, where a pedal is used.

3. Evaluating children's ability to hear differences in tone quality between instruments of the orchestra

a. Distribute Music Cue charts.

b. Tell children you will play a recording of eight instruments. Tell them to circle the instrument they hear as you call "one," "two," and so on. Play each instrument's solo from the RCA Victor recording *Instruments of the Orchestra*

Music Cue Chart

1. Violin	Cello	Trumpet	Tuba
Flute	Clarinet	Snare drum	Bass drum
2. Violin	Cello	Trumpet	Tuba
Flute	Clarinet	Snare drum	Bass drum
3. Violin	Cello	Trumpet	Tuba
Flute	Clarinet	Snare drum	Bass drum
4. Violin	Cello	Trumpet	Tuba
Flute	Clarinet	Snare drum	Bass drum
5. Violin	Cello	Trumpet	Tuba
Flute	Clarinet	Snare drum	Bass drum
6. Violin	Cello	Trumpet	Tuba
Flute	Clarinet	Snare drum	Bass drum
7. Violin	Cello	Trumpet	Tuba
Flute	Clarinet	Snare drum	Bass drum
8. Violin	Cello	Trumpet	Tuba
Flute	Clarinet	Snare drum	Bass drum
9. Violin	Cello	Trumpet	Tuba
Flute	Clarinet	Snare drum	Bass drum
10. Violin	Cello	Trumpet	Tuba
Flute	Clarinet	Snare drum	Bass drum

Rhythmic Concepts

Level I

Materials Needed
1. Rhythm instruments
   a. Rhythm sticks, maracas, and triangles
   b. Enough other rhythm instruments so that each child has an instrument
2. Copy of "Going to a Party"
3. Three large, laminated charts, approximately twelve by eighteen inches, modeled after the following:

4. Opaque projector and screen, if used
5. Illustrations for related arts
6. Music Cue charts

Instrumental Activity
Playing rhythm instruments

Related Musical Activities
1. Bodily movement
2. Music reading

Conceptual Understandings
1. The rhythm of music is related to bodily movements: some music "walks," some "runs," some suggests "giant steps," and so on.
2. These durations (notes) are related:

Behavioral Objectives
1. To demonstrate ability to understand and notate the relationship between

2. To help create simple accompaniments, using rhythm instruments

Related Arts
Observing durational relationships found in visual objects, such as those in figure 4.11

Procedure
1. Using bodily movement to explore the relationship between the eighth, quarter, and half notes.
   a. Display three cards showing eighth, quarter, and half notes.
   b. If children know these notes, review them quickly, then proceed to section c of this exercise. If not, hold up each card and do the following:
      (1) Let children discuss it, focusing on what it reminds them of and how each note differs from the others. (For example, a quarter note looks like a golf club. It is unlike the eighth note because it has no flag, unlike the half note because it is filled in.)
      (2) Tell the name of each note.
      (3) Tell bodily movement associated with each note.

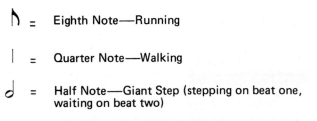

      (4) Have a child illustrate the bodily movement associated with each note, as you accompany him, using these or similar instruments:
         (a) Eighth notes—maracas
         (b) Quarter notes—rhythm sticks
         (c) Half notes—triangles
         Carefully maintain an exact pulsation, so the relationship between notes is apparent. Make certain child understands how to step the half note.
   c. Let other children demonstrate as you accompany. Select three children to be leaders for each note value.
   d. Divide the class into three groups: group one to walk, group two to run, group three giant step, as you accompany on selected instruments. Have the children line up behind their leaders. Give each leader the card representing his note value. (In order to allow groups to move freely without losing their designation, the teacher may distribute different colored ribbons to each group. For example, group one might wear yellow ribbons, group two red, group three blue.)
   e. Have children listen until they hear the accompaniment for their note, move until it stops, then "freeze."
   f. Play the walking accompaniment until walkers are moving easily in rhythm, then stop. Play

Figure 4.11
Three chocolate cakes, photograph by David Rosenthal

accompaniment for other notes, continuing long enough for children to have the feeling for the note. Continue, alternating notes, trying to "catch" children, until they respond easily.

2. Observing durational relationships, found in music, in visual objects
   a. Display figure 4.11 on a projector, cards, or draw it on the board.
   b. Have children describe it. (three chocolate cakes, all cut differently: in quarters, halves, and one is whole)
   c. Tell children the bottom cake, which is not cut, is a half note, and each time you point to it, they are to count "one-two." Tell them the middle cake, cut into two pieces, represents two quarter notes, and each time you point to that cake, they are to count "one-one." The top cake, which is cut into four pieces, represents eighth notes, to be counted "one and, one and."
   d. Point to each cake many times, initially counting with children, then gradually having them count alone.
   e. Ask children how many eighth notes it takes to make one quarter note. (two) How many eighth notes makes a half note? (four) How many quarter notes makes a half note. (two)

3. Exploring durational relationships between the quarter note, eighth note and half note by playing a game, using rhythm instruments
   a. Divide the class into three groups: one to play eighth notes (maracas); two, quarter notes (rhythm sticks or tone blocks); and three, half notes (triangles or finger cymbals).
   b. Write the following on the board, omitting the numbers and Kodaly counting symbols.

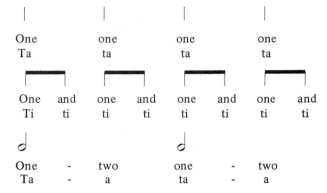

One	one	one	one
Ta	ta	ta	ta

One	and	one	and	one	and	one	and
Ti	ti	ti	ti	ti	ti	ti	ti

One	-	two	one	-	two
Ta	-	a	ta	-	a

   c. Have the children clap and count each.
   d. Tell the children playing rhythm sticks to play when you point to quarter notes; children playing maracas to play when you point to eighth notes; and children playing triangles to play when you point to half notes.
   e. Point to each line several times, changing order, until children can respond accurately and easily.
   f. Tell children you are going to make it more difficult. Write the following on the board, omitting the numbers.

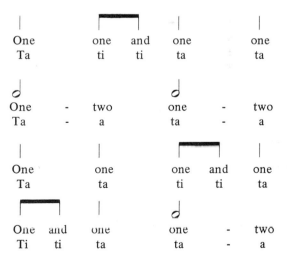

One	one	and	one	one
Ta	ti	ti	ta	ta

One	-	two	one	-	two
Ta	-	a	ta	-	a

One	one	one	and	one
Ta	ta	ti	ti	ta

One	and	one	one	-	two
Ti	ti	ta	ta	-	a

   g. Have children clap and count all lines, maintaining a steady beat.
   h. Tell children playing rhythm sticks to play each quarter note, children playing maracas to play

each eighth note, and children playing triangles to play each half note.

   i. Have children play patterns several times as you point to notes, until they can play easily, maintaining a steady beat.

4. Exploring durational relationships between quarter, eighth, and half notes by playing rhythm instruments to accompany a rhythmic dramatization

   a. Tell the class you will tell a story about children who went to a party. They are to tell you which used eighth, quarter, and half notes to get there.

      A group of children were playing in the school playground. They were talking, as they played, about a party at Betty's house. Betty lived about two blocks from the school, and as soon as the 3:30 bell rang, they would start for the party.

      As they were playing, John said to Jerry, "Let's go ahead. Mary, Joan, and the others are so slow!"

      "Great," said Jerry.

      "Well," said Joan, "I overheard what you said. You run ahead. We may walk slowly, but we take bigger steps, and we'll get there just as fast as you—you'll see! Besides, if you think we walk slowly, what about Bruce and Adrienne? We're much faster than they."

      Bruce and Adrienne didn't like what they heard. Immediately Bruce was at Joan's side. He was angry. He wanted to punch her, but he simply said, "What's your rush, big shot? The way you walk, you'd think you were going to a fire. You'll see, Adrienne and I will get there just as soon as you."

      Just then the 3:30 bell rang—and all the children took sides. Those who wanted to run lined up behind John and Jerry; those who wanted to walk, behind Joan and Mary; those who wanted to walk slowly, behind Bruce and Adrienne. And off they went.

   b. Ask the children which group would move to eighth notes, (the runners) quarter notes (walkers) and half notes (the slow walkers).

   c. Have volunteers demonstrate each type of movement, as you accompany.

   d. Select children to run to the party, some to walk and others to walk slowly. Have each group practice moving in the rhythm you play.

   e. Select volunteers to play accompaniments with you: a child playing maracas for runners (eighth notes); one playing rhythm sticks for walkers (quarter notes); another playing triangles for slow walkers (half notes).

   f. Group the instrument players near you, and the movers in a straight line at one end of the room. Remind them to listen and move toward Betty's house (at the other end of the room) when they hear their accompaniment. Tell the previous story. When you reach "And off they went," continue as follows:

First John, Jerry, and their friends ran off. (Play eighth notes on maracas, then stop. If children run faster than you play, stop them and have them run in exact rhythm to your beat.)

Next Joan, Mary and their friends began walking in a moderate tempo. (Play quarter notes on sticks, then stop.)

Next went the slow walkers—Bruce and Adrienne and their friends. (Play half notes on triangles, then stop.)

   g. Continue, alternating groups, playing the same number of measures for each, so that groups arrive at the other end of the room at approximately the same time.

   h. Discuss with the class. If all started at the same time, would they have arrived at the same time? (Yes, Although the half and quarter notes seem slower than the eighth, they are longer in duration—require larger steps—and therefore cover as much space as eighth notes.)

5. Evaluating children's ability to understand the relationship between these durations

   a. Reproduce and distribute this Music Cue chart.

Music Cue Chart

1.	$\mid$ $\mid$ $\mid$ $\mid$	♫ ♫ ♫ ♫	♩ ♩
2.	$\mid$ $\mid$ $\mid$ $\mid$	♫ ♫ ♫ ♫	♩ ♩
3.	$\mid$ $\mid$ $\mid$ $\mid$	♫ ♫ ♫ ♫	♩ ♩
4.	$\mid$ $\mid$ $\mid$ $\mid$	♫ ♫ ♫ ♫	♩ ♩
5.	$\mid$ $\mid$ $\mid$ $\mid$	♫ ♫ ♫ ♫	♩ ♩
6.	$\mid$ $\mid$ $\mid$ $\mid$	♫ ♫ ♫ ♫	♩ ♩

   b. Ask the class to listen carefully and after each number, circle the notes you play. Explain that instead of using a different instrument for each note you will use a drum for all.

   c. Using a drum, play one group of notes for number 1. Repeat, for all six numbers.

   d. Discuss the answers with children, clarifying any misunderstandings they have.

Instrumental Experiences That Focus on Rhythmic Concepts

Level I

Using Rhythm Instruments to Focus on Rhythm Patterns of Words
Question and Answer Improvisation

1. Children should have many experiences clapping, chanting, and playing the following on the drum: their names, favorite foods, television programs, and so on. (Make certain they articulate each syllable.)
2. Distribute rhythm instruments.
3. Explain the question-and-answer game. You will ask a question on the drum, and each child will have the opportunity to answer, on his instrument.
4. Chant the following, beating the exact rhythm of the words on the drum.

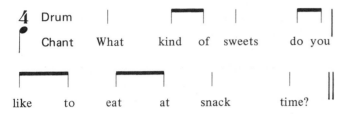

5. Ask volunteers to answer, making positive comments. Since this is a preparatory experience, children might give short answers: ice cream, licorice, chocolate cake, and so on. Later, ask children to give answers the same length as your question.

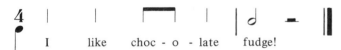

6. Give children additional experiences, using questions of interest to them. Eventually they will enjoy this in abstract form, as follows:

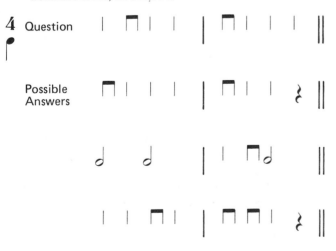

Questions should have a note value on the fourth beat of the second measure, answers end on the first or third beat of the second measure.

Level I

Focusing on Rhythm Patterns by Using Rhythm Instruments to Accompany a Chant
"Pit, Pat, Well-a-Day"

1. Distribute rhythm instruments. Tell children to listen, then echo, as you chant and clap the following:

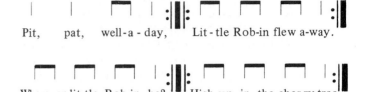

2. Tell children you will play a drum as you chant. Select a volunteer to echo on his instrument as the class chants with him.
3. Repeat, letting others play their instruments, individually, as the class chants the echo.
4. Ask for volunteers to join you, playing their instruments and chanting, as the rest of the class echoes. Add children to your part until parts are equally divided—half leading, chanting, and playing, half echoing.
5. When the class knows the rhyme, have them
   a. Form a circle, carrying instruments
   b. Step the basic beat in circle formation
   c. On your signal, begin chanting the rhyme
   d. Continue marching silently at conclusion of the rhyme
   e. On your next signal, say the rhyme inside as they play the word rhythms on instruments

Level I

Focusing on the Basic Beat by Using Rhythm Instruments to Accompany a Song
"Yankee Doodle"

1. Make certain that children know the first verse and chorus.
2. Distribute rhythm instruments. Group together children playing similar instruments.
3. Have the children sing, clapping on strong beats only.
4. Ask the class which part of the song would sound best as a solo. (the verse) Which would sound best played together. (the chorus)
5. Let the class decide which instruments will play the solos during verses. One class chose the following:

sand blocks	maracas	drums
triangles	tone blocks	cymbals

6. If possible, use a piano or recording for remainder of experience. Play "Yankee Doodle," while children play their choice of instruments during verses and the entire class plays accented beats during choruses.
7. Children will enjoy selecting a conductor to maintain steady rhythm.

Level I or II

Using Rhythm Instruments to Accompany Basic Bodily Movements

Before this experience children should have explored all basic bodily movements.

1. Display rhythm instruments.
2. List kinds of "walks" on the board. Ask what instrument would best accompany each, allowing children to discuss and experiment. Write instruments selected on the board.
   a. Walking slowly, when tired: large drum
   b. Walking quickly, late for school: rhythm sticks
   c. Walking lightly, like an elf: finger cymbals
   d. Walking like mother, high heels: rhythm sticks
   e. Walking like father, large strides: large drum
3. Ask children to clap as you play the instrument selected for each rhythm. Play each, emphasizing contrasts.
4. Select a child to play rhythm for the first walk, while several other children walk.
5. Select children to play each of the accompaniments as groups demonstrate different walks.
6. Encourage exploration of instrumental accompaniments for other basic bodily movements (running, jumping, etc.) in the same way.

Level II

Focusing on the Dotted Quarter by Playing a Song on the Recorder
"Marching Along"

1. Review the quarter note by counting and by playing rhythm sticks. Ask if anyone knows the name for these notes:

| *Sticks* | tap | tap | tap | tap | tap | tap | tap | tap |
| *Count* | one | one | one | one | one | one | one | one |

or

| | ta | ta | ta | ta | ta | ta | ta | ta |

2. Have a volunteer draw the note on the board:

3. Select volunteers to walk the quarter note rhythm as you play.

4. Tap and count a series of dotted quarter and eighth notes, tapping on "one," moving sticks down and to the left on the "dot" and tapping again on the "and."

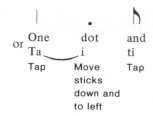

or	One	dot	and
	Ta	i	ti
	Tap	Move sticks down and to left	Tap

5. Ask the class what notes you tapped, and if anyone can draw them on the board. If necessary, explain: the dot increases the value of a note by one half. Thus, in 4/4 meter, a quarter note is held for one beat, a dotted quarter for a beat and a half.
6. Ask for volunteers to tap and count the pattern, then have the entire class count and clap the pattern.
7. Let children experiment with finding a "walk" that corresponds to the rhythm of the dotted quarter and the eighth. One group found:

| One | dot | and |
| Step with right foot | Bend right knee | Step lightly with left foot |

8. On the board write the words and music to "Marching Along."
9. Have the children clap and chant, using either number notation or Kodaly counting, then sing, using letter names and syllables.
10. Ask for volunteers to play the song on recorders. Then have the entire class play it.

Level II or III

Focusing on Rhythm Patterns in 4/4 Meter by Using Rhythm Instruments

1. Tell children to echo the rhythm patterns on page 199.
2. Distribute rhythm instruments, grouping instruments that play together.
3. Ask children to echo the same patterns, playing instruments instead of using rhythmic movements. Explain that specific instruments will play when you snap, clap, patschen, and stamp, as follows:

Teacher Movement	Instrument Played
Snaps fingers	Finger cymbals, cymbals
Claps	Tone blocks, rhythm sticks
Patschen (slaps thighs)	Tambourines, jingle bells, maracas
Stamps	Drums

4. Repeat, in slow tempo, the patterns in number 1, as children echo on instruments.

Marching Along

Lois Raebeck and Lawrence Wheeler

Fais Do Do

Old French Song

Level II or III

Focusing on Strong and Weak Beats in 3/4 Meter by Learning a Song on the Recorder
"Fais Do Do"

1. Put the following on the board, omitting the notation beneath lines:

$$\frac{3}{4}$$ | | | | | | | | | | | |

One one one   one one one   one one one   one one one
Ta   ta   ta   ta   ta   ta   ta   ta   ta   ta   ta   ta

2. Explain this is four measures in 3/4 meter. Ask children to clap and count, using the rhythmic counting most familiar to them, accenting the first note in each measure.
3. Ask which is the strong beat of each measure (first beat) and which are the weak beats (second and third).
4. Select a volunteer to play the triangle on strong beats as you play the song on the recorder. Repeat, one child playing the triangle on strong beats, others playing the tone blocks on weak beats.
5. Put "Fais Do Do" on the board. Have the class identify the strong and weak beats, steps, skips, repeated notes, and similar phrases.

6. Play the song as a child points to notes on the board and children accompany on triangles and tone blocks.
7. Invite a few children at a time to join you in playing the song.

Melodic Concepts

Level III

Materials Needed
1. Copy of "Six Boys," on a large card or prepared for a projector
2. A set of resonator bells or similar melody instrument
3. Eight eight-ounce water glasses and ample water to fill them
4. Illustrations showing focus and no focus
5. Music Cue charts and music for evaluation procedure

Instrumental Activities
1. Playing resonator bells
2. Playing tuned water glasses

Related Musical Activities
1. Singing
2. Creating scales (major scale and tone row) from tuned water glasses
3. Music reading
4. Creating a song based on the tone row

Six Boys

Lois Raebeck

Introduction for Bells

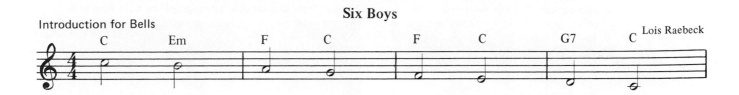

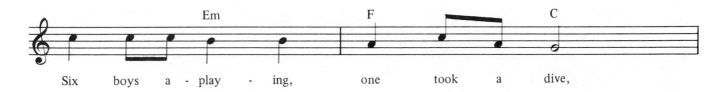

Six boys a - play - ing, one took a dive,

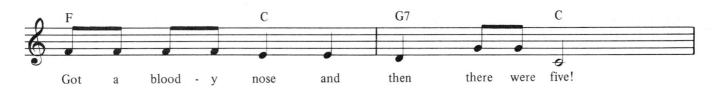

Got a blood - y nose and then there were five!

Bells

2. Five boys a-sleeping,
   One began to snore,
   The others shoved him out,
   And then there were four!

3. Four boys a-swimming,
   Happy as can be;
   One swam away,
   And then there were three!

4. Three boys a-hiking,
   One lost a shoe,
   Couldn't go on hiking,
   And so there were two!

5. Two boys a-camping,
   Camping in the sun,
   One went home
   And then there was one!

6. One boy a-reading,
   He was having fun,
   Along came the ice cream man,
   And then there were none!

Conceptual Understandings
1. All melodies are organized in some kind of scale.
2. A major scale has eight tones and a tonal center.
3. A tone row has no tonal center.

Behavioral Objectives
1. To sing and play more difficult interval relationships, including number, syllable, and letter names of the C scale
2. To hear the difference between music that has focus (tonal center) and no focus

Related Arts
Observing focus (tonal center) and no focus (no tonal center) in the visual arts, by using figures 4.12 and 4.13

Procedure
1. Learning the number, letter names, and syllables of the C scale, using resonator bells and the song "Six Boys"
   a. Hold up resonator bells and play high C. Tell children this is number one, sometimes called eight. Ask a volunteer to play number seven (B).

Figure 4.12
No focus. Daffodils, photograph by Lois Raebeck

Figure 4.13
Focus. Tree and clouds, photograph by Lois Raebeck

b. Play C and B. Ask a volunteer to play six (A). Continue in this manner until children have played down to one (C).

c. Ask the class to sing numbers up and down the scale as you play the notes on resonator bells.

d. Tell children one is also called C. Remind them that the musical alphabet moves from A up to G only. Ask a child to play one and two (C and D) on resonator bells.

e. Help children discover and sing additional letter names of the scale, ascending and descending.

f. Remind children that all major scales have a tonal center. Ask which tone in the C scale is the tonal center. (C) Have the class listen as a volunteer plays the scale, ascending and descending.

g. Have children examine the notation of "Six Boys" and discover descending (introduction) and ascending (postlude) scale passages. Teach the song by having children play scale passages on resonator bells, as an introduction and interlude between verses, as you sing. This gives children the opportunity to hear and follow the score several times before singing it.

2. Observing focus and no focus in the visual arts

a. Ask children to define the word focus. (a center of activity or attention)

b. Ask them where the focus is in a baseball or tennis game. (on the ball)

c. Ask where the focus is when they are watching a symphony orchestra. (on the conductor or a soloist)

d. Ask them where the focus is when they are watching a play on television. (on the person speaking, unless another character is doing something unusual)

e. Display figures 4.12 and 4.13.

f. Ask children to examine these pictures to see which has more focus. Encourage children to give their reactions. If necessary, ask questions.

   (1) Is there any center of attention in the picture of the daffodils? (no)

   (2) Does one flower seem more important than another? (no)

   (3) Why does the picture of the tree branches seem to have focus? (Children will describe either the tree or the clouds as the focus.)

   (4) If the picture of the tree had been limited to the clump of branches in the upper right, would it have had focus? (No. It would be much the same as the picture of daffodils, a repetition without pattern.)

g. After having seen these pictures, ask the class if they can define *focus* and *no focus* more clearly. One class volunteered the following:

   (1) Something with focus seems to have a point. Something with no focus has no real point.

   (2) Focus seems to mean that one thing is more important, other things are less important. In no focus nothing is more important than the other things.

h. Tell children that they will hear music that has focus and no focus.

3. Creating a major scale using tuned water glasses

a. Arrange eight water glasses in a row. Have a full water pitcher available.

b. Remind children of their experiences with the C scale.

c. Ask if any children have ever created a C scale with water glasses. If they have, ask for volunteers to explain the procedure and the scientific principles which make this activity possible. If not, explain, focusing on the following:

(1) In any musical instrument something must vibrate.

(2) On stringed instruments it is the string. On drums it is the drumhead.

(3) The longer or larger the vibrating material, the lower the tone.

(4) By filling water glasses with different amounts of water, we get larger or smaller amounts of vibrating material, which creates different pitches.

d. Have a child play middle C on a melody instrument. Ask another child to strike one of the empty glasses. Have the class compare pitches. Which is higher, the glass or the tone C?

e. Ask the class if they think the lowest tone in the C scale would require a great or small amount of water. (great)

f. Have a child fill the glass with water, checking the pitch by having another child strike the glass, as a third child plays C. Continue until middle C sounds on the glass.

g. Follow the same procedure for the other notes of the scale.

h. When scale is complete, let individual children play it ascending and descending, as the class sings, first letter names, then number names and syllables.

i. Let the class experiment with different striking objects (felt-covered mallets, pencils, and so on) to hear the different qualities of sound produced.

j. Encourage children to play simple patterns or phrases from familiar songs.

4. Creating a song for resonator bells, based on the tone row

a. Remind children that the major scale is but one kind of scale. Music uses scales in minor, pentatonic, and various modes. Another scale is the tone row. It is different in that it has no tonal center or focus.

b. Help children build a tone row, using notes from the resonator bells.

(1) Have them gather all notes (black and white) of the resonator bells between middle C and B.

(2) Have a child arrange them so they are not in order.

(3) Have a child play the arranged notes, making changes desired by the class.

c. Write the selected notes on the board on a musical staff, in the order decided. Assume the following was selected.

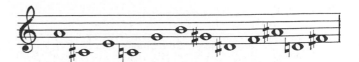

d. Write this on the board, omitting the counting beneath notes:

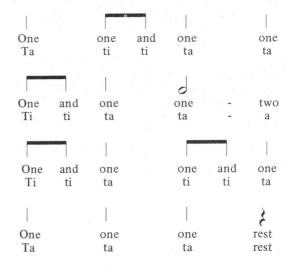

e. Have the class clap and count until they are familiar with the rhythm.

f. Explain that they are going to create a song using this rhythm pattern and notes in a tone row. The rules are

(1) They must use notes in the order they appear.

(2) They may start at the beginning, middle, or end.

(3) They may move forward or back.

Make certain the class understands the rules.

g. Select a volunteer to play the first phrase on tone row. Check the rhythm by having the class clap and chant the phrase again. Select volunteers to play other phrases. One class created the following:

5. Evaluating children's ability to hear the difference between music with a tonal center and music without a tonal center

a. Distribute Music Cue charts.

b. Tell children that you will play four melodies—one for each number on their papers. Tell them to circle the phrase that best describes each melody, tonal center or no tonal center. Play the following:

Melody 1
(tonal center)

Melody 2
(no tonal center)

Melody 3
(no tonal center)

Melody 4
(tonal center)

c. Discuss answers with children, clarifying any confusion about music with or without a tonal center.

Instrumental Experiences That Focus on Melodic Concepts

Level I

Focusing on Melodic Direction through Internalizing Activities
"All the Rain"

This type experience may be given on any level, using appropriate song material.

1. Teach children "All the Rain."

All the Rain

Lois Raebeck

All the rain goes drip, drip, drip, drip.

All the drops go skip, skip, skip, skip.

2. Show a child how to play the two-measure pattern on song bells.
3. Have the class sing the song as a child plays song bells.
4. Ask the class which notes are repeated most. (G's) Have them sing the song internalizing (thinking only, not singing) G's as child plays song bells.
5. Ask the class to listen for the melodic direction of "All the rain goes" as they sing, internalizing these notes.
6. Continue having the class internalize selected notes to focus on direction.

Level II

Focusing on Melodic Direction by Playing a Game with a Familiar Melody

This type experience may be given on any level, using appropriate song material and instrument.

1. Review "Scotland's Burning" by having children play it on the recorder as they follow the notation on the board.
2. Tell the class to play the song again, omitting the circled words. (Circle any phrase— "Fire! Fire! Fire! Fire!" for example.) Give children a signal to begin, and point to the notes as they play.

Scotland's Burning

Traditional Round

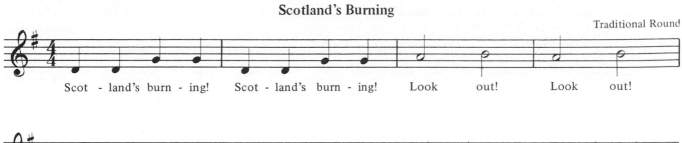

Scot - land's burn - ing!   Scot - land's burn - ing!   Look   out!   Look   out!

Fire!   Fire!   Fire!   Fire!   Pour   on   wa - ter!   Pour   on   wa - ter!

Old German Folk Tune

3. Ask what direction the notes in the omitted phrase move: up, down, or stay on same level.
4. Repeat, each time circling a different phrase.

Level II or III

Learning to Play Tonal Patterns from the C Scale
1. Place the notation for the "Old German Folk Tune" on a transparency. Ask children ways a melody can move: up, down, or stay in the same place; by step or by skip.

2. Ask children to examine the notation for "Old German Folk Tune" and find any phrases where notes step up. (phrases one and three) Ask for volunteers to play these phrases. Teach the class to play them.
3. Ask whether phrase number two steps or skips. (skips) Ask if it is like any other phrase. (Phrase six is similar but uses different note values.) Select volunteers to play phrases two and six. Teach entire class to play these phrases.
4. Ask what phrase, number one or two, most resembles phrase number four. (Phrase number two begins the

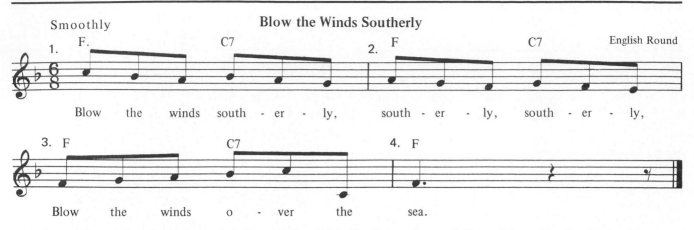

Blow the Winds Southerly

Smoothly

English Round

1. F.   C7   2. F   C7

Blow   the   winds   south - er - ly,   south - er - ly,   south - er - ly,

3. F   C7   4. F

Blow   the   winds   o - ver   the   sea.

Adapted from arrangement from *Heritage Songster* by Dallin and Dallin © 1966 by Wm. C. Brown Company Publishers, Dubuque, Iowa. (in public domain)

same.) Ask for a volunteer to play phrase four. Teach the class to play it.

5. Ask the class to play the first line of the song.
6. Ask which phrase resembles phrase number eight. (Phrase number four is similar except the note values are different.) Select a volunteer to play phrase eight, then teach the entire class to play it.
7. Have the class play all phrases learned as you play phrase five.
8. On another day, teach class to play phrase five, which will complete the song.

Level II or III

Focusing on Melodic Direction through Recorder Improvisation

1. Tell children you will play a question and answer game, using the recorders as "voices."
2. Explain that you will ask a question on your recorder, using the notes D, C, B, A, and G. They are to be ready to play an answer, using the same notes, in a different way. Their answer should be the same length as yours.
3. Play a simple melody similar to the following:

4. Immediately after playing your question, signal the entire class to play an answer, conducting for two measures to maintain the beat and help the class feel the duration of the two-measure phrase.
5. Tell the class that you would like volunteers to answer. Proceed as follows:
   a. Select one child to answer your question.
   b. Play a two-measure question.
   c. Signal him to answer, conduct unobtrusively as he plays his two measures. (If he has difficulty,

simply conduct and then continue without comment.)
   d. Select another child to answer, and continue as before. If children have difficulty improvising with these notes, limit the improvisation to the notes B, A, and G, until they improvise easily. Children will gradually acquire confidence and competence in improvising.

Level II or III

Focusing on Stepwise Progressions while Discovering an Autoharp Chording Plan
"Blow the Winds Southerly"

1. Place the notation and words of the song on the board or transparency.
2. Ask the class to examine the melody, and tell whether it moves by step or skip. (almost entirely by step)
3. Have the class sing the song, using letter names, then words.
4. Encourage volunteers to play the song on a melody instrument.
5. Write F and C7 on the board, explaining these are the chords needed to accompany the song.
6. Write F over the first note of the song.
7. Tell the class to sing as you strum the F chord and to raise their hands when it no longer blends with their singing. (Children should hear dissonance on the first use of the word *southerly*. If they do, ask on which word you should change the chord and select a volunteer to write C7 over *southerly*. If not, continue through the second measure and stop. Repeat, playing the F chord louder on *southerly* to stress the dissonance.)
8. Continue in this way, until children discover appropriate chords for the song; then have two children accompany (one child strumming, one child pressing buttons), as the entire class sings. If one child is capable of strumming and pressing buttons, let him do so.

Textural Concepts

Level II or III

Materials Needed
1. Recorder for each child
2. Copy of "Poet and Peasant"
3. Autoharp
4. Rhythm instruments, including a triangle and pair of rhythm sticks
5. Photographs depicting texture
6. Music Cue charts and music for evaluation procedure

Instrumental Activities
1. Learning to play "Poet and Peasant" in two parts on the recorder
2. Learning to play an Autoharp accompaniment to "Poet and Peasant" (a two-chord song, one child strumming and pressing buttons)
3. Creating an accompaniment for "Poet and Peasant" using rhythm instruments

Related Musical Activities
1. Music reading
2. Singing

Conceptual Understandings
1. Songs are generally accompanied by a group of related sounds produced simultaneously (chords), which must be changed to correspond to the melody.
2. Some songs can be accompanied by two chords.
3. Certain chordal progressions appear in many songs: I, V_7, I.

Behavioral Objectives
1. To play more complex songs on the recorder
2. To accompany a two-chord song on Autoharp, one child accompanying, independent of the teacher
3. To create more complex rhythmic accompaniments using rhythm instruments
4. To hear the difference between melody alone, a two-part song and a two-part song with accompaniment

Related Arts
Observing texture in the visual arts by using figure 4.14

Procedure
1. Observing texture in the visual arts
   a. Display figure 4.14.
   b. Ask children to explain the difference between the two pictures. (in figure 4.14a there are two children, in 4.14b, three)
   c. Ask if they can describe the effect created by photographing them one on top of the other instead of side by side. (We tend to see them all

Figure 4.14
a, Layers; b, layers plus, photographs by Sidney Hecker

a

b

at once, as one unit, rather than observing them one at a time, moving our eyes from left to right.)
   d. Ask if they can think of anything in music that resembles these pictures. (Figure 4.14a, could be

compared to two tones being sung or played at the same time; 4.14b could be compared to three tones being played or sung at the same time. In each case we hear the tones simultaneously, as in the pictures we see the faces simultaneously.)

  e. Ask what kind of picture would resemble a single tone in music. (one child)

  f. Ask children to identify the technical words in music that describe a series of single tones heard one at a time (melody) and several tones sounded simultaneously (harmony).

2. Learning how to play a two-part song on the recorder (adaptation of "Poet and Peasant")

  a. Write this notation on the board, omitting indications for syllables below the notes.

Harmony for "Poet and Peasant"

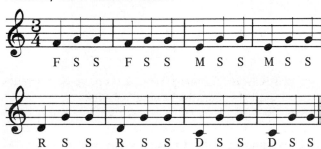

  b. Have children sing the notes, using letter names and syllables.

  c. Ask if there is any pattern to this melody. (The second and third beats of each measure are G's, or sols. The first note of alternate measures steps down.)

  d. Have volunteers play this phrase, then have the entire class play it.

  e. Tell the class they have been playing an accompaniment (harmony), and now you will play the melody, as they play harmony. Select a child to lead the class. Remind them to keep exact rhythm and to play their part three times. Give the signal to begin. Start the melody on the first repetition of the harmony. If children have difficulty, do not drill. Let them practice the harmony before playing it with the melody.

  f. Put the melody on the board. Discuss, focusing on the following:

    (1) Similar phrases: the first and third phrases are similar.

    (2) Stepwise progressions.

    (3) Scale-type progressions.

    (4) Notes moving by skip: only one interval moves by skip.

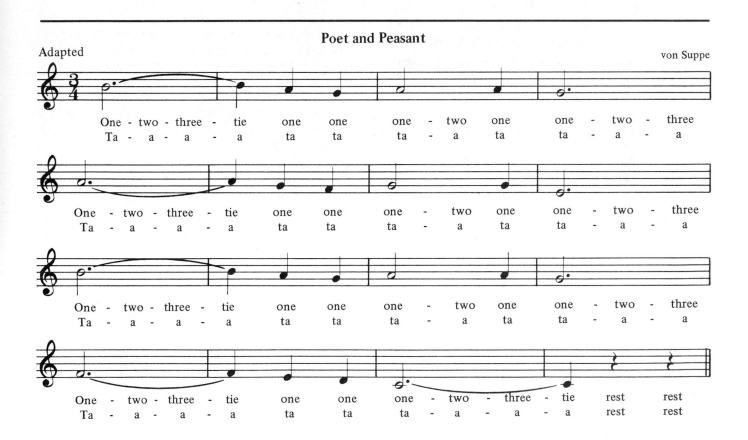

Poet and Peasant

(5) The "tie" between the first two notes in each line and between the last two notes.

(6) The meter and movement of the piece.

   g. Have the class count and clap the song, using number or Kodaly counting.

   h. Ask the class to sing the song, using letter names.

   i. Ask children to follow notes on the board, as you play. Play the melody several times, stopping in different places, asking children to identify the note on which you stopped.

   j. Ask for volunteers to play the first phrase, then ask the entire class to play it.

   k. Have the class examine the last phrase of each line and discuss the difference in rhythm and movement. (They are almost alike rhythmically. Melodically, the last phrase moves in a scalewise progression down to C.)

   l. Ask volunteers to play each of these phrases and teach them to the class.

   m. Ask for volunteers to play the entire melody.

   n. Select a child to lead the class playing the harmony, as you lead several children playing the melody.

   o. Divide parts equally and play.

3. Learning to play an Autoharp accompaniment to "Poet and Peasant"

   a. Place the following on the board, omitting chord markings above the melody.

   b. Ask children if they can identify this musical phrase. (It is the harmony part for "Poet and Peasant.")

   c. Explain that the two groups of notes are chords that accompany "Poet and Peasant." The first is the G_7 chord, the second is the C major chord.

   d. Have children identify the notes in each chord.

   e. Tell children that by examining the notes in each measure they can discover which chord fits it.

Help children decide which chords would best fit, and write their decisions above the first note of each measure.

   f. To check the accuracy of their decisions, ask a volunteer to play the selected chords on the Autoharp, as one child plays the recorder. Make changes, if needed.

   g. Select several children to play the melody to "Poet and Peasant," several to play the harmony, and one to play the Autoharp. Have the Autoharp play an introduction, and signal the melody part to begin.

4. Creating an accompaniment for "Poet and Peasant" using rhythm instruments

   a. Put the following on the board. Omit the number notation beneath the stick notation.

   b. Have the class clap and count each group of notes until they get the "swing" of each.

   c. Ask which group of notes feels like the rhythm of "Poet and Peasant."

   d. Ask if one of the notes felt stronger than the others. (first note)

   e. Display the rhythm instruments. Ask which instrument would best play the strong beat. (Assume they select a triangle.)

   f. Select a child to play the triangle on the first beat, as the class claps and counts "one, one, one" until the rhythm is established.

   g. Ask the class which instrument might sound best on the two weak beats. (Assume the class selects a tone block.)

   h. Select a child to play the tone block on weak beats, as the triangle plays on the first beat, and the class claps and counts.

   i. Let many children experiment with playing this pattern. Then select children to play the following:

     (1) Harmony part to "Poet and Peasant" on the recorder

     (2) Melody part to "Poet and Peasant" on the recorder

(3) Autoharp accompaniment to "Poet and Peasant"

(4) Triangle and tone block part to "Poet and Peasant"

j. Tell the class the sequence.

(1) Harmony: Autoharp, triangle, and tone block begin by playing the introduction.

(2) Melody begins on the repetition of harmony part.

(3) Harmony: Autoharp, triangle, and tone block repeat parts as a postlude.

k. Signal each part to begin and help them by conducting unobtrusively. If children have difficulty, select leaders where needed, clarify any misunderstandings and repeat.

5. Evaluating children's ability to hear differences in texture

a. Distribute copies of the following Music Cue chart.

Music Cue Chart

1. Melody alone	Two parts	Two parts with harmonic accompaniment
2. Melody alone	Two parts	Two parts with harmonic accompaniment
3. Melody alone	Two parts	Two parts with harmonic accompaniment
4. Melody alone	Two parts	Two parts with harmonic accompaniment

b. Tell children you are going to play a piece of music. They are to close their eyes, listen, then circle the phrase that best describes the music, after number 1. Play number 1 or a similar phrase.

c. Continue similarly for numbers 2, 3, and 4, using the music from this section or music of your own choice. Have the class compare their answers to the correct answers. Through discussion, clarify any misunderstandings. (The teacher may want to prepare a cassette.)

1. Melody alone

Arrangement from Mozart

2. Two parts

Old Song

3. Two parts with harmonic accompaniment

Arrangement from Mozart

4. Two parts

Instrumental Experiences That Focus on Textural Concepts

Level I

Creating an Original Composition for Rhythm Instruments

Read the experience outlined on page 229 "Focusing on Expressive Concepts by Creating a Composition for Rhythm Instruments" and adapt to focus on concepts related to texture.

Level II

Creating a "Symphony" for Rhythm Instruments
"America"

1. As the class sings "America" (page 212), have them do the following:
   a. Clap the melodic rhythm of "America"
   b. Step in place the metrical rhythm of "America"
   c. Step the metrical rhythm as they clap the melodic rhythm
2. When the class can do this, select volunteers to play the metrical rhythm on a drum and the melodic rhythm on tone blocks, as the class sings, steps, and claps.
3. Discuss ways rhythm can be varied. (strong and weak beats, long and short notes, fast and slow notes, loud and soft notes)
4. Invite children to experiment with different rhythm patterns to create a rhythm "symphony" for "America." Ask volunteers to demonstrate their ideas. Let the class decide on the patterns and instruments they prefer. One class created the following:

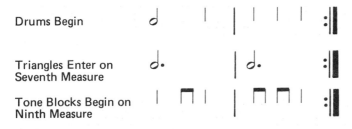

Drums Begin

Triangles Enter on Seventh Measure

Tone Blocks Begin on Ninth Measure

Figure 4.15
a, Texture or no texture? Photograph by Lois Raebeck. **b**, Creating texture. Photograph by Elizabeth Wheeler.

Level II

Discovering which Picture Illustrates Music with Texture and which Illustrates Music without Texture

1. Display figure 4.15, without showing the figure legend.
2. Ask children to examine each picture carefully to determine if they illustrate texture.
3. Discuss. (Figure 4.15a does not illustrate texture. The boy is using the same fingering on both recorders, thus playing the same melody. Children in 4.15b are playing different notes simultaneously, thus creating texture.)

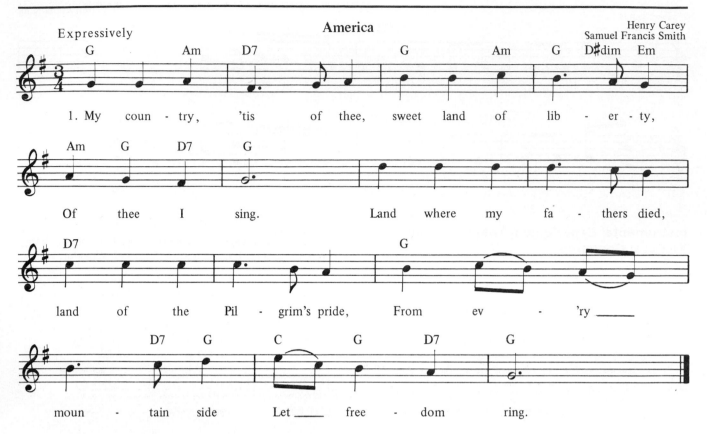

America

Henry Carey
Samuel Francis Smith

Expressively

1. My coun-try, 'tis of thee, sweet land of lib-er-ty,
Of thee I sing. Land where my fa-thers died,
land of the Pil-grim's pride, From ev-'ry _____
moun-tain side Let _____ free-dom ring.

2. My native country, thee, land of the noble free,
Thy name I love.
I love thy rocks and rills, thy woods and templed hills,
My heart with rapture thrills
Like that above.

3. Let music swell the breeze, and ring from all the trees
Sweet freedom's song.
Let mortal tongues awake, let all that breathe partake,
Let rocks their silence break,
The sound prolong.

4. Our fathers' God, to Thee, Author of liberty,
To Thee we sing.
Long may our land be bright with freedom's holy light,
Protect us by Thy might,
Great God, our King!

Adapted from *Heritage Songster* by Dallin and Dallin, © 1966 by Wm. C. Brown Company Publishers, Dubuque, Iowa. (in public domain)

Level II

Creating a Second Part by Ear for Song Bells
"Rig-a-Jig-Jig"

1. Have the class review the song by clapping two beats to each measure as they sing.
2. Tell them that by listening carefully to the song bells, they can create a second part for the song.
3. Ask a volunteer to play C in the rhythm previously clapped as the class sings softly. Tell the children to raise their hands when they hear a note on song bells that sounds wrong.

4. On this word, ask children which of the notes closest to C (B or D) they want played. Write the note selected on the board.
5. Ask children to sing the song again, continuing until another discord occurs. Continue until children have created a second part. One class created the following:
CC/CC/BB/CC/
CC/CC/BB/CC/
CC/CC/BB/CC/
CC/CC/BB/CC/
BB/CC/BB/CC/
CC/CC/BB/CC/

Rig-a-Jig-Jig

Animated

U. S.

As I was walk - ing down the street, Heigh - o, heigh - o, heigh - o, heigh - o! A pret - ty girl I chanced to meet, Heigh - o, heigh - o, _____ heigh - o!

Chorus

Rig - a - jig - jig and a - way we go, a - way we go, a - way we go, Rig - a - jig - jig and a - way we go, Heigh - o, heigh - o, _____ heigh - o! Heigh - o, heigh - o, heigh - o, heigh - o, heigh - o, heigh - o, heigh - o! Rig - a - jig - jig and a - way we go, Heigh - o, heigh - o, _____ heigh - o!

2. I said to her, "What is your trade?"
   Heigh-o, heigh-o, heigh-o, heigh-o!
   Said she, "I am a weaver's maid."
   Heigh-o, heigh-o, heigh-o!

Arranged from *Heritage Songster* by Dallin and Dallin, © 1966 by Wm. C. Brown Company Publishers, Dubuque, Iowa. (in public domain)

Canoe Round

My pad - dle's keen and bright, Flash - ing with sil - ver,
Dip dip and swing her back, Flash - ing with sil - ver,

Fol - low the wild goose flight, Dip, dip and swing!
Swift as the wild goose flies, Dip, dip and swing!

Level II

Learning to Press the Button and Strum the Autoharp for a One-Chord Song
"Canoe Round"

1. Have the class review the song as you accompany on the Autoharp, using two strums per measure.
2. Ask the class which hand pressed the button (left) and which strummed (right). Ask them to raise the finger of the left hand that pressed the button (index).
3. Invite children to accompany the "Canoe Round" at their desks by doing these things:
    a. Imagining their desks are Autoharps
    b. Placing their left index fingers firmly on their desks for the D minor chord
    c. Strumming their imaginary Autoharps with their right hands as they sing "Canoe Round," and you play the Autoharp
4. Select a volunteer to press the D minor chord and strum the Autoharp, as class sings, strumming on their "desk" Autoharps. Give other children the opportunity to accompany class singing.
5. The teacher may want to focus attention on the syncopation in the first three notes of the song by having children chant and clap.

Clap

Chant   syn - co - pah

Level II or III

Creating an Autoharp Accompaniment for a Two-Chord Song
"Lone Star Trail"

For a copy of this song, see chapter 3.

1. Review the song by having the class sing and strum imaginary Autoharps on their desks.
2. Tell the class they are going to discover how to accompany the song on the Autoharp. Explain that two chords are used, F and C_7, and the F chord begins the song. Write the following on the board:
F
started
3. Explain that this song begins on an upbeat and you will play a one-chord introduction before singing. Ask children to raise their hands when they hear a discord. Sing the first two phrases, or until children raise their hands. (They should raise their hands on "punch" in the second line. If they do not, repeat, strumming louder on the word "punch" to emphasize the discord.) Write on the board:

F	F				C7
1 Sing	— — started-ed	— —	— —	— —	punch-ing

4. Repeat song and continue beyond the C_7 chord until children hear another dissonance. (They should hear a dissonance on the word "Lone.")
5. Continue until the chord plan has been worked out and is on the board.

```
F                                    C7
1 Sing |— —|— —|— —|— —|— —|
       |start-                       |punch-
       |ed                           |ing

       F           C7          F
—  —|— —|— —|— —|— —|
   |Lone |   |Ki-|   |yay

                   C7    F
—  —|— —|— —|— —|— —|—  ‖
         |yip-  |yay.
         |pi
```

6. Have children pretend they have Autoharps on their desks and have them play this accompaniment, using their index fingers for the F chords and middle fingers for the C₇ chords. Divide the class into two groups, one group to sing as the other group plays. Remind children to watch the chart so they know when to change chords. Have a volunteer point to each beat as the class sings and plays.

7. Repeat, reversing groups.

8. Select children to play available Autoharps. If children have had experience pressing buttons and strumming, one child may play alone. If this is too difficult, two children may be assigned to each Autoharp, one to strum, the other to press buttons.

9. Give many children the opportunity to accompany as the class sings.

Level III

Creating a Descant for the Refrain of a Familiar Song, Using Song Bells
"Sweet Betsy From Pike"

This experience is best for accelerated classes or musically gifted children.

1. Ask children to sing "Sweet Betsy from Pike" (page 216), clapping on the refrain. (They will probably clap either on the first beat or on every beat of each measure.)

2. Explain that you will play each note of the C chord on song bells. Play C, E, and G.

3. Ask the class which chord note they would like as a first note of the descant, to accompany the refrain. (Suggest they limit themselves to one tone per measure.) When a child makes a suggestion, have him play his note as the class sings the measure.

4. Have the class experiment. When they choose a note, write it on a staff on the board.

5. Suggest that the next note of the descant may be discovered by repeating the same note or by using the note above or below it. Have children experiment as follows:

   a. *Class sings* Singing/too ra li/oo ra li
      Child plays   X   X
                        (First   (Repeat)
                        note)

   b. *Class sings* Singing/too ra li/oo ra li
      Child plays   X   X
                        (First   (Note above)
                        note)

   c. *Class sings* Singing/too ra li/oo ra li
      Child plays   X   X
                        (First   (Note below)
                        note)

6. Have the class decide upon the second note of the descant and write it on the staff on the board. Continue until they create a descant for the refrain. Have children decide about these things:
   a. Whether to add more notes per measure
   b. Words to sing for the descant

7. Have several children practice playing descant as the class sings the refrain. Later, select volunteers to sing descant with song bells as the class sings the melody.

8. One class created this.

Sing-ing too ra li oo ra li

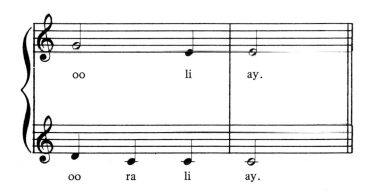

oo ra li ay.

Sweet Betsy from Pike

Crisply

Western U. S.

1. Did you ev - er hear of sweet Bet - sy from Pike, Who

crossed the wide prai - ries with her hus - band Ike, With

two yoke of ox - en, a big yel - low dog, A __

tall Shang - hai roost - er, and one spot - ted hog. Sing -ing

too ra li oo ra li oo ra li ay.

2. One evening quite early they camped on the Platte,
   Up close to the road on a green grassy flat;
   Poor Betsy, sore footed, lay down for repose,
   And Ike sat and gazed at his Pike County rose.
   Singing too ra li oo ra li oo ra li ay.

3. The alkali desert was burning and bare,
   And Ike cried in fear, "We are lost, I declare!
   My dear old Pike County, I'll come back to you!"
   Vowed Betsy, "You'll go by yourself if you do."
   Singing too ra li oo ra li oo ra li ay.

4. Their wagon broke down with a terrible smash,
   And over the prairie rolled all kinds of trash;
   Poor Ike got discouraged, and Betsy got mad;
   The dog drooped his tail and looked terribly sad.
   Singing too ra li oo ra li oo ra li ay.

5. 'Twas out on the desert that Betsy gave out,
   And down in the sand she lay rolling about;
   Poor Ike, half distracted, looked down in surprise,
   Saying, "Betsy, get up, you'll get sand in your eyes!"
   Singing too ra li oo ra li oo ra li ay.

6. Then Betsy got up and gazed out on the plain,
   And said she'd go back to Pike County again,
   But Ike heaved a sigh, and they fondly embraced,
   And they headed on west with his arm 'round her waist
   Singing too ra li oo ra li oo ra li ay.

7. They swam the wide rivers and crossed the high peaks;
   They camped on the prairie for weeks upon weeks;
   They fought with the Indians with musket and ball,
   And they reached California in spite of it all.
   Singing too ra li oo ra li oo ra li ay.

Arranged from *Heritage Songster* by Dallin and Dallin, © 1966 by Wm. C. Brown Company Publishers, Dubuque, Iowa. (in public domain)

Level III

Playing Thirds Below Melody, Using Song Bells: Preparation for Singing the Second Part
"He's Got the Whole World in His Hands"

For a copy of this song, see chapter 3.

1. Write the song on the board. Select several children to sing as the class follows the score. As they sing, play the notes a third below on song bells.
2. Ask the class if they can tell from the score which notes you played.
3. Ask the class to name the notes in the first phrase of the harmony part. Write letter names under the notes on the board, asking these, or similar questions:
   a. Is the second note on the same space as the first or does it move up or down? (same)
   b. Does the third note change? (yes) Does it step or skip, up or down? (skips down)
4. When they have named the lower notes of the first phrase, ask a volunteer to play on song bells. Have the class make corrections, if necessary. Give several children an opportunity to play the phrase.
5. Ask if the phrase is repeated any other place in the song. (yes, third phrase)
6. Help children discover notes and interval relationships in phrases two and four in a similar way. When children have identified and can play the entire second part on song bells, select volunteers to sing the harmony part, using letter names, then words, as a child accompanies on song bells.
7. Repeat, adding to the harmony group, until half the class can securely sing the harmony, accompanied by song bells, as the other half sings the melody.
8. Switch parts.

Level III

Discovering by Ear an Autoharp Chording Plan for a Three-Chord Song
"Michael, Row the Boat Ashore"

For a copy of this song, see chapter 3. Students should be familiar with Autoharp chords.

1. Write the words of the first verse on the board.
2. Remind the class that the three chords most often needed for a simple folk song are the I, IV, and V_7 chords. Write C notation on the board.

3. Ask children if, by knowing the chord root of the I chord, they can write the chord roots of the IV and V_7 chords. Select volunteers to write chord roots for IV and V_7, as follows:

4. Tell children these three chords can be used for a chording plan for "Michael, Row the Boat Ashore." Tell them the song begins on the C (I) chord. Write C over the word "Michael."
5. Explain the following will be used to discover the chords:
   a. You will play the C (I) chord as they begin singing and continue until they hear a discord, at which time they are to raise their hands.
   b. They will tell you on which word they hear the discord.
   c. They will sing again. On the word the discord occurs you will change to the G_7 (V_7) chord. They will decide if this chord blends with their singing.
   d. If it blends, a volunteer will write G_7 over the proper word on the board. If it does not, then it must be the F (IV) chord. They will test this by singing as you play the chord on the appropriate word.
6. Follow the same procedure until the children create a chording plan similar to the following:

C				F	
Mich-ael,	row the boat a-	shore, al-le	lu	-	

C			F		G7	C
ia. Mich-ael	row the boat a-	shore, al-le	lu	-	ia.	

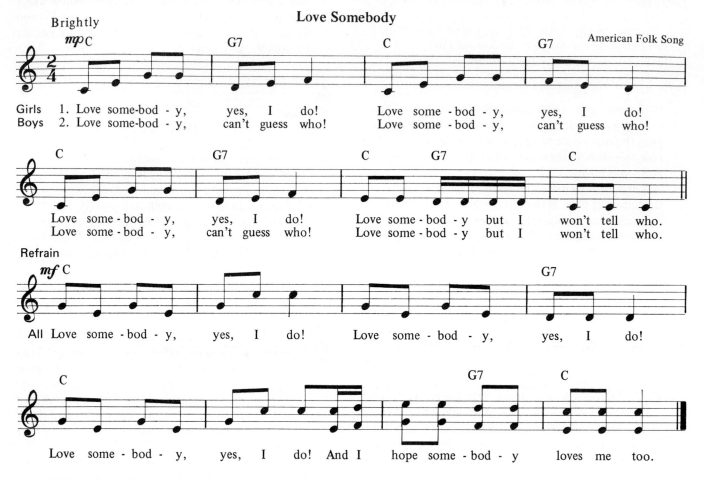

Love Somebody

Brightly

American Folk Song

Girls 1. Love some-bod-y, yes, I do! Love some-bod-y, yes, I do!
Boys 2. Love some-bod-y, can't guess who! Love some-bod-y, can't guess who!

Love some-bod-y, yes, I do! Love some-bod-y but I won't tell who.
Love some-bod-y, can't guess who! Love some-bod-y but I won't tell who.

Refrain

All Love some-bod-y, yes, I do! Love some-bod-y, yes, I do!

Love some-bod-y, yes, I do! And I hope some-bod-y loves me too.

Girls
3. Love somebody's eyes of blue. (three times)
   Love somebody but I won't tell who.

Boys
4. Love somebody's smile so true. (three times)
   Love somebody but I won't tell who.

All
5. Repeat first stanza.

Level III

Creating a Chordal Accompaniment Using Resonator Bells

"Love Somebody"

1. Write the C scale on the board and ask children to build a chord over each note. Remind them chords are built by placing notes on three consecutive lines or spaces.

2. Distribute resonator bells and have children play the chords they built on the C scale. (Three children will play each chord.)

3. Tell children they are going to accompany a familiar song, using resonator bells. Have them examine the

song, focusing on chords necessary to accompany it (C and G₇). Write these chords on the board. Have children tell the notes in each chord.

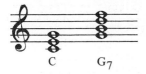

C   G₇

4. Ask for volunteers to play notes in each chord. (The G bell will be used in both chords.) Distribute resonator bells.
5. Through discussion and experimentation, have the class decide:
  a. If the song swings in twos or threes (twos)
  b. Which accompaniment they prefer:

    (1) *Chord*   C   C   G₇   G₇
           Beat   1   2   1   2
    (2) *Chord*   C   G₇
           Beat   1   2   1   2

  c. A chording plan for the song

C —	G₇ —	C —	G₇ —
Love	yes	Love	yes
C —	G₇ —	C G₇	C —
Love	yes	Love body	won't
C —	C —	C —	G₇ —
Love	yes	Love	yes
C —	C —	C G₇	C —
Love	yes	hope body	loves

6. The children holding the bells should play an accompaniment in a previously determined rhythm, and count one-two, one-two to maintain a steady rhythm. Remind them to play with a ringing sound and to hold mallets securely.
7. When they are ready have the children play the accompaniment, as the class sings.

Level III

Creating an Accompaniment to a Pentatonic Song
"There's a Little Wheel"

Children should know this song before this experience.

1. Ask children to suggest movements to accompany the song (page 220). One class suggested the following:

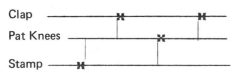

Clap
Pat Knees
Stamp

2. Have children sing the song using the rhythmic movements decided upon.
3. Have children suggest an ostinato pattern (a four quarter-note melodic pattern) using the notes F, G, A, C, or D, which will be played on the bells as an accompaniment to the song. One class suggested this:

4. Select a child to play the ostinato. Make certain he can play the correct notes and rhythm.
5. Before performing the song, tell the class they will begin with the patschen accompaniment, joined (two measures later) by the song bells, both of which continue as the singing begins two measures later. Perform the song.
6. Ask children to suggest another ostinato pattern that sounds pleasant with the first. One class selected this:

7. Select a child to play the second ostinato, and let him practice with the first child.
8. Explain that the class will begin the patschen accompaniment, the instruments will join two measures later, and the class will begin singing two measures later. Perform the song.
9. Ask children to suggest a third ostinato pattern that sounds pleasant with the first two. One class suggested the following:

10. Select a child to play the third ostinato and let him practice with the first two children.
11. Have the class perform as in number 8: patschen accompaniment beginning first, the three instruments beginning two measures later, singing beginning two measures after that.
12. If desired, still another ostinato pattern can be added.

There's a Little Wheel

Lively

mp

F

Spiritual

1. There's a lit - tle wheel a - turn - ing in my heart, ____
2. There's a lit - tle song a - sing - ing in my heart, ____
3. Oh, I feel so ver - y hap - py in my heart, ____

B♭   F

There's a lit - tle wheel a - turn - ing in my heart,
There's a lit - tle song a - sing - ing in my heart,
Oh, I feel so ver - y hap - py in my heart,

B♭   C7

1-3. In my heart, _____ in my heart, _____

F   C7   F

There's a lit - tle wheel a - turn - ing in my heart.
There's a lit - tle song a - sing - ing in my heart.
Oh, I feel so ver - y hap - py in my heart.

Used by permission of American Book Company.

Concepts Related to Form

Level II

Materials Needed
1. *Rhythm instrument for each child*
2. *Recorders*
3. *Illustrations for ABA and rondo form*
4. *Recording of "Amaryllis" by Gys, RCA Victor Basic Record Library for Elementary Grades* recording WE90
5. Music Cue charts
6. Music for evaluation procedure

Instrumental Activities
1. Playing rhythm instruments
2. Playing recorders

Related Musical Activities
1. Music reading
2. Listening

Conceptual Understandings
1. Some music is written in ABA form, which consists of three sections, the first and third similar, the second contrasting.
2. Rondo form is a musical form consisting of two or more sections alternating with section A (ABACA or ABACADA).

Behavioral Objectives
1. To identify ABA form through an experience using the recorder
2. To identify rondo form by creating an accompaniment to an orchestral composition, using rhythm instruments

Related Arts
Observing ABA and rondo form in the visual arts, using *The Plantation,* figure 4.16

Procedure
1. Observing form in the visual arts

Figure 4.16
American Painting (ca. 1825) American Artist, Unknown,
The Plantation. The Metropolitan Museum of Art, Gift of
Edgar William and Bernice Chrysler Garbisch, 1963.

a. Ask children what kind of musical forms they have experienced. Write their answers on the board. Encourage them to remember experiences with AB, ABA, and ABACA forms. Write these forms on the board.
b. Display figure 4.16.
c. Tell children to examine the picture carefully and decide which form it suggests. (ABA) If they have difficulty, ask the following or similar questions:
  (1) Into how many sections is the picture divided—one, two, three, or more? (Three)
  (2) What are they? (Have volunteers point to each section. They should see: the tree on the left, the hill with the house on top, and the tree on the right. The water at the bottom does not appear to be a separate section.)
  (3) If we call the trees *A* (since they are similar) what would we call the hill with the house on top? (*B*) Thus, we have ABA form.
d. Ask children to examine the A sections to see what techniques the artist used to make the two trees similar. (The artist could have painted two

trees so different in style that there would be no ABA effect.) Help them see the following:
  (1) Both trees are the same height.
  (2) Both have branches stretching toward the center.
  (3) Though different types, both trees have leaves made of similar brush strokes.
  (4) Clustered near each tree are houses (on the hill), further emphasizing the ABA form.
e. Ask the class what music creates ABA form (a song or musical composition in which the first and last sections are similar and the middle section is different)
2. Using the recorder to create an ABA form
  a. Write this on the board.

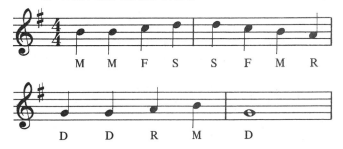

b. Have the class sing the melody, using letter names and syllables.
c. Discuss the melody.
   (1) Does it have any intervals that step? (Have a child point to the steps.)
   (2) Does it have any intervals that skip? (Have a child point to the skip between the last two notes.)
   (3) Are there places where a note is repeated? (Have a child point to these places.)
d. Tell children you are going to play the melody on a recorder and that you will stop anywhere. Ask them to follow the music so they can identify the stopping place. Do this several times, stopping at different places.
e. Ask volunteers to play the melody.
f. Ask the entire class to play the melody.
g. Present some internalization activities.
   (1) Circle one measure. Tell the class to "think inside" the circled notes and *play* all other notes. Repeat, circling different measures.
   (2) Ask the class to play the first and last notes and to internalize other notes, maintaining the exact rhythm throughout.
   (3) Ask the class to play only on high D's, internalizing all other notes, in rhythm.
h. Ask the class to help create an ABA form, using this melody as A. Explain that B will be created by the class in the following way:
   (1) The entire class will play A.
   (2) A volunteer will improvise B, using the notes D, C, B, A, and G in a different order and rhythm but retaining the basic pulsation and length as A.
   (3) The entire class will play A again.
i. Select a volunteer to play B. Tell him to play A with the class, then play B. Signal the class to begin and conduct unobtrusively, signaling B to be played at the proper time and A to be played again.
j. Repeat several times, allowing other children the opportunity to improvise B and helping the class to play more expressively.

3. Using rhythm instruments to focus on modified rondo form, while listening to "Amaryllis" by Joseph Gys
a. Remind children that music can change the way we feel. It can make us feel happy or sad, lively or lazy.
b. Play the recording of the first melody only.
c. Ask children how it makes them feel. Have them give this melody a name. They may think of "Happy Tune," "Dancing Tune," "Hopping Tune," "Ballet Tune," and so on. Let us assume they choose "Happy Tune." Write it on the board.

d. Tell children as the recording plays, they are to raise their hands each time they hear this tune.
e. Each time they raise their hands write "Happy Tune" on the board.
   Happy Tune   Happy Tune   Happy Tune
f. Ask the class if they heard another melody in addition to "Happy Tune." Have them vote on a name for it and write it on the board to the right of "Happy Tune." Assume they called the second tune "Forceful Tune."
g. Tell children as the recording plays, they are to stand when they hear "Forceful Tune." Play the recording and write "Forceful Tune" on the board when children stand.
   Happy   Forceful Happy   Forceful Happy
   Tune   Tune   Tune   Tune   Tune
h. Ask the class if they heard still another tune. Have them vote for a name for the third tune. Assume they name this "Graceful Tune." Write it on the board.
i. As the recording plays again, they are to raise both hands on the third tune. Play the recording and write "Graceful Tune" on the board when they raise both hands.
   Happy   Forceful Happy   Graceful Forceful
   Tune   Tune   Tune   Tune   Tune
j. Display rhythm instruments and ask the class which would best accompany "Happy Tune." Let them demonstrate suggestions as the recording plays and then vote for the one they prefer.
k. Distribute instruments selected for "Happy Tune" and as the recording plays, have children accompany "Happy Tune" sections.
l. Repeat for "Forceful Tune" and "Graceful Tune."
m. Have children exchange instruments. Repeat until all have had the opportunity to accompany each tune.
n. On another day, help children create bodily movements for the three tunes. Some children can move as others accompany.

4. Evaluating children's ability to recognize the difference between ABA and rondo form
a. Distribute the following to children.

Music Cue Chart

1. ABA		ABACA
2. ABA		ABACA
3. ABA		ABACA
4. ABA		ABACA

---

b. Tell children you are going to play four short pieces on the recorder. Ask them to decide if each is in ABA or rondo form (ABACA) and circle the form after numbers 1–4. Play pieces 1–4.

c. Discuss answers with children. Repeat any number to clarify misunderstandings.

1. ABA

2. ABACA

continued on page 224

3. ABACA

4. ABA

Au Clair de la Lune

French Folk Song

In the shin - ing moon - light, My dear friend Pier - rot,

Came to ask a fa - vor, But I told him no.

He came far too late, and I had gone to bed.

"Come a - gain to - mor - row. Ask me then in - stead."

Adapted from arrangement from *Music Skills for Classroom Teachers* by Robert Winslow and Leon Dallin, © 1958 by Wm. C. Brown Company Publishers, Dubuque, Iowa. (in public domain)

Instrumental Experiences That Focus on Concepts Related to Form

Level II

Learning to Play a Song in AABA Form on the Recorder
"Au Clair de la Lune"

Children should be able to play the notes A, G, F, E, D, and middle C on the recorder before this experience.
1. Write notation of the song on the board.
2. Give children the experience with "Au Clair de la Lune" described in the section "Notational Concepts: Music Reading" later in this chapter. Have them examine the score to focus on the similar and dissimilar phrases and the form they create. If they are familiar with the AABA form, they will recognize it. If not, help them discover that lines one, two, and four (A) are alike and line three (B) is different.
3. Ask for volunteers to play the first line. Have the class play the first, second, and fourth lines as you play the third line.

4. Select a volunteer to play the third line. Have the class play the first, second, and fourth lines as the volunteer plays the third line. Repeat, having other children play the third line.
5. Children will enjoy adding a percussive accompaniment. Instruments selected for A play lines one, two, and four; instruments selected for B play line three.

Level II or III

Using Rhythm Instruments to Create a Canon
1. Distribute rhythm instruments. Tell the class to listen, then echo you, using percussion instruments. Play the following music. If the class follows easily, proceed to steps 2 and 3. If they have difficulty, repeat on subsequent days until successful.

Drum

2. Remind the class of their experiences with rounds. Ask them to listen until you nod your head, then begin at the beginning and follow one measure after you, always repeating what they hear as they listen to the pattern you play.

3. Signal the class to enter on the second measure (marked with asterisk) as you do the following:

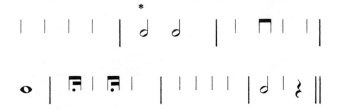

Expressive Concepts

Level II or III

Materials Needed
1. Recorder for each child
2. Rhythm instruments
3. Copy of "Happy Are They"
4. Copy of the haiku "A Fluttering Swarm"
5. Recording of Largo and Finale from *New World* Symphony by Dvorak
6. Copy of themes from Largo and Finale from *New World* Symphony
7. Picture of English horn
8. Piano or other melody instrument
9. Printed sheets for focusing on expressive concepts
10. Recordings: "Hobby Horse," "Sick Doll," and "My Daughter Lidi," all from *Album for the Young* by Tchaikovsky, Bowmar *Orchestral Library* recording BOL 081; "Stars and Stripes Forever" by Sousa, Bowmar *Orchestral Library* recording BOL 54/#067
11. Music Cue charts

Instrumental Activities
1. Creating an accompaniment on rhythm instruments to haiku (poetry)
2. Learning to play "Happy Are They" on the recorder
3. Learning to play a theme from a symphonic movement on the piano or other melody instrument

Related Musical Activities
1. Music listening
2. Bodily movement
3. Singing

Conceptual Understandings
1. Music may have many different moods.
2. Our voices and the instruments we play may be used in different ways to produce differences in tone quality and mood.
3. The nature of the rhythm, tempo, dynamics, and instrumentation affects the expressive qualities of a musical composition.

Behavioral Objectives
1. To create a definite mood by singing and playing the recorder and rhythm instruments
2. To create an expressive accompaniment to a poem using rhythm instruments

Related Arts
Experiencing changes of mood through haiku, by Sadaiye, translated by Harold G. Henderson, "A Fluttering Swarm"

Procedure
1. Experiencing changes of mood in poetry
   a. Through discussion, help the class focus on ways that elements of a poem can change its mood and emotion. Include the following:
      (1) Its rhythm may be even or uneven, punctuated or flowing.
      (2) Its phrases may be long or short, defined or indefinite.
      (3) It may or may not rhyme.
      (4) The sound of its words may suggest various moods.
      (5) The words may suggest different images.
   b. Remind children of previous experiences with the Japanese poetry form, haiku, and the structure and intent of this form.
      (1) An haiku is a very short poem.
      (2) It expresses and elicits emotion that may be happy, sad, serious, playful, and so on.
      (3) It often describes the essence of a moment in nature.
      (4) Because of its brevity, much of its effect comes from the suggestive power of its words. Thoughts and feelings are condensed.
      (5) When written in Japanese, haiku often has three lines: the first five syllables long, the second seven syllables, the third five syllables.
   c. Tell children you are going to read a translation of an haiku, and you would like them to think of the images it evokes. Read the following:

   A fluttering swarm
      of cherry petals—and there comes,
      pursuing them, the storm![2]

2. Harold G. Henderson, *An Introduction to Haiku* (New York: Doubleday & Company, Inc., 1958).

d. Ask for reactions. Children will probably think of a grove of cherry trees, whose leaves are being blown away by a storm.

e. Ask for volunteers to dramatize rhythmically, in the flow of the poetry, the ideas suggested by the class, as you recite the poem. Let many demonstrate and the class select the dramatizations they prefer. One class suggested having a group of children flutter (using arms, hands, entire body) away from another group who are moving toward them using aggressive, stormlike motions.

f. When the class has developed a dramatization, display rhythm instruments and ask what instruments would most effectively represent the cherry petals. Let the class experiment, as they say the poem with you. (One class chose finger cymbals and jingle bells played in a rapid, fluttery rhythm.)

g. Let the class experiment and select instruments to dramatize the storm. One class developed the following:

(1) Jingle bells and finger cymbals begin fluttering and continue until the end of the poem.

(2) Drums begin softly immediately after the bells and quickly crescendo until they hit a fortissimo, one strongly accented beat, after the word *storm*.

h. Select children to do the following:

(1) Recite the haiku

(2) Perform the rhythmic dramatization

(3) Accompany, using rhythm instruments

i. Have the class discuss the performance and make any changes desired.

j. Repeat, letting children take different parts.

2. Focusing on expression by singing and playing "Happy Are They" on the recorder

For copy of this song, see chapter 2.

a. Teach children to play the song on the recorder, using suggestions found in the section "Notational Concepts: Music Reading" later in this chapter.

b. Have the class play the song again, focusing on feelings aroused. Discuss. Select a predominate feeling and play the song again, expressing this feeling through tones produced on the recorder. (Children generally select sad feelings because of the minor mode.)

c. Discuss other ways to change the mood. (dynamics) Ask the class if certain parts of the song suggest playing louder or softer. (They may decide the second and third phrases, which move from the notes A to D, would sound better louder.) Let the class play the song again, incorporating their ideas.

d. Have the class sing the song first in unison, then as a round. Ask them if hearing the text changes their emotions.

e. When children decide how they want to perform the song, divide the class into two groups: one group to sing the song as a round, the other to perform the song on the recorder using dynamics and expressive qualities decided upon.

f. Have children combine groups, performing the song together, first in unison, then as a round. Ask children how the expressive qualities of the song change when performed together. Does the song sound fuller, richer, bigger? Are there new tone colors? Repeat, incorporating any new ideas.

3. Listening to Largo and Finale from *New World* Symphony by Antonin Dvorak, to focus on expressive concepts

Theme from Largo
New World Symphony

Antonin Dvorak

Theme from Finale
New World Symphony

Antonin Dvorak

a. Let a child learn these themes on a melody instrument.
b. Tell the children this story.

Many years ago, as railroads were being built across our country, a man named Antonin Dvorak came here from Czechoslovakia. He was so impressed with the spirit of growth and freedom, the strength of the pioneers, and the beauty of a new country being formed that he wrote the *New World* Symphony. In it he tried to express some of his feelings about America. Two movements from this symphony are Largo and Finale. The main theme of "Largo" is from the familiar American folk tune, "Goin' Home."

c. Have a child play the Largo theme several times. Encourage children to hum the melody.
d. Continue the story.

Dvorak used this melody as the main theme. The English horn played it (show picture), then violins, then the English horn again. As we listen, think of the different feelings about America that Dvorak tried to express, and the musical means he used to express them.

e. Play Largo. (Unless the class is really concentrating on the music, stop the recording at the end of the first theme, just before the violins begin the second theme.)
f. Ask children to describe the music in musical terms. Is it fast or slow, loud or soft, legato or staccato, smoothly flowing or uneven in rhythm?
g. Explain that the main theme of the Finale is different and have children listen for the feelings Dvorak tried to express and the musical means he used to express them.
h. Play the recording, turning the volume down slowly if the class begins to show signs of restlessness.
i. Ask class to describe the music. Is it fast or slow, legato or staccato, smoothly flowing or uneven rhythmically, loud or soft, stately or lively?
j. Remind children that the musical elements that create expression in music create images in our minds. Tell them that you would like to see what images were created by these two contrasting movements. Distribute sheets similar to that in the next column.
k. Tell children to listen to Largo and to circle the phrases that describe the music, pointing an arrow in the direction of the word Largo as follows:

Largo   **Finale**

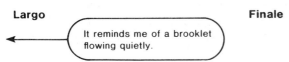

Largo   **Finale**

It reminds me of a skyscraper.

It reminds me of a powerful machine.

It makes me think of rolling plains.

It makes me think of rivers flowing.

It reminds me of the Grand Canyon.

It reminds me of a quiet meadow.

It reminds me of New York City.

It makes me think of people sitting under a tree on a summer day.

It makes me think of huge mountains.

It makes me think of a beautiful sunset.

It makes me think of brilliant colors like red, purple and orange.

It makes me think of walking down a quiet country road.

It makes me think of a calm, blue sky.

l. Play Largo as children circle phrases.
m. Play Finale as children circle phrases.
n. Collect papers and discuss answers, noting that there are differences of opinion. Focus on the musical elements that create the images.
4. Evaluating children's ability to hear expressive elements of music
a. Distribute copies of the following.

Music Cue Chart

1. Loud	Soft	Fast	Slow	Smooth	Detached
2. Loud	Soft	Fast	Slow	Smooth	Detached
3. Loud	Soft	Fast	Slow	Smooth	Detached
4. Loud	Soft	Fast	Slow	Smooth	Detached

b. Tell children you will play four musical compositions, and they should circle the expressive element in each that is the most important in creating the mood. Play the following:
(1) "Hobby Horse" from *Album for the Young* by Tchaikovsky (fast)
(2) "Sick Doll" from *Album for the Young* by Tchaikovsky (detached)
(3) "My Daughter Lidi" from *Album for the Young* by Tchaikovsky (soft)
(4) "Stars and Stripes Forever" by Sousa (loud)
c. Discuss answers. Clarify misunderstandings.

Instrumental Experiences That Focus on Expressive Concepts

Level I or II

Focusing on Expressive Concepts by Creating a Composition for Rhythm Instruments

1. Discuss the ways music can be changed to create differences in mood and feeling. For example:
   a. Rhythm (even, uneven, legato, staccato)
   b. Tempo (fast, slow)
   c. Dynamics (loud, soft)
   d. Phrase (long, short)
   e. Instrumentation (tone color)
2. Distribute rhythm instruments, having children playing like instruments sit together.
3. Ask children to help create a composition using musical elements to change the mood. Tell them to play only when and how you, as the conductor, indicate: fast or slow, loud or soft, staccato or legato, long or short phrases, and so on. Tell them to continue until you indicate otherwise. Experiment by having one instrument—triangles, for example—play slowly until they establish a definite mood, then signal them to stop.
4. Have another instrument play a different rhythm, tempo, and dynamics. For example, tone blocks may play the following:

   Have other instruments experiment: cymbals clash, jingle bells jingle softly, tambourines shake or be struck, finger cymbals tinkle softly, and so on.
5. When children understand and can follow easily, begin. Signal several instruments to play. Triangles might begin, followed by tone blocks, ending one short section with cymbals. Other instruments might gradually be added to create a long, slow crescendo, ending with a forte.

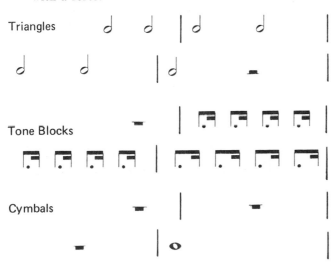

6. Keep building the composition in this way, creating differences in mood and expressive qualities so that children begin to understand how to create these differences with instruments.

Level I or II

Focusing on Expressive Concepts by Creating a Soundscape for Rhythm Instruments

1. Draw this on the board:

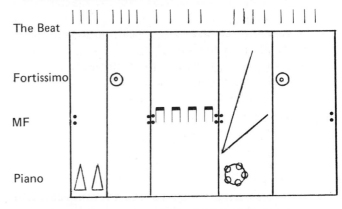

2. Ask children if they can explain the various words, lines, and pictures on the chart. Through discussion, help them understand the symbols.
   a. The Beat: The rhythm is grouped in fours. Have them count the rhythm: one, one, one, one; or ta, ta, ta, ta. Have them count the measures. (five)
   b. Fortissimo: *Fortissimo* means very loud. Anything printed high, where fortissimo is printed, should be played very loud.
   c. MF: *MF* means moderately loud. Anything printed in the middle of the chart should be played moderately loud.
   d. Piano: *Piano* means soft. Anything printed very low on the chart should be played softly.
   e. ⟁ This symbol refers to triangles. They play on the first and third beats of the first measure.
   f. ⊙ This refers to the cymbals, which play on the first beat of the second and fifth measures.
   g. ⊓ This refers to the rhythm sticks and tone blocks, which play eighth notes in the third measure.
   h. ⌘ This refers to the tambourines, which begin shaking on the first beat of the fourth measure and crescendo throughout that measure.
   i. : At this point one should return to the two dots facing the opposite direction and

repeat that entire section. Thus, measures one and two are repeated, the third measure is repeated, and measures four and five are repeated.

3. Have each instrument practice alone, reminding the class to observe the dynamics and rhythm indicated.
4. Tell all instruments to be prepared for their part so that they can begin on the exact beat intended and use the dynamics indicated. Signal the triangles to begin. Conduct, indicating beat, dynamics, and entrances.
5. Discuss with children and repeat, making improvements the class suggests.
6. On another day, help the class create their own soundscape for rhythm instruments.

Level I or II

Focusing on Expressive Concepts by Listening to a Recording
"Tubby the Tuba"

1. Collect pictures of the following instruments and mount each on large cardboards: tuba, oboe, piccolo, violin, flute, trumpet, cello, bassoon, French horn, xylophone, trombone, celesta.
2. Ask children to describe a tuba. During the discussion, mention that it is the largest instrument of the orchestra's brass section and plays the lowest tones. Show the picture of the tuba.
3. Ask the class to listen carefully to a recording you will play, so they can tell what happens to Tubby the Tuba and other characters.
4. Play the recording. Ask the following or similar questions.
   a. What kind of voice did Tubby have?
   b. How did he get in trouble with the orchestra?
   c. Who was his best friend? Does he have a high or low voice?
   d. Who taught Tubby a tune he could play with the orchestra?
   e. What were some of the other members of the orchestra? What kind of voices did they have?
5. Ask the class if they recognize the different instruments. Distribute pictures of instruments. Tell children to raise the appropriate picture when they hear the instrument. Play the recording.
6. Children may enjoy dramatizing "Tubby the Tuba."

Level I, II, or III

Focusing on Expressive Concepts by Playing Rhythm Instruments to Interpret Words
This experience is directed toward level I. By changing words, it can be adapted for level II or III.

1. Distribute rhythm instruments. Tell the children you will call specific instruments (triangles, for example) and a word (ringing, for example). The children holding the instrument are to play the word sound. (Children holding triangles should try to make a ringing sound.)
2. Use words that suggest movement and sound. For example:
   a. Rhythm sticks: running or bouncing
   b. Triangles: ringing
   c. Tambourines: shaking
   d. Finger cymbals: snowing or sparkling
   e. Maracas: laughing
   f. Drums: marching
   g. Tone blocks: ticking
3. Make positive comments about the more successful renditions of the words, but do not discourage children who have difficulty.

Level II or III

Focusing on Expressive Concepts by Creating a Composition for the Recorder
1. Through discussion, decide what type of song children would like to create.
   a. What kind of mood: gay, sad, quiet, or other?
   b. What tempo will create this mood: fast, slow, moderate?
   c. What rhythm will create this mood: even, mostly quarter or half notes; or uneven, dotted quarter notes and eighth notes?
   d. Should the song begin high and move down, or low and move up?
2. Have children experiment with their own ideas. Select a volunteer to play his idea for a first phrase on the recorder. Let others try until the class selects a phrase they like.
3. Notate it on the board and have the class play it. Explain you will choose a volunteer to play a second phrase, preceded by the class playing the first phrase. Select a volunteer. Signal the class to play the first phrase and the volunteer to continue. Give several children the opportunity to play a second phrase.
4. After the class votes for the second phrase they like, notate it on the board.
5. Continue until the song is complete. These hints may help:
   a. When a child plays a phrase that fits well with previous phrases, mention this to the class. When it does not, suggest that you like the phrase but it doesn't fit with those preceding.
   b. If the song is becoming too lengthy and fragmented, suggest it be kept short. Generally, songs of eight or sixteen measures are most successful.
6. When the song is complete and notated on the board, have the class practice until they can play it well.

Chinese Mystery

Fine

D. C. al Fine

Created by Fourth Grade Music Club, North School, N. Merrick, New York

Children will enjoy any of the following:
   a. Playing it from notation as a child points to notes on the board
   b. Notating it on a large card and displaying it on the bulletin board
   c. Choosing appropriate rhythm instruments for accompaniment
   d. Playing it for other classes
   e. Tape recording it
   f. Writing words for it
7. One fourth-grade class composed "Chinese Mystery" for a concert.

Notational Concepts: Music Reading

Level I

Materials Needed
1. Drum
2. Rhythm instruments
3. Song bells
4. Copy of "Engine Number Nine"
5. Music Cue charts
6. Music for evaluation

Instrumental Activities
1. Playing rhythm instruments from notation
2. Playing song with easy skips and steps on song bells

Related Musical Activities
1. Singing, with hand signals

2. Bodily movement (quarter notes, eighth notes and half notes)
3. Music reading

Conceptual Understandings
1. The direction of a melody when heard is related to the contour created when it is notated on the staff.
2. There is a relationship between different durations, which may be seen in notation.
3. The relationship between numbers, syllables, or letter names used in a singing experience may be notated on the musical staff.

Behavioral Objectives
1. To play simple passages on melody instruments
2. To begin to differentiate between contrasting melodic directions and phrases
3. To accurately sing back intervals using sol, mi, la, do, and re

Related Arts
The teacher may wish to give children an experience similar to that suggested on pages 58 and 60, in which children relate the contour suggested by mountain tops in a painting to the contour suggested by music when it is notated.

Procedure
1. Focusing on rhythmic relationship between quarter, eighth, and half notes through bodily movement related to a freight, express, and commuter train

a. Notate the following on the board, omitting number notation and Kodaly counting:

♩	♩	♩	♩
One - two	one - two	one - two	one - two
Ta - a	ta - a	ta - a	ta - a

b. Explain this is the notation for the rhythm of a slow-moving freight train. Have the class clap and count this pattern, clapping on the first beat, moving clasped hands upward on the second.

c. Select a volunteer to lead the children moving in the freight train rhythm, stepping on the first beat of each half note and bending their knees slightly on the second beat as you play the drum. If children have difficulty feeling the rhythm of the repeated half notes, help them by demonstrating it or having a child demonstrate.

d. When children moving in rhythm of freight train are successful, have them sit.

e. Write this on the board:

One	one	one	one	one	one	one	one
Ta	ta	ta	ta	ta	ta	ta	ta

f. Tell children this is the notation for the rhythm of a commuter train. Have them clap and count the pattern.

g. Select a volunteer to lead other children moving in the commuter train rhythm, stepping on each beat of the drum. When they can move easily to this rhythm, have them sit.

h. Write this on the board:

one and	one and	one	and	one and	one and	one and	one and	one and
ti ti	ti ti	ti	ti	ti ti	ti ti	ti ti	ti ti	ti ti

i. Tell children this is the notation for an express train, moving rapidly across the country. Have them clap and count this pattern:

j. Have a volunteer lead other children moving in the express train rhythm, stepping on each note as you accompany on the drum.

k. When children are moving easily in rhythm of the drum, have each group stand in a different corner of the room, behind their leaders. Tell them to listen to the drum and, when they hear the rhythm of their train, to move. They are to stay in line, as a train, and move precisely with the drum.

l. Begin playing the rhythm of one of the trains and continue until the children can move in rhythm. Switch to another train rhythm. When each group

has had the opportunity to move, begin changing rhythms more rapidly, forcing children to concentrate and to respond more quickly.

m. When children are responding quickly and easily, have them switch groups and repeat the exercise.

n. When children have had many such experiences, see if they can move simultaneously, as follows:

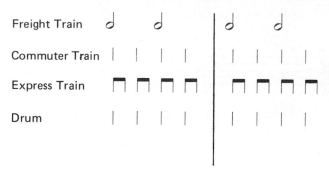

2. Focusing on the rhythmic relationship between the quarter, eighth, and half notes through a game, using rhythm instruments

a. Put the following on the board, omitting the number notation and Kodaly counting:

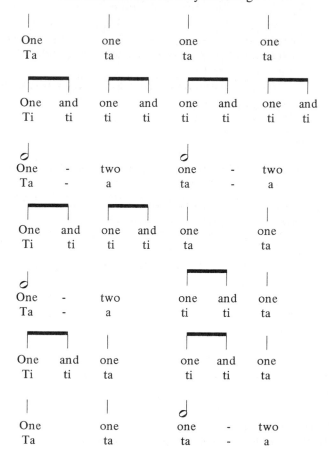

Engine Number Nine

Steadily

Music by Jean Hoover
Old Rhyme

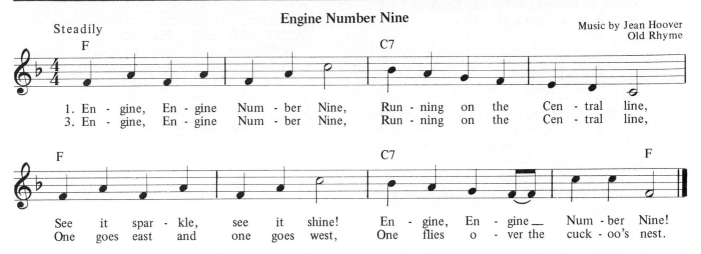

1. En - gine, En - gine Num - ber Nine, Run - ning on the Cen - tral line,
3. En - gine, En - gine Num - ber Nine, Run - ning on the Cen - tral line,

See it spar - kle, see it shine! En - gine, En - gine __ Num - ber Nine!
One goes east and one goes west, One flies o - ver the cuck - oo's nest.

b. Remind children of their experiences with the freight, commuter, and express trains. Ask which notes represent the commuter train. Select a volunteer to point to these notes. Ask which notes represent the freight and express trains and select volunteers to point to these notes.

c. Have the class clap and count the entire pattern.

d. Distribute rhythm instruments. Ask the class which instruments would best play each note. One class selected the following.

Quarter Notes: tambourines and tone blocks

Eighth Notes: rhythm sticks and maracas

Half Notes: triangles and finger cymbals

e. Make certain that the children understand exactly which note value they are to play. Have them follow the notation on the board so they are ready to play at proper times. Signal instruments playing quarter notes to begin. Point to notation in a steady rhythm.

f. Clarify, through discussion, any confusion about when and how to play, by doing one of the following:
   (1) Having a child from each group play the pattern
   (2) Having each group practice alone, internalizing the other notes and playing only when their notes appear

3. Focusing on melodic notation by using song bells to play short phrases in "Engine Number Nine"

a. Have the class echo, singing syllables and using hand signals, until children know each phrase.

D M D M   D M S   F M R D

T₁ L₁ S₁   D M D M   D M S

F M R D   S S D

b. Ask if the phrases they have sung remind them of a familiar song. ("Engine Number Nine")

c. Ask the class to help notate the song on the board. Notate F as follows, hold up song bells, and play F.

d. Ask the class to determine the direction the melody moves by singing the first phrase with hand signals and syllables.

e. Ask what direction the phrase moves from the first note (up) and select a volunteer to play the first two notes. Remind him that the second note may step or skip up.

f. Add A to the notation on the board and ask a child to play these notes.

g. Ask the class to sing the first phrase again, using hand signals and syllables, to hear whether the pattern is repeated in the melody or another pattern is introduced. When they discover that the pattern is repeated three times, add to the notation on the board. Have a child play this group of notes.

h. Have the class sing the first phrase and discover that the last note of the phrase skips up to C. Add this note to the notation on the board and have a child play the entire phrase.

i. Have children clap and count the phrase.
j. Continue helping children discover and play notation for the second and fourth phrases, focusing on the differences in contour created by the passages that step.
4. Evaluating children's ability to recognize steps, skips, and direction (up and down) from musical notation
   a. Distribute Music Cue charts to children.

Music Cue Chart

1. Step	Skip	Up	Down
2. Step	Skip	Up	Down
3. Step	Skip	Up	Down
4. Step	Skip	Up	Down

---

b. Tell children to study the musical notation you show them to determine the following: Does it step or skip? Does it move up or down? One at a time, show the notation for numbers 1–4. Have them circle the words that best describe each.
c. Discuss the answers. Clarify any misunderstandings by having children listen to the phrases played on song bells.

1.

2.

3.

4.

Instrumental Experiences That Focus on Notational Concepts

Level II

Learning to Play a Song on the Recorder, Using the C Scale
"I Had a Little Guppy"

1. Notate middle C on the board. Ask children what note is the next step up. (D) Notate D on the board. Continue until the C scale is on the board.

2. Tell children this combination of notes is called the C scale.
3. Ask a volunteer to play the scale. Have several children play the scale.
4. Tell children many songs are created by using the scale. Show the notation for "I Had a Little Guppy," on the board or a previously prepared chart.
5. Ask children if the scale in the song begins at the bottom or the top. (bottom)
6. Ask if the song goes directly up or if it repeats notes. (repeats each note)
7. Ask how many different notes are used in the first line. (two)
8. Ask the names of these notes. (C and D)

I Had a Little Guppy

Lois Raebeck

I had a lit - tle gup-py; His name was Ti - ny Tim. He

jumped in - to the wat - er, and he be - gan to swim. He

swam a - cross the o - cean; He swam a - cross the sea; And

can't catch me!" Hee hee hee hee hee hee hee hee. _____

9. Focus on syncopation and the dotted quarter followed by the eighth. If the class has had experience with these, proceed to the next step.
10. Ask for volunteers to lead the class by playing the first line on the recorder.
11. Continue helping children discover how to play lines two, three, four, and five.

Level II

Playing More Complex Phrases from a Song on Song Bells
"Au Clair de la Lune"

See the copy of this song earlier in this chapter.

1. Ask the class which number is higher, one or two? (two) Notate F on the board.

2. Tell children this is note 1. Ask who can place note 2 beside it. Select a volunteer to do so. Number notes 1 and 2. If children have difficulty placing G, remind them from a space to a line is one step.

3. Ask another volunteer to place note 3 (A) beside note 2. Write 3 below the note.

4. Ask the class to sing the number of each note as you point to it. Have children sing combinations of these notes. Some combinations are:

1 2 3 2 1   1 1 2 2 1   1 3 2 2 1   1 3 3 2 1   1 2 2 3 2 1

5. Show the notation of "Au Clair de la Lune." Tell the class there are many combinations of 1, 2, 3 notes in the song. Ask on which lines they are found. (lines 1, 2, and 4)

6. Ask for volunteer to play line one. Do the following:
   a. Line 1: Class sings, song bells accompany
      1 1 1 2 3 2   1 3 2 2 1
   b. Line 2: Class sings, song bells accompany
      1 1 1 2 3 2   1 3 2 2 1
   c. Line 3: Teacher sings alone
      2 2 2 2 6 6   2 1 7 6 5
   d. Line 4: Class sings, song bells accompany
      1 1 1 2 3 2   1 3 2 2 1
7. When class can sing tune using number names easily, have them sing words.

Level II

Focusing on Compound Meter (6/8) and its Notational Aspects, by Using Percussion Instruments
"Happy Are They"

For a copy of this song, see chapter 2.

1. Display rhythmic notation for "Happy Are They" and have children follow the score as you clap and count the rhythm of the round.

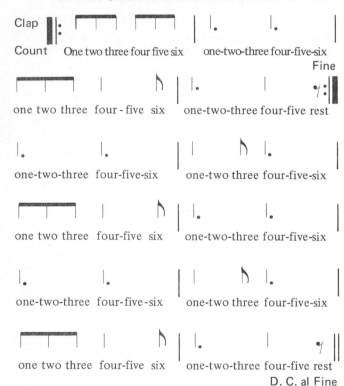

D. C. al Fine

2. Ask children if they noticed something different about your counting. Explain the following:
   a. In 6/8 meter the eighth note represents the basic beat.
   b. There are six, eighth notes (or six beats) to a measure.
   c. Six-eighths meter is called compound meter, i.e., it has two principal accents, the first beat and the fourth beat, giving the feeling of two groups of threes in each measure.
3. Ask children to watch the score as you clap, and note where you stop clapping. Begin, stopping in the middle of the song. Ask where you stopped. Repeat, until they can follow the rhythmic score.
4. Let a child point to notes as you clap and count the rhythm. Let volunteers clap and count each phrase.
5. When children are familiar with the rhythm of the round, help them select appropriate rhythm instruments to play each phrase. One class selected the following:
   a. Lines 1 and 2 (repeated): Rhythm sticks and tone blocks
   b. Lines 3, 4, 5, and 6: Triangles and finger cymbals
6. Divide the class into two groups, choosing a leader for each group. Have them perform the round, using rhythm instruments instead of singing.
7. Have the class say the words of the round in rhythm, no instruments.
8. Teach the melody and have the class sing.

Level II or III

Focusing on Notational Concepts by Transposing a Familiar Song from the Major Scale to the Twelve-Tone Scale
"Are You Sleeping"

For a copy of this song, see chapter 6.

1. Clap the rhythm of "Are You Sleeping." Ask what song you clapped.

2. Explain that music is written in different scales: major; minor; and others, such as the twelve-tone scale (sometimes called tone row).
3. Tell children we are going to alter "Are You Sleeping," using a twelve-tone scale.
4. Distribute the first twelve bells of the chromatic scale, beginning with middle C. Have children with resonator bells arrange themselves in a row so that bells are *not* in normal sequence. Starting at the beginning

of the row, have each child play his note (in the rhythm of "Are You Sleeping"), until the first twelve notes of the song have been played. In one class the result was the following:

5. Explain that since each note has been used, we must start at the beginning and play the notes in the same order, in the rhythm of the song. Once the order is established, no tone can be repeated until all twelve notes have been played. Have children continue until song is completed.

6. Have children write their notation for "Are You Sleeping" on the chalkboard. After they sing it, ask the following questions:
   a. Are there many skips? (Have a child point to skips.)
   b. Are there many steps? (Have a child point to steps.)
   c. Is the melody in the low, middle, or high range?
   d. What kind of notes are used in it? (quarter, eighth, half)
7. Children may enjoy orchestrating it, using poly-rhythms.
   Drums 1 2 3 4 1 2 3 4 1 2 3 4
   Claves 1 2 3 1 2 3 1 2 3 1 2 3

Level III

Focusing on Notation by Playing Themes, Using Song Bells

"Andante Cantabile" from String Quartet op. 11 no. 1, by Tchaikovsky

1. Display the theme of "Andante Cantabile."

2. Explain that Tchaikovsky, working in his study, heard a plasterer whistling this Russian folk tune, and he used it in one of his string quartets.
3. Tell children to examine the melody to see where it skips and steps. Ask individuals to point to skips, steps, and notes that stay the same.
4. Ask the class if there is anything unusual about the meter signature. (begins in 2/4, changes to 3/4, then back to 2/4)
5. Ask volunteers to play the first two measures, then all four measures, having the class help correct any errors.
6. Tell the class you will play the recording of "Andante Cantabile" from the String Quartet. Ask them to raise their hands when they hear the theme.
7. Play the recording. The theme, which we will call A, occurs as follows: A A A B B A A Coda. Children should recognize this as an ABA form.
8. Have the children discuss and give their reactions to the music.

Individualizing Instrumental Experiences

Listed below are activities that will help children reinforce concepts previously experienced in a large group.

Level I

Recordings for Individualizing Instrumental Experiences
For one child or a small group

Children can follow these recordings with little or no help from the teacher. All are available from Educational Record Sales, 157 Chambers St., New York, N.Y. 10007.

Exploring the Rhythm Instruments
Introducing the Rhythm Instruments
Our First Rhythm Band, vols. 1 and 2

Level II

Finish the Song Game
For one child

Duplicate, then distribute "Finish the Song Game" (page 238). Copy the Answer Sheet on heavy cardboard, then laminate it.

Finish the Song Game

Fill in the missing notes, using the letters beneath the staff and the rhythmic notation above the staff as a guide. Check your work with the Answer Sheet. Then practice playing the song until you can play it for the class.

B   B   A A G
Rock my soul,   Rock-a-long, Rock-a-long,

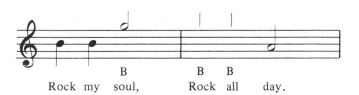

B   B   B
Rock my soul,   Rock all   day.

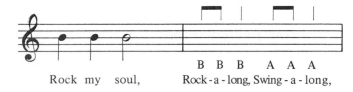

B   B   B   A   A   A
Rock my   soul,   Rock-a-long, Swing-a-long,

B   A   G
Rock my   soul,   All of the   day.

Answer Sheet

Level II or III

Scrambled Words Game
Instruments of the Orchestra

Ditto or mimeograph the following. Copy the Answer Sheet on heavy cardboard and laminate. Have children check their own work.

Scrambled Words Game

Beside each scrambled word, put the correct spelling of the instrument of the orchestra; it will be one of the instruments listed below. Check your answers with the Answer Sheet.

1. lartenic	6. aviol	11. phar
2. buta	7. shligne rhon	12. lesceta
3. locel	8. petrumt	13. colpico
4. ephoxason	9. ipitamn	14. bylcams
5. eboo	10. teflu	15. brontemo

Instruments harp, tuba, piccolo, trumpet, clarinet, oboe, English horn, cymbals, timpani, cello, flute, viola, saxophone, trombone, celesta

---

Answer Sheet

1. clarinet	6. viola	11. harp
2. tuba	7. English horn	12. celesta
3. cello	8. trumpet	13. piccolo
4. saxophone	9. timpani	14. cymbals
5. oboe	10. flute	15. trombone

Level III

Creating an Orchestration for a Rock Composition
For one child or a small group

1. Select a popular rock record.
2. Listen to the record.
3. Experiment playing rhythm patterns with three different instruments such as drum, tone block, and tambourine, until an orchestration has been created.
4. Notate orchestration in a manner similar to the following:

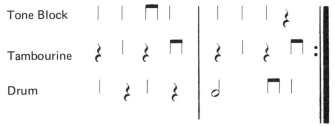

5. Perform for the entire group, using other children, if necessary.
6. Ask the class for positive suggestions for improving the orchestration.
7. Revise, if necessary.

Chairs to Mend

Round

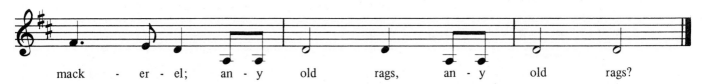

Chairs to mend, old chairs to mend; Mack - er - el, fresh

mack - er - el; an - y old rags, an - y old rags?

From *Guitar in the Classroom* by Timmerman and Griffith, © 1971 by Wm. C. Brown Company Publishers. (in public domain)

Level III

Learning to Play a Guitar Accompaniment for "Chairs to Mend"

For a small group or club activity

1. Review fingering for the D major chord, figure 4.17.

Figure 4.17
D major chord

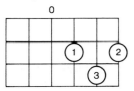

2. Place the following on the board:

3. Have children finger the D chord with their left hands, then strum, in rhythm, brushing the thumb of their right hands gently downward across the strings, over the sound hole.
4. Ask children if it would sound better to them if one of these strokes were stronger. Let them experiment.
5. Ask children to strum the first stroke for each pattern slightly louder, as you sing "Chairs to Mend."
6. Teach children a new strum. On the first and third beats, pluck the fourth string (D) with the thumb. On the second and fourth beats, flick fingernails down across the first three strings.

7. As children are learning these accompaniments, invite them to sing with you.

Level III

Learning to Alternate the A and E₇ Chords on the Guitar to Accompany "The Big Corral"

For a small group or club activity

Figure 4.18
a, A major chord; **b,** E₇ chord

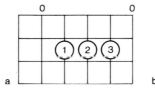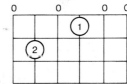

1. Review the fingering for the A major and E₇ chords by having children finger them as they strum, changing chords when you indicate. Have children play in patterns similar to the following:

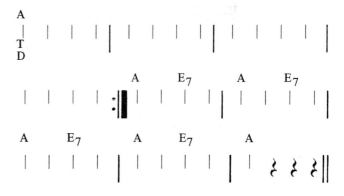

The Big Corral

2. The chuck we get ain't fit to eat.
   Press along to the big corral.
   There's rocks in the beans and sand in the meat.
   Press along to the big corral.

3. The wrangler's out a-scourin' the hills.
   Press along to the big corral.
   So hop in your britches and grease up your gills.
   Press along to the big corral.

Adapted from arrangement from *Folk Songster* by Dallin and Dallin © 1967 by Wm. C. Brown Company Publishers, Dubuque, Iowa. (in public domain)

2. When children can easily play the exercise in number 1, tell them to watch and listen as you sing and play the accompaniment for "The Big Corral," focusing on the words on which chords change.

3. Ask children these questions: What is the beginning chord? (A major) When do you change to E₇? (on the last syllable of *corral*) When do you change back to A? (on the word *should*) When do you change to E₇ once again? (on *big*) Continue until the end of the song.

4. Tell children to accompany the song with you, always being mentally prepared to change chords before the change occurs. When changing, they should move their fingers as a unit.

5. Divide the class into two groups, half to accompany as the others sing. Reverse group roles.

6. When children have mastered chord changes, invite them to experiment with more difficult strums, such as the following:

Level III

Learning to Accompany "Rio Grande" on the Guitar, Using D Major, G Major, and A₇ Chords
For a small group or club activity

Figure 4.19
a, D major chord; **b**, G major chord; **c**, A₇ chord

D Major

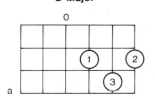

a

G Major

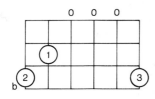

b

A₇

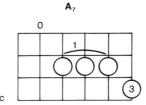

c

1. Review the fingering of the D major, G major, and A₇ chords.

2. Write the first verse of the song on page 242 (with chord markings) on the board. Ask children to sing it and clap on the first and fourth beat of each measure.

```
6  1  2  3  4  5  6
8
   Clap        clap
```

3. Discuss the chord changes, reminding children that they should keep strumming on one chord until a change is indicated above the words.

4. Have them do the following: finger the D chord; as an introduction, play two strums downward with the thumb; then sing, strumming twice for each measure. Remind them to be prepared for chord changes and to move their fingers as a unit when changes occur.

5. Select children to accompany as the class sings. Repeat, changing accompanists, until the class has some facility in playing. When children have mastered chord changes, they may enjoy learning the lope as follows. They will play two patterns per measure as they accompany the song.

Beat 1 Thumb strums gently down to the left of the hole.

Beat 2 Thumb moves upward to the right of the hole.

Beat 3 Close brush. (All fingers of the right hand brush down across the strings, then stop the strings with the palm of the hand.)

Level III

Focusing on the Dotted Eighth- and Sixteenth-Note Pattern by Learning an Accompaniment on the Guitar
"Michael Row the Boat Ashore"
For a small group or club activity

1. Put the following pattern on the board, omitting notation below it:

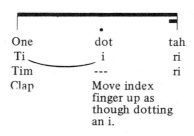

One	dot	tah
Ti	i	ri
Tim	---	ri
Clap	Move index finger up as though dotting an i.	

Rio Grande

Vigorously

American Chantey

1. O say, were you ev-er in Ri-o Grande? A-
   way, _____ Ri-o. ____ It's there that the riv-er runs
   down gold-en sand, And we're bound for the Ri-o Grande. ____

Chorus

And a-way, _____ Ri-o, ____ A-
way, _____ Ri-o, ____ So fare___ you well, my
bon-nie young girl, And we're bound for the Ri-o Grande. ____

2. Oh, New York City is no place for me, away, Rio.
   I'll pack my bags, and then I'll go out to sea.
   We're bound for the Rio Grande.

3. The anchor's aweigh and the sails they are set.
   The girls we are leaving we'll never forget. etc.

4. So pack up your sea bag and get under way.
   Perhaps we'll return again another day. etc.

5. A jolly good mate and a jolly good crew,
   A jolly good ship and a good skipper, too, etc.

6. Now you lovely ladies, we would let you know
   That the time has come, and we're about to go. etc.

7. Sing goodby to Sally, and goodby to Sue,
   And to all you listening, it's goodby, too. etc.

Arranged from *Heritage Songster* by Dallin and Dallin, © 1966 by Wm. C. Brown Company Publishers, Dubuque, Iowa. (in public domain)

Michael, Row the Boat Ashore

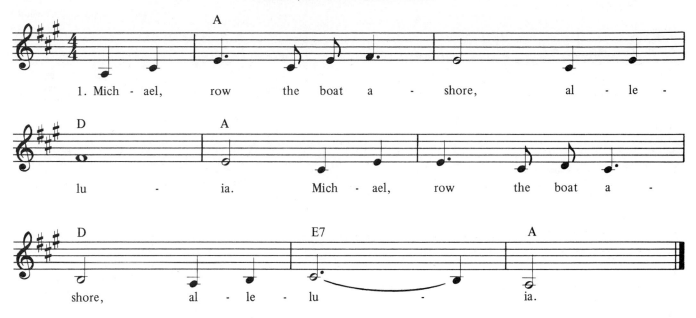

1. Mich - ael, row the boat a - shore, al - le -
lu - ia. Mich - ael, row the boat a -
shore, al - le - lu - ia.

2. Sister, help to trim the sail, alleluia, (twice)
   (Repeat verse 1 after each verse.)
3. River Jordan's deep and wide, alleluia, (twice)
4. River Jordan's chilly and cold, alleluia, (twice)

Adapted from arrangement from *Folk Songster* by Dallin and Dallin, © 1967 by Wm. C. Brown Company Publishers, Dubuque, Iowa. (in public domain)

2. Ask if anyone can name the two notes used in this pattern and demonstrate how they would be clapped. Explain, if necessary, that this pattern is a dotted eighth and sixteenth note and in 4/4 meter the dotted eighth note gets three-quarters of a beat, the sixteenth note gets one-fourth of a beat, the entire pattern one beat.
3. Have the class clap and count the pattern, using the counting most familiar to them.
4. Explain that this pattern is a good guitar accompaniment for many songs. Demonstrate, using chords from the song "Michael, Row the Boat Ashore."
5. Show the class how to strum: lightly rest four fingers of the right hand just below the sound hole. Gently strum down with the thumb, in the rhythm of the strum.

Thumb   Thumb
down   down

Level III

Focusing on 3/4 Meter by Learning Accompaniment on the Guitar
"Streets of Laredo," for a small group or club activity

1. Write this on the board. ¾
2. Ask where it is found. (at the beginning of a composition) Ask what it means. (The top number indicates three counts to each measure. The bottom number indicates a quarter note gets one beat.)
3. Teach the class a guitar accompaniment using the D major, G major, and A₇ chords. Use this entire sequence (the lope) for each chord.
   Beat 1 Thumb strums gently down to the left of the hole.
   Beat 2 Thumb moves upward to the right of the hole.
   Beat 3 Close brush. (Close brush means to brush all fingers of the right hand down across the strings, then stop the strings with the palm of the hand.)
4. When the class can play these chords, using the lope and moving easily from one chord to another, teach "Streets of Laredo" (page 244), as they accompany.

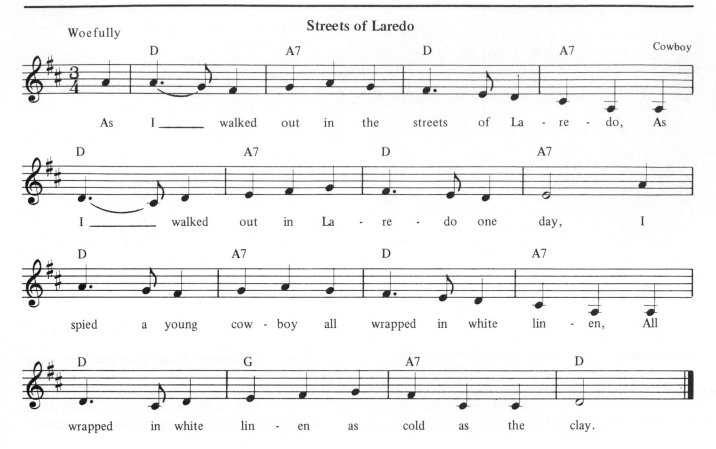

Streets of Laredo

Woefully

Cowboy

As I _____ walked out in the streets of La - re - do, As I _____ walked out in La - re - do one day, I _____ spied a young cow - boy all wrapped in white lin - en, All wrapped in white lin - en as cold as the clay.

2. "I see by your outfit that you are a cowboy,"
   These words he did say as I boldly stepped by;
   "Come, sit down beside me and hear my sad story,
   I'm shot in the breast, and I'm going to die."

3. "Now once in the saddle I used to go dashing,
   Yes, once in the saddle I used to be gay;
   I'd dress myself up and go down to the card-house,
   I got myself shot, and I'm dying today."

4. "Get six husky cowboys to carry my coffin;
   Get ten lovely maidens to sing me a song;
   And beat the drum slowly and play the fife lowly,
   For I'm a young cowboy who knows he was wrong."

5. "Oh, please go and bring me a cup of cold water
   To cool my parched lips, they are burning," he said.
   Before I could get it, his soul had departed
   And gone to its Maker—the cowboy was dead.

6. We beat the drum slowly, and played the fife lowly,
   And wept in our grief as we bore him along;
   For we loved the cowboy, so brave and so handsome,
   We loved that young cowboy although he'd done wrong.

Adapted from *Heritage Songster* by Dallin and Dallin, © 1966 by Wm. C. Brown Company Publishers, Dubuque, Iowa. (in public domain)

Additional Enrichment Activities

Experiences with rhythm, melody, accompanying, and band and orchestral instruments can be enriched when the teacher encourages children to play and use their knowledge of these instruments in combination with each other and other musical activities. When they create an accompaniment for a song learned on the recorder or select an effective rhythm pattern and instrument to accompany a song, not only is musical learning encouraged, but enjoyment as well. When they discover that they can use a recorder or song bells to play a phrase from a song or a theme from a listening experience, they see the relatedness of musical activities and mentally form musical concepts. Knowledge of chordal construction, derived from experiences with Autoharp, guitar, and other accompanying instruments, provides another skill, enabling them to help create a second part for recorder or song bells, based on the notes in Autoharp or guitar chords. As children learn to play melody and accompanying instruments in duets, trios, and ensembles they gradually become aware of one of music's most rewarding experiences, that of making music with other people.

The following list includes other enriching activities:

1. Listening to children or adults play instruments in the classroom or in assembly programs
2. Collecting pictures of instruments for a music notebook
3. Drawing illustrations of favorite instruments for the bulletin board or creating a mural to show instruments of the orchestra
4. Asking children who play instruments to accompany the class as they sing or play themes from listening experiences
5. Attending a concert, preferably for children, given by a band or orchestra

Discussions and Reports

1. Discuss the merits of the child playing rhythm, melody, and accompanying instruments to promote growth in conceptual understanding. Explain a creative approach by which these instruments can hasten the child's perception of musical concepts: rhythm, melody, texture, form, expression, and music reading.
2. Explain how singing, accompanied by melody instruments, helps children understand notation in the score.
3. Discuss ways that elementary-school children can explore and use a piano for musical growth and enjoyment.
4. Discuss ways to introduce rhythm instruments, so that children become aware of the distinctive tone qualities of each.

5. Discuss ways to use related arts to encourage specific conceptual understandings related to rhythm, melody, texture, form, expression, and music reading.
6. Write a report indicating advantages and disadvantages of combining many different musical activities (singing, rhythms, listening, instrumental experiences, and so on) with related arts, to focus on musical concepts.
7. Compare the contributions of the following to adult appreciation, understanding, and participation in musical activities: experiences with rhythm instruments, melody instruments, accompanying instruments, and band and orchestral instruments.
8. Compare and contrast the approach you would use for children age nine and those age six, to help them distinguish between the tone produced by violin, cello, trumpet, French horn, flute, oboe, bassoon, and tuba.
9. Explore ways to use guitar and Autoharp to help develop conceptual understandings related to texture.
10. Examine the Music Cue charts. Discuss changes that would help focus more precisely on the musical concepts under consideration.
11. Discuss this chapter, focusing on creativity versus rigidity.
12. Using the "Instrumental Activities Evaluation Chart," keep a log of all instrumental activities. This may be a basis for an expanding source of instrumental activities for future use.

Activities to Develop Skills and Practice in Initiating Musical Experiences

1. Be prepared to teach the class one or two songs from any available elementary songbook, using the guitar or Autoharp to accompany.
2. Prepare a strategy for introducing the Autoharp, song bells, or recorder. Indicate the age level for which the experience is planned as well as materials needed, related musical activities, conceptual understandings, behavioral objectives, and related arts.
3. Examine the Music Cue charts. Create several alternative ways of evaluating children's perception of a specific conceptual understanding. Write a plan for presenting one alternative to the class. Initiate and guide the experience. Evaluate through discussion.
4. Select a two-chord song from any available elementary songbook. Assuming the class is a fourth grade, initiate an experience in which they create a chording plan for the song, following a procedure similar to that suggested for "Poet and Peasant" ("Textural Concepts").
5. Prepare a set of water glasses to play the C scale. Introduce and initiate an experience in which the class learns to play a simple tune on the glasses.

6. Find a poem (haiku or other) that suggests sound effects that could be made by rhythm instruments. Prepare a plan similar to that suggested in this chapter ("Expressive Concepts") listing conceptual understandings, behavioral objectives, and specific suggestions to involve children. Initiate and guide the experience. Evaluate through discussion.

7. Prepare and initiate an experience for creating a second part for song bells, using guitar or Autoharp chord markings as an aid. Use an approach similar to that suggested for "Rig-A-Jig-Jig."

8. Using the outline suggested for each of the musical concepts, prepare a strategy for notational concepts (music reading), in which the recorder is used in relation with some other musical activity (singing, rhythms, listening).

9. Prepare a strategy for using rhythm instruments in conjunction with singing, listing age level, specific materials needed, related musical activities, conceptual understandings, behavioral objectives, and related arts.

10. Create a song for recorder or song bells. Prepare a teaching plan and initiate your plan.

11. Initiate an experience in which you guide the class as they create a song based on the tone row, similar to that suggested in the section, "Melodic Concepts."

12. Plan and initiate an experience in which the class identifies the instruments of the orchestra, using a composition from *Nutcracker* Suite. Be sure that you are familiar with the sequence in which the instruments play.

13. Prepare an experience for using both Autoharp and song bells (or recorders) to accompany class singing. Initiate and evaluate through class discussion.

14. Compile a list of songs, from available elementary songbooks, that can give additional experience playing tonal groups on the recorder (BAG, CBAG, or DCBAG, for example). Make a plan for teaching one of these on the recorder. Initiate and evaluate results.

15. Make a list of one-chord, two-chord, and three-chord songs, from the available elementary songbooks, that may be accompanied on Autoharp or guitar. Make a teaching plan for one of these songs. Initiate and guide the experience with the class. Evaluate results through discussion.

16. Prepare a music learning packet for Autoharp similar to that suggested for piano. Evaluate through discussion.

Instrumental Activities Evaluation Chart

Level	Song, If Used	Record, If Used	Instrumental Activity					Conceptual Understandings	Behavioral Objectives	Related Arts	Evaluation
			Rhythm Instruments	Simple Melody	Recorder	Accompanying	Band or Orchestral				

Supplementary Publications for Experiences with Instruments

Guitar Publications

Title	Author	Publisher
Alfred's Basic Guitar Method, 6 books	d'Auberge and Manus	Alfred Music Co.
Music through the Guitar, 4 vols.	Nance and Golda	Neil Kjos Publishers
Teaching Guitar	University of the State of New York	Bureau of Secondary Curriculum Development

Piano Publications

All About Music through the Keyboard	Sevush and Freidman	Lyre Publishing Co.
Music for the Classroom	Pace	Lee Roberts Music Publishers

Recorder Publications

Method Books

Basic Recorder Technique, 2 vols.	Orr	BMI Canada Ltd.
Bernard Krainis Recorder Method	Krainis	Galaxy Music Corp.
Breeze-Easy Method for Recorders, One and All	Richardson	M. Witmark
Classroom Recorder, The soprano, bks. 1 and 2	G. and S. Burakoff	Consort Music
Comprehensive Recorder Method—Singing and Playing with Orff Instruments (four children's books and accompanying teacher's manuals)	L. Wheeler and E. Wheeler	Belwin-Mills
Elementary Method for Soprano Recorder	G. Burakoff	Hargail Music Press
First Recorder Book (soprano)	M. Dubbe	Magnamusic Baton, Inc.
It's Recorder Time	d'Auberge and Manus	Alfred Music Co.
Music Making in the Elementary School (children's and teacher's editions)	G. Burakoff and L. Wheeler	Hargail Music Press
Music Making in the Elementary School, Vol. 2 (children's and teacher's editions)	L. Wheeler and E. Wheeler	Hargail Music Press
New Recorder Tutor, book 1 (soprano)	S. Goodyear	Belwin-Mills
Playing the Recorder (soprano or alto)	White and Bergman	E. B. Marks
School Recorder, book 1 (soprano)	Priestly and Fowler	E. J. Arnold, Ltd. (Leeds Music)

Solos

An Elizabethan Songbag (soprano)	Raebeck	E. B. Marks, Belwin-Mills
Easy Pieces of the Seventeenth and Eighteenth Centuries (soprano)	Kaestner and Lechner	B. Schott's Sohne
Folksongs from England (soprano)	Bixler	Magnamusic-Baton
Music Around the Year (soprano)	Chazanoff	Hargail Music Press
Nineteen Folksongs (soprano)	Dinn	Oxford University Press
Very First Favorites for the Soprano Recorder	Hofstad	G. Schirmer

Duets

Beginners Method for Soprano and Alto Recorders, part 1 and 2	G. and S. Burakoff	Hargail Music Press
Children's Song Book for Soprano Recorder	Newman and Kolinski	Hargail Music Press
Duet Recorder, The, books 1 and 2	G. Burakoff and W. Strickland	Consort Music
Elementary Duet Book for Soprano Recorders	G. Burakoff	Hargail Music Press
Ensemble Recorder	L. Wheeler	Consort Music
Tunes for Children	Kuhlbach	Peripole, Inc.

Ukulele Publications

Learn to Play the Alfred Way, Ukulele	Manus	Alfred Publishing Co.

Autoharp Publications

Autoharp Accompaniments to Old Favorite Songs	Fox	Summy-Birchard
Classroom Teacher's Guide and Score for the Musical Fun Books	Staples	Follett
Colors and Chords for the Autoharp	Ludwig	Carl Van Roy (Peripole)
Harmony Fun with the Autoharp	Krone	Niel A. Kjos
How to Play the Autoharp	Hall	Boston Music
Instructor for the Autoharp		Oscar Schmidt-International
Many Ways to Play the Autoharp, The, vols. 1 and 2	Peterson	Oscar Schmidt-International
Melody, Rhythm and Harmony	Slind	Belwin-Mills
More Melody, Rhythm and Harmony	Slind	Belwin-Mills
Sing and Strum	Snyder	Belwin-Mills
Teaching Music with the Autoharp	Nye and Peterson	Music Educators Group

Recordings and Filmstrips for Band and Orchestral Instruments

Title	Label	Elementary Grade Level
An Introduction to Musical Instruments	Lerner	Upper
Instruments of the Orchestra	RCA ·	Upper
Meet the Instruments	Bowmar/ Noble	All
Old King and His Fiddlers Four, The (strings)	Bowmar/ Noble	All
Tom the Piper (Woodwind)	Bowmar/ Noble	All
Young Person's Guide to the Orchestra (Britten)	Holt, Rinehart & Winston	Upper

Picture Sources for Band and Orchestra Instruments

Bowmar/Noble Inc., 4563 Colorado Blvd., Los Angeles, Ca., 90039
Conn, 1101 E. Beardsley St., Elkhart, Ind., 46514
Jam Handy Filmstrips, Prentice Hall Media, ServCode MM, 150 White Plains
    Rd., Tarrytown, N.Y. 10591
G. Schirmer, Inc., 609 Fifth Ave., New York, N.Y. 10017

Listening Experiences 5

Listening precedes any musical learning. It is the sense most needed to participate successfully in musical experiences and to achieve musical growth. Equally important, however, listening can be one of music's most satisfying experiences for the child, for here she can gain emotional satisfaction and a means of relating more successfully to herself and the world. The capacity for innate creativity also grows as she acquires a most enjoyable leisure activity.

Listening is not new to the child. As an infant, she discovered her world through touching, smelling, looking, tasting, and listening. She listened to rattles that came into the crib and sounds made by people and things. Slowly she began to discriminate. She learned the voices of mother and father; sometimes mother's voice sounded happy, sometimes stern, other times sad. She learned to imitate sounds and, through speaking, to communicate needs and feelings. Listening helped the child take the first steps toward role assumption and verbal communication.

Thus, when the child enters the elementary school, she has had listening experience. When she is offered an opportunity to participate in a relevant activity, she wants to listen. The teacher who recognizes and respects this attitude will plan his lessons to guide the child to more discriminate listening in music. He will focus the child's attention on the exciting, enjoyable elements in music and help her understand and participate in musical experiences through rhythm, melody, texture, form, and expression.

Aims of Listening Experiences

1. To keep the child's ear receptive through relevant listening experiences that she can participate in, understand, and enjoy.
2. To help the child discover the beauty and enjoyment she can experience through listening.
3. To help the child achieve conceptual understandings and behavioral objectives related to listening experiences. (For a list of conceptual understandings and behavioral objectives related to each age level, see the "Growth and Sequence Chart" at end of chapter 1.)

Listening Activities

Listening activities are most rewarding for the child when they follow her natural growth pattern, when they move gradually in sequence from the world of her experience to abstract music.

What does this imply for the teacher planning listening experiences? It suggests the necessity of knowing many avenues through which children can enjoy listening.

1. Nonmusical sources (sounds of the environment, poetry, literature, works of art), which can encourage more perceptive and imaginative listening habits
2. Experiences with singing, instruments, bodily movement, and music reading, which reinforce listening skills
3. Experiences with listening to all types of music: contemporary and classical; pure or abstract and program; music enjoyed for its own sake and music that provides new understandings about different people and cultures

It implies that the teacher must be able to plan experiences based on the maturity of the children involved—their attention span, conceptual ability, and sophistication level. He must be aware, too, that music becomes enjoyable through understanding and familiarity, which depend on repeated meaningful listening. Ultimately the teacher must hear the expressive elements in music (rhythm, melody, texture, form, and expression) and form concrete ideas for helping children hear and express their individual responses to them through active participation.

Through this process, the child gradually acquires a basis for developing an intelligent criteria for evaluating music. As she senses and begins to verbalize responses to the varied types of music she hears, music can become her own and act as a creative, positive force in her life.

To what specific kinds of music listening activities do children respond? Children in the elementary grades can respond to:

1. Story music: music written with the intent of telling a story, without words
2. Mood or picture music: music written to convey a mood or call up images
3. Abstract music
4. Opera and operettas.

Although children on any level can respond to these listening experiences, when they are tailored to the appropriate maturity level, the teacher will usually find that children in the early grades respond most naturally to story music. Because the child on this level experiences life through her own responses (which tend to be physical rather than verbal), and because she needs to relate all activities to her own life experience, she has a natural affinity for music that tells a story.

To give children on any age level the optimum experiences however, the teacher will want to do more than simply tell the story and have children listen. He will want to ask himself these questions.

1. What conceptual understandings and behavioral objectives can be achieved through this experience? How can my plans encourage them?
2. What musical concepts or elements (tempo, dynamics, melody, rhythm, tone color, expression, or other) are important to the story? How do they contribute?
3. How can I present the recording so that children hear and respond to these elements through active participation?

Through thoughtful answers to these questions the teacher can give children meaningful experiences.

As the child gradually learns to relate to other people, other ideas, and more abstract concepts, her potential for listening expands. She is better prepared to enjoy music that expresses a mood or paints a picture, more able to respond to subtle shades of emotion, and more apt to think of situations related to distant places and people. She also knows the musical elements used to reproduce these. It becomes easier to verbalize what she feels and sees. Consequently, experiences with mood and picture music not only help her experience new musical growth and enjoyment, they also help crystallize her feelings about life.

As in all listening activities, the child's experience with mood or picture music should be a reciprocal adventure; that is, the child should be helped to hear the composer's intent and should be encouraged to make her own response. To accomplish this, it is helpful to approach experiences with mood and picture music in two ways.

1. Experiences in which the title helps establish the mood or picture
2. Experiences in which children associate with the music independent of the title

In the first, the title is enough to stimulate the imagination: "The Moldau"—a river in Czechoslovakia. Where does it go? What does it pass on its way? What people, what events? How will the music tell us about these? When the child has explored the possibilities inherent in the title and the musical elements that might be used to articulate these ideas, she will listen eagerly not only to hear which of her ideas are expressed in music, but also

to see whether she has overlooked any ideas of the composer. In the second, the teacher will want to elicit the imagination of the child in hearing, feeling and seeing what the music is trying to convey through its rhythm, melody, texture, form, and expressive qualities, before revealing the title.

How does abstract music differ from mood and picture music? All music conveys a mood and all music, to some listeners, suggests a story or picture. Abstract music is music that fits the following:

1. It is composed without the intent of telling a story.
2. The focus of attention is on the themes used, musical forms created, and use of expressive musical elements to create these themes and forms.

Thus, mood and picture music can also be considered abstract music when the focus is on the themes or form rather than the mood or picture suggested.

Abstract music presents a greater challenge to the teacher than any other phase of listening activities. In no other phase is it quite so important for the teacher to give careful thought and planning to what he says and does. His attitude and method of presenting an experience will strongly influence the child's attitude toward abstract music.

Why is the teacher's attitude so important? The child approaching adolescence needs to be like his contemporaries. In music, unfortunately, this often means automatic rejection of abstract music. The teacher who accepts this attitude as normal for the child, and on that basis, refuses to fight it, will gain a foothold in developing the kind of relationship that allows him to help the child appreciate the richer experiences in music. In a practical sense, this means that the teacher must accept the child's right to her convictions in music, as in all other areas—even when these convictions run counter to those of an experienced and knowledgeable adult.

This does not mean that the teacher must reject the role of guide. On the contrary, it is important for the teacher to remember his role and to state his convictions honestly. When this is done with an attitude that accepts differences of opinion and encourages a spirit of mutual exploration, the child will come to believe that all music has something to offer—music from his world as well as music from the adult world. If, in addition, she sees the teacher incorporating and relating aspects of popular music into the listening experience and, indeed, occasionally finding classroom time to play recordings she loves, her attitude toward abstract music from the classical repertoire will become more accepting.

This can be further encouraged by the teacher who finds ways of letting children explore the elements that create music—helping them create mini-musical compositions that use the different types of scales (major, minor, whole tone, tone row), textures (harmony, polytonality, atonality, use of tone clusters), and rhythms (polyrhythms, irregular and shifting meters) as part of an overall experience in which he hears these elements used by composers in major compositions.

When children have been exposed to an approach that accepts their views and encourages an imaginative, unbiased exploration of classical music, they can adopt an attitude that encourages enjoyment of abstract music and growth in conceptual understandings.

Because in such an approach it is implicit that each experience must grow out of each unique combination of children, teacher, and classroom situation, it is impossible and undesirable to set rigid criteria for all procedures. It is possible, however, to set up guide lines that remind us of the conceptual understandings we hope to bring to children—whatever our method of proceeding.

Three points are important to remember in planning any experience with abstract music.

1. The child must be given a clear idea of what to listen for.
   a. The themes and resultant form
   b. The use of rhythm, melody, texture, form, and expressive elements to implement the themes and form
2. The child must be allowed to participate in one of the following ways:
   a. Through learning to recognize the themes
      (1) Hearing and seeing them
      (2) Learning to sing them or play them on a melody instrument
   b. Through learning to follow the themes as they occur in the composition
      (1) Using theme cards
      (2) Using skeleton or miniature scores
   c. Through responding to the thematic materials and the form of the composition
      (1) Creating rhythmic accompaniments
      (2) Creating dance forms or rhythmic dramatizations
3. Listening experiences must take into account the child's attention span. When the teacher needs to present a selection that is too long in its entirety, he should find a shortened version or stop the selection at an appropriate place. There is no reason to deprive children of the enjoyment and learning to be gained from a musical composition because of a feeling that it must be all or nothing.

Although the teacher's attitude and method of presenting abstract music are probably more important than the specific types of music chosen, he will want to know the various types of abstract musical compositions children in the elementary school enjoy.

1. Experiences with themes and simple musical forms
   a. ABA form
   b. Rondo
   c. Theme and variations
   d. Fugue
2. Experience with various types of musical compositions
   a. March
   b. Waltz
   c. Minuet
   d. Overture (in connection with the opera)
   e. Suite
   f. Symphony

The teacher will know whether his attitude, method of presentation, and choice of music are correct by observing the class during abstract music experiences. When children look forward to the experience, are eager to participate, freely express likes and dislikes, and discuss abstract music with the same seriousness as popular music, the teacher may feel assured they are accepting a source of enjoyment that can remain a positive force.

What about experiences with opera and operettas? The teacher initiating experiences with opera and operettas should be aware that children as well as adults are often unreceptive to opera. Hearing deeply felt emotions and a story expressed in a foreign language is not a pleasant experience. The feeling of inadequacy generated by an experience of this kind often turns to active dislike before time is taken to analyze the reasons for the reaction.

A fifth-grade child watching a teacher write *opera* on the board responded with, "I hate opera." The first impulse of the teacher is to respond negatively. It is not pleasant, after having spent time preparing for an experience, to have such a statement as an overture.

It is essential, however, for the teacher to understand the statement as an honest, although naive, expression of feeling. This feeling can result from being forced to listen to a static ridden performance of an opera for which she had no background for understanding and to which she should not have been expected to listen.

It is helpful to remember that an attitude can and does change. Knowing the story of an opera, understanding the gist of the words sung, and being aware of the emotions expressed can change the nature of the experience into an exciting adventure. Remember that the child in the elementary grades has a limited attention span and cannot respond positively to music that expresses feelings she does not understand. Yet, this child can enjoy exploring opera.

What does a child enjoy about opera? She enjoys those parts of the music that express feelings she can understand. She enjoys the story, when endless details are omitted. She enjoys the mechanics of opera: the scenery, costumes, and so forth. She even enjoys using adult words: aria, recitative, overture. Let the child sing a recitative and she begins to find that opera is fun. The teacher who can vividly portray these parts of opera, allowing the hesitant child to participate when she is ready, will open the world of opera to many for whom it might otherwise remain an unpleasant mystery.

Rhythmic Concepts

Level I or II

Materials Needed
1. Rhythm instruments
2. Illustrations of rhythmic concepts
3. The following recordings:
   a. "Bydlo" from *Pictures at an Exhibition* by Moussorgsky, RCA *Adventures in Music* grade 2, vol. 1, LES 1001 or Bowmar *Orchestral Library* recording BOL 097
   b. Minuet in F by Gluck, RCA Victor *Record Library for Elementary Grades* recording WE 75
   c. March from *Summer Day* by Prokofieff, RCA *Adventures in Music* grade 1, vol. 1, LES 1000
   d. "Waltz of the Doll" from *Coppélia* by Delibes, RCA *Adventures in Music* grade 1, vol. 1, LES 1000
   e. "Valsette" by Borowski, RCA Victor *Record Library for Elementary Grades* recording We 71
   f. March in F Major by Anderson, RCA Victor *Record Library for Elementary Grades* recording We 71
4. Music Cue charts

Listening Activities
1. An experience with mood and picture music: "Bydlo" from *Pictures at an Exhibition* by Moussorgsky
2. An experience with abstract music: Minuet in F by Gluck

Related Musical Activities
1. Bodily movement
2. Playing rhythm instruments

Conceptual Understandings
1. Rhythm may swing in twos or threes.
2. Rhythm is made up of many different durations.
3. These durations are related.

$$ | \quad = \quad \sqcap $$

Behavioral Objectives
1. To demonstrate the ability to hear the difference between music that swings in twos and music that swings in threes

---

Figure 5.1
a, Eight apples; b, one whole, two halves; c, threes; d, twos or threes; e, twos. Photographs *a, b, c,* and *e* by David Rosenthal; photograph *d* by Margaret Kelsey.

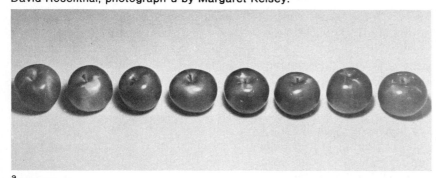

a

c

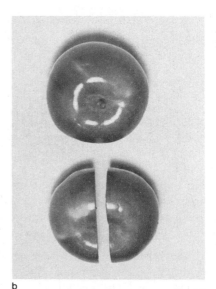

b

2. To demonstrate the ability to hear and reproduce the relationship of these durations:

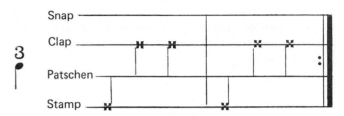

Related Arts
Observing rhythm that moves in twos and threes and the relationship of two halves to a whole, in the visual arts (using figure 5.1a–d)

Procedure
1. Focusing on the difference between rhythm that moves in twos and threes, by using bodily movement related to the visual arts and by playing rhythm instruments
   a. Tap feet in a slow, steady beat. Ask the class to join you.
   b. When children are tapping steadily, begin clapping twice as fast as the beat of your feet. Ask children to join you.
   c. When they are coordinating both rhythms, stop and show the pictures in figure 5.1.
   d. Ask which picture describes what they were doing. (picture b) Explain that two halves of an apple make a whole and two, eighth notes make a quarter note. Draw notation on the board and explain that their feet were tapping quarter notes, their hands tapping eighth notes.

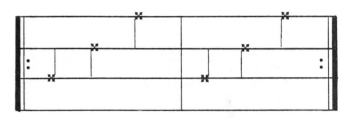

e. Have them tap their feet and hands again, as they observe the notation on the board.
f. Ask children to echo you in the following:

Continued on page 254

d

e

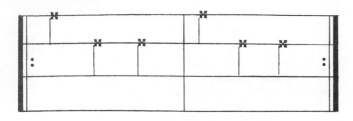

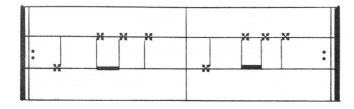

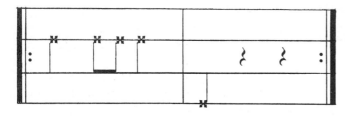

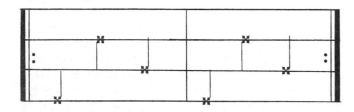

g. Distribute tambourines, tone blocks, triangles, and rhythm sticks. Have children playing like instruments sit together. Tell children that when you stamp, all children playing tambourines will play, echoing the stamping; when you patschen, tone blocks will play; when you clap, triangles will play; and when you snap your fingers, sticks will play. Therefore, on the first pattern the following will occur:

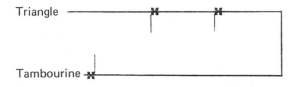

h. In a slow tempo, repeat the echo patterns in instruction f, so that children can echo successfully.

i. When successful, ask which picture illustrates what they were doing. (three and four) Explain that the rhythm patterns echoed were moving in threes, just as the apples are grouped in threes and the girl is stepping in threes.

2. Focusing on music that moves in twos, by using music that suggests a picture ("Bydlo" from *Pictures at an Exhibition* by Moussorgsky)

a. Tell children to tap their feet or hands to fit the beat. Play "Bydlo." Some children may hear the basic meter in twos. Others may hear the slow but steady eighth notes. Help, if necessary, by tapping quarter notes with your foot and clapping eighth notes.

b. Continue until children show signs of restlessness. Turn the volume down.

c. Ask children to look again at the pictures of fruit. Ask which pictures apply to this music. (Picture one is similar to the movement of eighth notes in "Bydlo." Picture two shows the relationship between quarter notes and eighth notes in "Bydlo." Picture five moves in twos, as does the rhythm of "Bydlo.")

d. Ask the class what kind of picture the music describes. If they have difficulty, ask these or similar questions:

   (1) Is the music describing something that moves slowly or quickly?

   (2) Do you think this is an animal, machine, or person?

   (3) What is the animal, machine, or person doing? Where is it going?

   (4) Where are we in relation to this object?

   (5) How does the music describe these things? Through its tempo, dynamics, instrumentation, melody, or rhythm?

e. As children express their ideas, encourage them to demonstrate. One class thought of a parade of tired soldiers approaching. As they came closer, the music grew louder. After they passed the music grew softer, until they disappeared.

f. As children individually dramatize their ideas, ask for suggestions for improving or expanding. Continue until all ideas have been explored and dramatized.

g. The class will enjoy comparing their story with the composer's story of his music.

"Bydlo" (bid-loh) is one of ten pieces in a suite called *Pictures at an Exhibition,* written by Moussorgsky as musical pictures of a number of sketches by an artist friend, Victor Hartmann. . . .

One of the pictures that interested him was a sketch of an old Polish wagon, or cart, drawn by a team of oxen. The big cart had giant, wooden wheels, and a driver dressed in peasant clothes sat on the box. The title, "Bydlo," is the Polish word for cattle, here referring to a cart drawn by oxen.[1]

3. Focusing on music that moves in threes, by using abstract music (Minuet in F by Gluck)
   a. Tell children to join you in bodily movement as they listen to Minuet in F by Gluck. Do the following, with the music:

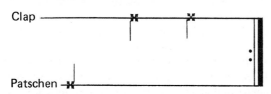

   b. When children are doing the pattern easily, turn the volume down. Ask how the music moves, in twos or threes. (threes)
   c. Tell children to listen, feel rhythm inside and raise their hands each time they hear the first tune, A. As they raise their hands, write on the board: ∧ ∧ ∧.
   d. Ask if anyone can think of bodily movement to fit the A section. Let children experiment as recording plays. Have the class vote on the movement preferred.
   e. Have volunteers do the movement for A as the class raises their hands when they hear the B section. Place on the board: A A B A.
   f. Have children experiment and vote on a movement for B.
   g. Have the class form a circle and dance as the recording plays. One class decided on the following movements:
      (1) A All face inward and alternate the following steps:
         (a) Step with the right foot; slide the left foot toward the right, simultaneously flinging the arms to the right.
         (b) Step with the left foot; slide the right foot toward the left, simultaneously flinging arms to the left.

1. From the Teacher's Guide, *Adventures in Music* grade 2, vol. 1, LES 1001, by Gladys Tipton and Eleanor Tipton © by Radio Corporation of America, 1961.

      (2) B All move to the right in a circle, alternating the following steps:
         (a) Step forward on the right foot; slide the left foot toward the right.
         (b) Step forward on the left foot; slide the right foot toward the left.
      (3) A Repeat A.
4. Evaluating children's ability to hear the difference between music that moves in twos and music that moves in threes
   a. Distribute the Music Cue chart to children.

Music Cue Chart	
1. Twos	Threes
2. Twos	Threes
3. Twos	Threes
4. Twos	Threes

   b. Tell children to listen and feel inside the way the music moves. If it moves in twos, they are to circle *twos* after number one. If it moves in threes, they are to circle *threes*. Play the recording for number one, have children circle the word that applies, and continue in the same manner for the other numbers.
      1. March from *Summer Day* by Prokofieff (twos)
      2. "Valsette" by Borowski (threes)
      3. "Waltz of the Doll" from *Coppélia* by Delibes (threes)
      4. March in F Major by Anderson (twos)
   c. Compare children's answers with correct answers. Clarify any misunderstandings.

Listening Experiences That Focus on Rhythmic Concepts

Level I

Creating a Rhythmic Dramatization of Music that Suggests a Picture
"To a Water Lily" by Edward MacDowell, RCA Victor *Basic Record Library for Elementary Grades* recording WE 79

1. Tell children the title and this background information: There once lived a man named Edward MacDowell who loved the woods, with its tall trees, rambling brooks, quiet lakes, and lovely wild flowers. He decided one day to compose some musical pictures describing the woods. One of the musical pictures he composed was about a water lily, entitled "To a Water Lily."

2. Discuss the water lily: What is it? Where does it grow? What color is it? How large is it?

3. Ask the class how music might sound when it is portraying a water lily gently swaying: Would it be fast or slow, even or uneven, loud or soft? What instrument could be used?

4. Play the recording. Discuss the picture painted by the music. (The lily seems to sway gently, then become agitated as though rocked by a boat or wind, then sway gently again.)

5. Ask the class how music painted a picture. (Music played on a piano begins slowly and steadily, becomes agitated and uneven, then returns to the original slow, steady rhythm.)

6. Play the recording again and ask children to sway their arms with the music, pretending they are water lilies. (Help them stay in rhythm with the music by swaying with them.)

7. Select individual children to be a boat or wind agitating the water as the recording plays, and children in their seats sway gently as a water lily.

8. Select individual children to be water lilies, boat, or wind. Let them dramatize as the recording plays.

Level I

Responding to Music that Suggests a Picture through Rhythmic Movement and Creating an Accompaniment
"The Bee" by Francois Schubert, RCA Victor *Basic Record Library for Elementary Grades* recording WE 79

1. Discuss with class ways that music can paint a picture. Some questions to guide the discussion can be: What kind of music would best paint a picture of an elephant? (slow, deep, low, heavy) A bird flying? (fast, light) A parade? (loud, marching)

2. Tell the class that a man named Schubert wrote a piece called "The Bee." Ask them to listen to hear what the bee is doing and what instrument portrays the bee. Play the recording and discuss: What instrument plays the bee? (violin) What is the bee doing? Flying? Fast or slow?

3. Ask children to think about how they could show the movement of the bee with their fingers. Play the record and let children experiment moving their fingers to music.

4. Ask the class to show the movement of the bee with their feet. Would they walk or run, fast or slow, with big or little steps?

5. Let one child experiment. Discuss it with the class. Let other children experiment as the recording plays.

6. Ask which instrument (maracas, sticks, triangles) would best show the movement of the bee.

7. Play the recording as one child experiments with the instrument selected, other children try other instruments, and a few children move as the bee.

Level II

Creating a Rhythmic Dramatization of Music that Tells a Story
"Of a Tailor and a Bear" by MacDowell, RCA Victor *Basic Record Library for Elementary Grades* recording WE 78

1. Tell the class this story.

Once upon a time a happy tailor sat cross-legged on a big table in his shop. He whistled a gay little tune to himself as he snipped and sewed. Suddenly he was startled to hear a commotion outside. As he looked up he saw the door swing open. A huge, shaggy bear shambled in, growling and rocking awkwardly from side to side as he glared about him. Frightened and trembling the poor tailor threw aside his sewing, jumped from his table, and started to run away as fast as he could. He paused abruptly, however, as he noticed a broken strand of rope hanging from a collar around the bear's neck. Of course—it must be a tame bear that had escaped his keeper! Tame bears are usually dancing bears, he thought. I wonder if he would dance to my music? Still shaking with fright he reached for his violin which he always kept nearby to play when he was tired. He tucked it under his chin, tuned it quickly, and played a dance tune. Sure enough, the bear stood on his hind legs and began to dance ponderously and clumsily. He could not move as fast as the tune, however, so he growled fiercely and lumbered threateningly toward the tailor. The tailor hastily tuned his violin once more, and this time played his piece more slowly. It was just right, for the bear kept exact step as he shuffled and swayed.

In the meantime the keeper had been searching frantically for his bear, up one street and down the next. Noticing the crowd of spectators gathered outside the tailor's shop and hearing the strains of music, he was certain his chase had ended. Elbowing his way through the crowd he rushed into the shop and seized the rope on the bear's collar. The bear knew it was time to go, so he sank down on all fours. But he had been having such a wonderful time he wanted to stay and dance forever to the tailor's beautiful music! His keeper tugged on the rope, but, growling angrily, the bear pulled the other way as he was half-led and half-dragged down the street. Never had the little tailor been so relieved as when he finally saw his uninvited visitor led out the door. He drew in a deep breath and put his violin away. Picking up his sewing and whistling to himself, because he was so happy to be safe and sound, he stitched away until time to lock his shop for the night.[2]

2. From Notes for Teachers, *Basic Record Library for Elementary Grades,* Album WE–78 by Miss Lilla Belle Pitts and Miss Gladys Tipton, © Radio Corporation of America, RCA Victor Division, 1947.

2. Ask children to listen for the story as it is told by the instruments of the orchestra. Play the recording.
3. Ask these or similar questions: What instruments play the part of the bear? (stringed basses) How does the music tell us the bear is dancing clumsily? (The rhythm is uneven.) How does the music tell us the bear is growling at the tailor for playing too fast? (The bass fiddles growl.) What is the difference between the music for the bear and the tailor?
4. Ask the children to raise their hands each time they hear the bear. Play the recording. Play it again, asking children to raise their hands when the tailor tunes his violin.
5. Select children to be the bear, tailor, and keeper. Discuss actions of the three characters, eliciting ideas from the class. Play the recording as children dramatize it. Discuss positively the better aspects of the performance. Select other children to dramatize.

Level II

Creating a Rhythmic Dramatization of Music that Tells a Story

"Can-Can" from *The Fantastic Toyshop* by Rossini, RCA *Adventures in Music* grade 2, vol. 1, LES 1001

1. Read or tell the story of "The Fantastic Toyshop."

. . . The scene is laid in a toyshop run by a shopkeeper and his young apprentice. Many people come in to examine the wonderful mechanical dolls which are featured by the shopkeeper. Among the curious are two families with children who drop in one day to see the dolls. The shopkeeper and his assistant wheel the toys in on a light trolley; they are wound up, and each dances in his own special way. There are two Italian dolls who dance a tarantella; four court card dolls, representing the Queen of Clubs, the Queen of Hearts, the King of Diamonds, and the King of Spades, who dance a stately mazurka; Cossack soldiers in brilliant uniforms who mark time and do a precise military drill; two dancing poodles, and many others.

None of these dancing toys quite satisfies the customers, however, and finally the shopkeeper brings out his favorite dolls—a pair of can-can dancers. As the two families watch, enthralled, a boy and a girl doll dance a fast stepping, hopping, whirling dance, ending in a pose, as their springs run down. The children immediately imitate the dolls, and the parents begin to argue about who shall buy them. Order is finally restored when each family agrees to buy one doll only. One family prefers the boy can-can doll, and the other is charmed by the girl can-can doll, so everyone is happy. They pay for them and leave, saying that they will call for their packages the next day. The shopkeeper and his assistant put the dolls back into their boxes and then close the shop for the night.

At the stroke of midnight, the dolls magically come to life, step out of their boxes, and have an hilarious party. Cossacks crouch and spring into the air; the poodles frolic and leap about; tarantella dancers whirl and stamp; toy ballet dancers glide and pirouette; and each of the can-can dancers performs a solo dance. Determined that the can-can dancers shall not be sold and thus separated from their friends, the Cossacks carry the girl dancer away, on crossed sticks held high, to hide her, and the boy dancer also finds a good hiding place. Finally, all join in a gay, syncopated cakewalk to end the merrymaking.

The next morning, after the toys are once again tucked away in their boxes, the shopkeeper and his assistant open the shop just in time to welcome the two families who have come for their dolls. The oblong boxes containing the can-can dolls are handed to them. They lift the lids and find—nothing! They turn angrily to the shopkeeper and berate him for trying to cheat his customers. Just then the dolls fantastically and magically come to life once more, and all of them proceed to drive the two families out of the shop. A little later, as the families peer into the shop window, imagine their astonishment when they behold the dolls gaily dancing around the shopkeeper, who is smilingly receiving a salute from the two can-can dolls.[3]

2. Tell the children you will play a recording that describes part of this story and to decide which part of the story the music tells. Play the recording.
3. Through discussion, compare each of their suggestions with music and encourage children to demonstrate their ideas as the recording plays. Have the class decide which ideas best fit the music. Let us assume that the class tells the story to where "their springs run down." Write the story ideas on the board with the melodies that suggest them.
   a. Introduction: The storekeeper opens his shop.
   b. Melody 1: People enter, and the assistant shows various dolls to customers. He runs with short steps. The shopkeeper follows, walking with more dignity. The shopkeeper asks the people if they like this or that doll that the assistant is showing them.
   c. Melody 2: The assistant brings out the can-can dolls. These impress all the customers.
   d. Melody 3: The dolls begin to dance, kicking first one leg and then the other, as they stand in place and then whirl.

3. From the Teacher's Guide, *Adventures in Music*, Grade 2, Vol. 1, LES 1001, by Gladys Tipton and Eleanor Tipton © by Radio Corporation of America, 1961.

e. Interlude: The dolls bow and curtsy.

f. Melody 2: The dolls dance again, jumping once on both legs in place (on strong beat), then moving one arm and then the other across the body in rhythm.

g. Melody 3: The dolls kick one leg, then the other, standing in place and then whirling.

h. Interlude: The dolls curtsy.

i. Melody 1: Finale: All dolls join can-can dolls in dancing; their springs run down, and the music ends.

4. Prepare for a dramatization by discussing the exact steps the can-can dolls might do, and suggest that the entire class practice these steps.

5. Select two can-can dolls. Ask them to listen and begin dancing when their melody begins. Have the class help by listening and raising their hands when the can-can part begins. Play the recording as can-can dolls dance at proper times.

6. Select two children to be the apprentice and shopkeeper. Play the recording as the four children dramatize the story.

7. Let the class make suggestions for improvement. Repeat, with other children playing parts of dolls, apprentice, and shopkeeper.

Level II

Creating an Instrumental Accompaniment to Mood or Picture Music

"Dagger Dance" from *Natoma* by Victor Herbert, RCA *Adventures in Music* grade 3, vol. 1, LES 1002

1. Without telling the title, ask children to listen, and experiment clapping different rhythms as you play a recording. If they have difficulty hearing that the rhythm moves in fours, count one-two-three-four as they clap.

2. Ask volunteers to clap their patterns. Patterns similar to the following may be demonstrated:

a. | 𝄽 𝄽 𝄽   d. | | 𝅗𝅥

b. 𝅗𝅥 | | e. 𝅗𝅥 𝅗𝅥

c. | | | |

3. Let the class vote on three patterns they like best. Write them on the board.

4. Tell the class to do the following as the recording plays:

a. The first child whose pattern was chosen will begin clapping her rhythm with the recording. On your signal, the class will join her. At your signal, all will stop clapping.

b. The second child whose pattern was chosen will begin clapping with the recording. At your signal, the class will join her. On your signal, all will stop.

c. The third child whose pattern was chosen will begin clapping her pattern. On your signal, the class will join her. On your signal, all will stop.

5. Play the recording and call the signals; help the class clap rhythms, if necessary.

6. Display rhythm instruments and help children select the instruments most appropriate for each pattern. If they have chosen patterns similar to those in instruction 2, they might use any of these instruments: large drums, small drums, sticks or tone blocks, tambourines, and triangles or finger cymbals.

7. Let the three children whose rhythm patterns were selected play instruments suggested by the class, as follows:

a. Play the recording.

b. Signal the first child to begin.

c. Signal her to stop.

d. Do the same with the other two children.

8. Let the class decide how they will accompany the music.

a. Clapping patterns as children with instruments play them, one at a time

b. Dividing the class into three groups, each group playing the pattern assigned to them as the child playing the instrument leads

c. All three groups playing patterns simultaneously throughout the recording

d. All groups playing together at the beginning and end, one group playing alone in the middle

9. Write the plan on the board. Play the recording, helping the class stay together. Repeat, letting children change instruments and patterns. If desired, one child may conduct, bringing in each section at an appropriate time.

10. Children may enjoy knowing the name and background of the composition, found in the pamphlet that accompanies the album.

Level II

Learning the Minuet in an Experience with Abstract Music

Minuet from *Don Giovanni* by Mozart, RCA Victor *Basic Record Library for Elementary Grades* recording WE 75

1. Project the story that follows and ask children to read silently as the recording plays or, if you prefer, read the story aloud as children listen.

Imagine you are living in the time of George Washington—when men and women wore powdered wigs and clothes made of satins and velvets with collars and cuffs of lace.

This was a time when boys and girls bowed low and curtsied, when dancing in great ballrooms was a dignified affair—a time of the minuet. Mozart lived during this time. When he wrote his famous opera, *Don Giovanni*, he included a scene for Don Giovanni's ball where people danced the minuet.

2. Ask these questions: How does the music for this dance differ from the folk or square dances we know? How does the minuet differ from the waltz, march, polka, or current popular dances?
3. Ask children to think of words that describe the music. (slow, dignified, stately, graceful)
4. Play the recording.
5. Teach the class the dance. Have them form a double circle of partners, the girl at the boy's right, partners holding hands. Follow these steps:
   a. Touch the toes of the outside foot to the floor three times.
   b. Walk forward three steps, starting with the outside foot.
   c. Touch the toes of the inside foot to the floor three times.
   d. Walk forward three steps, starting with the inside foot.
   e. Repeat a and b.
   f. Face your partner, drop hands, and make a low bow.
   g. Repeat a through f using the opposite foot and direction.
   h. Take right hands, held high, tap the right foot three times.
   i. Drop hands and bow to each other.
   j. Take left hands and repeat h and i.
   k. Drop hands and bow to each other.
   l. Repeat h through l.[4]

Level II or III

Using Bodily Movement to Focus on the Themes in Abstract Music

"Unsquare Dance" by Dave Brubeck, *Exploring Music,* vol. 4, Holt, Rinehart and Winston, 1975, record 9; or Silver Burdett recording, *Learning to Listen to Music*

1. Write on the board, "Unsquare Dance." Ask how music for an unsquare dance might differ from music for a square dance.

4. Adapted from *The American Singer* (Second Edition) Book 5, by John W. Beattie, Josephine Wolverton, Grace V. Wilson and Howard Hinga. © 1955 by American Book Company. Used by permission.

2. Tell the children to listen, then echo. Do the following, repeating until children echo easily:

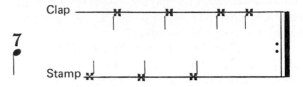

3. Write these words on the board: clapping, piano, bass viol, percussion.
4. Play "Unsquare Dance." Have the children listen for the four things written on the board and raise their hands when they hear each item. Have children circle the word on the board as they hear each.
5. Ask if they heard any repeated pattern. (The bass part is a six-measure ostinato, repeated throughout.)
6. Ask what happens between each of the bass notes. (After the first and second bass notes we hear one clap; after the third bass note we hear two claps, creating a grouping of beats in sevens.)

7. Ask the class to stamp the bass notes and clap with the clapping. Play the recording as children accompany.
8. When children can do the accompaniment, add the following:
   a. Drum playing the rhythm of the bass viol part
   b. Tone blocks playing on the claps
   c. A few children doing the following:

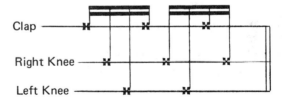

Melodic Concepts

Level II or III

Materials Needed

1. Recording of "Gavotte" from *Classical* Symphony by Prokofiev, Bowmar *Orchestral Library* recording BOL 088 or Holt, Rinehart and Winston *Exploring Music* recording 512
2. Rhythm instruments

3. Copy of "Hear the Beat of the Tom Tom" on chart or board
4. Melody instruments for playing themes
5. Music Cue charts
6. Music for evaluation procedure

Listening Activity
An experience with abstract music: "Gavotte" from *Classical* Symphony by Prokofiev

Related Musical Activities
1. Singing
2. Playing rhythm instruments
3. Music reading

Conceptual Understandings
1. The range of a melody is determined by its lowest and highest notes.
2. Melodies may move from low to high or high to low, by skip, step, or repeated notes.

Behavioral Objectives
1. To hear differences in range between melodies.
2. To differentiate between melodies that move from low to high, high to low, by step or by skip.

Related Arts
Exploring range through poetry in "Hear the Beat of the Tom Tom"

Procedure
1. Exploring range through singing, with hand signals:
   a. Tell the class to echo. Do the following, with hand signals:

b. Notate the entire range of their singing on the board omitting the words *low*, *middle*, and *high*.

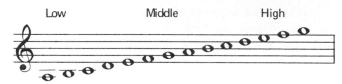

c. Have the class sing notes as you point, using letter names or a neutral syllable. Ask for volunteers to point to notes they think would be in the lower, middle, and high ranges. Write these words above the appropriate notes.
d. Discuss. Explain that the range of their singing is defined by the lowest and highest notes they can sing.
e. Review the method of determining from notation whether notes step or skip. Have a volunteer point to notes that step. As you point to notation, have the class sing intervals that step and skip.
2. Exploring range through an experience with poetry
   a. Display "Hear the Beat of the Tom Tom." Ask children to read it silently.

Hear the Beat of the Tom Tom

Hear the beat, beat, beat of the tom tom,
As it plays in the dark of the night.
Hear the boom of the drum in the dark of the moon,
Sounding low in the dimmest of light.

See the rays of the sun in the dawn's first glow,
Breaking slowly across the sky.
And the birds from their nests in the tall fir trees,
Venturing forth with a sharp little cry.

Feel the heat and the beat and the pulse of the day,
Growing loud in the glow of the sun.
Feel the heat, and the beat, and the pulse in your feet,
As the day breaks into a run.

Lois Raebeck

b. Tell children to listen, as you say the poem, and remember any images that come to mind. Recite the poem in this rhythm.

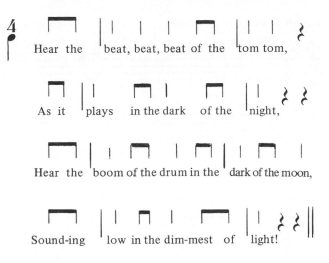

Hear the beat, beat, beat of the tom tom,

As it plays in the dark of the night,

Hear the boom of the drum in the dark of the moon,

Sound-ing low in the dim-mest of light!

c. Ask what images came to mind. Encourage children to express their ideas, without negative comments.
d. Explain that the words in poetry can suggest use of different vocal pitches. Write this on the board:
Low   Middle   High
e. Ask children to say the poem with you and think of the vocal range (low, middle, high) each verse suggests.
f. Discuss vocal range for each verse. Let them experiment. One class decided the following:
First verse   lower part of voice
Second verse   middle part of voice
Third verse   higher part of voice
g. Ask children if different parts of the poem seem to suggest different dynamics (louds and softs). Let them experiment, using their ideas. They may decide, as one class did, to start the poem softly, on the first verse, and gradually grow louder by the third verse.

h. Display rhythm instruments. Ask children to examine the instruments and decide which would best implement their ideas on range and dynamics. Let them experiment. One class decided the following:
First verse   Soft drums play on the beat.
Second verse   Drums on every beat; tone blocks on strong beats.
Third verse   Drums and tone blocks continue; triangles enter on first line, playing alternate beats; tambourines on second line, playing every beat; sticks and any other instruments on third line.
i. Children may enjoy exploring ways of adding interest to the poem: for example, having a few children say the first verse in a low range; adding other voices on the second verse in a middle range; and the entire class saying the third verse in a high range.
3. Exploring range, steps, and skips in a melody, through an experience with "Gavotte" from *Classical* Symphony by Prokofiev
a. Play the themes. Ask these questions:
(1) Which melody has the widest range? (Theme 1)
(2) Which melody skips most? (Theme 1)
(3) Which melody has the most repeated notes? (Theme 2)
(4) Which melody has the most steps? (Theme 1)
b. Ask children to raise their hands when they hear Theme 1. Play the recording.
c. Play Theme 2 on a melody instrument. Ask class to raise their hands when they hear Theme 2. Play the recording.

Theme 1

Theme 2

Themes from the "Gavotte" of the *Classical* Symphony by Prokofiev. Copyright 1926 by Edition Russe de Musique. Reprinted by permission of Boosey & Hawkes Inc., Assigness of the Copyright.

d. Ask which rhythm instruments would best accompany each theme. Have children experiment. Some possibilities are the following:

Theme 1   triangles or finger cymbals
Theme 2   tone blocks or sticks

e. Give instruments to volunteers. Let them experiment with rhythm patterns for each theme. The following may be suggested:

Theme 1

Theme 2

f. Play the recording. Let volunteers accompany each theme.

4. Evaluating children's ability to hear differences in range, skips, and steps in melody
   a. Distribute the Music Cue chart.

Music Cue Chart

1. Small range	Large range	Steps	Skips
2. Small range	Large range	Steps	Skips
3. Small range	Large range	Steps	Skips
4. Small range	Large range	Steps	Skips

b. Remind children of their experiences listening for range, steps, and skips in a melody. Ask them to listen, then circle the words that apply to number 1. Explain that they should circle two sets of words: small range or large range and steps or skips. Play melody number 1 on a melody instrument.

Melody 1 (small range, steps)

Melody 2 (large range, skips)

Melody 3 (large range, steps)

Melody 4 (small range, skips)

Listening Experiences That Focus on Melodic Concepts

Level I or II

Focusing on Melodic Concepts through an Experience with Picture Music
"Petite Ballerina" from Ballet Suite no. 1 by Shostakovich, RCA *Adventures in Music* grade 2, vol. 1, LES 1001

1. Give children an experience in vocal exploration as suggested in the section of chapter 3, "Melodic Concepts." Emphasize that their voices can make sounds in a high, middle, and low range and that we call all the notes they can sing, their range.
2. Tell children to listen and when they hear a melody in a high range, to put their hands on their heads, removing their hands when the melody changes to a lower range.
3. Play the recording. (High range occurs after the introduction and at the end.)
4. Ask children if they heard anything played in the middle and lower range. (Both are heard in the middle section.)
5. Ask what images came to mind as they listened. Play the recording again, if necessary.
6. Invite children to dramatize their ideas as they listen to the music again. Repeat until many children have had an opportunity to participate.

Level I or II

Focusing on Differences in Melodies through Listening to Two Selections of Picture Music

"Village Dance" by Liadov and Minuet by Mozart, Bowmar *Orchestral Library* recording BOL 066

1. Explain or elicit through discussion the fact that some melodies suggest fast, gay, rollicking movement, some melodies suggest slow, dignified movement. Some melodies are in a high range, some in a middle or low range.
2. Play "Village Dance." Ask the following questions. If necessary, play the recording again.
   a. Was the melody fast or slow? (fast)
   b. Was it gay and rollicking or dignified? (gay and rollicking)
   c. Was it in a high, middle, or low range? (medium and high)
3. Play Minuet by Mozart. Ask questions similar to those asked about "Village Dance."
4. Ask children which composition they would like to move to, and let them experiment improvising movement to the recording. When children have created movement to the music of their choice, encourage them to create a contrasting movement to the other selection.

Level II or III

Using Cues to Music Cards to Focus on Range, Steps, and Skips in Story Music

"Danse Macabre" by Saint-Saëns, Bowmar *Orchestral Library* recording BOL 072

1. Prepare cue cards similar to cards 1–16 in this section.
2. Teach a child to play skeleton and ghost themes on song bells.
3. Tell children that composers often use notes as authors use words to tell stories. Explain that you will tell them a story called "Danse Macabre," which they will soon hear told by music.
4. Tell the story of "Danse Macabre," holding up the cue cards at the proper times and playing, or having a child play the themes at appropriate times.
   a. Card 1:   As the music begins, we hear the clock striking twelve. It is midnight.
   b. Card 2:   It is time for the festivities to begin. We hear Death tuning his fiddle.
   c. Card 3:   Out come the skeletons, dancing a weird dance that gives us a clue that this will be a night of strange festivities. (Play or have a child who has previously practiced play the theme on song bells.)

d. Card 4:   Here come the ghosts to join the eerie assemblage. (Play or have a child play the theme on song bells, having class hum tune.)
e. Card 5:   The dance continues as the skeletons' bones rattle, played by the xylophone.
f. Card 6:   The ghosts begin a dance that forms strange patterns in the night. The strings play a little fugue to accompany them.
g. Card 7:   The song of the witches is heard as the woodwinds play in a high register.
h. Card 8:   Death plays a wailing solo on the violin, accompanied by the harp.
i. Card 9:   The skeletons laugh hilariously as their theme appears again, played by the low strings.
j. Card 10:   The dance becomes more wild as the trombones and strings play the ghost theme.
k. Card 11:   The strings play a descending chromatic scale as the witches fly excitedly above the eerie scene.
l. Card 12:   Death tunes his fiddle once more and plays a strange solo. Then the winds howl.
m. Card 13:   The skeletons and ghosts dance excitedly to both their themes.
n. Card 14:   The eerie scene becomes bedlam.
o. Card 15:   Suddenly the cock crows. It is dawn, time for all spirits to depart.
p. Card 16:   Day breaks. We are returned to the world of reality.

5. Play the recording of the composition and show Cues to Music cards at appropriate times.
6. Ask children which scene they like most and why.
   a. Death tuning his fiddle
   b. Skeletons dancing
   c. Ghosts dancing
   d. Witches flying
7. Discuss the themes in terms of the following:
   a. Which theme is in the highest range? Middle? Lowest?
   b. Which theme has most steps? Skips? Repeated tones?
8. Distribute Cues to Music cards to individual children. Explain that they are to stand in the order the cues are heard. As each cue is played on the recording, the child holding the cue should raise it. Other children in the class are to watch and raise their hands if a child misses her cue. The child who is first to raise her hand to correct a cue will receive the card for that cue.
9. Play the recording, having children hold up the cards.
10. Repeat, letting all children have the opportunity to hold a card.

11. As an enriching activity, children might enjoy one of the following activities.
   a. Telling the story and playing the recording, using the Cues to Music cards, for another class or an assembly program
   b. Making a set of their own Cues to Music cards
   c. Making a film strip to be used on the opaque or overhead projector
   d. Creating a rhythmic dramatization
12. An excellent way of challenging children further can be as follows:
   a. Prepare substitute cards for these:
      (1) Card 5: Omit the musical notation of the themes and the words, *Skeleton Theme*. Place the words *What Theme?* on the card.
      (2) Card 6: Omit the theme and the words *Ghost Theme* and *Ghosts Form Patterns in the Night*. Place *What Theme?* on the card.
      (3) Card 8: Omit the theme and the words *Ghost Theme*. Place *What Theme?* on the card.
      (4) Card 10: Omit the notation and words *Ghost Theme*. Place *What Theme?* on the card.
   b. Distribute Cues to Music cards except numbers 5, 6, 8, and 10. Remind children to hold up their cards every time their cue is heard, and those watching to raise hands when they see a missed cue. Play the recording, as children hold up cards. When cues for cards 5, 6, 8, and 10 occur, hold up substitute cards as the child holding card with original theme holds up her card. (Do not tell children with original themes when to hold up their cards. If a child misses a cue, select another child who perceives the error and raises her hand, to take the card.)

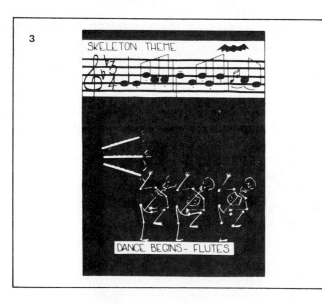

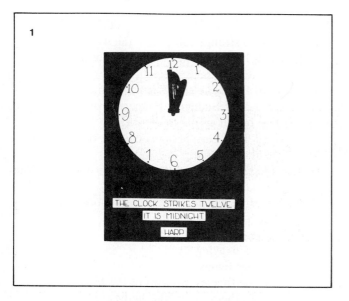

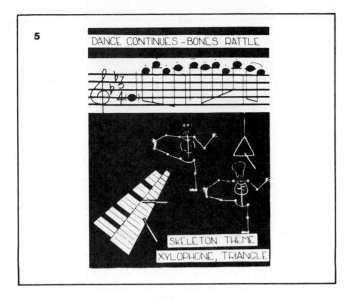

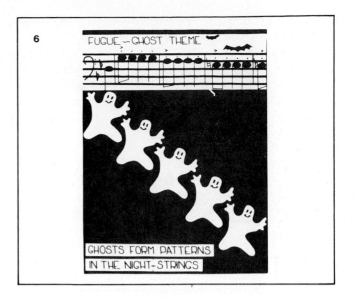

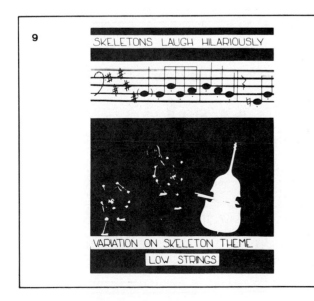

11 WITCHES FLY ABOVE THE EERIE SCENE

STRINGS

12 DEATH, ONCE MORE, TUNES HIS FIDDLE AND PLAYS A SOLO...

THEN ...THE WINDS HOWL...

STRINGS

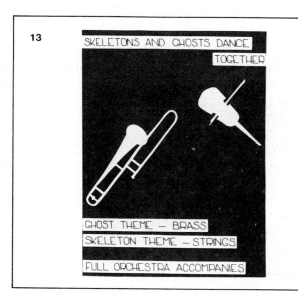

13 SKELETONS AND GHOSTS DANCE TOGETHER

GHOST THEME — BRASS
SKELETON THEME — STRINGS

FULL ORCHESTRA ACCOMPANIES

14 THE EERIE SCENE BECOMES BEDLAM

VIOLINS

15 SUDDENLY... THE COCK CROWS, GREETING THE DAWN
OBOE

THE DANCERS DISPERSE QUICKLY
STRINGS, TIMPANI

16 DAY BREAKS ...AND RETURNS US TO THE WORLD OF REALITY

VIOLIN PLAYS A NEW THEME

Using Cues to Music Cards to Focus on Range, Steps, and Skips in Story Music

"Till Eulenspiegel's Merry Pranks" by Richard Strauss,
Bowmar *Orchestral Library* recording BOL 096 or Holt,
Rinehart and Winston *Exploring Music* recording 513

1. Prepare cue cards similar to cards 1–26 in this section.
2. Select gifted children to play themes. (Children should be allowed to copy themes from cue cards, take them home and practice.)
3. Ask the following questions:
   a. What is a mischievous person?
   b. Why does a person go through life playing pranks?
   c. Do you think music can describe a person such as this? How?
   d. Do you think music can describe all the pranks such a person might play? How?
   e. What kind of melody might describe a mischievous person?
   f. What kind of rhythm would describe a mischievous person?
4. Tell the class you will play a recording of a musical composition that tells one version of a classic folktale describing a prankster whose greatest joy in life was playing pranks. Since Richard Strauss composed the music, this prankster was German, and his name was Till Eulenspiegel. Let the class pronounce *Till Eulenspiegel*.
5. Tell the class that Richard Strauss, through using all the instruments of the orchestra, musical ideas, and rhythms, composed one of the most humorous tales ever written in music.
6. Tell the story as you display Cues to Music cards, playing or letting a child play themes as they occur.
   a. Card 1: The strings play a lovely melody to begin this story of Till and his pranks.
   b. Card 2: Till's theme is announced by the horn and repeated by the oboe, bassoon, and strings.
   c. Card 3: A clarinet solo introduces Till's prank theme.
   d. Card 4: The strings, playing rhythmic staccato notes, indicate that Till has mounted his horse and galloped down the road.
   e. Card 5: As he nears the marketplace, the music tells us that he is creeping up on the unsuspecting people to frighten them. Strings and flute play very soft staccato notes.
   f. Card 6: Cymbals crash! Till has completely wrecked the marketplace, scattering pots and pans everywhere. The ladies scream and the chickens scurry.
   g. Card 7: He gallops away, chuckling to himself. (Ask children what the picture on the card indicates—a cloud of dust.)
   h. Card 8: Till has disguised himself as a clergyman and he rides through the town. The violas and bassoon create this scene.
   i. Card 9: Till fears he may come to a bad end by playing this kind of prank. The strings play the fear theme and the violin plays a descending glissando.
   j. Card 10: Till has fallen in love. The strings and woodwinds play lovely melodies.
   k. Card 11: Loud trumpet and trombones indicate that his love is rejected.
   l. Card 12: Till meets some scholars and pretends to be one of them. Jerky rhythms played by bassoon and clarinet depict the scholars.
   m. Card 13: Till laughs to think how easy it is to fool wise men. Different instruments play the prank theme many times, indicating that he thinks himself quite a successful prankster.
   n. Card 14: Till again rides along his merry way, whistling his street song.
   o. Card 15: Till wonders if he should continue playing pranks. The strings and woodwinds melodiously ask this question.
   p. Card 16: Repetition of Till's theme tells us he is having a difficult time making up his mind as to whether he should reform.
   q. Card 17: He decides, however, that he enjoys being a prankster and he rides toward the village.
   r. Card 18: No sooner does he reach the village than he is caught by the arresting officials. Full orchestra plays loudly.
   s. Card 19: The repetition of the clergy theme tells us Till's fears have now become real.
   t. Card 20: The loud drum roll and the brasses and strings playing loud chords indicate that he is taken before the court.
   u. Card 21: In defiance, Till whistles (prank theme) and the judge reprimands him (court theme), but he whistles again (prank theme). Clarinet solo plays prank theme.
   v. Card 22: The judge sentences him to be hanged!
   w. Card 23: Suddenly, Till realizes he has gone one step too far. Wailing brass and strings play the fear theme.

x. Card 24: Till is hanged. Trombone plays a descending leap, and the woodwinds play a soft ascending passage indicating Till is gone.

y. Card 25: Softly plucked strings tell us that Till is no more.

z. Card 26: An epilogue repeats the introductory theme, which seems to say, "And this was the story of Till Eulenspiegel."

7. Play the recording, holding up Cues to Music cards at proper places. Ask children these or similar questions:

a. Which prank was easiest to see?

b. Which part of the story do you think Strauss told best?

c. Do you remember the instruments that told this part?

d. Do you remember how the theme sounded?

8. Distribute the Cues to Music cards and ask children to arrange themselves in numerical order of the cards.

9. Tell those holding cards that they are to hold them down until they hear their cue, at which time they are to hold their card high. Remind the class to watch carefully, follow the cues, and raise their hands if someone misses a cue. Explain that the child who corrects a missed cue will take the card for that cue.

10. Play the recording as the children hold up their Cues to Music cards.

11. Repeat as often as children desire, letting all children have the opportunity to hold a card.

12. As an enriching experience, children might enjoy these activities.

a. Telling the story and playing the recording, using Cues to Music cards, for another class or for an assembly program

b. Making their own set of Cues to Music cards

c. Making a filmstrip for the opaque or overhead projector

13. To challenge children further, follow up this experience with this activity.

a. Prepare substitute cards for these.

(1) Card 13: Omit theme and replace the words *Prank Theme* with *What theme?*

(2) Card 16: Omit theme and the words *Repetition of Till's Theme*. Add the words *What theme?*

(3) Card 19: Omit notation. Add the words *What theme?*

(4) Card 26: Omit the theme and add the words *What theme?*

b. Distribute Cues to Music cards, except 13, 16, 19, and 26. Remind children to raise cards every time they hear their cue. Remind children watching to raise their hands when they see a missed cue. Play the recording as children raise cards. When cues for cards 13, 16, 19, and 26 occur, hold up substitute cards as child holding original theme raises the card. If a child misses a cue, select another child who perceives the error, to take the card.

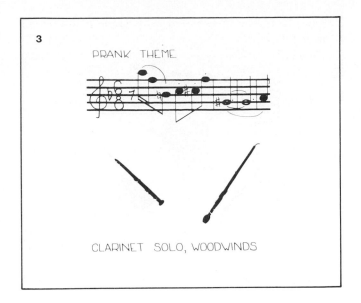

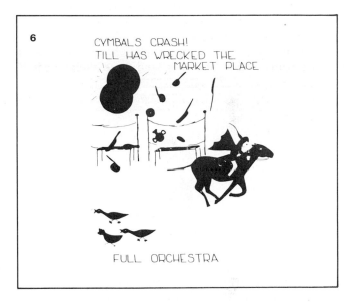

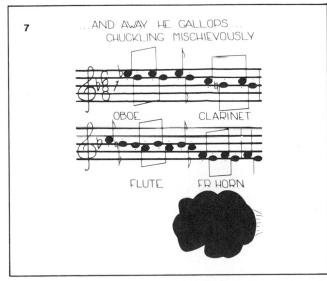

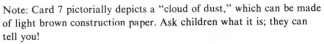

Note: Card 7 pictorially depicts a "cloud of dust," which can be made of light brown construction paper. Ask children what it is; they can tell you!

9 TILL FEARS HE MAY COME TO
   A BAD END – FEAR THEME

STRINGS, BRASS

DESCENDING GLISSANDO – SOLO
VIOLIN

10 TILL FALLS IN LOVE

STRINGS AND WOODWINDS
PLAY LOVELY MELODIES

11 ...BUT HE'S REJECTED

BRASS – FULL ORCHESTRA

12 TILL MEETS SOME SCHOLARS
    AND PRETENDS TO BE ONE OF
    THEM

BASSOON AND
CLARINET
PLAY SLOW,
JERKY
RHYTHMS

13 TILL LAUGHS AND THINKS,
    "HOW EASY TO FOOL WISE
    MEN!"

PRANK THEME PLAYED MANY
TIMES BY VARIOUS INSTRU-
MENTS

14 TILL IS AGAIN ON HIS MERRY
    WAY, WHISTLING HIS STREET
    SONG

STRINGS – WOODWINDS

15

AS TILL RIDES, HE WONDERS, "SHOULD I CONTINUE PLAYING PRANKS?"

STRINGS - WOODWINDS

16

TILL CANNOT DECIDE!

REPETITION OF TILL'S THEME

17

TILL DECIDES: "A SHORT AND MERRY LIFE" AS HE RIDES TOWARD THE VILLAGE

HORNS

18

UPON REACHING THE VILLAGE, TILL IS CAUGHT!

ORCHESTRA PLAYS LOUDLY

19

TILL CANNOT ESCAPE!

BRASSES - FULL ORCHESTRA ACCOMPANIES

20

TILL IS TAKEN BEFORE THE COURT - COURT THEME

DRUM ROLLS; BRASSES AND STRINGS PLAY LOUD CHORDS

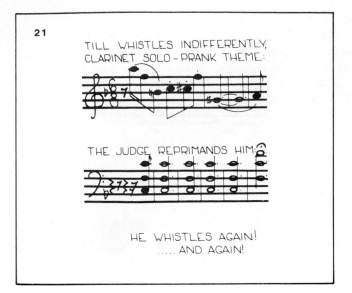

21

TILL WHISTLES INDIFFERENTLY,
CLARINET SOLO - PRANK THEME:

THE JUDGE REPRIMANDS HIM:

HE WHISTLES AGAIN!
..... AND AGAIN!

22

THE JUDGE SENTENCES TILL
TO BE HANGED IMMEDIATELY!
COURT THEME

ORCHESTRA PLAYS LOUDLY

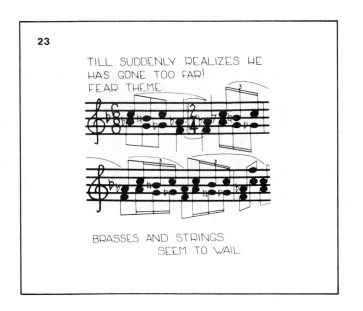

23

TILL SUDDENLY REALIZES HE
HAS GONE TOO FAR!
FEAR THEME:

BRASSES AND STRINGS
SEEM TO WAIL

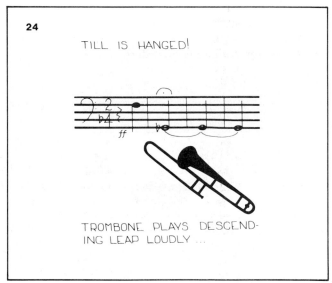

24

TILL IS HANGED!

TROMBONE PLAYS DESCEND-
ING LEAP LOUDLY ...

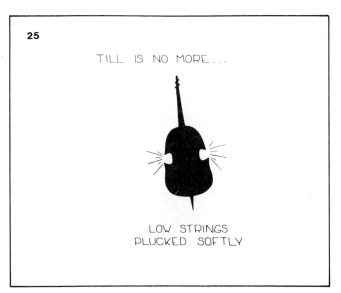

25

TILL IS NO MORE...

LOW STRINGS
PLUCKED SOFTLY

26

"AND THIS IS THE STORY
OF TILL EULENSPIEGEL"
(EPILOGUE)

STRINGS

Textural Concepts

Level III

Materials Needed
1. Rhythm instruments
2. Miscellaneous objects for collage
3. Two melody instruments
4. The following recordings:
   a. "Pacific 231" by Honegger
   b. "Sarabande" from Suite for Strings by Corelli and Pinelli, RCA *Adventures in Music* grade 6, vol. 2, LES 1008
   c. "Devil's Dance" by Stravinsky, Bowmar *Orchestral Library* recording BOL 081
   d. Menuetto no. 1 from Divertimento no. 17 in D by Mozart, RCA *Adventures in Music* grade 5, vol. 2, LES 1007
   e. "Col. Bogey March" by Alford, Bowmar *Orchestral Library* recording BOL 067
5. Music Cue charts
6. Music for evaluation procedure

Listening Activities
1. An experience with music that suggests a picture, using "Pacific 231" by Honegger
2. An experience with abstract music, using "Sarabande" from Suite for Strings by Corelli and Pinelli

Related Musical Activities
1. Playing rhythm instruments
2. Singing
3. Music reading
4. Playing melody instruments

Conceptual Understandings
1. When music has a key center, it has tonality; when music has no key center, it is atonal.
2. Music that has two different key centers is bitonal; music that has two or more key centers is polytonal.

Behavioral Objectives
1. To hear and understand the difference between music that is tonal and music that is atonal
2. To hear and understand the difference between music that has one tonality and music that is bitonal

Related Arts
Exploring texture through the visual arts, using figure 5.2 *a–e,* page 274.

Procedure
1. Using rhythm instruments and classroom objects to create collages that illustrate tonality and atonality
   a. Display rhythm instruments on a table in front of the room. Ask what they have in common. (They are all instruments that can play rhythm patterns.)
   b. Ask children to gather objects from the room—objects that are not related to each other, for example: a book, a ruler, a coin, a water glass, an eraser, an article of clothing.
   c. Ask a volunteer to define texture, tonality, and atonality.
   d. Explain that you would like the class to help you build a collage showing texture with tonality (or focus) and a collage showing texture without tonality, i.e., atonal (without focus). The articles gathered will be used to make these collages.
   e. Clear a space on the table and define the area in which the collage will be built. (A large rectangle or square may be marked with masking tape or a chalk line.)
   f. Ask the class for ideas, for using the materials to build a collage showing no texture. There are several ways of doing this. Children may suggest any of the methods shown in figure 5.2 *a, b,* or *c.*
   g. Discuss ideas suggested, emphasizing that no texture implies a single idea presented at any given moment—no overlapping of images. Thus, the rhythm sticks in *a* lead the eye from one to another but do not interrelate.
   h. Ask the class for ideas for building a collage using texture with tonality (focus). Emphasize that texture implies images (or sounds) seen (or heard) simultaneously and that tonality means a key center in music or a focus in the visual arts. Encourage children to discuss and experiment with ways they can achieve texture and tonality. One class decided to make a picture similar to figure 5.2*d.*
   i. Ask the class to build a collage, using objects on the table, to illustrate texture with no tonality or focus (atonal). Encourage discussion and experimentation until the class clearly understands that no tonality means no focus. One class made a collage similar to figure 5.2*e.*

Figure 5.2
a, Rhythm sticks in a straight line; b, one object placed in a space; c, several different objects placed in a row; d, texture with tonality (focus); e, texture without tonality—atonal (no focus). All photographs by David Rosenthal.

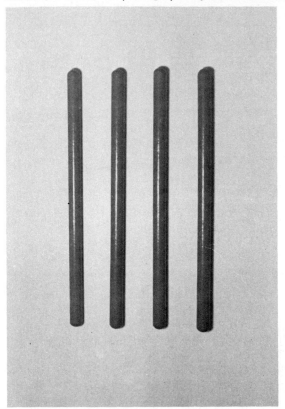

a

b

c

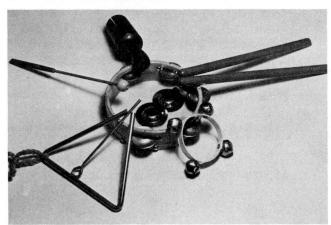

d

e

2. Exploring texture (bitonality) by using a familiar tune to create a bitonal composition
   a. Drawing on previous knowledge and experience, discuss the different ways music can be written. Focus on tonality and bitonality.
   b. Place the following melody on the board. Have volunteers identify the key (G) and play the song on a melody instrument.

   c. When a child can play it easily in rhythm, have the class sing, first with words, then a neutral syllable, as the child accompanies. Discuss with the class, helping them become aware of the feeling of tonality in the song.
   d. Explain that you will demonstrate how this familiar melody can become a musical experience in bitonality. Notate the following on the board:

   e. Have the class identify the key (F) and ask for a volunteer to play it on the second melody instrument.
   f. When a child can play it in a steady rhythm, have the class sing it as child accompanies. Discuss with class, emphasizing that this, too, has a key (or tonal) center, but it is different from the first version.
   g. Have children play their parts simultaneously, as you conduct unobtrusively. Divide the class in half; half to sing with the child playing in the key of G, half to sing with the child playing in the key of F.
   h. Discuss other ways of experiencing bitonality: combining melodies in different keys; playing a melody in one key, accompanied by chords from another key; playing tone clusters as accompaniments to a melody; and so on. This is an example.

Melody in the Key of G Major

Accompaniment: Chords in G♭ Major

3. Exploring texture by listening to picture music ("Pacific 231" by Honegger) and abstract music ("Sarabande" from Suite for Strings by Corelli and Pinelli)
   a. Remind children of previous experiences exploring tonality, atonality, and bitonality, not only in music but in the visual arts.
   b. Write the following on the board:
      Tonality Bitonality Atonality
   c. Ask children for words that describe these three textures. Write their ideas on the board. They may be similar to the following:

Tonality	Bitonality	Atonality
Things seem to fit together.	One seems to be pitted against the other.	Things don't seem to fit together.
It makes sense.	It's off balance.	Things seem out of tune.
It seems focused.	Two things are happening at once.	It's hard to hear a beginning, middle, and end.
It seems to have a beginning, middle, and end.		One thing doesn't have much to do with the other.

   d. Have children copy the list on paper at their desks.
   e. Tell children you are going to play a recording, and they should write the letter P in front of all the words and phrases that describe this composition. Play "Pacific 231."
   f. Tell children you will play a different recording, and they should write the letter S in front of the words or phrases that describe this composition. Play "Sarabande."
   g. Discuss their answers. If necessary, play either of the compositions a second or third time until children understand.
   h. Children will enjoy knowing the names and interesting facts about these compositions. For example, Honegger loved trains and wrote this in 1923 when trains were in their prime. He wanted to depict the feeling of a train. Corelli frequently included the sarabande—a dignified dance popular in the seventeenth century—in his sonatas.

4. Evaluating children's ability to hear the difference between music that is tonal, atonal, and bitonal
   a. Review the meaning of these three types of texture: tonal, atonal, and bitonal.
   b. Distribute the following Music Cue chart.

Music Cue Chart

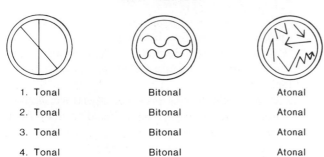

1. Tonal	Bitonal	Atonal
2. Tonal	Bitonal	Atonal
3. Tonal	Bitonal	Atonal
4. Tonal	Bitonal	Atonal

   c. Tell the class you are going to play a recording and to circle the term tonal, bitonal, or atonal under the circle that seems to describe the music. Play music for numbers 1–4.
      (1) "Col. Bogey March" by Alford (tonal)
      (2) "Devil's Dance" by Stravinsky (atonal)
      (3) Menuetto no. 2 from Divertimento no. 17 in D by Mozart (tonal)
      (4) "Three Blind Mice" (arranged bitonally)

Listening Experiences That Focus on Textural Concepts

Level I or II

Experiencing Textural Concepts by Creating a Rhythmic Interpretation

"Ballet of the Unhatched Chicks" from *Pictures at an Exhibition* by Moussorgsky, RCA *Adventures in Music* grade 1, vol. 1, LES 1000 or Holt, Rinehart and Winston *Exploring Music* recording 411

1. Write *texture* on the board. Explain that whenever more than one sound is heard in music, we have texture. Ask children to try to think of ways they have experienced texture and list them on the board. They may think of singing a round; playing rhythm instruments; singing a song with an accompaniment (guitar, Autoharp, piano, and so on).

2. Tell children to listen for type of texture and the feelings created by the instruments used. Play "Ballet of the Unhatched Chicks." Discuss texture, instruments heard, and feelings expressed.
3. Ask questions similar to the following:
   a. Does the music make you think of large or small things?
   b. Does it remind you of people, animals, or machines?
   c. Are they moving or standing still?
4. Let several children experiment as the recording plays, then let class guess what each child was dramatizing. Let other children explore ways of interpreting the music.

Level II

Focusing on Texture through an Experience with Electronic Music
"Bowery Bum" by Mimaroglu, Holt, Rinehart and Winston *Exploring Music* book 4, 1975, p. 149, recording 11

1. Through discussion remind children of their experiences with various types of texture. Play "Bowery Bum."
2. Ask these or similar questions:
   a. Was it music or noise? (Because it is organized, most musicians would call it music.)
   b. How was it created? (By recording the plucking and scraping of a rubber band at one speed, then playing it back, while rerecording at another speed. In addition, one set of sounds was superimposed on another, sounds were rerecorded, played backwards, and so on.)
   c. What do we call this method of creating music? (It is called electronic music—all sounds produced are generated through electronic means.)
3. As children listen again, they may enjoy these activities:
   a. Creating an abstract drawing illustrating the music
   b. Interpreting the music rhythmically
4. On other days, children might enjoy hearing other electronic music. One source is *Eight Electronic Pieces* by Rod Dockstader, Folkways recording FM 3434.

Note: The following may be of interest to the teacher: *The New World of Electronic Music* by Walter Sear, Alfred Publishing Co., N.Y., 1972; and *Guide to Electronic Music*, EAV Recording 8RB514, Pleasantville, New York.

Level III

Focusing on Texture through an Experience with Story Music
Petrouchka by Stravinsky, Bowmar *Orchestral Library* recording BOL 095

This experience should be extended over several music periods.
1. Write these words on the board: tone cluster, dissonance, polytonality, shifting melodies, rhythms, accents, and meters.
2. Ask the class whether these words describe contemporary music or music from the time of Mozart or Haydn. (contemporary)
3. Discuss each word or phrase, using experiences similar to the following:
   a. To illustrate the tone cluster, have a child simultaneously play E, F, G, and A, on the piano.
   b. To illustrate polytonality, have one child play "Hot Cross Buns" on the recorder or other melody instrument in one key (G) as another child plays the same tune in another key (F) and a third child plays it in still another key (C).
4. Explain that the experiences above create what we call dissonance. Encourage children to tell what—in light of these experiences—this word means to them.
5. To illustrate shifting meters, give children a clapping experience similar to the following. To maintain a steady rhythm, give children a cue—nod your head or signal with your right hand—on the last beat of each pattern you clap.

6. Tell children they will hear music that uses some of the devices discussed. Announce the title, *Petrouchka* by Stravinsky. Relate the story, displaying and playing themes. Play the recording. Discuss the various musical devices heard in the texture.

Concepts Related to Form

Level I

Materials Needed
1. Recording of March from *Nutcracker Suite* by Tchaikovsky, RCA Victor *Basic Record Library for Elementary Grades* recording WE 72
2. Copy of "Kye Kye Kole" and "Kum Ba Yah"
3. Copy of *St. Severin* by Robert Delaunay
4. Rhythm instruments
5. Music Cue charts
6. Music for evaluation procedure

Listening Activity
An experience with abstract music, using March from *Nutcracker* Suite by Tchaikovsky

Related Musical Activities
1. Singing
2. Playing rhythm instruments
3. Bodily movement

Conceptual Understandings
1. Music often consists of phrases. Each one is a musical idea and ends with a cadence.
2. In any one musical composition, there may be some phrases that are alike and some that are different.
3. Repeated sections (phrases) give meaning, form, to music.

Behavioral Objectives
1. To begin to hear and respond to a phrase in music
2. To begin to hear similar phrases in music

Related Arts
Focusing on concepts related to form through the visual arts, by using *St. Severin* by Robert Delaunay (figure 5.3)

Procedure
1. Focusing on phrases that are similar and different by singing "Kye Kye Kole" and "Kum Ba Yah"
   a. Teach children "Kye Kye Kole" by having them echo you, imitating both voice and actions. (Note that each phrase is repeated. For a copy of the song see chapter 3.)

b. Ask a volunteer to take your place. Explain that she must change actions for each new phrase, the action must be simple, and she must stay in the same place.
c. Repeat, using different leaders, until children know the song.
d. Ask children if phrases are all alike or different. (Each phrase was sung twice.)
e. Ask children if they remember another song from Africa, "Kum Ba Yah." Have them sing it with you. (For a copy of the song see chapter 3.)
f. Explain that songs consist of phrases. Just as a story has sentences, music has phrases to make it easier to understand.
g. Ask children to see if they can hear how many phrases there are in this song. Have them close their eyes and listen as you sing the song. Tell them to put their hands on their heads for the first phrase, and on a different part of their body (ears, chin, shoulders, hips, and so on) for each new phrase. Sing "Kum Ba Yah."
h. If children demonstrate they can hear the four phrases, continue. If not, have them open their eyes and repeat step g, helping them by putting your hands in different places for each phrase.
i. Ask children how they could tell when one phrase ended and a new phrase began. (The music sounds similar to the end of a sentence.) Explain that in music instead of having a period we have a cadence.
j. Ask children if all the phrases sounded alike or were some alike and some different. Tell children to listen carefully to the first phrase as you sing it. Tell them that each time they hear it they are to put their hands on their heads. Sing the song. (Children should have their hands on their heads for the first and third phrases.)
k. Ask if any other phrases are repeated. (no) Through discussion and experimentation, encourage children to discover a clapping pattern for three types of phrases. One class decided on the following:

Phrases 1 and 3

Phrase 2

Phrase 4

1. Have the class sing the song, using patterns decided upon.
2. Focusing on concepts related to form through the visual arts
   a. Display a picture similar to that in figure 5.3.
   b. Remind children of their experiences with phrases that are alike and different in music. Explain that the artist uses other devices, such as similar and contrasting lines, shapes, and colors to give meaning to paintings. Ask children to look at the picture and tell their reactions. Help, if necessary, by asking questions and having children point to the answers in the picture.
      (1) Do you see any slightly curved lines?
      (2) Do you see any arches?
      (3) Are these repeated?
      (4) What does the repetition of these lines and arches make you think of?
      (5) Which direction do all the lines and arches seem to move? (up and into the center of the picture)
      (6) Would the picture give the same feeling if the repeated shapes were squares and circles?
      (7) Would it give the same feeling if there were no repeated lines or shapes?
   c. Children might enjoy creating their own drawings, deciding upon a few shapes and lines, and repeating them to create a meaningful drawing.
3. Focusing on phrases that are similar and different through an experience with abstract music (March from *Nutcracker* Suite by Tchaikovsky)
   a. Through discussion, remind children of previous experiences in which the following ideas were explored:
      (1) Music is made up of phrases, like sentences.
      (2) Each phrase ends with a combination of notes, called a cadence, which make it sound like the end.
      (3) Phrases in music are repeated and contrasted to create meaning (form). In a painting, lines, shapes and colors are repeated and contrasted to create meaning. In a story, ideas about people, animals, or life are repeated and contrasted to give meaning.
   b. Tell children to decide on a word that they think best describes the music they hear—jolly, sad, marching or other. Play the first phrase (fanfare) of March. Ask for a word describing it. Assume they say marching.

Figure 5.3
St. Severin by Robert Delaunay. 1927 (after a painting of 1909). Lithograph, 22 ⅜ × 17″. Collection, The Museum of Modern Art, New York. Abby Aldrich Rockefeller Fund.

   c. Explain each time they hear marching they are to pat their thighs in rhythm. When they hear something else, they are to clap their hands. Play the recording. Each time children pat thighs, put *marching* on the board as follows:

marching   marching
marching   marching
marching   marching
marching   marching

   d. Ask if they heard a phrase different from marching. Ask them to name it and decide on a movement for it. Assume they decide on rolling.
   e. Tell children to pat their thighs whenever they hear marching and to pat their shoulders when they hear rolling. Play the composition and add rolling to the list on the board each time it occurs. The following should result:

marching   marching   rolling
marching   marching   rolling
marching   marching   rolling
marching   marching   rolling

f. Ask children what bodily movement fits marching. Let individual children experiment, moving to marching whenever it occurs, as you play the recording. Let the class choose the movement (or movements) they like best, and select children to do these movements as you play the recording.

g. Repeat step f to find a movement for rolling.

h. Have the class decide which rhythm instruments would best fit each tune, as they listen to the recording.

i. Encourage children to experiment with their ideas and select instrumentation and rhythm they prefer. One class suggested the following:

Marching

Tone Blocks, Rhythm Sticks, and Drum | | | |

Rolling

Triangles ♩ ♩

Tambourines ○ Strike on *one;* shake on *two-three-four.*

j. When children can play instruments with music successfully, divide the class into four groups and have them perform as the recording plays.

Group one	moving to marching
Group two	moving to rolling
Group three	playing instruments on marching
Group four	playing instruments on rolling

4. Evaluating children's ability to identify similar and dissimilar phrases

a. Distribute Music Cue charts.

Music Cue Chart

1.	Same	Different
2.	Same	Different
3.	Same	Different
4.	Same	Different

---

b. Tell children you are going to play two different phrases. If they are the same, they are to circle the word *same* after number 1. If they are different, they are to circle the word *different*. Play the first two phrases for number 1. Continue playing appropriate phrases for numbers 2–4.

Phrase 1, Number 1

Phrase 2, Number 1   (same)

Phrase 1, Number 2

Phrase 2, Number 2   (different)

Phrase 1, Number 3

Phrase 2, Number 3   (different)

Phrase 1, Number 4

Phrase 2, Number 4   (same)

c. Discuss the correct answers with children, clarifying any misunderstandings by doing the following things:
   (1) Playing the phrase again
   (2) Having children sing it on a neutral syllable
   (3) Focusing on direction (up or down) and predominance of skips or steps
   (4) Focusing on rhythmic characteristics

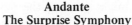

Andante

Franz Joseph Haydn

Surprise Chord

Listening Experiences That Focus on Concepts Related to Form

Level II

Focusing on Concepts Related to Form through an Experience with Abstract Music

Andante from *The Surprise* Symphony by Haydn, RCA Victor *Basic Record Library for Elementary Grades* recording WE 80 or Holt, Rinehart and Winston *Exploring Music* recording 27

1. Write the theme from the Andante on the board, a large cardboard, or a transparency.
2. Let a gifted child learn to play a theme on a melody instrument.
3. Tell children you would like to tell them a story about a composer who had a sense of humor. Tell this story:

People loved Franz Joseph Haydn so much that they often called him Papa Haydn. He lived over two hundred years ago, but he wrote such delightful music that people enjoy it today.

Haydn played every night at the court of a count. The ladies and gentlemen of the court had a large meal before they came to hear Haydn's music and they often got a little sleepy.

Though Haydn was a friendly, jolly person, it did irritate him to see people asleep as he and his musicians played. He thought about this problem and one day had an idea for waking them. He laughed as he thought of the joke he would play on these sleepy people and immediately set to work writing a new symphony.

When he and his musicians had carefully rehearsed, they decided it was time for the joke. The ladies and gentlemen came in from their dinner one evening and sat comfortably in their chairs, ready for their little catnap.

The music began. The first part of the symphony went as usual. But suddenly, in the middle of the Andante, crash! The drums, cymbals, and brass played together on one chord. What a noise it made!

Everyone jumped out of his seat as if a clap of thunder had sounded. Haydn and his musicians laughed to themselves when they saw that the response was exactly what they had hoped it would be.

If you haven't already guessed the name of this symphony, it is called *The Surprise* Symphony.

4. Display the theme.
5. Have the class find the surprise chord.
6. Have the child who learned the theme on the melody instrument play it.
7. Ask children if any of the phrases were repeated. (The first phrase is repeated, with a different ending.)

8. Ask children how many different melodies (sections) they heard (two) and what form they think this might be, AB or ABA. (AB) Focus on the introduction of a new melody immediately after the surprise chord.
9. Play the recording, asking children to raise their hands when they hear the surprise chord.
10. Let the class decide what rhythm instrument would best play the surprise chord. (probably cymbals)
11. Select children to play the surprise chord with instruments.
12. Play the recording, letting them play the surprise chord.
13. Help children experiment and decide upon instruments to accompany both A and B sections. Play the recording as they accompany.
14. Children may enjoy learning to conduct the Andante.

Level II or III

Focusing on ABA Form through an Experience with Abstract Music

March from *Nutcracker* Suite by Tchaikovsky, Bowmar *Orchestral Library* recording 071 or Holt, Rinehart and Winston *Exploring Music* recording 28

1. Play recording of Fanfare only.
2. Ask children to choose a colored card (from four or five large colored cards available) that best fits the melody. Assume they choose red.
3. Select a child to raise the card each time she hears the melody and ask the class to raise their hands when they hear the red melody. The form of the March is as follows:

A	B	A
fanfare and running passage, repeated six times	repeated four times	fanfare and running passage, repeated six times

4. Play the recording. Write *red* on the board each time children raise their hands.

red	red
red	red
red*	red*
red*	red*
red	red
red	red

*Children may hear these two sections as different tunes. If so, have them select another color and proceed as if it were a different tune, written in rondo rather than ABA.

5. Ask if they heard a different melody. Assume they hear the running passage of A.
6. Ask children to choose a card for the running passage. Assume they choose blue.

7. Play the recording as a child raises the red card on the red melody, another raises the blue card on the blue melody, and the class raises their hands when they hear the blue melody. Write the following on the board:

red–blue	red–blue
red–blue	red–blue
red–blue	red–blue
red–blue	red–blue
red–blue	red–blue

8. Ask if they heard another melody (B). Ask them to choose a card for B melody. Assume it is yellow. Select a child to hold up the card when the yellow melody is heard. Play the recording as all participate, and write this on the board:

red–blue	yellow	red–blue
red–blue	yellow	red–blue
red–blue	yellow	red–blue
red–blue	yellow	red–blue
red–blue		red–blue
red–blue		red–blue

9. Tell children that any composition with this pattern is called ABA form. Help the class create a rhythmic accompaniment for March.

Level III

Focusing on the Theme and Variations Form through an Experience with Abstract Music

Variations on the Theme "Pop! Goes the Weasel" by Cailliet, RCA *Adventures in Music* grade 4, vol. 1, LES 1004

1. Prepare five Cues to Music cards like the following:

White Card Introduction and Theme

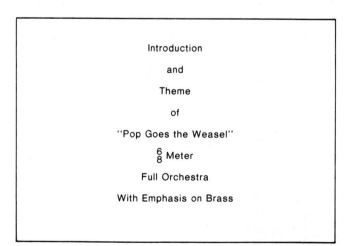

Introduction

and

Theme

of

"Pop Goes the Weasel"

$\frac{6}{8}$ Meter

Full Orchestra

With Emphasis on Brass

Orange Card Variation 1

Fugue

(little flight)

Clarinet

Drum

Horn

Clarinet

Trombone and Low Strings

Violins

Full Orchestra

(each plays a part of the theme)

Pink Card Variation 2

Minuet (or Waltz)

$\frac{3}{4}$ Meter

Theme is Played by

Brass below the Strings

Strings Play a Different Melody

Blue Card Variation 3

Adagio

Minor Scale $\frac{4}{8}$ Meter

Solo Violin Plays

Introduction then

Theme Appears in

the Strings

Rich Harmonies

Yellow Card Variation 4

Waltz

$\frac{3}{4}$ Meter

"Wa Wa" Introduction

Played by Trumpet

"Ump pa pa" Accompaniment

Played by Full Orchestra,

with "Jazzy" Effect

2. Be sure that children know the tune "Pop! Goes the Weasel."
3. Display the five Cues to Music cards.
4. Tell children that in a theme and variations a composer first presents a simple theme and then proceeds to vary it in several ways:
   a. Changing notes in the melody
   b. Changing the tempo (fast and slow)
   c. Using different instruments
   d. Using different harmonies
   e. Using different meters
5. Tell children that the composer used "Pop! Goes the Weasel" for the theme.
6. Tell them that they will first hear the introduction and theme, and immediately after the theme, they will hear four variations on this tune. They should decide which card matches each variation.
7. Discuss each Cues to Music card in the following order. (This is not the order they appear on the recording.)

a. Pink card
   (1) Discuss how a waltz or minuet swings. (in three, 1–2–3)
   (2) Clap the rhythm (1–2–3).
   (3) Call attention to the fact that the theme will be heard below the strings.
b. Orange card
   Tell the class that fugue means flight. Different voices or instruments play the theme or part of the theme in quick succession. In this variation, the following instruments play the theme.
   (1) Clarinet
   (2) Drum
   (3) Horn
   (4) Clarinet
   (5) Trombone and low strings
   (6) Violins
   (7) Full orchestra

c. Yellow card
  (1) Discuss how a trumpet makes the sound *wa wa.* (by using a mute)
  (2) Where might a mechanical *ump pa pa* accompaniment be heard?
  (3) What might be the difference in this variation and the other waltz variation? (instrumentation—wa wa introduction and ump pa pa accompaniment)
d. Blue card
  (1) Discuss the meaning of *adagio.* (slow)
  (2) Discuss the difference in mood between major and minor.
e. White card
  This one states the introduction and theme.

8. Tell class that as they hear each of the four variations that follow the introduction and theme (white card), they are to write down the order heard by indicating the color of the card. They may copy this from the board.

| Variation 1 | Variation 3 |
| Variation 2 | Variation 4 |

9. Play the recording. Have the class write the correct colors. If there is confusion about where variations begin, the teacher may try the following:
  a. Play the recording again, having children raise their hands at the beginning of each variation.
  b. Discuss further cues listed on cards.
  c. Play the recording as many times as necessary to clarify points listed on cards.

10. These are the correct colors for each variation.

| Variation 1 | orange | Variation 3 | blue |
| Variation 2 | pink | Variation 4 | yellow |

11. Discuss children's answers and clarify any misunderstandings.

Expressive Concepts

Level II or III

Materials Needed
1. The following recordings
  a. *The Sorcerer's Apprentice* by Dukas, Bowmar *Orchestral Library* recording BOL 072
  b. Prelude to Act I from *Carmen* by Bizet, Bowmar *Orchestral Library* recording BOL 093
  c. "En Bateau" by Debussy, Bowmar *Orchestral Library* recording BOL 066
  d. "Farandole" from *L'Arlesienne* Suite no. 2 by Bizet, RCA *Adventures in Music* grade 6, vol. 1, LES 1009
  e. "Fantasia" on *Greensleeves* by Vaughan Williams, RCA *Adventures in Music* grade 6, vol. 2, LES 1008

Figure 5.4
The Blue Window by Henri Matisse. (1911, autumn). Oil on canvas, 51 ½ × 35 ⅝". Collection, The Museum of Modern Art, New York. Abby Aldrich Rockefeller Fund.

2. Copy of proverbs
3. Copy of paintings
4. Music Cue charts

Listening Activity
An experience with story music, *Sorcerer's Apprentice* by Dukas

Related Musical Activities
1. Singing (vocal exploration)
2. Music reading (rhythmic notation)

Conceptual Understandings
1. The expressive qualities of music are changed by changes in instrumentation, tempi, and dynamics.
2. Our voices may be used in different ways to produce differences in tone quality and mood.

Behavioral Objectives
1. To hear ways in which differences in tempo, dynamics, and instrumentation affect the expressive qualities of music

Figure 5.5
Northeaster by Winslow Homer. The Metropolitan Museum
of Art. Gift of George A. Hearn, 1910.

2. To use our voices in different ways to produce differences in tone quality and mood

Related Arts
Exploring expressive concepts through the visual arts
1. *The Blue Window* by Matisse (figure 5.4)
2. *Northeaster* by Homer (figure 5.5)

Procedure
1. Exploring expressive concepts through the visual arts
   a. Display copies of the two paintings so that children can see them.
   b. Ask children to describe the difference between moods expressed in each. Encourage their thinking by asking the following:
      (1) Which picture makes you think of something calm and thoughtful?
      (2) Which picture makes you think of something exciting and turbulent?
   c. Ask children how a composer would create these moods in music. Would *The Blue Window* use full orchestra, playing forte, and in a fast tempo;

or would it be orchestrated for muted violins and woodwinds, playing piano (soft) and in a slow tempo? How would *Northeaster* be orchestrated?
   d. Ask children to examine *The Blue Window* and try to decide how the artist, Henri Matisse, created its mood of tranquility. Encourage children by asking the following:
      (1) Are the lines predominately pointed and sharp or curved and flowing?
      (2) Is violent activity suggested by any image?
      (3) What lines and shapes suggesting softness and stillness are repeated in the picture?
   e. Ask children to look carefully at *Northeaster* and decide how the artist, Winslow Homer, created its mood of turbulence. Encourage children by asking questions similar to the following:
      (1) Are the images violent or peaceful?
      (2) Are the lines predominately sharp and jagged or soft and curved?
      (3) How did the artist make it clear that the big, white shape billowing on the left is not a gentle cloud, but a tremendous wave

breaking against the rocks? (by making the rocks that break the wave much darker, sharply pointed, and clifflike, as they jut out from the water)

    f. Ask children what colors would be used in each picture to further develop the mood. (If possible, get a color reproduction of these pictures and let children compare their ideas.)

2. Exploring expressive concepts through vocal exploration, using proverbs in contrasting dynamics

    a. Write this on the board.

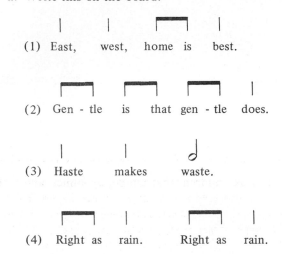

(1) East, west, home is best.

(2) Gen - tle is that gen - tle does.

(3) Haste makes waste.

(4) Right as rain. Right as rain.

    b. Have children chant and clap the proverbs, first with words, then with number notation.

    c. Ask children for examples of four different kinds of dynamics for each of these proverbs. Assume these are their answers and write them on the board:

        (a) loud   (c) crescendo
        (b) soft   (d) decrescendo

    d. Tell children you would like to explore the way differences in dynamics can change the expressive quality (mood) of each proverb.

    e. Divide the class into four groups and give each group a number and a letter, for example; 1a, 2b, 3c, and 4d.

    f. Explain that group 1a will say the first proverb in the dynamics indicated by a (loud); group 2b the second proverb in the dynamics indicated by b (soft); group 3c the third proverb using the dynamics indicated by c (crescendo); and group 4d the fourth proverb using dynamics suggested by d (decrescendo). Let each group practice.

    g. When each group can say its proverb in the dynamics assigned, have children recite all four proverbs, without missing a beat. Signal group 1 to begin and each group to enter.

    h. Tell children that you would like each group to say its proverb with different dynamics, and assign as follows:
Group 1 b (soft)
Group 2 c (crescendo)
Group 3 d (decrescendo)
Group 4 a (loud)
Let each group practice, then have them say all proverbs, as in step f.

    i. Ask children how changing the dynamics changed the feelings expressed. For example, how did saying "Gentle is that gentle does" with a crescendo differ from saying it softly?

    j. Have children experiment, singing the proverbs and using different dynamics, to feel changes in expressive qualities. Tell them to echo you, with hand signals.

(Softly)

S   M   S S   M
East,   west,   home is   best.

(Crescendo)

S L S M S L S
Gen - tle is as gen - tle does.

(Decrescendo)

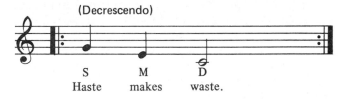

S   M   D
Haste   makes   waste.

(Loudly)

S S D^1 S S D^1
Right as rain.   Right as rain.

3. Exploring concepts related to expression through an experience with music that tells a story (*The Sorcerer's Apprentice* by Dukas)
The teacher should be familiar with the recording.

    a. Read the story to the class.

    The scene is laid in the workshop of Pancrates, a famous sorcerer. His apprentice, young Eucrates, speaks: "Ah, at last the old magician's gone away!

Gone and left me master over all the spirits. I have watched him working wonders, listened to his charms and passwords. Now, I, too, will make some magic!

> Water, Water, set in motion
> Little waves that from a distance
> Come in streams and flowing, swelling,
> Quickly fill the bath and basins.

Now, you old broom in the corner, come and stir your wretched carcass! Long enough you've been a servant, and today you'll do my bidding. Now then, stand up on two legs there. Head on top and take the pail, sir, for today you fetch the water. And see to it that you hurry!

> Water, Water, set in motion
> Little waves that from a distance
> Come in streams and flowing, swelling,
> Quickly fill the bath and basins.

See, he runs down to the river! He has reached the bank already! Back again as quick as lightening, then a second time returning! Hooray, how the water's rising in the master's bath and basins! Stop now, stop! Your gifts have served us quite enough. Oh, gracious heavens, what's the word? I've clean forgotten! Oh, that word! That word of magic which alone can stop this deluge! There, he's running to the river, fetching yet more pails of water! Oh, a hundred hateful rivers now are pouring in upon me! No, I cannot, will not bear it! 'Tis a demon, and its glances drive me almost mad with terror!

Oh, you villain! Oh, you devil! Do you really mean to drown me? See, the water's crossed the threshold! Oh, mad creature, stop, I pray you, be a broom just as you once were! So you won't leave off? I'll fix you, Wooden Head, with my sharp hatchet!

See, he's coming, slipping, slopping—Now you goblin, now you'll catch it! Crash! There goes my valiant hatchet. Right in two he's cut. Thank Heaven! Once again I can breathe freely!

Can it be that both the pieces now are standing up and moving? Two slaves now to carry water, Oh, ye Gods above, protect me!

Off they go, and wet and wetter grow the steps and all the workshop now is flooded. Master, Master, hear my cry, my plight is ghastly! I have summoned evil spirits and I know not how to stop them!"

The old Sorcerer suddenly appears and speaks:

> "In the corner, broom! Be still now.
> And you, boy, had best remember
> That the master summons spirits
> Only for some worthy purpose!"[5]

5. From *A Listener's Anthology of Music*, vol. II, by Lillian Baldwin, © 1948, Silver Burdett Company.

b. Write this on the board:

Scene	Tempo	Dynamics	Instruments
1. Apprentice saying magic words			
2. Broom beginning to walk			
3. Broom beginning to run			
4. Water rising			
5. Apprentice cutting broom in half			
6. Both parts of boom beginning to carry water			
7. Sorcerer saying magic words			
8. Brooms stopping			

c. Ask children what tempo, dynamics, and instruments might best depict these scenes from *The Sorcerer's Apprentice*. Encourage children to explore possibilities for each scene. Write the majority opinion on the board. For example, would the broom probably begin walking slowly or immediately run? If it begins walking slowly, would the music be loud or soft? If it is soft, would it be played by violins or trumpets?

d. Ask children to raise their hands when they hear the music for each scene, as a volunteer points to the scene on the board. Play the recording. If children miss a scene, you point to it.

e. Discuss the music with the class, helping compare the composer's use of tempo, dynamics, and instruments in each scene with those voted on and listed on board.

f. Children will enjoy hearing the recording several times as different children point to the scene titles. They will also enjoy these enriching experiences.

(1) Illustrating a section or sections of the story: This can be in the form of large illustrations, which could be developed into Cues to Music cards, or smaller illustrations, which can be made into a filmstrip and shown on a projector.

(2) Seeing the filmstrip (published by Jam Handy).

(3) Creating a rhythmic dramatization, which could be developed into an assembly program.

4. Evaluating children's ability to hear differences in tempo, dynamics, and instrumentation

a. Distribute Music Cue charts.

Music Cue Chart

1. Mostly fast	Mostly slow	Mostly loud	Mostly soft	Which instrument plays first melody?	_____
2. Mostly fast	Mostly slow	Mostly loud	Mostly soft	Which percussion instrument plays accents?	_____
3. Mostly fast	Mostly slow	Mostly loud	Mostly soft	Which instruments play first theme?	_____
4. Mostly fast	Mostly slow	Mostly loud	Mostly soft	Which instruments are heard playing the melody?	_____

b. Tell children to circle the words that apply to the music you will play, and answer the question for each number. Play the following:

Number 1: "En Bateau" by Debussy (first part).
(*Answers:* Mostly slow   Mostly soft   Flute plays first melody.)

Number 2: Prelude to Act I from *Carmen* by Bizet (band one only).
(*Answers:* Mostly fast   Mostly loud   Cymbals play accents.)

Number 3: "Farandole" from *L'Arlesienne* Suite no. 2 by Bizet (first theme only).
(*Answers:* Mostly fast   Mostly loud   Full orchestra, oboes, clarinets and violins, bassoons, French horns and low strings all play theme.)

Number 4: "Fantasia" on *Greensleeves* by Vaughan Williams (first part only).
(*Answers:* Mostly slow   Mostly soft   Violas and violins play melody.)

c. Discuss the answers with children, focusing on how tempo, dynamics, and instrumentation create changes in expression. If children desire, play selections again and explore other devices that create the mood.

Listening Experiences That Focus on Expressive Concepts

Level II

Focusing on Expressive Concepts through an Experience with Story Music

"Beauty and the Beast" from *Mother Goose* Suite by Ravel, Bowmar *Orchestral Library* recording BOL 070, or RCA *Adventures in Music* grade 5, vol. 1, LES 1006

1. Read or tell story of "Beauty and the Beast."[6]

Once upon a time a traveler lost his way in a deep wood. The man was tired and very hungry. He tried first one path, then another, but he could not find his way out. Just as he was about to give up in despair, he noticed a strange and beautiful house ahead of him. As

---

6. Adapted from *Music for Young Listeners, The Green Book*, by Lillian Baldwin. © 1951, Silver Burdett Company. Reprinted by permission.

---

he came nearer he saw that the house stood in a lovely garden. Although it was midwinter, flowers were blooming and birds singing gaily in the sweet, warm air. No human creature was to be seen.

The man went into the house, hoping to find food and a place to rest, and someone to tell him the way home. The house was as deserted as the garden, but in one of the rooms was a table spread with the most delicious-looking food. The man was so hungry that he sat down and ate a hearty supper. Then he spied a comfortable couch that seemed to be waiting for him. So he stretched his weary bones upon it and fell fast asleep. When he awoke he again searched the house, but not a soul could he discover.

"What a strange place." said the man. "I do not like to go away without thanking my host for my good supper and my good bed."

He went into the garden again. On both sides of the path grew the most beautiful roses the man had ever seen.

"How my daughter, Beauty, would love these roses." said the man. "I shall take one home to her. Surely one rose will not be missed among so many."

But just as he started to pick the rose, a terrible beast appeared and bellowed in a most terrible voice, "What do you mean by picking my roses? For this you shall pay with your life!"

The man hastened to beg the Beast's pardon. He said he had meant no harm. He had only wanted to take one rose to his daughter who loved flowers dearly. The Beast replied that all that made no difference to him. He was most particular about his roses and whoever touched them must be punished.

"Go on home," he growled. "Take the rose to your daughter. But at the end of one month either one of your daughters must come to live in my house, or you must die."

The poor man went sorrowfully home and told his story.

"Well, Father," said Beauty, "since you got into all this trouble by picking a rose for me, I must be the one to go to the Beast's house."

So, at the end of the month, Beauty said good-by to her brothers and sisters and set out for the Beast's house. It was very brave of her; for although the Beast's house was a wonderful place, the Beast himself was too terrible for words.

All day long Beauty had everything a girl could dream of to make her happy. But every evening after supper the Beast would come shuffling in and ask in his terrible voice, "Beauty, will you marry me?"

Beauty would always answer, as politely as she could, of course, "No thank you, Beast."

Every night Beauty would dream of a charming prince who begged her to rescue him from a cruel spell that bound him. The prince also urged her not to think too much about the way people looked. He said that a lot of people looked much worse than they really were— all of which is solemn truth. Beauty could not understand what it all meant. But after a while this prince of her dreams seemed very real to her. So real that she loved him.

As the days went by, Beauty found that she really didn't mind the old Beast so much. He couldn't help his beastly looks and he certainly was kind and tried to give her a good time. He even sent Beauty off for a visit with her family, after she promised that she would come back to him in two months. But Beauty had such a good time visiting that she was late in coming back to Beast's house. When she did return, she found the poor fellow lying under a rosebush, all but dead. The doctor said he was suffering from a bad case of broken promises. It is a terrible disease. Even beasts curl up and die of it.

"Oh," cried Beauty, "this is all my fault! I am so sorry!"

Her pity seemed like magic medicine. The beast felt better at once. He was soon able to get up and waddle off.

That evening after supper he came to Beauty's parlor to ask his usual question. A little bird, who was eavesdropping on the window sill, reports this conversation.

Beauty: (still feeling sorry) "When I think of your kind heart, Beast, you don't seem quite so ugly to me."

Beast: (sighing) "Yes, lady, it is true; I've a kind heart, but still I am a monster."

Beauty: (still feeling sorry) "There are many men who are worse monsters than you!"

Beast: (gratefully) "How kind you are. If I were clever, I would pay you a fine compliment by way of thanks, but I'm only a Beast. Beauty—will you be my wife?"

Beauty: (politely) "No, thank you, Beast."

Beast: (with a sigh that almost split his hide) "Then I might as well die. But I shall die happy because I have had the joy of seeing you once more, my Beauty."

When the Beast mentioned dying, something happened to Beauty's heart. She knew she could never be happy without the Beast.

Beauty: (eagerly) "No, no, dear Beast, you must not die! Live, and I will marry you!"

With that, the Beast disappeared and in his place stood the charming prince of her dreams.

We all know—without the little bird telling us—the end of the story. For, of course, Beauty and her Prince lived happily ever after.

2. Discuss the story, eliciting children's ideas about beauty and humanistic values. Stress that often things and people are ugly on the surface but have real beauty as we get to know them.

3. Explain that Ravel wrote a composition that describes the conversations between Beauty and the Beast. The clarinet is the voice of Beauty and the double bassoon the voice of the Beast. (At this point the teacher may want to play the themes of Beauty and the Beast from charts accompanying the Bowmar recording or from *Music for Young Listeners: The Green Book* by Lillian Baldwin, Silver Burdett Company, publishers.)

4. Explain further that their conversation starts simply but grows more excited as the music progresses. The Beast pleads with Beauty, his voice growing louder and louder, and Beauty answers with *no's* that are just as excited. Finally, however, the harp plays a magic tune, and the Beast seems to dissolve as the Prince appears. In the end the music seems to tell of the joy Beauty and the Prince will have together.

5. Tell children to raise their hands when they hear the following:
   a. The first time Beauty speaks
   b. The first time the Beast speaks
   c. The voices of Beauty and the Beast talking to each other
   d. The harp announcing the transformation of the Beast into the Prince

6. Play the recording. If children have difficulty hearing these voices help by indicating when each occurs.

7. Discuss the music, asking questions similar to the following:
   a. Why do you think Ravel chose the clarinet to play the voice of Beauty and the bassoon to play the voice of the Beast?
   b. How do the tempo and dynamics change as the conversation gets more excited?
   c. What other expressive devices help tell the story?

8. On another day children may enjoy dramatizing "Beauty and the Beast."

Level II

Focusing on Expressive Concepts through an Experience with Mood or Picture Music
Carnival of the Animals by Saint-Saëns, Bowmar *Orchestral Library* recording BOL 064, or Holt, Rinehart and Winston *Exploring Music* recording 28

1. Explain that composers sometimes write music with the intent of painting musical pictures of people, animals, or things. In *Carnival of the Animals,* for example, Saint-Saëns has drawn musical pictures of the animals.

2. Write on the board the names of the animals described. Do not list numbers on the board.

Fleet-Footed		Hens and Cocks	(2)
Animals	(3)	Aquarium	(7)
Cuckoo in the		Fossils	(12)
Deep Woods	(9)	Elephant	(5)
The swan	(13)	Turtles	(4)
Lion	(1)	Aviary (birds)	(10)
Kangaroos	(6)	Long-Eared	
Pianists	(11)	Personages	(8)

3. Discuss ways that the composer might describe each.
   a. Would the bird's music be best played by a bass tuba or violin?
   b. Would the lion's music be slow or fast, loud or soft?
   c. Would the rhythm of the hens and cocks be uneven, slow and steady, or fast and detached?
   d. Would the music of the swan be legato or staccato?
   e. What kind of melody would the cuckoo have? Ask children to count the number of times they hear the cuckoo.
   f. What kind of melody would describe personages with long ears?
4. Tell the class the animals are not listed in the order they will be heard. The first child to recognize the animal described by the music will place number 1 by the correct animal, and so on, throughout the composition.
5. Play the recording, letting children number the animals.
6. Distribute drawing paper and crayons. As children illustrate their favorite sections, play the five or six most popular sections.
7. Play the recording once more, asking children to come to the front of the room and show their drawings as the section they illustrated is playing.
8. Children might enjoy illustrating favorite animals for a bulletin board display.

Level II or III

Focusing on Expressive Concepts through an Experience with Mood or Picture Music
"Hornpipe" from *Water Music* by Handel and "Departure" from *Winter Holiday* by Prokofieff, RCA *Adventures in Music* grade 2, vol. 1, LES 1001

1. Write the following on the board:
   Carnival Funeral Homecoming Hornpipe Departure
2. Ask children to define each word.
3. Ask children to imagine they are composers and to tell you what instruments, tempo, and dynamics they would use to create music depicting each word on the board.

4. Have them write on paper the titles "Hornpipe" and "Departure."
5. Tell them to write their ideas for instruments, tempo, and dynamics of music to go with each of these titles.
6. Tell the class to (a) underline the words on their papers that describe the music and (b) add any other words, not already on their papers, that describe instrumentation, tempo, or dynamics used by the composer, underlining these twice.
7. Play "Hornpipe."
8. Ask children to share with the class the words they underlined and the new expressive devices they heard. Clarify any misunderstandings. Explain that there are many different ways of creating music for "Hornpipe"; thus, their answers may differ.
9. Follow the same procedure for exploring expressive devices in "Departure."

Level III

Exploring Expressive Concepts through an Experience with Story Music
"The Firebird" by Stravinsky, Jam Handy recording and filmstrip

1. Ask the class the following questions:
   a. What is a firebird?
   b. What might it look like?
   c. What might it do?
   d. What kind of music might be written for a firebird?
2. Tell children the story of the Firebird:

"Firebird" is a Russian folk tale. The Firebird, a beautiful bird—half bird, half woman—is caught by the young prince, Ivan Tsarevitch, as she is plucking golden apples off the silver trees in the orchards of the evil Kastchei. Begging to be released, the beautiful bird is freed. Before flying away, she gives Ivan one of her shining feathers for his kindness to her.

As Ivan wanders through the orchard, he sees thirteen beautiful maidens dancing among the silver trees. He immediately falls in love with the most beautiful of them. The maidens, who are prisoners of the evil Kastchei, beg Ivan to depart in haste, lest Kastchei cast an evil spell over him and turn him to stone. Refusing to leave the beautiful maidens to Kastchei's mercy, Ivan encounters grotesque slaves, including the terrible Kastchei himself. However, the Firebird's golden feather protects Ivan against the wicked powers of Kastchei.

Suddenly the Firebird appears. Flying among them, the Firebird engages Kastchei and his slaves in a dance that grows so wild that all the participants fall to the ground in exhaustion. The Firebird tells Ivan about the egg that is the source of Kastchei's power. Ivan searches for the egg, and upon finding it, breaks it. Kastchei dies, the castle vanishes, the spell over Kastchei's slaves is broken. Ivan wins the most beautiful princess of all, Tsarevna, and a joyous celebration takes place.[7]

3. Ask the class how music describing the following characters would sound:
   a. The Firebird: fast or slow, light or heavy, high or low, loud or soft
   b. Ivan: fast or slow, light or heavy, high or low, loud or soft
   c. The princesses: fast or slow, light or heavy, high or low, loud or soft
   d. Kastchei: fast or slow, light or heavy, high or low, loud or soft
4. Ask the class what instrument or instruments the composer might use to depict the following actions:
   a. The Firebird plucking apples
   b. Ivan catching the Firebird
   c. Ivan seeing the thirteen beautiful maidens
   d. Ivan entering the castle
   e. The Firebird leading the frenzied dance of Kastchei and his slaves
   f. The dancers falling in exhaustion
   g. The destruction of the egg
   h. The joyous celebration that follows
5. Ask the children to listen carefully to the kind of music Stravinsky wrote to tell the story. Play the recording and show the filmstrip simultaneously.
6. Compare children's ideas with those of Stravinsky. (Play the recording and show the filmstrip again to clarify points in the discussion.)
7. Have the class plan a series of illustrations to depict the story. Divide the class into groups and assign each group a different illustration.
8. This experience can be enriched by these activities:
   a. Make an original filmstrip by using the illustrations that children create. (Illustrations must be the proper size for the projector.)
   b. Use illustrations as Cues to Music cards.
   c. Create a rhythmic dramatization that can be enacted for another class or an assembly program.

Level III

Exploring Expressive Concepts through an Experience with Mood or Picture Music
"Circus Music" from *The Red Pony* by Copland, RCA *Adventures in Music* grade 3, vol. 1, LES 1002

1. Appoint a small group to give a report on Aaron Copland, stressing that:

7. Story of "Firebird" adapted from the sound filmstrip series "Music Stories," a Jam Handy presentation for Prentice Hall Media, Inc., Tarrytown, N.Y. Used by permission.

a. He is an American composer, born in Brooklyn, New York.
b. His music often uses well known American folk tunes.

2. Discuss the various expressive devices available to a composer to create different moods and pictures in music.
   a. Dynamics
   b. Tempo
   c. Pitch
   d. Rhythm and meter
   e. Instrumentation
   f. Texture
   g. Tonality (tonal or atonal)
   h. Form
3. Tell the class to guess what the music is about, basing their decisions on listening for expressive devices.
4. Play the recording. Discuss its expressive devices.
5. Ask children if they can guess what the music depicts. Encourage them through asking questions similar to the following. Play the recording again, if necessary.
   a. Is it large or small?
   b. Is it fast or slow?
   c. Is it real or imaginary?
   d. What picture does it depict?
6. Children will probably discover that it is about something large, fast, both real and imaginary; there is dissonance, it is in ABA form, and it suggests a circus.
7. On another day children may enjoy dramatizing "Circus Music" or hearing the background for the music as described in the booklet accompanying the recording.

Level III

Focusing on Expressive Concepts by Relating Visual Arts Techniques to Abstract Music
Polka from *The Age of Gold* by Shostakovitch, and "Cries in the Street" by Mompou, RCA Victor *Basic Record Library for Elementary Grades* recordings WE 82

1. Collect pictures illustrating these contrasting moods.
   a. Mood 1   b. Mood 2
      (1) Quiet   (1) Bold
      (2) Peaceful   (2) Boisterous
      (3) Calm   (3) Active
      (4) Restful   (4) Discordant

Note: Pictures should be large. They can be obtained from the art consultant, brought to school by children, or collected from magazines. In addition, permission may be obtained from the Museum of Modern Art, 11 West 53rd St., New York, New York 10019, or the Metropolitan Museum of Art, New York, New York 10028 to enlarge small reproductions on the projector.

2. The following pictures are suggested:
   a. Mood 1
      (1) *Lady at the Piano,* Renoir
      (2) *The Music Lesson,* Metsu
      (3) *La Seine a Lavacourt,* Monet
      (4) *The Blue Window,* Matisse
   b. Mood 2
      (1) *Three Musicians,* Picasso
      (2) *Rhythm and Melody,* Cerney
      (3) *Agony,* Gorky
      (4) *Demon above the Ships,* Klee
      (5) *Listen to Living,* Matta
3. Distribute sheets upon which these words appear: bold, quiet, boisterous, cartoonlike, peaceful, dance-like, pretty, humorous, active, calm, sweet, lively, solemn, flippant, discordant, restful.
4. Ask children to look at the pictures to see how they differ in mood and to give you any adjectives that describe each. Write the adjectives on the board near each picture.
5. Discuss the ways the artists created the moods described by the chosen adjectives. For example, to create a mood of calmness, would an artist use bright colors or subdued colors? Soft lines or angular lines? Clearly defined figures or hazy figures?
6. Tell children that a composer can do the same thing through music. Ask the following questions:
   a. To create the mood of calmness, would a composer use a fast or slow tempo? Would the music be loud or soft? Generally, what instruments would give the calmest feeling?
   b. To create the mood of agitation, would a composer use even or uneven rhythm patterns? What kind of melody would he or she write, notes that move by step or skip? Would the music be loud or soft? Would many or few instruments play?
7. Tell the class you will play a piece that has a definite mood ("Cries in the Street"). Tell them to circle the words that best describe the mood. (Do not tell them the title.) Play the recording twice, if necessary.
8. Tell them you will play another piece ("Polka") with a different mood, and this time they are to check (X) the words that best describe "Polka." (Do not tell them the title.)
9. Collect the papers. Read the words from a few of the papers. Discuss the moods conveyed in each piece and compare with the moods of the pictures.
10. Children may enjoy enriching the experience by hearing the background information for each composition from the pamphlet that accompanies the record.
11. Other ways of using pictures to emphasize mood in music follow:

   a. Display one picture, play two contrasting selections, and let the class decide which composition best fits the picture and why.
   b. Display two pictures, play one composition, and let the class decide which picture best fits the composition.

Notational Concepts: Music Reading

Level III

Materials Needed
1. Copy of echo canon
2. Copy of theme from Little Fugue in G Minor by Bach
3. The following recordings and theme charts
   a. "Little Fugue in G Minor" by J. S. Bach, RCA *Adventures in Music* grade 6, vol. 1, LES 1009
   b. "Minuet" by Mozart, Bowmar *Orchestral Library* recording BOL 066 and accompanying theme chart
   c. "German Waltz—Paganini" *(Carnaval)* by Schumann and Glazounov, Bowmar *Orchestral Library* recording BOL 066 and accompanying theme chart
   d. "En Bateau" by Debussy, Bowmar *Orchestral Library* recording BOL 066 and accompanying theme chart
   e. "Gavotte" *(Mlle. Angot* Suite) by Lecocq, Bowmar *Orchestral Library* recording BOL 066 and accompanying theme chart
4. Rhythm instruments
5. Melody instrument
6. Music Cue charts

Listening Activity
An experience with abstract music; Little Fugue in G Minor by J. S. Bach

Related Musical Activities
1. Playing rhythm and melody instruments
2. Singing
3. Music reading
4. Rhythm (echo) canon

Conceptual Understandings
1. There is a rhythmic relationship between different durations of sounds that may be notated.

2. Chords played on the Autoharp (or other accompanying instruments) are often outlined in the notation of a melody.
3. The direction of a melody when heard (up, down, same, by step or skip) is related to the contour on the staff.
4. The rhythm of music is usually divided into measures, separated by bar lines.
5. Time signatures indicate the number of beats to a measure and the kind of note that gets one beat.
6. Key signatures are related to the scale in which the song is constructed.

Behavioral Objectives
1. To recognize and reproduce rhythmically the relationship between these durations

Durations

2. To recognize these from notation: chord outlines, melodic direction moving up and down by step and skip, the division of music into measures
3. To see the relationship between bar lines and meter
4. To see the relationship between the key signature and tonality

Related Arts
The teacher may wish to initiate an experience similar to that in chapter 4, "Rhythmic Concepts."

Procedure
1. Internalizing the relationship between durations of sound through an experience with echo canon
   a. Review the round by having class sing "Frere Jacques."
   b. Tell the class that another term for *round* is *canon*, and they will experience a rhythmic canon. Explain it will be a real challenge, for they must watch you, and when you nod your head, begin clapping what they just heard you clap. They will continue this throughout.
   c. Begin clapping the following and nod your head on the first beat of the second measure.

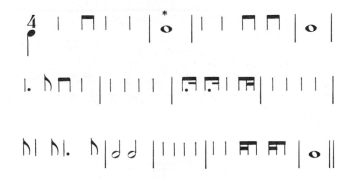

*Children begin first measure.

2. Focusing on rhythmic notation through an experience with rhythm instruments
   a. Put the following (rhythmic notation of Little Fugue in G Minor by Bach) on the board, omitting number and Kodaly counting.

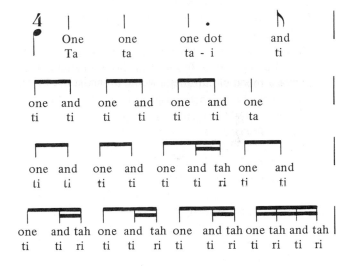

   b. Have the class clap and count notation using number or Kodaly counting. Repeat until they are thoroughly familiar with each measure.
   c. Ask the class if they have memorized the first measure. If they have, erase it, then have them clap the entire pattern, starting with the first measure. Tell them to look at the second measure, then erase it. Have them clap the entire pattern. Continue erasing the measures and having them clap the entire pattern.
   d. Ask who can write the notation on the board for the first measure. Select a volunteer to do so. Ask for volunteers to write the notation for measures two, three, and four, giving help when needed.
   e. Divide the class into four groups, one group to clap each duration.
      Group 1 quarter notes
      Group 2 dotted quarter
      Group 3 eighth notes
      Group 4 sixteenth notes

Theme
Little Fugue in G Minor

f. Explain that each group is to clap, in a steady rhythm, only the note assigned. Conduct one measure of 4/4 meter, signal the group clapping quarter notes to begin.

g. If children have difficulty, practice these parts at a slower tempo.

h. Ask children which rhythm instruments would fit each note value. Vote. One class selected these:
   Group 1 (quarter notes) hand drums
   Group 2 (eighth notes) maracas
   Group 3 (sixteenth notes) tone blocks
   Group 4 (dotted quarter note) triangle

i. Have the class perform rhythm pattern using instruments.

3. Focusing on notational concepts through an experience with abstract music (Little Fugue in G Minor by J. S. Bach)

   a. Select a gifted child to play the theme on a melody instrument.

   b. Tell children the following:
      (1) Fugue means flight.
      (2) This composition was given its title because the main idea (theme) flies from part to part, resulting in the simultaneous sounding of many melodies (also known as counterpoint).

   c. Ask children to examine the theme. Then ask:
      (1) On what note values does the theme begin?
      (2) What note value does it change to?
      (3) On what note value does it end?
      (4) What chord do the first three notes outline? (G minor)
      (5) What chord do the ninth, tenth, and eleventh notes outline? (D major)
      (6) Where do you see skips between notes?
      (7) Where do you see steps between notes?
      (8) How many beats are there in a measure?
      (9) What is the meter?
      (10) In this music, how many quarter notes comprise a measure? Eighth notes? Sixteenth notes?
      (11) What is the tonality?

d. Ask the class if they can lightly tap the rhythm of the theme as a child plays it on a melody instrument.

e. Ask a volunteer to clap the rhythm of the theme as you point to the notes in a slow tempo.

f. Ask the class to clap as you point to the notes.

g. Ask the class to sing the theme on a neutral vowel (loo) as you play it.

h. Tell the class to count the number of times they hear the entire theme. Play the recording.

i. Ask how many times they heard the theme. (nine times in full, once in fragment)

j. Ask the class to describe the theme. Write their descriptive adjectives on the board. (regal, stately, beautiful, and so on)

k. Write these on the board:
   Clarinet
   English horn
   Violas, bass clarinet, and bassoons
   Bass clarinet, bassoons, and other low strings
   Oboes, English horn, and trumpets
   French horns
   Bass clarinet, bassoons, and other low strings
   Violins, piccolos, flutes, and oboes
   Bass clarinet, bassoons, French horns, trombones, and others

l. Tell the class that the theme is played by the instruments in the order listed. Ask them to raise their hands as they hear each instrument entrance.

m. Play the recording. Identify the theme fragment so that children do not confuse it with a full theme.

n. This activity can be enriched by the following activities:
   (1) Create a dance. One class divided into nine groups—one group for each statement of the theme. Each group created a movement, which in their minds reflected the mood and rhythm of the theme, and began moving upon the entrance assigned to them. They

continued until all nine groups were moving simultaneously in the same rhythm but with different motions.

(2) Listen to other fugues such as Bach's Prelude and Fugue in C Minor, Columbia, *Switched-On Bach;* or McBride's "Pumpkin Eater's Little Fugue," RCA *Adventures in Music"* grade 2, LES 1011.

4. Evaluating children's ability to recognize a musical selection from its notational aspects

a. Display theme charts for the following selections, with titles printed above each selection.

(1) Theme 1, Minuet by Mozart

(2) "German Waltz—Paganini" *(Carnaval)* by Schumann and Glazounov

(3) Theme 1, "En Bateau" by Debussy

(4) "Gavotte" (*Mlle. Angot* Suite) by Lecocq

b. Discuss notational aspects of each theme, using these questions:

(1) On what note value does the theme begin? Who can clap the first measure?

(2) Does anyone see notes that move by step or skip, or the outline of a chord in the melody? (Have children point out examples of each.)

(3) What is the meter? What kind of note gets one beat? How many beats are there in one measure?

(4) How many measures are in the theme?

(5) Does the theme appear to have a tonality? Does anyone know what it is?

c. Distribute the Music Cue chart.

Music Cue Chart

1.	Minuet	Gavotte	En Bateau	German Waltz—Paganini
2.	Minuet	Gavotte	En Bateau	German Waltz—Paganini
3.	Minuet	Gavotte	En Bateau	German Waltz—Paganini
4.	Minuet	Gavotte	En Bateau	German Waltz—Paganini

d. Tell children you will play a recording of the theme from one of the compositions discussed. They are to decide from examining the notation which theme is being played, then circle the appropriate name. Play numbers 1–4 as children circle the titles. Repeat any piece that seems difficult for the children.

(1) Theme 1, Minuet by Mozart (Theme 1 is played twice.)

(2) "German Waltz—Paganini" *(Carnaval)* by Schumann and Glazounov (Play Theme 1; it is played twice.)

(3) Theme 1, "En Bateau," by Debussy (Play first theme only. Repeat, if necessary.)

(4) "Gavotte" (*Mlle. Angot* Suite) by Lecocq (A short introduction precedes theme, which is played twice.)

e. Discuss answers. Play any selection to clarify misunderstandings.

Listening Experiences That Focus on Notational Concepts

Level II or III

Focusing on Notational Concepts by Creating a Rhythmic Accompaniment to Abstract Music
Rondo from *Eine Kleine Nachtmusik* by Mozart

1. Place this theme on the board:

2. Play the theme on song bells, piano, or recording. Have the class sing, using syllables and hand signals.

3. Ask a child to point to the notes on the board as the theme is played again.

4. Play the recording, having children raise their hands when they hear the theme. (three times)

5. Have several children suggest and demonstrate rhythm patterns that they believe would best accompany the theme. (Play the theme for them as they demonstrate.)

6. Have the class vote for the rhythm pattern they like best and, if possible, notate it on the board, in blank notation. One of the following may be suggested.

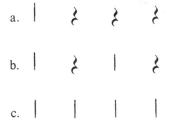

7. Have several children suggest and demonstrate rhythm instruments to accompany the theme, using the rhythm pattern decided upon.

8. Select a child to accompany on rhythm instrument, using the pattern chosen. Remind her to play only when the theme is heard.

9. Play the recording.

10. Distribute instruments to other children and let them accompany.

11. Repeat until all children have had the opportunity to participate.

12. If desired, children may create rhythmic accompaniments for the other themes of the composition.

Focusing on Notational Concepts through an Experience with Picture Music

Carnival of the Animals by Saint-Saëns, Bowmar *Orchestral Library* recording BOL 064

1. Display the theme cards (which accompany the recording) for the following sections: "Royal March of the Lion," "Hens and Cocks," "Elephant," and "Aquarium."

2. Compare the notation of the various themes, guiding the exploration through questions such as these:
   a. Which theme is in the lowest register? ("Elephant")
   b. How many beats would the eighth note get in "Elephant"? (One beat for each eighth note. It is in 3/8 meter.)
   c. Which theme has sixteenth notes? ("Elephant")
   d. Which theme starts in the highest register? ("Aquarium")
   e. Who can play the first measure of "Royal March of the Lion"? "Hens and Cocks"? "Elephant"? "Aquarium"?
   f. Who can sing the first two measures of "Royal March of the Lion"? "Aquarium"?

3. When children have explored notation for these themes, tell them that you will play a composition and when someone recognizes the theme, to raise her hand. Play "Royal March of the Lion." Since there is an introduction and children may have difficulty hearing the entrance of the theme, indicate when the theme begins.

4. Continue in a similar way for "Hens and Cocks," "Elephant," and "Aquarium," encouraging children to associate the proper theme card with the music.

Level III

Focusing on Notational Concepts through an Experience with Picture Music

"The Moldau," *(My Fatherland)* by Smetana, Bowmar *Orchestral Library* recording BOL 073, or Holt, Rinehart and Winston *Exploring Music* recording 611

1. Prepare Cues to Music cards 1–11.
2. Let children learn to play the themes on a melody instrument.
3. Ask the following questions:
   a. What rhythm would best describe a peacefully flowing river? (legato, smooth, flowing)
   b. What rhythm would best describe a river going over rapids? (rough, uneven, detached)
   c. What things or activities might a river pass?
   d. What type melody and rhythm, tempo and dynamics would describe each of these things or activities?

4. Let children find the Moldau River on the map. (It is called the Vltava River on most maps.)

5. Explain to children that you would like to tell them, with the help of the Cues to Music cards, what they will hear in the music. Tell the story of the Moldau as it is told on the cards. Play or let a child play the themes on a melody instrument.
   a. Card 1: As the music begins, the flute tells us that a warm, rippling stream is flowing along and is soon joined by a cool, peaceful stream, played by the clarinet.
   b. Card 2: These two streams unite and become the mighty Moldau (or Vltava) River. The Moldau theme is played by full orchestra.
   c. Card 3: As the Moldau passes through the forest, we hear the hunter's horns.
   d. Card 4: Now we hear a gay dance tune played by the full orchestra, which tells us the Moldau is passing a wedding festival.
   e. Card 5: It is night, and the violins, flutes, and harp tell us that the nymphs are dancing on the moonlit water.
   f. Card 6: In barely audible voices, the woodwinds tell us that the river is flowing toward the rapids.
   g. Card 7: As the river approaches the rapids, we again hear the Moldau theme.
   h. Card 8: When the river reaches the rapids, the full orchestra, playing loudly, indicates the violently churning river.
   i. Card 9: After passing the rapids, the river flows majestically. We hear the Moldau theme in the major mode.
   j. Card 10: A triumphant theme tells us the river is flowing past the ancient fortress of Vysehrad.
   k. Card 11: As the music ends, soft strings indicate that this great river flows toward the city of Prague.

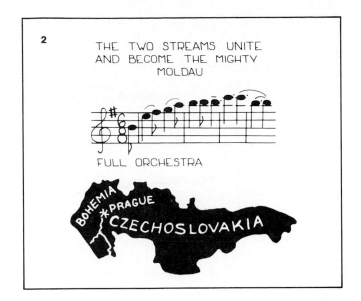

2 THE TWO STREAMS UNITE AND BECOME THE MIGHTY MOLDAU

FULL ORCHESTRA

3 HUNTERS' HORNS ARE HEARD IN THE FOREST

4 THE RIVER COMES UPON WEDDING FESTIVITIES WHERE THERE IS DANCING

FULL ORCHESTRA (STRINGS)

5 NIGHT... NYMPHS DANCE ON THE SHINING WATER

VIOLINS, FLUTES, HARP

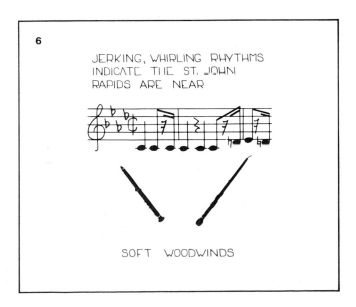

6 JERKING, WHIRLING RHYTHMS INDICATE THE ST. JOHN RAPIDS ARE NEAR

SOFT WOODWINDS

7 RUSHING ON TOWARD THE RAPIDS, THE MOLDAU THEME IS HEARD AGAIN

FULL ORCHESTRA

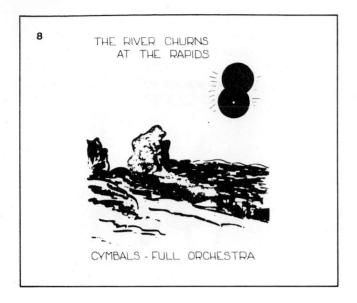

8 THE RIVER CHURNS AT THE RAPIDS

CYMBALS - FULL ORCHESTRA

9 AFTER PASSING THE RAPIDS, THE RIVER FLOWS MAJESTI-CALLY ON

MOLDAU THEME, MAJOR MODE - FULL ORCHESTRA

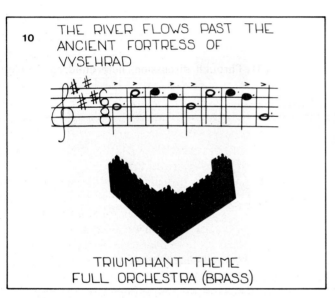

10 THE RIVER FLOWS PAST THE ANCIENT FORTRESS OF VYSEHRAD

TRIUMPHANT THEME FULL ORCHESTRA (BRASS)

11 THE MOLDAU FLOWS ON TOWARD PRAGUE

SOFT STRINGS

6. Tell children as each cue appears in the music, you will raise the appropriate card. Play the recording, holding up cards at proper times.
7. Ask the class these questions:
    a. How could you tell that the two streams united?
    b. Do you remember which instruments played to depict the moonlight shining on the river?
    c. Which part did you like best? Why?
8. Discuss the themes:
    a. Which has the widest range?
    b. Which is in the highest part of the range? Lowest?
    c. Which has the most steps? Skips? Repeated notes? Eighth notes? Sixteenth notes? Half notes?
    d. How many are in 6/8 meter? 2/4? 4/4?
9. Continue experience in a way similar to that described earlier in the chapter for "Danse Macabre"

and "Till Eulenspiegel's Merry Pranks." Enrich the experience as follows:
    a. Make drawings for a filmstrip.
    b. Make a set of original Cues to Music cards.
    c. Read the story of "Vltava" from *A Listener's Anthology of Music,* vol. 2 by Lillian Baldwin, Silver Burdett Company.
    d. Prepare substitute cards for 7 and 9. Have children hold up all other cards (omitting 7 and 9). When these two cards occur in the music, have the children raise the new cards for those numbers.
       (1) Card 7: Omit musical notation of the theme. Replace the words *The Moldau Theme is Again Heard* with *What Theme?*
       (2) Card 9: Omit the musical notation of the theme. Replace the words *Moldau Theme— Major Mode* with *What Theme?*

Listening Experiences with Opera and Operetta

Level II or III

Materials Needed
1. Elementary songbooks available
2. Rhythm instruments
3. Separate cards imprinted with these words: overture, aria, chorus, orchestra, recitative, ballet, act, scene, costumes, scenery, conductor, duet, trio, quartet.

Listening Activity
Listening activities involved in creating an opera, using familiar songs

Related Musical Activities
1. Singing
2. Playing rhythm instruments
3. Bodily movement

Conceptual Understandings
1. An opera is a drama set to music.
2. An opera contains many small musical forms: overture, recitative, aria, chorus, duets, trios, quartets, and ballets.

Behavioral Objectives
1. To become acquainted with opera as a musical form
2. To participate in some of the forms used in opera

Procedure
1. Exploring opera through discussion of the musical forms and other elements (costume, scenery, orchestra, and so on) that create the opera
   a. Tack cards on the bulletin board.
   b. Discuss the words on the cards as they relate to opera.
      (1) *Overture:* a musical composition played by the orchestra to convey the mood of the act that follows it.
      (2) *Recitative:* a song-speech (half sung, half spoken) sung by one person. It quickly conveys ideas important to the action of the story.
      (3) *Aria:* a solo sung by one person conveying feeling rather than fact.
      (4) *Chorus:* a song sung in parts, by a group, reflecting a feeling or attitude.
      (5) *Duet:* two people singing different parts together.
      (6) *Trio:* three people singing different parts together.
      (7) *Quartet:* four people singing different parts together.
      (8) *Ballet:* a dance.
      (9) *Act:* one of the main divisions of an opera.
      (10) *Scene:* a part of an act.
      (11) *Costumes* and *Scenery:* help establish the time, place, and mood, and add color and interest to the story.
      (12) *Orchestra:* plays the overture and accompanies the opera.
      (13) *Conductor:* keeps the music of the orchestra and the singers together.
2. Exploring opera by creating an opera based on familiar songs
   a. Ask children to select five or six familiar songs, making sure that songs suggest a theme or plot for the opera.
   b. Help children create a plot as follows:
      (1) List the songs selected on board.
      (2) Ask them to think of a story suggested by these songs. (This should be a simple plot. The important aspect of creating a plot is not plot construction, but giving children some familiarity with operatic construction.
      (3) Through discussion, help children develop details of the story.
      (4) Have children decide where each song will be sung and in what form (aria, chorus).
      (5) If children think of other songs, let them substitute or add if they are more suitable or would enhance the plot.
      (6) Add dialogue needed to develop the plot. This can be done as follows:
         (a) Examine the first idea in the plot.
         (b) Ask children what needs to be said and by what character to convey this idea.
         (c) Select children for parts in this section of the opera and let them practice.
         (d) Continue until dialogue has been created.
         (e) Encourage children to sing the dialogue in a recitative style (half sung, half spoken). Remember that it need not sound polished or professional.
   c. Review songs that have been chosen for the opera. (Words can be changed or new verses written to make the song more adaptable.)
   d. Have children create an overture by adding a rhythmic accompaniment to several of the songs. These can be played on the piano as a medley.
   e. Have children choose the song most suitable for a simple ballet. Select dancers and let them practice.
   f. Select children for these parts.
      (1) Singers for the chorus
      (2) Musicians for the orchestra (overture)
      (3) Conductor for the orchestra and chorus
      (4) Announcer for each act

g. Have them make these decisions:
   (1) Location of the stage
   (2) Location of the orchestra
   (3) Location of the chorus
   (4) Selection of props or other physical details important to the plot
h. Let them enact the opera.
i. Discuss sections that need improvement.
j. Children might like to polish their opera (adding scenery and costumes) and give it for another class or an assembly program.

An Opera Created by a Fifth-Grade Class

1. Songs used as a basis for the plot
   a. "Mama Don't 'Low," from Silver Burdett Book 5, *Music,* p. 4
   b. "I'm Gonna Walk," from Silver Burdett Book 5, *Music,* p. 6
   c. "Rain," from Macmillan Book 5, *The Spectrum of Music,* p. 91
   d. "Nobody Knows the Trouble I've Seen," Macmillan Book 5, *The Spectrum of Music,* p. 85
   e. "This Land is Your Land," from Silver Burdett Book 5, *Music,* p. 225
2. Characters

Bob	Joan	Jean
Mother	John	Ballet dancers
Kim	Elaine	Chorus

3. Acts
   Act 1: Bob's home, in the living room
   Act 2: A city street
   Act 3: A cave in the woods
4. Ballet
   Performed by ballet dancers (city street people) at the end of Act 2, to the music "I'm Gonna Walk."
5. Plot

   Bob is in his living room, playing his guitar. His mother enters and scolds him for not doing his homework. They argue. A chorus of girls and boys sings "Mama Don't 'Low." Act 1 ends with Bob walking off angrily.

   Act 2 begins with Bob walking down a street singing "I'm Gonna Walk." At the end of the song, he meets his friend Kim. Bob invites him along, and they leave. Almost immediately they meet John, who also joins them, and soon after, Joan, Elaine, and Jean join the boys. As the entire group, joined by the chorus, sings "I'm Gonna Walk," the ballet dancers do a lively dance.

   Act 3 finds the girls and boys in a cave. It is raining. Elaine stands at the entrance singing "Rain." The other girls join her and all sing "Rain." The girls

tell how unhappy, cold, and wet they are, and when Bob comes to the entrance, they tell him they want to go home. He replies that he's too unhappy at home and sings "Nobody Knows the Trouble I've Seen" as all join in. The other girls and boys convince Bob to give his mother another chance, to do his homework so he can play the guitar, and to go home to see if it will work. They start to leave the cave, singing "This Land is Your Land."

6. The opera (in detail)

Overture to act 1: *"This Land is Your Land," is played on the piano and orchestrated with percussion instruments, guitars, and Autoharp.*

Act 1 Bob's home, in the living room
Bob is playing his guitar. Mother enters.

Mother *(recitative):* Robert, you should be studying.
Bob *(recitative);* I'm practicing. Leave me alone.
Mother *(recitative):* You have homework to finish.
Bob *(recitative):* I'll do it later. Leave me alone.
Mother *(recitative):* You didn't do it last night. You'll fail!
Bob *(recitative):* Leave me alone!
Mother *(recitative):* Robert! Do your homework!

[Chorus *(girls singing Mother's part, boys singing Bob's part) sings "Mama Don't 'Low" as Mother pantomimes scolding Bob, he indicating he doesn't care.]*
(Act 1 ends as Bob angrily leaves.)

Act 2 A city street
Bob is walking down the street singing an Aria— "I'm Gonna Walk." Kim enters from opposite direction as Bob finishes song.

Bob *(recitative):* Hi, Kim.
Kim *(recitative):* What 'ya know?
Bob *(recitative):* I'm on the run. Wanna come?
Kim *(recitative):* Sounds like fun!

(Both sing "I'm Gonna Walk" and walk across stage, but are stopped by John, entering from opposite side.)

John *(recitative):* Hi guys. What 'ya know?
Bob and Kim *(recitative):* We're on the run. Wanna come?
John *(recitative):* Sounds like fun!

(All sing "I'm Gonna Walk" and walk across stage, but are stopped by Joan, Elaine, and Jean.)

Joan, Elaine, and Jean *(recitative):* Hi guys. What 'ya know?

Bob, Kim, and John *(recitative):* We're on the run. Wanna come?

Joan, Elaine, and Jean *(recitative):* Sounds like fun!

(All sing "I'm Gonna Walk" and walk across and around stage as dancers perform a lively dance. Act 2 ends with cast and chorus singing "I'm Gonna Walk," with ballet.)

Act 3 A cave in the woods
Elaine is standing at the entrance to a cave. As she sings "Rain," the other girls come to the entrance of the cave. Elaine, Joan, and Jean sing trio of "Rain." As the girls begin to sing the recitatives, the boys come, one by one, to the entrance of the cave.

Joan *(recitative):* I'm scared. I want to go home.

Elaine *(recitative):* It's cold.

Jean *(recitative):* And wet.

Joan *(recitative):* I'm scared. I want to go home.

Elaine and Jean *(recitative):* Me too. Let's go.

Bob *(recitative):* But I hate to go home. I never get to play my guitar.
My mother's always crabbing. I'm unhappy at home.

(Bob sings aria, "Nobody Knows the Trouble I've Seen." One by one, the others join until all are singing.)

Elaine *(recitative):* If you'd do your homework, she wouldn't crab.

Joan *(recitative):* She's not that bad!

Kim *(recitative):* We'll all talk to her!

John *(recitative):* Maybe we can convince her!

Elaine *(recitative):* Please Bob.

Joan *(recitative):* I'm cold.

Jean *(recitative):* I'm wet.

Girls *(together):* Please Bob, let's go home.

Bob *(recitative):* OK, but I'd better be able to play my guitar!

John *(recitative):* We'll talk to her.

Kim *(recitative):* She'll let you—if you just study.

Joan *(recitative):* After all, it's a free country.

Jean *(recitative):* It's your home too!

Elaine *(recitative):* She'll let you—if you just do your homework.

Bob *(recitative):* OK, we'll go talk to her. You're right. It is a free country.

(One by one they come out of the cave. Bob begins singing, joined gradually by the others, the chorus, and the percussive group in "This Land is Your Land.")

Additional Experiences with Opera and Operetta

Level III

A General Survey of Opera
Selections from *Amahl and the Night Visitors* by Menotti, *Carmen* by Bizet, and the *William Tell* Overture by Rossini

1. In addition to the recordings, collect pictures relating to opera (singers, stage manager, costume mistress, ballet dancers, electricians, and so on).
2. Display pictures showing opera scenes. Ask children to examine the pictures. Discuss each picture as it relates to opera.
3. Write the word *opera* on the board and ask children to define it. (It is a play that is sung.)
4. Ask children why people began setting plays to music. Why not speak instead of sing?
5. Explain the sequence of writing and producing an opera.
   a. The words sung by each character are written and arranged into acts and scenes, called a *libretto*. (Show the class a libretto, passing it around so all can see it.)
   b. The music is written for the libretto including music for singing, dancing, and the orchestra. Each character's part is written, in addition to the parts for the instruments of the orchestra. This is called the *score*.
   c. Scenery, lighting, and costumes are created or developed, the singers selected, and the opera rehearsed so that all involved know what to do.
   d. Performance night arrives. The audience are in their seats, the house lights dim, the conductor steps to the podium, and what do we hear?
6. Explain the following:
   a. Write *overture* on the board and define it. (An overture is meant to set the mood for the opera. Many of the opera's melodies are included in the overture. Thus, when the curtain goes up, the audience is prepared for the opening scene.)
   b. Tell children you will play the overture to the opera, *William Tell* by Rossini. Ask them to imagine what the story of this opera might be.[8]
   c. Play recording, then ask for children's ideas about the opera.
   d. Write *recitative* on the board and explain its meaning. (A recitative is a song-speech, part

8. Time permitting, tell or have a child tell the story of William Tell. Lillian Baldwin, *Music for Young Listeners: The Blue Book* (Morristown, New Jersey: Silver Burdett Co.) If the story is told before the recording is played, discussion after the recording can focus on what the class thinks was described in the overture.

sung, part spoken; it is often used to convey ideas or facts important to the action of the story.) If time permits, let children create recitatives using ordinary classroom conversation.

e. Tell children you will play a short section from *Amahl and the Night Visitors.* Explain they will hear Amahl's mother scolding him for annoying the kings. Play the first part of side 2 (through Amahl singing "Yes, Mother").

f. Write *aria* on the board. Ask children to pronounce it, and define it for the class. (It is an elaborate song. It is used to express strong feelings such as love, anger, and sadness.)

g. Write *chorus* on the board and explain its use in opera. (The chorus reflects attitudes and feelings toward the events taking place.)

h. Tell children you will play an aria and chorus from *Carmen.* This aria is called the "Toreador Song." Escamillo, a bullfighter who is in love with Carmen, sings it. In it he tells the thrills and dangers of being a bullfighter, including the overthrow of the picador, the man on horseback who throws darts into the bull to make him angry. He tells of the spectators' fright and the roar of the angry bull. Ask children to listen for the chorus singing after each verse, as though to clarify what Escamillo has just sung. Play the recording of the "Toreador Song."

Level III

Exploring the Opera Carmen, *by Bizet*

1. The following selections from *Carmen* will be needed for this experience.

Overture to act 1	"Toreador Song"
"Street Boys' Parade"	Overture to act 4
"Habanera"	

2. Prepare two large cardboards with the following:

Main Characters in Carmen	*Music from Carmen*
Carmen: a gypsy girl	Overture to act 1
Don Jose: a young soldier	"Street Boys' Parade"
	"Habanera"
Micaele: a girl from Don Jose's home town	"Toreador Song"
	Overture to act 4
Escamillo: a toreador	

3. If possible, have illustrations of the main characters from *Carmen.*

4. Select three or four children to read the story of *Carmen* and one child to play the recording. Have them practice so that they know their cues.

5. Review the words *opera, aria, chorus, overture,* and *ballet.*

6. Display illustrations of main characters and lists of characters and music.

7. Introduce opera by telling children they will hear the story of a famous opera, *Carmen,* which takes place in Spain near Seville. Call attention to the main characters and the music listed on cardboards. Remind them that the first music they hear will be the Overture to act 1. Play the Overture.

8. Have several children read the story, interspersing music as indicated.

Bong! Bong! Bong! The bell strikes noon across the sunny square in Seville, Spain. Children stop in their play to count the strokes of the factory bell. The soldiers count the strokes too, for it signals the changing of the guard. The orchestra plays a military march as the soldiers change, and the children march down the street after them. (Play recording of "Street Boys' Parade.")

Across the square we see the cigarette factory door open. Out stream the factory girls. Among them is Carmen, a beautiful gypsy girl with dark hair. Look! She has a red rose in her hair. The soldiers all admire her and try to attract her attention. Carmen loves to tease the soldiers, and she sings for them, telling them that her love is like a wild bird that cannot be tamed. (Play "Habanera.")

Only Don Jose ignores Carmen, and this makes her angry, since she is not used to being ignored. Just before returning to the factory, she tosses him the red rose from her hair.

As Don Jose holds the rose and thinks about this beautiful gypsy girl, Micaele (Mik-ah-ay-lah), a girl from his home town, enters with a message from his mother.

Suddenly noise comes from the factory. The door is thrown open and out come the girls, shouting and screaming, "It was Carmen, she's the one, she began the quarrel." Carmen's temper has gotten the best of her and now she is in trouble. She slapped another girl. Don Jose is ordered to take the wild Carmen off to prison. But Carmen is not an easy prisoner. Left alone with Don Jose, she teases him and coaxes him to let her go. She promises to meet him at a nearby inn for dancing and singing if he will release her. Finally, Don Jose unties her wrists. Off she runs. Don Jose is arrested for letting Carmen escape.

Act 2 takes place at the inn. Carmen and her gypsy friends are dancing and singing. Escamillo enters. He is a popular bullfighter. He sings the famous Aria, "Toreador Song." (Play "Toreador Song.") Escamillo and the gypsies leave the inn. Carmen stays behind waiting for Don Jose. She wants him to join the band of smugglers. Soon, he arrives. He has just been released from prison and is anxious to see Carmen. As Carmen coaxes him to join the smugglers, a bugle is heard, calling him back to the army. Don Jose starts to leave. Carmen is furious with him and tries to persuade him to stay. At that moment, one of his captains enters. He, too, likes Carmen and orders Don Jose back to the barracks. This makes Don Jose jealous and he starts a fight with the captain. A gypsy friend of Carmen's stops the fight, but it is too late. Don Jose cannot go back to the army for he is now guilty of insubordination; so he does the only thing he can do, he stays with Carmen and the band of smugglers.

Act 3 takes place in a wild mountain pass. Don Jose is with the smugglers. He is left to guard the pass as the smugglers go to the border. Don Jose sees someone climbing the mountain and fires a shot to scare the intruder. Although he is not aware of it, there are two climbers, Micaele and Escamillo. Micaele is frightened by the shot and hides. Escamillo, who is looking for Carmen, finally reaches the pass and immediately engages Don Jose in a bitter fight. Luckily, Carmen arrives in time to stop the fight. Escamillo starts down the mountain, reminding his friends to attend his next bullfight. As he leaves, Micaele is discovered. She tells Don Jose his mother is dying and wants to see him. Carmen sarcastically tells Don Jose to go to his mother. Although Don Jose hates to leave Carmen, he decides he must go. Don Jose leaves. In the distance, as he descends the mountain, we can hear Escamillo singing the "Toreador Song." (Softly play a portion of the "Toreador Song.")

Act 4 takes place outside the arena in Seville. (Play the Overture to act 4.) It is a beautiful day for a bullfight and it seems that the entire city has come to see Escamillo fight. The streets are filled with people dressed in their finest clothing, men selling candy and flowers, and street bands playing martial music. The officials, picadors, Escamillo, and Carmen arrive. Carmen is dressed in her most beautiful clothing. Escamillo tells Carmen that she will be proud of him today, and she assures him of her love.

Carmen leaves the arena and goes to the square. She has heard that Don Jose is nearby and wants to talk with her. She has no use for him but she wants to settle the quarrel with him. Don Jose comes up to Carmen. He is a changed man. No longer a soldier, he is dirty, bedraggled, and sad. He begs Carmen to return to him. He has sacrificed everything for her. He begs in vain, for Carmen is now only interested in Escamillo. "All is over," she cries.

Carmen hears the excited crowd crying "Ole" in the arena and wants to return and watch Escamillo. Don Jose becomes furious and draws a knife and strikes Carmen. She falls and dies. Don Jose kneels beside Carmen, heartbroken at what he has done and cries, "I have killed her, you may arrest me!" The curtain closes.[9] (Play a short section of the Overture to act 4, slowly bringing the volume down until it becomes inaudible.)

9. May Andrus, "Story of Bizet's *Carmen*," *Keyboard Jr.: Music Magazine for Children* Oct., Nov., Dec., 1957; Jan., 1958. Adapted. Used by permission.

Level III

Using a Libretto to Follow the Story of an Opera
Amahl and the Night Visitors by Menotti

In addition to the recording of the opera, a libretto for each child will be needed; published by G. Schirmer, Inc., New York City.
1. Distribute librettos.
2. Select individuals to read parts. The rest of the class may read in unison the parts of the shepherds and villagers.
   a. Amahl
   b. Amahl's mother
   c. Kaspar, a king
   d. Melchior, a king
   e. Balthazar, a king
   f. The Page
3. Using librettos, have children read the opera as a play.
4. Discuss the music.
   a. How might the music sound when Amahl's mother tells him it is time to go to bed?
      (1) Would the melody be high or low?
      (2) Would the mother's singing be fast or slow?
      (3) Would many instruments be used?
      (4) Would the music be loud or soft?
      (5) What would the general mood of the music be?
   b. As he describes the sky would Amahl's singing be quiet or excited? Fast or slow?
   c. When his mother becomes irritated with Amahl, would the orchestral music be loud or soft? Fast or slow?
   d. How might the music sound as the kings are heard in the distance and as they progress to the hut?
      (1) Would the music be sad, happy, or mysterious?
      (2) Would the music be fast or slow?
      (3) What scale might be used to depict the mood?
      (4) As the kings advance toward the hut, would the music get louder or softer?
      (5) Would the rhythm of the kings' march be even or uneven?
      (6) Might any special percussive effects be used to depict the kings' procession to the hut?
   e. During the shepherds' arrival song, they bring food and gifts to the kings. What kind of music would best depict the shepherds? (folklike music)
   f. When Amahl takes his first steps, would the music be fast or slow? Would the rhythm be even or uneven?
5. Play the recording as children follow the libretto.

Enriching Listening Experiences

The most successful enrichment experiences will flow so naturally from the listening experience that neither teacher nor child will be aware of the separation. As children respond to the music, they will be enriching the experience.

The teacher who encourages and acts upon children's suggestions will find the students eager and able to experience music in many different ways. The teacher will be more able to use suggestions and plan listening experiences, when he is aware of the possibilities for enrichment.

Though the suggestions following are divided according to the type of music (story, mood or picture, abstract, operas and operettas), they can also be used to enrich different categories. There are many ways to enjoy music, and the teacher who finds that a child is making a story from an abstract listening experience, for example, should not be concerned. Each child grows at her own speed, and there is no reason to be stringent about when and how each child should enjoy music of any type.

Story Music

1. Pantomiming or shadow pantomiming the story as the music plays: This is a fruitful experience when the story is clearly delineated, the selection is not too long or complicated, and there is an obvious way of pantomiming the action. Pantomiming several musical stories, with narration added to unify the whole, can make an effective assembly program.
2. Creating a rhythmic dramatization: This means enacting the story in the rhythm of the music. By adding costumes and simple scenery to several musical stories, along with a narration to unify them, an assembly program is created.
3. Illustrating the story: The children can draw or paint illustrations of various scenes from the story. If desired, the illustrations can depict the entire story and be made to fit an overhead projector, then shown in sequence as the story unfolds. Illustrations can also be made as Cues to Music cards by adding the theme, pictures of instruments that play the theme, and a word description of the actions suggested by the theme.

Mood and Picture Music

1. Drawing or painting illustrations of the music. This can take several forms.
   a. Abstract designs portraying the mood
   b. Realistic pictures suggested by the music
   c. Cues to Music cards
   d. Abstract or realistic drawings based on the blank notation of the themes
2. Creating a rhythmic dramatization: Rhythmic dramatizations should respond to definite musical ideas, that is, changes in rhythm, tempo, melody, mood, or instrumentation. When done in this way, both learning and enjoyment are greatly enhanced.
3. Creating a rhythmic accompaniment: When the musical selection is not too long, and different sections are clearly defined, children enjoy and gain much from creating rhythmic accompaniments to music.
4. Creating dances: This differs from rhythmic dramatization in that no story is involved. Children decide what dance steps or rhythmic movement fit each section of the music. This type of experience is more apt to succeed when the selection is not too long and each section is clearly defined melodically and rhythmically.
5. Writing stories: It is but one step from seeing a picture in music to thinking of a story. Children in the lower grades enjoy telling stories they think of, while children in the intermediate and upper grades can write them. Children like hearing themselves on tape, telling their story as the music plays.

Abstract Music

1. Drawing abstract designs to illustrate themes or form: When more than one theme has been stressed (as in all ABA experiences) children enjoy creating contrasting abstract designs to portray each theme. Some classes make a large drawing upon which all three sections of an ABA form are represented.
2. Rhythmic interpretation of different themes or sections: This is rewarding when the themes of a composition can be clearly defined rhythmically and when they are not too long for children to grasp. Working on one section at a time brings an easier and more profitable experience.
3. Creating a rhythmic accompaniment: This is especially beneficial and enjoyable when the composition has clearly defined sections that children can easily hear. When children are allowed to select the instrument and the rhythmic pattern, they are apt to become more involved with the music.
4. Creating Cues to Music cards: The benefit and procedure for doing this is explained earlier in this chapter.

Operas and Operettas

1. Let children draw a stage setting or create dioramas.
2. Take children to see an opera or operetta after they have studied it in class.
3. Let children tell the story of an opera, do one of the dances, and sing one or two songs. Add recordings and illustrations of characters and give as an assembly program.

Other Activities That Enrich Listening Experiences

1. Have children, individually or in small groups, prepare reports on the life and music of a composer and play recordings of his or her music.
2. Let children learn to play on melody instruments themes of compositions heard in class.
3. Have children report on recent musical programs heard on television or at concerts.
4. Have children find pictures that depict the mood of compositions heard in class.
5. Plan with children a concert in which musically gifted children and other members of the community perform for the class.
6. Have a favorite record day. Let children bring in their favorite records, tell why they like their records, and play them for the class.
7. Plan a classroom concert of favorite records and invite other classes or parents to attend.
8. Let children compile a class musical scrapbook that includes all their musical activities. This might also be an individualized or small group activity.
9. Let children plan and execute a mural based on a musical story, opera, or favorite composition.
10. Let children plan and prepare a bulletin board based on favorite listening experiences, using illustrations and reports.

Individualizing Listening Experiences

Listed below are activities that will help individual children reinforce concepts already experienced in a large group. In addition, the teacher may wish to use outstanding television programs as a resource for individualized activities. Some teachers distribute weekly listings and require children to write short reports of programs heard.

Level I

Listening to a Recording
First Listening Experiences (for one child or a small group)

This recording is structured so that children can follow with little or no help from the teacher. It is available from Educational Record Sales, 157 Chambers Street, New York, New York 10007.

Level III

Listening for Musical Elements in an Operetta
Down in the Valley by Kurt Weill (for one child)

Reproduce the following. Have child listen to the record, then answer the questions on the sheet. Since a wide variety of answers may be correct, the teacher will have to check the child's answers.

Note: A similar individualized experience may be given using *Amahl and the Night Visitors* or *The Telephone*, both by Menotti.

Down in the Valley by Kurt Weill

1. What section of the music is most expressive of the dramatic situation taking place? _____

2. What musical elements are used to achieve the dramatic effectiveness of the story: tempo, dynamics, orchestration, rhythm, melody, or texture? _____

3. What forms from opera or operetta do you find in this composition: recitative, aria, chorus, overture, ballet, duets, trio, quartets, scenes, or acts? _____

Level III

Famous Composers: Scrambled Words Game
For one child

Reproduce the following. Put the Answer Sheet on large cardboard and laminate. Have children check their own work. (The list may be changed to include composers with which children are familiar.)

Famous Composers: Scrambled Words

Find the composer in each scrambled word and write the answer to the right of the word. Composers may include: Ravel, Tchaikovsky, Schubert, Mendelssohn, Schumann, Debussy, Chopin, Brahms, Saint-Saëns, Liszt, Wagner, Bach, Beethoven, Handel, and Ibert.

1. TEOENRVFH	6. LVARE	11. BESYSUD
2. TESBUCHR	7. RBETI	12. ZTLSI
3. HABC	8. DLAEHN	13. NHCSUANM
4. YTAHKSVICOK	9. OHNICP	14. AISTN SANSE
5. GAEWRN	10. SRBHMA	15. LOSHNDEMNSE

Answer Sheet

1. Beethoven	6. Ravel	11. Debussy
2. Schubert	7. Ibert	12. Liszt
3. Bach	8. Handel	13. Schumann
4. Tchaikovsky	9. Chopin	14. Saint Saëns
5. Wagner	10. Brahms	15. Mendelssohn

Level III

Music in Concert: Scrambled Words Game
For one child

Reproduce the following. Prepare the Answer Sheet on large cardboard and laminate. Have children check their own work.

Music in Concert: Scrambled Words

Find these words in the list below and write the appropriate word next to each scrambled word: audience, band, cantata, chorus, concerto, conductor, encore, opera, operetta, orchestra, overture, program, soloist, symphony, usher.

1. preoa	6. reenoc	11. magprro
2. reotapet	7. roetevru	12. shucro
3. hersu	8. loostis	13. asothrecr
4. actanta	9. netoorcc	14. nadb
5. psoyhnym	10. cedunaie	15. trococund

Answer Sheet

1. opera	6. encore	11. program
2. operetta	7. overture	12. chorus
3. usher	8. soloist	13. orchestra
4. cantata	9. concerto	14. band
5. symphony	10. audience	15. conductor

Discussions and Reports

1. Discuss the concept that music listening experiences in the elementary school should help children focus on the elements in music they can enjoy, and help them understand and participate through rhythm, melody, texture, expressive elements, and notation rather than be structured as music appreciation lessons.

2. Discuss and clarify the aims of listening experiences.

3. Write a report outlining the ways children can enjoy listening to music; explore nonmusical as well as musical activities, and the implications of these for the teacher planning listening activities.

4. Write a report discussing how listening relates to rhythmic, singing, instrumental, and music-reading experiences.

5. Through discussion, differentiate story, mood or picture, and abstract music.

6. Write a paper comparing the type of mood or picture music suitable for level I with that suitable for level III. Show how, with maturity, the child's responses to music change, the conceptual understandings and behavioral objectives develop, and the nature of participation changes.

7. Write a paper discussing the importance of the teacher's attitude in presenting abstract music to children. Assuming the class to be a fifth or sixth grade (level III) list possible ways of helping them be receptive to experiences with abstract music.

8. Write a paper describing your background in abstract listening experiences. Describe the positive as well as negative influences and explain how you, as a teacher, would avoid negative influences.

9. Assume you are planning to initiate an experience with a fifth-grade class, giving them a general background in opera. Write a paper describing how you would introduce the experience to obtain the most positive reaction from the class. Outline a procedure for making the experience a successful one.

10. Prepare a strategy for level I or II, focusing on either rhythmic or melodic concepts through a listening experience. Include related musical activities and a related arts experience. List specific conceptual understandings and behavioral objectives.

11. Discuss ways to make music listening more enjoyable and productive through use of rhythmic interpretations and dramatizations; rhythm instruments to create orchestrations; Cues to Music cards; related arts; illustrations; and story writing. List advantages and limitations of each.

12. Write a paper listing the concepts related to rhythm, melody, texture, form, expression, and music reading you think most suitable for focus in listening experiences. Give reasons.

13. Through discussion, define the following characteristics of contemporary music: polytonality, bitonality, atonality, shifting rhythms and meters, twelve-tone scale.

14. Discuss various ways of introducing electronic music in the elementary grades.

15. Write a paper discussing various ways of individualizing listening experiences. Evaluate the relative merits of each.

16. Observe a listening experience in an elementary classroom. Write a description of the approaches, materials, activities, and children's responses to each. Tell how you might improve and expand the experience.

17. Discuss the general suggestions throughout this chapter in relation to creativity versus rigidity, and explain how they may be used creatively in an actual teaching situation.

18. Utilizing the "Listening Activities Evaluation Chart" keep a log of all successful listening activities. This chart may be a basis for an expanding source of possible listening activities for the elementary school.

Activities to Develop Skills and Practice in Initiating Listening Experiences

1. Study the strategy for level I or II, "Rhythmic Concepts" in which "Bydlo" from *Pictures at an Exhibition* and Minuet in F are the focus. Make any changes you believe would improve the plan. Initiate and guide this experience with the class. Evaluate in terms of the response, the degree to which the conceptual understandings and behavioral objectives were achieved.

2. Select one of the experiences suggested in the section, "Listening Experiences That Focus on Rhythmic Concepts." Create a strategy with this as the basic listening experience. State specific conceptual understandings and behavioral objectives. Add other musical experiences (singing, rhythms, instrumental, or music reading) and an experience with related arts. Initiate and guide experience with the class. Evaluate results through discussion.

3. Study the strategy for level II or III, "Melodic Concepts," in which the "Gavotte" from the *Classical Symphony* is the focus. Make any changes you think would improve the plan. Initiate and guide the experience. Evaluate class response and achievement of conceptual understandings and behavioral objectives.

4. Select one of the experiences suggested in the section, "Listening Experiences That Focus on Melodic Concepts." Create a strategy with this as a focus, using related arts and experiences with other areas of music. State the conceptual understandings you will encourage.

5. Study the strategy for level II, "Textural Concepts" in which "Pacific 231" is the listening experience. Using the same format, devise your own strategy, with different music, appropriate conceptual understandings and behavioral objectives, related musical activities, and related arts. Present it to the class. Evaluate through discussion.

6. Study the experience using Cues to Music cards for "Till Eulenspiegel's Merry Pranks" ("Listening Experiences that Focus on Melodic Concepts"). Prepare a strategy for level II, using this as the focus, but including other musical activities and related arts. List specific conceptual understandings and behavioral objectives. Initiate and guide the experience.

7. Examine the Music Cue charts suggested for evaluating learning for each of the conceptual focuses (rhythm, melody, texture, form, expression, and music reading). Select the one you think most effective. Make any changes desired and present it to the class. Discuss ways of improving its effectiveness.

8. Select a recording for level III from the list of music for abstract listening. Decide on the concept focus, behavioral objectives, and procedure for presenting the music so that the class will enjoy participating. Develop a related arts activity that will enhance the experience. Present it to the class as a prelude to the listening experience. Evaluate both through discussion.

9. As a group activity, create a set of Cues to Music cards for any composition, similar to those for "The Moldau" or "Till Eulenspiegel." Follow the suggestions given in this chapter. Prepare a presentation plan, using the Cues to Music cards. Have a member of the group initiate and guide the experience. Through discussion, evaluate: Were the cues (themes) chosen important and appropriate? Were all important cues included? Was each step of the plan valid?

10. From the list of mood and picture music at the end of this chapter, select a recording. Prepare a strategy for presenting this experience to the class using an appropriate technique suggested in this chapter. State specific conceptual understandings and behavioral objectives, related musical activities, and related arts. Present it to the class. Evaluate through discussion.

11. Examine the experience with electronic music, which uses "Bowery Bum" ("Listening Experiences That Focus on Textural Concepts"). After studying the conceptual understandings related to expression listed in the "Growth and Sequence Chart" in chapter 1, prepare a strategy for teaching this composition, focusing on expressive concepts. Initiate and guide the experience. Evaluate results, focusing on the way a different conceptual focus can change the listening experience.

12. Examine the suggestions for individualizing listening activities. Select several that you believe would be effective. Try them on your classmates. Evaluate, through discussion, the effectiveness of each and make suggestions for improving.

13. Prepare an individualized listening experience for level III. Present it to fellow students. Evaluate results.

Listening Activities Evaluation Chart

Level	Recording	Type of Music				Conceptual Understandings	Behavioral Objectives	Related Musical Activities	Related Arts	Evaluation
		Story	Mood or Picture	Abstract	Opera or Operetta					

Recordings and Filmstrips for Listening Experiences

Teachers should be aware of suggestions for integrated listening that appear in many of the elementary song series, and adapt such suggestions to techniques found in this chapter.

Recordings and Filmstrips of Story Music

Title	Composer	Recording
"American in Paris"	Gershwin	
"Ballet Petit"	Donaldson	BOL 53/066
"Barcarolle" (Tales of Hoffman)	Offenbach	RCA LES–1002
"Berceuse" (Firebird Suite)	Stravinsky	RCA LES–1000
Billy the Kid	Copland	
"Can-Can" (The Fantastic Toyshop)	Rossini	RCA LES–1001
"Clowns" (Midsummer Night's Dream)	Mendelssohn	RCA WE 71
"Conversations of Beauty and the Beast" (Mother Goose Suite)	Ravel	RCA LES 1006
"Danse Macabre"	Saint-Saëns	BOL 59/072 and RCA LM 2056
"Departure" (Winter Holiday)	Prokofiev	RCA LES–1001
"Desert Water Hole" (Death Valley Suite)	Grofe	RCA LES–1004
Firebird Suite	Stravinsky	
"Flight of the Bumblebee"	Rimsky-Korsakov	BOL 52/065
Johnny Can Sing Too, vols. 1, 2, and 3	Raebeck	CM 1014, CM 1026 and CM 1052
Let's Sing and Act Together	Raebeck	CM 1057
"Little White Donkey" (Histoires, no. 2)	Ibert	RCA LES–1001
"March of the Dwarfs" (Lyric Suite)	Grieg	BOL 52/065 and RCA WE 79
"March of the Gnomes" (Christmas Tree Suite)	Rebikoff	RCA WE 79
"March of the Little Lead Soldiers"	Pierne	BOL 54/067 and RCA WE 77
"March—Trumpet and Drum"	Bizet	BOL 53/066 and RCA WE 77
"Night on Bald Mountain"	Moussorgsky	
Nutcracker Suite	Tchaikovsky	HRW 28 BOL 58/071

Note: Sources of recordings are given only when compositions have been recorded by companies whose materials are most commonly used in the elementary schools. Compositions of importance in teaching and easily available from commercial recording companies are listed without reference to company or record number because of the frequency with which these change.

"Of a Tailor and a Bear"	MacDowell	RCA WE 78
Once Upon a Time Suite	Donaldson	BOL 52/065
Peer Gynt Suite	Grieg	
"Petrouchka"	Stravinsky	
"Phaeton"	Saint-Saëns	BOL 59/072
"Pizzicato" *(The Fantastic Toyshop)*	Rossini and Respighi	BOL 53/066
Prelude (Act 3, *Lohengrin*)	Wagner	RCA LES–1009
"Ritual Fire Dance" *(El Amor Brujo)*	Falla	
"Rodeo"	Copland	
Scheherazade, op. 35	Rimsky-Korsakov	
"Season Fantasies"	Donaldson	BOL 52/065
Sorcerer's Apprentice	Dukas	BOL 59/072
"Street in a Frontier Town" *(Billy the Kid)*	Copland	RCA LES–1009
Swan Lake	Tchaikovsky	
"Three Bears, The"	Coates	BOL 67
"Till Eulenspiegel's Merry Pranks"	Strauss	BOL 81 HRW 513
"Waltz of the Doll" *(Coppelia)*	Delibes	

Filmstrip with Recording

Coppelia	Delibes	Jam Handy
Firebird Suite	Stravinsky	Jam Handy
Hansel and Gretel	Humperdinck	Jam Handy
Midsummer Night's Dream	Mendelssohn	Jam Handy
Nutcracker Suite	Tchaikovsky	Jam Handy
Peer Gynt Suite	Grieg	Jam Handy
Peter and the Wolf	Prokofiev	Jam Handy
Scheherazade	Rimsky-Korsakov	Jam Handy
Sleeping Beauty	Tchaikovsky	Jam Handy
Sorcerer's Apprentice	Dukas	Jam Handy
Swan Lake	Tchaikovsky	Jam Handy
William Tell	Rossini	Jam Handy

Recordings of Mood and Picture Music

"*Air Gai (Iphigenia in Aulis)*	Gluck	RCA LES–1000
"American Salute"	Gould	RCA LES–1006
"An Evening in the Village" *(Hungarian Sketches)*	Bartok	RCA LES–1007
"Argonaise" *(Le Cid)*	Massenet	HRW 610 and RCA LES–1000
"Ball, The" *(Children's Games)*	Bizet	RCA LES–1000
"Ballet of the Sylphs" *(Damnation of Faust)*	Berlioz	RCA LES–1000
"Ballet of the Unhatched Chicks" *(Pictures at an Exhibition)*	Moussorgsky	RCA LES–1000
"Barcarolle" *(Tales of Hoffman)*	Offenbach	RCA LES–1002
"Berceuse" *(Dolly, op. 56, no. 1)*	Faure	RCA LES–1001
"Berceuse" *(Firebird Suite)*	Stravinsky	RCA LES–1000
Billy the Kid	Copland	
"Butterfly Etude"	Chopin	RCA WE 81
"Bydlo" *(Pictures at an Exhibition)*	Moussorgsky	RCA LES–1001

"Can-Can" *(The Fantastic Toyshop)*	Rossini and Respighi	RCA LES–1001
Carnival of the Animals	Saint-Saëns	BOL 51/064 and HRW 28
"Caucasian Sketches"	Ippolitov-Ivanov	
Children's Corner Suite	Debussy	
"Children's Dance" *(Merry Mount* Suite)	Hanson	RCA LES–1002
Children's Games	Bizet	
Children's Symphony, Third Movement	McDonald	RCA LES–1001
"Chopin" *(Carnaval)*	Schumann and Glazounov	BOL 53/066
"Circus Music" *(The Red Pony)*	Copland	RCA LES–1002
"Circus Polka"	Stravinsky	BOL 51/064
"Clair de Lune"	Debussy	BOL 52/065 (Excerpt RCA WE 81)
"Clock, The"	Kullak	RCA WE 73
"Clown"	MacDowell	RCA WE 79
"Clowns"	Mendelssohn	RCA WE 71
"Cortege of the Sardar"	Ippolitov-Ivanov	BOL 54/067
"Cradle Song" *(Children's Games)*	Bizet	RCA LES–1000
"Cries in the Street"	Mompou	RCA WE 82
"Dagger Dance" *(Natoma)*	Herbert	RCA LES–1002
"Dance of the Chinese Dolls" *(Christmas Tree* Suite)	Rebikoff	RCA WE 80
"Dance of the Comedians" *(Bartered Bride)*	Smetana	BOL 56/069
"Dance of the Gnomes"	Liszt	RCA WE 82
"Dance of the Little Swans" *(Swan Lake)*	Tchaikovsky	RCA LES–1000
"Dance of the Mosquito"	Liadov	BOL 52/065
"Danza" *(Brazilian Impressions)*	Respighi	RCA LES–1007
Death Valley Suite	Grofe	
"Departure *(Winter Holiday)*	Prokofiev	RCA LES–1001
"Elfin Dance"	Grieg	RCA WE 78
"En Bateau"	Debussy	BOL 53/066 and HRW 110
"Espana" Rhapsody for Orchestra	Chabrier	RCA LES–1006
"Evening Bells"	Kullak	RCA WE 78
"Fairies and Giants" *(Wand of Youth)*	Elgar	RCA LES–1002
"Farandole" *(L'Arlesienne* Suite no. 2)	Bizet	RCA LES–1009 and HRW 68
"Father of Waters and Huckleberry Finn" *(Mississippi* Suite)	Grofe	HRW 511
Finale *(William Tell* Overture)	Rossini	HRW 68 and RCA LES–1002
First Listening Experiences	Schumann, Grieg, etc.	CM 1038
"Flight of the Bumblebee"	Rimsky-Korsakov	BOL 52/065
"Fountain Dance" *(Wand of Youth)*	Elgar	RCA LES–1001
"From Uncle Remus and of Br'er Rabbit" *(Woodland Sketches)*	MacDowell	

"Gavotte"	Handel	HRW 18
"Gnomes"	Reinhold	RCA WE 71
"Golliwog's Cakewalk"	Debussy	RCA WE 78
Grand Canyon Suite	Grofe	BOL 61/074
"Harbor Vignettes"	Donaldson	BOL 53/066
"Hoe-Down" *(Rodeo)*	Copland	BOL 55/068, HRW 512 and RCA LES–1007
"Hornpipe" *(Water Music)*	Handel	HRW 59, RCA LES–1001
"Hungarian Dance" no. 1	Brahms	RCA LES–1007
"Hungarian Dance" no. 5	Brahms	BOL 55/068 and RCA WE 82
"Hurdy-Gurdy" *(Adventures in a Perambulator)*	Carpenter	RCA LE/LES 1007
"Hurdy-Gurdy Man, The" *(Kaleidoscope)*	Goossens	RCA WE 78
"Jack-in-the-Box" *(Mikrokosmos* Suite no. 2)	Bartok	RCA LES–1001
"Laranjeiras" *(Saudades do Brazil)*	Milhaud	RCA LES–1001
"Leap Frog" *(Children's Games)*	Bizet	RCA LES–1000
Lieutenant Kije Suite	Prokofiev	
"Lincoln Portrait"	Copland	
"Little Hunters, The"	Kullak	RCA WE 78
"Little Train of Caipira" *(Bachianas Brasileras* no. 2)	Villa Lobos	RCA LES–1002
"Little White Donkey, The" *(Histoires* no. 2)	Ibert	RCA LES–1001
"Lullaby"	Brahms	RCA WE 77
March *(Soirees Musicales)*	Rossini	RCA LES–1000
March *(Summer Day* Suite)	Prokofiev	RCA LES–1005
March *(The Love for Three Oranges)*	Prokofiev	BOL 54/067 and RCA WE 76
"March and Comedians' Gallop" *(The Comedians)*	Kabalevsky	RCA LES–1002
"March Little Soldier" *(Memories of Childhood)*	Pinto	RCA WE 77
"March of the Dwarfs"	Grieg	BOL 52/065 and RCA WE 79
"March of the Tin Soldiers"	Tchaikovsky	RCA WE 73
"March of the Toys" *(Babes in Toyland)*	Herbert	RCA LES–1001
"March Past of the Kitchen Utensils" *(The Wasps)*	Williams	RCA LES–1002
"Military March"	Schubert	BOL 54/067
Mississippi Suite	Grofe	
Mother Goose Suite	Ravel	BOL 57/070
"Moldau, The" *(My Fatherland)*	Smetana	BOL 60/073 and HRW 611
"Music Box, The *(The Musical Snuff Box)*	Liadoff	RCA WE 81
Norwegian Dance, op. 35, no. 2	Grieg	RCA WE 75
Once Upon a Time Suite	Donaldson	BOL 52/065
"On Muleback" *(Impressions of Italy)*	Charpentier	RCA LES–1006
"On the Steppes of Central Asia"	Borodin	RCA LES–1009
"Pacific 231"	Honegger	
"Pantomime" *(The Comedians)*	Kabalevsky	RCA LES–1000
Papilloons, no. 8	Schumann	RCA WE 73
"Parade" *(Divertissement)*	Ibert	RCA LES–1000
"Pastoral"	Milhaud	HRW 511
"Petite Ballerina" *(Ballet* Suite no. 1)	Shostakovich	RCA LES–1001
"Phaeton"	Saint-Saëns	BOL 59/072
Pictures at an Exhibition	Moussorgsky	HRW 411
"Pines of the Villa Borghese" *(The Pines of Rome)*	Respighi	RCA LES–1004
"Pizzicato Polka" *(Ballet* Suite no. 1)	Shostakovich	RCA LES–1000
"Play of the Waves" *(La Mer)*	Debussy	RCA LES–1008
"Plow that Broke the Plains, The"	Thomson	HRW
Polka *(Age of Gold)*	Skostakovich	HRW 27 and RCA WE 82
Polka *(Bartered Bride)*	Smetana	
"Polovtsian Dances"	Borodin	
Prelude (Act 3, *Lohengrin*)	Wagner	RCA LES–1009
"Puss-in Boots and the White Cat" *(Sleeping Beauty)*	Tchaikovsky	RCA LES–1002
"Ritual Fire Dance" *(El Amor Brujo)*	Falla	
Rosenkavalier Suite	Strauss	RCA LES–1009
"Royal March of the Lion"	Saint-Saëns	BOL 51/064 and HRW 28
Scenes from Childhood	Schumann	HRW 18
"Season Fantasies"	Donaldson	BOL 52/065
"Shepherd's Dance"	Menotti	RCA LES–1005
"Skater's Waltz"	Waldteufel	BOL 55/068 and RCA WE 74
"Spanish Dance" no. 1 *(La Vida Breve)*	Falla	RCA LES–1009
"Spanish Serenade"	Bizet	RCA WE 76
"Sparks"	Moszkowski	RCA WE 71
"Spinning Song"	Kullak	RCA WE 78
"Street in a Frontier Town" *(Billy the Kid)*	Copland	RCA LES–1009
"Swan, The" *(Carnival of the Animals)*	Saint-Saëns	BOL 51/064, HRW 28 and RCA LES–1003
"Swan of Tuonela, The" *(Four Legends)*	Sibelius	
"To a Water Lily" *(Woodland Sketches)*	MacDowell	RCA WE 79
"To Spring"	Grieg	RCA WE 82
"Traumerei" *(Scenes from Childhood)*	Schumann	RCA LES–1005
"Turkey in the Straw"	Guion	RCA WE 75
"Under the Big Top"	Donaldson	BOL 51/064
"Viennese Musical Clock" *(Hary Janos* Suite)	Kodaly	RCA LES–1001
Waltz *(Les Patineurs)*	Meyerbeer	RCA LES–1001
"Waltzing Doll"	Poldini	RCA WE 78
Waltz no. 1 *(Faust Ballet Music)*	Gounod	RCA LES–1002
"Waltz of the Doll" *(Coppelia)*	Delibes	RCA LES–1000
"White Peacock, The," op. 7, no. 1	Griffes	RCA LES–1009
"Wild Horseman, The"	Schumann	RCA WE 78
"Witch"	MacDowell	RCA WE 79
"Witch, The"	Tchaikovsky	RCA WE 73

Recordings of Abstract Music

ABA Form

"Andante Cantabile"	Tchaikovsky	
"Ballet of the Sylphs" (Damnation of Faust)	Berlioz	RCA LES–1000
"Berceuse" (Firebird Suite)	Stravinsky	RCA LE/ LES–1000
"Bourree and Menuet II" (Royal Fireworks Music)	Handel	HRW 110 and RCA LES–1003
Children's Symphony, First Movement	McDonald	HRW 27 and RCA LES–1003
Children's Symphony, Third Movement	McDonald	RCA LES–1001
"Chinese Dance" (Nutcracker Suite)	Tchaikovsky	HRW 28 and BOL 58/071
"Dance of the Flutes" (Nutcracker Suite)	Tchaikovsky	HRW 28 and BOL 58/071
"Dance of the Little Swans" (Swan Lake)	Tchaikovsky	RCA LES–1000
"En Bateau"	Debussy	BOL 53/066 and HRW 110
"Folk Dances" (Somerset)	V. Williams	BOL 56/069
"Fountain Dance" (Wand of Youth)	Elgar	RCA LES–1001
"Gavotte"	Kabalevsky	BOL 55/068
"Grand Waltz"	Lecocq	BOL 56/069
"Hungarian Dance" no. 1	Brahms	RCA LES–1007
"Hungarian Dance" no. 5	Brahms	BOL 55/068
"Lapland Idyll"	Torjussen	BOL 60/073
"Laranjeiras" (Saudades do Brazil)	Milhaud	RCA LES–1001
"Le Secret" (Intermezzo)	Gautier	RCA WE 90
"March Past of the Kitchen Utensils" (The Wasps)	Williams	RCA LES–1002
"March of the Dwarfs" (Lyric Suite)	Grieg	BOL 52/065 and RCA WE 79
"Mazurka"	Khatchaturian	BOL 55/068
Minuet	Mozart	BOL 53/066
Minuet (Don Giovanni)	Mozart	HRW 511 and RCA WE 75
"Norwegian Dance," op. 35, no. 2	Grieg	RCA WE 75
"Pizzicato Polka" (Ballet Suite no. 1)	Shostakovich	RCA LES–1000
"Rataplan"	Donizetti	RCA WE 90
"Serenata"	Moszkowski	RCA WE 90
"Tambourine" (Cephale et Procris)	Gretry	RCA LES–1001
"Traumerei" (Scenes from Childhood)	*Schumann	RCA LES–1005
"Tritsch-Tratsch Polka"	Strauss	BOL 56/069
Waltz (Les Patineurs)	Meyerbeer	RCA LES–1001
Waltz (The Fantastic Toyshop)	Rossini	BOL 56/069
"Waltz of the Flowers" (Nutcracker Suite)	Tchaikovsky	BOL 58/071 and HRW 28
"With Castanets"	Reinecke	RCA WE 90

Other Forms

Adagio and Allegro (Divertimento in B Flat)	Mozart	HRW 19
"A Ground"	Handel	BOL 53/066
Allegretto Scherzando (Second Movement, Symphony No. 8 in F)	Beethoven	RCA LES–1009
"Amaryllis" (Old French Rondo)	Ghys	RCA WE 90
"An Evening in the Village"	Bartok	RCA LES–1007
"Badinerie" (Suite no. 2 in B Minor)	Bach	RCA LES–1002
"Berceuse" (Dolly, op. 56, no. 1)	Faure	RCA LES–1001
"Bourree and Minuet" (Fireworks Music)	Handel	HRW 110
"Bydlo" (Pictures at an Exhibition)	Moussorgsky	RCA LES–1001
Canon for String Quartet	Schoenberg	HRW 59
Canzona no. 2 for Brass and Organ	Gabrieli	HRW 38
"Changing of the Guard" (Carmen Suite no. 2)	Bizet	RCA LES–1003
Classical Symphony	Prokofiev	HRW 512
Clock Symphony no. 101 in D	Haydn	
"Col. Bogey March"	Alford	BOL 54/067
Concerto no. 25 (Water Music)	Handel	HRW 59
"Cradle Song" (Children's Games)	Bizet	RCA LES–1000
"Dagger Dance" (Natoma)	Herbert	RCA LES–1002
"Departure" (Winter Holiday)	Prokofiev	RCA LES–1001
Egmont Overture	Beethoven	HRW 610
Eine Kleine Nachtmusik	Mozart	
"Entrance of the Little Fauns"	Pierne	BOL 54/067
"Farandole" (L'Arlesienne Suite, no. 2)	Bizet	RCA LES–1009 and HRW 68
"Gavotte" (Mlle. Angot Suite)	Lecocq	BOL 53/066
"German Waltz—Paganini"	Schumann and Glazounov	BOL 53/066
Gigue (Cephale et Procris)	Gretry	RCA LES–1000
Gigue (Suite no. 3 in D Major)	Bach	RCA LES–1000
"Girl I Left Behind Me" (Irish Suite)	Anderson	RCA LES–1007
"Jack-in-the-Box" (Mikrokosmos Suite no. 2)	Bartok	RCA LES–1001
"Jesu, Joy of Man's Desiring"	Bach	RCA LES–1006
"Juba Dance"	Dett	RCA WE 76
Little Fugue in G Minor	Bach	RCA LES–1009
March (Summer Day Suite)	Prokofiev	RCA LES–1000
"March of the Toys" (Babes in Toyland)	Herbert	RCA LES–1001
"March—Trumpet and Drum"	Bizet	BOL 53/066
Melody in F	Rubenstein	RCA WE 78
"Morning in the Hills" (Ozark Set)	Siegmeister	
"My Lady Hunsdon's Puffe"	Dowland	HRW 68
New World Symphony (Symphony no. 9)	Dvorak	
"Pantomime" (The Comedians)	Kabalevsky	RCA LES 1000
"Parade" (Divertissement)	Ibert	RCA LES–1000
Polka	Lecocq	BOL 53/066
Polka (Bartered Bride)	Smetana	
Polka and Fugue (Schwanda the Bagpiper)	Weinberger	
"Polovtsian Dances"	Borodin	
"Pomp and Circumstance" no. 1	Elgar	BOL 54/067
"Pop! Goes the Weasel"	Cailliet	RCA LES–1004
Prelude (Act 3, Lohengrin)	Wagner	RCA LES–1009

Prelude to *Hansel and Gretel*	Humperdinck	RCA LES–1007
"Rhapsody in Blue"	Gershwin	
"Romanze" *(Eine kleine Nachtmusik)*	Mozart	RCA LES–1004
"Rondeau" *(The Moor's Revenge)*	Purcell	HRW 19
Rondo for Bassoon and Orchestra (Andante and Rondo)	Von Weber	HRW 37
Rosenkavalier Suite *(Der Rosenkavalier)*	R. Strauss	RCA LES–1009
"Russian Sailors' Dance" *(The Red Poppy)*	Gliere	RCA LES–1008
"Semper Fidelis"	Sousa	HRW 110 RCA LES–1003
"Scherzo" (Septet in E Flat, op. 20)	Beethoven	HRW 110
"Slavonic Dances"	Dvorak	
Sonata in D Minor, First and Third Movements	Rosenmueller	HRW 19
"Stars and Stripes Forever"	Sousa	BOL 54/067, HRW 59 and RCA LES–1005
String Quartet no. 10 in C Major, K. 170, First Movement	Mozart	HRW 410
Symphony no. 8, Second Movement	Beethoven	RCA LES–1009
Toccata for Percussion, Third Movement	Chavez	HRW 38
Toy Symphony	Haydn	
"Valse Triste"	Sibelius	
"Village Dance"	Liadov	BOL 53/066
Violin Concerto in D Major, op. 61, Third Movement	Beethoven	HRW 411
"Walking Song" *(Acadian Songs and Dances)*	Thomson	RCA LES–1000
"Waltz of the Doll" *(Coppelia)*	Delibes	RCA LES–1000
Water Music Suite and *Royal Fireworks*	Handel	
Western Symphony	Kay	

Recordings and Filmstrips of Operas and Operettas

Aida (excerpts)	Verdi
Amahl and the Night Visitors	Menotti
Carmen (excerpts)	Bizet
HMS Pinafore (highlights)	Gilbert and Sullivan
Pirates of Penzance (highlights)	Gilbert and Sullivan
Telephone, The	Menotti

Filmstrips

Aida	Verdi	Jam Handy
Barber of Seville, The	Rossini	Jam Handy
Bartered Bride, The	Smetana	Jam Handy
Lohengrin	Wagner	Jam Handy
Magic Flute, The	Mozart	Jam Handy
Mastersingers, The	Wagner	Jam Handy

BOL—Bowmar/Noble Orchestral Library recording
CM—Classroom Materials Company recording
HRW—Holt, Rinehart and Winston Exploring Music recording
Jam Handy—Prentice Hall Media
RCA LES—RCA Victor *Adventures in Music* Series recording
RCA WE—RCA Victor *Basic Record Library for Elementary Grades* Recording

Notational Experiences: Music Reading 6

The child who is beginning to read music is also—in a very real sense—beginning to make music his own, for he has begun to internalize the concepts basic to an understanding of music and to recognize their symbols in notation.

To the extent that the child is successful in interpreting the musical score, music can become an activity he is able to pursue by himself. No longer need he be a semipassive participant in an activity instigated and guided by someone else. The child senses this profound change within himself as he begins to interpret notation on the musical staff, and the excitement of the experience carries him to more complex music-reading experiences.

It behooves teachers to help sustain this enthusiasm by keeping experiences with music reading as successful and enjoyable as possible. This means that prior to introducing music reading experiences teachers must give extensive opportunities to experience and internalize the basic elements of music through appropriate musical activities—rhythms, singing, listening, playing instruments, creating. It means that prior to introducing any musical symbol in notation teachers must know that the child understands the relevant concepts. (See lists of conceptual understandings in the "Growth and Sequence Chart" of chapter 1.) It means that teachers must have acquired demonstrable evidence that the child can:

> Hear and reproduce the basic beat in duple and triple meter.
> Hear, reproduce (through clapping and chanting number notation), and notate simple rhythm patterns in duple and triple meter.
> Hear, sing, reproduce (with appropriate hand signals), and notate simple melodic patterns.
> Hear and respond through bodily movement to differences in melody, rhythm, and meter.
> Verbalize differences in melodic and rhythmic movement.
> Use syllables, letters, or numbers in reading tonal relationships.

With this evidence, what is the best procedure for beginning music-reading experiences? There are many ways. The authors will suggest a general, eclectic approach, incorporating some of the principals of Kodaly.

With this approach, the child's first introduction to notation can be through singing, or through playing, from notation, a short melodic pattern on a melody instrument. Initially, the experience should be short, easily grasped, and from the board, rather than from a music book.

When children have had many such experiences, and the idea of notation has become familiar, the teacher should prepare them to use books. She will want to do this with all the enthusiasm and care possible, so that children will feel that using the musical score, as musicians do, is an exciting experience, one worth any effort needed to master it.

The teacher will want to keep music books for special events, used to help read music. They should not become a meaningless accoutrement to the teacher's singing, or a means of looking at the words or accompanying pictures for songs. When children use books, we want them to feel that *they* are using the notation.

We can encourage this, if we do the following:

1. Begin with an overview of the score, rather than focusing on minute details. Does it have a melody that moves up and down or stays mainly in the same place? Is the rhythm even or uneven? Are there similar phrases? What are the highest and lowest notes?
2. Focus on notation for which children have a solid conceptual background for understanding.
3. Use concrete associations to help children understand. (When quarter notes are moving at a *walking* tempo, eighth notes will *run* and half notes will take *giant steps*.)
4. Emphasize relationships in rhythm and melody. (*This* note is twice as long as *that* note. It takes two of these notes to equal one of those. This note is moving up by step; that note stays in the same place as the preceding note; this note is skipping one note as it moves downward, and so on.)
5. Focus on scale passages (5–4–3–2–1) and melodies that outline a chord (1–3–5) as well as repeated rhythmic and melodic patterns and phrases.
6. Make frequent use of the system chosen for naming tonal and rhythmic relationships (syllables, letters, or numbers, for the melody; Kodaly or number counting for the rhythm).

7. Use new skills in reading notation in *all* musical experiences: singing, listening, experiences with instruments, rhythms, experiences creating songs and accompaniments, and so on.
8. Relate notational concepts (moving up or down, by step or skip) to other arts.

Aims of Reading Experiences

Guiding children in experiences with music reading is perhaps the most challenging aspect of teaching music. Music-reading experiences can become tedious, burdensome activities to both children and teacher. They can, on the other hand, be growth-producing and satisfying, when children acquire a language that opens a new world for them, the world of music.

The basic aim of notational experiences must be, then, to help children see music reading as an exciting skill that they would like to develop, and to help them acquire the conceptual understandings and behavioral objectives necessary for each stage of this development.

Music-Reading Activities

Children learn to read music by participating in a musical activity in a way that helps them associate what they are hearing and doing with what they are seeing. Music reading can begin through participation in activities similar to the following:

Rhythmic Experiences
1. Rhythmic movement associated with notation.

Walking

Running

Giant Steps

2. Clapping (from notation) the rhythmic notation of familiar rhymes, proverbs, and name chants.
3. Internalizing activities.
   a. Singing the song inside (from notation) and clapping the rhythm of words, or the basic beat.
   b. Observing notation and
      (1) Clapping or playing quarter, eighth, half, or whole notes on rhythm instruments, different children and instruments assigned to different note values.
      (2) Clapping only first and last (or underlined) measures aloud, internalizing the rest.

4. Identifying familiar songs or chants from rhythmic notation.
5. Taking rhythmic dictation involving familiar and unfamiliar rhythm patterns. (Teacher claps and counts; children echo, then notate what they heard.)
6. Playing rhythm games that involve clapping and chanting notation.

Singing Experiences
1. Singing with hand signals, by rote, then by note, from the board, beginning with sol, mi, then adding la, do, re, fa, and ti

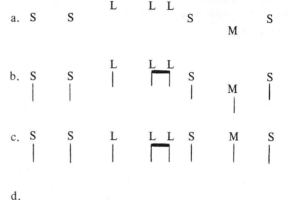

d.

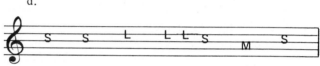

e.

f.

2. Drawing contour of melodies on the board
3. Learning to recognize the following, sung first by rote, then observed and performed from notation
   a. Scale passages
   b. Outlines of chords
   c. Steps and skips
   d. Melody and rhythm patterns

4. Internalizing activities
   a. Singing a familiar song inside, then notating it
   b. Hearing an unfamiliar melody, singing it inside, then aloud, then notating it
   c. Seeing notation for unfamiliar song or rhythm: internalizing, singing, playing, then notating it
5. Identifying a familiar song from the following:
   a. Notation
   b. Letter names of notes
   c. Hearing song played
6. Following the notation of a song played or sung by the teacher; when she stops in the middle of the song, identifying the final note sung

Instrumental Experiences
1. Associating rhythm patterns played on rhythm instruments to notation.

2. Playing rhythm games, using notation and rhythm instruments. (Rhythm patterns are written on the board. Sticks play quarter notes; maracas, eighth notes; triangles, half notes; and so on.)
3. Playing melody instruments from notation (simple, then more complex phrases) and singing syllables, letter names, or words.
4. Hearing a familiar song or part of a song played on an instrument, singing it inside, then notating it.
5. Seeing notation of an unfamiliar song or rhythm, reading it inside, playing it, notating it.

Listening Experiences
1. Examining notation for themes in listening experiences, learning to play them, listening for them in a recording.
   a. Do they move up or down, or both?
   b. Are there steps? Skips?
   c. Is there a tonal center? What is it?
   d. What is the meter? What does it indicate?
   e. Are there mostly quarter notes? Eighth notes? Half notes? Other?
2. Comparing themes for several different selections; discussing them in terms of questions a-e; playing them, when possible; listening to them as they occur in recordings.
3. Observing notation of themes on Cues to Music cards; discussing it, playing it, when possible; holding cards as themes (cues) occur on the recording.

For teachers of very young children, Madeleine Carabo-Cone and Beatrice Royt have suggested ideas for specific music-reading experiences in their book, *How to Help Children Learn Music,* published by Harper and Row, Inc., New York.

For many of the experiences suggested in their book, a floor staff must be constructed. The authors suggest constructing it in this manner: (1) get a nine-by-twelve foot linoleum rug; (2) apply two coats of white deck paint; (3) paint horizontal black, enamel lines on it; (4) make two, five-line staves of the grand staff, with a pencil line, to indicate the invisible leger line of middle C; (5) paint the bass and treble clefs at the left; (6) cover with several coats of clear shellac.

Once this is available, many experiences suggest themselves. A few are listed here.

Tightrope Walk
Each staff line represents a rope. Children line up left of the bottom (G) line of the bass staff and follow the leader across it, one foot in front of the other, arms outstretched for balance. As they walk, they hum the sound of the line to the teacher's piano accompaniment. When the line ends, they walk around the outside of the staff, counterclockwise, and begin the next line, B, again from the left.

Shuffleboard
With a yardstick, each child pushes a black paper note across the floor staff. A child plays the caller. If the caller calls *line* the pusher must land his note onto a line; if the caller calls *space* the note must land in a space.

Beanbag Game
A child throws a beanbag at the staff, calling *line* if he thinks it will land on a line or *space* if in a space. If he calls correctly, he gets a second throw. The child wins still another throw if he can name the line or space upon which it lands. (A staff can be placed nearby to help identify lines and spaces.)

For older children, the teacher will want to ask children to name the specific note the beanbag lands on, as well as the specific line or space upon which the bag lands.

Rhythmic Concepts

Level I

Materials Needed
1. Illustrations and poem for related arts
2. Copy of "Clap Your Hands"

Chart of Rhythmic Counting and Clapping

Quarter Notes ♩ — **Quarter Rest** 𝄽

Notation	|	|	|	|	
Count	One Ta	one ta	one ta	one ta	
Clap	Clap	clap	clap	clap	Rests are indicated by touching pointer finger to the lips or tapping fingers on shoulders.

Eighth Notes ♪

Notation	⊓		⊓		⊓		⊓		
Count	One Ti	and ti	one ti	and ti	one ti	and ti	one ti	and ti	
Clap	Clap	clap	clap	clap	clap	clap	clap	clap	Clapping should be approximately half the height of the clapping for the quarter note.

Half Notes 𝅗𝅥

Notation	𝅗𝅥		𝅗𝅥		
Count	One Ta	two — a	one ta	two — a	
Clap	Clap	Move clasped hands upward	Clap	Move clasped hands upward	Clapping should be twice the height of the clapping for the quarter note.

Dotted Half Notes 𝅗𝅥.

Notation	𝅗𝅥.			𝅗𝅥.		
Count	One Ta	two — a	three (or dot) — a	one ta	two — a	three (or dot) — a
Clap	Clap	Move clasped hands upward	Move clasped hands upward	Clap	Move clasped hands upward	Move clasped hands upward

Whole Notes 𝅝

Notation	𝅝			
Count	One Ta	two — a	three — a	four — a
Clap	Clap	Move arm clockwise over the head in a large, circular motion		

Triplets

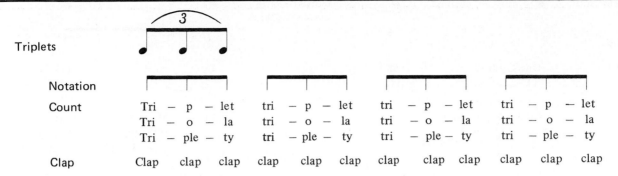

Notation											
Count	Tri	– p –	let	tri	– p –	let	tri	– p –	let	tri	– p – let
	Tri	– o –	la	tri	– o –	la	tri	– o –	la	tri	– o – la
	Tri	– ple –	ty	tri	– ple –	ty	tri	– ple –	ty	tri	– ple – ty
Clap	Clap clap clap			clap clap clap			clap clap clap			clap clap clap	

(For musical purposes, the word *triplet* has been changed to a three-syllable word (tri p let), the middle syllable to be pronounced *puh,* with a slight emphasis on the first syllable.)

Rests

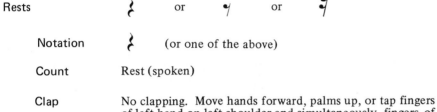

Notation	𝄽 (or one of the above)
Count	Rest (spoken)
Clap	No clapping. Move hands forward, palms up, or tap fingers of left hand on left shoulder and simultaneously, fingers of right hand on right shoulder.

Sixteenth Notes

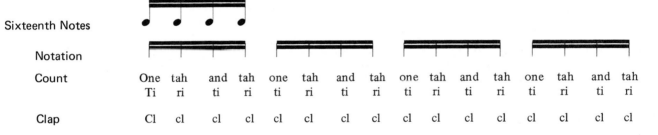

Notation																
Count	One	tah	and	tah	one	tah	and	tah	one	tah	and	tah	one	tah	and	tah
	Ti	ri	ti	ri	ti	ri	ti	ri	ti	ri	ti	ri	ti	ri	ti	ri
Clap	Cl	cl	cl	cl	cl	cl	cl	cl	cl	cl	cl	cl	cl	cl	cl	cl

Combinations of Eighth and Sixteenth Notes

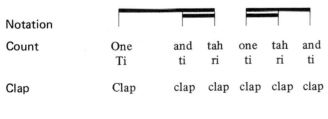

Notation						
Count	One		and	tah	one	tah	and
	Ti		ti	ri	ti	ri	ti
Clap	Clap		clap	clap	clap	clap	clap

Ties

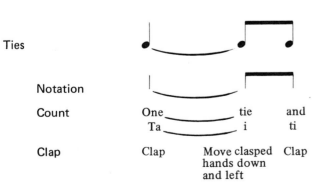

Notation			
Count	One_____	tie	and
	Ta_____	i	ti
Clap	Clap	Move clasped hands down and left	Clap

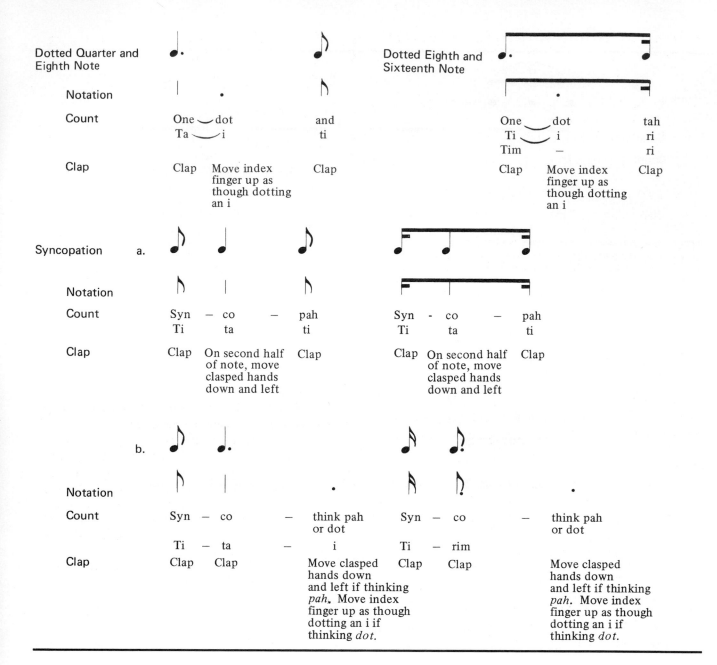

				Dotted Eighth and Sixteenth Note		
Dotted Quarter and Eighth Note						
Notation						
Count	One — dot		and	One — dot		tah
	Ta — i		ti	Ti — i		ri
				Tim —		ri
Clap	Clap	Move index finger up as though dotting an i	Clap	Clap	Move index finger up as though dotting an i	Clap

Syncopation   a.

Notation						
Count	Syn — co	—	pah	Syn - co	—	pah
	Ti	ta	ti	Ti	ta	ti
Clap	Clap	On second half of note, move clasped hands down and left	Clap	Clap	On second half of note, move clasped hands down and left	Clap

b.

Notation						
Count	Syn — co	—	think pah or dot	Syn — co	—	think pah or dot
	Ti — ta	—	i	Ti — rim		
Clap	Clap Clap		Move clasped hands down and left if thinking *pah*. Move index finger up as though dotting an i if thinking *dot*.	Clap Clap		Move clasped hands down and left if thinking *pah*. Move index finger up as though dotting an i if thinking *dot*.

3. Rhythm instruments
4. Music Cue charts

Music-Reading Activities
1. Rhythmic dictation
2. Focusing on rhythmic notation of a phrase from a song

Related Musical Activities
1. Bodily movement (clapping)
2. Singing
3. Playing rhythm instruments

Conceptual Understandings
1. Durational relationships demonstrated in rhythmic counting and clapping may be notated.
2. Rhythm patterns may be seen in notation as well as felt while clapping, chanting and singing.

Behavioral Objectives
1. To notate rhythm patterns using these symbols:

2. To recognize notation of rhythm patterns (in a song) formerly clapped

Related Arts
1. Focusing on durational relationships through an experience with a poem
2. Focusing on patterns through an experience with visual arts
   a. *Broadway Boogie Woogie* by Piet Mondrian (fig. 6.1)
   b. *Rhythm without End* by Robert Delaunay (fig. 6.2)

Procedure
1. Focusing on durational relationships through an experience with a poem
   a. Write these words on the board: cat, sat, room, broom, it, bit, brown, town.
   b. Ask children to say the words with you, listening for long and short sounds.
   c. Ask which words sound long and which sound short, and list on board.

Short	Long
cat	room
sat	broom
it	brown
bit	town

   d. Tell the children you will recite a poem and they should listen for the longest sounds.

   There once was a cat named CROON,
   Who was born in the month of JUNE;
   He loved to creep near the big oak tree
   And dance by the light of the MOON.

   e. Ask children to listen again and raise their hands whenever they hear a long sound.
   f. Display triangles and rhythm sticks. Ask children which has the longest sound, letting them experiment.
   g. Ask volunteer to play triangle on long sounds as the class says the poem.
   h. Remind children that music also has long and short sounds.
2. Focusing on rhythmic concepts through echo clapping, using number or Kodaly counting
   a. Tell the children to echo you. Do the following:

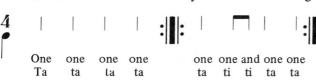

One one one one one one and one one
Ta ta ta ta ta ti ti ta ta

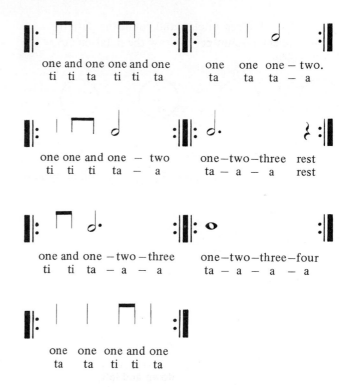

one and one one and one   one one one — two.
ti ti ta ti ti ta   ta ta ta — a

one one and one — two   one—two—three rest
ti ti ti ta — a   ta — a — a rest

one and one —two —three   one—two—three—four
ti ti ta — a — a   ta — a — a — a

one one one and one
ta ta ti ti ta

   b. Ask children if they heard any long sounds. (They should hear the whole note, dotted half note, and half note, identifying them through the type of counting used, if they do not yet know the note values.) Ask children which sounds were shortest (the eighth notes, "one and" or "ti ti" notes). (Children should have many similar experiences, using these durations in different combinations.)
3. Focusing on the notation of durational relationships through a circle game
   a. Use beat board (see chapter 1, page 5) or draw four circles on the board.

   b. Put your hand on your heart. Ask children to do the same, until they feel the beat of their hearts. Explain that the lines in the circles represent the heartbeats and that you will tap a pattern on these circles. Tap the following pattern:

c. Ask children to clap and count the pattern.
d. Select a volunteer to draw the notation below the circles.

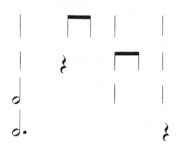

e. Follow the same procedure for the following patterns:

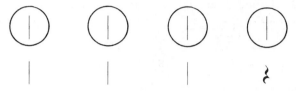

4. Focusing on patterns through an experience in related arts
   a. Ask children what a pattern is, focusing on the definition of pattern as a design or repeated motif.
   b. Ask children to name some things that have patterns in them. They may think of dress fabrics, dishes, wallpaper, and floor coverings.
   c. Explain that many things have patterns—music and art both use patterns to give meaning and form.
   d. Display the pictures in figures 6.1 and 6.2 or some similar to these.
   e. Ask children to look at *Broadway Boogie Woogie* to discover whether there are any patterns in the picture. Ask them to share their ideas with the class. They may see the repetition of these elements.
      (1) Black squares, in groups of threes
      (2) Grey squares, sometimes single, sometimes in groups of twos
      (3) Black rectangles, in various shapes
      (4) White squares and rectangles, in similar and dissimilar shapes
   f. When children have explored their ideas they may enjoy knowing the definition of *boogie woogie*: a primitive style of playing the piano, in which a bass rhythm is repeated, with a melody in the upper register.

Figure 6.1
Broadway Boogie Woogie by Piet Mondrian. 1942–43. Oil on canvas, 50 ×50″. Collection, The Museum of Modern Art, New York.

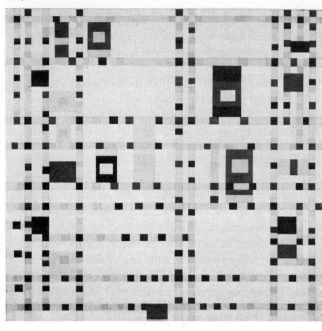

Figure 6.2
Rhythm without End by Robert Delaunay. (1935). Gouache, brush and ink, 10⅝ × 8¼″. Collection, The Museum of Modern Art, New York.

Clap Your Hands

Clap, clap, clap your hands, Clap your hands to - geth - er;

Clap, clap, clap your hands, Clap your hands to - geth - er.

g. Ask children to examine *Rhythm without End* for patterns. They may see these elements.
   (1) The repetition of curved lines (half circles) to the right and left of the center (vertical) line
   (2) The repetition of blacks, greys, and whites filling in the half circles
   (3) The full circles formed by the half circles
   (4) The repetition of vertical lines to the left and right of the center line
5. Focusing on rhythm patterns in the notation of a song
   a. Write the following on the board, omitting the notation below.

one one one and one
ta ta ti ti ta

   b. Have children clap and count the pattern, using number or Kodaly counting.
   c. Remind children of other experiences with patterns in music and related arts. Explain that this is a rhythm pattern that they will hear in a song you will sing. Tell children to listen and put their hands on their heads when they hear this pattern. Sing the song, "Clap Your Hands." (Children should put their hands on their heads on "Clap, clap, clap your hands.")
   d. Ask children the words that used this rhythm pattern. Invite them to sing and clap this pattern each time it occurs, as you sing the song.
   e. Display rhythm instruments and ask which instrument would best accompany pattern. Let children experiment and vote on the one they prefer.
   f. Select a child to play the pattern each time it occurs and another child to point to the notation on the board. Have the rest of the class sing the pattern as you sing the entire song.

g. Ask children if they heard another pattern. They may have heard the repetition of "Clap your hands together."

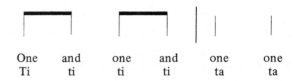

One and one and one one
Ti ti ti ti ta ta

   h. Follow the same procedure for helping children explore this pattern.
6. Evaluating children's ability to recognize and notate rhythm patterns using familiar durations
   a. Distribute Music Cue charts to the class.

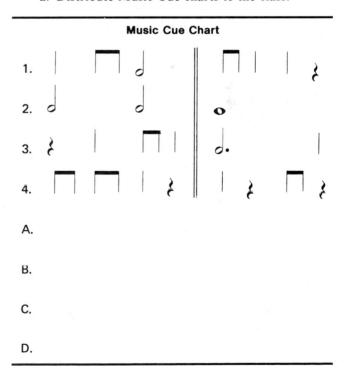

Music Cue Chart

1.
2.
3.
4.
A.
B.
C.
D.

b. Remind children of their experiences recognizing and notating rhythm patterns. Tell them to listen, then circle the pattern they hear you count and tap, after number 1. Tap and count either pattern on the beat board. Continue in the same way for numbers 2–4.

c. Tell children to notate the pattern you tap, after letters A–D. Tap these on the beat board.

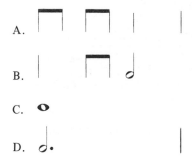

A.

B.

C.

D.

Music-Reading Experiences That Focus on Rhythmic Concepts

For additional experiences see the sections in each chapter entitled "Focusing on Notational Concepts."

Level I

Focusing on Notation through Basic Bodily Movements

This experience is outlined on page 62, chapter 2, "Rhythmic Experiences."

Level I

Focusing on the Rhythmic Notation of the Quarter Rest by Notating a Chant
"Little Fred"

Children should know the chant before having this experience.

1. Put the words of the chant on the board. Tell children to pat their knees and say *beat* as you say the chant and simultaneously put the notation above the words, as follows:

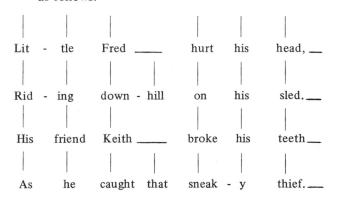

Lit - tle Fred _____ hurt his head, __
Rid - ing down - hill on his sled. __
His friend Keith _____ broke his teeth__
As he caught that sneak - y thief. __

2. Ask children if they noticed places where there were no sounds. Ask them to say the chant again to discover where rests occur. Repeat, putting in rests.

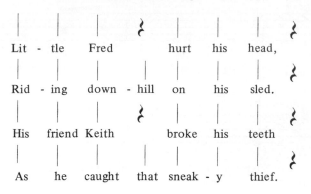

Lit - tle Fred hurt his head,
Rid - ing down - hill on his sled.
His friend Keith broke his teeth
As he caught that sneak - y thief.

Level I, II, or III

Focusing on Rhythmic Notation by Playing a Number Game

1. On a large card, print notation suitable for the level desired. (See sample on top of page 323.)
2. Have the class clap each pattern, using number or Kodaly counting.
3. Ask volunteers to clap patterns, without using numerical order (1, 8, 3, 4, and so on).
4. Ask volunteers to clap the following: 12 (number 1, followed immediately by number 2); 58 (5, followed by 8); 73; 46; 123; 654; 876; 1823; 4756.
5. If desired, teams may be formed, girls playing against boys. Score one point for each pattern correctly clapped. The team scoring ten points first wins the game.

Level I, II, or III

Focusing on Rhythmic Notation by Clapping a Rhythmic Ostinato to a Chant or Song

1. Notate this on the board:

1. | | | ‰   7. | ‰ ‰ |
2. | ‰ | ‰   8. ‰ | | |
3. | ‰ | | 9. ‰ | ‰ |
4. | | ‰ | 10. ‰ | | ‰
5. | ‰ ‰ ‰   11. ‰ ‰ ‰ |
6. | | ‰ ‰   12. ‰ ‰ | ‰

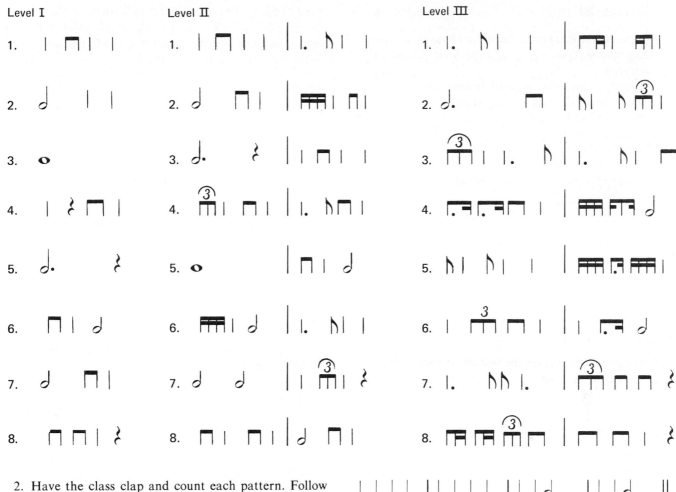

2. Have the class clap and count each pattern. Follow these instructions for the level desired.

    Level I Have the class select one pattern (3, for example) and clap this as an accompaniment to a familiar song or chant that swings in twos.

    Level II Have the class select two patterns (2 and 7, for example) and clap these patterns, one immediately after the other, as an accompaniment to any familiar song that swings in twos.

    Level III Have the class select any four patterns (4, 5, 11, and 12, for example) and clap these patterns as an ostinato accompaniment to any familiar song.

Level I, II, or III

Focusing on Rhythmic Notation through Internalizing Activities for a Familiar Song

1. Select any song with familiar rhythmic notation. (For example, level I would be familiar with notation for "Are You Sleeping.")
2. Write rhythmic notation on the board. If "Are You Sleeping" is used, it would be as follows:

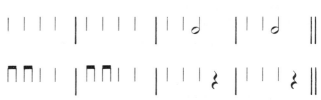

3. Have the class clap and chant, using number of Kodaly counting.
4. Tell the class you will circle part of the notation, and that they are to clap and count everything except the notation circled, which they are to feel inside, maintaining a steady beat. Perhaps you will circle the following:

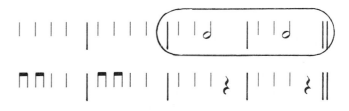

5. Erase the circle around the phrase; circle another phrase and repeat.

Level I, II, or III

> *Focusing on Rhythmic Notation through an Experience Notating a Familiar Song, Chant, or Proverb*

1. Have the class select a familiar song, chant, or proverb. (A level II class, for example, might select the song "My Lord, What a Morning.") (For copy of the song, see chapter 3, *"Singing Experiences."*)
2. Have the class sing and clap any section with familiar notation using number or Kodaly counting; for example, the chorus of "My Lord What a Morning."

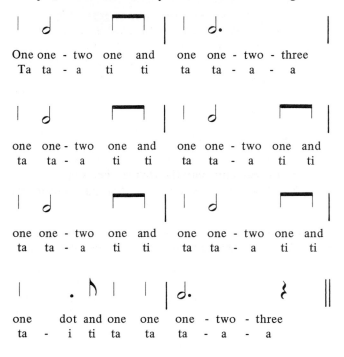

3. Ask volunteers to write rhythmic notation of first and subsequent phrases on the board. Have the class help by clapping each phrase until they discover the correct notation.

Level II

> *Focusing on the Notation of Rhythm Patterns in a Song*
> "Chairs to Mend"

For copy of song, see chapter 4, "Experiences with Instruments."

1. Read the text of the song. Ask children who they think sings this song. Explain that in some parts of the world it is quite common for people to go down the street calling out their wares in order to attract customers.
2. Write the following on the board, omitting the number notation.

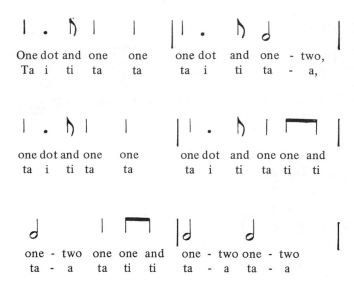

3. Tell children you are going to clap the rhythm of one phrase and you would like them to tell you which phrase you clapped. Clap and count the rhythm of the dotted quarter followed by the eighth and quarter notes. (As you say *dot,* bring your clasped hands down to the left or, if you prefer, point your right index finger forward.)
4. Ask a volunteer to point to the phrase you clapped and counted.
5. Have the class count the number of times this appears in the song (three). Select a child to point to the places it appears.
6. Ask the class to clap and count the phrase with you, then clap and count the entire song, as you point to the notes. Clarify any difficult phrases by repeating them.
7. Ask children which patriotic songs they know use this pattern. ("America the Beautiful"—on the word *beautiful:* "America"—on the words *tis of thee.*)
8. Tell the class as you sing the song you would like them to clap the rhythm softly. Sing the song as the class claps.
9. Ask the class which rhythm instrument might play the dotted quarter followed by the eighth and quarter notes. Let children demonstrate suggestions as the class sings the song. Then let them vote for the instrument they prefer.
10. Ask which instrument might play this rhythm when it occurs in the fisherman's song, and help class select the instrument, as in number 9.
11. Select children to play the rhythm pattern for both the chair mender's song and the fisherman's song. Let them play the pattern each time it occurs, as class sings. Repeat, letting different children accompany.
12. Encourage children to find the pattern in other songs.

Level II

    Focusing on Notation, through a Clapping Game and Chant

This experience has been outlined on page 63, chapter 2, "Rhythmic Experiences."

Level II or III

    Focusing on Rhythmic Notation through an Experience with Speech Canon
    "Coins"

1. Write the following on the board:

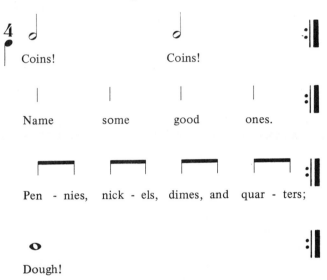

2. Ask for volunteers to clap and chant each line. Have the class chant the entire rhyme.
3. Ask for ideas as to which percussion instruments would best play each line. One class selected:
   Coins: finger cymbals and triangles
   Name some good ones: rhythm sticks and tambourines
   Pennies, nickels, dimes, and quarters: hand drums and jingle bells
   Dough: cymbals
4. Select volunteers to play instruments for each line as children internalize the words.
5. Divide the class into four parts.
   a. Part 1 begins clapping and chanting, accompanied by instruments throughout.
   b. Part 2 begins clapping and chanting when part 1 reaches the first word in the second line.
   c. Part 3 begins when part 2 reaches the first word in the second line.
   d. Part 4 begins when part 3 reaches the first word in the second line.
6. Children may enjoy the following sequence:
   a. Instruments play the rhyme, then stop.
   b. Class does speech canon in four parts (no instruments).
   c. Instruments play the rhyme.

Level II or III

    Focusing on Rhythmic Notation through an Experience with Singing and Basic Bodily Movements
    "Rally Song"

Rally Song

Balkan
Four Part Round

From *The Ditty Bag* © 1946 by Janet E. Tobitt. Used by permission.

1. Place the following on the board or overhead transparency:

   a. ♩ ♫ ♩ ♫ ♩   mil-ha bi-lou lou-bi: phrase 2, measure 1

   b. ♩   ♩   ♩   mil-ha bi: phrase 1, measure 1; phrase 3, measure 1; phrase 4, measure 1

   c. ♩   ♩.   shem-bel: phrase 2, measure 2

   d. ♩ ♫ ♩   ♩   lou lou-bi shem-bel: phrase 1, measure 2; phrase 3, measure 2; phrase 4, measure 2

2. Clap one of the foregoing. Ask the class to identify the pattern.
3. Continue until children can identify all patterns.
4. Have children clap patterns until they can clap them in any sequence. (For example: 1 followed by 3, then 1, 4, 2, 3, and so forth.) (Interest can be maintained by having children stamp, clap hands, pat knees, and snap fingers. Rhythm instruments can also be used.)
5. Show children the notation of the song. Have them find pattern a.
6. Play, or have child play pattern a on a melody instrument.
7. Have children sing this pattern, with instrumental accompaniment.
8. Follow a similar procedure for each pattern.
9. Have children sing the song, accompanied by instrument.
10. Children will enjoy singing and moving to the song as a two-, three-, or four-part round.

Movement

Phrase One

(Move to right)	1	2	3	4
	Right Foot	Left Foot (Left foot always crosses behind right foot)	Right Foot	Left Foot (Just touch)

(Move to left)	5	6	7	8
	Left Foot	Right Foot	Left Foot	Right Foot (Close)

Phrase Two

(Move to left)	1	2	3	4
	LF	RF	LF	RF (Touch)

(Move to right)	5	6	7	8
	RF	LF	RF	LF (Close)

Phrase Three

(Move forward)	1	2	3	4
	RF	LF	RF	LF (Touch)

(Move back)	5	6	7	8
	LF	RF	LF	RF (Close)

Phrase Four

(Move back)	1	2	3	4
	LF	RF	LF	RF (Touch)

(Move forward)	5	6	7	8
	RF	LF	RF	LF (Close)

Position of Groups for Four-Part Round

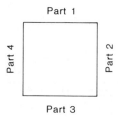

Level II or III

Focusing on Rhythmic Notation by Creating an Accompaniment for a Song Played on the Recorder
"Turn the Glasses Over"

1. Teach children to play the first eight measures of "Turn the Glasses Over" on the recorder.
2. Write this on the board:

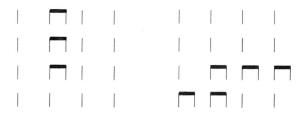

3. Have the class clap and count the patterns.
4. Ask the class if they can guess the name of this familiar song.
5. Ask how many different rhythm patterns they see. (four)

Turn the Glasses Over

Adapted from arrangement from *Folk Songster* by Dallin and Dallin, © 1967 by Wm. C. Brown Company Publishers, Dubuque, Iowa. (in public domain)

6. Display percussion instruments. Ask children for suggestions for instruments to play each pattern. Let them experiment and vote for instruments they prefer. One class decided on the following:

Tone Blocks

Hand Drum

Rhythm Sticks

Tambourine

7. Select volunteers to play instruments.
8. Divide the class and perform the song.
   a. Group 1 plays the song on recorders.
   b. Group 2 sings the song.
   c. Group 3 accompanies, using rhythm instruments.
9. On another day, teach the remainder of the song.

Level III

Focusing on Rhythmic Notation by Creating Words to a Favorite Rock Song

1. Ask the class to vote on their favorite rock song.
2. Guide them in creating a new set of words for the song. The following may help:
   a. Through discussion, help the class decide on a topic for the song.

Notational Experiences   327

b. Try to help them decide exactly what they want to convey.

c. Ask for ideas for a first line; have the class sing each to see if it fits the music.

d. When a first line has been chosen, have the class sing it, and volunteers sing a second line alone.

e. Continue developing ideas for the song in this manner.

3. When words for the entire song have been created, put them on the board. Have the class clap the rhythm as they sing the song.

4. Working phrase by phrase, ask for volunteers to notate on the board the rhythms suggested by their words. Give the help needed to achieve an accurate notation of the song.

Melodic Concepts

Level II

Materials Needed
1. Illustration for concepts related to scale passages
2. Copy of "Four Monkeys"
3. Recorders or song bells
4. Recording of "Turtles" from *Carnival of the Animals* by Saint-Saëns, Bowmar *Orchestral Library* recording BOL 064
5. Melody instrument

Music-Reading Activities
1. Singing syllables from the board
2. Playing intervals from a major scale from the song "Four Monkeys"
3. Reading and singing scale passages from a theme from "Turtles" from *Carnival of the Animals*

Related Musical Activities
1. Singing
2. Playing recorders and song bells
3. Listening

Conceptual Understandings
1. All melodies are organized in some kind of scale.
2. Melodies written in the major scale have their own unique sound.
3. The end of a melody is marked by a cadence.

Behavioral Objectives
1. To recognize scale passages in the notation of a song
2. To recognize major scale construction, from notation
3. To hear a cadence at the end of a melody
4. To hear and follow a theme in an abstract listening experience

Related Arts
Focusing on concepts related to scale passages through an experience with the visual arts, using figure 6.3, *Steps,* and 6.4, *More steps*

Procedure
1. Focusing on interval relationships in the major scale through echo singing, using hand signals
   Previous to this experience, children should have had many experiences echo singing intervals in the following combinations and sequence.

   Sol and mi
   Sol, mi, and la
   Sol, mi, la, and do
   Sol, mi, la, do, and re
   Sol, mi, la, do, re, and fa
   Sol, mi, la, do, re, fa, and ti

   a. Tell children to echo you, and sing the following, using hand signals.

   b. Ask children the following questions:
      (1) Did you hear any scale passages? (yes)
      (2) Did it sound like you were singing in major or minor? (major) (If children are not familiar with the major and minor scales, the teacher should play each.)
      (3) What syllable is the home tone? (do)
      (4) Did you hear a sequence of notes that sounded as though the singing had come to an end? (yes) (If children know the word *cadence,* use it. If not, explain it is a point of rest.)
      (5) Where did you hear these notes? (the cadence, or last three notes)

2. Focusing on notation of interval relationships in the major scale, through singing syllables with hand signals
   a. Write this on the board:

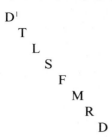

   b. Have the class sing these notes, with hand signals, both ascending and descending.
   c. Ask what it is. (a major scale)
   d. Ask which is the home tone, or key center. (do)
   e. Have children sing these notes, using hand signals, as you point to them in various combinations.
   f. When children have had experience singing these notes in many combinations, give them the following sequence of experiences, using these notes.
      (1) Write this on the board; have children count and clap the rhythm, then sing the syllables, using hand signals.

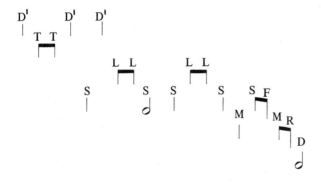

      (2) Write this on the board; have children count and clap the rhythm, then sing syllables, using hand signals.

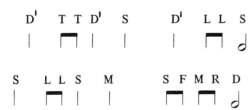

      (3) Ask individual children to notate the following on a staff. If children have had previous experience listening for and finding a cadence in the notation of a song, ask them to point out cadence in this notation. If not,

Figure 6.3
Steps, photograph by Lois Raebeck

ask what notes seem to indicate the ending (g, f, e, d, and c). Explain that this is called a cadence.

3. Focusing on melodic concepts through an experience with the visual arts
   a. Display figure 6.3.
   b. Ask children what, in music, this reminds them of. If they have difficulty, ask them to listen as you sing and to raise their hands when they hear something that reminds them of the picture. Sing the following melody. Children should raise their hands as you sing the last two measures—a descending C major scale. If they do not, repeat, pointing to each step (fig. 6.3) as you sing the syllables. (You should be on the sidewalk when you reach the bottom do.)

Figure 6.4
More steps

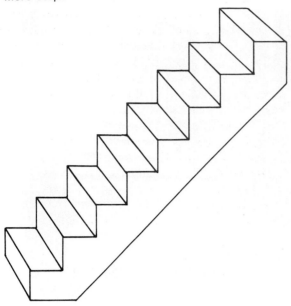

c. Draw steps on the board, or enlarge the picture (fig. 6.4) using a projector. Ask children to assume the sidewalk is bottom do, top step high do. Have them sing syllables, with hand signals, as you point to each step.

d. Remind children that melodies move up and down, by step and skip, just as many things in life reflect similar motion.

4. Focusing on the notation of interval relationships in the major scale by learning to play a song on the recorder or song bells

   a. Write the song "Four Monkeys" on the board, omitting number counting, syllable notation, and verses.

   b. Have children count and clap the rhythm. Ask volunteers to sing each measure, using syllables and hand signals. Place the syllable below each note as it is sung correctly.

   c. Have the class sing the melody, using syllables and hand signals. Erase syllables. Have the class sing the melody again.

   d. Have the class sing the melody, using letter names of notes.

   e. Ask the class what scale is used. (C major scale)

   f. Ask the child to circle notes that form the cadence. (last four notes)

   g. Ask for volunteers to play the song on song bells or recorder. If recorders are available, encourage the entire class to play.

   h. On another day, help children create a percussive accompaniment for the song and perform as follows:

      (1) Group 1 sings the song.

      (2) Group 2 plays on the recorder.

      (3) Group 3 plays a percussive accompaniment.

5. Focusing on scale passages in an experience with abstract music ("Turtles" from *Carnival of the Animals* by Saint-Saëns)

   a. Display theme card for "Turtles," which accompanies the recording.

Copyright 1922 Durand et Cie. Used by Permission of the Publisher, Theodore Presser Company, Sole Representative, U.S.A.

Four Monkeys

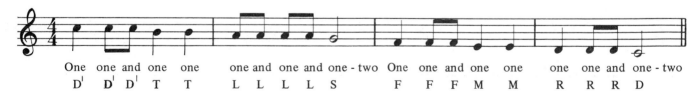

1. Four monkeys playing, playing in a tree,
   One took a fall, and then there were three.

2. Three monkeys dancing, dancing near some glue,
   One missed his step, and then there were two.

Note: Children may enjoy creating other verses, telling how the other two monkeys disappear.

b. Explain that this notation is the theme for "Turtles." Ask children to examine the notation, to find steps, skips, scale passages, home tone, and perhaps a cadence. (The presence of a cadence may be more easily heard than seen.) Encourage children to express their ideas. Correct any misunderstandings that can be clarified by examining notation.

c. Select a volunteer to point to notation as you play the theme.

d. Ask children to sing the last eight notes, using syllables and hand signals (do do¹ ti la sol fa mi re).

e. Tell children to raise their hands when they hear this theme in the recording of "Turtles." Play "Turtles."

f. Ask children if the themes sounded exactly the same both times. (No. The first time it sounds exactly as written on the card. The second time there is a different ending.)

g. Tell children you will play the recording again, and this time to raise their hands each time they hear the cadence. If children are confused, review the definition of cadence. Have a volunteer point to the cadence on the chart (last eight notes).

h. On another day, children may enjoy creating a rhythmic interpretation of "Turtles."

6. Evaluating children's ability to recognize scale passages from notation

a. Distribute Music Cue charts.

b. Ask children to examine each of the phrases notated in numbers 1–4, and to circle scale passages. Make certain they understand that a scale passage is any group of notes moving stepwise up or down. Explain further that if one note is repeated, the group of notes still remains a scale passage.

c. When children have circled scale passages, discuss and clarify misunderstandings.

Music Cue Chart

Notational Experiences That Focus on Melodic Concepts

For additional music reading experiences see the sections in each chapter entitled "Notational Concepts: Music Reading."

Level I

Focusing on Notation of Melodic Relationships through Singing a Nursery Rhyme
"Donkey, Donkey, Old and Grey"

This experience may be adapted to any nursery rhyme and expanded to include the notes re, do, sol, la, and mi.

1. Have the class learn the rhyme, using a patschen— clap accompaniment, and echoing each phrase.

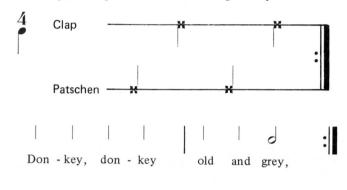

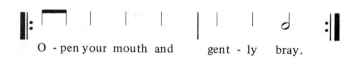

O - pen your mouth and   gent - ly   bray.

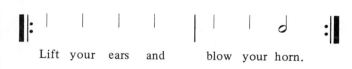

Lift your ears   and   blow your horn.

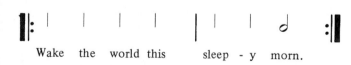

Wake the world this   sleep - y morn.

2. When children know the words, sing the rhyme, using sol, mi, and la, with hand signals. Ask them to echo you.

Don - key, don - key   old   and grey,

O - pen your mouth and   gent - ly bray.

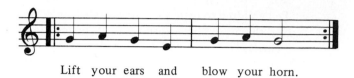

Lift your ears   and   blow your horn.

Wake the world this   sleep - y   morn.

3. Encourage children to assist in notating song by (a) writing the first syllable on the staff, and (b) having the class sing each phrase to help volunteers discover the correct notation. The following should occur:

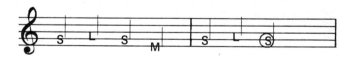

Are You Sleeping?

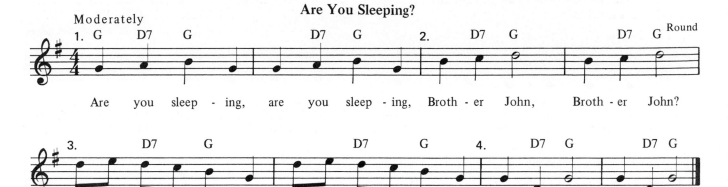

Moderately

Are you sleep - ing, are you sleep - ing, Broth - er John, Broth - er John?

Morn - ing bells are ring - ing, morn - ing bells are ring - ing, Ding, ding, dong; ding, ding, dong.

Frère Jacques, Frère Jacques,
Dormez-vous, dormez-vous?
Sonnez les matines, sonnez les matines,
Din, dan, don; din, dan, don.

Adapted from arrangement from *Heritage Songster* by Dallin and Dallin, © 1966 by Wm. C. Brown Company Publishers, Dubuque, Iowa. (in public domain)

Level I

Focusing on Melodic Notation of Skips by Learning a Song
"Are You Sleeping"

1. Write notation for "Are You Sleeping" on the board.
2. Tell the class you will play the bell sounds for "ding, ding, dong" on a melody instrument.
3. Ask how many times "ding, ding, dong" occurs in the song. (twice)
4. Let a child point to where it occurs.
5. Ask the class to examine the melody of "ding ding, dong." (G, D, G)
6. Ask if they can show the melodic direction with their hands. Help, if necessary, by pointing to the notes and simulating intervals with large arm movements or hand signals.
7. Play "ding, ding, dong" again, showing how the melody moves down, then back up.
8. Teach a child to play "ding, ding, dong."
9. Sing the entire song as a child plays and the class joins in on "ding, ding, dong."
10. Repeat, having other children play until the class knows the song.

Level I

Focusing on Melodic Notation of Sol, Mi, and Do by Learning a Song
"I'm a Person"

This experience is outlined on page 98, chapter 3, "Singing Experiences."

Level I or II

Focusing on the Notation of Scale Passages by Singing and Playing a Song on the Song Bells or Recorder
"Stepping"

1. Place notation of the song (see page 334) on the board, omitting number and Kodaly counting.
2. Have a volunteer, then the entire class, clap and count the first two measures.
3. Ask if any of the other phrases have the same rhythm.
4. Have the class clap and count the entire song, as you point to the notation.
5. Repeat, having a child point to the notation.
6. Ask the class to name the first note of the song. (middle C)
7. Ask how the song moves in the first four measures: up or down, by step, skip, or repeated tones?
8. Ask the class to examine the first four measures carefully to discover what familiar note sequence occurs. (C major scale)
9. Ask a volunteer to play the first four measures. Let him practice, then have the class sing as a child accompanies.
10. Follow the same procedure for helping the class sing and play the last four measures.

Stepping

Lois Raebeck

Stepping, stepping up-ward, Now it's time to stop,
one and one and one one one and one and one - two
ti ti ti ti ta ta ti ti ti ti ta - a

Climb-ing, climb-ing high-er, Now we reach the top.
one and one and one one one and one and one - two
ti ti ti ti ta ta ti ti ti ti ta - a

Step-ping, step-ping down-ward, Watch us as we go,
one and one and one one one and one and one - two
ti ti ti ti ta ta ti ti ti ti ta - a

Step-ping, step-ping down-ward, Now we land on "do."
one and one and one one one and one and one - two
ti ti ti ti ta ta ti ti ti ti ta - a

Jingle at the Window

Gaily

American Singing Game

Pass one win-dow, ti - de - o, Pass two win-dows, ti - de - o,

Pass three win-dows, ti - de - o, Jin-gle at the win-dow, ti - de - o.

Ti - de - o, ti - de - o, Jin-gle at the win-dow, ti - de - o.

Used by permission of the Follett Publishing Co.

Level II

Focusing on Notation of Do, Re, and Mi by Learning to Play and Sing a Song
"Au Clair de la Lune"

This experience is outlined on page 225, chapter 4, "Experiences with Instruments"

Level II

Focusing on Notation of Melody Patterns by Learning a Song
"Jingle at the Window"

1. Play the notes E, D, and C (mi, re, do) on song bells. Ask children to name songs that begin with these notes. ("Hot Cross Buns," "Three Blind Mice," "Mary Had a Little Lamb")
2. Hold the song bells vertically, with low notes on the bottom. Tell children that E is 3, or mi. Ask what numbers and syllables the notes below would be. (D is 2, or re. C is 1, or do.)
3. Have children sing the 3, 2, 1 pattern using numbers, then syllables, indicating melodic direction with hand signals.
4. Tell children to sing it again, adding a second "1" (3, 2, 1, 1). Help by playing and singing with them.
5. Have children sing the letter names E, D, C, C, and syllables mi, re, do, do.
6. Tell the class you will sing a song, and each time they hear 3, 2, 1, 1 to sing these numbers. Sing "Jingle at the Window." (Children should sing 3, 2, 1, 1 on "ti-de-o," which occurs in the last measure of each line.)
7. Draw a staff on the board. Ask children how many lines there are on the staff (five) and how many spaces (four). Write 3, 2, 1, 1 on the staff:

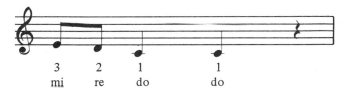

8. Explain that this is the notation for the phrase they just learned. Sing the song again as children sing "ti-de-o" each time it occurs, and you point to the notation.
9. Follow a similar procedure for teaching children the following patterns in the song:

Level II or III

Focusing on Melodic Notation by Learning to Play a Song on the Recorder
"Kum Ba Yah"

For a copy of the song, see chapter 3, "Singing Experiences"

1. Teach class "Kum Ba Yah," using syllables and hand signals.
2. Tell the class that the first note (do) is C. Ask volunteers to write notes for each phrase on a staff on the board. Have the class sing as many times as necessary, until the following is on the board.

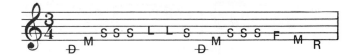

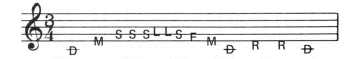

3. Ask the class to clap the rhythm of each phrase as they sing, to determine the note values. Help, if necessary, by telling them the first two notes are eighth notes. Ask volunteers to write the rhythmic notation for the song, helping them by having the class clap rhythm as they sing each phrase. The following should result:

4. Have a volunteer play the first phrase on a recorder. Have the entire class play the first phrase.
5. Continue in the same manner until the class can play the entire song.

Level III

Focusing on Melodic Notation through a Listening Experience
Little Fugue in G Minor by J. S. Bach, RCA *Adventures in Music* grade 6, vol. 1, LES 1009

This experience may be found outlined on page 294, chapter 5, "Listening Experiences."

Level III

Focusing on Melodic Notation through a Listening Experience

"En Bateau," by Debussy, Bowmar *Orchestral Library* recording BOL 066

1. Notate the following on the board:

2. Ask how many beats there are in a measure (six) and what kind of note gets one beat (eighth note). How many beats does a dotted half get? (six) A dotted quarter? (three)
3. Have the class clap and count the rhythm.
4. When they can achieve this, have them sing the melody, with syllables and hand signals.
5. Erase the melody. Display the first theme card that accompanies the recording and play the notes on a melody instrument.
6. Select a volunteer to raise the theme card whenever that theme is heard on the recording. Have the class listen carefully to see that the theme card is held up at the appropriate time, and to try to guess what the composer was trying to express. Play the recording.
7. Discuss, focusing on three repetitions of the theme: twice at the beginning, once at the end. Encourage reactions. Explain that the title means "In a Boat." Children may suggest that the music reminds them of waves, a boat rocking or sailing, a storm brewing, and so on.

Level III

Focusing on Melodic Notation of Chord Tones While Learning a Song

"Love Somebody"

For copy of this song, see chapter 4, "Experiences with Instruments."

1. Make a large copy of the song on a card. Have the children examine the song to discover which resonator bells are needed to play the song. Give these bells to individual children and have them sit in this order: C, D, E, F, G, A, B, C, D, E.
2. Ask children holding middle C, E, and G (C chord) to play, one note at a time as the class sings letter names.
3. Ask the class to find the notes of this chord and the number of times they appear in the song. (three times, on the words "Love somebody")
4. Have children holding the bells play the notes C, E, G, G, as they occur with "Love somebody."
5. Ask the class if the word "yes," skips, or steps, up or down, and to what note.
6. Have the class sing letter names, as the bells play "Love somebody, yes."
7. Follow the same procedure for discovering interval relationships and letter names for "I" and "do."
8. Have the class sing letter names as the bells play "Love somebody; yes, I do!"
9. Ask the class if the same notes appear with "yes, I do!" in any other place.
10. Ask how the "yes, I do!" at the end of line one differs. (Its notes move downward—F, E, D.)
11. Have the class sing letter names, as individuals play the bells, from the beginning of the song to the middle of second line, ending on "yes, I do!"
12. Follow the same procedure to discover how to sing and play the entire song. Have the bells play and the class sing letter names, then words.

Textural Concepts

Level III

Materials Needed
1. Illustrations of texture and no texture
2. Copy of "Blow the Winds Southerly"
3. Autoharp
4. Three melody instruments
5. Copy of recording and theme charts for "Petrouchka" by Stravinsky, Bowmar *Orchestral Library* recording BOL 095.
6. Copy of music and Music Cue charts for evaluation

Music-Reading Activities
1. Learning to sing a three-part round from notation
2. Learning to play and sing a theme in three parts, in connection with a listening experience

Related Musical Activities
1. Singing
2. Playing melody instruments
3. Playing the Autoharp
4. Listening

Conceptual Understandings

1. Music may be homophonic (a melody accompanied by chords) or polyphonic (two or more melodies sounded simultaneously) as in a round or canon.
2. A sequence of tones suggesting part of a scale can often be found in the notation of a melody.

Behavioral Objectives

1. To recognize from notation the difference between music that is homophonic and polyphonic
2. To recognize scale passages in a melody, from notation

Related Arts

Focusing on texture through an experience with visual arts, using pictures of hamburgers (fig. 6.5)

Procedure

1. Focusing on texture through an experience with the visual arts

   The teacher may wish to substitute the experience comparing *Homage on the Square* to *Birds Eye View of the Great New York and Brooklyn Bridge* as described in chapter 2, "Rhythmic Experiences."

   a. Display figure 6.5a and b.
   b. Discuss the differences between the two pictures, asking questions similar to the following:
      (1) Which gives a feeling of a single layer?
      (2) Which suggests several layers?
      (3) Which suggests a single image?
      (4) Which suggests a single taste sensation?
      (5) Which suggests more than one image?
      (6) Which suggests more than one taste sensation, experienced almost simultaneously?
   c. Ask children the following questions:

   Note: The teacher may want to illustrate each question by playing an example on the piano or other instrument.

      (1) Which illustration is most like a single melody?
      (2) Which is most like a song with more than one part?
      (3) If each layer in *b* represented a sound, how many sounds would we be hearing as we looked at it? (five)
   d. Continue discussing the illustrations in relation to music with texture, until children understand that as our eyes see life about us in terms of single and multiple images, our ears *hear* music that is sometimes a single sound, sometimes many sounds simultaneously (which we call texture).
2. Focusing on notational concepts related to texture by learning to sing a round from notation
   a. Notate the first part of "Blow the Winds Southerly" on the board, omitting number counting but printing the words.

Figure 6.5
a, Hamburger; **b**, hamburgers; photographs by Lois Raebeck

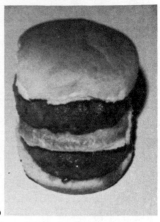

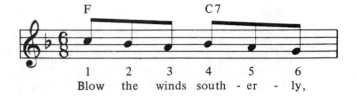

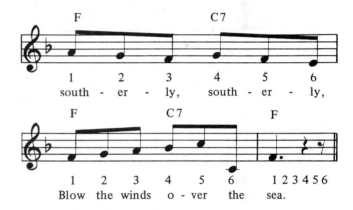

   b. Ask children how many melodies they see. (one)
   c. Have children examine the time signature to discover the type of note that gets one count (eighth note) and the number of beats to a measure (six).
   d. Have the class clap and count the song.
   e. Ask if they see any scale passages.
   f. Ask where do is. (F)
   g. Ask where sol is. (C)
   h. Ask a volunteer to sing the first measure, using syllables and hand signals. Have the entire class sing. (If children have not had adequate experience in singing syllables with hand signals, the teacher may help by teaching the first and second measures.)
   i. Continue exploring the remainder of the song, focusing on movement by steps, except for the last three tones.

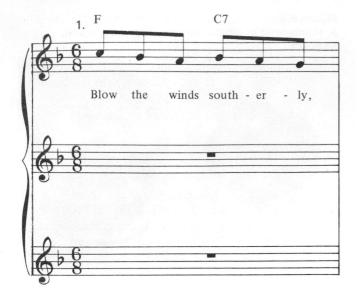

Blow the winds south - er - ly,

sea.

Blow the winds o - ver the

south - er - ly, south - er - ly,

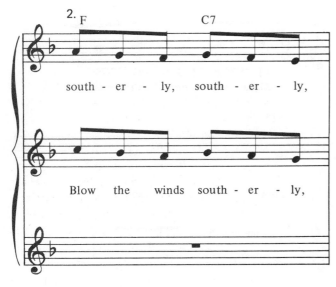

2. south - er - ly, south - er - ly,

Blow the winds south - er - ly,

sea.

Blow the winds o - ver the sea.

j. Select a volunteer to accompany on the Autoharp as children sing the words.

k. Tell children they have just experienced homophonic music (a melody accompanied by chords). Write the word on the chalkboard.

l. Write the second and third parts of the round on the board.

m. Ask the class how many melodies they see. Explain that this is polyphonic music.

n. Ask for a volunteer to point to the three melodies, so that children understand clearly on which staff each melody occurs.

o. Ask children if these three melodies are the same or different.

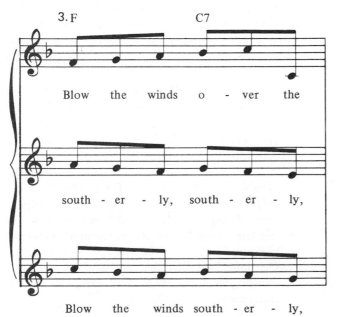

3. Blow the winds o - ver the

south - er - ly, south - er - ly,

Blow the winds south - er - ly,

p. Divide the class into three groups. Signal group 1 to begin. Conduct unobtrusively, bringing in groups 2 and 3 at appropriate times.

3. Focusing on notational concepts related to texture by learning to play and sing a three-part theme in a listening experience (Theme three, "Russian Dance" from *Petrouchka* by Stravinsky, Bowmar *Orchestral Library* recording BOL 095, band 4, side 1)

Note: Before presenting this experience, teach three children to play this theme on melody instruments, each playing one part.

a. Display the theme card that accompanies the record.

b. Ask the class to examine the notation. Ask the following questions:
   (1) Is this a single melody?
   (2) How many parts are being played simultaneously?
   (3) Are any familiar chords outlined? (C major, B minor, D minor, E minor, and A minor) Have a volunteer point to the chords outlined.
   (4) What do we call this kind of music: monophonic, polyphonic, or homophonic?
c. Select volunteers to clap and count the rhythm, then have the class do so.

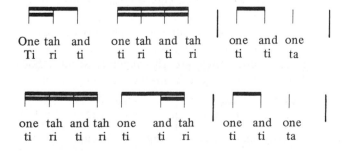

d. When the class can clap and count the rhythm, ask the child who learned the top line to play it for the class as another child points to the notation. Have the class sing it, using a neutral syllable, as the child plays it a second time and the other child points to the notation.
e. Use the procedure in step d to learn the middle line.
f. Divide the class into two groups, half to sing the top line, half to sing the middle line, as children accompany. Repeat until the class can sing both lines with accurate pitch and rhythm.
g. Follow the same procedure for teaching the bottom line, then divide the class into three groups: one to sing the top line on a neutral syllable; one to sing middle line; and one to sing bottom line, with three children accompanying.
h. Tell the class to listen for this theme in a piece of music. Explain that it will be played much faster, so fast they may not recognize it. Play the recording of "Russian Dance."
i. Ask questions similar to the following:
   (1) How many heard the theme?
   (2) Did you hear it many times?
   (3) Was it repeated exactly or with variations?
   (4) Were there other themes?
       (The theme is introduced by a narrator: "The puppets step down from their separate compartments and dance an energetic Russian dance." After two repetitions, many variations using similar rhythm patterns, occasional exact repetitions, and an apparent finale, it is repeated once again. The end is signaled by a series of chords, with a final tone sounded by the trumpet and the drums.)
j. Select a child to hold theme card and tell him to raise it when he hears the theme. Ask the class to raise their hands if a child holding a card "misses" a theme; then select another child to take the card.

4. Evaluating the children's ability to recognize, from notation, the difference between homophonic and polyphonic music
a. Distribute the Music Cue chart.
b. Ask children if they recognize, from notation, homophonic and polyphonic music. Review the definition of each term. Tell them to write the letter H in front of the homophonic phrases and P in front of the polyphonic phrases.
c. Discuss the answers: 1, H; 2, P; 3, P; 4, H.
d. Clarify any misunderstandings by playing the music and discussing the attributes of each phrase.

Music Cue Chart

1.

2.

3.

4.

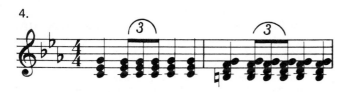

Notational Experiences That Focus on Textural Concepts

For additional music-reading experiences, see the sections in each chapter entitled "Notational Concepts: Music Reading."

Level I

Experiencing Texture by Playing Rhythm Instruments, from Notation, as an Accompaniment to a Chant
"Chickeree, Chickeree, My Little Pup"

1. Write the following on the board, omitting the number and Kodaly counting:

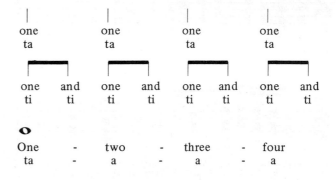

2. Ask for volunteers to clap and count each line, then have the entire class clap and count.
3. Display rhythm instruments. Help children explore which instruments sound best with each note. One class chose the following:

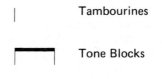

4. Divide the class into three groups: group 1 to play quarter notes; group 2, eighth notes; group 3, whole notes.
5. Have group 1 and group 2 practice playing together until stable, then add group 3. Let all three groups practice until they are rhythmically secure. Have them continue as you begin the following chant.

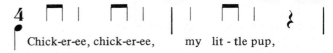

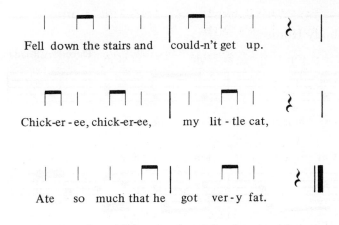

Fell down the stairs and could-n't get up.

Chick-er-ee, chick-er-ee, my lit-tle cat,

Ate so much that he got ver-y fat.

6. Select a few children to chant the rhyme with you as the three groups accompany.
7. Repeat, adding children to the chanting group until the class is equally divided into four groups and children can perform with rhythmic precision.

Level I

Focusing on Texture by Learning to Play, from Notation, a Chant as an Accompaniment to a Song
"Hey, Betty Martin"

For a copy of this song, see chapter 3, "Singing Experiences."
1. Write the following on the board:

Tip - toe, tip - toe

2. Tell the class, that the first note is do. Ask what the second is. (sol)
3. Have them sing the phrase, using syllables, then words, as you point to the notation. Repeat, having a child point to the notation and the class sing, using syllables and hand signals, then words.
4. Ask if anyone knows the letter names. (G and D)
5. Ask who can play these notes on melody bells. Select a child to play the ostinato and several to sing the chant as the class sings the song.

Level II or III

Focusing on Texture by Adding an Accompaniment to a Song
"Every Night When the Sun Goes Down"

1. Teach the song in a manner similar to that described on page 58.
2. Write the following on the board:

Guitar
Strings should be tuned as follows:

Xylophone

Metallophone
(or resonator bells)

3. Have the class examine the notation for each instrument and, through questions, focus on interval relationships.
   a. What chord is outlined by the notes in the bass and treble clefs in the guitar part? (If children have not had experience with the bass clef, the teacher should explain the function of this clef.)
   b. What chord does the xylophone outline?
   c. What syllables does it use, if the tone center is C? (do, sol, do¹, sol)
   d. What syllables does the metallophone part use? (do and sol; mi¹ and re¹)
4. Have the class count and clap each part.
5. Select volunteers to play each part and practice until they are rhythmically stable. Have the guitar begin, add the xylophone two measures later, metallophone four measures later. When all are playing together, have the class sing the song.

Level II or III

Focusing on Texture by Learning a Song in Two Parts from Notation
"He's Got the Whole World in His Hands"

For an additional experience with notation and a copy of this song, see pages 120–122.
1. Display the notation of the song. Ask the class how many parts they see.
2. Have a child point to the top part and another child to the bottom part.
3. Ask if any phrases are repeated. Ask if the melody moves by step, skip, or by repeated tones, and have children point out places where these occur in each part.

Hey, Ho! Nobody Home

Adapted from *101 Rounds for Singing*, published by World Around Songs. Used by permission.

4. Ask children to examine the top line and name the syllable that begins the song. (sol)
5. Ask a volunteer to sing the first phrase, using syllables. If children have difficulty, ask them the syllables, and write them on the board. Have the class sing the phrase using hand signals.

S   S   S   S   S
    M   M   M
        D

6. Help children discover syllables for the second and fourth phrases, until they can sing the entire melody.
7. Help children learn the harmony part in the same way. (The teacher may want to facilitate the process by having a child learn the harmony on a melody instrument, then play it as the class sings the newly learned melody. Gradually add children to the group singing the harmony part until the class is equally divided between melody and harmony.)
8. If there are guitar students in the class, they will enjoy adding another element of texture by accompanying the singing.

Level III

Focusing on Texture and Notation by Adding a Rhythmic Accompaniment while Learning a Song
"Hey, Ho! Nobody Home"

1. Notate this on the board:

(1)   (4)

(2)   (5)

(3)   (6)

2. Ask for volunteers to clap the following numbers: 1; 4; 643 (six, followed by four, followed by three); 5214; 531,246.
3. Write 531,246 on the board. Have the entire class clap this number. If they have difficulty, rearrange the patterns on the board.

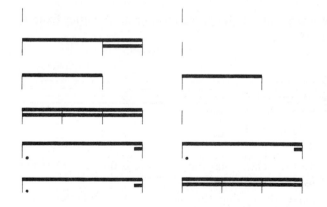

4. When the class can clap the notation, divide into two groups: group 1 to begin and continue clapping; group 2 to begin when group 1 is starting the second pattern. Explain that this is a rhythmic canon.
5. Ask the class to clap a basic beat as you sing "Hey, Ho, Nobody Home." Repeat the song, asking the class to sing with you.
6. Divide the class into two groups and sing the song as a round, clapping the basic beat softly.
7. Repeat, each group clapping the *word* rhythms as they sing.
8. Ask the class to sing the round in unison, as they clap the rhythm of the round as a second part. (Clapping begins when they sing "No-.")
9. Divide the class into two groups and repeat step 8. The second group begins one measure after the first (each group singing in unison, clapping the rhythm

of the round as a second part, which starts one measure behind the melody.)

10. If the class has difficulty, have one group sing and the other clap the rhythm as a second part.

11. Children will enjoy substituting percussion instruments for clapping.

Level III

Focusing on Texture and Notation while Learning a Two-Part Song
"Tina Singu"

1. Sing "Tina Singu" (page 344), accompanying yourself with one of the following:

2. Ask the class to open their books and listen to the part marked *Group,* at the end of first line. Sing these measures:

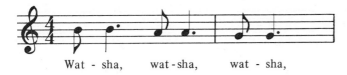

Wat - sha,   wat - sha,   wat - sha,

3. Ask the class to sing it with you.
4. Ask them how many times and where it occurs.
5. Ask these questions:
   a. Does it ascend or descend?
   b. What are the names of the notes?
   c. Can anyone play it on a melody instrument?
6. Select a volunteer to practice, then accompany the class as they sing.
7. Sing the entire song, with the class singing and instrumentalist playing that phrase.
8. Ask if there are other descending phrases in the song. (Yes. The lower part, line four, begins a sequence of three phrases, each of which starts descending on the second note: D, G, F♯, E, D, C; E, A, G, F♯, E, D; A, D, C, B, A, G.)
9. Select a volunteer to play these phrases on a melody instrument. When he can play them easily, have the class sing with him.
10. Ask the class if this sequence is repeated. (Yes. On the last measure of line five, the lower part.)
11. Let someone practice playing both the phrase and sequence described in steps 2–10. Sing the entire song as the class sings the words to these phrases.
12. Repeat, letting other children play the descending melodies as the class sings.

13. When the class knows the melody, teach the high part by singing it as the class sings the melody. Have the class identify the notes. Add individuals to the high part until a balance exists.
14. Children will enjoy creating a dance to accompany the singing.

Concepts Related to Form

Level II or III

Materials Needed
1. Copy of "Deep in the Woods"
2. Rhythm instruments
3. Flash cards
4. Recorders or melody instruments
5. Recording of Minuet by Mozart, Bowmar *Orchestral Library* recording BOL 066
6. Theme charts for Minuet by Mozart (These accompany the recording.)
7. Music Cue charts and music for evaluation procedure

Music-Reading Activities
1. Rhythmic notation of a poem (ABA and ABACA form)
2. Rhythmic and melodic notation from flash cards (AB, ABA, and ABACA form)
3. Rhythmic and melodic notation of themes from Minuet by Mozart

Related Musical Activities
1. Bodily movement—clapping
2. Playing rhythm instruments
3. Listening to music

Conceptual Understanding
AB, ABA, and ABACA (rondo) forms can be recognized from notation.

Behavioral Objective
To recognize AB, ABA, and ABACA (rondo) forms from notation

Related Arts
Focusing on form through an experience with related arts, using a poem, "Deep in the Woods"

Note: In addition, the teacher may want to give children an experience similar to one of the following: chapter 2, "Rhythmic Experiences," p. 46; chapter 3, "Singing Experiences," p. 124; chapter 4, "Experiences with Instruments," p. 221; chapter 5, "Listening Experiences," p. 279.

Introduction (first time only)

Tina Singu

Basutoland Africa

Ti - na sing - u le - lu - vu - tae - o, Wat - sha, wat - sha,

wat - sha, Ti - na, Tin - na sing - u le - lu - vu - tae - o,

wat - sha, wat - sha, wat - sha, wat - sha, la - la - la - la - la

Part 2.

Wat - sha, _____ wat - sha, _____ wat - sha,

la, la - la - la - la - la la, la - la - la - la - la la, la

wat - sha, wat - sha, _____ wat - sha, _____

la - la - la - la - la, la - la - la - la la, la - la - la - la - la

wat - sha, _____   wat - sha,   wat - sha,   wat - sha.

la,   la - la - la - la - la   la,   la - la - la - la - la - la.

Meaning: We are the burning fire; we burn; we burn. (*Tina* means *we*.) Transcribed from the singing of Kathleen Hill.

Procedure

1. Focusing on notational concepts related to form through an experience with related arts
   a. Write the following on the board, omitting the A, B, and A.

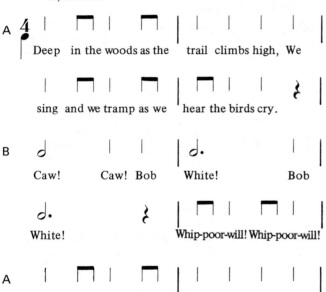

A

Deep in the woods as the trail climbs high, We

sing and we tramp as we hear the birds cry.

B

Caw!   Caw! Bob   White!   Bob

White!   Whip-poor-will! Whip-poor-will!

A

Deep in the woods as the trail end's near, We

shout and we run as we hear the birds cheer.

   b. Have the children clap and chant the poem, using number notation, then words.
   c. Ask the children the form of poem: AB, ABA, or ABACA. (ABA) Have a volunteer point to and label the A and B sections.
   d. Ask for ideas for creating an ABACA (rondo) form. (Children may think of other bird calls or sounds heard in the woods.) One class thought of:

C

Ket-a-ket! Ket-a-ket!   Coo!   Coo!   Ker-

onk!   Ker-onk!   Frahnk! Frahnk! Frahnk!

   e. Write the C and additional A sections on the board, beneath the ABA. Have the class clap and chant using numbers, then words.
   f. Display rhythm instruments. Help the class develop, through experimentation, an orchestration for the poem that reflects the form and expressive elements of each section. One class decided on the following:

A sections	Tone blocks, low drums, temple blocks
B section	Caw! Caw!—cow bell
	Bob White!—triangle
	Whippoorwill!—finger cymbals
C section	Ketakek!—rhythm sticks
	Coo! Coo!—bird whistle
	Keronk!—castanets
	Frahnk!—claves

   g. Have the class recite the poem, as children accompany, using the chosen orchestration. Remind the class to use their voices and instruments expressively.
2. Focusing on notational concepts related to form by creating AB, ABA, and ABACA forms
   a. Display the following flash cards.

(1)

(2)

(3)

  b. Ask the class to examine the three phrases carefully for skips, steps, repeated tones, scale passages, and so on.
  c. Ask who can arrange the cards in such a way that they will create an AB form. As children make different arrangements, play them on a melody instrument and discuss each one. Have children vote for the arrangement they like best. (In all likelihood, they will prefer the first, followed by the third phrase.)
  d. Ask who can arrange the cards for an ABA form. Play each arrangement suggested. Let children vote for the one they like best. (Probably they will like 1, 2, 1 or 1, 3, 1.)
  e. Select children to create an ABACA (rondo) form. Play each arrangement. Let children vote for the one they prefer. (In all likelihood, they will prefer 1, 2, 1, 3, 1.)

  f. When the class has selected arrangements in AB, ABA, and ABACA, teach them to play these on a recorder or other melody instrument.
3. Focusing on notational concepts related to form through a listening experience (Minuet by Mozart)
  a. Prior to this experience, teach two children to play Themes 1 and 2 on a melody instrument.
  b. Display theme charts that accompany the record:

Theme 1

Theme 2

  c. Have children examine notation for Theme 1, asking questions such as the following:
    (1) Are any chords outlined? (Have children play the outlined chords on a melody instrument.)
    (2) Do you see any skips? Where? (Have a child point to the skips.)
    (3) Do you see any steps? Repeated notes? (Have children point to these.)
  d. Have a child play the theme on a melody instrument.
  e. Have children examine Theme 2 and focus on interval relationships by asking questions similar to those in instruction c. (They will notice that scale passages predominate, with few skips or repeated notes.)
  f. Have a child play the theme on a melody instrument.
  g. Tell the class you will play a recording using these themes. Give the chart for each theme to two

children and ask them to raise their chart when they hear their theme played. Play the recording and, as children raise their charts, write the following on the board:

A   A   B   Interlude   A

   h. Ask the class the form of the Minuet.

   i. Children may enjoy creating a dance in the style of the Minuet.

4. Evaluating the children's ability to recognize AB, ABA, and ABACA forms from notation

   a. Distribute Music Cue charts.

Music Cue Chart

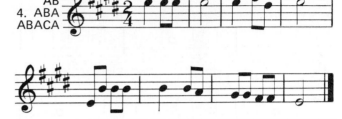

   b. Ask children to examine the notation for each number and circle the form used.

   c. Discuss the answers, clarifying any misconceptions: 1, AB; 2, ABACA; 3, ABA; 4, AB.

Notational Experiences That Focus on Concepts Related to Form

For additional music-reading experiences, see the section in each chapter entitled "Notational Concepts: Music Reading."

Level I

   Focusing on Notational Concepts Related to Form by Creating ABA and ABACA Forms

By using more difficult rhythm patterns, this experience may be used on levels II and III.

1. Write the following on the board, omitting number and Kodaly counting beneath stick notation:

2. Ask for volunteers to clap and count the phrase, using number or Kodaly counting.
3. Have the entire class clap and count the phrase.
4. Tell the class this is A. Write *A* above the phrase.
5. Have a volunteer clap a B phrase, immediately after the class claps A.
6. Repeat, letting other children clap B.

7. Let the class decide which B they like and write it on the board, labeling it *B*. Let us assume they chose the following:

B

8. Remind the class that ABA form consists of two like phrases divided by a phrase that is different. Select a volunteer to add a phrase that will create an ABA form on the board. The following should result:

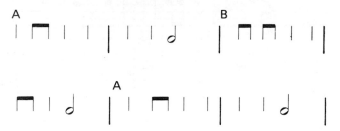

9. Follow a similar procedure for a rondo.
10. Children will enjoy creating an orchestration, using rhythm instruments, which emphasizes the differences between the phrases.

Level II

Focusing on Notational Concepts Related to Form by Creating an Orchestration for an ABA Form
"Africana"

1. Notate the following on the board, omitting syllables beneath the notation:

Africana

Lois Raebeck

L L S M   L L S M   L L T S   L

L L T S   L L T S   L D T S   L

L L S M   L L S M   L L T S   L

2. Have the class carefully examine and discuss the notation, focusing on similar phrases, skips, steps, repeated tones, or scale passages.
3. Ask children the form of this song: AB, ABA, or ABACA.
4. Ask children if there are any repeated patterns in line 1 (section A).
5. Ask volunteers to sing the first two measures, using syllables and hand signals. After several try, have the entire class do this.
6. Ask for volunteers to sing measures 3 and 4; then have the entire class sing.
7. Do the entire song, having the class sing A sections (lines 1 and 3), using syllables and hand signals. You sing the B section alone.
8. Ask for volunteers to sing line 2 with you, as the class sings A sections.
9. Display rhythm instruments. Ask for suggestions for instruments to accompany each section. Let the class experiment and decide on an orchestration they like. One class decided on the following:
   A sections sticks, temple blocks, drums, playing quarter notes | | | |
   B sections triangles, finger cymbals, playing half notes ♩ ♩
10. Ask the class to choose African-sounding words to replace the syllables for each section. One class decided on these:
    A sections Toom-ba, toom-ba, toom-ba, toom-ba, toom-ba, toom-ba, ba!
    B section Kuh-ruh, kuh-ruh, kuh-ruh, kuh-ruh, kuh-ruh, kuh-ruh, kuh!
11. Divide the class into four groups: group 1 to sing A sections; group 2 to sing B; 3 to play A sections; 4 to play B section.

Level II

Focusing on Notational Concepts Related to Form by Learning a Song in ABA Form
"Goodby, Old Paint"

For copy of song, see chapter 2, "Rhythmic Experiences."
1. Project the song from a transparency. (This song is in the public domain.)
2. Sing the chorus and first verse as a child points to the notation.
3. Discuss the text. Ask the class to listen for the number of melodies or sections in the song, as you sing it. (two)
4. Ask for volunteers to point to the two melodies. Discuss their notational differences. (The first melody, A, begins higher than the second, B. B has more repeated tones.)

5. Sing A again, as a child points to the notation.
6. Sing the chorus and first verse again, having the class raise their hands each time they hear A.
7. Tell the class you will sing all three verses. They should sing A with you each time it occurs.
8. Display tone blocks, rhythm sticks and triangles. Ask which might be used to accompany B melody. Let individual children experiment as you sing chorus and first verse, then let class vote on instrument they prefer.
9. Select child to play instrument on B as you sing entire song, class singing A melodies.
10. Ask boys if they know B well enough to sing it. Select several boys to sing, then sing entire song: entire class singing A, boys singing B, child accompanying on rhythm instruments.
11. Help class suggest other variations for singing song:
    a. Boys sing A, girls sing B.
    b. Soloists sing B.
    c. Different accompanying instruments for B.
    d. Adding accompanying instruments for A.
    e. Adding melody bells or recorders to either or both melodies.
    f. Using autoharp accompaniment.

Level III

Focusing on Notational Concepts Related to Form by Learning a Song on the Recorder
"Vesper Hymn"

1. Prepare the following flash cards.

2. Show the first card. Ask if there are any skips. Ask children how to tell whether notes move by step or by skip.
3. Select a volunteer to play the notes of the first card, on a recorder.

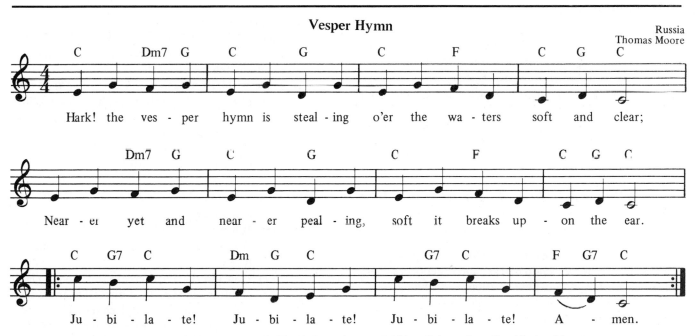

Vesper Hymn

Russia
Thomas Moore

Hark! the ves - per hymn is steal - ing o'er the wa - ters soft and clear;

Near - er yet and near - er peal - ing, soft it breaks up - on the ear.

Ju - bi - la - te! Ju - bi - la - te! Ju - bi - la - te! A - men.

Adapted from *Heritage Songster* by Dallin and Dallin, © 1966 by Wm. C. Brown Company Publishers, Dubuque, Iowa. (in public domain)

4. Show the other cards, asking for volunteers to play each one. Switch cards, until children can play them easily.
5. Place the flash cards on board railing (not in the order of the song).
6. Tell the class you will play the song, and they should tell you which card represents the notation for the first measure. Play the song.
7. Select a volunteer to put the appropriate card at the beginning.
8. Repeat the song, having children arrange the cards in appropriate order.
9. Have children play the song on the recorder.
10. Ask them how many melodies there are. (two) Have a volunteer point to each.
11. Ask the class to name the form. (AB)
12. Ask them how it could be made into ABA form. (by playing first four cards again, at the end)
13. Let children experiment playing the song in ABA form. They may enjoy creating an orchestration for percussion instruments.

Expressive Concepts

Level II or III

Materials Needed

1. Illustrations and poem, "I'm Nobody! Who Are You?" by Emily Dickinson
2. Chart for vocal exploration
3. Copy of "La Raspa"
4. Music Cue charts
5. Recordings
   a. "Running Horses," RCA Victor *Basic Record Library for Elementary Grades* recording WE 71
   b. "Chopin" from *Carnaval* by Schumann and Gla-zounov, Bowmar *Orchestral Library* recording BOL 066
   c. "Clowns" from *Midsummer Night's Dream* by Mendelssohn, RCA Victor *Basic Record Library for Elementary Grades* recording WE 71
   d. March from *Alceste* by Gluck, RCA Victor *Basic Record Library for Elementary Grades* recording WE 72

Music-Reading Activities

Exploring notation of expressive elements (pp, mp, mf, crescendo and decrescendo marks, and others) in experiences with a poem, vocal exploration, and singing

Related Musical Activities
1. Singing
2. Playing rhythm instruments
3. Listening

Conceptual Understandings
1. Our voices and the instruments we play may be used in different ways to produce differences in tone quality and mood.
2. The tempo, dynamics, and other expressive elements used in a musical performance may be notated.

Behavioral Objective
To begin to use expressive markings as a way of indicating dynamics, tempo, and other expressive qualities

Related Arts
Focusing on concepts related to expression through the visual arts and poetry
1. Illustrations figure 6.6a–d
   a. Happy
   b. Sad
   c. Soft
   d. *The Angler,* by Paul Klee
2. Poem, "I'm Nobody! Who Are You?" by Emily Dick-inson

Procedure
1. Focusing on the notation of expressive elements through an experience with the visual arts
   a. Ask children for adjectives that describe different types of music and list their suggestions on the board.

happy	forceful	slow (adagio)
sad	gentle	serious
loud (forte)	humorous	beautiful
soft (piano)	fast (allegro)	bouncy
		flowing

   b. Display pictures similar to those in figure 6.6.
   c. Ask which words on the board describe pictures *a, b,* and *c.* Remind children that music expresses emotions felt by all of us.
   d. Have children examine and discuss *The Angler* by Paul Klee. Ask questions such as those following:
      (1) What is happening in the picture?
      (2) What is unusual about the man?
      (3) On what is he standing, and how is it unusual?
      (4) What is unusual about the head, besides being large?
      (5) What kind of a day is it?
      (6) What word on the board describes this picture?
      (7) How did the artist create this mood? (Help children see the use of distortion and understatement of lines and shapes to create a very special mood related to a fisherman.)
   e. When children have explored *The Angler* fully, ask them to compare the way an artist creates different moods with the way a composer creates

Figure 6.6
a, Happy; **b,** sad; **c,** soft; photographs by Sidney Hecker.
d, *The Angler (Der Angler)* by Paul Klee, 1921. Watercolor, pen and ink, 18⅞ × 12⅜″. Collection, The Museum of Modern Art, New York. John S. Newberry Collection.

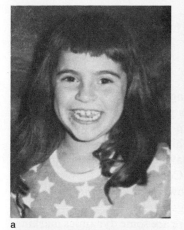
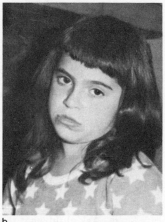

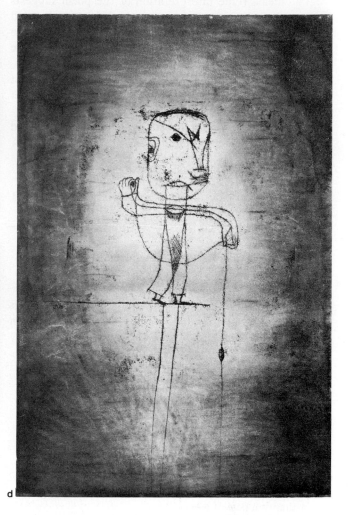

different moods. Write the comparison on the board.

Artist

Use of different kinds of lines, shapes, colors
Changing reality to create different feelings
Use of darks and lights
Exaggerating some things, de-emphasizing others

Composer

Use of different kinds of tempo, dynamics, rhythms, melodies, scales (major, minor, other), tonalities (or no tonality), instruments

2. Focusing on the notation of expressive elements through an experience with a poem ("I'm Nobody! Who Are You?" by Emily Dickinson)

a. Write the poem on the board.

> I'm Nobody! Who are you?
> Are you—Nobody—Too?
> Then there's a pair of us?
> Don't tell! they'd advertise—you know!
>
> How dreary—to be—Somebody!
> How public—like a Frog—
> To tell one's name—the livelong June—
> To an admiring Bog!
>
> by Emily Dickinson

Reprinted by permission of the publishers and the Trustees of Amherst College from *The Poems of Emily Dickinson,* edited by Thomas H. Johnson, Cambridge, Mass.: The Belknap Press of Harvard University Press, Copyright © 1955 by the President and Fellows of Harvard College.

b. Read the poem to children and have them say it with you.

c. Discuss the meaning with children, eliciting their ideas. (One interpretation of the poem suggests that there is such a universal drive to be well known—famous—that someone who is content to be a simple person is considered strange; but the poet considers being famous dreary.)

d. Ask the class if they think the poem would best be said allegro (quickly) or adagio (slowly). Let them experiment.

e. Write this on the board, omitting definitions, and ask children to define each:

pp　　*mp*　　*p*　　*mf*　　*f*　　*ff*

Very Soft　Moderately　Soft　Moderately　Loud　Very Loud
　　　　　Soft　　　　　Loud

Crescendo: Gradually　　　　Decrescendo: Gradually
Getting Louder　　　　　　　Getting Softer

f. Ask children which of these expressive markings they would like to use for each line of the poem (first verse). Let them experiment until they decide. Do the same for the second verse. One class chose the following:

pp

I'm Nobody! Who are you?

mp

Are you – Nobody -- Too?

mf

Then there's a pair of us?

Don't tell! they'd advertise -- you know!

mp

How dreary – to be -- Somebody!

mf

How public – like a Frog –

To tell one's name – the livelong June –

To an admiring Bog!

3. Exploring the notation of expressive elements through an experience with vocal exploration:
   a. Draw this on the board or a large cardboard.

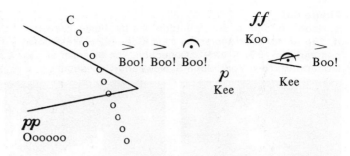

b. Explain the markings: a low-pitched voice should be used for sounds placed low; a middle-pitched voice for sounds in center; a high-pitched voice for sounds placed high.

c. As you conduct, have children make sounds, following the score. Continue until they can make sounds freely, following the dynamics and other notational markings easily.

d. Ask children if there are some dynamics markings or sounds they would like to change. Encourage them to experiment for the most expressive dynamics and sounds. (Children may wish to add more sounds.)

4. Exploring notation of expressive elements through singing and orchestrating a familiar song ("La Raspe")
(Children should know the song prior to this experience.)

a. Have children sing "La Raspe."

b. Ask if their singing expressed the text.
   (1) Was the tempo correct?
   (2) Were the dynamics appropriate?
   (3) Was the mood appropriate?

c. Through discussion and experimentation, help children decide how they want to sing the song.

d. Tell the class to notate the tempo and dynamic markings they chose. Place notation of the song on the board, and help children write appropriate expressive markings above it. One class decided on the dynamics shown for "La Raspe" in this section.

e. Have the class sing the song, following dynamic markings notated.

f. Display rhythm instruments. Encourage children to experiment with different instruments and rhythm patterns as they sing, until they create an orchestration that reflects the expressive qualities. One class chose the following:

First and second lines　castanets and maracas

End of first and second lines (final syllable of "tambourine" and "queen")　tambourines shake

La Raspe

Allegro

mf — G — D7 — Tr. Maurice Talbot

With click-ing of cas-ta-nets and jing-le of tam-bour-ine, All

work of the day for-got, and danc-ing to-night is queen, We're

danc-ing a dance from old Mex-i-co, La la la la la la; Our

steps light and gay and our hearts a-glow, La la la la la la.

Adapted from arrangement from *Heritage Songster* by Dallin and Dallin, © 1966 by Wm. C. Brown Company Publishers, Dubuque, Iowa. (in public domain)

Beginning of third and fourth lines ("dancing a dance from old Mexico" and "steps light and gay and our hearts a-glow") tone blocks and rhythm sticks

End of third and fourth lines ("La la la la la la") castanets and maracas

Sixth "la" in third and fourth lines tambourines shake

g. Divide the class into two groups, one to sing, one to accompany on rhythm instruments. Remind all to follow the markings notated. Give the signal to begin, and conduct.

h. Encourage children to make any changes in expressive qualities and repeat, having different children play the instruments.

5. Evaluating children's ability to relate notational symbols to expressive qualities of music
   a. Distribute Music Cue charts.

Music Cue Chart								
1.	*pp*	*mp*	*p*	*mf*	*f*	*ff*	*allegro*	*adagio*
2.	*pp*	*mp*	*p*	*mf*	*f*	*ff*	*allegro*	*adagio*
3.	*pp*	*mp*	*p*	*mf*	*f*	*ff*	*allegro*	*adagio*
4.	*pp*	*mp*	*p*	*mf*	*f*	*ff*	*allegro*	*adagio*

b. Make sure that children understand the notational symbols on the charts.

c. Tell children you will play four recordings, and they should circle the notational symbols that apply to each. For example, if the first recording is very loud and slow, they will circle *ff* and *adagio*. If it is moderately soft and fast, they will circle *mp* and *allegro*. Play the recordings. (The teacher may want to substitute other recordings for those listed.)
   (1) "Running Horses": primarily *mf* and *allegro*
   (2) "Chopin" from *Carnaval* by Schumann and Glazounov: primarily *pp* and *adagio*
   (3) "Clowns" from *Midsummer Night's Dream* by Mendelssohn: primarily *pp* and *allegro*
   (4) March from *Alceste* by Gluck: primarily *f* and *adagio*

d. Discuss children's answers, which may vary without being wrong.

Individualizing Music Reading

Listed below are activities that will help individual children reinforce concepts previously experienced in large groups.

Level II

> *Roll-a-Note Game*
> For two or three players

Copy the ("Roll-a-Note Game" and Answer Sheet) on heavy cardboard, then laminate.

Roll-a-Note Game

Instructions: Player 1 rolls the dice, then identifies the note indicated by the number on the dice. Other players check his answer. If he identifies the note correctly, he gets one point. Players alternate turns. The first player to win fifteen points wins the game.

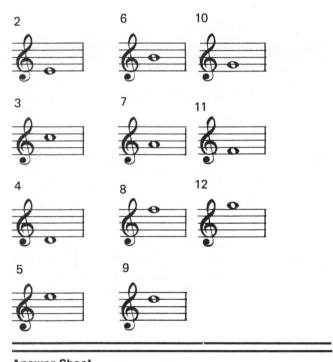

Answer Sheet

2. E	6. B	10. G
3. C¹	7. A	11. F
4. D	8. F¹	12. G¹
5. E¹	9. D¹	

Level II

> *Note Identification Game*
> For one child

Reproduce the following. Copy the Answer Sheet on heavy cardboard and laminate.

Note Identification Game

Instructions: Write the note names under each note. Each pattern spells a word. Check against the Answer Sheet. Write a story using ten words from these patterns. Play the words on a recorder, piano, or Orff instrument, as you read your story to the class.

Answer Sheet

1. Cafe	2. Baggage	3. Egg	4. Fad
5. Bee	6. Fade	7. Bead	8. Bed
9. Cabbage	10. Age	11. Dad	12. Badge
13. Cage	14. Bag	15. Bed	16. Deaf
17. Face	18. Cab	19. Deed	20. Ad
21. Feed	22. Beg	23. Add	24. Bad

Level II

Note-Writing Game

For one child

Reproduce the "Note-Writing Game." Copy the Answer Sheet on cardboard and laminate.

Note-Writing Game

Instructions: Place a whole note on the line or space each letter suggests. Check against the Answer Sheet. Make up a story using ten of the words on this sheet. Learn to sing or play the words on a melody instrument and perform them as you read the story to the class.

Answer Sheet

For a more advanced experience, the teacher may give children the following.

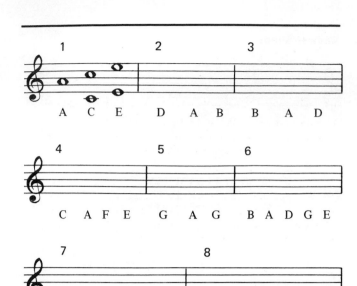

A C E D A B B A D

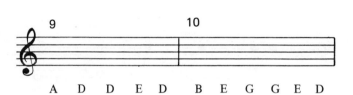

C A F E G A G B A D G E

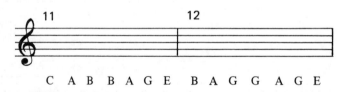

F A D E D F A C E D

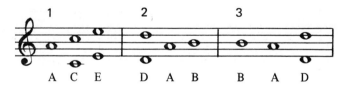

A D D E D B E G G E D

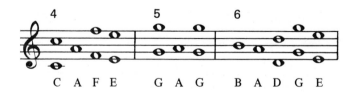

C A B B A G E B A G G A G E

Answer Sheet

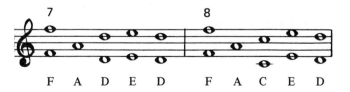

A C E D A B B A D

C A F E G A G B A D G E

F A D E D F A C E D

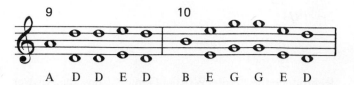

A D D E D B E G G E D

C A B B A G E B A G G A G E

Level II

Roll-a-Melody Game No. 1
For two or three players

Reproduce the following. Copy the Answer Sheet on heavy cardboard and laminate.

Roll-a-Melody Game No. 1

Instructions: Player 1 rolls the dice. If he can clap the rhythm of the pattern indicated by the number on the dice, he gets one point. If he can name the notes he gets one point. If he can play the melody on the recorder or melody bells he gets two points. Other players check answers. Players take turns. The first player with twenty points wins.

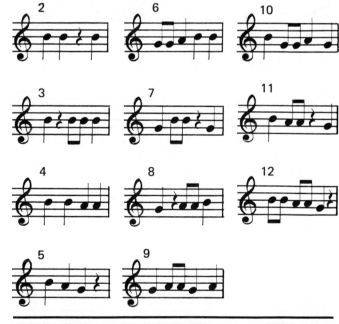

Answer Sheet

2. B B rest B
3. B rest BB B
4. B B A A
5. B A G rest

6. GG A B B
7. G BB rest G
8. G rest AA B
9. G AA G A

10. B GG A G
11. B AA rest G
12. BB AA G rest

Level II

Equal Values Game
For one child

Reproduce the following. Copy the Answer Sheet on heavy cardboard and laminate.

Equal Values Game

Instructions: Examine each note symbol. Indicate the number of notes (written out) needed to equal the value of the note symbol. Check against the Answer Sheet.
Example: =   2 half notes

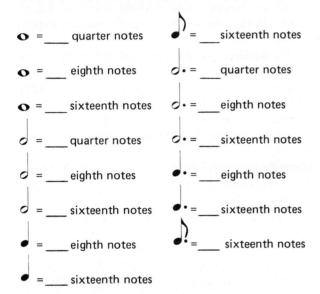

𝅝 = ___ quarter notes   ♪ = ___ sixteenth notes

𝅝 = ___ eighth notes   𝅗𝅥• = ___ quarter notes

𝅝 = ___ sixteenth notes   𝅗𝅥• = ___ eighth notes

𝅗𝅥 = ___ quarter notes   𝅗𝅥• = ___ sixteenth notes

𝅗𝅥 = ___ eighth notes   ♩• = ___ eighth notes

𝅗𝅥 = ___ sixteenth notes   ♩• = ___ sixteenth notes

♩ = ___ eighth notes   ♪• = ___ sixteenth notes

♩ = ___ sixteenth notes

Answer Sheet

𝅝 = _4_ quarter notes   ♪ = _2_ sixteenth notes

𝅝 = _8_ eighth notes   𝅗𝅥• = _3_ quarter notes

𝅝 = _16_ sixteenth notes   𝅗𝅥• = _6_ eighth notes

𝅗𝅥 = _2_ quarter notes   𝅗𝅥• = _12_ sixteenth notes

𝅗𝅥 = _4_ eighth notes   ♩• = _3_ eighth notes

𝅗𝅥 = _8_ sixteenth notes   ♩• = _6_ sixteenth notes

♩ = _2_ eighth notes   ♪• = _3_ sixteenth notes

♩ = _4_ sixteenth notes

Level III

Roll-a-Melody Game No. 2
For two or three children

Reproduce the following. Copy the Answer Sheet on heavy cardboard and laminate.

Roll-a-Melody Game No. 2

Instructions: Player 1 rolls the dice. If he can clap the rhythm of the pattern indicated by the number on the dice, he gets one point. If he can name the notes he gets one point. If he can play the melody on a recorder or melody bells he gets two points. Other players check the answers. Players take turns. The first player to get twenty points wins.

Answer Sheet

2. B AB CB A   6. GA BA G D   10. B G BC D
3. C GG C G   7. DC DC B B   11. D B CA G
4. AB CD CB A   8. D AA D rest   12. GA B DC D
5. D CB A G   9. D CD BA G

Level III

Total the Beats Game
For one child

Reproduce the following. Copy the Answer Sheet on a large cardboard and laminate. Have children check their own work.

Total the Beats Game

Instructions: Add the number of beats indicated by each pattern and put the number in the empty space to the right of the pattern. Check against the Answer Sheet.

Example   ♪| . + ▬ + ♩. = 7/7
                2 + 2 + 3 = 7/7

1. ♪| . + ♫ + ▬ = ___ .   11. ⊞ + ♫ + ⁶₄ + ♫³ = ___ .
2. ♩. + |. ♪ = ___ .   12. ⊞³ + ♩ + ▬ = ___ .
3. ⊞ + |. ⁷ + ♩ = ___ .   13. ♫ + | + ♩. = ___ .
4. ⁷ + ⊞³ + |. ♪ = ___ .   14. o + ♫ + | + ♫³ = ___ .
5. ♩ + ⊞ + |. ⁷ = ___ .   15. ⊞ + ♫ + ♫³ = ___ .
6. ⊞ + ♩ + ▬ = ___ .   16. |. ♪ + ⊞ + ♪³ = ___ .
7. ♫ + ▬ + |. ⁷ = ___ .   17. ▬ + ♫ + ⁷ ♪³ = ___ .
8. o + ⊞³ = ___ .   18. |. ⁷ + ⊞ + ♩ = ___ .
9. ⊞³ + ♩. + ⁷ = ___ .   19. o + ⊞ + |. ♪ = ___ .
10. ♫ + |. ♪ + ⊞³ = ___ .   20. |. ♪ + ⊞³ ♪ ⁷ = ___ .

Answer Sheet

1. 5	6. 5	11. 4	16. 5
2. 5	7. 7	12. 5	17. 4
3. 5	8. 5	13. 5	18. 5
4. 4	9. 5	14. 7	19. 7
5. 5	10. 4	15. 3	20. 4

Class Discussions and Reports

1. Discuss the theory that the child who has begun to internalize musical concepts is ready to begin learning to read music.
2. Write a report discussing experiences, understandings, and skills needed prior to the first experience with musical notation.
3. Discuss possible ways of introducing children to notation, giving the advantages and disadvantages of each.
4. Discuss the use of music books in learning to read music. Outline approaches that make optimal use of books, as well as approaches that produce negative results.
5. Write a report describing how you learned to read music.
6. Examine the list of music-reading activities. Discuss these, focusing on the following:
   a. The importance of internalizing activities involving rhythms, singing, and instruments
   b. Ways in which music-reading activities can be interwoven with other experiences so that music reading occurs slowly, without a feeling of drill, and in the context of enjoyable musical experiences
   c. The development of music reading in each activity (rhythms, singing, instrumental) from notation as a related concept, to notation as the primary focus.
7. Discuss the approaches of Madeleine Carabo-Cone and Beatrice Royt as an aid in teaching music reading.
8. Discuss ways to use experiences with notation to focus on concepts related to rhythm, melody, form, texture, and expression.
9. Prepare a strategy for level I or II, focusing on notational concepts related to melody, rhythm, or form. Include related musical activities, a related arts experience, a means of evaluation, and specific conceptual understandings and behavioral objectives.
10. Discuss various ways of individualizing experiences with musical notation.
11. Prepare an individualized activity.
12. Observe a music-reading experience in an elementary classroom. Describe the approach, materials, activities, and responses of children. Explain how you might improve the experience.
13. Discuss the general suggestions throughout this chapter in relation to creativity verses rigidity. Explain how they may be used creatively in a teaching situation.
14. Examine the Music Cue charts at the end of each conceptual focus. Discuss how they could be more effective as evaluation materials.
15. Using the chart that follows, log all successful music-reading activities. This may be a basis for an expanding source of music-reading activities.
16. Peruse *Orff and Kodaly Adapted for the Elementary School* by Lawrence Wheeler and Lois Raebeck (Wm. C. Brown Company Publishers, Dubuque, Iowa) for approaches in exploring notation. Discuss these with the class.

Activities to Develop Skills and Practice in Initiating Musical Experiences

1. Study the strategy for level I, "Rhythmic Concepts." Make any changes that would make the plan more effective. Initiate and guide this experience. Evaluate it in terms of the response and the degree to which conceptual understandings and behavioral objectives were achieved.

2. Select an experience suggested under "Notational Experiences that Focus on Rhythmic Concepts." Create a strategy with this as the music-reading experience. State the conceptual understandings and behavioral objectives. Add other pertinent musical activities and an experience with related arts. Initiate and guide the experience. Evaluate it through discussion.

3. Examine the sequence for singing intervals, using syllables and hand signals on page 328, "Melodic Concepts." Give your class an experience echo singing these intervals. Evaluate it through discussion, focusing on how it is valuable preparation for later sight-singing experiences.

4. Select a familiar song that has a short, repeated phrase and is appropriate for a beginning music-reading experience for level I. Prepare a plan for a reading experience in which children learn to play the repeated phrase on song bells or another melody instrument. Add related musical activities and a related arts experience, if appropriate. State conceptual understandings, behavioral objectives and materials needed. Initiate and guide the experience. Evaluate it through discussion.

5. Select a familiar song for level II in which the melody outlines a chord. Prepare a music-reading experience in which the guitar and Autoharp, or both, are used to help perceive the chord outline in the melody. State the materials needed, related musical experiences, conceptual understandings, behavioral objectives and a related arts experience. Initiate and guide the experience for the class. Evaluate it through discussion.

6. Prepare a reading experience for level III in which children learn to play or sing a theme prior to a listening experience. Interweave this with another musical experience (or experiences) and prepare a strategy stating materials needed, related musical experiences, conceptual understandings, behavioral objectives, a related arts experience and criteria for evaluation. Initiate and guide the experience. Evaluate it through discussion.

7. Select one of the experiences suggested in "Notational Experiences that Focus on Melodic Concepts." Create a strategy using related arts and other activities. State the conceptual understandings and behavioral objectives, materials needed, and evaluation procedure. Initiate and guide the experience. Evaluate it through discussion.

8. Examine the strategy for level III in which children focus on homophonic and polyphonic music. Make any changes needed to create a more effective experience. Initiate and guide the experience. Evaluate the results through discussion.

9. Examine the song experience using "Tina Singu." Using this as a focus, prepare a strategy for level III that incorporates related musical activities and a related arts experience. State conceptual understandings, behavioral objectives and materials needed. Initiate and guide the experience. Evaluate it through discussion.

10. Examine one of the strategies for level II or III in "Concepts Related to Form" or "Expressive Concepts." Make any changes needed to create a more effective experience. Initiate and guide the experience. Evaluate it through discussion.

11. Examine the suggestions for individualizing music-reading experiences. Select several that you believe would be effective. Create others. Use them with the class. Evaluate, through discussion, the effectiveness of each, and make suggestions for improvement.

Music-Reading Activities Evaluation Chart

Level	Music-Reading Activity				Conceptual Understandings	Behavioral Objectives	Related Arts	Evaluation
	Rhythmic Experience	Singing Experience	Instrumental Experience	Listening Experience				

Music in Special Activities
Special Clubs and Assembly Programs

7

Music cannot be departmentalized. It relates too persistently to other activities and areas of life. Though it fits naturally into the classroom as a subject in its own right, as well as a correlative of other subjects, its expressive qualities encourage its use outside the classroom. Because, for example, music can be such a satisfying medium for expressing feelings, we look for ways of insuring that the child will learn to use it as an expressive art throughout his life. The experience of belonging to a music group helps, to some degree, to accomplish this purpose. And so we take music out of the classroom and into special clubs such as chorus, guitar, ukulele, and recorder clubs, bands, orchestras, and small ensembles.

We discover that music can serve purposes which, though not primarily musical, are properly related to music. In school assembly programs, we see a prime example of this as music is used to (1) set a mood; (2) establish the character of a person; (3) express an emotion quickly; (4) add variety interest, and color to the program; and (5) give opportunities for individual and group participation.

The elementary school that encourages use of music in special clubs and assembly programs finds vitality added to its overall program. In addition, these activities fulfill certain needs of the participants, which may not be fulfilled in any other way. These will be discussed more thoroughly later. In general they provide the following:

1. An opportunity for individualized attention to musical interests and needs
2. An opportunity to experience music as an expressive art, on a more advanced level than is possible in the classroom
3. An opportunity to consolidate the feeling that music has a value and meaning of its own
4. The opportunity to experience the satisfaction and growth that comes from working with a cohesive group on a constructive project
5. An opportunity for individual musical expression

Special Clubs

In most schools it is the music consultant or specialist who organizes and directs clubs. It is he who must ultimately decide (1) what clubs are most desirable and feasible; (2) how to select members; (3) when and for how long these clubs should meet; (4) what, in general, should occur in the time allotted for club meetings; (5) how to deal with problems involving organizational operation; and (6) what the goals and growth objectives of each organization should be.

Although these questions should be discussed and policy developed with the school administrators, it is the responsibility of the music specialist to initiate special activities and to implement the policies formed.

Though there are many clubs that can be organized, recorder clubs and chorus are perhaps most useful to the child and, because of time limitation, are the ones most often found in the elementary school. Other clubs that are sometimes organized are sing clubs (to help the weak singer), guitar and ukulele clubs, and Autoharp clubs.

Chorus

While choruses exist in almost every elementary school, there are many questions to answer before organizing such a group. First and foremost, who should be allowed to join? Should the chorus be for talented children only, or for any child who wants to sing? Should it consist of children from the fourth, fifth, and sixth grades or from the latter two grades only? Should it include 50 or 150 members?

These questions must be answered by each teacher in a way that satisfies himself as well as the school policy. All answers evolve from the type of club it is to be: a special group that serves needs not met in the classroom, or a group that augments classroom activities.

The teacher who allows any child to join, gives chorus experience to many more children—some of whom may never have the opportunity to participate in such a club. There is a risk, however, of having an oversized group whose singing lacks quality and whose morale is hard to maintain because of this.

The teacher who has a very select group, chosen on the basis of demonstrated ability to sing in tune with precise rhythm, knows these children are receiving the opportunity for advanced singing experiences.

There are alternative solutions to this problem. One is to have two clubs, one for a talented group and one for all children who wish to join. These groups can be organized so that the large voluntary group is composed of

Chorus Audition Sheet

Teacher _____ Grade _____ Room _____

Child's Name	Rhythmic Aptitude	Intonation	Quality	Range	Tonal Memory	Part

fourth and fifth graders, while the select group is from the sixth grade. The select group may be part of the larger group, thus giving support to their singing; they would also meet alone once a week to learn more difficult songs.

Another alternative is to have sing clubs for each grade level. Sing clubs, organized to help weak singers who want to sing with a group, often improve and develop singing ability so that children can qualify for chorus membership. Either of these alternatives seems better than organizing only one group.

Singing two or three short songs can be the test for membership in a selected chorus. This test is usually sufficient, since it enables the teacher to determine whether each child can sing in tune with a steady, flowing rhythm. If further information about a child's musical ability is desired, the teacher may give an aural and rhythmic aptitude test. An audition chart, similar to the sample above, is helpful.

Chorus rehearsals are most enjoyable and productive when the group meets twice each week for forty to fifty minutes. It is possible, though difficult, to function with only one rehearsal a week. In such a case, it is necessary to arrange additional rehearsals for parts and soloists when preparing for a concert.

Most groups will enjoy vocalises that help improve their singing. There are many vocalises and ideas about development of vocal technic. Each teacher must decide which are most helpful. Standard vocalises, which can help improve range, tone quality, and strengthen the diaphragm, are found in this section. (Chords indicated are for piano.)

The nature of the music to be experienced varies with the type of group. The select chorus will enjoy singing fine art songs in unison, two-part songs, and an occasional three-part song. They will enjoy working in small groups (before and after school or during lunch periods) to write and practice original operettas and to rehearse solos and small ensembles. They will enjoy and be capable of giving excellent concerts and operettas.

The nonselect chorus, open to all, will vocalize, sing many unison songs, simple two-part songs, songs with descants and counter melodies, and songs with solo parts, for a well-balanced repertoire.

At best, the nonselect group is large (usually between 75 and 125) and organizational problems can interfere seriously with its work. As in all groups, it is well to give members opportunity to express their opinions about rules and regulations; however, the final decisions in matters of procedure and organization must be made by the teacher. What are some of these problems?

1. Finding a place for such a large group to meet
2. Getting members to and from rehearsals quickly and quietly
3. Establishing a seating plan that insures that members find their seats quickly
4. Arranging for the distribution and collection of music so that a minimum of rehearsal time is wasted

To Increase Range

Continue as high as children can sing (at least an octave), then descend chromatically as low as they can sing (at least to G below middle C).

To Improve Tone Quality

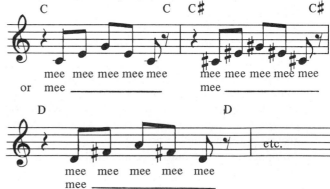

Continue to high G above high C, then descend. Other syllables that may be used: may, mah, mow, moo, any combination of these vowel sounds.

To Strengthen the Diaphragm

vah - ah ah hah hah hah hah

vah - ah ah hah hah hah hah etc.

Continue up to high C.

The teacher must insist upon having a large room in which a piano and chairs are placed in a satisfactory arrangement. When space is available and the administration knows the need, provision will normally be made for rehearsals.

How can chorus members get to and from rehearsals quickly and quietly? One good arrangement is to have the teacher, for the first few rehearsals, call for children from each class and return them after rehearsals, suggesting that they come and go in line, quickly and quietly. Since calling for children is time consuming, he should soon use monitors to help children come and go by themselves.

Should there be a seating plan? If so, how should it operate? Allowing children to sit where they please can create problems of many kinds. For example, part-singing becomes difficult when children change from one seat to another—and thus from one part to another, perhaps causing both themselves and those around them to sing off pitch. Precious hours are wasted as children respond negatively to lack of organization. How, then, can a seating plan operate to effectively organize a large group quickly? How can music be distributed efficiently?

Both these problems can be solved simply by providing each child with a folder upon which her name and number has been printed. These folders, containing the music to be rehearsed, can be placed on children's chairs before rehearsal.

Who prints the names on folders? Who places the folders on chairs and collects them so they are in proper order for the next rehearsal? Children, especially "problem" children, will be delighted to help when selected for this "most important" role.

Discipline of large groups can be a major concern unless the teacher solves the problems of organization. It can also be minimized when the teacher, with the group, devises a set of rules to be carefully and consistently followed. These rules must clearly state when children are allowed to talk, how they come to and from rehearsals, and so on. Children who are less cooperative can be given special tasks, such as collecting folders or moving the

piano, which make them feel needed and thus more cooperative. When this approach does not seem to help, a private conference with the child will often convey to her the necessity of her help and cooperation. If all approaches fail, the child may have to be warned about possible removal from the group.

The teacher will have to take responsibility for the goal of the chorus. He will want the children to perform for assemblies and at concerts. What, how, and why they sing depends very much on the teacher. When they sing music because they enjoy singing it, performances are valuable experiences and will remain vital memories throughout their lives. When other less valid motives are fostered, children sense and accept these as being proper values. It behooves the teacher to encourage children to accept the highest goal—the joy of singing beautiful music.

Recorder Clubs

Recorder clubs are best organized as an outgrowth of a program initiated in the third grade, wherein children are given basic instruction on the instrument. These clubs are generally organized to provide additional opportunities for children who show unusual interest and ability and are unable to nurture this skill by participating in other instrumental activities (band and orchestral instruments).

The objective of the third grade recorder program is to give every child the opportunity to participate. The objective of the fourth grade club, on the other hand, is to give further opportunity for the child who showed special interest and ability in the third grade.

The problem of selecting members for these groups is not difficult. The test given to determine eligibility need not be complex.

1. Have each child play whatever songs he may remember, with or without the use of a score.
2. Have each child answer a few questions that reveal her understanding and knowledge of note values and pitch names.
3. For children with no previous experience on recorder, give an aural test, having the child identify which is high and which is low of two notes played on a melody instrument. Also give a rhythmic perception test, having the child imitate rhythm patterns clapped by the teacher.

Children who are interested in playing the recorder, or have the innate ability to learn, will come to the attention of the teacher. Membership in these clubs must be limited. Fifteen children is generally sufficient.

A good schedule should provide for a meeting at least once a week of from thirty to fifty minutes duration, with fifty minutes being preferable.

What shall children experience at their meetings? This depends, of course, upon what they have experienced previously. Let us assume that the average child in the third grade learns to play songs in 2/4, 3/4, and 4/4 meter, using quarter, eighth, half, dotted half, and whole notes, all played at a moderate tempo. These meters and note values will be reviewed by the fourth grader, who will play songs at a faster tempo, with more agility. In addition, she will learn more complex songs: they will be lengthier, contain increasingly difficult skips, include sixteenth notes, and be in parts as well as in unison. Further, the club will be able to create songs, and perform solos and marching-in music for assembly programs. The particular music the children learn is not important when selection of music provides continued use of past knowledge, is challenging, of high calibre, musically interesting, and promotes feelings of success, enjoyment, and achievement.

Organizational problems for clubs such as these, which do not have large memberships, are not difficult. In general, it is helpful for the teacher to remember that fourth-grade children, while wanting to participate in planning, also appreciate clearly defined limits. Thus, children will appreciate having assigned seats. They will respond well when the teacher has very concrete suggestions concerning which songs might be learned and the best way to play them. On the other hand, fourth-grade children do enjoy having their ideas considered in these and all major decisions, and will cooperate more readily when the teacher asks for and uses their ideas.

The goal of the club will be strongly influenced by the teacher. Essentially, the problem is whether enjoyment of the club expeience itself or presentation of a musical program should be the goal.

Because of the need for enjoyable musical programs that demonstrate learning, it is easy for the goals to become distorted. It will, indeed, take much effort to prevent such goal distortion. It is unfortunate when the concert performance becomes the sole reason for the club's existence. Is it not better that children learn to practice and play for their own satisfaction and enjoyment? Performance then becomes a natural outgrowth of healthy, constructive activity. The child's attitude then becomes one of self-satisfaction and a wish to share his playing ability by performing for others.

Guitar Clubs

Guitar clubs are most successful when initiated on level III, at which time children have developed the physical maturity to hold and play the guitar without too much difficulty.

The teacher planning to organize a guitar club will have to answer the following questions:

1. How large should it be? It is well to keep the club small enough to enable the teacher to help tune each guitar and give individual help. Eight or ten children are suggested as a maximum number.
2. How long should it meet? Forty-five minutes is a minimum length, one hour preferable.
3. How does one supply children with good guitars? Guitars should be chosen for the comfort of the player: they should not be too large or small; they should strum easily; strings should be easily pressed to frets; the tone should be pleasing; they should be free of neck warpage. Arrangements can often be made with local merchants to rent or purchase suitable guitars.
4. How can children be helped to take care of guitars? Children should be advised to provide a case for the guitar, to avoid bumps and excessive temperature or moisture changes.
5. What is a good sequence to follow in teaching children how to play the guitar?
   a. An introduction to the guitar in the classroom. (See chapter 4.)
   b. Learning to tune the guitar:
      (1) Tune the sixth string to E, an octave and five notes below middle C.
      (2) Place a finger below (toward tuning pegs) the fifth fret of the sixth string. Play both fifth and sixth strings simultaneously. Match pitches.
      (3) Place a finger below the fifth fret of the fifth string. Play both fifth and fourth strings. Match pitches.
      (4) Place a finger below the fifth fret of the fourth string. Match pitches of the third and fourth strings.
      (5) Place a finger below the fourth fret of the third string. Match ptiches of the second and third strings.
      (6) Place a finger below the fifth fret of the second string. Match pitches of the first and second strings.
   c. Learning how to read a chord diagram: position the left hand to finger chords and strum an accompaniment to a one-chord song, using one or more of the chords in figure 7.3.

Figure 7.1
The strings of the guitar are numbered 1 to 6 beginning at the right as the guitar faces you. Match string 1 to the E on the piano above middle C or high E on a pitchpipe. Middle C is the C nearest the center of the piano, often near the lock. From *Guitar in the Classroom* by Timmerman and Griffith © 1971 by Wm. C. Brown Company Publishers, Dubuque, Iowa.

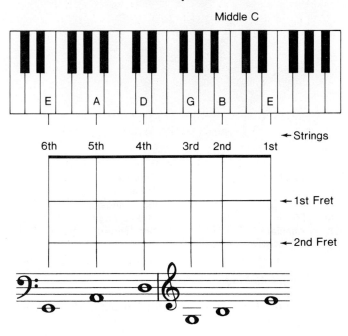

Figure 7.2
Left hand. Photograph by David Rosenthal. (Numbers above left-hand fingers will appear in chord diagrams.)

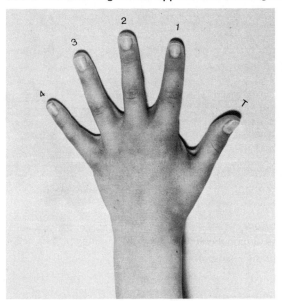

Figure 7.3
a, C chord; **b,** G chord; **c,** D chord; **d,** E minor chord. Numbers and letters on top of string symbols refer to the name and number of each string. Numbers in circles indicate which finger of the left hand should press the string at which fret. *O* above the string is an indication that the string should be played, along with strings on which fingering is marked.

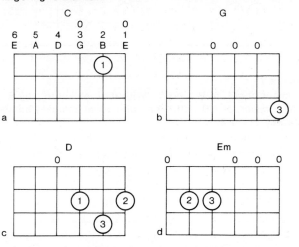

d. Learning how to alternate between C and G_7 chords and accompany a song using these chords.

Figure 7.4
G_7 chord

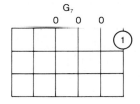

e. Learning how to play the A_7 chord: alternate between D and A_7 chords and accompany a song using these chords.

Figure 7.5
A_7 chord

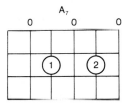

f. Learning to accompany three-chord songs in D major, using D, G, and A_7 chords.
g. Learning additional chords (fig. 7.6–7.8) and accompaniments that follow.

Figure 7.6

a, A major chord. **b,** E₇ chord. (With their ability to play D major, A major, and E₇, children may play songs in the key of A major.)

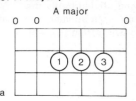
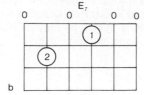

A major

E₇

a   b

Figure 7.7

a, A minor chord. **b,** B₇ chord. (With their ability to play E minor, A minor, and B₇, children can now accompany songs in the key of E minor.)

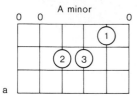
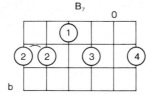

A minor

B₇

a   b

Figure 7.8

a, C major chord. **b,** D₇ chord. (With their ability to play G major, C major, and D₇, children can now accompany songs in the key of G major.)

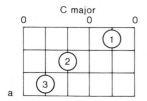
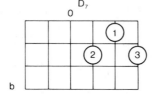

C major

D₇

a   b

Accompaniments

Down-up brush
Thumb brushes down, index finger up. (Brush only strings in the chord.)

Pluck-brush (Em chord)
Pluck the sixth string with the thumb.
Brush the fingernails down against the first five strings.
Pluck the fifth string with the thumb.
Brush the fingernails down against the first four strings.
(May be used with any chord in which all strings are played.)

Figure 7.9

Right hand. Photograph by David Rosenthal. (Right hand fingerings have been taken from the Spanish, where so much guitar music originated.)

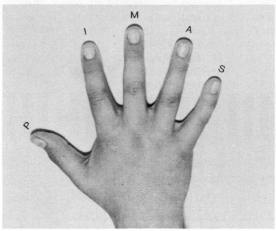

	Spanish	*English*
P	Pulgar	Thumb
I	Indicio	Index finger
M	Medio	Middle finger
A	Annular	Ring finger
S		Little finger

Finger picking

E minor (may be adapted for any chord that uses six strings)

A minor (may be adapted for any chord that uses five strings)

Vary the string plucked by the thumb to get variety. Experiment with variations on the basic style.

The Lope
This is a good accompaniment for songs in 3/4, when all strings are being used.

1	*2*	*3*
Thumb strums gently down to left of hole.	Thumb moves upward to right of hole.	Close brush.

(Close brush means to brush all fingers of right hand down across strings, then stop strings with palm of hand.)

The Golpe

This is a good accompaniment for Spanish and calypso songs. In Spanish *golpe* means to hit. All strings must be used.

	1	*and*	*2*	*and*
2	Slap heel	Move first	Move first	Move first
4	of palm	finger up	finger	finger up
	over sound	across	down	across
	hole.	strings.	across	strings.
			strings.	

Full House

This is a good accompaniment when a strong, full beat is needed and all strings are being used.

E Major

P Thumb Down · P Thumb Up · Brush · P Thumb Down · Close Brush

The following books may be helpful.

Title	Author	Publisher
Classic Guitar Technique, vol. 1	Schearer	Franco Colombo Publications (a division of Belwin Mills)
Guitar in the Classroom	Timmerman and Griffith	Wm. C. Brown Company
Mel Bay's Guitar Class Method		Mel Bay Publications, Inc.

Ukulele Clubs

Ukulele clubs may be organized for children on level II, following a similar procedure to that outlined for guitar clubs. Because of the comparative ease with which the ukulele may be played, a detailed introduction to this instrument will not be discussed. The teacher may wish to use a ukulele instruction book and adapt ideas for guitar to the ukulele. The following may be helpful.

Title	Author	Publisher
You Can Play the Ukulele	Ball	Associated Music Publishers, Inc.
Roy Smeck's Ukulele Method		Robbins Music Corp.

Figure 7.10
Baritone ukulele, photograph by David Rosenthal

Figure 7.11
Key of D major: **a**, D chord; **b**, G chord; **c**, A₇ chord

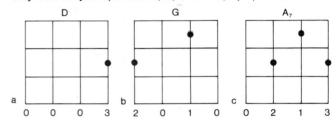

Figure 7.12
Key of D minor: **a**, D minor chord; **b**, G minor chord; **c**, A₇ chord

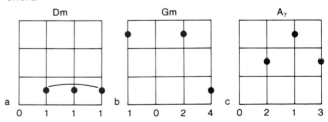

Figure 7.13
Key of G major: **a**, G chord; **b**, C chord; **c**, D₇ chord

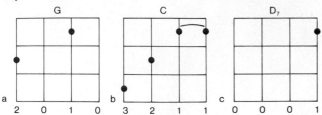

Figure 7.14
Key of G minor: **a**, G minor chord; **b**, C minor chord; **c**, D₇ chord

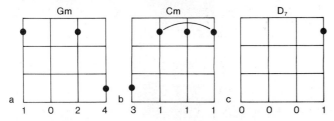

Figure 7.15
Key of A major: **a**, A chord; **b**, D chord; **c**, E₇ chord

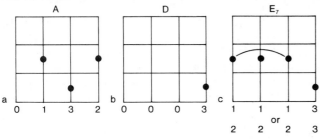

Figure 7.16
Key of A minor: **a**, A minor chord; **b**, D minor chord; **c**, E₇ chord

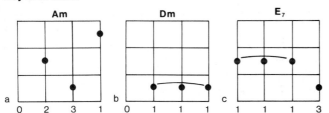

Music in Assembly Programs

Music increases the effectiveness of the assembly program even when it is used in a most simple way. Add an appropriate song, enthusiastically sung by a soloist, a small group, or an entire class, and the assembly program comes to life. Find a natural, meaningful way to use competent instrumentalists and singers, and their musical expressiveness results in deeper enjoyment of the program. Simultaneously, in these situations children enjoy the opportunity of expressing themselves musically.

The teacher may wonder how to find songs that relate to the theme of the assembly program, and where in the program these songs or instrumental selections fit naturally and effectively. Appropriate songs can be found without difficulty, providing the teacher makes use of all books of the elementary series available in the school. Though music books are graded, books designated for one grade often contain songs suitable for other grades. Thus, the teacher looking for songs appropriate for a *Moving West* theme should peruse the classified indexes of song books of several grades. By so doing, a wealth of material can often be found.

The problem of how to use the song (solo, ensemble, or entire class) and where to place it in the program so that it fits naturally into the sequence of events, should be planned cooperatively with the class involved. When these problems are approached with imagination and flexibility, it is a comparatively simple matter to find satisfactory solutions. This is particularly true if the teacher remembers that (1) musical selections are made more interesting by presenting them in a variety of ways (solo as well as group singing); (2) it is appropriate to adapt the program to incorporate musical selections; (3) when no place can be found in the program, it is often effective to present musical selections between acts. The teacher who explores the use of music in the assembly program will be rewarded by both the vitality added to the program and the enthusiastic response of the class.

Musical Assemblies

Music can be more than an attractive asset to an assembly program. It can, indeed, be the theme around which the program is built. Use of music in this way, as the focal point for an assembly, makes it possible to add a new dimension to the assembly program—the dimension of musical growth for those attending as well as for those participating.

For the teacher wishing to make music the major emphasis, a vast amount of material is available—material that in itself can suggest ideas for entertaining, educational programs.

Some specific possibilites for this type of assembly program follow.

1. Assembly sings
2. Song dramatizations
3. Rhythmic dramatizations of recorded music
4. Adaptations of program music and music from ballets
5. Dramatizations of song stories from music books and recordings
6. Operettas (original and published)
7. Adaptations of operas and operettas
8. Concerts by recorder clubs, chorus, band, orchestra, and small ensembles
9. Original plays based on social studies, using appropriate songs.
10. Plays adapted from books and recordings

Assembly Sings

Simple to organize but unusually effective when developed around an interesting theme, assembly sings are a good beginning for the teacher wishing to use music as the theme for an assembly. These assemblies take many forms.

1. A program by one class: the class presents the assembly, singing songs that relate to a particular theme (*Moving West, Greece, A Trip Across Our Country, Music of the West, Around the World in Song*).

   The songs used may be sung as solos, by small ensembles, or by the entire class. A narrator may introduce and give background for each song. If desired, simple scenery can be used as a backdrop. The class can sit in an attractive arrangement on stage. Simple rhythmic and melodic instruments can add interest. Stage lights can be used effectively to change the mood quickly. The audience can be asked to join in the chorus of one or two songs.
2. The entire assembly participating: the class presenting the assembly leads the singing, but with emphasis on participation of the entire assembly.

   This type of assembly can be handled exactly as the foregoing except that the entire assembly sings frequently with the class presenting the program. Songs must be chosen that are familiar to those attending. For variation, pictorial illustrations of songs, drawn in class, can be shown on the projector as the assembly sings.

How does the assembly sing evolve? Who selects the songs? The theme? In the primary grades, the teacher must take a very active part in all of these aspects. However, as children move into the intermediate grades they can help, and when they are in the upper grades they can often develop, with a minimum of guidance, an entire program.

The following plan was used by a sixth-grade class for an assembly sing. Children chose the theme, *Songs of Our Country,* and selected seven favorite songs, which

they knew were familiar to children in the fifth and sixth grades. The assembly program developed quite easily, as they followed these steps:

1. Decided on the best sequence for songs to provide contrast in mood while relating the idea
2. Decided which songs or sections of songs should be assigned to soloists, small ensembles, or the entire assembly
3. Wrote a narration explaining the background of each song and selected a narrator
4. Practiced, with the teacher's guidance, the songs and narration
5. Decided what to do with stage lighting
6. Decided where to sit on the stage
7. Decided on stage directions and use of the curtain
8. Practiced the program until they were satisfied that it would be smooth and expressive

An Assembly Sing for Grades Five and Six

Songs of our Country, written and presented by a sixth-grade class

Songs Used
"This Land is Your Land" from *Exploring Music,* Holt, Rinehart and Winston book 5
"Drill Ye Tarriers" from *This Is Music for Today,* Allyn and Bacon book 4
"If I Had a Hammer" from *Exploring Music,* Holt, Rinehart and Winston book 5
"The City Blues" from *Experiencing Music,* American book 5.
"I Ride an Old Paint" from *The Spectrum of Music,* Macmillan book 6
"Kuma Echa" from *The Spectrum of Music,* Macmillan book 6
"No Man Is an Island" by Whitney, Kramer and Ringwald, Shawnee Press

Narrator 1: Good afternoon, girls and boys. This afternoon our class would like to present a program entitled *Songs of Our Country.* We will sing several songs we know you like, and we hope you will sing with us. First let's begin with a song by one of our finest American folksingers—Woody Guthrie. The song is "This Land Is Your Land." Please sing with us! (All sing all verses.)

Narrator 2: People came to America from all over the world and helped to build our great nation. The next song is one that was written by some of the men who built the railroads connecting the east and west coasts of our country. If you haven't guessed, the song is "Drill Ye Tarriers." It was written by the Irish workmen, who were called tarriers. They worked hard, and to make things easier, they made up songs about their work. This song is the one they made up. We'd like the fifth grades to sing the verses with those of us on the stage and the sixth grades to join on the choruses. *(Class and fifth grades sing verses, all sing on the choruses.)*

Narrator 1: Here's another song that could have been sung by men as they worked on the railroad. It's called "If I Had a Hammer" and was written by two folksingers—Pete Seeger and Will Hays. We'd like to do it with our own orchestration, and we invite you to sing with us. *(Entire assembly sings four verses. Children improvise accompaniment using the following instruments.)*

    Verse 1 (hammer) tone blocks
    Verse 2 (bell) triangle
    Verse 3 (song) maracas
    Verse 4 all instruments

Narrator 2: Our next song is about the cities of our country. It was written by another folksinger—Jerry Silverman. Our accompanist for this song will be our own Don Pacay, playing a blues strum on the guitar. There's a lot of repetition in each verse, so if you want to sing, join in! *(Class sings "The City Blues.")*

Narrator 1: Another group who helped build our country was the cowboy. There have been many songs written about him. One of our favorites is "I Ride an Old Paint." It describes a cowboy going to Montana to throw down and brand steers. You might be interested in knowing the meaning of some of the words used in the song. *Houlihan* means to bring down steers for branding; *coulees* are small valleys; a *draw* is a watering hole; *dogies* are motherless calves. We'll be accompanied on the guitar by Chris Rivuto. Please sing the chorus. You'll enjoy it! *(Class sings "I Ride an Old Paint.")*

Narrator 2: The songs of our country come from all over the world, brought by people trying to find a better life here in the United States. Here's a song brought over from Palestine called "Kuma Echa." The words mean "Rise, my friends. Let's dance around and around, and work another day." *(Class sings "Kuma Echa.")*

Narrator 1: No matter where we live in this big country of ours, we need each other. The next song, "No Man Is an Island," reminds us of this. Everyone sing on this grand finale! *(Entire assembly sings.)*

Song Dramatizations

Creating an assembly program of song dramatizations is one step from the assembly sing. It can, in fact, evolve to include some basic ingredients of the assembly sing. It has only the added element of dramatization, which is appealing to children of all ages.

Songs suitable for dramatization suggest themselves frequently to one who is alert to this use of songs. Sometimes the dramatization is suggested by the text. Other times, though no story is implied, there is a strong suggestion for action or movement. Both types are suitable for dramatization, providing the rhythm suggests movement and the song itself is appealing to children. For example, "Train Is A-Coming" in Holt, Rinehart and Winston's *Exploring Music,* book 2, suggests a very definite story. The train is coming down the track. People are waiting at the station. They buy their tickets. The train leaves the station. On the other hand, "La Raspa" from *Discovering Music Together,* Follett, book 5, suggests a definite rhythmic movement, which could be used by having children create dance steps.

Presenting individual song dramatizations as an assembly program means that a theme must be found to relate the songs to each other and make the presentation meaningful and effective. The theme may be specific.

Songs about Halloween (Valentine's Day, Washington's Birthday)
Songs about Animals
Songs about People
Songs about Work
Funny Songs
Songs about the Sea (Mountains, Rivers)
Songs from France (America, England)

The theme may be, on the other hand, quite general and used simply as a means to unify the program.

Songs We Love to Sing
Songs We Like to Dramatize
Songs with Different Moods
Songs We Know

Interestingly enough, vague themes can often be more effective. Either type is effective when it is a direct outgrowth of the enthusiasm of the children and relates the songs to one another.

The teacher who plans to use the song dramatization as the basis for an assembly program should begin early in the school year presenting songs that can be effectively dramatized. Thus, children have the opportunity to gradually build a repertoire that can be used to create an assembly program. When children have had this background, the steps needed to create an assembly program are simple, and the teacher is more able to guide children in planning details for the program. One possible sequence for creating an assembly program built on song dramatizations is the following:

1. Learn many songs that can be dramatized and create a rhythmic dramatization of each.

2. Decide who will dramatize each part of each song and how.
3. Practice each dramatization until it is easily and effectively presented.
4. Select a theme that will relate the songs to each other.
5. Select narrators and decide what they will say to convey the theme and introduce each dramatization.
6. Decide what scenery, if any, should be used and who will make it.
7. Decide what costumes, if any, should be used and select a committee to make or obtain them.
8. Decide what lighting effects, if any, should be used.
9. Decide when the curtain should be open and closed.
10. Practice the entire dramatization on the stage until it is done effectively.

A Song Dramatization Assembly for Fourth Grade

Songs About the Sea, written and presented by a fourth-grade class

> *Songs Dramatized*
> "Banana Boat Loader's Song" from *Exploring Music*, Holt, Rinehart and Winston, book 4
> "Silent Sea" from *Music*, Silver Burdett, book 5
> "Song of the Fishes" from *The Spectrum of Music*, Macmillan, book 4
> "Round the Bay of Mexico" from *Investigating Music*, American Book Co., book 4
> "I Am the Monarch of the Sea" *from The Spectrum of Music*, Macmillan, book 6
> "Bound for the Rio Grande" from *Exploring Music*, Holt, Rinehart and Winston, level II

The curtain opens showing Narrator *dressed as a ship's captain, standing on a deck, where a few sailors are working. Below, half a dozen sailors are loading crates of bananas onto the boat.*

Narrator: Hello, everyone! Welcome aboard! *(To sailors on deck)* Mates, pull up the anchor and get ready to sail. We're off to sea! *(Looks down and notices men loading boat.)* But wait! What's this? The boat hasn't been loaded yet! Get on with it, men!

(The spotlight focuses on the sailors loading crates of bananas onto the boat. They are obviously exhausted. They work in the rhythm of the song, as all sing "Banana Boat Loader's Song." One sailor sings the verses. The captain struts back and forth, pantomiming orders to work harder, without interfering with the singing. The curtain closes slowly at the end of the song.)

Narrator: The sea has many moods. This is one of the reasons men and women are attracted to it. Here's a song that describes one of its quieter moods.

(The curtain opens. The children are sitting on their heels, on the floor. As the class sings "Silent Sea" they do motions similar to those described in book 5, Music. The curtain slowly closes during the last verse.)

Narrator: For a sailor who has been working hard all day, it's fun to sit on the deck at night, trying to outdo one's buddies in spinning a tall tale. Let's take a look at a group of sailors doing this.

(The curtain opens, showing a group of sailors sitting on the deck of a ship singing, as one accompanies with a guitar. Different sailors sing solos for each verse, competing with the previous singer. Other sailors patomime verses. The curtain slowly closes during the last verse.)

Narrator: One of the exciting things about a sailor's life is the opportunity to see the rest of the world. For a landlubber who has never been more than a few miles from home, it's a great thrill to sail into a foreign port. Here's a chantey that tells about a trip around the bay of Mexico.

(The curtain opens showing sailors leaning on one another's shoulders, singing "Round the Bay of Mexico." Children may want to create additional verses of the song, letting individuals sing solos. The curtain slowly closes during the last verse.)

Narrator: There have been hundreds of songs written about the sea. The next song is unusual, however, because it comes from an operetta—*HMS Pinafore*, by Gilbert and Sullivan. It's called "I Am the Monarch of the Sea."

(The curtain opens showing the captain surrounded by his sisters and his cousins and his aunts. All sing.)

Narrator: Please join us in singing our last song. This song takes us to the Rio Grande. The chorus is printed on the large cardboard to the right of the stage. Ready? Wait for Jonathan to begin the guitar accompaniment, and off we go!

(The curtain opens showing the entire class grouped around Jonathan, who is strumming a guitar. The class begins singing the chorus, and the narrator signals the audience to join. The class sings the entire song, the audience sings the choruses. The curtain closes slowly during the last chorus.)

Rhythmic Dramatizations of Recorded Music

A first-grade teacher, planning for an assembly program recently remarked, "I want this assembly to have value. We spend so much time preparing, I want the children to realize lasting value from the time and effort they spend on it."

The time and effort needed to develop an assembly program is indeed great. A program made up of rhythmic dramatizations, however, often takes less time and effort than other types of assemblies and is more rewarding. This is especially true when it is remembered that each rhythmic dramatization is a listening and rhythmic experience. The value of this opportunity to become intimately acquainted with several musical compositions cannot be overemphasized. It is through such experiences that the child learns to hear and interpret, in her own way, the expressive elements of music: rhythm, melody, tone color, texture, form, and expression. It is through such experiences with these expressive elements that she comes to understand and respond to music as a source of enjoyment. Because of these factors, the teacher who uses rhythmic dramatizations to develop an assembly program is capitalizing on an opportunity to help children grow musically while fulfilling the responsibility to present a program.

What is a good sequence for developing an assembly based on rhythmic dramatizations? As in the case of the assembly program based on song dramatizations, it is wise to think ahead to the date and prepare in advance by initiating experiences so that children develop rhythmic dramatizations of many musical compositions.

Through such a procedure, children have the opportunity to develop dramatizations gradually and without pressure. Their musical preferences and the effectiveness of each become evident as they create their dramatizations over a period of weeks. It is then a simple matter for them to select their favorite compositions for the program. (Children in the fourth, fifth, and sixth grades can develop a rhythmic dramatization for a musical composition of such length that one dramatization is sufficient for an entire assembly program. "An American in Paris" by Gershwin is one example. In the lower grades, because children need to work with short compositions of one to three minutes' duration, five or six compositions are needed.)

After the composition or compositions have been selected and effective dramatizations created, one possible sequence for developing a program can be the following:

1. Add costumes, when appropriate. (These can be made simply, by children.)
2. Determine the most effective sequence for the dramatizations.
3. Decide what should be said to introduce each, and select a narrator.
4. Decide if lighting effects or curtain changes should be used.
5. Decide where on the stage each dramatization will take place and where children will be when not performing. (When a large stage is available, it is often effective to keep all children on stage during the entire assembly. They can sit in semidarkness in the back and move to the front when it is time to perform.)
6. Practice the entire program on stage, using narrator, lighting, and curtain changes and finally, costumes, until children can perform easily and effectively.

Adaptations of Program Music and Music from Ballets

Program music and music from ballets offer the imaginative teacher a variety of ways to present stimulating assembly programs. One of these ways is the rhythmic dramatization discussed earlier.

Another way, however, of adapting program or ballet music for an assembly program is to emphasize the visual images they suggest. Children can be encouraged to create illustrations for overhead projector, depicting the story, mood, or pictures suggested by the music. These can then be projected on the screen as the music is played. A narrator can introduce various scenes or provide continuity.

In addition to projecting illustrations, children can draw poster-type illustrations that they display at the proper times, as announced by the narrator or heard in the music.

Another unusual adaptation of ballet or program music is using hand puppets, made by children, to enact a story. Pantomime or shadow pantomime (pantomime behind a sheet or screen with a light singing behind the actors to create a shadow) can also be effective in dramatizing the story as the music plays.

All of these approaches offer the teacher the opportunity to give children different kinds of experiences with music and encourage musical growth. At the same time, they help the assembly program to become something other than a stagnant, dull routine.

Dramatizations of Stories and Song Stories from Books and Recordings

Many music books and recordings contain stories or song stories that, with a little creativity and imagination, can be adapted for assembly programs.

When an appropriate story is available, the teacher may want to help children turn it into a musical by doing the following:

1. Add appropriate songs from music books or created by class.
2. Help children create appropriate rhythmic movement or dances.
3. Add soloists, small ensembles, or singing by the class.
4. Encourage children to play accompaniments or sound effects on rhythm instruments, guitar, or Autoharp.

Although, for children, perhaps the most valuable method of presenting the story is to create a dramatization and perform the singing, rhythmic movement, and accompaniments, these are other ways of creating an interesting program:

1. Encourage children to make small illustrations of a story, for use on the overhead projector. Have a narrator tell the story, and the class sing the songs as illustrations are shown.
2. Encourage children to create pantomimes, shadow pantomimes, or tableaux of story as the recording plays or children narrate and sing the songs.
3. Encourage children to make hand puppets and dramatize the story as the recording plays or children narrate and sing the songs.
4. Encourage children to create large illustrations of the story, which they display as children narrate and sing the songs.

Children on level I will have to learn the story and songs by rote, listening to a recording or the teacher sing and narrate. In addition, they will need guidance in creating a dramatization. Older children can use books, when available, and can contribute extensively to every aspect of the dramatization.

Original and Published Operettas

For many years, teachers in the elementary school have used operettas for assembly programs. *Hansel and Gretel,* by Humperdinck, for example, has been used countless times and rightly so, for it is a fine operetta. Other operettas such as this should continue to be used to develop assembly programs. However, here we will consider the original operetta—conceived and developed by children.

Original operetta—conceived and developed by *children?* Yes, it is quite possible for children to think of a story, develop a script, and write original songs. Moreover, the results are often more interesting than those created by adults. Certainly the enthusiastic response of children tells us that something dynamic is occurring.

What does happen in the process of writing an operetta to bring such a positive response? One possibility is that the child derives joy from knowing she can create a melody, a line of words, a story idea, part of the script, or any of the endless things that go into composing an operetta. She may also enjoy working with others to develop a truly creative project. Whatever the reason, it is obvious that children enjoy the process of writing their own operettas. Beyond all this, the child learns much from this experience. (See page 164, chapter 3 "Singing Experiences.")

When children have had adequate preparatory experience in dramatizing songs and stories, creating original words to songs, and writing original poems, melodies, and entire songs, they are ready to write an operetta. They realize that they have been able to write songs, and an operetta is "lots of songs." What, then, is a possible plan for proceeding? While there are many possible approaches, the authors have found the following to be successful.

1. Develop the plot.
   a. Children on level III can write a simple plot by themselves, after discussing the need for a plot complication and its solution. Have each member of the class write a simple plot. Discuss several you think best. Let the class decide which plot (or combination of ideas) they want to use. Select a small group of talented children to work with you, or follow the procedure suggested for younger children (1b, this section).
   b. Children on level I or II need much guidance. Through discussion, decide on a basic idea for a plot. Divide the plot into scenes. Assign parts for each scene, and let the characters (1) decide what must be said and done to tell the story and (2) enact the story until a script evolves.
2. Decide songs to be included. Discuss the entire plot and decide where songs might most effectively help tell the story, delineate a character, or underline a mood. Later decide which songs would best be sung as solos, duets, or small ensembles.
3. Create the songs, following the procedure suggested on page 164.
4. Add orchestrations.
   a. Ask the class to explore the idea of adding rhythmic accompaniments to some of the songs. These might be songs from which an overture could be developed or songs in which the mood would be enhanced by a rhythmic accompaniment.
   b. Guide children in creating orchestrations, using procedures suggested in preceding chapters.
5. Add dances.
   a. Have the class decide where a dance (solo or group) might be effective.
   b. Guide them in creating a dance to one of the songs.
6. Add accompaniments. Most songs children write suggest a very simple harmonic background. The teacher who cannot add this will need the aid of the music specialist or another teacher to notate or play accompaniments.
7. Select the cast. Though some teachers will wish to select their casts, it is most effective to let the children make the selection. This can be a morale builder and creates a fine group spirit. A procedure for this type casting follows:
   a. Decide what kind of tryout you like. This might be having children sing a short song or read a short selection.

Contestant's Name _____

For role of _____

Singing Ability: 1   2   3   4

Speaking Ability (volume and expressiveness) 1   2   3   4

Circle the number which best describes the contestant's ability. 1—Excellent, 2—Good, 3—Fair, 4—Weak.

b. Explain to the class that they are going to cast the operetta. Emphasize the importance of their making objective decisions, because this is their operetta, and they will want the best possible cast.

c. Guide children in establishing a criteria for auditioning. Slips of paper might be distributed for rating each child similar to the one above.

d. Let all children interested in leading roles try out. Tabulate the results in private. The child with the highest rating should be cast in the leading role; the child with the second highest rating in the next most important role; and so on. Announce the cast.

8. Decide on scenery, lights, props, curtains, and costumes. Through discussion, have the class or committees decide what they want in each of these areas and how to proceed to obtain it. The help of the art specialist, parents, and teachers can be solicited.

When all these aspects have been developed, rehearsals will begin. Following are a few helpful hints to make the production more effective and enjoyable:

1. Plot and songs should always be simple. The teacher can help children achieve simplicity by asking leading questions and making helpful comments as the script evolves, such as the following:

"You're losing me here. I don't quite understand what you mean."
"Let's not get too complicated."
"That's a good idea, but we could never do it on *this* stage."
"Let's remember that we're limited by the number of hours we can expect people to sit and watch."
"If you were in this situation, what would you do and say?"

These should always be given in the spirit of helpful advice.

2. Never tell children what to do. Let them discover what they want by asking questions that focus on the specific problem. Remember that if the production is to be worthwhile it must be theirs. If you help too much, they will sense this and resent it, and perhaps even withhold their own suggestions. Let it be imperfect, but above all, let it be their own.

3. Don't be a perfectionist. Be happy with whatever melodies children offer, especially in their first attempts. As they gain confidence and freedom, you may gradually initiate questions that will cause them to examine their work more closely, but this must be done with discretion.

When the teacher encourages children to express their ideas freely and reacts to each expression optimistically, children gain confidence. With each successful experience in song writing, their enthusiasm and skill grow until, when the operetta is complete, both children and teacher realize the satisfaction that comes from creating something valuable. Notice on page 375 two original songs from two operettas written by sixth-grade children.

Adaptations of Operas and Operettas

The assembly program's potential is greatly increased when the teacher is aware of the possibility of adapting operettas and operas. Although copyright laws must be observed, many works are in public domain, thus making it possible to adapt operas and operettas to meet the needs of the elementary school.

To take advantage of this, the teacher must accept the proposition that performing segments of a major musical composition is a valuable project. He must be willing to delete all but the most essential parts of the story and music, leaving only those parts necessary to tell the story and those parts children can successfully dramatize and sing. For the music lover, especially, this seems to be encouraging irreverence toward great works of music. However, when this sort of pruning is done in good taste and for good reasons, there is no need to feel that making such alterations desecrates a great work of art. Indeed, what it does do is to make it possible for youngsters to become acquainted with great music in the most dynamic way—by singing it. And what better way to develop a friendship with music, which will last a lifetime.

Exercise Song

One, two, up and down, Bend your knees and turn a-round. Three, four, touch the floor,

Do not tire for there is more. Five, six, for-ward bend, No help-ing hand we'll lend.

Sev-en, eight, swing your weight, Make it fast and don't be late! Jump, skip, hop, and run.

Come on San-ta, this is fun. Strut a-round like a hen. Nine, ten, be-gin a-gain.

From *Santa's Wait*, an operetta by the sixth-grade class of Camp Avenue School, N. Merrick, N.Y.

Bravissimo el Toreador

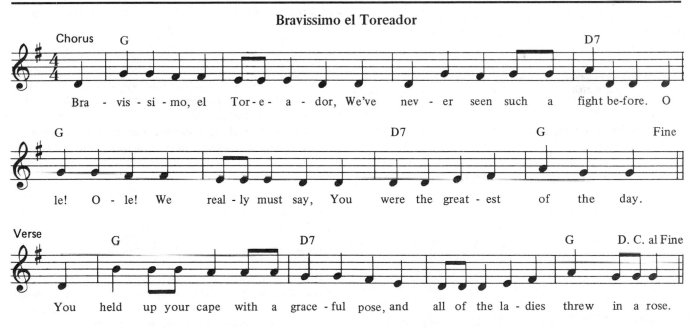

Chorus

Bra-vis-si-mo, el Tor-e-a-dor, We've nev-er seen such a fight be-fore. O

le! O-le! We real-ly must say, You were the great-est of the day.

Verse

You held up your cape with a grace-ful pose, and all of the la-dies threw in a rose.

2. You looked the bull into the eye,
   Thinking and hoping that he would die.
3. You took your sword and ran him through,
   If you hadn't he would have killed you!

4. The people were sitting at the end of their seats,
   Hoping and praying you'd make a great feat.

From *Mystery at the Mardi Gras*, an operetta by the sixth-grade class of North School, N. Merrick, N.Y.

Thus, *Carmen* can be given by ten- and eleven-year-olds when the story is simplified to its basic outline and when the music is restricted to the most familiar arias and choruses such as "Habanera" and "Toreador Song." Children can give a rousing, though cut, performance of Gilbert and Sullivan's *The Pirates of Penzance*, or *H. M. S. Pinafore,* omitting songs and deleting all but the essential elements of the story. Using a narrator makes it possible to span gaps in a story and to cover ground quickly. It is possible to cut an opera or operetta from a two-hour performance to a twenty or twenty-five minute performance and still retain its essential character. Children in level III can, thus, perform and enjoy operas and operettas that they otherwise might never hear.

Concerts by Chorus, Recorder Clubs, and Small Ensembles

For the music specialist, who most often has the responsibility for this type of assembly program, the school concert is the culmination of many months of concentrated involvement with music clubs. When this involvement has been a happy one, the children participating in the concert and the audience as well, will sense that something special is occurring. The something special is, of course, self-expression and re-creation. The atmosphere of the assembly changes because of the value that everyone unconsciously places on this special activity.

The wise teacher capitalizes on this attitude by planning the program to avoid the common pitfalls that destroy respect. Thus he might organize the program to evolve from a theme that relates each group of songs and helps the audience understand and enjoy the music. Further, he might use a narrator to introduce and relate the songs to the theme.

To avoid the error of making undue demands on the concentration of the audience, he might find ways to change the pace: alternating groups so that a singing group follows instrumentalists, or a soloist follows a group; alternating moods by following a rousing song with a soft, flowing song; varying the accompaniments, using *a cappella* singing, piano accompaniments, and instrumental or rhythmic accompaniments. Only the best taste in choices of music and interpretation should be employed.

The physical arrangement of the performing groups can create problems. Audiences squirm restlessly as large groups of children file on and off the stage. To avoid this, arrange groups so they move once—at the beginning of the program—to the place where they will perform. This may take planning, but it often determines the success of a program. When it is impossible to arrange groups to move only once, a concert must be planned so that the audience waits a minimum length of time as performing groups move.

Finally, the program must be kept short. It is a mistake to believe that the more children participating, the better the concert. Children as well as adults leave a performance with a bad impression of both music and concerts when they sit through a long, drawn out program. It is much better to have the audience leave wishing they could hear more than feeling relieved that the concert is finally over.

The outline of a concert with the theme *Music from Various Countries of the World* follows. It includes music ensembles of all sizes. Instrumental groups played between countries as the singers moved on a magic carpet from one part of the world to another.

CONCERT
presented by
Sixth-Grade Chorus
Fifth-Grade Chorus
Fifth- and Sixth-Grade Recorder Clubs
Fourth-Grade Recorder Club

Today's the Time for Singing . . . . Folk Melody
Entire Group
Narrator: We move to the Southern part of our country.
Go Down Moses . . . . Spiritual
Chorus and Soloists
Mister Banjo . . . . Arr. Harry Simeone
Ensemble, Autoharp Accompaniment
He's Got the Whole World . . . . Spiritual
Chorus and Soloists
Narrator: As we move on, we are entertained by musicians.
Blowin' in the Wind . . . . Boy Dylan
Five Hundred Miles . . . . Hedy West
Fifth- and Sixth-Grade Recorder Clubs
With Soloists from the Sixth-Grade Chorus
Narrator: We arrive in Spain along the Mediterranean Coast.
Shy Incognita . . . . Jurey
Both Choruses, Three Dancers
Accompanied by Maracas and Tambourines
Coasts of High Barbary . . . . British Folk Song
Choruses and Soloists (eight children dressed as pirates)
Narrator: Our magic carpet lifts us up once again. As we look down we see children singing and playing. Finally, they tire and go to sleep.
My Shadow . . . . Stevenson and Gearhart
Don't Slip . . . . .Gearhart
Musical Clocks . . . . .Gearhart
Children's Folk Songs, by Small Ensemble
Chinese Mystery . . . . Composed by Fourth-Grade
Recorder Club
Theme from *Surprise* Symphony . . . . .Haydn
Theme from *William Tell* Overture . . . . .Rossini
Lullaby . . . . .Brahms
Fourth-Grade Recorder Club
Assisted by Cymbals, Drums, and Soloists
Narrator: It's been a wonderful trip, but now we must start home.

The Happy Wanderer . . . . .Moller
Choruses with Descant on Refrain
Narrator: Finally, we return home to a rousing reception.
When the Saints Go Marching In . . . . .Spiritual
All Choral and Instrumental Groups

Sometimes it is effective to present a more formal concert, such as the following.

PROGRAM
I
This Land Is Your Land . . . . .Guthrie
Five Hundred Miles . . . . West
Shenandoah .Sea Chantey
My Little Pony . . . . .Orff
II
Zum Gali Gali . . . . Palestinian
No Man Is an Island . . . . Ringwald
Ezekiel Sow the Wheel . . . . .Spiritual
I'm Gonna Sing .Spiritual
Fourth-Grade Chorus
III
Now Is the Month of Maying . . . . Morley
Sheep May Safely Graze . . . . Bach
Bouree for Bach . . . . .Bach-Williams
Sourwood Mountain-Swing Low . . . . .arr. Wheeler
It's a Grand Night for Singing . . . . .Rodgers
IV
Marching to Pretoria . . . . Marais
Tumba . . . . .Visca-Oliver
With a Song in My Heart . . . . .Rodgers
Dance Song . . . . .Orff
Fifth- and Sixth-Grade Chorus

Original Plays with Music

Which shall I stress, the subject matter or the creative aspect of the experience? What teacher has not had this conflict. Shall he drill facts and figures or give the children experiences that will expand their creative powers? This is an eternal problem for the teacher who wants to give the child both knowledge and the ability to use it with imagination. It is well to remember, however, that the creative aspect of an experience often helps the child remember the facts and figures.

It is well to be aware, too, of the ways that acquisition of knowledge and creative experience can intermingle. When it is initiated because of enthusiasm and involvement in a particular area of study, creating a play can be one way of resolving the conflict. The sensitive teacher will easily perceive the times when this involvement is strong enough to act as a springboard for creating a play.

When he suggests this—as a natural outgrowth of studies that interest the class—they will respond eagerly. As they become involved in creating a play, they will, in turn, show renewed interest in the subject. Thus, the class studying community helpers might respond enthusiastically to the idea of creating a musical play that uses their knowledge of community helpers. A class studying Greece might eagerly write a play that uses their knowledge of this country and challenges them to obtain further knowledge to make their play more authentic. In both cases, it is quite natural to add songs and dances to emphasize the mood and story.

The alert teacher, who knows that his class must eventually give an assembly program, will constantly be aware of the curriculum as a source for the theme of an original play. When he and the class have agreed on a study area that might serve this purpose, he can suggest that children develop a plot using this study area as a basis. Older children are capable of writing plots independently. Younger children will need to verbalize the story rather than write it, and will need guidance (nondirective questions). The class will enjoy selecting from the stories a plot or combination of plots. Once they select it, a procedure for encouraging them to develop it into a play with music might be the following:

1. Through nondirective questions, let children decide into how many acts the story should be divided. (Encourage children to keep the action simple.)
2. Through discussion and questions, help children decide exactly what characters will be needed in each act, and what each character must do and say to tell the story.
3. Let children act out the plot until the dialogue and action make sense. (As an alternative, a small group can meet at special times to develop a script.)
4. Select, with the help of the class, children to play each character. Give them ample time to practice, using the class as helpers in improving the action and dialogue.
5. Select, or encourage children to select, songs from the available song series for the play.
6. Help children learn the songs. Decide which should be sung by the entire class, which by soloists, duets, and so on.
7. Ask children for suggestions for enriching the play (adding original dances, rhythmic accompaniments, and so on).
8. Incorporate children's suggestions into the play.
9. Let children give their ideas for improving the play.
10. With the help of the class, class mothers, and art consultant, arrange for costumes, scenery, and props.
11. Practice in the classroom until children are thoroughly familiar with the play.
12. Make certain that each child knows where she will be before, during, and after the play before going on stage.

13. Let the class decide what lighting effects they want, and when the curtain should open and close. Select children to be responsible for these duties.
14. Practice on stage several times, adding props, scenery, lights, curtain, and costumes gradually, so that children have ample time to adjust to each new change.

Research, Class Discussions, Reports, and Activities to Develop Skills and Practice in Initiating Musical Experiences

1. Discuss ways in which special clubs give individualized attention to the child's musical interests and needs. List specific experiences, skills, and growths that might result from an experience in a specific club.
2. Discuss the two methods of selecting members for clubs, emphasizing the advantages and disadvantages of each: membership through special tests and voluntary membership.
3. List specific attitudes and procedures that help the child retain the feeling that the activity of her club is more important than participating only for performance.
4. List ways that music might be added to a play to add interest.
5. Select a play. List specific songs and dances you would use to make the play more interesting, and where in the play you would use them.
6. Select a theme. Find seven or eight appropriate songs that might be simply dramatized. Write a plan for an assembly program based on these song dramatizations.
7. Guide the class in creating a song dramatization.
8. Create a song. As you do so, list the problems encountered. Write a paper discussing these problems as they would relate to children creating a song.
9. Guide the class in creating a song.
10. List problems and possible solutions that might present themselves to the teacher initiating the writing of an original operetta.
11. Discuss the relative merits for the child of each of the following: performing a published play or creating an original play; giving a published operetta or creating an original one; singing a solo or singing with a group.
12. Examine the suggested assembly programs in this chapter. Select the one that most appeals to you and write a short paper explaining why.
13. Recall your own experiences in elementary school assembly programs. Write a paper describing your reactions to these programs and outline the resultant implications for your future teaching philosophy.
14. Discuss ways to develop assembly programs into valuable educational experiences.
15. Select a social studies topic. Guide the class in developing a plot, dividing it into acts, deciding on words and actions for each act, and choosing songs.
16. Prepare a plan for an assembly sing using songs from the available songs series. Guide class in a rehearsal for this program. Through discussion, evaluate its strengths and weaknesses.
17. Discuss the general suggestions throughout this chapter in relation to creativity versus rigidity, and clarify how they may be used creatively in a teaching situation.
18. Discuss ways of using guitar and ukulele clubs for assembly programs and other musical activities.

Supplementary Publications for Music in Special Activities

Song Collections for Elementary School Chorus

Title	Arranger or Composer	Publisher
Choral Gems from the Masters	Grant	Boston Music
Choral Musicianship Series, book 1	Wilson	Silver Burdett
Choral Program Series, book 1	Wilson	Silver Burdett
Come Sing	Ringwald	Shawnee Press
Descants High Descants Low	Martin	Pro Art Publ.
Descants to Sing for Fun	Foltz-Murphy	Belwin-Mills
Elizabethan Songbag, An	Raebeck	E. B. Marks/ Belwin Mills
Festival Song Book, The	Bell	Belwin-Mills
Fun Songathon, A	Merman	Shawnee Press
Great Songs of Faith	Krones	Neil A. Kjos
Hello Tomorrow	Simeone	Shawnee Press
Here a Song, There a Song	Marsh	Shawnee Press
Hi and Lo	Ehret-Gardner	Staff Music
Little Folk Songs	Ades	Shawnee Press
Melody and Harmony	Ehret-Gardner	Staff Music
Mills First Chorus Album	Jurey	Belwin-Mills
More Descants to Sing for Fun	Foltz-Shelley	Belwin-Mills
More Partner Songs	Beckman	Ginn
Music from the Broadway Shows	Cassey	Ginn
Partner Songs (2 vols.)	Beckman	E. H. Morris
Prentice-Hall Choral Series, book 5	Wilson-Ehret	Prentice-Hall
Rise and Shine	Simeone	Shawnee Press
Rodgers and Hammerstein Showtime	Rodgers	Williamson Music
Run and Catch the Wind	Hayward	Shawnee Press
Salt and Pepper	Hayward	Shawnee Press
Salute to Music	Wilson-Ehert	Boosey and Hawkes
Singing Bee, A	Gearhart	Shawnee Press
Singing is Fun	Rhea	Bourne, Inc.
Sugar and Spice	Ades	Shawnee Press
They Came Singing	de Cesare	Sam Fox

Time for a Folk Song, vols. 1 and 2	Churchill	Belwin-Mills
Time for Singing, A	Hoggard	Shawnee Press
Treasured Ten	Zanzig	Summy-Birchard
Treble Chorister	Douglas	Pro Art
Treble Ensemble	Martin-White	Hall-McCreary
Two for the Song	Ades	Shawnee Press
Youthful Chorister, The	Ehret	E. B. Marks

J. W. Pepper and Son, Inc., P. O. Box 850, Valley Forge, PA 19482 issues classified guides for choral music of all publishers and offers an *on approval* service.

Books and Sources for Music Materials

Basic Elementary Song Series

Aubin, Neva; Beer, Alice S.; Beethoven, Jane; Crook, Elizabeth; Hayden, Erma; Hoffman, Mary E.; McNeil, Albert; Reimer, Bennett; and Walker, David S. *Music*. Morristown, N.J.: Silver Burdett Company, 1974, 1978. Books for K–8, teachers' guides, accompaniments, recordings, filmstrips, and spirit masters.

Boardman, Eunice, and Landis, Beth. *Exploring Music*. New York: Holt, Rinehart & Winston, Inc., 1971. Books for grades 1–6, teachers' guides with accompaniments and recordings.

Choate, Robert A.; Berg, Richard C.; Kjelson, Lee; and Troth, Eugene W. *New Dimensions in Music*. Cincinnati: American Book Company, 1970, 1976. Books for early childhood, K–6, teachers' editions, accompaniments, and recordings.

Landeck, Beatrice; Crook, Elizabeth; and Youngberg, Harold C. *Making Music Your Own*. Morristown, N.J.: Silver Burdett Company, 1971. Books for grades K–6, teachers' guides with accompaniments and recordings.

March, Mary Val; Rinehart, Carrol; Savage, Edith; Beelke, Ralph; and Silverman, Ronald. *The Spectrum of Music*. Riverside, N.J.: Macmillan Publishing Co., Inc., 1974. Books for grades K–8, teachers' guides with accompaniments and recordings.

Sur, William R.; Fisher, William R.; Tolbert, Mary R.; and McCall, Adeline. *This Is Music for Today*. Rockleigh, N.J.: Allyn and Bacon, Inc., 1971. Books for grades K–8, teachers' editions, accompaniments, and recordings.

Books on Listening for the Teacher

Baldwin, Lillian. *A Listener's Anthology of Music*. 2 vols. New York: Silver Burdett Company, 1948.

Baldwin, Lillian. *Music to Remember*. New York: Silver Burdett Company, 1951.

Baldwin, Lillian, *Music for Young Listeners*. 3 vols. New York: Silver Burdett Company, 1951.

Bulletins and Curriculum Guides

Association for Supervision and Curriculum Development, NEA. *Teaching Music in the Elementary School: Opinion and Comment*. Washington, 1963.

Benson, Warren. *Creative Projects in Musicianship*. Washington: Music Educators National Conference, 1967.

Boyle, J. David, compiler. *Instructional Objectives in Music*. Reston, Va.: Music Educators National Conference, 1974.

Gary, Charles L., and Landis, Beth. *Comprehensive Music Programs*. Washington: Music Educators National Conference, 1972.

Henry, Nelson B. "Basic Concepts in Music Education." *The Fifty-seventh Yearbook of the National Society for the Study of Education*. Chicago: University of Chicago Press, 1958.

Kansas State Department of Education. *Guidelines for the Development of a Comprehensive Music Curriculum for Elementary and Secondary Schools*. Topeka, 1973.

Meske, Eunice B., and Rinehart, Carrol, compilers. *Individualized Instruction in Music*. Reston, Va.: Music Educators National Conference, 1975.

Music Educators National Conference. *Electronic Music*. Washington, 1968.

Music Educators National Conference. *Facing the Music in Urban Education*. Washington, 1970.

Music Educators National Conference. *Music Books for the Elementary School Library*. Washington, 1972.

Music Educators National Conference. *Music Education for Elementary School Children*. Washington, 1960.

Music Educators National Conference. *Music in Everyday Living and Learning*. Washington, 1960.

Music Educators National Conference. *Study of Music in the Elementary School: A Conceptual Approach*. Washington, 1967.

New York State Department of Education, Bureau of Elementary Curriculum Development. *Music K–6, Rhythm, Melody, Harmony,* experimental edition. Albany, 1972.

New York State Department of Education, Bureau of Elementary Curriculum Development. *Words, Sounds and Pictures about Music: A Multimedia Resource Listing for Teachers of Music in Grades K–6*. Albany, 1972.

New York State Department of Education, Division of Humanities and the Arts, Report on Conference in Albany. *The Role of Music in the Special Education of Handicapped Children*. 1971.

Thomas, Ronald. *Manhattanville Music Curriculum Program Synthesis*. Bardonia, N.Y.: Media, Inc., 1971.

U.S. Department of Health, Education, and Welfare, Office of Education. *Music in Our Schools: A Search for Improvement,* Bulletin OE–33033, #28. Washington, 1964.

The University of the State of New York, The State Department Bureau of Secondary Curriculum Development. *Music in Modern American Society (Contemporary Music): A Guide for a High School Elective Course*. Albany, 1973.

Charts

Kidd, Eleanor. *Threshold to Music,* 2d. ed. Belmont: Fearon Publishers, 1975. Experience charts for early childhood, with teachers' guides; levels I, II, and higher grades. (Vol. 1 and 2, 1974. Higher grades, 1975.)

Lewis, Aden G. *Listen, Look and Sing,* 4 vols. Morristown, N.J.: Silver Burdett Company, 1971, 1972, 1976, 1979. Charts with teachers' guides.

Professional Books for the Teacher

Adam, Jeno. *Growing in Music with Movable Do*. Highland Park: Kossuth Foundation, 1971.

Andrews, Francis M., and Cockerille, Clara E. *Your School Music Program*. Englewood Cliffs: Prentice-Hall, Inc., 1958.

Andrews, Gladys. *Creative Rhythmic Movement for Children*. Englewood Cliffs: Prentice-Hall, Inc., 1954.

Aronoff, Frances Webber. *Music and Young Children*. New York: Holt, Rinehart & Winston, Inc., 1969.

Athey, Margaret, and Hotchkiss, Gwen. *A Galaxy of Games for the Music Class*. West Nyack: Parker Publishing Company, Inc., 1975.

Bachman, Tibor. *Reading and Writing Music*, children's and teacher's editions. Elizabethtown: Continental Press, Inc., book 1, 1968; book 2, 1969; book 3, 1971.

Beer, Alice A., and Hoffman, Mary E. *Teaching Music: What, How, and Why*. Morristown: General Learning Press, 1973.

Bennett, Michael D. *Surviving in General Music*. Memphis: Pop Hit Publishing, 1974.

Bergethon, Bjornab, and Boardman, Eunice. *Musical Growth in the Elementary School*. 3d ed. New York: Holt, Rinehart & Winston, 1975.

Betten, Bette, and Manning, Ardelle. *Basic Music for Retarded Children*. 2d ed. Palo Alto: Ardelle Manning Productions, 1960.

Biasini, Americole; Thomas, Ronald; and Poconowski, Lenore. *MMCP Interaction, Early Childhood Music Curriculum*. Bardonia, N.Y.: Media Materials, Inc. 1970.

Burnett, Millie. *Melody, Movement and Language*. San Francisco: R. and E. Associates, 1973.

Carroll, Jean, and Lofthouse, Peter. *Creative Dance for Boys*. London: Macdonald & Evans Ltd., 1969.

Cheyette, Irving, and Cheyette, Herbert. *Teaching Music Creativity in the Elementary School*. New York: McGraw-Hill Book Co., 1969.

Crews, Katherine. *Music and Perceptual-Motor Development*. New York: Center for Applied Research in Education, Inc., 1975.

Darazs, Arpad, and Jay, Stephen. *Sight and Sound*. Oceanside: Boosey and Hawkes, Inc., 1965.

Dietz, Betty Warner, and Olatunji, Michael. *Babatunde, Musical Instruments of Africa*. New York: John Day Company, 1965.

Doll, Edna, and Nelson, Mary Jarman. *Rhythms Today!* Morristown: Silver Burdett Co., 1965.

Dorson, Richard M., ed. *African Folklore*. Garden City: Anchor Books (Doubleday), 1972.

Driver, Ann. *Music and Movement*. New York: Oxford University Press, 1966.

Dwyer, Terence. *Composing with Tape Recorders*. New York: Oxford University Press, 1974.

Findlay, Elsa. *Rhythm and Movement, Applications of Dalcroze Eurhythmics*. Evanston: Summy-Birchard Co., 1971.

Fyfe, Joan Z. *Back to Music Basics*. Floral Park, N.Y.: Dynamite Publications, 1978.

Fyfe, Joan Z. *Personalizing Music Education: A Plan for Implementation*. Sherman Oaks, Ca.: Alfred Publishing Co., 1978.

Gary, Charles L., ed. *Music in Therapy*. New York: The Macmillan Co., 1968.

Gelineau, R. Phyllis. *Experiences in Music*. 2d ed. New York: McGraw-Hill, 1976.

Glass, Henry. *Exploring Movement*. Freeport, N.Y.: Educational Activities, Inc., 1966.

Greenberg, Marvin, and MacGregor, Beatrix. *Music Handbook for the Elementary School*. West Nyack, N.Y.: Parker Publishing Co., 1972.

Hackett, Layne C. *Movement Exploration and Games for the Mentally Retarded*. Peek Publications, 1970.

Hall, Doreen. *Teacher's Manual, Orff-Schulwerk Music for Children*. Mainz, Germany: B. Schott's Sohne; Clifton, N.J.: European-American Music, distributors, 1956.

Hardy, Donna Dee. *Music Mixtures*. Pittsburgh: Volkwein Bros., Inc., 1977.

Hardy, Gordon, et al. *Julliard Repertory Library*. Cincinnati: Canyon Press Inc., 1970.

Hickok, Dorothy, and Smith, James A. *Creative Teaching of Music in the Elementary School*. Boston: Allyn and Bacon, Inc., 1974.

Hotchkiss, Gwen, and Athey, Margaret. *Treasury of Individualized Activities for the Music Class*. West Nyack, N.Y.: Parker Publishing Co., 1977.

Jaques-Dalcroze, Emile. *Rhythm, Music, and Education*. London: The Riverside Press, 1967.

Jones, Archie N. *Music Education in Action*. Boston: Allyn and Bacon, Inc., 1960.

Jones, Bessie, and Hawes, Bess Lomax. *Step It Down*. New York: Harper & Row, 1972.

Jones, Genevieve. *Seeds of Movement*. Pittsburgh: Volkwein Bros., Inc., 1971.

Konowitz, Bert. *Music Improvisation as a Classroom Method*. New York: Alfred Publishers, 1973.

Kurutz, Marian, and Resver, Grace. *Music Fun*, 3 vols. Buffalo: Kenworthy Educational Service, 1964.

Lament, Marylee M. *Music in Elementary Education*. New York: Macmillan Publishing Co., 1976.

Landis, Beth, and Carder, Polly. *The Eclectic Curriculum in American Music Education: Contributions of Dalcroze, Kodaly, and Orff*. Washington: Music Educators National Conference, 1972.

Landon, Joseph W. *How to Write Learning Activity Packages for Music Education*. Costa Mesa, Ca.: Educational Media Press, 1973.

Landon, Joseph W. *Leadership for Learning in Music Education*. Costa Mesa, Ca.: Educational Media Press, 1975.

Leonard, Charles, and House, Robert W. *Foundations and Principles of Music Education*. New York: McGraw-Hill Book Co., 1972.

Livingston, James A.; Poland, Michael; and Simmons, Ronald E. *Accountability and Objectives for Music Education*. Costa Mesa, Ca.: Educational Media Press, 1973.

Mariott, Alice, and Rachlin, Carol K. *American Indian Mythology*. New York: Mentor Books (Times Mirror New American Library), 1972.

Marsh, Mary Val. *Explore and Discover Music*. Toronto: The Macmillan Co., 1970.

Mettler, Barbara. *Materials of Dance as a Creative Art Activity*. Tucson: Mettler Studios, 1971.

Monsour, Sally; Cohen, Marilyn; and Lindell, Patricia. *Rhythm in Music and Dance for Children*. Belmont: Wadsworth Publishing Co., Inc., 1966.

Mulligan, Mary Ann. *Integrating Music with Other Studies*. New York: Center for Applied Research in Education, 1975.

Nash, Grace; Jones, Geraldine; and Potters, Barbara. *The Child's Way of Learning*. Sherman Oaks, Ca.; Alfred Publishing Co., 1977.

Nordoff, Paul, and Robbins, Clive. *Music Therapy in Special Education*. New York: John Day Co., 1971.

Nye, Robert E., and Nye, Vernice T. *Essentials of Teaching Elementary School Music*. Englewood Cliffs: Prentice-Hall, Inc., 1974.

Nye, Robert E., and Nye, Vernice T. *Music in the Elementary School*. Englewood Cliffs: Prentice-Hall, Inc., 1970.

Nyquist, Ewald, and Hawes, Gene, eds. *Open Education*. New York: Bantam Books, 1972.

Orff, Carl, and Keetman, Gunild. *Music for Children*, 5 vols. English adaptation by Doreen Hall and Arnold Walter. Mainz, Germany: B. Schott's Sohne; Clifton, N.J.: European-American Music, distributors, 1956.

Orff, Carl, and Keetman, Gunild. *Music for Children*, 5 vols. English adaptation by Margaret Murray. Mainz, Germany: B. Schott's Sohne; Clifton, N.J.: European-American Music, distributors, 1950 through 1967.

Paynter, John, and Aston, Peter. *Sound and Silence, Classroom Projects in Creative Music*. Cambridge: Cambridge University Press, 1970.

Regner, Herman, coordinator. *Music for Children*. Orff-Schulwerk American Edition, vol. 2, Primary, 1977; vol. 3, 1979. Clifton, N.J.: Schott Music Corp., European-American Music.

Reynolds, Jane L. *Music Lessons That Are Easy to Teach,* West Nyack, N.Y.: Parker Publishing Co., 1976.

Reynolds, Jane L. *Music Lessons You Can Teach*. West Nyack, N.Y.: Parker Publishing Co., 1970.

Richards, Mary Helen. *The Child in Depth*. Portola Valley, Ca.: Mary Helen Richards, 1969.

Richards, Mary Helen. *Language Arts through Music, A Trilogy*. Portola Valley, Calif.: Richards Institute of Music Education and Research, 1971.

Rosenstrauch, Henrietta. *Percussion, Rhythm, Music, Movement*. Pittsburgh: Volkwein Bros., 1970.

Runkle, Aleta, and Eriksen, Mary L. *Music for Today, Elementary School Methods*. 3d ed. Boston: Allyn and Bacon, Inc., 1976.

Russell, Joan. *Creative Dance in the Primary School*. London: Macdonald & Evans, 1970.

Sandor, Frigyes, ed. *Music Education in Hungary*. London: Barrie and Rockliff, 1966.

Sear, Walter. *The New World of Electronic Music*. Port Washington: Alfred Publishers, 1972.

Silverman, Jerry. *How to Play the Guitar*. Garden City: Doubleday & Co., Inc., 1968.

Smith, Robert B. *Music in the Child's Education*. New York: The Ronald Press, 1970.

Standifer, James A., and Reeder, Barbara. *Source Book of African and Afro-American Materials for Music Educators*. Washington: Music Educators National Conference, 1972.

Swanson, Bessie R. *Music in the Education of Children*. San Francisco: Wadsworth Publishing Co., 1969.

Swanson, Bessie, R. *Planning Music in the Education of Children*. Belmont: Wadsworth Publishing Co., 1965.

Tillman, Rix W. *Music Educator's Guide to Personalized Instruction*. West Nyack, N.Y.: Parker Publishing Co., 1970.

Way, Brian. *Development through Drama*. Atlantic Highland, N.J.: Humanities Press, 1973.

Weyland, R. H. *A Guide to Effective Music Supervision*. Dubuque, Iowa: Wm. C. Brown Co. Publishers, 1961.

Wheeler, Lawrence, and Raebeck, Lois. *Orff and Kodaly Adapted for the Elementary School*. Dubuque, Iowa: Wm. C. Brown Co. Publishers, 1977.

Winslow, Robert W., and Dallin, Leon. *Music Skills for Classroom Teachers*. Dubuque, Iowa: Wm. C. Brown Co. Publishers, 1970.

Young, J. E., and MacKnight, C. B. *Reading and Playing Musical Patterns*. Elizabethtown: The Continental Press, 1972.

Zimmerman, Marilyn. *From Research to the Music Classroom #1: Musical Characteristics of Children*. Reston, Va.: Music Educators National Conference, 1971.

Sources for Music Materials

This list includes sources for audiovisuals, cassettes, instruments, records, tapes, and transparencies.

Alfred Music Co., Inc., Sherman Oaks, CA, 91403

Audio Visual Teaching Materials, Educational Audio Visual Inc., Pleasantville, NY, 10570

Belwin/Mills Publishing Corp., Melville, NY, 11746

Bowmar/Noble Publishers, Inc., 4563 Colorado Blvd., Los Angeles, CA, 90039

Classroom Materials, 93 Myrtle Dr., Great Neck, NY, 11021

Educational Activities, Box 461, Coram, NY, 11727

Educational Record Sales, 157 Chambers St., New York, NY, 10007

Folkways Records, 43 W. Sixty-first Street, New York, NY, 10023

Folkways Scholastic Records, 50 W. Forty-fourth St., New York, NY, 10036

Gamble Hinged Music Co., 312 S. Wabash Ave., Chicago, IL, 60604

Hargail Music Press, 51 East Twelfth St., New York, NY, 10003 (Specialists in recorders and recorder materials)

Jam Handy Filmstrips, Prentice-Hall Media, Serv Code MM, 150 White Plains Road, Tarrytown, NY, 10591

Keyboard Publications, 1346 Chapel St., New Haven, CT, 06511

Kodaly Musical Training Institute, 23 Main St., Watertown, MA, 02172

Lyons, Inc., 430 Wrightwood Ave., Elmhurst, IL, 60126

Musitronic, Inc. (Piano Labs), 2125 Fourth St., NW, P.O. Box 441, Owatonna, MN, 55060

Pepper, J. W. & Son, Inc., P.O. Box 850, Valley Forge, PA, 19482

Peripole Products, Inc., P.O. Box 146, Lewistown Rd., Browns Mills, NJ, 08015

RCA Records, Educational Department, 1133 Avenue of the Americas, New York, NY, 10036

Rhythm Band, Inc., P.O. Box 126, Fort Worth, TX, 76101

Scholastic Records, 906 Sylvan Ave., Englewood Cliffs, NJ, 07632

Schwann Record Catalog, 137 Newbury St., Boston, MA, 02116

Sesame Street Records, 1 Lincoln Plaza, New York, NY, 10023

Shawnee Press, Delaware Water Gap, PA, 18327

Sing 'n Do Company, Inc., P.O. Box 279, Brooklyn, NY, 11227

Up with People, 3103 N. Campbell Ave., Tucson, AZ, 85719

Materials and Charts for Individualized Learning

Biographical Material

Music Questionnaire

1. Name your three favorite songs.

    1. _____

    2. _____

    3. _____

2. Name your three favorite TV shows; include day and time.

    1. _____

    2. _____

    3. _____

3. How do you like to spend your free time? _____

    _____

4. What are your hobbies? _____

5. What do you like most about music? _____

6. What do you like least about music? _____

7. Check the instrument(s) you would like to play.   1. guitar _____   2. ukulele _____

      3. recorder _____   4. Autoharp _____

8. What are your ideas for musical activities in the classroom? _____

    _____

9. Do you collect records?   yes _____   no _____

10. Name some of your favorite records. _____

    _____

(continued)

11. Do you play an instrument? yes _____ no _____ If so, what instrument? _____

12. Were you in band or chorus last year? band _____ chorus _____ both _____

Diagnostic Tests

Teacher's Guide and Answer Sheet

I. Rhythm

Teacher Claps   *(pause)*   *Answer*

A.   Ⓢ D

B.   S Ⓓ

C.   S Ⓓ

D.   Ⓢ D

E.   S Ⓓ

F.   Ⓢ D

II. Pitch

Teacher Plays Each Twice   *Answer*

A.   H Ⓛ

B.   Ⓗ L

C.   Ⓗ L

D.

III. Melody

Teacher Plays

IV. Meter

Circle the Correct Meter for Each

A. $\frac{2}{4}$ $\frac{3}{4}$ $\frac{4}{4}$ $\frac{6}{8}$

B. $\frac{2}{4}$ $\frac{3}{4}$ $\frac{4}{4}$ $\frac{6}{8}$

C. $\frac{2}{4}$ $\frac{3}{4}$ $\frac{4}{4}$ $\frac{6}{8}$

V. Note Letter Name Identification

A. Write the letter name.

B. What words do these notes spell?

VI. Note and Rest Value Identification

A. Match

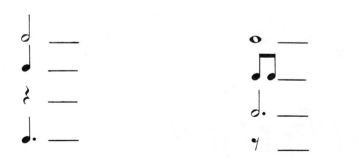

a. two eighth notes
b. dotted quarter note
c. whole note
d. quarter note
e. half note
f. quarter rest
g. eighth rest
h. dotted half note

B. In $\frac{4}{4}$ meter, tell how many beats each note or rest receives.

Students' Answer Sheet

Name _____ Date _____

Grade _____ Classroom _____

I. Rhythm

Are these rhythms the same or different? Circle [S] if they are the same. Circle [D] if they are different.

A. [S] [D]   D. [S] [D]

B. [S] [D]   E. [S] [D]

C. [S] [D]   F. [S] [D]

II. Pitch

Two tones will be played. If the *second* tone is higher than the first, circle [H] If the second tone is lower,

circle [L] Each example will be played twice.

A. [H] [L]   D. [H] [L]

B. [H] [L]   E. [H] [L]

C. [H] [L]   F. [H] [L]

III. Melody

Are these melodies the same or different? Circle [S] if both are the same. Circle [D] if they are different.

A. [S] [D]   D. [S] [D]

B. [S] [D]   E. [S] [D]

C. [S] [D]   F. [S] [D]

Note: For answers to sections I–III, see pp. 386 and 387.

IV. Meter

Circle the Correct Meter for Each

A. 2/4 3/4 4/4 6/8 ‖ 4/4

B. 2/4 3/4 4/4 6/8 ‖ 2/4

C. 2/4 3/4 4/4 6/8 ‖ 3/4

V. Note Letter Name Identification

A. Write the letter name.

E   C   G   E   F   B   D   F   A

B. What words do these notes spell?

B A G   D A D   F E E   C A F E   A D

E D G E   C A B   B E D   E D G E

VI. Note and Rest Value Identification

A. Match

a. two eighth notes
b. dotted quarter note
c. whole note
d. quarter note
e. half note
f. quarter rest
g. eighth rest
h. dotted half note

B. In $\frac{4}{4}$ meter, tell how many beats each note or rest receives.

 2

♩ 1

♪ ½

▬ 4

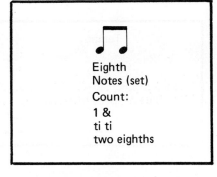 1½

𝄾 1

♫ 1

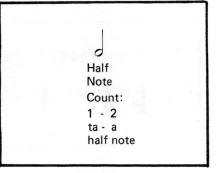 4

𝄿 ½

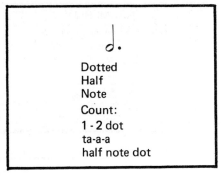 1

Suggestions for Charts

These charts should be permanently displayed in the room for peripheral and concrete learnings. Charts can be colorfully made and laminated. They can be used on bulletin boards or hung from the ceiling or lighting fixtures. Use both sides of the charts.

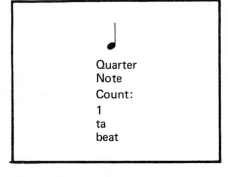

Quarter
Note
Count:
1
ta
beat

Eighth
Notes (set)
Count:
1 &
ti ti
two eighths

Half
Note
Count:
1 - 2
ta - a
half note

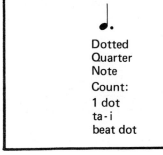

Dotted
Quarter
Note
Count:
1 dot
ta - i
beat dot

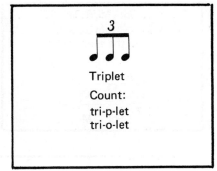

Triplet
Count:
tri-p-let
tri-o-let

Dotted
Half
Note
Count:
1 - 2 dot
ta-a-a
half note dot

Sixteenth
Notes (set)
Count:
1 tah & tah
ti-ri-ti-ri

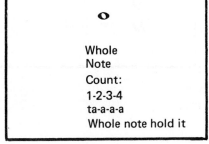

Whole
Note
Count:
1-2-3-4
ta-a-a-a
Whole note hold it

Count:
ti   ta   ti
syn-co - pah

Count:
one tah &
ti   ri   ti

Count:
one   &   tah
ti   ti   ri

Count:
ti   ta   ti
syn-co - pah

Repeat Signs

Tempo

Rate of speed in music

Sol—Mi Rule:
When sol is around the
line, mi is around the
line below.

Sol   Mi

Sol—Mi Rule:
When sol is in a space,
mi is in the space below.

Sol   Mi

Sol—Mi—Do

Sol Mi Do

Dynamics

p   soft
mf   medium loud
ff   very loud

Note Values Chart

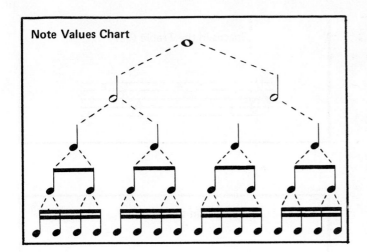

Rest Values Chart

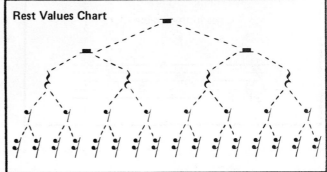

Fermata	Accent	Time Signatures
⌢	>	$\frac{2}{4}$ $\frac{4}{4}$ $\frac{5}{4}$ $\frac{6}{8}$
Hold the note.	Stress or emphasize the note.	Top number tells number of beats in a measure. Bottom number tells the kind of note that receives one beat.

Dots

A dot after a note (or rest) receives one-half the value of the note it follows. Example:

1 + ½ = 1½ beats

Crescendo

Gradually becoming louder

Decrescendo

Gradually becoming softer

Ritardando

Gradually becoming slower

Accelerando

Gradually becoming faster

Dynamics

f	forte	loud
$f\!f$	fortissimo	very loud
$s\!f$	sforzando	sudden emphasis
p	piano	soft
$p\!p$	pianissimo	very soft

Slur

Indicates notes should be connected smoothly, one flowing into the other.

Repeat Signs

Indicates everything between the dots should be repeated.

Tie

Indicates two or more notes are to be sung or played as one long note.

Lines in the Treble Clef

Spaces in the Treble Clef

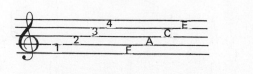

Lines in the Bass Clef

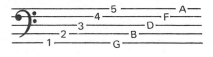

Spaces in the Bass Clef

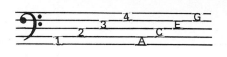

Minor Scales

Any minor scale is a group of seven tones arranged in a pattern of whole and half steps. There are three forms of the minor scale: natural, harmonic, and melodic. (D minor scale is used to illustrate in the following.)

Natural Minor Scale

In the natural minor scale the half steps are between the second and third, and fifth and sixth, degrees of the scale. It descends in the same notation as it ascends.

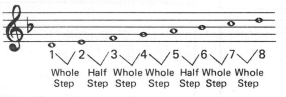

A sharp (♯) raises a tone ½ step.

A flat (♭) lowers a tone ½ step.

A natural (♮) cancels a sharp or flat.

Major Key Signatures

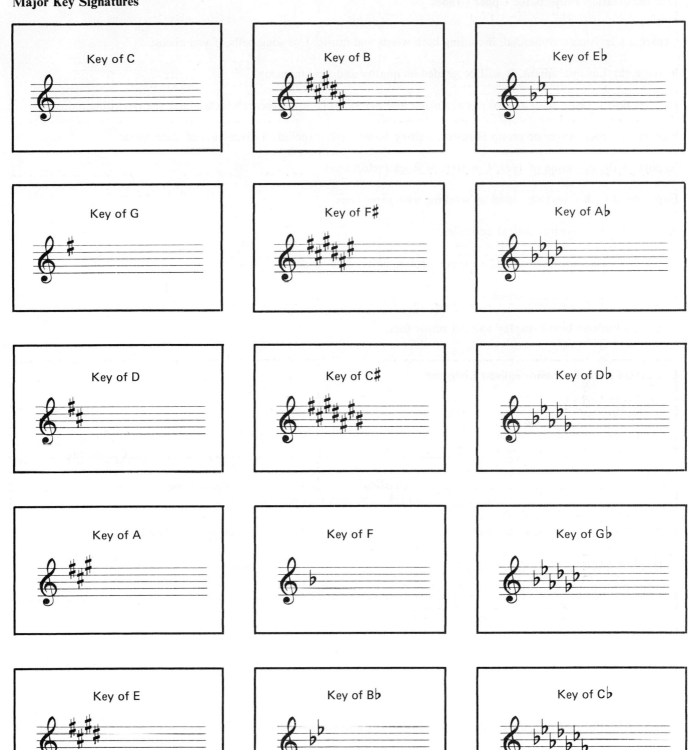

Individualization Projects for Upper Grades

Create a television commercial, including both words and music. Use song bells, if you choose.

Make a rhythm instrument. It will be graded on quality and workmanship.

Explain how rock or other recordings are made and marketed (sold). Research facts about the recording industry.

Report on a rock singer or group (Beetles, Rolling Stones, etc.). Include a discussion of their music.

Report on the evolution of Jazz, Country, or Rock (select one).

Experiment with sound on sound by working with tape loops.

Report on your favorite musical activities.

Report on music written using 12-tone row, polytonality, or bitonality.

Create musical games or puzzles.

Prepare a bulletin board display using a music topic.

Evaluation Form for Individualized Listening

Listening Station

Name _____ Classroom _____

Pop-rock _____ Classical _____ Record and filmstrip _____
                                              (check appropriate category)

Listen to the recording several times. If you need help, ask a member of your team or the teacher.

Recording _____

Composer _____

Melody

Is there an introduction? _____

Is it singable? _____

Is it smooth and flowing? _____

Does it have changing dynamics? _____

Is it divisible into phrases (has stopping points—cadences)? _____

Does it work toward a climax? _____

Is it major or minor? _____

Rhythm

Is it quiet? _____

Is it vigorous? _____

Does it have regular accents? _____

What is the meter? _____

Are two or more rhythms playing at the same time (polyphonic)? _____

Does it use repeated rhythmic patterns (ostinato)? _____

Instruments Used _____

Tempo

Is the tempo fast, medium, or slow? _____

Does it have any changes of tempo (speed)? _____

Harmony

Does it have many or few harmony changes? _____

Does it use counterpoint? _____

Form

Is the theme repeated? _____

Does it have a contrasting section? _____

Does it have a sense of order? _____

Expressive Qualities

How does the music make you feel? _____

What does it seem to describe? _____

_____

What is the outstanding feature of the music? _____

_____

General comments: _____

_____

_____

Glossary

Abstract Music: (also called absolute music) music that neither tells a story nor depicts a scene

Accidental: signs of alteration introduced for individual notes in a specific measure that are not included in the key signature of the song or composition. These include the following:
Sharp ( ): raises a tone a half step
Flat ( ): lowers a tone a half step
Double sharp (X): raises a tone a whole step
Double flat ( ): lowers a tone a whole step
Natural ( ): cancels a sharp or flat in a specific measure, thus the note is neither sharped nor flatted

Accompaniment: an instrumental or vocal part designed to support or enrich a melody

Action Song: a song in which bodily movements or dance steps are indicated or suggested by the words

Atonality: a composition with no key or tonal center

Bitonality: a composition in which two different key centers are played or sung simultaneously

Cadence: a point of rest or semirest in the melody or harmony of a song

Canon: a composition in two or more voice parts in which the second part exactly imitates the first; exact imitation of one voice by another

Chant: a short, recurring melodic figure sung as a background or accompaniment to a song or melody

Chromatic: tones foreign to a given chord or scale

Coda: a little tail; thus, a short passage added to conclude a song or composition

Counter Melody: an independent part generally written below the melody

Counterpoint: melody against melody; hence, two or more independent melodies played or sung simultaneously

Crescendo: gradually growing louder; increasing in volume

Decrescendo: gradually growing softer; decreasing in volume

Descant: a name for the highest voice part; often an independent melody sung by a few voices as an addition to the melody and harmony of a song

Dissonance: a combination of clashing sounds

Duration: the length of time a note or rest receives

Dynamics: varying degrees of loudness and softness of musical sound

Echo Song: echolike repetition of a melodic figure or phrase of a song

Electronic Music: music produced by electronic means

Form: organization of music in a meaningful arrangement

Harmony: several tones sounding together simultaneously; generally a triad or chord

Improvisation: the spontaneous creation of rhythm or melody

Instrumentation: choice and use of instruments in a musical composition

Internalization: ability to hear rhythms or melodies without assistance of sound

Interval: distance between two notes determined by counting upward every line and space from the lower (bottom) note to the top note

unison 2nd 3rd 4th

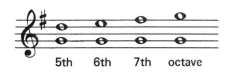

5th 6th 7th octave

Intonation: the production of tone in singing or playing an instrument with relation to the accuracy of pitch

Key Center: the scale around which a composition is created

Legato: in a smooth, connected manner; no breaks between tones

Libretto: words of an opera, operetta, oratorio, or other vocal work

Measure: the music appearing between two bar lines

Melodic Figure: a short, easily recognized succession of notes, often repeated

Melody: a meaningful succession or arrangement of sounds; a succession of single tones generally relating to a tonal center

Meter: rhythmic structure denoting the division of notes into measures and consisting of a uniform number of time units or beats

Musical Score: the printed music and verse for voices or instruments

Notation: method of representing musical sounds by a system of symbols

Ostinato: repetition of a melodic or rhythmic pattern

Patschen: patting the knees, usually in a sequence with other body sounds such as clapping, snapping, and stamping

Pentatonic Scale: a five-tone scale that can be reproduced by playing only the black keys on the piano

Phrase: a natural division of the melodic line; a short musical thought not necessarily complete in itself

Pitch: the highness or lowness of a tone

Polytonality: a composition with two or more key or tonal centers

Program Music: music that tells a story or depicts a scene

Progression: succession of tones or chords

Refrain: a phrase or section that recurs at the end of each stanza

Rhythm: regularity or flow of movement; organization of time in music through recurring pulses or patterns

Rhythm Pattern: a short, easily recognized metrical succession of notes, often repeated

Rote: learning a song in a mechanical, routine way by numerous repetitions of each phrase

Round: exact imitation of one voice by another on the same pitch level

Scale Passage: a succession of notes, ascending or descending by step or half step, to the next letter name in the scale

Singing Game: earliest type of group dance, often suggested by the words, which may include a game, movement, and singing

Skip: a succession of two notes, ascending or descending, but not to the next letter name of the scale

Solmization: the method of teaching scales and intervals through syllables

Staccato: short, detached, disconnected tones

Staff: five parallel lines upon which modern musical notation is written

Step: a succession of two notes, ascending or descending, to the next letter name of the scale

Suite: a composition consisting of a series of pieces, often using various dance forms

Syncopation: displacement of the accent from a strong to a weak beat

Tempo: rate of speed of a composition

Timbre: tone color or quality of tone

Tonality: loyalty to a tonic; the key scheme of a composition that establishes a relationship between tones

Tone Cluster: three or more adjacent tones sounded simultaneously as a chord

Tone Quality: unique sound characteristics of a voice or instrument

Twelve-Tone Scale: (also called serial music) a scale in which twelve tones from the chromatic scale are arranged in an arbitrary manner, with no one tone serving as a tonal center

Volume: loudness or softness of pitch

Whole-Tone Scale: scale made up of six notes with a whole tone interval between each interval

Song Index

Subject Index

fast and slow beats, 83
form, 48, 222, 347
homophonic and monophonic music, 339–40
melodic contour and rhythm, 143
melodic direction, 37, 97
melody and accompanying instruments, 191
musical notation, 234–35, 295, 321
music reading, 61, 353
music that moves in twos and threes, 255
range, 262
similar and dissimilar phrases, 280
skips and steps, 262
strong and weak beats, 29
Music reading
activities evaluation chart, 360
activities related to rhythms, singing, instruments, listening, 314–15
activities to develop skills in initiating, 359
basic aims of, 314
Carabo-Cone, Madeleine; and Royt, Beatrice, ideas, 315
chart of rhythmic counting and clapping, 316–18
class discussions and reports, 358
experiences preliminary to, 313
focusing on
expression, 350–53
form, 343–50
melodic concepts, 328–36
rhythmic concepts, 57–58, 64, 231–33, 315–28
textural concepts, 336–43
individualizing experiences, 354–58
initial experiences, 313
instrumental experiences, 178–81, 193–95, 198, 201–3, 233–37
listening experiences, 253, 263–72, 281–82, 292–99
singing experiences, 139–50
Music specialist, 8
Music supervisor, 9

Notational experiences. See Music reading
Number Game, to focus on rhythmic notation, 141, 322–23

Offenbach, Jacques, Tales of Hoffman, 124, 126
Opera and operettas
Amahl and the Night Visitors (Menotti), 301–2, 303
for assembly programs, 373–76
Carmen (Bizet), 302–3
created by children, 299–301
guidelines for presenting, 251–52, 299
Orchestral instruments
to focus on expressive concepts, 134, 230, 288–92
introduction to, 192–93
picture sources for, 248
recordings and filmstrips, 248
related to listening experiences, 256–57, 263–72, 282–84, 286–88, 289–90

Orff
echo canon, 45
echo clapping, snapping, patschen, and stamping, 30, 41–43, 106–7, 198–99, 253–54, 277
orchestrations, 44, 83, 111, 219, 341
rhythmic accompaniment, 93–94, 109, 112, 129, 134
rhythmic canon, 44–45
Overhead projector, 5, 164, 194, 205, 326

Part-singing
chants, 103, 111–12
chord roots, 104, 117
counter melodies, 103, 117
descants, 103, 117
echo songs, 103, 106–9, 112–13
to focus on
form, 123–32
textural concepts, 103–23
guide for teaching, 103–4
harmonizing
cadences, 103, 117
by ear, 104, 122–23
thirds and sixths, 104, 120
rounds and canons, 103–4, 114–15
vocal chording, 104, 120–22
Pass the Beat, game, 92
Pentatonic song, accompaniment for, 219
Physical and psychological characteristics of child
level I, 14
level II, 16
level III, 18–19
Piano
in the classroom, 189–90
learning packet for piano instruction, 190
music for rhythmic experiences, 73
publications for, 247
Pierne, Henri, "Entrance of the Little Fauns," 64
"Pit, Pat, Well-a-day," chant, 197
Plans for musical experiences, 9–10, 79
Plays with music, 377
"Poet and Peasant," 209
Poetry and music
to focus on durational relationships, 319
haiku, 226–27
"Hear the Beat of the Tom Tom," 260–61
"I'm Nobody! Who Are You?" (Dickinson), 351–52
"There Once Was a Cat Named Croon," 319
Pop-rock, 238
Problems in teaching music, 11–12
Program music for assembly programs, 372
Prokofieff, Serge
"Departure" from Winter Holiday, 290
"Gavotte," from Classical Symphony, 259, 261–62
March from Summer Day, 252, 255

Range, exploring, 77, 260–62, 263–72
Ravel, Maurice, "Beauty and the Beast" from The Mother Goose Suite, 288

Recorder
clubs, 361, 363
concerts by, 376
creating original composition for, 230–31
to experience
ABA form, 221–22
internalizing activities, 204
melodic improvisation, 206
texture, 208–9
experiences with, 179–85
to focus on
C scale, 234–35
dotted quarter followed by eighth, 198
expressive concepts, 227, 230–31
rhythmic notation, 326–27
strong and weak beats, 200
to play tonal patterns, 205–6
publications for, 247
strategy for introducing, 181–83
Recordings. See also suggested experiences in each chapter
as an aid in teaching a song, 163
for band and orchestral instruments, 248
for listening experiences, 308–12
for rhythmic experiences, 69–75
for singing experiences, 169–70
Related arts, focusing on
expression, 54, 132, 226–27
form, 46, 125, 220–21, 279, 345
instrumental experiences (timbre), 173, 195
melodic concepts, 36, 96–97, 177–78, 202, 260–61, 327–30
music reading, 58–60, 140–41
rhythmic concepts, 27, 28, 80–81, 194, 195, 253–54, 319
singing experiences, 80
texture, 40, 106, 207–8, 211, 273–74, 337
Resonator bells, 101, 200–203, 218–19
Rhythmic canon, 45, 225, 293
Rhythmic concepts
instrumental experiences, 194–200
level I, 15
level II, 17–18
level III, 19–20
listening experiences, 252–59
music-reading experiences, 315–28
rhythmic experiences, 26–35
singing experiences, 79–94
Rhythmic dramatizations
for assembly programs, 371–73
to enrich singing, 152–55
to experience
expressive elements, 55, 226–27
form, 48, 50–53
to focus on notation, 62
guidelines for developing, 25
music for, 25
related to
melodic concepts, 38
rhythmic concepts, 32–34, 81–83, 255–58
sequence for developing, 24
types, 24
value to child, 24–25

Rhythmic experiences
  activities evaluation chart for, 69
  activities to develop skills in initiating, 68
  as an aid to singing experiences, 79
  basic aims of, 21
  basic bodily movements, 22. *See also* Basic
    bodily movements
  behavioral objectives for, 15, 18, 20
  clapping rhythmic ostinato to song, 322–23
  class discussions or reports regarding,
    67–68
  defined, 21–22
  dramatizations, 24–26. *See also* Rhythmic
    dramatizations
  focusing on
    concepts related to form, 45–53
    expressive concepts, 53–57
    melodic concepts, 35–40
    notational concepts, 57–65, 342
    rhythmic concepts, 26–35
    textural concepts, 40–45
  free movement, 24. *See also* Free
    movement
  interpretations, 22–24. *See also* Rhythmic
    interpretations
  piano music for, 73
  recordings for, 69–75
  related arts for, 28, 36, 40–41, 46–47, 54,
    58–60
  related to
    music reading, 313
    other musical activities, 21
  rhythmic movement and notation chart, 23
  types of activities, 14, 16, 19, 21–22
Rhythmic interpretations
  guidelines for teacher, 22–26
  related to
    rhythmic concepts, 29
    texture, 276
  sequence for developing, 22–24
  value to child, 22
Rhythm instruments
  to accompany
    basic bodily movements, 198
    a chant, 197, 340
    a song, 93–94, 197
  chart of types, 172
  for creating
    an accompaniment for mood or picture
      music, 258
    an original composition, 229
    a rhythmic canon, 225–26
    a soundscape, 229
    a "symphony," 211
  to experience
    form, 125–27, 222, 225, 279–80, 345
    twos and threes, 253–54
  to focus on
    compound meter, 236
    expressive concepts, 133–34, 226–27,
      229–30
    notation, 293–94, 321
    rhythm patterns, 198–99
  guidelines for using, 171–72
  how to make, 174–75

related to
  instrumental experiences, 194–96
  music reading, 233
  other activities, 172
  rhythmic experiences, 28, 51, 54, 64
rhythm band, 172
with rock, 150
strategy for introducing, 173–74
used with question and answer
  improvisation, 197
"Right, Right, I Think I Did Right," rhyme,
  34
Rimsky-Korsakov, N.A., *Flight of the
  Bumble Bee,* 80, 83
Rock, used to focus on musical concepts, 150,
  327–28
Rossini, Gioacchino, "Can-Can" from *The
  Fantastic Toyshop,* 257–58
Round-clapping, 43, 63
"Running Horses," recording, 350, 353

Saint-Saëns, Camille
  Carnival of the Animals, 26, 29, 55,
    289–90, 296–98, 330–31
  "Danse Macabre," 263–66
Schubert, Francois, "The Bee," 256
Schumann, Robert
  "Soldier's March," 26, 29
  "Traumerei," 80, 83
Schumann-Glazounov
  "Chopin" from *Carnaval,* 350, 353
  "German Waltz—Paganini" from
    Carnaval, 243, 292
"Shadows" (Schytte), 173–74
Shostakovich, Dmitri
  "Petite Ballerina" from *Ballet* Suite no. 1,
    262
  "Pizzicato Polka" from *Ballet* Suite no. 1,
    52, 54–55
  "Polka" from *The Age of Gold,* 291–92
Singing experiences. *See also* Vocal
  exploration; Weak singer
  activities, 14, 16–17, 19
  activities evaluation chart for, 167
  activities to develop skills in initiating, 166
  aids in teaching a song, 163–64
  basic aims of, 77
  behavioral objectives for, 16, 18, 20
  class discussions or reports regarding, 165
  enrichment of, 150–56, 165
  focusing on
    concepts related to form, 123–32
    expressive concepts, 132–39
    melodic concepts, 94–103
    notational concepts, 234–37
    rhythmic concepts, 79–94
    textural concepts, 103–23
  guidelines for teaching a song, 78
  individualized activities for, 156–59
  motivating interest in a song, 78
  recordings for, 169–70
  related arts for, 80–81, 96–97, 105–6, 125,
    132, 140
  related to
    conceptual understandings, 78
    other musical experiences, 79

rock, to experience conceptual
    understandings, 150
  selecting the song, 77
  sequence for teaching a song, 78–79
  song collections, 167–69
Singing soundscape, 106
Smetana, Bedrich, "The Moldau," 296–98
Song bells
  creating a descant with, 215
  creating a second part by ear for, 212–13
  experiences with, 175–78
  to focus on melodic notation, 230, 233–34,
    235–36
  to help learn to sing a second part, 217
  playing themes for listening experience,
    237
Song books for children, 381
Song collections, list of, 167–69
Song dramatizations for assembly programs,
  370–71
Songs, alphabetical index of, 401–2
"Stamp, Clap," rhyme, 44
Stories, dramatized for assembly programs,
  372–73
Story music
  defined, 249–50
  experiences with, 256–58, 263–72, 277–78,
    286–89, 290–94
  guidelines for presenting, 250
Strauss, Richard, "Till Eulenspiegel's Merry
  Pranks," 267–72
Stravinsky, Igor
  "Devil's Dance," 273, 276
  "Firebird, The," 290–91
  Petrouchka, 277, 336, 339
Syllables, experiences with, 94–95, 98–102,
  105–6, 137, 144–45, 148, 158–59,
  221–22, 233–34, 260, 328–29

Tchaikovsky, Peter
  Album for the Young, 228
  "Andante Cantabile" from *String Quartet*
    no. 1, 237
  March from *Nutcracker* Suite, 26, 28
Teacher. *See also* Classroom teacher; Music
  consultant; Music specialist; Music
  supervisor
  professional books for, 381–83
Tests
  diagnostic, 386–90
  for evaluating musical growth. *See* Music
    Cue charts
Texture
  conceptual understandings related to, 15,
    17, 19–20, 40–45, 103–23, 186,
    207–19, 273–78, 336–43
  experienced through
    instrumental experiences, 207–19
    listening experiences, 273–78
    music-reading experiences, 336–43
  focusing on, through illustrations, 211
  monophonic, homophonic, and polyphonic
    music explored, 109–11
  related to
    rhythmic experiences, 40–45
    singing experiences, 103–23